Barriers to European Growth

Barriers to European Growth
A Transatlantic View

ROBERT Z. LAWRENCE
CHARLES L. SCHULTZE
Editors

THE BROOKINGS INSTITUTION
Washington, D.C.

Copyright © 1987 by
THE BROOKINGS INSTITUTION
1775 Massachusetts Avenue, N.W., Washington, D.C. 20036

Library of Congress Cataloging-in-Publication data:

Barriers to European growth.

Papers presented at a conference.
Includes bibliographical references and index.
1. Europe—Economic conditions—1945–   —Con-
gresses. 2. Europe—Economic policy—Congresses.
I. Lawrence, Robert Z., 1949–   . II. Schultze,
Charles L.   III. Brookings Institution.
HC240.B297   1987   338.94   87-26900
ISBN 0-8157-7770-1
ISBN 0-8157-7769-8 (pbk.)

9 8 7 6 5 4 3 2 1

THE BROOKINGS INSTITUTION is an independent organization devoted to nonpartisan research, education, and publication in economics, government, foreign policy, and the social sciences generally. Its principal purposes are to aid in the development of sound public policies and to promote public understanding of issues of national importance.

The Institution was founded on December 8, 1927, to merge the activities of the Institute for Government Research, founded in 1916, the Institute of Economics, founded in 1922, and the Robert Brookings Graduate School of Economics and Government, founded in 1924.

The Board of Trustees is responsible for the general administration of the Institution, while the immediate direction of the policies, program, and staff is vested in the President, assisted by an advisory committee of the officers and staff. The by-laws of the Institution state: "It is the function of the Trustees to make possible the conduct of scientific research, and publication, under the most favorable conditions, and to safeguard the independence of the research staff in the pursuit of their studies and in the publication of the results of such studies. It is not a part of their function to determine, control, or influence the conduct of particular investigations or the conclusions reached."

The President bears final responsibility for the decision to publish a manuscript as a Brookings book. In reaching his judgment on the competence, accuracy, and objectivity of each study, the President is advised by the director of the appropriate research program and weighs the views of a panel of expert outside readers who report to him in confidence on the quality of the work. Publication of a work signifies that it is deemed a competent treatment worthy of public consideration but does not imply endorsement of conclusions or recommendations.

The Institution maintains its position of neutrality on issues of public policy in order to safeguard the intellectual freedom of the staff. Hence interpretations or conclusions in Brookings publications should be understood to be solely those of the authors and should not be attributed to the Institution, to its trustees, officers, or other staff members, or to the organizations that support its research.

Foreword

IN THE early 1970s, after more than two decades of unparalleled performance, the economies of the major European countries began to falter. Economic growth slowed sharply during the remainder of the 1970s as inflation and unemployment both rose. In the first half of the 1980s growth slowed further, and though inflation eventually subsided, unemployment grew even more rapidly.

While economic performance deteriorated in all industrial countries after 1973, the distinguishing feature of the European experience has been the behavior of unemployment. For Europe as a whole it has risen in almost every year since 1973, now standing at 11 percent of the labor force.

This study reports on a joint undertaking by American and European economists and other experts to examine the principal European economies in an effort to understand the causes of the high unemployment and to offer some suggestions for policy. An initial planning conference was held in February 1986. Eight American authors then prepared papers on various aspects of the European economies. The papers were presented at a conference held at Brookings in October 1986, where they were discussed and evaluated by a group of European economists and government officials. The papers, the formal comments, and summaries of the general discussion are presented in this volume. The volume is introduced by an overview chapter, written by the editors, that summarizes the major findings of the study and, building on those findings, offers a number of suggestions about the causes and remedies for European unemployment.

The editors of the volume, Robert Z. Lawrence and Charles L. Schultze, are senior fellow and director of the Brookings Economic Studies program, respectively. During the course of the project, all the American authors visited Europe, where government officials, university economists, and many research organizations gave them extensive help. In particular, the editors and authors wish to thank the many staff members of the Commission of the European Communities and the Organization for Economic Cooperation and Development who steered them to data sources, provided institutional lore, and offered useful analytic suggestions.

Barbara de Boinville, Caroline Lalire, Jeanette Morrison, and James R. Schneider edited the manuscript; Victor M. Alfaro, Gregory I. Hume, Carl L. Liederman, Dale B. Thompson, and Almaz S. Zelleke verified its factual content; and Florence Robinson prepared the index. Research assistance to the editors was provided by Tamara Giles, Gregory I. Hume, and Carl L. Liederman. Evelyn M. E. Taylor assisted the editors in arranging both conferences, and Anita G. Whitlock managed the flow of manuscripts and correspondence in preparing the final volume.

This project was supported by the German Marshall Fund of the United States and the Rockefeller Foundation, for which Brookings is very grateful.

The views expressed in this volume are those of the authors and discussants and should not be attributed to the people and organizations whose assistance is acknowledged above, or to the trustees, officers, or other staff members of the Brookings Institution.

BRUCE K. MACLAURY
President

September 1987
Washington, D.C.

Contents

MACROECONOMIC CONSTRAINTS

Tables

Figures

ROBERT Z. LAWRENCE
CHARLES L. SCHULTZE

Overview

AFTER the initial reconstruction from the damage of the Second World War, Europe experienced twenty-five years of unparalleled economic performance. Labor productivity grew at a rate more than three times its average in the previous eighty years. Investment was extraordinarily high, and new technology was introduced into the production process at a very rapid rate. Yet the labor force adjusted smoothly; unemployment stayed year after year at very low levels. And while inflation occasionally became a problem, for the most part it was kept under control.

In the early 1970s, however, Europe's economic performance began to deteriorate on almost every count: GNP growth, productivity, unemployment, and inflation. Although performance also deteriorated elsewhere in the industrial world, the difference was that in Europe unemployment kept on rising all through the 1970s and early 1980s not with a cyclical rhythm but monotonically. Indeed, unemployment accelerated its upward move after 1980. By 1986 unemployment among the European members of the OECD stood at over 11 percent, 2 percentage points higher than it had been at the height of the 1982 recession, and 4 percentage points higher than it was in the United States. Explanations for the problems are complex and policy prescriptions contradictory. But both Left and Right agree that Europe faces a serious economic problem, even if its precise nature and the appropriate remedies remain hotly debated.[1]

---

1. The prevailing view is captured by the titles of studies such as Andrea Boltho, ed., *The European Economy: Growth and Crisis* (Oxford University Press, 1982); Ralf Dahrendorf, ed., *Europe's Economy in Crisis* (Holmes and Meier, 1982); Kenneth Dyson and Stephen Wilks, eds., *Industrial Crisis: A Comparative Study of the State and Industry* (St. Martin's Press, 1983); "Europe's Technology Gap," *Economist* (November 24, 1984), pp. 93–98; Assar Lindbeck, "What Is Wrong with the West European Economies?" *World Economy*, vol. 8 (June 1985), pp. 153–70; and Peter Gourevitch and others, *Unions and Economic Crisis: Britain, West Germany and Sweden* (London: Allen and Unwin, 1984).

1

From an American perspective Europe's central economic problem has been its failure to provide sufficient jobs for its labor force. The growth of output per worker has slowed, but it has also slowed in Japan and the United States, and at the present time output per worker seems to be growing more than twice as fast in Europe as in the United States. What improves productivity growth eases the problem of excessive real wages and makes it possible to pursue expansionary policies further than would otherwise be the case. And so we are concerned with both efficiency and resource utilization, but our main attention is still focused on the latter.

This volume presents an American viewpoint on the causes of and possible remedies for Europe's economic problems. It contains papers by American economists on various aspects of the European economy that were initially presented at a conference held at the Brookings Institution in October 1986. There they were subjected to critical evaluation and discussion by a number of European economists and policymakers. The evaluations and summaries of the discussions are included along with each of the papers.

This overview chapter starts with a capsule description of the major hypotheses—partly conflicting, partly complementary—that have been prominently put forward in Europe to explain its economic difficulties. Next it summarizes the findings of each of our authors and synthesizes from their results and from the discussions at the conference an overall assessment of the causes of Europe's economic difficulties, in particular its high unemployment. It closes with some recommendations for economic policy.

Alternative Diagnoses

Our reading of the economic literature suggests that analysts have concentrated on four strands of causation, intertwined in different ways, to explain Europe's current predicament: impediments to growth result-ing from shifts in structural growth patterns, the debilitating effects of the welfare state, inappropriate prices in the aggregate supply function, and the interaction of exogenous shocks and macroeconomic policies. In what follows we provide a flavor of each as seen by its advocates. Counterarguments follow later.

The Changed Structure of Growth

The forces behind postwar European growth have run their course: since 1973 there has been a sea change in the nature of growth, one that European institutions are ill-equipped to deal with.[2]

European expansion in the 1950s and 1960s reflected unusually favorable conditions in the markets for factors of production. Indeed, as Angus Maddison has shown, the growth rates achieved in this period were far higher than those in Europe's historical experience.[3] An abundant supply of workers streaming into industry from agriculture and from neighboring countries to the east and south kept wages in check. Oil discoveries in the Middle East and the dominance of certain major oil companies (the so-called seven sisters) ensured secure supplies of cheap energy. U.S. technologies enabled the relatively backward European economies to realize rapid improvements in productivity. Rising real incomes enlarged markets at home, while the removal of trade barriers through the actions of the European Community (EC), the European Free Trade Association, and the various multilateral trade rounds, along with improvements in communications, opened up markets abroad. For several European nations, undervalued currencies contributed to export-led growth. Secure in their expectations of cheap production inputs and growing markets, European entrepreneurs invested heavily with funds supplied by high domestic savings rates and, after 1958 when European currency convertibility revived international capital markets, supplemented by foreign borrowing.

Growth followed traditional patterns. Immediately after World War II it was concentrated in infrastructure, construction, and such basic industries as steel and chemicals; later it extended into transportation equipment, machinery, and consumer electronics. Industrial policies strengthened and enlarged firms to exploit economies of scale and to make them competitive with American counterparts. Except in the United Kingdom, success was widespread. Economic strategies ranging

2. See Business Round Table Ad Hoc Task Force, "Job Creation: The United States and European Experience, Analysis of the Issues of Economic Growth and Job Generation," staff working paper (Washington, D.C.: Business Round Table, December 12, 1984).

3. By contrast, growth rates in the United States were only about 20 percent higher than those in its historical experience; see Angus Maddison, "Growth and Slowdown in Advanced Capitalist Economies: Techniques of Quantitative Assessment," *Journal of Economic Literature*, vol. 25 (June 1987), pp. 649–98.

from the social market economy in Germany to the *dirigiste* approach of France all seemed to work.

But in the early 1970s conditions changed. The movement of labor from the farms to the cities had run its course, while immigration from southern Europe was bringing with it considerable social problems. The baby boom generation entered the labor market with rising expectations and weaker commitments to the work ethic. Labor relations deteriorated, and labor militancy increased. In 1973 OPEC ushered in what was to be a decade of expensive and insecure energy supplies. Exchange rates adjusted to raise European labor costs toward parity with those of its foreign competitors. Former growth sectors of the economy—standardized manufactured products such as steel, automobiles, and ships—experienced sluggish demand and increasing competition from Japan and the newly industrialized countries of Asia.[4] Unfortunately, Europe had specialized in these medium-technology products. In the information industries that were becoming the locus of global industrial growth European firms performed poorly.[5]

The European economies had exhausted the benefits of relative backwardness, and they now experienced problems in graduating from a catch-up economy to one on the frontier of technology. In a catch-up economy the avenues of growth are known, and government, management, and labor can follow fairly set formulas to achieve given results. But at the frontier, flexibility and the capacity to cope with uncertainty and risk are crucial. Europe has failed to adapt its management systems, labor relations, capital market institutions, and government policies to those of a postindustrial economy.

Competitiveness at the frontier depends on innovation rather than the adoption and adaptation of existing technologies. The commercial exploitation of new technologies hinges not simply on committing resources to research and development (in which Europe far outspends Japan) but on the close collaboration between scientific institutions and industry (which Europe does poorly).

The new modes of production call for reallocation of labor within

4. See for example, Robert B. McKersie, *Job Losses in Major Industries: Manpower Strategy Responses* (Paris: OECD, 1983).

5. See "Europe's Technology Gap." See also Pari Patel and Keith Pavitt, "Measuring Europe's Technological Performance," draft for a chapter in Henry Ergas, ed., *A European Future in High Technology?* (Brussels: CEPS, forthcoming); and OECD, *Industry in Transition: Experience of the 1970s and Prospects for the 1980s* (Paris: OECD, 1983).

companies and across the economy. Old work rules must be abolished, even though Europe's strong unions resist such changes. Workers must have general training to adapt to new tasks, and European education, which has encouraged apprenticeships that provide specific skills, must adapt. The labor force must also be able to move easily to where the jobs are. The United States and Japan have successfully reallocated their labor forces, the former by relying principally on the market, the latter by shifting workers within firms. But heavy sales taxes on European housing, cultural traditions, slow-moving large corporations, and poorly functioning labor markets inhibit such reallocation.

Small firms and entrepreneurs will have to take a greater part in the new European economy. Entrepreneurs willing to take large risks must be encouraged and financed and the entry of new businesses facilitated. This change of attitude will not be easy. Harsh bankruptcy laws like those in Germany induce excessively conservative decisions. New firms, which cannot rely on capital from earnings or from banks on the basis of long-standing relationships, must be able to raise equity in active venture capital and over-the-counter markets. But with the exception of the United Kingdom, these options remain relatively undeveloped in Europe. The European policy of creating large "national champion" industries has badly misfired, the market power conferred on them having shielded them from new rivals and the pressures to leave declining industries. Competitive pressures must be allowed to force innovation and adaptation.[6]

Employment must grow in business services, finance, communications, and retail trade, but in many European sectors, state monopolies and regulation inhibit new business ventures. In addition, firms must strive to create markets of continental size: the fixed costs of R&D in the development of telecommunications, for example, are so great that only through access to a large market with common standards can firms sustain them. But the uncommon market, in which each nation seeks to advance its own national champions in pursuit of a "diversified production base," precludes the emergence of companies with genuinely European strategies.[7] Indeed, with a few exceptions, only the American

6. See Paul A. Geroski and Alexis Jacquemin, "Corporate Competitiveness in Europe," *Economic Policy*, no. 1 (November 1985), pp. 169–218.

7. As noted in Geoffrey Shepherd, François Duchêne, and Christopher Saunders, eds., *Europe's Industries: Public and Private Strategies for Change* (Cornell University Press, 1983), Western Europe's larger countries are in the worst of all worlds. Their

and Japanese multinationals have pan-European strategies. As the *Economist* notes, "Testing and certification requirements, differing standards, border delays and restraints on trade in services all take their toll on trade between EEC countries."[8]

Above all, these structural changes have major political consequences for the distribution of social power; the beneficiaries of the old order must yield to the new. Unions and regions wedded to the old industries must give way to accommodate the interests of new firms and labor force entrants. In the 1950s and 1960s, growth was built without the need for clearing away the old order and outmoded industrial capacity: that had been accomplished by the war. And employing new entrants such as refugees and displaced farmers was relatively easy. But the growth patterns of the 1980s and beyond will require reallocating productive factors from activities in which they are entrenched and comfortable. Inducing displaced industrial workers into the service sector is considerably more difficult.

The inadequate adjustment of its industry has reduced Europe's ability to compete in global markets. Domestic demand and supply are increasingly mismatched. Domestic expansion spills abroad, with little effect on the home economy. Poor trade performance has in turn damaged the industrial base and severely reduced employment opportunities in industry.

The Excessive Role of the State

A different, although not necessarily contradictory, view attributes Europe's economic problems to the rapid growth and large size of the welfare state. Over the course of the postwar period, European nations vastly increased their commitments not simply to maintain full employment but to maintain employment in specific regions, firms, and even jobs. They sought not simply to provide basic benefits for the poor but to provide broad support for housing, education, day care, and retirement for the middle class. Such traditional regulatory objectives as safety on the job were expanded to ensure worker participation in management

---

home markets are too small, but their illustrious histories provide them with pretensions to be full-range producers.

8. "Europe's Technology Gap," p. 95. See also Commission of the European Communities, "Completing the Internal Market," white paper from the Commission to the European Council (Brussels, June 1985).

decisionmaking and government oversight of plant closures and layoffs. Because market forces often seemed unfair or inadequate states began to allocate credit, encourage mergers, and nurture national champion firms, eventually becoming full-fledged entrepreneurs operating state-owned industries responsible for a wide range of products. And they aimed not simply to redistribute income through the tax system but to do so indirectly by minimum wage legislation, agricultural support programs, and price controls. In its efforts to ensure economic security, the welfare state advanced to the point that it stifled initiative, stimulated waste, and curtailed growth.[9]

As a result of excessive state intervention the link between achievement and reward has been severed. Failing firms are bailed out by subsidies, nationalizations, and trade protection; failing workers by employment subsidies, extensive unemployment and disability benefits, and training programs.[10] Disability and sickness benefits are available without adequate proof of illness.[11] At the same time, confiscatory marginal tax rates penalize successful entrepreneurs and productive workers.[12] State intervention also burdens employers. Firms are reluctant to hire new workers because of the difficulties of firing them if they do not work out, and they are reluctant to take on part-time workers because of distortions from social security taxes. They also hesitate to expand beyond certain levels because they then become susceptible to costly administrative requirements.

The taxes, transfer payments, and minimum wage legislations of the welfare state have also meant that wages and prices do not reflect supply and demand. Despite increased unemployment among younger workers in Sweden, the United Kingdom, and France, wages for youth relative

9. See, for example, Theodore Geiger, *Welfare and Efficiency: Their Interactions in Western Europe and Implications for International Economic Relations* (Washington, D.C.: National Planning Association, 1978); Per-Martin Meyerson, *Eurosclerosis: The Case of Sweden* (Stockholm: Federation of Swedish Industries, 1985); Herbert Giersch, ed., *Reassessing the Role of Government in the Mixed Economy: Symposium 1982* (Tubingen: J. C. B. Mohr, 1983); and Herbert Giersch, "Eurosclerosis," Kiel Discussion Papers 112 (Kiel Institute for World Economics, October 1985).

10. See OECD, *High Unemployment: A Challenge for Income Support Policies* (Paris: OECD, 1984).

11. According to Herbert Giersch, in Germany 70 percent of sick days are taken on Monday or Friday and only 4 percent on Wednesdays. See "Eurosclerosis," p. 8.

12. In 1983, for Europe as a whole, a single-earner married couple with two children and the income of an average production worker paid the equivalent of 42.5 percent of its income in taxes and had a marginal tax rate of 59 percent. See OECD, *Structural Adjustment and Economic Performance: Synthesis Report* (Paris: OECD, 1987), p. 14.

to those of adults rose substantially between the mid-1960s and the early 1980s because of collective bargaining practices and legislated youth-specific minimum wage rates (which in Germany, however, have remained fairly constant).[13] The availability of free health care, day care, and other benefits encourages waste, as allocation occurs through rationing rather than by marginal cost-pricing. Political pressures instead of rates of return determine the allocation of capital. Regulatory and other political pressures stifle competition. Government procurement discriminates not only against foreign firms but also against those too small to be perceived as potential national champions. Restrictions on business hours prevent the expansion of specialized retail stores. State-controlled transportation services use cross-subsidization to drive up the prices of services that are actually cheap in order to subsidize the prices of those that are not.

Coincident with the expansion of government commitments has come the expansion of systems to deliver the benefits and increases in taxes to pay for them. As a result, public spending has taken an ever-larger share of gross national product.[14] The increased tax burdens have rapidly raised marginal tax rates, damaging incentives to work harder and earn more. And the European political systems have promised more than they can pay for, sacrificing the future for the present.[15] Despite significant reductions in public investment, government deficits have burgeoned; increased taxes have financed only part of the spending spree.[16]

The explosion in state spending in the 1970s has given way to painful attempts at retrenchment in the 1980s, and European governments have been unwilling to add to the deficits to reflate their economies. Thus in addition to inhibiting microeconomic adjustments, large structural deficits have prevented the use of countercyclical fiscal policies.

13. See *OECD Employment Outlook* (Paris: OECD, September 1984), chap. 5, for an excellent treatment of this question.

14. See Peter Saunders and Friedrich Klau, *OECD Economic Studies: The Role of the Public Sector*, no. 4 (Spring 1985, *special issue*), p. 12.

15. On promises see, for example, "The Burden Imposed by Social Security Contributions since the Beginning of the Seventies," *Monthly Report of the Deutsche Bundesbank*, vol. 38 (January 1986), pp. 16–23; on sacrificing the future, see Michel Albert and James Ball, *Toward European Economic Recovery in the 1980s: Report to the European Parliament*, Georgetown University, Center for Strategic and International Studies, Washington Papers 109 (Praeger, 1984), esp. pp. 8–20.

16. See for example, Michael Emerson, "The European Stagflation Disease in International Perspective and Some Possible Therapy," in Emerson, ed., *Europe's Stagflation* (Oxford University Press, 1984), pp. 195–228.

Aggregate Supply Imbalances

The third source of current European economic problems stems from distortions in aggregate supply relationships. Real wages and profits do not reflect what is appropriate to full employment,[17] and aggregate demand policies have contributed to the insensitivity of wages to unemployment.

First, the battle over income shares in the late 1960s sent real wages soaring to levels incompatible with a return to previous employment levels. Shortly thereafter the economies of Europe, like those throughout the world, were afflicted with a series of unfavorable, price-raising supply shocks, the oil price increases in 1974 and 1979–80, and a sharp slowdown in productivity growth. Some argue that to these shocks should be added the loss of competitiveness to Far Eastern nations. As a consequence, the path of real wages that was consistent with the maintenance of high employment fell to a lower level and grew more slowly. But the real wages paid to workers did not adjust accordingly. Instead, wages increased at the expense of profits. Consequently, investment slumped, and what investment there was attempted to save labor expense rather than expand capacity. As capacity stagnated, a shortage of capital coexisted with an excess supply of labor. The full use of capital corresponded to higher and higher levels of unemployment. This situation implied that efforts to restore full employment would result in more inflation. The natural rate of unemployment had shifted upward secularly because real wages were high and because of an inadequate capital stock.[18]

17. See Jacques Artus, "The Disequilibrium Real Wage Rate Hypothesis: An Empirical Evaluation," and Leslie Lipschitz and Susan M. Schadler, "Relative Prices, Real Wages, and Macroeconomic Policies: Some Evidence from Manufacturing in Japan and the United Kingdom," *International Monetary Fund Staff Papers*, vol. 31 (June 1984), pp. 249–302, 303–38; Jeffrey D. Sachs, "Real Wages and Unemployment in the OECD Countries," *Brookings Papers on Economic Activity, 1:1983*, pp. 255–304; and Dennis Grubb, Richard Jackman, and Richard Layard, "Wage Rigidity and Unemployment in OECD Countries," *European Economic Review*, vol. 21 (March–April 1983), pp. 11–39.

A more skeptical view is to be found in Robert J. Gordon, "Wage-Price Dynamics and the Natural Rate of Unemployment in Eight Large Industrialized Nations," paper presented to OECD Workshop on Price Dynamics and Economic Policy (September 1984).

18. For a discussion of the relationship between capacity utilization and unemployment, see Friedrich Klau and Axel Mittelstadt, "Labour Market Flexibility and External Price Shocks," Working Paper 24 (Paris: OECD, September 1985).

Aggregate Demand Policies and the Response to Shocks

A fourth view assigns an important part of the blame for Europe's unemployment problem to deficient aggregate demand, caused principally by macroeconomic policies that remained too restrictive for too long and exacerbated by weakness in the private demand for investment goods.

To stem the inflationary consequences for their own economies of the two OPEC price hikes and the Reagan administration's economic program, European monetary authorities were compelled to follow tight policies.[19] While some attempted to avoid such contractions (for example, Sweden's bridging policies after the 1973–74 oil shock and François Mitterrand's expansionary program in the early 1980s), the strong interdependence of the European economies rendered such strategies impotent. In principle, fiscal policies might have been used to offset some of the contractionary impulses in the 1980s, but structural deficits prevented their use.

The aggregate demand shocks left a serious and persistent legacy. They damaged the ability of labor markets to function and destroyed investor confidence. Displaced workers became discouraged and their skills outmoded. They have been disenfranchised from their unions, which no longer take account of their employment opportunities when pressing for higher wages.

European investors have also been affected. Before the 1970s they assumed that growth could be sustained. In 1974, however, they learned how vulnerable growth was to sudden inflationary shocks. The slump damaged their confidence and contributed to the fall in investment. Moreover, much of Europe's productive capacity had been constructed on the assumption of much faster growth. Only when such capacity was utilized would investment recover. The interaction of the destruction of investor confidence and the slump in aggregate demand created a cumulative process of recession. Declining profit margins typify cyclical declines; with sufficient demand stimulus these profit margins would

19. See especially, James Tobin, "Unemployment in the 1980s: Macroeconomic Diagnosis and Prescription," in Andrew Pierre, ed., *Unemployment and Growth in the Western Economies* (New York: Council on Foreign Relations, 1984), pp. 79–112; and Andrea Boltho, "Economic Policy and Performance in Europe since the Second Oil Shock," in Emerson, ed., *Europe's Stagflation,* pp. 10–32.

recover. Declining productivity growth is also primarily the result of the aggregate demand shock.[20]

Policymakers in Europe refuse to pursue more expansive policies for some combination of three reasons—all of them unwarranted according to those who argue that a Keynesian expansion would work. First, policymakers believe that excessive real wage aspirations and structural rigidities would convert demand stimulus not principally into additional output but into higher inflation. Second, having spent the better part of the past six years reducing their budget deficits, with varying degrees of success, they (and apparently their voters) are reluctant to reverse course. And third, there is a widespread belief that only export-led growth generated by the rest of the world appears an acceptable means of reestablishing growth. In particular, this concern is so strong in the key German economy that policymakers seem to believe it impossible to raise aggregate demand sufficiently to absorb the excess supply of labor, and those nations more willing to expand cannot do so without German expansion because their exchange rates will depreciate.

Interactions

Independently, none of these four strands adequately explains Europe's economic problems, but together they interact to create circles of stagnation. For example, the exhaustion of old growth opportunities should have occurred gradually; it is difficult to explain how, on their own, structural changes have caused the sudden erosion in European growth and the rise in unemployment observed after 1973. Again, the constraints presented by the growth of the welfare state would not have been binding if the nature of structural change had not shifted or if aggregate growth in demand had been sustained. The commitment to particular employment opportunities remained relatively inexpensive as long as growth followed predictable and stable patterns; but when structural change required deemphasizing politically powerful heavy industries, commitments to maintain jobs in these sectors became extremely expensive. Similarly, the welfare state could afford generous unemployment benefits as long as unemployment remained low, and

20. See John F. Helliwell, Peter H. Sturm, and Gerard Salou, "International Comparison of the Sources of Productivity Slowdown, 1973–82," *European Economic Review*, vol. 28 (June–July 1985), pp. 157–91.

could pay for annual increases in living standards as long as rapid productivity growth continued.

But when the supply shocks of the 1970s hit the European economies and when the nature of structural change shifted, government spending exploded. This led to increased taxes, which further raised labor costs and discouraged investment. The declines in productivity growth and the deterioration in terms of trade and competitiveness made the process of wage determination yield inappropriate factor prices—an outcome reinforced by the provisions of the welfare state. Inappropriate factor prices in turn implied that efforts to stimulate aggregate demand became increasingly inflationary, inducing the need for much tighter aggregate demand policies.

Sluggish demand also induced a conservative and pessimistic view of structural change. Workers accustomed to changing jobs in an environment of excess demand found that layoffs meant long spells of unemployment. Accordingly, unions became more rigid in demanding limits on layoffs. Because innovation, too, depended on strong demand, productivity growth slowed in the sluggish environment. Thus the four strands can be interwoven almost without limit, and the complex interrelationships of the problems suggest that growth cannot be restored unless all four are attacked simultaneously—hence the despair sometimes termed Europessimism.

Some Conceptual Issues

In the first paper in this volume Paul Krugman sets out to provide an analytical framework within which to examine the issues involved. He identifies the most important European problem as the rise in unemployment since 1973 and observes that while excessively high real wages are the mechanism that has brought it about, this fact does not explain the underlying causes. The paper raises questions about the explanations for European unemployment and the policy prescriptions advocated to reduce it.

Krugman considers a variant of the argument that the rise in unemployment has been primarily caused by the very nature of the structural change that has occurred. Although he discusses the claim of those made uneasy by technological innovation that accelerating automation (labor-saving technology) and expanding trade with developing countries have dramatically reduced labor demand at any given wage rate, he rejects this view because it is inconsistent with the data. If technological change is highly labor-saving, labor demand should be reduced; but output per employed worker should rise and profits should increase as a share of value added. In fact, however, output per employed worker has not accelerated in Europe (labor productivity growth has decelerated) and the share of production costs attributable to labor has increased.

The persistence of unemployment over the medium run cannot, Krugman argues, be ascribed simply to insufficient aggregate demand. To be sure, there is insufficient demand for labor at existing wage rates, but the reason is that European policymakers are prevented from increasing aggregate demand by the fear of rekindling inflation. The primary problem thus lies on the supply side, in the increase of the unemployment rate associated with stable inflation. The trade-off between inflation and unemployment has clearly worsened. Inflation rates in the mid-1980s are similar to those of the 1960s, but unemployment is now much higher.

Krugman feels that explanations blaming the market-stifling impact of the welfare state, so-called Eurosclerosis, offer some important insights. Restrictions that discourage the firing of employees may account for the particularly high proportions of long-term and youth unemployment. But other aspects of this explanation are troublesome. He argues that, in principle, the net effect of such restrictions on employment at any given real wage is ambiguous: restrictions impede flows both in and out of unemployment. And the timing of the European slowdown seems inconsistent with the view that the welfare state brought on Eurosclerosis: the welfare state was already highly developed in the 1960s. Why did a social system that seemed to work extremely well in the 1960s become increasingly ineffective thereafter? Krugman quotes Assar Lindbeck's view that the deterioration in adjustment capabilities brought about by the welfare state had long been occurring but only revealed itself in the face of the shocks of the 1970s.

Krugman also raises some issues about the empirical relevance of studies of real wages. Simply comparing the growth of real wages with that of labor productivity, he cautions, may provide misleading estimates of the extent of disequilibrium. Labor productivity is not independent of real wages since changes in real wages induce the substitution of capital for labor. Similarly, shifts in income shares between labor and capital may be misleading indicators of the extent to which wages are excessive.

Such shifts could be the result of an equilibrium when production functions or technological change have particular characteristics. Krugman concludes that we should be skeptical of even the most sophisticated econometric estimates of the appropriate real wage.

He also considers the argument that the shocks of the 1970s led to unemployment, which in turn raised the nonaccelerating inflation rate of unemployment (NAIRU)—the so-called hysteresis explanation. Hysteresis can result if slow growth reduces capital formation, thereby lowering the marginal product of labor compatible with any given level of employment. It can also occur if the economy writes off workers who have been unemployed too long, either because they lose skills and become discouraged, as Layard and Nickell emphasize, or because they become disenfranchised from the wage-setting process, as the insider-outsider models predict. Krugman observes that perhaps generous unemployment and government support for unions contributes to the hysteresis process. But, he asks, if European unions worry only about insiders, why was Europe able to increase employment in the 1960s?

Although he is skeptical of technotrade pessimism as an explanation for Europe's rising unemployment, Krugman notes that one response to it could be to accept stagnant employment, and to take labor demand as given and ration work instead of trying to improve the functioning of labor markets or reducing real wages. But he points out that this solution may keep output unnecessarily low. An alternative approach would reduce wages, so as to increase employment, and offset the distributional impact by profit sharing or by redistribution through the tax system.

Krugman is also skeptical of prescriptions to raise aggregate demand to reduce unemployment rates to their previous levels. He suggests that virtually all economists believe the European NAIRU has shifted upward. Indeed, he observes that the aspirations of European policymakers, even those left of center, to achieve fuller employment have become very limited. If the root cause of the change in NAIRU is overexpansion of the welfare state, he cautions, increasing demand will simply lead to inflation. The appropriate solution is to make the economy more flexible, presumably by scaling back welfare state benefits. He notes, however, that with the exception of the government of Margaret Thatcher, no government has summoned the political will to undertake such measures on a large scale. Krugman therefore considers second-best options such as subsidizing employment, removing the social security financing burden from labor costs, and tying wages more closely to profits.

However, he cautions that such measures may not succeed if those who are employed have no interest in allowing the unemployed to obtain work. Krugman draws on the work of Jeffrey Sachs to argue that in the face of hysteresis unemployment can be reduced only by permanently increasing inflation and inflation reduced only by increasing unemployment.

These pessimistic considerations suggest that new policy tools must be developed—selective job creation might be an example. And despite their poor track record, incomes policies may be worth trying. Krugman notes that the previous hysteresis of the 1930s was only ended by the Second World War. A dramatic change in policy regimes seems called for.

Findings of This Study

We found it useful to distill from the public debate and the economic literature four broad hypotheses about the sources of Europe's economic slowdown and the obstacles to its future growth. Paul Krugman's discussion of analytical issues considers variants of these hypotheses. But to use additional empirical evidence and economic analysis to separate fact from fancy and unsupported assumption from reasoned judgment, we found it necessary to organize the remainder of the investigation somewhat differently. The other studies in this book develop the implications of each hypothesis for six major aspects of the European economies, and then, within each area, confront the implications of the various hypotheses with the data and the analysis.

The first of these areas is the *performance of labor markets*. Each of the hypotheses implies something about labor markets. And two of the four—the damage done by excessive real wages and insufficient demand—have to be evaluated principally through an analysis of labor markets. The papers by Gary Burtless, Robert Flanagan, and Charles Schultze are concerned with the labor market.

The second area of analysis, in the paper by Robert Lawrence, is the *performance of firms and industries in international markets*. Lawrence seeks to determine whether European industries are afflicted with inadequate competitiveness characterized especially by a sluggish response to changes in international markets. ·

The *performance of financial markets* is the subject of Robert Aliber's paper. How efficiently and cost effectively did European financial markets allocate funds from savers to investors? Did poor performance in financial markets lead to less saving, to less investment, to misallocated investment?

These investigations of labor markets, product markets, and financial markets share a common concern with the causes of Europe's slower growth and higher unemployment. They seek to identify current barriers to faster growth and higher employment by asking why growth slowed and unemployment rose in the first place. The next three areas of investigation are concerned with various macroeconomic features of the European economies, partly because they have been blamed by some as the cause of Europe's slower growth but more importantly because even if they are not responsible, they may nevertheless be obstacles to better performance in the future.

Therefore the fourth area of investigation, *government budget and fiscal policies,* is taken up by Paul Courant. While Courant deals with the proposition that excessive levels of taxation and spending by European countries have dulled initiative and reduced investment and so been an important cause of sluggish growth, his principal concern is fiscal policy. In particular he investigates the issue of whether fiscal policy in any or all of the European countries is so constrained that it cannot be used as an expansionary measure, even granted the existence of room for some demand stimulus.

The next subject area is closely related, and in his paper on *national saving and investment* Charles Schultze considers three questions. What has happened over the past twenty years to national rates of saving and investment (public and private) and what has caused the changes? Are current rates of private investment sufficient, from a supply-side standpoint, to support a reasonable growth of economic potential in the major European countries? To what extent would an expansion of aggregate demand relative to potential GNP increase national saving and investment rates?

Finally, Richard Cooper investigates *potential constraints on growth from the balance of payments.* When any one European country expands relative to the others, its imports rise relative to exports. To the extent it cannot attract an inflow of foreign capital, the resulting current account deficit will depreciate its currency. How important is the balance-of-payments constraint? How necessary is it that any pan-European expansion be jointly coordinated among all individual European countries?

The European economy is vast, complex, and diverse. To investigate the economy of each country in detail would require a study of much greater scope than is feasible here. Accordingly, although they draw on the experience of other countries, these papers focus primarily on the three largest: France, Germany, and the United Kingdom. In addition, they consider Sweden to gain insight into a smaller country and one that does not belong to the European Community. And a few papers consider still other countries.

The pages that follow summarize and then attempt to integrate the findings of the authors. They present findings about specific problems, offer some policy recommendations, and necessarily leave some unresolved puzzles. In addition, as will gradually become evident, several very general themes emerge. First, the evidence and the analyses will not support the conclusion that any one of the four hypothesized elements is the dominant cause of Europe's slow growth and high unemployment. The sources of the problem are manifold, not monolithic, and involve both cyclical and structural elements. Second, some although by no means all of Europe's worsened economic performance—with respect to such indicators as productivity growth, unemployment, investment, and profitability—is not so much a sign of deeply rooted economic problems as the result of an inevitable return to normality from an earlier performance that was outstanding but unsustainable. Third, the evidence fails to support a number of specific factors that have been widely cited as responsible for Europe's slower growth. Fourth, the major structural sources of Europe's problems appear to be concentrated in its labor markets. The authors could not trace any substantial part of Europe's economic growth problems to inefficiencies in its financial markets, a lack of industrial flexibility, or a failure to be competitive.

Performance of Labor Markets

Classified very broadly there are four potential sources of the great increase and sustained high level of European unemployment: the Keynesian problem of deficient aggregate demand; the neoclassical problem of rigid wage aspirations that failed to adjust sufficiently to the supply shocks and reduced productivity growth of recent years; structural maladjustments in labor markets, including work disincentives from overly generous unemployment insurance systems, that interfered with the efficient allocation of labor supplies to labor demands; and the phenomenon of *hysteresis*—that as unemployment rose and remained high, it lost some or all of its capacity to moderate wage increases.[21]

UNEMPLOYMENT COMPENSATION. Two sets of observations have given rise to the belief that the relatively generous unemployment insurance systems of most European countries have created work disincentives that have caused rising unemployment. First, virtually all microeconomic studies of the subject have concluded that both the level of unemployment benefits relative to the wage of employed workers and the length of time benefits are available increase the average length of unemployment. Second, the United States, with a much less generous compensation system than is found in European countries, has suffered a much smaller rise in unemployment; and much of the difference in unemployment experience is due to the substantially shorter duration of unemployment in the United States.

Gary Burtless starts his assessment of unemployment compensation systems in Germany, France, the United Kingdom, and Sweden with an analytical description of their major characteristics. Because the systems differ significantly, he develops a set of comparable indexes along a limited number of dimensions. In brief, he finds that all the European systems are more generous than those in the United States along the two most important dimensions: the replacement ratio—the average ratio of benefits to prior wages—and the length of time benefits are available. He also finds that, measured by average expenditures per unemployed worker, the systems in Sweden and France have become more generous since the 1970s, the system in Germany less generous (after 1975), and that in the United Kingdom gradually more generous until the mid-1970s and slightly less so thereafter.

Burtless quickly disposes of the naive argument that the generosity and substantial growth of unemployment insurance in European countries relative to the United States explains the difference in unemployment behavior between the two. In the 1960s the unemployment rate in the United States was much higher than in Europe, while unemployment compensation was much less liberal. Europe's unemployment compensation systems were relatively generous long before its unemployment started to grow. Moreover, among European countries themselves there is no relationship between changes in the liberality of benefits and

21. *Hysteresis* is a technical term that, when applied to any economic variable—such as exports or unemployment—means that when the variable rises (falls), it will create conditions that tend to keep it high (low).

changes in unemployment. The system become more generous in the past ten to fifteen years both in France, where unemployment rose sharply, and in Sweden, where unemployment rose very little. The worst increase in joblessness has occurred in the United Kingdom, where the overall generosity of the compensation system has probably decreased since 1975.

A more sophisticated argument proposes that when major shocks from either the demand or supply side drive up unemployment, high levels of jobless pay reduce workers' incentives to adjust, lengthen the average duration of unemployment, and thus contribute to the overall rise in the unemployment rate. Burtless notes that almost without exception the published studies have found statistically significant relationships between the duration of unemployment and the level of benefits available. Burtless argues, however, that the effect of unemployment depends on the state of the labor market. In a tight labor market, where the number of vacancies is high relative to the number of unemployed, generous jobless benefits will indeed induce the unemployed to search longer, which will cause the average duration of both unemployment and vacancies to rise and the unemployment rate to increase. But in a relatively loose labor market, where vacancies are not so plentiful, any job turned down by an unemployed person getting benefits will be snapped up by someone without such benefits. The composition of the unemployed will change—more of them will be drawing benefits—but neither the average duration nor the overall rate of unemployment will be substantially affected. Ironically, making compensation more generous may increase unemployment when it is low but is not likely to add much to unemployment when it is at the levels it has been in Europe for some time now. Moreover, using data from Britain and the United States, Burtless shows that even if effects derived from microeconomic studies are applied to the overall duration of unemployment, the changes in the generosity of the British system relative to that in the United States would account for only a tiny fraction of the rise in U.K. unemployment relative to that in the United States in recent years.

Burtless concludes that liberal unemployment compensation may have slowed the reemployment of jobless workers in France, the United Kingdom, and Germany, but the effect is too minor to have constituted a significant contribution to increased unemployment in those countries.

STRUCTURAL PROBLEMS IN LABOR MARKETS. Robert Flanagan starts with the observation—based on a number of earlier studies, and supported in Charles Schultze's paper on wages in this volume—that the rise in European unemployment has been greater than can be explained either by low aggregate demand or by excessively high wage growth. Excluding, for the moment, the existence of hysteresis phenomena, this observation implies that for one reason or another structural problems in European labor markets interfere with the smooth balancing of labor demands and supplies.

Increased structural problems in European labor markets are directly evidenced by the fact that Beveridge curves have shifted upward. (The curve plots the inverse relationship between unemployment and unfilled job vacancies. In a tight labor market unemployment is low while unfilled vacancies are high; in a loose market the opposite is true.) An increase in unemployment due to deficient aggregate demand and an increase due to excessive real wages share the common characteristic that they lead to movements along a given Beveridge curve because employers have fewer jobs to offer while the number of workers without jobs increases. A rise in structural maladjustments, however, causes an upward shift of the curve. When adjustment is poor, large numbers of unemployed exist simultaneously with large numbers of unfilled jobs.

Flanagan marshalls evidence to show that many explanations offered to account for the growth of structural unemployment in Europe are either invalid or, if valid, not very important quantitatively. One proposed explanation, for example, asserts a growing mismatch between the skills and locations of unemployed workers and skill requirements and locations of potential new jobs. This mismatch could have arisen because the pace of industrial change increased while European labor market institutions adjusted inefficiently and sluggishly. Or it could be that European labor markets became more inefficient because of the spread of job protection laws or restrictive union agreements or the increasing rigidity and compression of relative wages.

Flanagan finds that the interindustry dispersion of employment growth rates (a measure of the pace of structural change) did rise in the 1960s and early 1970s but declined in the second half of the 1970s and, except for the United Kingdom, into the 1980s. On this measure, therefore, the pace of structural change slowed rather than quickened. Flanagan also finds that the growing ratio of vacancies to the number of unemployed in many European countries was spread among all industries and regions. Thus whatever the reason for the upward shift of the Beveridge curve,

Flanagan concludes structural failures of European labor markets did not stem from an accelerated pace of structural change, nor did they show up as a skewed mismatch between labor surpluses in certain declining industries and regions and excess labor demands in other industries and regions.[22]

Decreasing worker mobility in Europe is also often cited as responsible for structural maladjustments and higher unemployment. In turn this lack of mobility is sometimes attributed to the marked compression of relative wages, which presumably reduces the incentives for workers to change jobs. Flanagan finds that European mobility did decrease, but it also decreased substantially in Sweden and the United States, where, of course, unemployment behaved quite differently. Further, he presents evidence that the causation goes the other way—lower demand for labor and higher unemployment in Europe reduced workers' willingness to leave one job to try for another. An empirical analysis of mobility in France suggests that relative wage compression did decrease mobility but that most of the reduction was caused by the decline in labor demand. Flanagan also argues that the effect of European job protection laws may have been less to raise the level of unemployment than to concentrate its incidence among "outsiders"—young people, women, new entrants.

Thus Flanagan finds only limited evidence for barriers to growth on the supply side of labor markets. But he does observe some striking characteristics of the rise in unemployment that leads him to suggest an alternative explanation. He himself finds (or cites the work of other authors) that in France, Germany, and the United Kingdom, for any given vacancy rate, there has been a decline in the rate at which people leave unemployment but no increase in the rate at which people move into unemployment. That is, the upward shift in the Beveridge curve— higher unemployment at any given vacancy rate—is associated not with a greater propensity of workers to lose jobs but is accounted for by longer durations of unemployment and a smaller probability of finding a job for those who are unemployed.

Gary Burtless, as we saw, found no evidence that the longer duration of joblessness arose because more generous unemployment compensation made workers choosier about the jobs they were willing to take. That increased duration must therefore have arisen because firms became

22. While this story is widely correct in the 1970s, there did appear to be some growth in industrial, but not regional, mismatches between workers and jobs in 1981 and 1982 (when Flanagan's data ends).

choosier about hiring workers. Flanagan associates this increased unwillingness to hire with the growing compression of European intrafirm wage differentials. Employers want willing and qualified workers who will stay with the job. Turnover is costly, and stability of the work force improves productivity. Screening applicants to determine if they will stay with the firm and remain productive is costly, however, and even when done well is highly imperfect. Paying low wages to new workers but providing generous wage increments with seniority thus establishes a self-screening mechanism. By initially accepting low wages, workers in effect post a bond that they will stay with the firm and perform effectively. But Flanagan offers evidence that solidaristic wage policies—at least in Sweden, France, and Italy—have substantially reduced these intrafirm wage differentials. Moreover, while job protection measures, formal and informal, may not have played a large direct role in raising unemployment, they may have made it more difficult for employers to use trial-and-error methods of selecting employees. All of this, according to Flanagan, has effectively raised the cost of hiring and has made firms more reluctant to take on new workers. The result has been similar to an increase in labor costs, but an increase confined to new employees. At the margin, firms are reluctant both to hire new outside workers and to fire valued insiders. The consequence, says Flanagan, is an increase in the duration of unemployment, a concentration of unemployment among inexperienced outsiders,[23] and a reduced willingness on the part of firms to respond to changes in the market environment whenever those changes require a more rapid pace of new hiring and firing.

REAL WAGES AND REAL WAGE ASPIRATIONS. Perhaps the most widely held view about the cause of Europe's high unemployment is that it stems from excessively high and downwardly rigid real wages. They first got out of line in the late 1960s when, as already noted, there was a virtual explosion of European wages. The gap between real wages and what the economy could pay while still maintaining full employment got further out of line in the years that followed, when oil prices rose sharply and productivity growth fell, while the path of real wages did not adjust downward accordingly. Reacting to the excessive wages, firms reduced

23. In Germany, for example, Flanagan finds that, controlling for the vacancy rate, there has been a decline in the probability of men but not women being fired, while the declining probability that an unemployed person will find a job has been more heavily concentrated among women than men.

output and produced that output with more capital-intensive methods.[24] An extensively used measure of the extent of the real wage excess is the "wage gap," the cumulative excess of the growth of real product wages over the cyclically adjusted growth in productivity since some base period, usually the mid-1960s. An equivalent measure is the growth in labor's share of income (again, adjusted to remove the effects of cyclical changes in productivity).

Until recently most of the discussion about wage gaps centered on manufacturing. Using data from the Commission of the European Communities that allocates self-employment income between wages and return to capital, Charles Schultze calculates wage gaps for the total nonfarm business sector in the United States, the United Kingdom, Germany, France, and Italy. He finds that in Germany, Italy, and the United Kingdom positive wage gaps did appear in the 1970s but have subsequently disappeared (in the United States they have remained very low). In France and Italy, however, a wage gap emerged in the business sector as a whole in the 1970s. It subsequently diminished in both countries but remains at a substantial level in France. In the manufacturing sector, wage gaps opened up in all countries in the 1970s, but except in Germany, where the gap remains large, and to a lesser extent in the United States, the gaps have disappeared.[25]

More fundamentally, Schultze argues that observing the actual course of real wages will not be a useful guide to the role of excess wage aspirations in causing unemployment. In the context of the ongoing or expected rate of inflation, employers bargaining formally or informally with their employees set nominal wages presumably designed to produce some desired real wage. But these real wage aspirations are not the same

24. If firms' marginal cost curves slope upward and if in the long run prices are set equal to or proportional to marginal costs, then a rise in unemployment, whatever its cause, will ultimately be associated with a growth in real wages relative to what they would have been at full employment. Thus the effect on unemployment of a rise in the Beveridge curve could be offset by a sufficient decline in real wage aspirations. But we have reserved the term "excess real wages" to refer to the more limited hypothesis that real wage aspirations first rose autonomously in the late 1960s and then got further out of line when they failed to adjust downward to the falling productivity growth and the oil price increases of the 1970s.

25. Robert Gordon has also developed wage gap measures for the total economy aggregated across eleven European countries and finds that the real wage gap rises only very slightly between 1973 and 1975 and then declines almost continuously to a value, in 1984, well below the 1973 level. See Robert J. Gordon, "Productivity, Wages, and Prices Inside and Outside of Manufacturing in the U.S., Japan, and Europe"(Cambridge, Mass.: National Bureau of Economic Research, November 1986).

thing as real wage outcomes. If, for example, the rate of productivity growth falls and other supply shocks occur, while the growth of real wage aspirations does not moderate, inflation will begin to rise, and cannot be halted without a higher unemployment rate. The nonaccelerating inflation rate of unemployment (NAIRU) will have increased. Macroeconomic policy may initially tolerate escalating inflation but will not accept it in the long run: restrictive policies will eventually be introduced to halt the rise. Actual unemployment will then increase to meet the NAIRU, and—since the monetary authorities will probably want to reverse some of the initial rise in inflation—may rise above the NAIRU. In broad outline this is what happened in Europe during the 1970s and early 1980s. As Stephen Nickell points out in his comment on Gary Burtless's paper, if, in the short and medium run, employers set prices by applying a constant markup to standard unit costs, the path of real wages would adjust to the lower path of trend productivity growth. No real wage gap, as conventionally calculated, would be observed. Yet excess wage aspirations would have been the underlying cause of the rise in unemployment.

In the long run as well, real wage outcomes may not tell anything about whether real wage aspirations have been excessive. If the elasticity of substitution in the production function is less than one—and a number of studies suggest that in manufacturing, at least, it is—then in the normal course of economic development real wages will rise faster than trend productivity, even when there is full employment. Schultze also argues that adjustments in real exchange rates can alter the competitive environment and demand elasticity facing monopolistically competitive domestic firms, alter their markups over marginal costs, and thus change real wages without necessarily leading to a rise in unemployment.

WAGE DETERMINATION IN EUROPE AND THE UNITED STATES. Since real wage aspirations, and not ex post real wages, are the relevant exogenous variable that interacts with other economic variables and economic policy to determine employment, Schultze turns to an analysis of the determinants of wages. He develops and fits augmented Phillips curve equations for the total nonfarm business sectors in the United States, Germany, France, Italy, and the United Kingdom. These equations have the following special characteristics. First, the unemployment rate is not used to measure excess labor demand or supply. Since the Beveridge curves have shifted upward significantly in Europe and to a lesser extent in the United States, the level of unemployment associated with zero excess labor demand has risen, so that use of the unemployment rate to measure excess demand or supply will give misleading results. On grounds that the trend of output would tend to reflect long-term changes in NAIRU, Schultze uses the deviation of actual from trend output (the gap) as a measure of excess labor demand and supply.[26]

Second, Schultze posits that the upward path of workers' wage norms or aspirations, which employers take into account in setting wages, does not adjust quickly or automatically to changes in productivity growth or other supply considerations but that eventually it will. Wage norms may also shift exogenously, as appears to be the case during the wage explosion of the late 1960s. An increase in the pace at which wage norms are rising relative to productivity growth will accelerate inflation and set in motion the process described earlier. Schultze allows for changes in wage aspirations through shifts in the constant of his wage equations. He finds evidence that wage norms did shift upward in the four European countries at the end of the 1960s. After 1973 productivity growth declined, increasing still further the gap between wage aspirations and the capability of the European economies to meet those aspirations while simultaneously providing high employment. The NAIRU rose, as did unemployment and inflation. By the early 1980s, in response to restrictive macroeconomic policies, actual unemployment had risen above the NAIRU and inflation declined. Finally, in the early 1980s wage norms or aspirations did appear to be declining.

From these wage equations and estimates of the current trend level of productivity growth Schultze calculates the natural rates of output— the level of the gap at which inflation will not rise or accelerate above its current rate—and finds that in Germany, France, and Italy actual output was some 2 to 3 percent below the natural level in 1985. In the United Kingdom, however, the equations imply that output in 1985 was somewhat above the level at which inflation should begin rising.

Through Okun's law equations, which relate the level of the gap to the level of unemployment, estimates of the 1985 natural rate of output were translated into estimates of the NAIRU. These are given below for

26. From 1976 on, Schultze extends the previous trend of output with movements in the capital stock adjusted to take account of a long-term upward drift in the capital-output ratio. This is a very conservative measure of the gap. The growth of the capital stock has slowed sharply since the 1970s, and some of that slowdown may have reflected not only increases in the NAIRU but also a Keynesian deficiency of effective demand. To that extent the gap measure understates the degree of economic slack.

Germany, France, and Italy under both the standardized definition of unemployment used by the OECD and that used by the United States. (Italian actual unemployment, under the OECD definition, is for 1985.)

	OECD definition			U.S. definition (BLS)		
	Germany	France	Italy	Germany	France	Italy
NAIRU	6.5	9.2	9.9	6.0	9.5	5.7
Actual (1986)	8.3	10.3	10.5	7.6	10.7	6.2

From the wage equations Schultze also estimates how much of the rise in the NAIRU since the late 1960s is due to excess wage aspirations. These are measured as the algebraic sum of three components: the rise in aspirations in the late 1960s, plus the decline in the trend rate of productivity growth after 1983, less the decline in wage aspirations in the early 1980s. The results suggest that in the four European countries most of the net rise in the NAIRU between the late 1960s and the mid-1980s was not due to excess wage aspirations but either to hysteresis effects or to upward shifts in the Beveridge curve reflecting structural problems in labor markets.

In Germany and the United Kingdom, the two countries where the relevant data are available, regressions of the unemployment rate on the vacancy rate provide strong direct evidence for upward shifts in the Beveridge curve, shifts that were particularly large in the United Kingdom. Rising Beveridge curves in turn may reflect structural changes in labor markets. They may also reflect hysteresis to the extent that the phenomenon arises either from an obsolescence of the skills of unemployed workers or from the increasing concentration of unemployment among young or inexperienced outsiders.

If hysteresis phenomena are important, a rise in unemployment will only temporarily exert a moderating influence on wages. The standard statistical test for hysteresis, therefore, is to see whether a lagged unemployment term in a standard wage equation has a significant positive coefficient to offset the negative coefficient on current unemployment. Schultze finds that for Germany, Italy, and the United Kingdom there are indeed significant positive coefficients on lagged unemployment, ones almost as large as the initial coefficient. But he and his discussant Charles Bean argue that given the virtually monotonic rise in European unemployment over the past twelve to fifteen years, the positive coefficient on lagged unemployment may simply be reflecting the effect of a rising NAIRU. Under circumstances that have prevailed in Europe, it is impossible statistically to distinguish the two phenomena. Nevertheless, Schultze argues that on the weight of the evidence developed or cited by Flanagan, it is impossible to believe that the huge apparent upward shift of the Beveridge curve in the United Kingdom could have stemmed solely from structural changes in the demand for labor among regions, industries, or occupations. In a much weaker way the same can be said of the other three countries. By elimination, therefore, hysteresis may be playing a role in sustaining employment at high levels in the United Kingdom, and, with less certainty, in other European countries.

Product Markets and Trade Performance

Pessimism about Europe's international trade performance has become widespread. Trade is seen not only as a major constraint on expansion but also as the source of deindustrialization. Robert Lawrence questions some of these views. Using a system of trade equations to determine the foreign and domestic growth rates compatible with balanced trade at unchanged terms of trade, he finds that Sweden, France and Germany can keep trade balanced while matching 3 percent GNP growth rates in the rest of the OECD. Without an increase in its oil exports, however, the United Kingdom will be able to grow at no more than half that rate.

Lawrence also finds that real devaluations are usually effective in improving trade balances, but his estimates of import and export price elasticities tend to be low. Devaluation is thus no panacea. European countries are so open that even if trade flows are fairly price elastic, the terms-of-trade costs of output growth more rapid than the rest of OECD could be considerable. Each 1 percent rise in British GDP for example, increases imports by 2 percent. Thus even if British exports and imports both had unitary price elasticities, the change in the terms of trade needed to keep trade balanced in the face of a 1 percent rise in growth above the warranted rate would reduce real income by 0.5 percent. In the short run, individual European countries may borrow readily, but over the medium term they will only be able to deviate from the growth rates of their trading partners by undergoing considerable changes in their terms of trade. The external linkages will keep most European countries growing at similar rates.

Lawrence uses his equation system to account for the trade performance of his four sample countries. He argues that the rise in oil prices rather than a fundamental deterioration in manufacturing competitiveness (see the remarks by Armin Gutowski) was primarily responsible for the German current account deficit in 1979 and 1980. He also finds that in 1986, starting from a very large trade surplus, Germany had room to grow more rapidly than its trading partners without reducing its current account surplus below its historic average.

The real depreciation experienced by Sweden since the mid-1970s was required not to offset an erosion in manufacturing performance but to compensate for the service costs of increased international indebtedness and higher oil import bills. In the absence of such shocks in the future, Sweden should be able to grow at its long-run potential rate without shifting its terms of trade.

Despite French alarm in the early 1980s about the need to reconquer its domestic market, Lawrence finds that higher oil prices were the major source of the deteriorating French trade balance. His analysis, however, does point to problems in French export behavior after 1980. In particular, manufactured goods exports have performed poorly despite real devaluations, increased profit margins, and excess capacity.

The external performance of the United Kingdom has been poor throughout the period. In the absence of its oil bonanza the United Kingdom would require considerable real depreciation if it were to match the growth rate of its trading partners. Moreover, manufacturing competitiveness has been severely eroded over the past fifteen years in a manner that cannot be neatly explained by its price competitiveness.

Lawrence's paper calls into question the argument that the peculiar nature of the structural changes after 1973 damaged European competitiveness and adversely affected growth. It has been alleged that in several European countries supply and demand became increasingly mismatched, which would presumably have increased marginal import propensities. But in his tests on Germany and France, Lawrence finds no change in the response of imports to domestic demand growth, either before or after 1974. Nor have exports seemed to respond differently to global demand. He does, however, find a small increase in import propensities in the United Kingdom.

Europeans have attributed the declining share of manufacturing employment to poor trade performance. Lawrence emphasizes that, particularly since 1980 but with the notable exception of the United Kingdom, trade has actually exerted a positive influence on the share of the industrial sector. Weak domestic demand associated with slow overall growth and particularly poor investment has been the major reason for the fall in manufacturing employment. Lawrence also finds that patterns of domestic use rather than trade performance (that is, competition with developing countries) are the dominant reason for the shrinkage in low-technology industries. The restoration of demand rather than increased competitiveness is the key to sustaining manufacturing growth.

It is difficult to confirm arguments linking poor European trade performance with the extent of structural change or the mix of products produced or traded. The structure of European employment and industry changed as much in the decade before 1973 as it did in the decade following. The composition of production is remarkably similar between major European economies and those of the United States and Japan. And the trade structure of the United Kingdom resembles that of Germany and the United States. The degree of structural change is not clearly related to performance. While the product structure of Japanese manufacturing changed the most, the second largest shifts took place in the United Kingdom. Germany achieved its strong trade performance despite the smallest structural shifts in industry. The data also fail to demonstrate a clear association between rates of new business formation and industrial growth and trade performance. The United Kingdom has the highest rates of firms entering the marketplace.

Lawrence notes that France, the European country with the most distinctive industrial policies, actually has the least distinctive trade structure. The industrial composition of its manufactured exports is highly correlated with the composition of its imports. He also argues that shifts in François Mitterrand's industrial policies have either been caused by or resulted in a marked deterioration in French manufacturing export performance.

Lawrence questions the notion that improvements in high-technology competitiveness are essential if trade performance is not to constrain European growth. He notes that in Sweden and France high-technology exports actually increased more rapidly than imports between 1970 and 1983. Although the growth of German high-technology imports has exceeded exports, Germany retained a considerable surplus in such trade in 1983. A continuation of these trends, Lawrence demonstrates, is unlikely to pose a serious threat to German trade performance in the medium term.

Performance of Financial Markets

The inadequate nature of European financial institutions has been perceived as a structural problem limiting European growth. The focus in Robert Aliber's paper is to determine whether the sluggishness of business investment in Europe is better explained by the high cost of capital to European firms or by the low level of anticipated profitability of investment in Europe. Aliber presents evidence that the performance of European financial markets has not been an important reason for sluggish growth. While the shortcomings of European financial market arrangements may have raised interest rates, these effects have been overshadowed by the complication of higher levels of saving and the lower levels of anticipated profitability on new European investment. Using data on direct foreign investment by American and European firms, Aliber argues that those headquartered in Western Europe have a cost-of-capital advantage over American firms. These firms could have invested more domestically if the domestic market had appeared more profitable, but they did not do so despite their cost-of-capital advantage.

Aliber's paper systematically analyzes the determinants of the cost of capital. Savings rates have been higher in Europe than in the United States, and real interest rates on government securities in Europe have been lower. Potentially, the costs of financial intermediation could offset these lower real rates in the cost of capital to corporate borrowers: limited competition between banks and the failure to fully realize economies of scale because of the national segmentation of markets could increase the difference between the returns obtained by investors and the costs paid by borrowers. In addition, the illiquidity of European markets and limited information about borrowers could induce investors to demand a large spread between the interest rates charged nongovernmental borrowers and those charged governmental borrowers.

In exploring these possibilities Aliber notes that European and American banks pay investors similar rates when they compete in Eurocurrency and bond markets. He also points out that since large borrowers and large investors can choose between offshore and domestic markets, the wedges between interest rates paid and interest rates received by these borrowers and investors in domestic markets cannot differ substantially from those in offshore markets. Similarly, competition keeps the costs of raising money from banks and from markets closely linked for large borrowers. The coexistence of these sources of funds implies that for large participants unhindered by capital controls competition limits the room for large differences among countries in the size of intermediate wedges. Aliber cautions that smaller borrowers and investors may have greater difficulty using offshore markets and could face larger wedges. Indeed, transaction costs of buying securities differ across national markets for small investors. But Aliber finds that these are not large enough to offset the advantage of lower European real interest rates.

Aliber's explicit examination does not indicate that the costs of intermediation of bank finance (the ratios of operating costs to assets) are higher in Europe than the United States. His data on the ratio of equity prices to book value suggest lower costs of capital in Germany than in the United States, while in other European countries, with the exception of the Netherlands, equity capital costs seem similar to those in the United States.

Investor expectations of the higher profitability of investments in the United States have been borne out. Aliber finds that by 1985 manufacturing rates of return in the United States were considerably higher than they were in Western Europe.

Performance of Budget and Fiscal Policy

At the risk of ignoring some important differences of timing and emphasis, one can say that the various European governments have exhibited a common pattern of fiscal policy. During the 1970s and the early 1980s government expenditures as a share of GDP rose substantially. In the past few years that trend has been halted and, in some countries at least, marginally reversed. Until 1979 or 1980 revenues did not keep pace; deficits in most countries became quite large. Since then, in virtually all countries fiscal policy has become restrictive; budget deficits have been reduced and, after cyclical adjustments, many countries have achieved a structural budget surplus. From the standpoint of fiscal policy the swing toward restrictive practices has been both pervasive and substantial and has been pursued in the face of rapidly mounting unemployment. As of the middle of 1987 there is little sign that any European government will relax these policies.

Paul Courant's chapter on budget and fiscal policy analyzes these trends for Germany, France, Sweden, and the United Kingdom, and then frames one central question: given some economic slack in these countries (with the possible exception of Sweden) and considering that they have made marked progress in consolidating their budget deficits, why are the governments unwilling to relax fiscal policy as a means of generating additional growth in aggregate demand?

Courant considers several reasons. The first is the problem of "solvency." The governments of Western Europe do not have to worry about solvency in the sense of being unable to pay their bills, but they do have to assume they cannot pursue policies that lead to an indefinitely continuing rise in the ratio of government debt to GNP. Hence if the continuation of current budget policies implies a rising ratio of government debt to GNP, taxes will eventually have to be raised or expenditures reduced to ensure solvency. Governments whose budgets are at or near the margin where solvency, so defined, is in doubt will naturally be reluctant to relax fiscal policy to stimulate their economies, since the relaxation cannot be sustained and will eventually require tax increases.

Because interest on the public debt is a component of budget expenditures, the higher the interest rates and the higher the ratio of debt to GNP, the larger the surplus of revenues will have to be to ensure solvency. The lower the expected growth rate of GNP, the smaller the tolerable growth of debt, and the larger the revenue requirement for solvency. But Courant's examination of the current budget positions of Germany, France, Sweden, and the United Kingdom finds that, even when conservative assumptions about interest rates and growth rates are used, the problems of solvency are not a constraint on expansionary fiscal policy.[27]

A second and more serious constraint on relaxing fiscal policy is the problem of long-run "crowding out." National saving as a share of GDP fell substantially over the past two decades in all four countries. Some of the decline is cyclical, but even when corrections are made, the decline remains significant. Most of it can be accounted for by a fall in government saving as budget surpluses turned into deficits while investment outlays declined. In the United Kingdom during the early 1970s and in Sweden from 1978 to 1982, foreign borrowing made it possible to

---

27. There is a dark spot in this rosy picture. In Germany, and to a lesser extent in France and the United Kingdom, the effect of demographic changes on the social security systems will generate increases in the ratios of government debt to GNP over the next twenty-five years, assuming no changes in the budget policy. And in the United Kingdom, North Sea oil revenues will eventually run out. But, Courant argues, the necessary corrections in future budgets—because of the higher debt-GNP ratio—will not have to be significant.

sustain domestic investment temporarily in the face of a decline in national saving. But over the period as a whole declining government saving led to lower domestic investment.

On the basis of this analysis Courant concludes that even though some demand stimulus may be warranted—again, Sweden aside—a permanent increase in the fiscal deficit would lower even further the already low levels of domestic investment. Would a temporary fiscal stimulus then be effective, and if effective, would it be useful? Courant argues that just as fiscal stringency in recent years reduced output, fiscal expansion could be expected to raise it. But would the effects of temporary stimulus disappear once it was withdrawn? Would the economy be left no better off in the long run and with a higher level of government debt? Courant suggests that the answers depend on the extent to which hysteresis is present.

If hysteresis is at work, high unemployment would tend to perpetuate itself by creating conditions in the labor market that are unfavorable for economic expansion. By the same token, however, an initial increase in demand, with its attendant fall in unemployment, could create the more favorable labor market conditions that would make it possible for unemployment to stay lower. According to Courant, the state of economic knowledge is not sufficient to determine whether a temporary fiscal stimulus could set in motion this benign chain of events and produce a permanent improvement in the economy. But if the judgment were made that labor market hysteresis does indeed describe a real phenomenon, that would greatly strengthen the case in favor of expansive fiscal action.

Courant also points out that government investment has plummeted. To the extent that public investment opportunities with decent rates of return are available, a temporary stimulus concentrated in such expenditures would match the resultant increase in government spending with an increase in productive assets, so that even if the fiscal effects of such a stimulus did wear off, national wealth would have been permanently increased with the use of national resources that would otherwise have lain idle.

Turning from fiscal policy, Courant examines the effects on investment of taxing capital income in the four countries. While the effective tax rates on capital income are substantial in each, they have not risen in the past several decades and in some countries have declined. It is difficult, therefore, to blame taxes for the fall in domestic investment.

Moreover, empirical studies suggest that tax policy is not very effective at inducing investment.

Courant does note, however, that in each country capital income is taxed differently, depending on the type of asset, the kind of owner, and the means of financing. These differences are enormous and introduce substantial distortions into the economic structure. Although recent literature suggests that the measurable improvement in national output from eliminating these distortions may not be huge, Courant argues that in this situation the direction of the effect is unambiguous. Tax reforms aimed at reducing these distortions would clearly make the economies of Europe more efficient and responsive to consumer preferences.

Saving and Investment

In his second paper Charles Schultze looks further at the decline in national rates of saving and investment examined by Courant. Covering Germany, France, Italy, and the United Kingdom, Schultze suggests that the fall in investment as a share of GNP since the 1960s is not the result of a crowding-out process, whereby declining national saving drove up interest rates and thereby discouraged investment, but rather proceeded independently of the fall in saving and indeed may have caused it.

According to Schultze, the 1950s and 1960s were a period of disequilibrium and catch-up. The best available technology was far ahead of what was incorporated in Europe's capital plant, although management and workers were perfectly capable of operating on the frontier of innovation. The profits to be earned from investing in this new technology were large relative to the cost of capital, and this induced a heavy volume of investment. But as the capital stock grew rapidly, the output-capital ratio fell, and profitability gradually declined. For the business sector as a whole, in France and Italy the fall in profitability was exacerbated by declining profit margins. But in other countries, decreasing profitability was chiefly associated with a deterioration in the output-capital ratio. As profitability declined so did investment. And, after 1980, the accelerator effects of the sharp reduction in output growth came to play an important role. As one side effect of the steadily falling output-capital ratios that characterized most European countries over the past several decades, a higher investment share of GDP is now required to produce any given rate of growth in the capital stock.

It is quite probable that the fall in investment demand during the 1970s, as it weakened the growth in aggregate demand, called forth from governments a more relaxed fiscal policy, which was principally responsible for the decline in national saving. For Germany, France, Italy, and the United Kingdom, Schultze estimates the private business investment that would be required, from a supply-side standpoint, to provide a growth of economic potential large enough to absorb the projected growth in the labor force and to generate productivity gains roughly in line with the current trend. He finds that the current level of investment in all four countries is below the "required" level, but not by a large amount.

Schultze calculates that if in the next several years France and Germany grew about 1 percent faster than their long-term potential and Italy about 0.75 percent faster—which would be possible without inflationary pressures if calculations of the NAIRUs in Schultze's paper on real wages are roughly correct—the resulting improvement in profitability and the accelerator effect of reducing the gap would increase investment demand enough to make the growth of the business capital stock roughly consistent, on the supply side, with the estimated growth of potential business GDP.

Schultze also finds that the cyclical sensitivity of national saving, principally through cyclical variations in the budget deficit, is substantial. He estimates that a catch-up increase in output of the magnitude suggested earlier would raise the national saving rate in Germany and France by roughly enough to match the increase in required investment. Partly because of the modest size of the catch-up allowed for Italy in the above scenario, its saving rate would still remain a little below the required level.

Finally, Schultze points out that the German current account surplus will shrink in the next several years. The surplus was 4 percent of GDP in 1986; if it levels off at 1.5 percent of GDP, that, together with a catch-up, would provide room both for the needed expansion of domestic investment and for a deficit-raising fiscal stimulus.

Constraints on Growth from Balance of Payments

The consequences of expansionary demand policies for balance of payments have been said to represent a major constraint on stimulative aggregate demand policies in economies as open as those in Europe.

Richard Cooper challenges this view. He argues that now, in contrast to the immediate postwar period when exchange rates were fixed and international borrowing capacities limited, the external constraint is unimportant. European economies now enjoy widespread opportunities for international borrowing. In addition, they have greater flexibility to adjust their exchange rates.

Cooper presents six case studies in which severe external constraints allegedly limited growth. In late 1976 the United Kingdom arranged a loan and an adjustment program from the International Monetary Fund. This arrangement did not, Cooper argues, result from a fundamental impairment of Britain's creditworthiness, but was actually used by Chancellor Denis Healey to generate external support and pressure for a policy that was controversial domestically. Nor were the problems experienced by Italy, when it borrowed from the IMF in 1977, related to a failure in its economic policies. Instead, capital outflows were driven by the political crisis associated with the increasing popularity of the Communist party. In addition, like Britain, Italy found it helpful to use the disciplinary pressure of the IMF in implementing such domestic policies as the reform of methods for adjusting wages to inflation, which were highly controversial.

Despite weakness in the German economy, in early 1981 the Bundesbank tightened monetary policy in response to a perceived critical deterioration in the balance of payments. But Cooper finds that these measures were self-imposed rather than compelled by an externally imposed constraint on German policy. Germany was quite able to finance its current account deficit by private foreign borrowing—indeed capital inflows responded promptly to increased German interest rates. But German concerns about rising public debt and the desire to be a net exporter of capital induced policies to lower fiscal and current account deficits.

The speculative run on the French franc in 1983 prompted the Mitterrand government to accompany currency devaluation with fiscal austerity and official restraints on wages and prices. Cooper points out that the government's nationalization policies had caused unusually large amounts of capital flight. Nonetheless, he notes that in 1983 commercial banks remained eager to lend to France. He argues, therefore, that French policy was dictated by domestic constraints—an economy actually close to full employment; the desire to remain in the European monetary system; and a concern about the conditions associated with the buildup in foreign debt.

Cooper cites the success of Swedish devaluation policies in the early 1980s as an example of the ability of a small open European economy (that is willing to absorb the inflation and tolerate a deterioration in its terms of trade) to use improved competitiveness to expand in the face of sluggish global demand. He concludes from his case studies that unlike developing countries, European countries were in no case denied access to external credit. Instead, domestic policymakers' desires to change economic strategies were the principal reason for policy choices. Cooper also cites evidence indicating considerable autonomy in setting interest rates exists in major European economies, although he cautions that interest and exchange rates may not be adjusted independently.

Any European country that wants to expand can do so, he concludes. If it runs a current account deficit by expanding, it can permit its currency to depreciate to eliminate the deficit. Alternatively, by an appropriate policy mix—for example, expanding fiscal policy and tightening monetary policy—it can increase activity without currency depreciation because the higher interest rates associated with such a mix will induce sufficient external borrowing to cover the current account deficit. Openness in an economy thus creates new opportunities as well as imposing new constraints. Real currency depreciation is a means of stimulating domestic output and employment not available in a closed economy; appreciation is an additional tool for reducing inflation; and the ability to borrow abroad permits a divergence between spending and production decisions. Cooper cautions, however, that not all countries can exercise such options simultaneously.

While arguing that European economies can act independently, Cooper also points to the benefits of coordinated actions. Expanding together with trading partners will result in smaller current account deficits than expanding alone. This reduces the need for foreign borrowing or depreciation. In most European economies fiscal expansion, even when accompanied by accommodating monetary policy, will not be very effective under fixed exchange rates. Simulation exercises indicate that much of the impact leaks abroad. Fiscal multipliers can, however, be increased through collective action.

Cooper cautions, though, that coordinated action is difficult to implement. Small countries often find it comfortable to await actions from their larger trading partners, and most countries seem to prefer export-led rather than domestically generated growth. Moreover, collective error could be more damaging than independent and partly offsetting national actions.

Additional Reflections on Market Rigidities

Reflection on the papers and comments in this volume, especially those dealing with the labor market, suggests several additional lines of thought about the sources of European unemployment. The first has to do with the possibility of hysteresis-like phenomena in the Beveridge curve. The second involves the possibility that some of the recent declines in real wages relative to productivity may, paradoxically, reflect a worsening of the aggregate supply curve.

HYSTERESIS IN THE BEVERIDGE CURVE? There is one important development that, in varying degrees, characterizes the labor markets of all the large European countries. It is recognized recurrently in Robert Flanagan's paper and in other sources, and it contrasts strongly with labor market developments in the United States. European workers simply move less frequently among firms and into and out of unemployment than was formerly the case and than is now the case in the United States. As Flanagan notes, any lessening of demand for labor, even if unaccompanied by increased labor market rigidities, will tend to reduce mobility. When vacancies are few, workers are less likely to quit to look for a better job. Fewer jobs to be filled means less hiring as well as fewer separations. But in Europe labor mobility appears to have decreased even after the decline in labor demand is taken into account. Flanagan presents evidence for this in the case of France. He also shows that, after controlling for vacancies, the flow out of unemployment into employment in Germany has decreased. Firms are reluctant to hire because hiring has become more costly and because firing has become more difficult. Thus even though vacancy rates are low—reflecting the lack of demand for labor—they are still significantly higher relative to unemployment than earlier relationships would have suggested. And while employers find the various job protection laws costly, they are, says Flanagan, anxious to hold onto their increasingly valued insiders. Germany, Italy, and the United Kingdom have thus experienced sizable declines in both the rate of hiring and the rate of separations, in contrast to the United States, where both increased even as unemployment drifted upward.[28] John Martin, in his comment on Flanagan, presents data showing that the proportion of jobs held for less than two years has fallen, while the proportion held for ten years or more has risen. In 1982,

---

28. *OECD Economic Outlook*, no. 36 (December 1984), pp. 56–57.

when the overall unemployment rate in the United States was higher than in Europe, only 17 percent of the unemployed in the United States had been out of work for a year or more, compared with 45 to 65 percent in Germany, France, and the United Kingdom.

These developments reflect a European labor market that has become increasingly rigid and is characterized by institutional devices and other forces that seek to lock insiders into current jobs and protect their wages while freezing out new entrants and those who have lost their jobs. But these developments may themselves be the products of a long period of slow growth and high unemployment. When unemployment continues to rise and employment falls or stagnates for a long time, the resulting environment breeds protective responses among workers and in the political arena that yield the phenomena noted.

High unemployment may feed on itself in another way. Changes in the international competitive environment and in technology continue throughout a period of high unemployment. The economy does gradually adjust, but it adjusts to the mix of output and employment that goes with slow growth and declining employment, not to the mix that would accompany higher growth and full employment. As a consequence, the longer unemployment lasts and the smaller the turnover rate among the unemployed, the wider the gap between the skills and locations of the unemployed and the potential requirements of a high-employment economy. The actual mismatch may be modest, but the potential mismatch can be much larger. When vacancies do begin to rise, the economy moves along a more unfavorable Beveridge curve. And, of course, a similar sequence of events produces an aggregate level and a composition of industrial capacity inadequate to a high-employment economy. The latter problem can be overcome by vigorous investment, but it limits the pace of any recovery.

Thus in the sense that a long period of rising unemployment itself begins to produce rigidities and imbalances in labor markets, there exists another kind of hysteresis—a hysteresis of the Beveridge curve.

THE MEANING OF RECENT REAL WAGE MODERATION: A PESSIMISTIC HYPOTHESIS. According to Flanagan, the combination of compression in pay scales within firms and institutional and legal constraints on layoffs raises the cost of both hiring and firing. And as Jacques Drèze points out in his comments on Paul Krugman's paper, the more such costs increase, the more hiring decisions become akin to long-term investment decisions: uncertainty about future demand and labor costs increases the risk premium on expansion. In Drèze's words, "It is precisely because anticipation regarding demand and labor cost remains guarded and uncertain that European firms today are investment shy and hiring shy."

In analytical terms the consequences of the increase in the fixed costs of hiring workers and increased uncertainty is not merely to raise the cost of labor but to steepen the slope of the aggregate supply curve. Because of their greater reluctance to take on added inputs, firms meet an increase in aggregate demand less with a rise in output and more with an increase in markups. Charles Schultze's wage equations suggest that, in the short and medium run at least, the rise in prices is not fully captured by higher wage demands in the next round. Thus, ex post, real wages fall relative to productivity. But the moderation does not generate more employment. If this is true, greater rigidity in the labor market can combine with an increase in uncertainty about the future to reduce the output and employment gains that could be achieved without renewing inflationary pressures.

DOES AUSTERITY BREED FLEXIBILITY? With perhaps a few exceptions neither the papers in this volume nor other research studies suggest that the long period of restrictive macroeconomic policies, slow growth, and high unemployment in Europe has resulted in substantial progress toward more flexible labor markets in Europe. Some of the macroeconomic evidence on mobility and job turnover is a few years out of date, but as far as it goes none implies movement toward more mobility. When we were able to formulate Beveridge curves, none showed any evidence of shifting down. With respect to government actions toward liberalizing the economy there have been more promises than results. For the EC as a whole, government spending as a share of GNP has continued to rise: in 1985 it was 6 percentage points higher than in 1980. And as the 1987 OECD economic survey of Germany diplomatically put it, "So far, Government action in the field of deregulation has been modest. . . ."[29] In an environment of high unemployment and stagnant employment opportunities, it is hardly surprising that governments consider the immediate and tangible costs of economic liberalization in terms of greater job insecurity as outweighing their longer-term and intangible benefits, however much larger those benefits are.

The Schultze wage equations show some evidence of a downward shift in wage aspirations that may have been produced by the sustained

29. *OECD Economic Surveys, 1986–87: Germany* (Paris: OECD, 1987), p. 58.

period of high unemployment. But insofar as rigidities in the labor market are concerned, while we are not confident of our ability to assign causality and are even less confident about prescribing specific cures, we think it demonstrable that a strategy of slow growth and sustained austerity has not reduced them.

A Summary of Conclusions

The papers in this volume, we believe, help narrow the choices among explanations for Europe's unemployment problems and among policy recommendations to deal with them. First, the contributors have presented evidence that heavily discounts the importance of some explanations given for Europe's problems. Whatever the difficulties caused by the large size and growth of European welfare states, we could not find evidence that their generous unemployment compensation schemes were a major cause of the rise in unemployment. Similarly, while Paul Courant argues strongly in favor of reforming the taxation of capital income, he does not find that current European tax systems have played a significant role in the reduction of European investment that has occurred over the past twenty years. The evidence brought to bear directly and by citation in the papers by Robert Flanagan and Robert Lawrence does not support the view that Europe was confronted with an increased pace of change in the structure of the labor demand or in its international competitive environment. Paul Krugman rejects the argument that automation and trade with developing countries have caused rising unemployment. Robert Aliber finds that Europe was not penalized during the period by relatively high real interest rates or inefficient and costly financial markets. Paul Courant concludes that the reluctance of European governments to adopt more expansionary fiscal policies cannot be rationalized on grounds of endangering solvency. And finally, Richard Cooper argues that any one government could, if it wished, expand domestic demand and find the means of financing the accompanying trade deficit without a serious deterioration in its exchange rate. (Lawrence points out, however, that while this may be true in the short run, it is not in the long run.)

Not only can certain explanations be discounted but the relative importance of others can be roughly assessed. In Germany, France, and Italy the actual unemployment rate is now above the NAIRU—there is

room to expand aggregate demand without running into serious inflationary problems. But the Keynesian component of the unemployment
problem is not very large. And in the United Kingdom, however, we
could find no evidence that wage inflation has recently been behaving in
a way that would indicate a natural rate of unemployment below the
actual rate. In Germany, France, Italy, and the United Kingdom the
component of unemployment due to the explosion of real wage aspirations in the late 1960s and the subsequent failure of aspirations to adjust
fully downward as productivity growth slackened in the 1970s is no
longer large.

Most of the rise in unemployment stems, we believe, from two sources
with unknown relative importance: hysteresis effects in the determination of wages (especially in the United Kingdom but possibly in other
countries) and increasing structural rigidities in European labor markets,
characterized by a reduction of labor force flows among firms, industries,
and regions and into and out of unemployment. Decreased mobility was
reflected in a rising Beveridge curve, which might itself be partly
hysteretic in nature. That is, Europe's sustained experience with high
and rising unemployment may have led to protective mechanisms and
rigidities that helped perpetuate the unemployment.

That we do not ascribe an important part of Europe's current unemployment to a continuing failure of real wage aspirations to adjust
downward in the face of the supply shocks of the 1970s does not imply
that real wage moderation is unimportant. Even if rigidities and immo-
bilities in the labor market persist, reductions in real wage aspirations
relative to productivity growth can help offset the consequences of those
rigidities and make possible higher employment. Moreover, to the extent
that real wages fail to moderate further, or do so sluggishly, removing
impediments to rapid adjustment in product markets could help raise
employment by increasing efficiency and productivity, thereby raising
the warranted real wage.

While moderation in real wage aspirations is important, it must be
accompanied by appropriately expansive economic policies to be effective. Sometimes the arguments in favor of real wage moderation seem
to suggest that the principal gain will be to induce the use of more labor-
intensive means of production, thus generating additional employment
without any increase in output. In fact, the room for expanding employment, with constant output, through a change in the ratio of wages to

capital costs is likely to be limited.[30] A large employment increase will require a large output increase. The major advantage from lower real wage aspirations is not principally that they would induce more labor-intensive means of production but that they would increase the rate at which aggregate demand and output could expand without inflationary consequences. Wage moderation will permit but does not itself generate that expansion. For that, complementary macroeconomic policies of expansion are required.

Strategies for the Future

One possible strategy for dealing with unemployment can be rejected out of hand. That would be to accept today's high unemployment and current rigidities in the labor market as inevitable and to search for the best ways of living with the situation—through sharing jobs, for example. For reasons given below this approach is not only premature but potentially dangerous.

On the basis of the conclusions the contributors to this volume have reached and the judgments made earlier, we urge a two-pronged strategy. First, structural reform in both labor and product markets must be a central component of any programs to reduce unemployment. Neither our authors nor we have developed a list of targets for legislative and institutional reform. But they are numerous. There are institutional barriers to greater wage flexibility and mobility such as the legal arrangements in Germany by which union agreements can be made mandatory on nonunion firms and workers. And although Robert Flanagan argues that the impact of European job protection laws on employment has been exaggerated, they do exist and they do raise the cost and the risks of hiring. Easing the burden of these laws is a bit like tax reform—attempts to measure the quantitative result often suggest the magnitudes are small, but they are unambiguously in the right direction.

---

30. On the standard Cobb-Douglas and competitive pricing assumptions (with the capital-income share labeled α,) the real wage elasticity of employment, assuming output is allowed to vary while the stock of capital remains fixed, is $1/\alpha$. With a typical value for α of 0.30, the elasticity is 3.3. But if output is fixed and capital is allowed to vary, the elasticity is not $1/\alpha$ but α, which is only one-eleventh as great. See James Tobin, "Comment," and Martin Neil Baily's comments in "General Discussion" of Robert M. Coen and Bert G. Hickman, "Keynesian and Classical Unemployment in Four Countries," *BPEA, 1:1987*, pp. 198–205, 206.

Removal of barriers to the flow of goods, services, people, and ideas within and among European countries could indirectly alleviate unemployment by raising the warranted real wage and inducing more investment.[31] And since competitive forces can be brought to bear by movements in goods and services as well as by movements in factors of production, the liberalization of inter-European trade, especially in services, would be an indirect means for unemployed outsiders to exert pressure on the insider labor market. As for specific decisions needed to meet the target for a "boundary-free" common market by 1992, removing the barriers to a free flow of services within Europe, dismantling the formal and informal barriers to trade that have grown up in specific industries such as textiles, automobiles, and semiconductors, and opening up public procurement to international competition represent some of the steps that should be taken.[32] On the domestic front, continuing the recent progress in reducing industrial subsidies and pursuing meaningful deregulation, especially in transportation, communications, and finance, would—as in the United States—not only improve efficiency but increase wage flexibility in a number of key industries.

Tax reform, especially to reduce distortions in the tax treatment of different kinds of investment and to reduce marginal effective tax rates on investment income, while producing no bonanza, would also improve efficiency and again indirectly help employment by raising the warranted real wage. Most important, the kinds of reform needed involve process—improving the efficiency and speed with which resource flows adjust to changes in the economic environment. What should be avoided are government attempts to impose through subsidies, regulation, or investments in national champions a specific set of outcomes and a specific industrial structure.

Second, the structural reforms should be coupled with the introduction of more expansive macroeconomic policies designed to raise the growth of GDP for several years significantly above the growth of long-term potential. The bulk of recent research, including the relevant parts of this study, conclude that there is some economic slack in most European

31. For a catalog of the barriers that still exist within Europe, see Commission of the European Communities, "Completing the Internal Market."

32. General government purchases of goods and services amounted to 9 percent of European (EC) GDP in 1985. Commission of the European Communities, "Annual Economic Report, 1986–1987," communication from the Commission to the European Council (Brussels, October 1986), p. 127.

countries. Some of the current unemployment would effectively be absorbed by a higher level of aggregate demand without substantial inflationary consequences.

If our argument for more expansive policy rested solely on this ground, however, we would have little to say to European policymakers that they have not heard—and ignored—many times before. The case for a carefully administered dose of expansion rests on two additional grounds. First, we think the balance of the evidence favors the proposition that sustained high unemployment loses some of its force to moderate real wage aspirations—the corollary of which is that an expansion in aggregate demand will have more unemployment-lowering and less inflation-raising consequences than predicted by the standard analysis. Even more important, perhaps, we are convinced that structural improvements in labor markets are much more likely to occur when an economy is expanding than in the current environment of highly restrictive policy and slow growth. However necessary the recent restrictive policies may have been to reduce inflation and to moderate real wage aspirations, there is little evidence they have improved the flexibility and adaptability of the European economies. Indeed, our discussion of the possible hysteretic component to labor market rigidities suggests that slow growth may have made matters worse.

European unemployment has lost some of its force to moderate wages, and it may be exacerbating labor market rigidities. To some extent high unemployment creates the conditions for its own perpetuation. If so, an initial successful effort to lower unemployment could pay multiple dividends and help turn a vicious circle into a virtuous one through its effect in improving the structural characteristics of Europe's labor markets.

The argument that hysteretic components have contributed significantly to unemployment is admittedly speculative. Several participants in this study offered reasons why, in the context of monotonically rising unemployment, hysteresis in wage determination could not be demonstrated from time series data. And our argument for the existence of a hysteretic component to labor market immobility has been inferred from bits and pieces of evidence. But the existence of some Keynesian slack—even if modest—provides insurance. Stimulative action to expand aggregate demand and produce an initial reduction in unemployment, taken one step at a time, should not increase inflation unduly even if our twin conclusions about hysteresis are wrong. The effect of the recent and prospective reduction in the U.S. trade deficit, by creating additional slack in Europe, adds still more insurance.

The approach outlined here meets the basic difficulty identified by Paul Courant that a permanent fiscal stimulus runs the danger of crowding out sorely needed business investment, while a temporary stimulus may give only temporary results. If structural reforms are put in motion simultaneously, and if we are right that lower unemployment will itself help reduce rigidities, then the improved growth prospects on the supply side would induce higher investment and raise the growth of private demand.

Though Richard Cooper has argued that any of the major countries of Europe could finance the balance-of-payments consequences of a unilateral speed-up in growth, the chances of achieving a sustained improvement would be far greater if these countries acted together. While countries can for a time secure financing for a current account deficit, they are unlikely to be able to continue indefinitely. They could, of course, offset the tendency for current accounts to deteriorate by currency depreciation, but they would be better off if expansion by their trading partners allowed them to avoid the effects of depreciation on their price levels and terms of trade.

As Europe's strongest economy, Germany has a key role to play in the expansion. In mid-1987 Germany remains far within its external and internal constraints. Robert Lawrence argues that despite the appreciation of the deutsche mark through mid-1987, Germany could grow 1 percent a year faster than the OECD for three years without driving its current account into deficit. Charles Schultze's conservative estimates put German unemployment at almost 2 percent above the level at which inflation will accelerate, before allowing for the possibility of hysteresis.

The alternative to this mixed strategy of stimulating demand and encouraging structural reform is to continue the present neoclassical and conservative policy of steady-as-you-go. Our fundamental objection to such an approach is only partly that it eschews stimulating demand while we recommend it. The objection also arises from other sources. The conservative view holds that rigidities and inflexibilities in labor and other markets will only be wrung out by persistent discipline and that expansionary macroeconomic policies at the present time would relax that discipline before the cure was affected. But we believe the prospects for structural reform through liberalizing markets and increasing the mobility of resources will be much more favorable—politically and economically—in an environment of growing output and employment.

It is, in the best of circumstances, difficult to convince people that the indirect and long-term benefits from reducing protective barriers outweigh what they perceive as an immediate and direct threat to job security. That difficulty, we think, rises and falls in direct proportion to the growth in overall job opportunities. In the past ten years, liberalizing measures seem to have been much easier to promote in the U.S. environment of job growth than in the European environment of job stagnation. The discipline of the last six or seven years has indeed moderated wage aspirations and brought down inflation in Europe, but there is little evidence to suggest discipline has improved the adaptability and flexibility of European labor markets or permitted the large-scale enactment of liberalizing laws.

A steady-as-you-go policy poses another danger. Recession and supply shocks have not been banished from the world economy. Can we be confident that the liberal political and economic institutions of Europe would come unscathed through a recession or new supply shocks, given the current European unemployment rate of more than 11 percent? Moreover, the attitude that avoids on principle any role for expansionary macroeconomic policies may carry over from an environment of 2.5 percent growth in demand—where the policy is at least debatably appropriate—to an environment of much slower growth, where by any standards the policy is harmful. In the transition period when the U.S. trade deficit is likely to be falling sharply, such a policy could ratchet unemployment upward even more.

A Final Observation

Throughout the conference at which the papers in this volume were presented, one caveat was reiterated by both American and European participants: a large and inherently irreducible uncertainty attaches to any quantitative estimate either of the natural rate of unemployment or the real wage gap. Economists cannot and should not expect to convince policymakers to alter their views or to adapt new policies on the basis of such estimates. We are fully aware of that. But neither does the uncertainty about measurements of the natural rate or the wage gap warrant continuation of a conservative, steady-as-you-go policy. In either case one takes a not insignificant risk of being wrong. It is the likelihood of a positive relationship between employment growth and a reduction of rigidities that is at the core of our preference for a policy combining expansionary macroeconomic policies with structural reform.

PAUL R. KRUGMAN

Slow Growth in Europe: Conceptual Issues

THIS PAPER reviews some of the main issues in the debate over European economic performance. Its aim is not to provide answers but to organize the positions in a systematic way, sorting through the sometimes confusing discussion of Europe's economic problems to isolate the major themes. What are the major competing explanations of the poor record of European growth and employment? How do these explanations differ, and what sort of evidence could be used to distinguish among them? What policies make sense if a particular diagnosis of the problem is correct?

The assessment of positions in the debate on Europe is aided by making two kinds of distinctions. The first is the distinction among time periods, and the second is the distinction between the mechanisms that generate unemployment or slow growth and the underlying causes that drive these mechanisms. Much of the confusion in the discussion of Europe's growth problems arises from a failure to make one or both of these distinctions.

The issues of concern regarding European growth fall into three time frames, two of them retrospective and one of them prospective. First is the long sweep, since roughly 1973, over which growth has been disappointing, employment almost stagnant, and unemployment increasing almost steadily. Second is the shorter period, since about 1980, when growth fell to still lower levels and unemployment began rising much more rapidly than before. Finally, there is the very short run—macroeconomic performance over the next year or so.

The important questions at issue concern the long sweep and the

I would like to thank Olivier Blanchard and Assar Lindbeck for helpful comments on early drafts of this paper.

further deceleration since 1980, not current macroeconomic performance. Yet this point is often lost. For example, in early 1986 participants in the study that generated the present volume heard representatives of the German government use forecasts of fairly brisk near-term growth in their economy to deny vehemently that Germany was suffering "Eurosclerosis." Their forecasts were not fulfilled, but even one year's good growth would not have answered the fundamental question of why the past thirteen years, or even the past six years, have been so disappointing, nor would it have offered reassurance about the next six years. In principle, it is possible to have quite different explanations for the generally poor performance since 1973 on one hand and the especially poor performance since 1980 on the other. Such distinctions are at the heart of current policy debates. Some economists argue that the rise in unemployment before 1980 was essentially classical, correctable only through difficult structural changes, whereas the rise since 1980 is Keynesian and can simply be reflated away. Others strongly disagree.

The distinction between mechanisms and ultimate causes may be illustrated by considering the most important example. Many economists have argued that persistent unemployment in Europe reflects real wages that provide too much incentive for firms to economize on labor—the so-called disequilibrium real wage hypothesis. This hypothesis, if correct, describes the *mechanism* by which unemployment has been generated. However, it does not tell us why normal market forces have not corrected the situation. Why haven't real wages fallen in the face of mass unemployment? Among analysts who share the disequilibrium real wage view, there are widely differing opinions about what keeps real wages up. Some point to the rigidities and disincentives created by a too-generous welfare state; others argue that Europe was simply unlucky enough to encounter shocks too large for market forces to cope with. As I argue below, the diagnosis of ultimate causes is crucial for policy advice.

The paper is in four parts. The first part reviews the dimensions of Europe's problems. Most of this is familiar ground, over which I move quickly. I have tried, however, to supplement the usual macroeconomic indicators with some attention to other indicators that have concerned lay audiences. Most notable of these are concerns over international competitiveness, deindustrialization, and Europe's perceived failure in the competition to develop advanced technology.

The second part of the paper turns to the question of the mechanism that has produced slow growth in Europe. Inevitably the main issue is stagnant employment and high unemployment in the labor market. I review first the dispute over the relative importance of aggregate supply and demand factors, then turn to the most worked-over part of the discussion, the debate over the disequilibrium real wage hypothesis. The discussion concludes with disaggregative labor market issues, such as "rigidity" in intersectoral wages and restrictions on hiring and firing.

The third part turns to the "bigthink" debate: what are the underlying causes of European problems? I argue that there are three main positions here. The first is a position that is not popular with professional economists but is highly influential among other groups, a view that I call "automation and the third world." On this view, basic structural changes in the world economy, arising both from technological change and the spread of industrialization, have undercut the sources of employment growth. A second view already has a catchy name: "Eurosclerosis." I interpret this as the view that rigid real wages and other sources of poor performance are the revenge of the welfare state, which taxes away incentives and regulates away flexibility. The third view, "hysteresis," is the newest. This view holds that market economies in general are not as adaptable as economists usually imagine—given bad luck or bad management or both, any economy can find itself in a low-employment trap. On this view, Europe's predicament is just one of those things that happens now and then.

The fourth part closes the paper with a discussion of policy implications. The analyses I describe have *interpreted* the world in various ways; the point, however, is to *change* it. Does it make a difference for policy whether the source of unemployment is demand deficiency or disequilibrium real wages? Or whether wages stay high because of unemployment benefits or union power? There has been surprisingly little discussion of the relationship between diagnosis and prescription, so this section of the paper is more creative than the rest.

The Dimensions of Europe's Economic Problems

Dissatisfaction with European economic performance is multidimensional. This section reviews the two undeniable facts of poor growth and

Table 1. *Annual Growth Rates of Real GDP and Employment, European Community and the United States, 1961–85*
Percent

| | Real gross domestic product | | Employment | |
Period	European Community	United States	European Community	United States
1961–73	4.8	4.1	0.3	1.9
1973–80	2.8	2.6	0.1	2.0
1980–85	1.2	2.1	−0.5	1.6

Source: "Annual Economic Review, 1986–87: Statistical Annex," *European Economy*, no. 29 (July 1986), pp. 141, 144.

rising unemployment, together with more controversial concerns about international competitiveness and technology.

Growth

Europe has experienced a progressive reduction in growth rates since the early 1970s (table 1). At first, during the mid- to late 1970s, this slowdown could be rationalized as something normal and expectable. After all, Europe's growth in the 1950s and even to some extent the 1960s represented in part a recovery from World War II. Furthermore, although Europe could benefit from U.S. technology as long as Europe was playing catch-up, the opportunity became smaller as the gap in productivity and technology narrowed. Finally, Europe's slowdown was shared by the United States and Japan, which suggested that common factors such as energy prices were really the key. Since 1980, however, the contrast between continuing growth in the United States and Japan and near-stagnation in Europe has made such explanations implausible.

Nonetheless, growth as such is not the aspect of Europe's performance that causes the most concern. Rather, it is the fact that growth has been achieved almost entirely through gains in productivity, with hardly any expansion of opportunities for the employment of a growing work force.

Employment and Unemployment

From 1973 to 1980, employment in Europe was nearly stagnant, and since 1980 it has declined (table 1). The unemployment rate has risen steadily since 1973, and especially rapidly after 1980 (figure 1). This performance has been poor in comparison with that of the 1950s and

Figure 1. *Unemployment Rates in the United States and the European Community, 1961–85*[a]

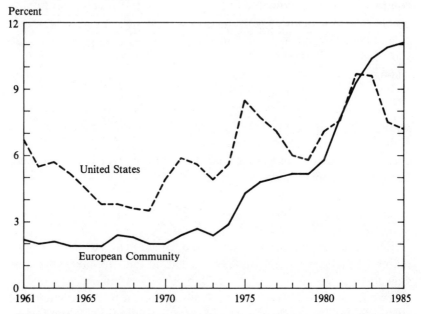

Percent

Source: "Annual Economic Review, 1985–86: Statistical Annex," *European Economy*, no. 29 (July 1986), p. 142.
a. European Community without Greece.

1960s in Europe. It has also been poor in comparison with the performance in the 1970s and 1980s in the United States, where the addition of more than 20 million jobs accommodated an expansion of the labor force much greater than Europe's.

Unemployment in Europe was extraordinarily low during the 1960s. Since then there has been a massive secular rise in the unemployment rate throughout Europe. Because unemployment rates in the 1960s were so low, this rise did not bring European unemployment to levels long regarded as normal in the United States until the late 1970s. By the mid-1980s, however, the unemployment rate in Europe had become persistently higher than the U.S. rate.

A number of observers have noted that the aggregate level of unemployment in Europe masks two features that may aggravate its social consequences. First is the large share of long-term unemployed. In the United States, economists frequently point out that 1930s-style unemployment, where workers lose their jobs and remain unemployed for years at a stretch, is a small part of the current unemployment problem.

Typically, the long-term unemployed in the United States are a small fraction of the unemployed except in years of severe recession. By contrast, the long-term unemployed are a substantial fraction of Europe's problem.[1] This condition presumably increases the human and social cost of the aggregate level. It also has a bearing on our diagnosis of the sources of labor market failure. Second, the rate of unemployment among youth in Europe has risen sharply, suggesting that many young people never manage to get work at all.

The timing of the changes in unemployment is a key issue in interpreting the European problem. Unemployment in Europe was very low in the 1960s; any explanation of its rise in the 1970s must either point to changes in the structure of Europe's economy during the intervening years or to changes in external conditions. Why else would a system that worked so well in one decade work so badly in another? The sudden rise in unemployment after 1980 poses still more problems. Thus, the interpretation of timing is central to the policy debate.

International Competitiveness

The current account balances of the largest European economies since 1973 fail to suggest any serious problem of international competitiveness (table 2). Germany has on average run substantial surpluses, while the United Kingdom, after large deficits in the mid-1970s, has run surpluses since 1978. Only France has been consistently in deficit, and except for 1982 these deficits have not been large. When compared with the performance of the United States in this regard, the international competitiveness of European economies seems to be satisfactory.

In fact, however, many Europeans do see themselves as facing an international competitive problem. This view partly reflects concern over "strategic" high-technology industries, which I discuss a little later. There are also less exotic concerns, however, which vary from country to country.

UNITED KINGDOM. In the United Kingdom, the perceived competitive problem is that of deindustrialization. Current account surpluses have been achieved with the help of North Sea oil—the movement from deficit to surplus in energy has more than offset a substantial movement of

1. Donges reports that the average duration of unemployment has tripled over the last fifteen years. Juergen B. Donges, "Chronic Unemployment in Western Europe Forever?" *World Economy*, vol. 8 (December 1985), p. 356.

Table 2. *Current Account Balances as Percent of GDP,*
Four European Countries and the United States, 1973–85

Year	France	Germany	Italy	United Kingdom	United States
1973	0.5	1.3	−1.7	−2.0	0.5
1974	−0.2	3.1	−4.6	−4.6	0.3
1975	−2.3	1.0	−0.2	−2.1	1.2
1976	0.0	1.1	−1.5	−1.7	0.3
1977	−1.5	0.9	1.2	−0.1	−0.7
1978	−0.7	1.4	2.4	0.4	−0.7
1979	0.6	−0.8	1.7	0.0	−0.1
1980	0.0	−1.7	−2.5	1.6	0.2
1981	−1.4	−0.7	−2.3	2.4	0.2
1982	−3.0	0.5	−1.6	1.5	−0.2
1983	−1.7	0.7	0.2	0.8	−1.0
1984	−0.6	1.0	−1.0	0.3	−2.6
1985	−0.8	2.2	−1.1	0.8	−2.9

Source: "Annual Economic Review, 1986–87," p. 157.

manufacturing trade in the opposite direction. Conventional economic analysis finds nothing wrong in this; but many in the United Kingdom— as in the United States—believe that manufacturing is the bedrock of the whole economy and that the decline of manufacturing competitiveness therefore harms the whole economy.

Industry, and particularly manufacturing, possesses certain growth-inducing characteristics that other sectors of the economy do not have. . . . if industry contracts, the whole economy may well contract too in a vicious circle downwards, owing to the dependence of many service sectors on industry and to the dependence of trade and the balance of payments on manufacturing output.[2]

Behind this belief lies a vaguely formulated but influential Kaldoresque view that increasing returns in the manufacturing sector give it a uniquely dynamic role in economic growth.

GERMANY. It is somewhat startling to find concerns over international competitiveness in Germany, which has in recent years run manufacturing trade surpluses second only to those of Japan. Nonetheless, conversations with German officials almost invariably lead to a discussion of international competitiveness as a growth problem.

The Germans appear to worry about competitiveness over two time

2. A. P. Thirlwall, "Deindustrialization in the United Kingdom," *Lloyds Bank Review,* April 1982, pp. 26–27.

frames. First, they view the prospect of deficits in the current account as a constraint on demand expansion. Although the current German surplus is large, the experience of 1979–81 appears to have unnerved German policymakers. At the Bonn summit of 1978, Germany agreed to help lead a concerted reflation; soon after, it found itself with a brief but unprecedentedly large current deficit. The Ayatollah Khomeini, through the second oil crisis, may have had something to do with the sudden deficit; nonetheless, the experience seems to have left German policymakers profoundly fearful of expansionary policies.

For the longer term, Germans share, in muted form, some of the concerns of U.K. observers about industrial competitiveness and growth. Despite large manufacturing surpluses in the last few years, the experience of the 1970s seems to have left an enduring impression on German concerns. In the 1960s the mark was widely viewed as undervalued and was thereby thought to allow a "virtuous circle" of export-led growth. German government officials sound surprisingly like Cambridge Group economists in describing this era. With the floating of the mark in 1973, it came to an end. By 1980 German labor compensation per hour was the highest in the industrial world, 25 percent above that of the United States.[3] Although this situation was soon reversed (and now has been re-reversed), German policymakers feel that the age of export-led growth in manufacturing has passed.

FRANCE. The problems France has had with its balance of payments are more conventional than those of Germany or the United Kingdom. Since 1981, France has been persistently, though usually mildly, in deficit on its current account. In 1982 the perceived balance of payments constraint thwarted the macroeconomic program of the Mitterrand government.

France is also the country in which concerns over competition in advanced technology are most strongly expressed. This, however, warrants a separate discussion.

Technology and Productivity

Technological change and labor productivity are among the most confused elements in the discussion of Europe's economic problems. It

3. Otto Eckstein and others, *The DRI Report on U.S. Manufacturing Industries* (Data Resources, 1984), p. 57.

Table 3. *Change in Manufacturing Productivity, Four European Countries and the United States, 1960–84*
Percent

Period	France	Germany	Italy	United Kingdom	United States
GDP per employee					
1960–73	4.9	4.1	5.8	2.9	1.9
1973–80	2.6	2.5	1.7	0.9	−0.1
1980–84	1.7	1.9	0.5	2.5	1.0
Output per hour					
1960–73	6.5	5.9	7.3	4.3	3.2
1973–80	4.6	3.8	3.7	1.0	1.2
1980–84	4.7	3.1	3.5	5.3	4.0

Source: Molly McUsic, "U.S. Manufacturing: Any Cause for Alarm?" *New England Economic Review*, January–February 1987, p. 10.

is fitting, therefore, that the evidence on how Europe is doing in these areas is also confusing: although Europe clearly did not do as well after 1973 as it did before, the certainty ends there.

One way to approach the data is to consider the aggregate productivity numbers (table 3), which show that growth of labor productivity in Europe slowed after the early 1970s. However, except for the United Kingdom, where productivity was nearly stagnant between the oil shocks, Europe's performance remained more favorable than that of the United States. (One influential school sees *excessive* growth in productivity as part of the problem; for this group the fact of lower growth should pose something of a puzzle.) Since 1980, the growth of productivity in the United Kingdom has approached the 1960–73 pace, but the data do not indicate whether this is a fundamental shift in trend. Interestingly, critics of the British government as well as some officials argue that an important part of the poor performance from 1973 to 1980 reflected labor hoarding and that much of the post-1980 upturn reflects a one-time shedding of excess labor.

Thus, while the growth of productivity in Europe has declined, the problem has not been worse than that in the United States, and certainly not a problem for Europe's international competitiveness. But concern in Europe is focused less on aggregate performance than on new industries, especially those involving microelectronics, where its performance has indeed been markedly weaker than that of either the United States or Japan.

Some of this disparity is visible in trade statistics concerning high-technology products, that is, goods for which the cost of research and development is a large fraction of sales. Both the United States and Japan have substantially higher shares of world exports of high technology than they do of manufactures generally; correspondingly, Europe remains relatively reliant on traditional manufacturing. More specifically, few European firms are major players in the cluster of industries based on microelectronics. Semiconductor technology is dominated by the United States (microprocessors) and Japan (memories); computers by the United States, with competition coming from Japan and Korea; and software by the United States.

Europe's most visible effort to challenge the United States in advanced technology has been Airbus Industrie, a subsidized manufacturer of commercial aircraft. While Airbus products are highly regarded, European confidence has not been much bolstered by the market results: unsubsidized Boeing, in the face of a very high exchange value for the dollar, has retained the dominant position in the market.

The Mechanism of Slow Growth

As argued above, a distinction should be made between the mechanism generating slow European growth and the underlying causes driving this mechanism. The dispute over mechanism is narrower and more technical than that over ultimate causes, but there remain several key issues: the roles of aggregate supply and demand; the importance of disequilibrium real wage levels; and the importance of other "rigidities" in the labor market.

Aggregate Supply and Demand and the NAIRU

It is probably safe to say that most professional economists view the slowdown in European growth from the pre-1973 period to about 1980 as essentially a problem of aggregate supply, while they are divided about the sources of slowdown since then. However, the nature of the presumed supply problem breaks down some equivalences that are usually made in macroeconomics. Economists usually associate growth in aggregate supply with growth in the economy's resources or in the productivity with which it uses those resources, and they associate changes in aggregate demand with fluctuations in the level of utilization of resources. In other words, aggregate supply equals potential output, and the effect of demand is measured by the output gap. In the European case, however, most of the growth slowdown, and by definition all of the rise in unemployment, represents a decline in utilization. Calling this a supply problem thus runs counter to our usual intuition.

Also, it is clear that workers and firms have experienced the problems of the European economies as demand failures, not as supply constraints: workers cannot find jobs or are laid off, and firms cannot sell their output. Why cannot one conclude from this ground level experience that the problem is one of demand, not supply?

Noneconomists, and economists outside the mainstream, often seem confused about the nature of the argument that places the main weight for Europe's problems on supply. Some have argued that economists are simply ignoring the demand side. This is not fair. The essence of the orthodox position is that over the longer run, aggregate demand is controlled by governments. If governments have not provided enough stimulus to prevent unemployment from growing, it is because they find that the supply side of the economy does not let them.

To understand the argument of orthodox economists, one needs to invoke the concept of the NAIRU—the nonaccelerating inflation rate of unemployment. It is now almost universally accepted in the economics profession (which does not mean that it is true) that at any given time an economy has a unique rate of unemployment consistent with stable inflation. If a government stimulates demand enough to push unemployment below this rate, it will accelerate inflation, and if it reduces demand enough to raise unemployment above the NAIRU, it will reduce inflation. This formulation does not deny that, at any given time, demand drives fluctuations in output and unemployment. It does say that the actions of a government that is concerned about inflation will be constrained by the level of the NAIRU.

The orthodox story is that the NAIRU in Europe has risen, and this has induced governments to restrict demand. Governments, the story goes, found that attempting to keep unemployment at the levels of the 1960s produced accelerating inflation. They thus tightened monetary and fiscal policy until unemployment rose sufficiently to bring inflation under control. In a proximate sense, then, demand restriction is the source of rising unemployment, and participants perceive the immediate problem as one of insufficient demand. Nonetheless, in a deeper sense the problem is one of supply. In interpreting what happened in Europe, the details of monetary and fiscal policy are therefore not the main point.

In any given year, demand management dominates, but over the longer run demand is what it has to be to control inflation.[4]

For the present debate, the key point of the orthodox view is that essentially all of the rise in average unemployment rates from the 1960s to the post-1973 period can be attributed to a rise in the NAIRU. The reason is simple: European inflation rates in the mid-1980s are not much lower than they were in the late 1960s. If the unemployment rate over the past fifteen years had been consistently above the NAIRU, one would expect to have seen accelerating deflation by now.

This view seems to leave little room for demand-side policies to reduce unemployment. However, economists associated with the Centre for European Policy Studies have argued that changes in the inflation rate over time suggest that the current unemployment rate is above the NAIRU, allowing some scope for expanding demand.[5] The argument is portrayed schematically in figure 2. The argument grants that Europe's NAIRU has been rising over time (although perhaps leveling off, as discussed below). However, the argument is that during the 1970s the actual unemployment rate lagged behind the NAIRU, which is consistent with the accelerating inflation of that period; and that since 1980 the unemployment rate has risen above the NAIRU, producing a disinflation. On average the gap between the NAIRU and the actual rate has been zero, but at the moment there is room for demand expansion.

The policy implications of this argument will be discussed below, but a quantitative point should be made here: even the proponents of this assignment concede that the gap between the actual unemployment rate and the NAIRU is small. Thus Layard and the other CEPS economists, while strongly arguing the case for demand expansion, expect such expansion to reduce unemployment by only a fraction of the rise since 1973.[6]

4. Layard and Nickell give a particularly clear exposition of this view, using it to explain why they neglect demand in their study. As they point out, dismissing demand as a secondary problem does not imply that the government always gets the unemployment rate it wants. "The central mystery," they say, "is why, at present levels of unemployment, wage inflation is not falling." Richard Layard and Stephen Nickell, "The Performance of the British Labour Market," paper presented at the Conference on the British Economy, Sussex, May 18–21, 1986, p. 1.

5. See in particular Richard Layard and others, "Europe: The Case for Unsustainable Growth," in Olivier Blanchard, Rudiger Dornbusch, and Richard Layard, eds., *Restoring Europe's Prosperity: Macroeconomic Papers from the Centre for European Policy Studies* (MIT Press, 1986), pp. 33–94.

6. Ibid., pp. 35–36.

Figure 2. *Schematic Representation of View That the Current Employment Rate Is above the Nonaccelarating Inflation Rate of Unemployment*

Unemployment rate

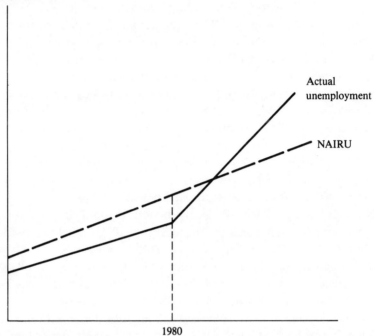

Actual
unemployment

NAIRU

1980

The Disequilibrium Real Wage Hypothesis

If Europe's NAIRU has risen, the question becomes why. As already noted, the question can be separated into one of mechanism and one of ultimate cause. Leaving causation aside for the moment, the most influential answer about the mechanism is that the real wage is in disequilibrium—it is too high.

The concept of the disequilibrium real wage is illustrated in figure 3. The real product wage is on the vertical axis, and employment is on the horizontal axis. The demand curve, D, represents the number of workers who would be hired if firms were able to sell as much as they wanted. L^f is full employment, and the equilibrium real wage is w^f. The figure shows that if the real wage is above the equilibrium level, say at w^d, firms will not be willing to employ everyone who wants to work, even if there is

Figure 3. *Schematic Representation of View That the Real Wage Rate Is in Disequilibrium*

Real wage

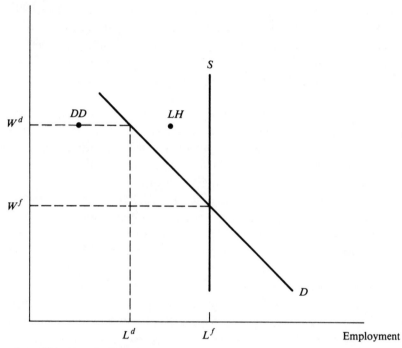

Source: Richard Layard and others, "Europe: The Case for Unsustainable Growth," in Olivier Blanchard, Rudiger Dornbusch, and Richard Layard, eds., *Restoring Europe's Prosperity: Macroeconomic Papers from the Centre for European Policy Studies* (MIT Press, 1986), p. 40.

sufficient demand. Thus, if an attempt is made to expand employment above L^d, firms will respond by raising prices instead of output. As long as workers receive the real wage w^d, the NAIRU will be $L^f - L^d$. This does not deny that demand can also play a role in unemployment: if firms cannot sell all they would like to, employment can be less than the NAIRU rate, for example, at point *DD*—for double disequilibrium. (An argument relating to point *LH* will be made shortly.) Nonetheless, if one adopts the orthodox view, then a rise in the NAIRU accounts for most of Europe's rise in unemployment. So disequilibrium real wages must, a priori, be given a central role. Although this simple presentation neglects some technical points—for example, high real wages need not represent a demand by workers; they could be an unintended consequence of nominal wage stickiness in the face of falling markups by firms—such points are not the main problem. The question is whether evidence actually supports the disequilibrium real wage view.

At first sight, testing the view might seem simple: just compare increases in the real wage with productivity growth. If real wages have risen faster than productivity, one concludes that real wage disequilibrium exists. Calculations of this sort are often made, but they are neither necessary nor sufficient indicators of a disequilibrium real wage.[7] The main reason is that the very substitution of capital for labor that is supposed to be induced by a real wage increase plays havoc with this interpretation of productivity growth, as follows. If, for some reason, workers suddenly demand higher real compensation, firms will substitute capital for labor, reducing labor demand. The capital-deepening, however, will raise the productivity of workers that remain. Thus a comparison of real wage growth with productivity growth will at best understate the size of the excess real wage increase. Indeed, if the scope for capital–labor substitution is large enough (elasticity of substitution greater than one), a rise in real wages will raise productivity by more than the real wage increase. This case is perhaps unlikely, but the point is that the comparison of the real wage with productivity does not convey very much information by itself.

On the other side, the substitution of capital for labor is a normal process even when real wages are not in disequilibrium, and except in the borderline case of Cobb-Douglas technology, this will lead to disparities between increases in the real wage and productivity growth. For example, an economy that is engaged in capital-deepening because of a high savings rate will also experience rising real wages, and ordinarily these real wages will rise faster than productivity. In Japan the labor share of income rose significantly from the late 1960s to the mid-1980s. Was this an equilibrium or a disequilibrium rise? Because unemployment remained negligible, the guess has to be that equilibrium was maintained.

Technological change further confounds the issue. Technology will ordinarily shift not only the productivity of the economy but its equilibrium distribution of income. Over a span of fifteen years, who is to say that technological change did not cause large divergences between productivity growth and warranted growth of real wages?

The technically correct way around these conceptual difficulties is to estimate production functions in which the role of capital, labor, energy,

7. See, for example, *European Economy*, which annually offers estimates of the real wage gap.

technology, and so on is considered. By most accounts the best such study is that by Artus, which confirms that large real wage gaps exist in Europe.[8] A review of the Artus study provokes two reactions: admiration for the care and effort involved, and skepticism about the reliability of any conclusions based on such an intricate mix of assumptions and estimation.

Fundamentally the disequilibrium real wage view has received wide acceptance, not because of overwhelming evidence but because it is logically tidy. Faced with a persistent failure of the labor market to clear, economists have little alternative but to conclude that the real wage is too high. The data do not fly in the face of this conclusion—as they might if, for example, real wages had consistently risen by *less* than productivity had. It would be wrong, however, to imagine that the disequilibrium real wage hypothesis is strongly supported by solid evidence.

This brings me to a final point: is the disequilibrium getting better or worse? Recent data suggest that while real wages may have outpaced productivity during the 1970s, they have not done so in the 1980s. Examination of this evidence, plus more sophisticated calculations, has led several economists, including Dornbusch and Bruno, to argue that the disequilibrium has in fact been reduced.[9] This conclusion dovetails nicely with the view, described above, that the rise in unemployment since 1980 largely has been a problem of demand rather than supply.

Unfortunately, the evidence that the gap has narrowed is by no means clear. For one thing, the calculations are subject to all the difficulties just reviewed. In addition, many observers, at least in the United Kingdom, believe the unemployment rate had to rise, even with a constant real wage gap, because of labor hoarding: firms were unwilling to fire workers or were legally prevented from doing so during the 1970s. Thus, in terms of figure 3, employment during the late 1970s was actually to the right of the labor demand curve, say at point *LH*. Over time, employment was reduced through attrition and bankruptcies. This view says that the rise in unemployment represented a movement to the labor

8. Jacques R. Artus, "The Disequilibrium Real Wage Rate Hypothesis: An Empirical Evaluation," *International Monetary Fund Staff Papers,* vol. 31 (June 1984), pp. 249–302.

9. Rudiger Dornbusch, "Macroeconomics and Unemployment in Europe," *Challenge,* forthcoming; and Michael Bruno, "Aggregate Supply and Demand Factors in OECD Unemployment: An Update," Working Paper 1696 (Cambridge, Mass.: National Bureau of Economic Research, September 1985).

demand curve, not a movement off it—and therefore no room for demand expansion exists after all.

The question of labor hoarding leads to the next issue, one that is frequently associated with the concept of real wage disequilibrium: rigidities in the labor market imposed by regulations and other institutional features.

Rigidities and Unemployment

The view has been advanced with special force in Germany that government labor policies and trade union power are as important as excessive real wages in causing unemployment.[10] In this view, the government and unions have created "rigidities" in the labor market, such as wage differentials that are fixed across sectors, regions, and occupations; impediments to the movement of workers out of depressed areas; and restrictions on the hiring and firing of workers.

The argument about fixed wage differentials may be expressed by the remark, often heard in Germany, that everyone's wage is determined by the chemical workers in Stuttgart. Union wages throughout Germany are keyed to wage settlements in the most prosperous sectors and regions. Law and custom then ensure that these wages are matched in nonunion sectors. Is this argument separate from that of disequilibrium real wages? At an aggregate level, the two would be hard to distinguish. Suppose that wages throughout the economy are based on those in the most successful area; then for the country as a whole real wages will be too high to clear markets. Only by looking at the detail would one be able to say that workers were demanding too high a wage relative to their compatriots, rather than relative to the cost of living. Perhaps it would be least confusing to say that relative wage inflexibility is an explanation of real wage disequilibrium, rather than a distinct cause of unemployment.

A similar remark could be made about the immobility of labor. If workers are unwilling or unable to move from depressed areas to affluent ones, the pressure on real wages in the affluent areas is kept down. If the wage increases are then matched nationwide, the result is to aggravate unemployment. Again, however, it is perhaps best to think of immobility as a source of real wage disequilibrium, not a distinct problem.

10. See Donges, "Chronic Unemployment"; and Herbert Giersch, "Eurosclerosis," Discussion Paper 112 (Kiel Institute for World Economics, October 1985).

Restrictions on firing impose true nonwage costs on firms. In much of Europe the firing of workers requires either a difficult legal process or costly severance payments or both. Many authors have observed that in an uncertain world, raising the cost of firing will make firms less willing to hire. It is thus widely accepted that the regulation of firing is an invisible cost to employment that is a source of disequilibrium distinct from high real wages.

But while restrictions on firing clearly reduce hiring at any real wage, they also reduce firing. Thus the impediments reduce flows both into and out of unemployment. Simple algebraic examples suggest that the net effect on employment at any given real wage is ambiguous. The reduced flexibility of firms reduces somewhat the efficiency of the economy, but efficiency is not a major question for Europe.

Restrictions on firing can, however, help explain the high levels of long-term unemployment and of youth unemployment in Europe: when flows into and out of jobs are low, unemployment is likely to be relatively prolonged, and new job-seekers—who are mostly the young—will have a hard time finding jobs.

Underlying Causes

More fundamental than the question of what mechanism produces rising unemployment and slow growth in Western Europe is the question of what drives the mechanism. At the risk of oversimplifying, I divide holders of opinions on this matter into three groups. The first group locates the problem in *technology*: both the direction of technological change within Europe and the spread of technology abroad have weakened Europe's ability to provide jobs. The second group locates the problem in *politics*: the growth of the welfare state has eliminated economic incentives and flexibility. The third group locates the problem in *accidents*: a combination of adverse shocks and bad management pushed the European economies into a low-level equilibrium trap called "hysteresis."

Automation and Third World Competition

A view widespread in the general population and among prominent and influential thinkers but shared by few economists attributes Europe's woes to a combination of technological change and increased foreign competition. The technological part of the argument is strongly reminiscent of the debate in the United States during the 1950s over automation. New technology, it is argued, removes much of the demand for labor. For example, W. W. Rostow worries that "the character of the new technologies coming forward, combined with the erosion of the older manufacturing industry, [will] render a significant margin of the working force unemployable."[11] In a similar vein, Peter Drucker argues that "in the industrial economy . . . production has come 'uncoupled' from employment" and further argues that "we are facing a new, sharp acceleration in the replacement of manual workers by machines."[12] In other words, new technology has moved in a strongly labor-saving and capital-using direction and has thus tended to reduce the level of employment at any given real wage. Some authors have argued that the labor-saving effects of new technology are so great that new investment, which facilitates the introduction of technology, will actually lower employment instead of raising it.[13]

The international part of this view is that the rise of the newly industrializing countries has deprived Europe of markets and of the industries that have migrated to those countries. This argument is also one about technology, in this case about the spread of traditional technology to the third world. In terms of economic analysis, trade with labor-abundant countries raises the demand for capital while lowering that for labor. The result is a fall in the real wage to restore full employment, or equivalently a reduction in employment at a given real wage. In both a formal and an economic sense, trading with a more labor-abundant country is similar in its effects to a strongly labor-saving technological change.

This pair of arguments seems to have persuaded many Europeans that a sort of "speed limit" prevents their economies from growing faster than about 3 percent per year.[14] The story also has an environmental-

---

11. W. W. Rostow, "Technology and Unemployment in the Western World," *Challenge*, vol. 26 (March–April 1983), p. 6.

12. Peter F. Drucker, "The Changed World Economy," *Foreign Affairs*, vol. 64 (Spring 1986), pp. 768, 778.

13. See, for example, Terry Barker, "Long-Term Recovery: A Return to Full Employment?" *Lloyds Bank Review*, January 1982, pp. 19–35.

14. Where the estimate of 3 percent comes from is unclear. See, however, the arguments described in David Fairlamb, "Europe's Grim Job Outlook," *Dun's Business Month*, September 1984, pp. 133–36.

resource twist to it. Despite falling prices for raw materials in recent years, many still fear that such prices will rise again, especially if growth is too fast. Rostow argues that rising prices for materials require heavy capital investment and thus block job creation.[15] In informal discussions, Europeans sometimes cite environmental limits to growth such as the problem of acid rain.

The view that sees Europe's problems in terms of automation and third world competition has some obvious empirical difficulties. If either rapid technological change or the loss of labor-intensive industries were causing unemployment, rapid growth in productivity would be expected among those still employed. Yet as noted earlier, productivity growth has actually been slower since 1973 than it was before. Also, despite assertions that labor has become an unimportant factor of production, the share of production costs attributable to labor has risen since the 1960s. To a U.S. economist used to hearing that the United States is losing jobs because of inadequate productivity, the European complaint of job loss because of excessive productivity is ironic. Nonetheless, whether the automation-competition view makes sense or not, it is influential and a force to be reckoned with.

Eurosclerosis

Among economists who study Europe, it seems clear that the most popular explanation of economic problems is that it is the fault of governments. Herbert Giersch, who coined the term "Eurosclerosis," argues that the welfare state inhibits economic adjustment in a variety of ways. Generous unemployment compensation removes the incentive for discharged workers to seek new employment and removes pressure on still-employed workers to moderate their demands. Restrictions on hiring and firing prevent adjustment and (perhaps, as noted above) reduce employment. Industrial change is blocked by protection and industrial policy. Heavy charges for social insurance raise employment costs relative to take-home pay. Legal restrictions on wage competition reinforce the market power of trade unions. All these factors together prevent market forces from working and thus lead to the European problems of low employment and slow growth.[16]

15. Rostow, "Technology and Unemployment," pp. 7–8.
16. For a passionate statement of this case, see Giersch, "Eurosclerosis." For an

This view has much to recommend it. First, it is internally consistent, and second it can account for the simultaneous rise in unemployment and fall in productivity growth. Third, it fits the preconceptions of economists, who as a professional matter prefer to assume that markets work. Fourth, it is in keeping with the current political spirit, with its hostility to government activism.

The main difficulty with the Eurosclerosis hypothesis is one of timing. Although details can be debated, no strong case exists that Europe's welfare states were much more extensive or intrusive in the 1970s than in the 1960s, and no case at all exists that there was more interference in markets in the 1980s than in the 1970s. Why did a social system that seemed to work extremely well in the 1960s work increasingly badly thereafter?

A leading advocate of the Eurosclerosis hypothesis, Assar Lindbeck, has tried to deal with the timing question. His answer has two parts. First, he argues that the disincentive effects of government policies took time to be fully felt. For example, the government commitment to full employment increased the market power of unions; but it took years of experience of full employment before unions realized just how large their power was and became bold enough to exploit it. Lindbeck states that "the previous success of the full-employment policy to some extent carried the seeds of its own destruction."[17]

Second, Lindbeck argues that the nature of the rigidities produced by Eurosclerosis is such that the economies of Western Europe functioned well as long as the news was good. In the favorable technological and international environment of the 1960s, an inability to adjust to adversity did not matter. Only when the world became less friendly did the failings become apparent:

A problem with the hypothesis of a *gradual* deterioration in the basic mechanisms of the West European economies is that the increase in unemployment, and the slowdown of output and productivity growth, occurred quite *abruptly* during the 1970s. But the point is that, as long as the requirements for rapid adjustments in the allocation of resources were not large (perhaps apart from the contraction of agriculture), existing rigidities did not pose severe problems. And, as long as the economy was not exposed to drastic supply

---

earlier statement, and the origins of the term, see Assar Lindbeck, "Emerging Arteriosclerosis of the Western Economies: Consequences for the Less Developed Countries," *India International Centre Quarterly*, no. 1 (1982), pp. 37–52.

17. Assar Lindbeck, "What is Wrong with the West European Economies?" *World Economy*, vol. 8 (June 1985), p. 155.

)

shocks, downward rigidities in real wage rates did not create severe unemployment problems, for firms could afford to "hoard" labor during short recessions. But when abrupt changes in relative costs and international competition required a large and rapid reallocation of resources, the rigidities started to become a severe disadvantage to the West European economies. And when a drastic drop occurred in productivity growth, and strong inflationary cost impulses emerged, the demand for compensation from employees not only accentuated inflation; it also created a severe threat to the opportunities for employment.[18]

On this view, then, the apparently solid prosperity of the 1960s was in fact precarious: it depended on consistent good news. The balance was upset by the first oil shock and perhaps also by a wave of labor militancy following the student risings of the late 1960s.[19] The further deterioration after 1980 is then to be attributed to the second oil shock, and perhaps also to the "third oil shock" effect of high U.S. real interest rates and the strong dollar.[20] The basic point, however, is that these shocks only served to reveal a fundamental deterioration in the economic system that had been going on over a much longer time.

While the advocates of Eurosclerosis are thus able to rationalize the suddenness of economic deterioration, it remains true that the timing issue at least makes their case less strong. Very recently, a new concept called hysteresis, in which the adverse shocks of the 1970s and 1980s are given much more weight, has become popular; according to this view, the shocks did more than simply unmask the economy's long-term problems—they actually created these problems.

Hysteresis

The concept of hysteresis begins with the observation that estimates of the NAIRU seem to move parallel to the actual unemployment rate.

18. Ibid., pp. 155–56.

19. Donges, in "Chronic Unemployment," emphasizes exogenous political pressure as a key source of deterioration.

20. The rise of the U.S. dollar could have aggravated Europe's disequilibrium through at least two channels. First, if Europeans insisted on receiving normal growth in real consumption wages in the face of deteriorating terms of trade, the result would be a rise in real product wages. This is the channel emphasized in Martin Feldstein, "U.S. Budget Deficits and the European Economies: Resolving the Political Economy Puzzle," Working Paper 1790 (Cambridge, Mass.: National Bureau of Economic Research, January 1986). Alternatively, Fitoussi and Phelps have argued that the strong dollar allowed firms in Europe to raise markups, with negative effects on employment. Jean-Paul Fitoussi and Edmund Phelps, The Slump in Europe (Oxford: Basil Blackwell, forthcoming).

Sachs has noted that this could represent causation running from the NAIRU to the actual rate: as explained above, inflation-conscious governments may rein in demand as the NAIRU rises.[21] Proponents of hysteresis have maintained that causation can also run the other way: high current unemployment can raise the NAIRU.

Two basic channels have been suggested by which current shocks can raise the equilibrium unemployment rate in the future. First is the effect of recessions on capital formation. If a recession leads to lower investment, this will ordinarily lower the labor demand curve in the future. If a disequilibrium real wage already exists at the time of the shock, perhaps because of Eurosclerosis, these effects could be quite large.[22]

More fundamental in its implications is the argument that the economy tends to write off workers who have been unemployed too long, so that any sustained bulge in unemployment gets built into the NAIRU. This argument is known as the "insider–ousider" model and comes in two variants. One, emphasized by Layard and Nickell among others, emphasizes the effect of unemployment on the unemployed themselves. The other, associated both with Lindbeck and Snower and with Blanchard and Summers, emphasizes the influence of the unemployment rate on the behavior of those still employed.[23]

In the view of Layard and Nickell, those who have been long unemployed simply come to be regarded as unemployable. Rightly or wrongly, they are perceived as having lost the work skills and attitudes that are needed for employment. As a result, the long-term unemployed

21. Jeffrey D. Sachs, "High Unemployment in Europe: Diagnosis and Policy Implications," Working Paper 1830 (Cambridge, Mass.: National Bureau of Economic Research, February 1986).

22. The importance of capital formation in generating persistent unemployment has been emphasized by Edmond Malinvaud, *Mass Unemployment* (Oxford: Basil Blackwell, 1984). The extent of its possible importance in a disequilibrium setting may be seen from the following example. Suppose that half of any fluctuation in output is invested, and that the capital–labor ratio is 2. If the real wage is rigid, then a temporary shock that reduces GNP by 1 percent for one year will permanently reduce the GNP associated with the NAIRU by 0.25 percent.

23. Layard and Nickell, "Performance of the British Labor Market"; Assar Lindbeck and Dennis Snower, "Wage Setting, Unemployment, and Insider–Outsider Relations," *American Economic Review*, vol. 76 (May 1986, *Papers and Proceedings, 1985*), pp. 235–39; and Olivier J. Blanchard and Lawrence H. Summers, "Hysteresis and the European Unemployment Problem," in Stanley Fischer, ed., *NBER Macroeconomics Annual 1986* (MIT Press, 1986), pp. 15–78.

are not effectively competing for jobs with the employed, and the greater the number of long-term unemployed, the higher the NAIRU.

In the insider–outsider view, wages are set by trade unions that represent workers who are employed or only recently fired. Workers who have been unemployed for a long time become disenfranchised. Thus if an unexpected shock leads to higher long-term unemployment, unions after a while will show no interest in wage restraint that allows the chronically unemployed to find new jobs.[24]

In either of these views, temporary shocks assume far more importance than economists usually give them. OPEC power and union militancy may have passed, but their legacy lives on; the shocks of the 1970s have essentially led to the permanent exile of millions of workers from employment.

An appealing feature of the hysteresis theory is its suggestion that Europe's current problems are not unique. Blanchard and Summers note that the interwar period in Britain and the 1930s in the United States present the same puzzle as does the current situation in Western Europe: why did not wages fall in the face of mass unemployment? They argue that essentially the same process of disenfranchisement of the unemployed was at work. The interwar unemployment problem, of course, came to an end with World War II; this has some disturbing implications for the present, as I argue below.

Perhaps one need not choose between hysteresis and Eurosclerosis. A neat if perhaps too-pat synthesis is that Eurosclerosis removes the adjustment mechanisms that prevent hysteresis. In this formulation, generous unemployment compensation and government support for trade unions prevent firms from breaking their unions when unemployment is high; this in turn allows the unions to disregard the plight of the unemployed. Then one arrives at Lindbeck's formulation: the European economic system worked well as long as the shocks were favorable but was prone to upward ratcheting of the unemployment rate whenever an unfavorable shock came along.

Finally, the hysteresis theory of unemployment in Europe, like the other views I have discussed, faces at least one awkward fact, in this case a fact about the 1960s. If European unions take no interest in the provision of jobs for outsiders, how did Europe manage to achieve a

24. Lindbeck and Snower, in "Wage Setting," point out that a similar tendency of employment to stick wherever it is can result from hiring and firing costs to firms even where workers are unorganized.

rapid increase in nonagricultural employment during the 1960s? If the system protects the interests of insiders but not of outsiders, why were real wages kept low enough to facilitate the absorption, not only of millions of domestic farmers, but of large numbers of migrant workers from southern and eastern Europe? The newness of the theory means that its proponents have not yet come to grips with its problems. Since the idea of hysteresis is rapidly growing in popularity, however, we can expect to see some clever answers soon.

Policy Implications

This section assesses the policies that would be appropriate to each of the four theories about the cause of slow growth in Europe.

Supply versus Demand

An unrepentant Keynesian, observing Europe's unemployment, would call for massively expansionary government policies. One of the surprising features of the European intellectual scene is that such unrepentant demand-siders are nowhere to be found. Virtually all economists are adherents of some version of the NAIRU view, which necessarily implies that little or no room exists for demand expansion. Important currents of thought exist outside the mainstream of economics, but they are marked by a technological determinism that does not encourage the belief that simple fixes can reduce unemployment.

The only proposals for demand stimulation that have any currency are those that call for a small amount and those that call for selective job creation aimed at the long-term unemployed. If one accepts the view represented in figure 2, there is room for a little bit of demand expansion to make up some of the rise in unemployment since 1980. But the amount cannot be regarded as more than a secondary part of a policy that must be aimed primarily at reducing the NAIRU.

In the United Kingdom, support is growing for selective employment measures inspired by the hysteresis theory and aimed at the long-term unemployed. In accordance with the theory, proponents of the measures believe that the long-term unemployed do not exert any influence on wage settlements, and therefore aid policies would not be inflationary. Furthermore, with success the measures could bring some exiled workers back into the fold, permanently lowering the NAIRU. The aspirations of policymakers seem to have become remarkably limited. A Labour party adviser in the United Kingdom was fairly typical in suggesting that his party's program might aim to lower unemployment from 3 million to 2 million over five years or so.

Technological Pessimism

Suppose that the technological view of Europe's problems is right: automation and third world competition are undercutting employment growth. What policies are indicated? The most popular response among adherents of this view is to accept stagnant or declining employment and spread it around. Proposals for work-sharing, or at least reduced work weeks, have received wide support.[25]

Several logical alternatives to this response are possible. One is simply to cut real wages enough to preserve full employment. Of course if one believes in the capital-using bias of technology, this approach might involve very large cuts, especially if capital–labor substitution possibilities are small.[26] To mitigate the effects on the distribution of income, one might want some form of profit-sharing arrangement. In any case, it is hard to conceive of a situation in which the expansion of employment is impossible.

Eurosclerosis

If an overexpanded welfare state is the root of Europe's problems, two policy rules seem to follow quite naturally.

The first rule defines what not to do. If unemployment is high because incentives are distorted or lacking, then attempting to correct the unemployment with demand stimulus will only translate into inflation, not higher employment. So Eurosclerosis implies conservatism on the demand side.

Second, the best solution to unemployment is to make the economy more flexible. In the Eurosclerosis view, this precept means scaling back

25. For a discussion of the work-sharing concept, see Jacques H. Drèze, "Work-Sharing: Some Theory and Recent European Experience," *Economic Policy*, no. 3 (October 1986), pp. 561–602.

26. Advocates of the technology view have not commented on this directly, as far as I know. It seems inevitable, however, that they would be elasticity pessimists if they were to address the issue.

the European welfare states by reducing unemployment compensation, lifting restrictions on firing, and in general undoing the whole set of rules that creates rigidity.

The political willingness to follow this advice is clearly lacking except in the United Kingdom, and if estimates of a steadily rising NAIRU in the United Kingdom are correct, then the Thatcher government has not succeeded. The political strategy advocated by Giersch is a long-term one, and surprisingly idealistic in content. It envisages the establishment of a citizen's right "to sue in court all those legislative bodies and government agencies which have imposed legal and regulatory barriers to entry, and all those private organizations which are resorting to restrictive practices. The result would be . . . a broad citizen's initiative to free the initiative of citizens."[27]

If the best solution is so difficult to obtain, what is the second-best solution? The problem of a disequilibrium real wage indicates that a struggle over distribution of income has thwarted the role of the wage rate as a marginal signal. A second-best solution would try to uncouple distribution from the cost of labor.

How? One answer might be employment subsidies or, more modestly, shifting the financing of social insurance away from the wage bill. A more heterodox answer would be a Weitzman-style revision of the whole payment system, with profit-sharing traded off for reductions in the marginal cost of employment. The practical objections to either approach are matched by the practical objections to accepting double-digit unemployment forever; thus, even problematic schemes deserve serious attention.

A more devastating objection to the decoupling approach is that the employed have no interest in allowing the unemployed to find jobs. In this case a wage subsidy or profit-sharing scheme would simply be absorbed by the employed, with no gain in jobs, precisely what the hysteresis view would predict.

Hysteresis

A useful analysis of the implications of hysteresis for demand policy is provided by Sachs.[28] He notes that hysteresis imposes an especially

27. Giersch, "Eurosclerosis," p. 13.
28. Sachs, "High Unemployment in Europe."

nasty choice on policymakers. They can reduce inflation but only at the cost of permanently higher unemployment, or vice versa. It is unclear which choice is appropriate. If the inflation rate is high, it will make sense to bring it down with a period of high unemployment even at the expense of some permanent increase in the NAIRU. If the NAIRU is high, it may be worth bringing it down through a period of low unemployment even though this permanently raises the rate of inflation. The point is that hysteresis does not offer any presumption in favor of expansionary demand policies.

If demand policies alone offer such poor alternatives, other tools must be considered. The U.K. proposals for selective job creation are a mild example. The search by Blanchard and Summers for historical parallels, however, suggests that stronger measures might be appropriate. They argue that the interwar unemployment problem was at root similar to the current European problem. The earlier unemployment was ended by war: a massive demand expansion that did not cause inflation to explode because prices were controlled by the government. Economists have long derided the notion that wars and their concomitant price controls are necessary to end depressions. But if Blanchard and Summers are right, a peacetime demand expansion would not have worked. Without the price controls, such a demand expansion would have led to inflation instead of employment creation. Because peacetime price controls are notoriously ineffective, something like a wartime atmosphere may have been necessary after all.

Whether the moral equivalent of war is really necessary or not, the hysteresis view clearly provides a stronger case for an incomes policy than does traditional macroeconomics. Ordinary models require a permanent incomes policy to lower the NAIRU; temporary incomes policies can at best reduce the costs of a disinflation. In the hysteresis model, however, temporary price and wage controls could contribute to a permanent reduction in the unemployment rate—if they were to work.

Conclusions

I conclude this all-too-brief summary of a complex discussion with two remarks about the state of the debate. First, it would be helpful if researchers in this area were more frank about the fragility of their empirical foundations. A survey of the work on NAIRUs or on real wage disequilibriums reveals that the numbers thrown about are more nearly speculations informed by the data than estimates to be used with any assurance. There is nothing wrong with making such speculations—empirical leaps of faith are often necessary, especially when policymakers require an answer now. However, that the United Kingdom's NAIRU is 12 percent or that its real wage gap is 30 percent are statements that should be made with tongue firmly and visibly in cheek.

Second, while empirical statements should be made with more caution, policy analysis should be less timid. Both the Eurosclerosis view and the hysteresis view seem to point toward radical departures in policy, not small incremental shifts. Such departures may not happen soon, but economists do the world a disservice if they suppress ideas only because they are not yet politically acceptable. If the theory implies that the welfare state should be dismantled or that five years of massive public spending backed by Draconian price and wage controls are necessary, it should be said clearly. Forthrightness may or may not change policy, but it certainly improves the quality of the discussion.

Comment by Ralf Dahrendorf

Krugman's paper is a clear and useful summary of the debate on the subject of Europe's growth problems. In a more extensive critique, one would wish to examine details as well as the main argument. For example, when and why did the welfare state become unaffordable? Could it be that it was not the construction of the welfare state, as such, but the addition of apparently minor but in fact costly elements in the 1970s that broke the camel's back? And were these elements added as part of an initial bargain among government, industry, and labor to bring about the adjustments that continue to be necessary? Would the welfare state of the late 1960s therefore be workable, whereas the welfare state of the late 1970s is not? However, in the following four remarks, I pursue a different line of argument—and I do so as a noneconomist. Much of the comment is, moreover, inspired by my experience as chairman of the OECD High-Level Group, which recently produced a report on labor market flexibility.[29]

29. Organization for Economic Cooperation and Development, *Labour Market Flexibility: Report by a High-Level Group of Experts to the Secretary-General* (Paris: OECD, 1986).

First, Krugman is wise and certainly right in introducing the time dimension into his discussion. Clearly, the 1970s were a traumatic period in recent economic history. Arguably, those years mark a sea change, the effects of which will be with us for decades to come. But one has to distinguish between immediate and long-term effects. The immediate trauma of the 1970s was that of stagflation. But today this particular subject is not uppermost on people's minds. There is, indeed, little evidence of the phenomenon of "slow growth" in Europe, at least in the perception of Europeans. The dominant subject for them is a different one: how is it that considerable growth can go hand in hand with continuing unemployment at the present high rates? As a subject of public concern, the place of stagflation has been taken by jobless growth or boom unemployment. Is there really a boom? Krugman is right; one should not assume a built-in speed limit for growth. At the same time, 3 percent growth in GNP seems to most Europeans quite satisfactory and serves to focus attention less on growth than on unemployment or even on environmental side effects of growth.

Second, it is often useful to emphasize the obvious: who or what is Europe? There is the special development of the United Kingdom, where real growth is truly slow, inflation and unemployment appear together, regional differences are pronounced, and oil has produced a Mexico-type situation. But anyone writing about Europe has to deal above all with the special cases of Sweden, Austria, and Switzerland. It is misleading to lump them together, though in recent years all three have shown a combination of not inconsiderable growth, low inflation, and very low unemployment. The countries have certain factors in common: they are relatively small, but more important they have a limited number of economic actors—either a few large firms and a few strong unions, or more complex mechanisms of coordination, as in Switzerland. All three display versions of a corporatism that works, or has worked in the past. The story has to be be told, if only because the evidence seems to defy all other generalizations.

Third, my key comment on Krugman's paper has to do with the vantage point of analysis. It has to be recognized that (1) rigidities are from another point of view beneficial developments and that (2) such rigidities exist both in Europe and in the United States.

Take nonwage labor cost. It is often cited as one of the main sources of rigidity, not only of labor markets but of industrial adjustment and even of the welfare state itself. In fact, however, nonwage labor cost is merely a somewhat curious way of calculating contributions to the safeguarding of social citizenship rights; they are a social tax levied on the basis of employment. If one reduces nonwage labor costs, one of two consequences is certain: either social services have to be reduced or the money will have to be found elsewhere. Thus perfect, theoretical flexibility has a price, and the price may be considered too high by some.

There is a more dramatic way of making the same case. It has to do with real wages rather than with nonwage labor cost. It is often observed that, in Europe, real wages are particularly sticky. However, if one were to get them unstuck, the result would be similar to that which can already be observed in the United States. While few people (at least few widely publicized ones) who stay in their jobs have suffered an actual decline in their real income, many have been forced to leave fairly well paid jobs to take much less well paid ones. The net effect is an aggregate decline in real wages (often, incidentally, accompanied by a decline in social benefits accruing from negotiated nonwage labor cost). Wage levels as well as wage expectations take a downward turn.

This development probably accounts at least in part for the reversal of the secular decline in the proportion of Americans who fall below the official poverty line. By 1973 this proportion had declined to 11 percent, but by 1984 it had risen again to 15 percent.[30] This change is no less striking than the increase in unemployment in Europe since the mid-1970s and, more particularly, since 1979. One wonders whether poverty in America is the necessary equivalent of unemployment in Europe: either real wages are kept high at the cost of high unemployment, or real wages are allowed to fall at the cost of a growing number of working poor.

Fourth, which is worse? People have different views about this, but I for one would probably prefer to be unemployed in Europe than be poor in America. But this is a question that has much to do with prevailing values. In the United States, work is still more central to the self-image of people and to the contract between individual and society than it is in Europe. This is not to say that unemployment in Europe can be left as it is. Although its consequences are more indirect and more complicated than is often assumed—it affects the moral texture of societies more than their political structure—they are grave. Some redistribution of

30. U.S. Department of Commerce, Bureau of the Census, *Current Population Reports,* series P-60, no. 157, "Money Income and Poverty Status of Families and Persons in the United States, 1986" (Government Printing Office, 1987), pp. 3–4.

work, by changes in working time and other measures, is probably necessary. One may even wish to follow the German path of clandestine job creation programs, through extremely long initial education, through apprenticeships and vocational training, and through conscription. The underdeveloped nature of the service sector in some European countries is an important question too. Such a battery of programs would at any rate address themselves to the major issue of Europe's politico-economic debate.

The point of my remarks can be put in a nutshell: there is not just one model for the way in which modern economies can move forward. The fact that the textbook model of economists happens to be closer to the American than the European or Japanese experience does not mean that the American experience is uniquely suited to bring about effective adjustment and social satisfaction. In the OECD report on labor market flexibility, we argued that there are at least three models, and probably more. They are not just actual alternatives, but genuine alternatives in terms of effectiveness. Even growth can be achieved in more ways than one, let alone "balanced" or "socially acceptable" growth. From the debate about Eurogloom, from American self-doubt, and even from an incipient Japanese reappraisal, the awareness might yet emerge that each of the corners of the developed world has something important to offer the others.

Comment by Jacques H. Drèze

"Donkeys do not stumble twice on the same stone," says French popular wisdom. The same cannot be said of economists. Because the *milestones* of economics keep changing shape and location, economists sometimes fail to recognize old mistakes and stumble again. It is appropriate for Europeans at this time to look at the past twenty-five years (as I do in the first part of this comment) to identify problems that are still with them and on which they might stumble again unless they take appropriate action (of the kind outlined in the second part).

Looking Back

Over the first half of the past quarter-century, Europe demonstrated its ability to maintain a high rate of balanced growth (4.8 percent for the twelve nations now in the European Community). Favorable factors that contributed to this achievement are listed in the overview chapter to this volume. Over the second half of the same period, Europe demonstrated the following characteristics: (1) a high sensitivity to external shocks; (2) an amazing (and, to me, shocking) tolerance of persistent mass unemployment, in contrast to limited tolerance of sustained inflation, and no tolerance of external deficits (as shown by the premature abandonment of the German "locomotive" experiment and of the early Mitterrand policies); and (3) an alarming inability to coordinate policy (re)actions, in spite of the coming into being of the European Community, and of the lessons learned in the 1930s.

One is thus left to wonder whether Europe today is capable of resuming growth and of coping effectively with the new uncertainties of the day.

The difficulties that exploded in the mid-1970s were associated with three major shocks; the shocks, in turn, arrived in the wake of the two significant trends. The first was the industrial development of Japan and the newly industrialized countries (NICs). Between 1961 and 1973 the share of Western Europe in the exports of manufactures to destinations outside Western Europe and Asia declined from 41.3 percent to 36.6 percent, whereas that of Asia grew from 7.8 percent to 17.1 percent. The second trend was the development of the "welfare state" in Europe, which is reflected in the growth of social expenditures as a share of GDP. In 1981 that share was 18 percent in Japan, 21 percent in the United States, but about 30 percent in the major EC countries.[31]

The first purpose of the welfare state is to transfer income from the more privileged to the less privileged. (One example is pensions paid out of current contributions by the young, which transfer resources from the "richer" younger generation to the "poorer" older generations.) Its second purpose is to organize social insurance. This insurance includes both standard forms, such as health or life insurance, which are largely neutral at the macroeconomic level and are unrelated to cyclical fluctuations, and new forms of insurance, such as unemployment benefits, severance pay, and wage indexation, aimed directly at stabilizing the real incomes of workers. These new forms, especially the first two, were seen as "built-in stabilizers" that should reduce the sensitivity of an economy to aggregate shocks, in particular by stabilizing consumption. Unfortunately, they brought in their wake a number of contractual or regulatory rigidities that work in the opposite direction.

31. Organization for Economic Cooperation and Development, *Social Expenditure, 1960–1990: Problems of Growth and Control* (Paris: OECD, 1985), p. 21.

As for the shocks that occurred in the 1970s, it seems appropriate to emphasize three major surprises.

—The fluctuation in exchange rates that resulted from the abandonment of fixed parities. These fluctuations turned out to be more sizable than anticipated. Schultze, in his article on real wages elsewhere in this volume, is right in stressing the problem created by these fluctuations for real wage adjustments.[32]

—The two oil shocks.

—The demand shock of 1975, associated with the temporary sterilization of oil revenues, a marked decline in the growth rate of world trade, and a sharp decline in investment.

My reading of the historical record is that these shocks went beyond the adjustment capabilities of unprepared economic agents and institutions. In Krugman's terms, Europe was "unlucky enough to encounter shocks too large for market forces to cope with." Private agents (firms and labor unions), markets, and governments could not deal smoothly with the situation; it was simply too much for them! Of course, the difficulty was compounded by the standard problem of assessing the exact nature of observed developments; for instance, were the oil price increases transitory or permanent?

A major area of maladjustment concerned the formation of wages and prices. The growth of *real* wages over the period 1961–73 had been warranted but substantial—at an annual rate close to 5 percent for the twelve Community members, according to EC estimates. In several countries real wages continued to grow on trend, or even faster, in 1975 and 1976, a time when the worsened terms of trade and demand conditions would have called for a pause. The increases of those two years alone contributed some 10 to 12 percent to whatever "wage gap" may have developed in the 1970s. All participants in the wage bargaining process share responsibility for that untimely episode, which Europeans must study and understand to avoid its repetition.

A similar remark applies to prices. Inflation reached records, as the demand-pull element of the mid-1970s gave way to cost-push in the ensuing years. Signs of abatement did not come until 1982.

These developments reveal that private agents were slow in recognizing the need for adjustments and inefficient in bringing them about.

32. The "Annual Economic Report, 1986–87" of the EC sees this as an issue of current relevance: "Wage agreements should allow for rapid adjustments . . . to take account of the very marked changes—largely unpredictable—in the terms of trade." *European Economy*, no. 30 (November 1986), p. 57.

Governments were equally ineffective in designing appropriate policies. And markets, especially particular exchange markets, proved to be subject to overshooting.

With the benefit of hindsight, and some insight provided by recent theoretical contributions, it is now understood that market economies cannot be expected to weather such storms smoothly and that they remain vulnerable to similar occurrences in the future.

The resulting disequilibriums leave Europeans with a heavy legacy. The underutilization of resources, associated with the combination of insufficient aggregate demand, inadequate relative prices of capital and labor, and ill-suited production structures, has affected labor and capital differently. On the labor side, massive unemployment has resulted (11 to 12 percent for the EC, or 16 million people, at this time). The persistence of the phenomenon has led to the concentration of unemployment among weaker groups: the young, who do not benefit from employment relationships initiated in better times; the less skilled; and the other marginal groups (women, immigrants, aged workers). Long-term unemployment is now widespread among all these groups.

On the capital side, underutilization has led to low investment for new capacity and accelerated scrapping (often precipitated by bankruptcies), resulting in a serious contraction of the capital stock and productive capacities. The measurement of that phenomenon is less easy and less accurate than the measurement of unemployment. But the phenomenon is significant and is at the root of current fears that an insufficient number of work places stands in the way of a return to full employment and that insufficient capacity limits the scope for rapid growth.[33]

A further legacy is the accumulation of budget deficits, hence of interest charges on the public debt, which today amount to some 5 percent of GDP for Europe as a whole.

All these disequilibriums are undisputed, but their interrelationships are complex, and no simple one-sided explanation accounts for them satisfactorily. Instead, various channels though which employment and growth have been held back must be recognized; several effects must be added together or otherwise combined to account for the overall situation.

In this spirit, a search for the causes of unemployment and for the

33. See Jacques H. Drèze, "Underemployment Equilibria: From Theory to Econometrics and Policy," *European Economic Review,* vol. 31 (February–March 1987), pp. 9–34.

impediments to faster growth should not proceed from parallel investigations of specific explanations (from Eurosclerosis to hysteresis in Krugman's paper, from wage gaps to competitiveness in the later papers). Instead, one should compare the quantifications of the complementary influences under alternative models, to identify areas of convergence as well as discrepancies.

By way of illustration, let me quote from an article about Belgium by Sneessens and Drèze: "The observed level of unemployment for 1982 could be decomposed as follows":

Total unemployment (percent)	16.0
Due to: capital gap	4.7
structural mismatch	4.5
need to offset potential demand pressures	1.6
insufficient demand	5.2.

An important conclusion is that stronger demand could reduce unemployment (in 1982) by 5 percent without inflationary pressure, so long as the "distributive gap" (DG) remains close to zero. Another important conclusion is that "creation of additional capacity (to eliminate the capital gap) and better adjustment of supply to demand (to eliminate structural mismatch) would be needed to reduce unemployment (and the NAIRU) below 11 percent."[34] The analysis underlying these conclusions departs from most of the work presented at this conference in an important respect: it attaches significance to the capital stock and the associated number of work places as a determinant of employment and of the NAIRU. Yet the analysis remains too close to "mechanisms" rather than "ultimate causes" (in Krugman's terminology), in particular by treating investment and exports as exogenous.

Before turning around to look ahead, I wish to address briefly the question of Europe's uniqueness in the current recession. In doing so, I express my own views of the relevance of the alternative theories reviewed by Krugman.

A first remark is that one should not exaggerate the difference between developments in Europe and elsewhere over the past ten years. The unemployment rate during that period reached two digits in the United States and is still abnormally high at 7 percent. And the decline in output

---

34. Henri R. Sneessens and Jacques H. Drèze, "A Discussion of Belgian Unemployment, Combining Traditional Concepts and Disequilibrium Econometrics," *Economica*, vol. 53 (1986, *Supplement,*), p. S116.

growth as of 1975 relative to earlier years was just as marked in the United States and Japan as in Europe.

The main distinguishing fact about Europe all along has been the stagnation of employment—a stagnation that was a stabilizing factor in the 1960s and early 1970s, but that has turned into a growing destabilizing factor since then. Current levels of unemployment entail a huge social cost, in particular because youth unemployment is so high, depriving one out of every three or four young adults of the normal opportunities for self-realization, social integration, and personal development (through family, home, and the like).

In an international comparison, Europe's position is definitely weaker than that of Eastern Asia or the United States. As mentioned earlier, the shocks of the mid-1970s hit Japan and the NICs during a period of fast growth, fed by an increasing managerial ability to turn low-cost domestic labor into valuable exports. At the world level, producers in Japan and in the NICs enjoy low marginal cost; accordingly, their output should be less sensitive to fluctuations in aggregate world demand than output in regions, such as Europe and the United States, with higher marginal cost. But the United States has other comparative advantages: the bigger size of an integrated market and the greater autonomy of a less open economy, with a single currency and a single government. These advantages have enabled the United States to pursue a mix of fiscal and monetary policies not available to individual European countries acting on their own and not achieved by Europe as a whole because of insufficient integration and coordination.

This weaker position of Europe, which makes it most exposed to worldwide fluctuations, is still present today and is not apt to be remedied easily. Wage competitiveness relative to Japan and the NICs is not likely to improve, and additional countries with surplus labor will join these in managerial mastery—leaving the road of market integration, monetary integration, and policy coordination as the only promising alternative. That road has proved difficult to travel so far, and it is not clear how the difficulties will be overcome (see below).

Krugman identifies three main positions about the underlying causes of Europe's problems. Looking at these positions in the light of the foregoing discussion, I would first of all argue that "automation and the third world" provides one element, among several, of the overall explanation. Technology and trade are linked, because automation and capital-intensive, labor-saving technologies offer the only prospect for competitiveness with the NICs on world markets (of which European domestic markets are a part). And it is not easy to implement policies that simultaneously promote capital-intensive techniques in the sectors open to international competition and labor-intensive techniques in the service sector—all the more so when some service activities (banking, insurance, consulting, transportation) become more international.

The Eurosclerosis position puts much of the blame on the undesirable side effects of the welfare state and could easily be construed as an argument to dismantle it altogether. Krugman notes that the political will to do so seems to be lacking, Mrs. Thatcher not withstanding. Perhaps there are merits to the antiwelfare political attitude—even if it lacks overall consistency in failing to supply a workable alternative. I would tend to share the view expressed by Assar Lindbeck that the welfare state is an incomplete blueprint, the weaknesses of which were revealed by the recession of the late 1970s.[35] As already mentioned, one could have hoped that the welfare state had built automatic stabilizers into the Western European economies. In fact, it worked the other way around. A defensible conclusion is that the welfare state should be amended, not dismantled. For the motivation to create more individual security is certainly not diminished by recent experience—quite the contrary. To give up the goal altogether without attempting to find more effective means would suggest sclerosis of economists and policymakers. Later in this comment, I outline amendments, inspired by recent European experience, that retain the goals of promoting individual welfare through adequate collective insurance and that provide an approach to flexibility more imaginative than continuous clearing of spot markets.

As for hysteresis, I note that Krugman lists two channels through which underutilization of resources may tend to perpetuate itself: one is capital formation, and the other (of which he identified two variants) is the NAIRU. I have already expressed my conviction that the first channel (to which Krugman pays only lip service) is important. It is at the root of the view that current unemployment in Europe is in part "classical," reflecting the contraction of the capital stock and of the associated number of work places. Hysteresis is a novel, and in my opinion far-fetched, name for the obvious fact that low investment, advanced scrapping, and capital deepening lead to less potential employment.

35. Assar Lindbeck, "What Is Wrong with the West European Economies?" *World Economy*, vol. 8 (June 1985), pp. 153–70.

With reference to the NAIRU, I agree with Layard and Nickell that the effect of unemployment on wage settlements is nonlinear.[36] As unemployment increases, the dampening effect on wages of an additional percentage point of unemployment is bound to diminish, one good reason being the presence among the unemployed of an increasing fraction of discouraged workers. But I would hasten to add that, as unemployment increases beyond the NAIRU, this concept loses relevance, and the "hysteresis-through-the-NAIRU" story loses relevance as well.

The same stricture applies to the Blanchard and Summers variant, according to which unions negotiate wages without regard for job seekers.[37] If unions cared only about the employed, newcomers would always be excluded in a world of overlapping generations, in good times as well as in bad. Surely, more sophisticated answers to downward wage rigidities are possible (work-sharing is one example), and peacetime investment is a more appealing savior than war-like emergencies.[38]

Looking Ahead

The view that European unemployment is the result of a combination of influences, among which deficient aggregate demand and untimely wage increases figure prominently, is directly relevant to the question whether happier times lie ahead. That view suggests indeed that adequate, stable paths of both aggregate demand and labor costs are essential to the growth of output and employment. Such a view strikes me as entirely consistent with theoretical and empirical assessments of business behavior.[39] It is precisely because anticipation regarding demand and labor cost remains guarded and uncertain that European firms today are investment shy and hiring shy. Both adequate demand and cost competitiveness will be required over the medium run to ensure profitability of the investments in new capacity and new hirings. These

36. Richard Layard and Stephen Nickell, "The Performance of the British Labour Market," paper presented at the Conference on the British Economy, Sussex, May 18–21, 1986, pp. 25–28.

37. Oliver J. Blanchard and Lawrence H. Summers, 'Hysteresis and the European Unemployment Problem," in Stanley Fischer, ed., *NBER Macroeconomics Annual 1986* (MIT Press, 1986), pp. 15–78.

38. Jacques H. Drèze, "Work-Sharing: Some Theory and Recent European Experience," *Economic Policy,* no. 3 (October 1986), pp. 561–602.

39. For an exposition of the parallel short-run argument, see Olivier J. Blanchard and others, "Employment and Growth in Europe: A Two-Handed Approach," in Blanchard and others, eds., *Restoring Europe's Prosperity,* pp. 95–124.

investments are indispensable if Europe is to grow again at a rate exceeding the current forecast of barely 2.5 to 3 percent per year. Faster growth is needed to reduce unemployment; it is also needed to generate the export revenue and public revenue without which policy margins are too narrow to cope with even moderate shocks. It should be remembered, in this connection, that output growth of 2.5 to 3 percent per year has been needed to keep employment constant in Europe over the past twenty-five years. Under current forecasts, any reduction in unemployment requires faster growth.

The task of generating adequate and stable aggregate demand is particularly challenging. Surprisingly perhaps, the conceptual issues are less clearly defined in this area than in the area of incomes policies. The challenge is to understand how a consistent course of aggregate demand management could be steered, with due allowance for rapid adjustment to changing circumstances but without a fall into the delusion of fine tuning. Given the extent of current uncertainties, the unsuccessful record of recent experiences, recurring difficulties of policy coordination, and the constraints surrounding Europe's starting position, the challenge is formidable indeed.

The current uncertainties concern, in particular, the cost of energy, exchange and interest rates, and U.S. policies. I would place the external balance foremost among the constraints. If Robert Lawrence is right (and he seems to be) when he estimates in his paper that Germany could grow only 1 percent faster than the OECD while maintaining a balanced current account, the room for expansion is severely limited. (It remains to be seen what a similar calculation suggests for Europe as a whole.) I would place next on the list of constraints the public debt and deficits of some countries and the widespread desire to reduce the overall size of government and tax revenues—a desire that might well be invigorated by the new U.S. tax reform. The fact that current account surpluses accompany excessive public deficits in several countries (Benelux, Spain, and Portugal) poses a special challenge to policy coordinators. A third constraint is inflation, once the respite from improved terms of trade fades out.

In thinking about the demand management challenge, one cannot avoid raising the conceptual issue of goals. As I mentioned at the start, it is amazing that Europeans have proved so tolerant of unemployment and so touchy about external deficits and inflation. A credible demand stabilization promise calls for different priorities. The goal of current surpluses would need to be moderated, and a reasonable openness to capital inflows, or to the possibility of such inflows, should be accepted instead. As for inflation, the main issue today is one of accepting calculated risks. The pressing task of stimulating employment, and the forbidding prospect of seeing unemployment rise to new heights under inadequate aggregate demand, amply justify accepting some risk of inflationary pressures. Never accepting the need to balance risks of accelerating inflation against the prospect of persistent unemployment would deserve the stigma of intellectual sclerosis.

Is it feasible for Europe to steer a course of stable aggregate demand? A proper answer to that question could at best take the form of spelling out the implications of the required fiscal and monetary policies for the associated courses of real wages, exchange rates, and interest rates. The premise of stable exchange rates among major European currencies suggests itself, but there would be no reason to be dogmatic if it appeared that stable exchange rates imposed undue constraints elsewhere. The first step in an analysis that largely remains to be spelled out is to define operational guidelines for coordination, with the knowledge that coordination does not mean following parallel policies in the different countries but rather adapting the national policies to a common goal and to country-specific constraints. Such operational guidelines are not easy to define. The material assembled for this volume should prove helpful for that purpose, but a number of questions remain. One of them concerns the role and instruments of monetary policy. In his paper Paul Courant mentions short-run monetary stimulus as a means of reconciling short-term stimulus with higher rates of government saving. But precisely how should the monetary stimulus be engineered, and what is known about quantitative effects and response lags? Regarding fiscal policies, the case for coordination is obvious, but the operational means are not.

The next question concerns the choices of fiscal instruments. There seems to be unanimous agreement, both in Europe and among the contributors to this volume, in favor of public investment and of private involvement in ambitious public projects (the Channel tunnel, high-speed rail links, telecommunication). A more difficult question concerns the orientation of other fiscal measures toward investment stimulus or employment support. Capital-widening investment is the preferred candidate from the viewpoint of long-term growth. But no one quite knows how best to promote it. And special employment programs probably offer a higher and faster return in terms of jobs per dollar.

Turning to incomes policies and wage developments, I note that the relevant sections by Krugman (hysteresis aside) and the three interesting papers in that area by Schultze, Flanagan, and Burtless are far from sanguine. I was expecting sharper strictures passed on excessive real wage growth in the mid-1970s.

The objectives here seem to be as follows: (1) to prevent beggar-thy-neighbor policies of wage competition among European nations; (2) to generate confidence in realistic long-run developments of wages and labor costs, of the kind experienced in Europe in the sixties, with low risk of repeating the mistakes of the mid-seventies; and (3) to salvage the legitimate goals of the welfare state while pruning excesses and designing greater flexibility.

My own prescriptions, addressed to the conceptual issue but with an eye to a credible social compact, would proceed from the following principle: wage flexibility for employees under regular contract should not aim at following the vagaries of the marginal value product of labor but should instead aim at efficient risk sharing between workers and equity owners, with as much labor hoarding as would be allowed by implicit or explicit contracts. As for job seekers, who are not yet a party to labor-hoarding arrangements, their wages should display greater downward flexibility—but still within the provisions of efficient risk sharing, which sets limits to the downward flexibility.[40]

Some worthwhile innovations in keeping with that principle could go as follows.

—Replace full indexation of wages on the consumer price index, where it exists—or lack of indexation, where it exists—by a flexible scheme combining partial indexation on the CPI with partial indexation on nominal national income (a proxy for such a risk-sharing scheme is to index wages on a price index corrected for terms of trade and indirect taxes).

—Introduce more discrimination between the compensation of workers under contract and the compensation of newly hired workers at times of unemployment (thus allowing for wage equalization as soon as full employment is restored). By adding a regional or sectoral dimension to the measure of unemployment, one would open up additional avenues of flexibility of the kind emphasized in particular by Giersch.[41]

40. See Drèze, "Work-Sharing."
41. Herbert Giersch, "Economic Policies in the Age of Schumpeter," *European Economic Review,* vol. 31 (February–March 1987), pp. 35–52.

—Introduce exemptions into social security contributions in an amount corresponding roughly to minimum wages, on the grounds that the corresponding (minimal) social security benefits are by and large benefits accruing to all citizens and not reserved to workers. Recover the foregone contributions through general taxation (either direct or indirect as the case may be, but at any rate without an employment base) while continuing to levy social security contributions on that portion of compensation exceeding the exemption.

—Introduce procyclical variations in the remaining social security contributions as a means of reducing effective labor costs during recessions and raising them during booms, thereby bringing total labor costs closer to the marginal value product of labor at given levels of employment and net labor income.

Some Europeans are attracted to the profit-sharing scheme propounded by Weitzman.[42] One might suggest to them that they investigate an alternative whereby social security is no longer financed by taxes on wages but rather by profit shares computed in accordance with the Weitzman principle—that is, by taxes on profits at rates varying from firm to firm (presumably, in inverse proportion to their equity per employee).

This profit-based approach has two distinct advantages in comparison with the original scheme. First, the variable part of take-home pay would be reduced (or even eliminated), thereby reducing the undesirable income uncertainty imposed on workers by Weitzman's plan. Second, under the Weitzman scheme, new hirings lower the incomes of inside workers through division among more beneficiaries of a fixed share of total profits; insiders may thus resist new hirings. Under the profit-based approach, the bargaining would be transferred from the hands of unions (suspected of representing only insiders) to the hands of a public agency conscious of the social opportunity cost of labor and concerned with aggregate employment.[43]

42. Martin L. Weitzman, *The Share Economy: Conquering Stagflation* (Harvard University Press, 1984). This aspect is picked up by Krugman as well as by the EC's Annual Economic Reports.
43. In contrast to the four specific proposals listed earlier, this last suggestion is meant to stimulate a debate. It strikes me as definitely more attractive than the original profit-sharing scheme, but also as conducive to clearer identification of the difficulties surrounding implementation. I note with interest that whenever I have let out the suggestion in front of European audiences, it did indeed stir up debate at once, which was not the case at this conference.

All these suggestions are untested; the extent to which they are negotiable remains to be verified, and improvements are no doubt possible. If economists and policymakers in Europe are not victims of sclerosis, they should hasten to explore these similar suggestions.

My emphasis on the role of suitable expectations regarding both aggregate demand and labor costs should not be understood as total neglect of other factors relevant to hiring decisions. Additional supporting measures, in particular supply-side measures aimed at raising the labor-demand schedule, have been suggested in various places and need not be repeated here. I will simply note two small points in the spirit of this comment, which proceeds from the premise that hiring decisions are long-term decisions comparable to those regarding investment and typically involve the combination of labor with capital and energy. The first point is that long-term commitments are typically deterred by uncertainty. Measures that will reduce the uncertainties faced by European producers (about energy prices and exchange rates, in particular) would be welcome. Markets for longer-term options on oil prices and exchange rates would seem worth developing at this stage. The second point concerns the use and extension of capital. Measures helping to extend the rate of utilization of capital, for instance through more flexible working-time arrangements (multiple shifts, rolling week, and so on), would be welcome.[44] And measures reducing the cost of capital, for instance through greater efficiency of capital markets, would be equally welcome.[45]

Conclusion

Economists should look beyond the rise in the NAIRU to understand the causes of unemployment and the impediments to growth in Europe. The view reflected in Krugman's paper that a rise in the NAIRU accounts for most of the rise in unemployment has gained some popularity, but it is too narrow.

Krugman cogently explains the main argument behind the view: *if* governments are successfully pursuing demand management policies aimed at neutrality vis-à-vis the rate of inflation, then observed unemployment would correspond to the NAIRU, and changes in the unem-

44. See Drèze, "Work-Sharing."
45. See Franco Modigliani and others, "Reducing Unemployment in Europe: The Role of Capital Formation," paper no. 28 (Brussels: CEPS, 1986).

ployment rate would correspond to changes in the NAIRU. This argument has the merit of making economic policies endogenous, which is always desirable when possible.

The argument does not assert that demand management has aimed (successfully) at constant inflation. That assertion would be difficult to reconcile with observed vagaries in the rate of inflation and would negate the avowed objective of reducing inflation in the 1980s. Rather, the argument asserts that demand management has aimed at achieving a rate of unemployment which by itself would not cause the wage bargaining process to add to or subtract from existing inflationary pressures, such as those arising from changes in the terms of trade.

The assertion that policy aims over the relevant period are confined to that objective seems suspect. It neglects the weight of external constraints and of objectives stated directly in terms of budget deficits, public debt, or employment. And it seems more plausible to me that the planned and realized deceleration of inflation in the 1980s has pushed unemployment above the NAIRU.

Testing the assertion empirically requires knowledge that economists do not possess. Empirical estimates of the NAIRU must be based on complete models endogenizing the interactions among demand, supply, price formation, and wage formation. I am afraid that our models are not sufficiently reliable and consistent to generate the information that policymakers should have used to pursue successfully the assumed policies and that economists should use to test that assumption.[46] The truth of the matter is that economists do not have a precise estimate of the potential impact of aggregate demand stimulation on wage formation in Europe today. It may be that the current trend toward wage moderation is strong enough to persist at higher rates of output growth. It may also be that the wage restraint of recent years has built up latent pressures toward catching up, which might or might not be exacerbated by demand stimulation. I have little confidence that published estimates of the NAIRU provide a reliable answer to that question. As indicated earlier, I see no alternative to accepting a calculated risk that reflects normative priorities.

I thus heartily concur with Krugman in his concluding remarks: a

---

46. As noted by Krugman in his concluding remarks, "A survey of the work on NAIRUs . . . reveals that the numbers thrown about are more nearly speculations informed by the data than estimates to be used with any assurance."

greater amount of solid empirical analysis and bolder policy analysis is badly needed if the economists are to escape the disease of Eurosclerosis.

Comment by Armin Gutowski

First of all I want to congratulate the Brookings Institution on having undertaken the effort to look more deeply into the causes and effects of slow growth in Europe. The papers in this volume are written by Americans trying to determine the central problems facing Europe and the policies that would be best for Europe. This method avoids the self-serving nationalistic policy recommendations and mutual reproaches in which politicians and academics from both sides of the Atlantic have indulged. I appreciate the sober, thorough, and competent analyses in the papers for this conference. But the papers also show that there is still a long way to go before agreement can be reached on what should be done to improve economic performance in Europe.

Nevertheless, I agree with the concluding remarks in Krugman's stimulating paper: though we economists should make our empirical statements with greater caution, we should be less timid in analyzing policies and making policy recommendations. Policy decisions cannot wait for academic solutions. We have to use what empirical results we have got so far, combined with informed judgment, in order to help narrow the chances and risks of alternative policy decisions. But we should also modestly admit that the choice of policy strategies will always represent decisionmaking under uncertainty, with social and political traditions, as well as faith in certain ideologies and paradigms not easily captured in economic analysis, playing a major role.

Before I turn to the specifics of conceptual issues raised by Krugman, I will say a few words about the notion of "slow growth" in Europe. First, compared with growth in the United States, Europe's growth has not been slow. According to the OECD, in Europe GDP grew on average at 4.9 percent a year between 1969 and 1973; in the United States it was 3.3 percent. The average growth rate went down in Western Europe to 2.4 percent a year for the period 1974–79 and further down, to 1.4 percent, for the period 1980–86; in the United States, it went down to 2.6 percent and 2.1 percent in the two periods. Since 1980 the growth rate has declined in the United States from its 7.2 percent peak in 1984 to 2.5 percent in 1986; in Western Europe it went up to the same 2.5

percent from its 1.3 percent low in 1983. Indeed, if one looks at per capita growth, the average rates were lower in the United States than in Western Europe for the two previous periods and equal for the 1980–86 period, namely 1 percent a year. Given these figures, I would not subscribe to Krugman's formulation that since 1980 there has been a "contrast between continuing growth in the United States and Japan and near-stagnation in Europe."

I would not deny the existence of a growth problem in Europe. I am concerned about the rising unemployment and stagnating employment that exists in spite of the slowdown in productivity growth. By contrast, in the United States the much lower productivity increase has accompanied a remarkable rise in employment over the full range of the three periods. Moreover, Europe's productive potential has adjusted to the high unemployment level. The rates of growth of the European potential output have declined drastically. Unemployment is no longer a mere cyclical phenomenon. To remedy the situation, more job-creating investment, perhaps combined with more structural change, is urgently needed. I have severe doubts about Krugman's belief that in the European case "most of the growth slowdown, and by definition all of the rise in unemployment, represents a decline in utilization." It seems to me that the sluggish growth of potential production keeps capacity utilization fairly high.

At this point I will follow the outline of Krugman's paper. Regarding the international competitiveness of Germany, it is certainly wrong that the undervalued mark before 1973 produced an export-led virtuous circle of growth. Germany probably would have done still better if it had adjusted the deutsche mark's parity under the Bretton Woods regime faster and more often. This could be seen after 1973, when Germany moved rather quickly into substantial trade surpluses despite the first oil price hike and even though the mark strongly appreciated in real terms. The solution to this apparent puzzle is that Germany was not able under fixed exchange rates to fully use its potential advantage in the terms of trade. After 1973 Germany had just the right mix of export goods to offer. They were products in strong demand worldwide and their availability counted much more than price, so that the mark could appreciate without detrimental effects on exports. The situation was completely different after the second oil price shock. The demand stimulation resulting from the Bonn summit did not bring about the

German current account deficit. Rather, it was that production in the rest of the world was by then better matched to demand. So German exporters now faced price competition, and this time only a depreciation against the dollar brought Germany back into surplus on current account. This explains why Germany was concerned about its competitiveness in spite of its surpluses. Its share of high-tech commodities in total exports had declined, whereas the U.S. and Japanese shares had risen.

This concern is also not incompatible with the fact that, as Krugman rightly points out, Europe's productivity growth remained more favorable than that of the United States. It is not the average productivity increase that counts but the productivity growth in high-tech areas. And one has to be very careful, as Krugman has also discussed at length, in interpreting measured rates of increase in labor productivity. I certainly agree—it is not a disaster that Europe is quite reliant on traditional manufacturing, at least as long as productivity gains are high enough to prevent newly industrialized countries from exerting too much pressure on real wages. It is noteworthy that German industries no longer complain about a technology gap. But they might well be surprised about the extent to which their exports will depend on price competitiveness when the J-curve effect of the recent appreciation of their currency will have run out.

I can be brief in my remarks regarding the next two parts of the Krugman paper because I agree with much of what is said there. But I cannot suppress some remarks on the NAIRU and on the possibility of separating the issues of aggregate supply limits, disequilibrium real wage hypothesis, rigidities, and Eurosclerosis.

When I read about the NAIRU for the first time, I thought I had missed a famous Indian economist whose name was attached to an economic phenomenon he had discovered. I soon found that the NAIRU was only an expression for a simple and well-known phenomenon, which seems to have been invented to prevent policymakers and union leaders from understanding what is meant. After having gone through the elaborate descriptions of figures 1 and 2 in Krugman's paper, I am inclined to ask whether it would not have been much simpler to put it all under the broad heading of real wage disequilibrium and perhaps better to rename it real labor cost disequilibrium. Because it is such a complex matter, it is difficult, if not impossible, to measure anything like the NAIRU. The "wage gap" should rather be called a labor cost gap and include all risk elements for entrepreneurs, which definitely have cost equivalents. As long as the various calculations give very different results, one cannot know for sure whether there is room for demand expansion, or whether real labor costs are simply too high for full employment, or whether a combination of both would be an appropriate description of the present situation.

I believe that the simple textbook wisdom is indisputable: if labor costs are such that there is no point of full employment on the production function that can be reached and sustained (apart from purely cyclical movements), then either real labor costs have to be reduced (in general or for a part of the labor force) or restrictions on the production function— be they legal or institutional or because of union contracts—have to be removed. Otherwise, physical capacities will adjust to the lower level of profitable employment.

I suggest, without being able to prove it here and now, that all of the rigidities as well as the problems caused by technical progress and all the elements of Eurosclerosis enumerated in the Krugman paper (and in more detail in some of the other papers in this volume) can be shown either to have raised real labor costs or to have restricted the otherwise technically feasible production function. If this is so, the analysis is simpler, though not the measurement. Real labor costs in this broader sense have gone up quite substantially in the late 1960s and in the 1970s, even if one looks only at that part of them which can be measured. In the 1980s, wage increases were more moderate, and profits went up after the recession. Nevertheless, the employment situation continued to deteriorate until 1984, and improved afterward only rather slowly. But to derive from this that there is now substantial room for Keynesian pump priming means jumping to conclusions. In fact, impediments to growth did not cease to rise, first of all (as Assar Lindbeck pointed out)[47] because many of the cost-increasing and capacity-restricting legal and contractual measures have taken time to come to their full effect, and second because (at least in Germany) the judiciary tended to aggravate these effects by court rulings in favor of employees and their representatives.

Let me add a few remarks regarding the hysteresis hypothesis discussed in Krugman's paper. It seems true that the long-term unemployed sooner or later become disenfranchised by the unions, by the

47. See Assar Lindbeck, "The Recent Slowdown of Productivity Growth," *Economic Journal*, vol. 93 (March 1983), pp. 13–34.

employers, or probably by both. But before I would subscribe to the policy conclusions Krugman seems to draw from this phenomenon, I would like to ask why it should not be sufficient to exempt the unemployed, after a certain period of unemployment, from minimum wage requirements imposed either by legislation or by binding union contracts; or why it would not be sufficient to pay, if the former appears to be politically impossible, wage subsidies to those who hire these unemployed.

I must also warn against overstating the historical parallels that Krugman mentioned in his paper. Interwar Britain was suffering—especially during the 1920s—from a highly overvalued currency; I cannot find a parallel to that now. As competent a scholar as Joseph Schumpeter attributed the experience of the United States during the 1930s mainly to the efforts of the administration to cure the consequences of the great contraction of the late 1920s and early 1930s by supporting cartels and by vigorously promoting wage increases. The great contraction itself, which had caused the high unemployment, was brought about by an utterly restrictive monetary policy. Again I cannot see similarities to the current situation in Europe. Monetary policy in nearly all European countries can better be described as expansionary than as restrictive. Wages, especially the wages for unskilled labor, are certainly too high and labor law is too restrictive. But one will not find among the contemporary European governments any which believe—as the administrations of the 1930s did—that raising wages is the right way to raise employment.

Finally, the conclusion drawn from the observation that the employment problems of the 1930s came to an end with World War II and the then massive expansion of demand, combined with wage and price controls, leads us nowhere. Price and wage controls under peacetime conditions will always cause distortions, which can easily produce new and additional employment problems. A massive demand expansion in the present European situation would, when the spending ends, leave the countries with high accumulated debt without their having achieved anything that was worth the price. It is no accidental coincidence that Germany, for example, found its way out of its massive unemployment of the late 1940s and early 1950s just the other way around: by abolishing wage and price controls and by establishing sound monetary and fiscal policies.

These considerations have carried me to my concluding remarks on policy implications. These differ from the policy conclusions Krugman draws from his analysis of the causes for slow economic growth in Europe. I also, of course, do not believe that it would be feasible to cut real wages enough to achieve full employment. Although cutting real wages is a logically possibile way to regain full employment, it would probably greatly deteriorate the prospects for economic growth, at least for some time. Since it would mean substantial reductions in take-home pay, the incentive to work would further decrease. The alternative favored by unions in Germany and elsewhere in Europe, cutting work hours, is attractive to many who are employed only because it reduces net income far less than income before taxes. But tax rates and social taxes would have to be raised before long to accommodate further reductions of working time and more work-sharing and part-time work, because otherwise the level of government expenditures could not be upheld.

Some other possible measures, such as adding tax incentives for investment, sometimes even for selected industries, are also inappropriate. This would be like pouring oil into the engine after having thrown sand into its wheels—the engine might speed up for a while, but not for long, and it might go in the wrong direction.

Therefore, the best course is to reduce real labor costs without reducing disposable income, and to remove restrictions on the production function in order to stimulate supply by giving new incentives to work and to invest. But this must be done not by just trying to turn back the wheel of time, revoking all former legislation (though much of it has to be revised). What I have in mind are basic reforms, in particular of health care systems, of the existing old-age pension schemes, and not the least of the tax systems in Europe along the lines considered in the United States. I cannot go into details, but I am convinced that courageous reforms of that type could reduce gross labor costs substantially without diminishing the intended social protection of labor and the socially warranted redistribution of income. The prospects for the acceptance of reform proposals of this type by policymakers in Europe seem to be improving. For the economics profession, I strongly believe that it is at least as important to develop such reform schemes as it is to analyze the causes for slow growth and high unemployment in Europe. In concluding, let me say that such reforms, especially tax reforms, which increase the potential for growth, could be designed in a way that stimulates demand without rekindling inflation.

General Discussion

Is Europe's problem slow growth or high unemployment? Several participants suggested that Europe's unemployment problem is unique but that its growth problem is shared with Japan and the United States. It was argued that if one eliminates from the figures both the business cycle and the substitution effects of high wages, European productivity growth since 1972 has been as fast as Japan's and more than three times as fast as that in the United States. But another participant contended that Europe is faced with a growth-and-accumulation problem. Insiders—that is, employed workers—in Europe keep their real income rising through some restrictive practice, in which case they pay higher taxes to finance unemployment benefits (in the American system they can share their work with those who would otherwise be excluded and accept stagnant real income and lower taxes.) Outsiders (the unemployed) in the American system are subjected to a great deal of uncertainty about such elementary things as health care to induce them to accept dead-end jobs that provide at least minimum benefits. In Europe they are maintained at a reasonable level but are left unemployed. This, he argued, shows that Europe is primarily faced with a growth problem. But another participant disagreed. The data show that the deceleration of U.S. productivity growth after 1973 was not in any way attributable to the hiring of women, young people, and other outsiders.

Several troubling aspects of Europe's slow growth since 1973 were noted. First, the rate of productivity growth in manufacturing suddenly declined 2 to 4 percentage points after 1973. Second, the rate of growth of the manufacturing capital stock declined by 60 to 70 percent after 1973 (falling to zero in some countries). Third, the number of man-hours input into manufacturing declined by 30 to 50 percent after 1973. These statistics apply equally well to countries such as Sweden and Switzerland, where there has been practically no increase in unemployment, and to those such as France, Germany, and the United Kingdom, which have experienced large increases in unemployment.

The incidence of unemployment among the young was also emphasized. Except in Germany, typically 25 to 30 percent of youth are unemployed, and the duration of their unemployment is very long. The prospect of being unemployed for the rest of his or her life prevents a young person from looking ahead toward starting a family, buying a house, and establishing a career. Growth rates significantly higher than 2.5 to 3 percent are needed to reduce the pool of unemployed. It was noted that from an American viewpoint slow growth in Europe is a concern because it restricts U.S. export growth and could lead to the spread of mercantilism and protectionism through the rest of the world, with devastating effects.

Are European wages too high? One commentator argued that it is important to distinguish between manufacturing and nonmanufacturing sectors when making statements about productivity and wage gaps. The wage gap in manufacturing has been smaller in Europe than in the United States since 1981, and almost all the apparent increase in the European nonmanufacturing wage gap has been due to the shift out of self-employment (mostly farm employment and small shopkeeping).

But drawing policy implications from wage gap measures was noted as problematic. In most macroeconomic models, prices are simply a markup on wages. An increase in the wage rate in such models will immediately lead to inflation and, typically, a rise in unemployment. Because of normal inertia in the price equation, prices should lag a bit behind wages, and the real wage will increase. At this point there will indeed be a wage gap; however, the story is not over. To stabilize the inflation that has occurred, demand will be reduced and unemployment will increase. Because of the nature of the price-setting mechanism, when inflation has been stabilized, the price markup on wages will necessarily be the same as it was originally; hence the real wage will be unchanged. Excess wage pressure would have been the fundamental cause of the unemployment, yet real wages would not have risen. The overall point is that if price is nothing more than a markup on normal cost, however much people aspire to higher real wages, in the long run they get only unemployment. The disequilibrium real wage hypothesis—that the real wage is too high—thus would appear fallacious, given the way prices seem to be determined in European economies.

One participant pointed out that those who believed excessive real wages were the main problem should be specific about how lower real wages might improve European growth. Would a cut in real wages make a nation more competitive? First, while a fall in wage costs within a particular country would improve that country's international competitiveness, this policy would be ineffective if generalized. If every nation cut its wage costs, none would benefit. Second, the macroeconomic effects of a redistribution from wages to profits might dampen demand and thus discourage rather than stimulate investment. Third, if wage costs were reduced without cutting wage income, who would make up the revenue loss? If the reduction amounts to a tax cut, it would be a demand stimulus in disguise unless taxes were increased somewhere else. But if taxation of wage income and capital income were increased, investment would be unlikely to rise.

Another participant responded that a fall in real wages should, through the normal economic process, bring about a supply-side impetus and an increase in output. If this were not the case, if producers were pessimistic about their potential gains, then there would always be room for Keynesian demand-side policies. In other words, lower real wage pressures raise the rate at which the aggregate may be safely expanded, whether that demand is generated from the private or the public sector.

A German participant saw the need to clarify some matters concerning recent German economic policy. He said his experiences during the early 1980s had made him wiser. Large-scale deficit financing cannot support long-term growth in employment. The recent economic upturn in Germany is increasingly being stimulated by self-sustained domestic demand (consumer spending and private-sector investment), the precondition for which was a sustained reduction of budget deficits through cuts in government expenditure. For Europe as a whole he emphasized the need for fast-paced structural adjustment: the reduction of subsidies and tax benefits as well as adoption of tax systems more conducive to growth. He called for deregulation and liberalization as well as cohesion within the European internal market.

The hysteresis or persistence-of-unemployment theory had come under attack by Paul Krugman for being inconsistent with the experiences of the 1950s and 1960s. Indeed, it was pointed out that Summers' and Blanchard's version of the model implies that increases in the demand for labor result in higher wages rather than higher employment. But the Lindbeck-Snower model yields different results. It contains two demand curves for labor—one for insiders and one (further down) for outsiders. The difference between the two curves is determined, among other factors, by turnover costs and productivity effects when outsiders try to enter the work force. In this model, if there is a sufficiently large increase in the demand for labor, both insider and outsider demand curves move to the right. If the shift of the outsider curve is large enough, a number of entrants will join the work force and be employed. Hence this model is consistent not only with the experiences of the 1950s and 1960s but also with more recent experience.

One participant noted that people were often too ready to dismiss potential explanations for Eurosclerosis because of timing—the phenomena in question existed before the growth slowdown. But he pointed out that lags are a well-known economic phenomenon. Furthermore, economic relationships can be nonlinear, and there can be threshold effects.

One participant took exception to Krugman's suggestion that something as dramatic as a war might be necessary to lower the European unemployment rate permanently. Improving some of the factors that have led to the persistence of unemployment, such as the decline in the skills of displaced workers, the deterioration in the stock of physical capital, and the increase in firms' turnover costs, seemed to be a preferable policy. Another agreed, observing that the fall in British unemployment between 1933 and 1938 was substantial.

Labor, Product, and Financial Markets

GARY BURTLESS

Jobless Pay and High European Unemployment

OVER THE past fifteen years unemployment has risen in all major Western economies. The rise has been especially dramatic in Europe. Where West European economies once enjoyed unemployment rates that were low in comparison with the rate in the United States, they now struggle with rates that are sharply higher.

Different hypotheses have been advanced to explain the deterioration of the labor market in Europe. This paper examines the suggestion that generous income maintenance payments to the unemployed have created such severe work disincentives in Europe that economic adjustment has been delayed or prevented, thereby increasing structural unemployment. Many authors have argued that high jobless benefits are an important or even the main cause of high or rising unemployment. Minford, for example, claims that the rise in British joblessness since the early 1970s is attributable to a combination of high and rising unemployment benefit levels and unionization rates.[1] Several authors who have examined the time-series pattern of jobless pay and unemployment have concluded that earnings-replacement rates strongly affect the rate of unemployment.[2] In their examination of high British unemployment in the 1920s,

The author is grateful to Tony Atkinson, Johanna Gomulka, and Richard Layard of the London School of Economics and Christoph Büchtemann, Bernd Reissert, and Günther Schmid of the International Institute of Management in Berlin for help in assembling information for this paper.

1. Patrick Minford, *Unemployment: Cause and Cure,* 2d ed. (Oxford: Basil Blackwell, 1985).

2. Grubel and Maki found a high elasticity of U.S. unemployment with respect to benefit levels (the time-series elasticity was 6.0). See H. G. Grubel and D. R. Maki, "The Effects of Unemployment Benefits on U.S. Unemployment Rates," *Weltwirtschaftliches Archiv,* vol. 112 (1976), pp. 274–97. Maki and Spindler, in a time-series analysis of Britain, found a significant and very large effect of benefits on unemployment.

Benjamin and Kochin conclude that "the persistently high rate of unemployment in interwar Britain was due in large part . . . to high unemployment benefits relative to wages."[3] Not surprisingly, all the research just cited has been subject to intensive scrutiny and controversy.

In this paper I examine evidence on benefits and unemployment for five countries: Britain, France, West Germany, Sweden, and the United States. These countries differ markedly in the benefits they offer to unemployed workers. The paper describes the systems of jobless pay in the five countries and gives evidence on trends in generosity within national programs. The differences in generosity and in trends in generosity are then compared with the patterns of joblessness within and across countries. Comparisons of this type can give a basis for deciding whether generous unemployment pay in Europe is a plausible explanation for the sharply higher unemployment rates of recent years. The evidence can be used to address three questions: Do trends in the generosity of jobless benefits within each country correspond to trends in national unemployment? Do different levels of unemployment benefits across countries explain the cross-national pattern of joblessness? Do slack conditions in the labor market cause the adverse effects of jobless benefits to become larger or smaller?

For several reasons it seems inappropriate to analyze the evidence assembled here using formal econometric models. For one thing, the unemployment insurance data for the five countries are not always comparable and do not always extend over a lengthy period. Hence the use of the data in formal statistical models could be extremely misleading. For another, even where the data for a given country are unobjectionable, I am skeptical of the reliability of aggregate time-series methods in this application. The intense debate over the time-series evidence produced by Minford, Maki and Spindler, and Benjamin and Kochin reveals the tremendous sensitivity of the time-series results to changes in specification and the time period of analysis.[4] This sensitivity to specification

---

See Dennis Maki and Z. A. Spindler, "The Effect of Unemployment Compensation on the Rate of Unemployment in Great Britain," *Oxford Economic Papers,* vol. 27 (November 1975), pp. 440–54.

3. Daniel K. Benjamin and Levis A. Kochin, "Searching for an Explanation of Unemployment in Interwar Britain," *Journal of Political Economy,* vol. 87 (June 1979), p. 474.

4. For an exchange on Minford, see Stephen J. Nickell, "A Review of Unemployment:

changes should hardly be surprising. The usual economic model of response to unemployment insurance focuses on behavior and economic variables at the level of the individual. At the aggregate level, neither the behavior nor the economic variables are appropriately observed or measured.

The paper is organized as follows. The first section briefly summarizes the expected behavioral responses to jobless benefits. It highlights the major features of insurance systems that can adversely affect incentives for workers and employers. The second section describes systems of jobless pay in the five countries and trends in their generosity over time. This is followed by an analysis of trends in joblessness in the five nations and an assessment of the plausible effects of benefits on unemployment levels. The paper concludes with a brief summary.

Expected Effect of Insurance on Unemployment

Unemployment insurance can affect the level of aggregate employment and unemployment in four main ways. Jobless benefits can lengthen the average duration of unemployment spells by reducing the incentive for unemployed workers to accept new jobs. Insurance can also raise the number of spells of unemployment by affecting either the quit behavior of employed workers or the layoff policies of employers. The level of insurance benefits can influence the wage-bargaining behavior of unions and unionized workers, thus affecting the equilibrium real wage level and the rate of unemployment. Finally, the usual method of financing benefits—payroll taxes—can affect the cost of labor and hence the demand for labor by firms. I consider each of these potential effects in turn.

Probability of Leaving Unemployment

The impact of unemployment insurance on the search behavior of jobless workers is the effect that has attracted the most attention from

Cause and Cure," *Economic Journal*, vol. 94 (December 1984), pp. 946–53, and Patrick Minford, "Response to Nickell," ibid., pp. 954–59; for a critique of Maki and Spindler, see P. N. Junankar, "An Econometric Analysis of Unemployment in Great Britain, 1952–1975," *Oxford Economic Papers*, vol. 33 (November 1981), pp. 387–400; for critiques of Benjamin and Kochin, see the collection of comments in the *Journal of Political Economy*, vol. 90 (April 1982), pp. 369–436.

economists. The partial equilibrium impact seems straightforward, at least in theory. An unemployed worker determines a set of reservation conditions with which he or she compares any job offer that is received. For simplicity, most job search models focus on a single reservation condition—the reservation wage. If an offer that meets these conditions is received, it is accepted and the worker becomes employed or reemployed. Otherwise the offer is rejected, and the individual continues to search for a better offer. By supplementing a worker's income during spells of unemployment, jobless benefits permit the worker to establish a more selective set of reservation conditions. Other things being equal, this must reduce the probability that the worker will receive an acceptable offer within a fixed period, so the expected duration of a completed spell of unemployment will lengthen. Baily has suggested that jobless pay may affect not only a worker's reservation conditions but also the amount of effort devoted to job search.[5] If search intensity is reduced, the worker will receive fewer job offers per period. For this reason, too, the probability of becoming employed or reemployed falls.

Four aspects of an unemployment insurance system can affect the search behavior of jobless workers. Eligibility conditions for insurance benefits help to determine the potential scope of overall effects. If eligibility criteria are so strict that only a small proportion of jobless workers qualify for benefits, the aggregate effect of insurance must be small. The generosity of benefits can also have important consequences on job search efforts. If weekly benefits are high compared with typical earnings in employment, the financial cost of unemployment will be low. High benefits thus permit workers to establish stringent reservation conditions for an acceptable job. A third critical element in an insurance system is the duration of potential benefits. Payments that continue indefinitely place less pressure on jobless workers to find work than do payments limited to only a few weeks or months. Finally, an important but often overlooked aspect of an insurance program is the effort made by authorities to prevent malingering among insured job seekers. Most systems have rules requiring that those who collect benefits be available for work, make good faith efforts to find work, and accept suitable jobs when they are offered. If these rules were zealously and effectively enforced, the adverse effects of unemployment insurance on job search would be reduced.

5. Martin Neil Baily, "Unemployment Insurance as Insurance for Workers," *Industrial and Labor Relations Review,* vol. 30 (July 1977), pp. 495–504.

Much of the empirical literature on unemployment insurance has been devoted to measuring the influence of one or another of these four elements on the duration of a spell of unemployment. The most common subject of research is the effect of benefit levels on unemployment duration, where benefits are typically measured as a percentage of weekly earnings in the worker's most recent job. Using microeconomic data, economists determine the benefits available to individual workers and attempt to estimate the influence of benefits on the rate of job finding or the length of completed spells of unemployment. Virtually all these studies find evidence that job seekers eligible for higher-than-average benefits experience significantly longer unemployment, although the evidence is often not very robust.

It is widely—though erroneously—assumed that evidence of this type demonstrates a definite link between high jobless pay and high aggregate unemployment.[6] The expected effect on overall unemployment depends, however, on the nature of the labor market and the extent of eligibility for insurance benefits. Consider two types of labor market, one tight and the other slack. In the tight market vacancies are relatively plentiful and the insured unemployed are not queuing up for jobs. Vacancies remain open until a qualified applicant comes along whose reservation conditions are satisfied by the job. When this match occurs, there is one less vacancy and one less unemployed worker. Clearly, an increase in jobless benefits can raise overall unemployment in a tight labor market. Workers receiving increased benefits will set more stringent reservation conditions for an acceptable job. Thus they will reject some offers they would previously have accepted. If employers do not raise wage offers, job vacancies—especially low-wage vacancies—will remain unfilled longer than before the increase in benefits.

Uninsured job seekers, if they exist in this tight market, might benefit from the choosier job search strategy adopted by unemployed workers receiving increased benefits. Because low-wage jobs will remain vacant somewhat longer and hence will become more plentiful, workers with lower reservation wages should find jobs somewhat faster than before the increase in benefits. In the aggregate, however, the duration of spells of unemployment must increase because the average unemployed worker is more likely to reject the average job offer. The mean duration of a

6. See, for example, Kathleen P. Classen, "The Effect of Unemployment Insurance on the Duration of Unemployment and Subsequent Earnings," *Industrial and Labor Relations Review*, vol. 30 (July 1977), especially pp. 442–44.

typical vacancy will rise. This change in turn will encourage some employers to raise their wage offers and reduce their equilibrium level of employment. In this classical view of search behavior in a relatively tight labor market, the equilibrium number of vacancies and unemployed workers will rise in response to an increase in jobless benefits, the number of employed workers will fall, and the average wage in employment will rise.

In a slack labor market, an increase in insurance benefits might have almost no effect on overall joblessness. Suppose workers are queuing up for available jobs or, equivalently, that vacancies are short-lived because an army of unemployed is willing to accept jobs at the prevailing wage. In this labor market the longer job searches of insured unemployed workers after a benefit increase could be exactly counterbalanced by the shorter spells of unemployment experienced by uninsured or poorly insured job seekers.[7] Because generously insured workers are competing for jobs with uninsured and poorly insured workers, a job offer that is rejected by an insured unemployed worker will be readily accepted by a less well insured rival. According to this view, the composition of unemployment, but not its level, will be affected by an increase in insurance benefits. How jobless benefits affect overall unemployment thus depends on the state of the labor market as well as on specific characteristics of the insurance program.

This analysis suggests that an increase in unemployment benefits will more strongly affect unemployment in tight labor markets than in slack ones. The point is illustrated in figure 1, which shows the relation between vacancies and unemployment under two different benefit regimes. The curved, negatively sloped line AC shows the relation between job vacancies and unemployment in an economy with relatively low benefits, while line BC shows the relation in the same economy after benefits have been raised.[8] For reasons mentioned above, the effect of the benefit increase on unemployment is greater when vacancies are high (V_h) than when they are low (V_l). At a sufficiently low level of vacancies, here represented at point C, an increase in benefits may have no effect on unemployment. If this analysis is correct, it implies that the

7. This effect has been pointed out by Stephen J. Nickell in "The Effect of Unemployment and Related Benefits on the Duration of Unemployment," *Economic Journal*, vol. 89 (March 1979), pp. 34–49, and by A. B. Atkinson in "Unemployment Benefits and Incentives," in John Creedy, ed., *The Economics of Unemployment in Britain* (London: Butterworths, 1981), pp. 128–49.

8. This figure was suggested by Jules Theeuwes in his comment on this paper.

Figure 1. *Vacancy-Unemployment Relationship under Alternative Benefit Levels*

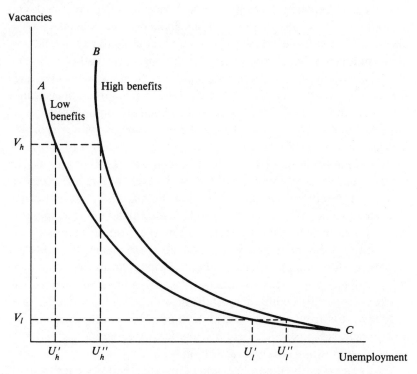

Vacancies

adverse effects of generous insurance on search behavior will be smaller during cyclical downturns, near point *C*, than during economic expansions, near points *A* and *B*.

Probability of Entering Unemployment

The discussion has thus far focused on the effects of jobless pay on the probability that unemployed workers will leave unemployment. In addition, unemployment insurance can raise the probability that workers will enter unemployment. There are several mechanisms through which this might occur. Workers who are assured of a comfortable income if they become unemployed might be more inclined to quit an unsatisfying job.[9] They might be less inclined to perform in a job to the best of their

9. If the laws and regulations governing eligibility for benefits exclude voluntary job leavers or establish a substantial initial waiting period of unemployment before benefits

ability. These attitudes can increase the number of workers entering unemployment because of quitting or dismissal for cause.

Baily and Feldstein have argued that the rate of temporary layoff unemployment can also be raised by the financing mechanism of jobless benefits.[10] Individual employers are seldom required to pay the full cost of unemployment benefits paid out to their temporarily laid-off workers. (That is, employers' premium payments for unemployment insurance are not fully "experience rated" to reflect their previous use of insurance benefits.) Only in the United States and Sweden are employers required to pay even part of the cost of these benefits. Jobless pay is typically financed by a proportional payroll tax levied on all employers or workers. Baily and Feldstein suggest that this financing arrangement provides an implicit subsidy for employers to engage in excessive layoffs because they pay for only a small part (if any) of the marginal cost associated with an added layoff. This subsidy will cause employers to respond to variations in final demand by laying off workers rather than adopting some strategy that on the margin is more costly to themselves and their employees, for example, accumulating extra inventories, reducing wage rates and product prices, or limiting weekly hours. Employers and workers essentially collude against the insurance fund to minimize their collective loss from a downturn in demand. The more generously the government sets insurance benefits, the less strenuously will workers resist the imposition of temporary layoffs.

Oddly, most of the theoretical and empirical studies of excess-layoff unemployment have been performed by Americans. All the empirical studies concentrate on the experience in the United States, where the implicit subsidy to temporary layoff unemployment is low by international standards. Virtually no attention has been given to this issue in Europe, where the implicit subsidy is essentially complete. Later I will consider whether the Baily-Feldstein hypothesis can explain different unemployment patterns in Europe and the United States.

---

begin (as is the case, for example, in many states of the United States), then the effect of the system in raising the incidence of quits will depend on how rigorously the regulations are enforced.

10. Martin Neil Baily, "On the Theory of Layoffs and Unemployment," *Econometrica*, vol. 45 (July 1977, *part 2*), pp. 1043–63; and Martin Feldstein, "Temporary Layoffs in the Theory of Unemployment," *Journal of Political Economy*, vol. 84 (October 1976), pp. 937–57.

Wage Bargaining and Tax Burdens

Jobless benefits can potentially affect unemployment by raising the equilibrium real wage. Of course, one reason for this is that higher benefits increase the average duration of job search, thus reducing the number of workers in employment. To the extent that workers spend less time employed and the average number of workers in employment falls, the marginal product (and wage) of employed workers will rise if there is a fixed capital stock. This effect of benefits, however, is really just a side effect of the mechanism described above. An alternative mechanism has been emphasized by Nickell and Andrews and Minford, who point out that the generosity of benefits may affect the bargaining stance of unions.[11] If benefits are high, the income losses arising from a reduction in union members' employment will be small. Hence unions may be tempted to be aggressive in bargaining over wages. To the extent they succeed in obtaining higher wages than warranted, employment will decline and unemployment rise.

Finally, taxes imposed to finance unemployment benefits can increase the employment costs borne by employers. Insurance is typically financed by a tax imposed on employer payrolls. When more generous benefits are financed with higher payroll taxes, the wage bill of the employer must rise, at least in the short run. One consequence may be reduced employment. (In the long run, some or all of the burden of the tax will be passed back to workers through lower net real wages.) The same analysis applies to other forms of social insurance financed through payroll taxes. Recently, several European countries have liberalized disability and old-age insurance programs, permitting older unemployed workers to retire before the normal age. Early retirees may not be counted as unemployed workers, but the cost of paying for their early retirement will nonetheless drive up payroll tax rates on the wages of workers who remain in employment. If the tax increases cannot be shifted back on workers in the short run, employers may cut back on employment.[12]

11. Stephen J. Nickell and M. Andrews, "Trade Unions, Real Wages and Employment in Britain, 1951–79," *Oxford Economic Papers,* vol. 35 (November 1983, *Supplement*), pp. 183–206; and Patrick Minford, "Labor Market Equilibrium in an Open Economy," ibid., pp. 207–44.

12. Nickell and Andrews, in "Unions, Real Wages and Employment in Britain,"

Comparing Jobless Pay across Countries

This section briefly describes the main features of jobless pay in four European countries and the United States. The survey concentrates on three aspects of individual insurance systems: the relation of benefits to earnings, the eligibility criteria for benefits, and the maximum duration of benefits. (Additional details about the national programs can be found in the sources identified in the data appendix.) Before starting this survey of unemployment insurance in the five countries, though, it is worth considering how the generosity of different programs can be compared.

The Replacement Ratio

A critical feature of any system of jobless pay is the relation of benefits to earnings. Because most national programs are complicated, it is difficult to obtain a single reliable index of the generosity of payments. Virtually all analysts of jobless pay have sought to define and measure some concept of an earnings-replacement rate. Unfortunately, there is little agreement about the proper definition of this concept. Competing measures of the replacement rate can show divergent trends in benefit generosity.

The most useful concept of a replacement rate for assessing microeconomic work incentives is the ratio of net benefits received in unemployment to net earnings received at work.[13] Yet this simple theoretical

---

and Minford, in "Labor Market Equilibrium," use econometric specifications that suggest they may have had this mechanism in mind. Within the context of an efficiency wage model of labor markets, Jeremy I. Bulow and Lawrence H. Summers, in "A Theory of Dual Labor Markets with Application to Industrial Policy, Discrimination, and Keynesian Unemployment," *Journal of Labor Economics*, vol. 4 (July 1986, *part 1*), pp. 376–414, suggest a similar mechanism through which higher unemployment benefits and tax rates can drive up unemployment via an effect on firms' wage-setting behavior. See especially p. 408.

13. A number of other broad definitions have been proposed, but some, such as the "gross" replacement rate, seem inappropriate as a measure of the consumption cost of lost employment. For comprehensive surveys, see Wayne Vroman, "State Replacement Rates in 1980," in National Commission on Unemployment Compensation, *Unemployment Compensation: Studies and Research,* vol. 1 (U.S. Government Printing Office, 1981); P. Roberti, "Unemployment Compensation Replacement Rates," in Organization for Economic Cooperation and Development, *High Unemployment: A Challenge for Income Support Policies* (Paris: OECD, 1984), pp. 98–120; and A. B. Atkinson and John Micklewright, *Unemployment Benefits and Unemployment Duration* (London: Suntory-Toyota International Centre for Economics and Related Disciplines, 1985).

concept is fraught with difficulty when it is applied to the computation of actual replacement rates. Most available measures are restricted to a comparison of past money wages with monetary benefits from unemployment insurance. But a comparison of this type can be misleading when either labor compensation or unemployment compensation includes such nonmonetary benefits as pension coverage or health insurance. In the United States, for example, health insurance is typically provided as a fringe benefit of employment, and it ceases soon after a worker loses his job. In European countries with nationalized health insurance, both employed and unemployed workers are covered by health insurance.

The most perplexing measurement problem arises in defining a suitable period over which replacement rates should be computed. One popular approach is to compute a worker's after-tax benefit during a week in which he is fully eligible and then divide this benefit by his net wage during a recent week in which he was employed. A problem with this definition is that it ignores those weeks in which no benefit was obtained (for example, because of waiting weeks or periods of disqualification). Another problem is the sensitivity of the net benefit and net wage to the expected duration of a spell of unemployment. For very short spells of joblessness, the worker will typically receive a full benefit during each week after the waiting period has elapsed. The benefit may later decline, for example, after the exhaustion of the regular insurance benefit and commencement of a lower assistance benefit. Similarly, net weekly earnings will vary depending on the fraction of a tax year spent in unemployment. Under a progressive tax system, the marginal tax on a worker's annual earnings falls as less and less of the year is spent in employment. For both these reasons, the weekly replacement rate falls with increases in the length of an unemployment spell. The replacement rate can thus be defined only in relation to a specified duration of joblessness.

One last problem is the appropriate measurement of net earnings in employment. Although it is customary to measure earnings loss as the net earnings in a worker's last job, this choice is sometimes questionable for measuring work disincentives. An older worker might receive a large wage premium as a result of his seniority. If this job were lost, the premium would disappear. The jobless benefit could represent a much higher fraction of *potential* earnings on a new job than of actual earnings on the job that was lost. Presumably the worker is deterred from accepting a new job because the potential wage is low relative to the weekly insurance benefit, regardless of the relation between the benefit and the wage on a *previous* job. This has two implications for interpreting replacement rates. First, if replacement rates are measured using actual wages on a past job, the average replacement rate may understate work disincentives for a worker whose past wage included a substantial seniority premium. Second, work disincentives will also be understated whenever there is a decline in the mean wage in the wage offer distribution.

The ideal measure of a nation's average replacement rate would reflect the benefits available to a representative sample of people entering unemployment during a specified period. The information needed for a measure of this type is seldom available, even in such countries as Sweden and the United States where detailed microcensus surveys are routinely conducted. In comparing replacement rates across countries, economists are therefore forced to rely on imperfect measures, and the reader should bear this in mind when comparing one benefit system with another.

The most careful international comparison of replacement rates has been performed by the Centre d'Etude des Revenus et des Coûts (CERC) in the French government.[14] Rather than compute replacement rates during an initial week of unemployment, CERC investigated the consequences of long-term unemployment on net family income in five European countries. Analysts in the Organization for Economic Cooperation and Development (OECD) replicated these computations using data for the United States, permitting a comparison of the replacement rates in the five countries included in this study. The computations were performed for wage earners at different earnings levels and in different family circumstances, but the cases selected were "representative" earners rather than actual earners from a randomly drawn sample of the unemployed or employed populations. CERC calculated net family incomes in and out of work for spells of a few months and one and two years.

Although these computations are useful, they do not permit economists to observe directly the effects of differences in the composition of unemployment across countries. For example, if unemployment is concentrated among poorly paid workers in one country but among well-

14. Centre d'Etude des Revenus et des Coûts, *L'Indemnisation du Chômage en France et à l'Etranger,* no. 62 (Paris: CERC, 1982).

paid workers in another, the question arises whether economists should compare the replacement rates available to average-wage workers in the two countries. If unemployment typically lasts three months in one country but twelve months in another, the one-year replacement rate may not be a reliable gauge of relative generosity.

Another shortcoming of the CERC and OECD calculations is that they do not permit economists to observe replacement rates over a long interval within any country. The CERC calculations cover unemployment benefits in 1980 and 1982 for five European countries. They have been updated to cover 1984 for a few of the same countries.[15] But CERC did not calculate the trend in replacement rates during the 1970s, when the systems in some countries (notably France and Sweden) were dramatically liberalized. To show the trend in replacement rates over a longer interval, I have relied on country-specific computations performed by several different authors. These computations are usually far less satisfactory than the detailed calculations performed by CERC. Individual analysts obtained some measure of the overall average benefit in unemployment and then divided this number by the average net earnings in employment, occasionally with some adjustment for the distribution of family types represented on the unemployment rolls. (The replacement rate trends reported later for Sweden and the United States are based on a more sophisticated methodology.)

These replacement rate trends are difficult to compare across countries because each analyst used a different method to calculate replacement rates in the country under study. To remedy this inconsistency, I have computed the trend in replacement ratios using an identical procedure for each country. My measure is the gross expenditure on insurance and assistance benefits for each recipient of benefits divided by the net earnings of an average production worker in manufacturing.[16] This crude approximation is far from ideal, but it permits a reasonably consistent comparison of benefit generosity over time.

Other aspects of unemployment insurance across countries are easier to compare. The duration of benefits and eligibility criteria for various

15. See CERC, *Changements Intervenus depuis 1982 dans les Systèmes d'Indemnisation du Chômage en France et dans Quatre Pays Etrangers* (Paris: CERC, 1984).

16. I use the average tax situation of a single person in computing the after-tax earnings of an average worker. The tax situation of average workers has been described in a series of OECD publications; for example, *The Tax/Benefit Position of Selected Income Groups in OECD Member Countries, 1972–76* (Paris: OECD, 1978), and *The Tax/Benefit Position of Production Workers, 1979–84* (Paris: OECD, 1986).

forms of insurance, for example, can be described fairly easily for systems in the five nations. The remainder of this section briefly describes the levels and trends in insurance in each of the countries.

United Kingdom

The main features of the British insurance system were established as far back as the 1930s, when the Unemployment Act of 1934 set up a dual-tier structure of benefits. The first tier of benefits is provided by the National Insurance unemployment benefit (UB), available to fully unemployed workers for as long as fifty-two weeks after an initial layoff. The second tier is provided by the means-tested supplementary benefit (SB), which is payable to income-eligible workers who have not become insured under UB or who have exhausted their claim to UB. New entrants into the labor market may thus be entitled to SB. Recipients of UB can also receive means-tested SB if their income and resources are low relative to their assessed "needs."

Among the countries surveyed, Britain is unique in paying weekly unemployment benefits that are essentially independent of workers' past average pay. A fully insured minimum-wage worker who is laid off is paid the same benefit as a laid-off executive. The basic unemployment benefit is supplemented for married men whose spouses earn less than a modest amount. Until 1984 the basic benefit was also supplemented by allowances for dependent children. The weekly benefit thus depends primarily on a breadwinner's family situation rather than on previous earnings, as in other countries. The means-tested supplementary benefit depends, of course, exclusively on a person's assessed needs, not on his or her previous earnings. The weekly UB or SB payment can therefore represent a large fraction of past weekly earnings for a poorly paid worker with a dependent spouse, but a very small percentage of lost earnings for a well-paid single worker.

Until recently many unemployed British workers received jobless benefits that were based on past average earnings. Between 1966 and 1982 the unemployment insurance system included an earnings related supplement (ERS), which was based on a worker's average covered earnings during a base year and was payable during the third to the twenty-eighth week of the fifty-two weeks covered by the basic UB benefit. In the mid-1970s about 60 percent of UB recipients unemployed between three and twenty-eight weeks qualified for an earnings related supplement.[17] The earnings related supplement was abolished in 1982, partly because of the Thatcher government's belief that overly generous benefits made insured unemployment too attractive. As a result, replacement rates for many moderately or well-paid workers have fallen.

The generosity of British jobless benefits in comparison with earnings at work has been the subject of heated and lengthy debate. Some observers claim that a substantial fraction of jobless workers have enjoyed a combination of UB, SB, and ERS benefits that is greater than the net income that could be earned in employment. Other analysts assert that the extent of this problem is greatly exaggerated.[18] CERC's calculation of replacement rates for representative workers, referred to earlier, sheds some light on this controversy.

The CERC findings about jobless benefits in the United Kingdom are reported in table 1. The results show the strong influence of the flat-rate benefit and dependents' allowances on replacement rates. Unemployed workers who previously earned twice the average wage have only a modest proportion of net earnings replaced. Workers who earned less than the average wage can enjoy high replacement rates, especially if they support dependents.[19] A comparison of the first and third columns in table 1 shows the effects of the 1982 legislative reforms. Replacement rates during the first year of unemployment were substantially reduced by the reforms, especially among the unmarried. Before 1982 an insured unemployed worker could expect a sharp drop in net income during the second year of his unemployment. The 1982 reforms dramatically reduced the falloff in income by reducing benefits available in the first year of joblessness, while leaving benefits in the second year untouched.

The CERC calculations are interesting, but they shed little light on the replacement rate received by the average worker in unemployment,

17. The remaining 40 percent of recipients earned too little during the base period to qualify. See Atkinson and Micklewright, *Unemployment Benefits and Unemployment Duration,* p. 96.

18. The first view is presented in Minford, *Unemployment: Cause and Cure,* while the latter view has been argued by Atkinson and Micklewright, *Unemployment Benefits and Unemployment Duration,* and John Micklewright, "On Earnings-Related Unemployment Benefits and Their Relation to Earnings," *Economic Journal,* vol. 95 (March 1985), pp. 133–45, among others.

19. It should be noted, however, that in November 1981 only 47 percent of the male unemployed were married and less than a quarter had child dependents. See Clive H. Smee, "Unemployment Compensation Replacement Rates: A United Kingdom View," in OECD, *High Unemployment: A Challenge for Income Support Policies* (Paris: OECD, 1984), p. 129.

Table 1. *Percentage of Previous Household Income Maintained during First and Second Years of Unemployment, United Kingdom, 1980, 1982*[a]

Earnings level and family situation	October 1980		July 1982	
	First year	Second year	First year	Second year
Two-thirds average earnings[b]				
Single	52	43	44	43
Married, 0 children	67	59	60	59
Married, 2 children	82	76	76	76
Average earnings[b]				
Single	37	28	28	28
Married, 0 children	48	40	40	40
Married, 2 children	61	54	54	54
Twice average earnings[b]				
Single	20	14	14	14
Married, 0 children	26	21	21	21
Married, 2 children	34	31	30	30

Source: Centre d'Etude des Revenus et des Coûts, *L'Indemnisation du Chômage en France et à l'Etranger* (Paris: CERC, 1982), pp. 63, 85, 87.

a. It is assumed that the breadwinner is the sole earner in household, is fully insured for unemployment benefits, and in the second year of unemployment meets the means test for supplementary benefit.

b. Average earnings of an adult full-time production worker in manufacturing.

nor do they show how replacement rates have varied over time. Dilnot and Morris, using microeconomic information from the Family Expenditure Survey, computed replacement rates among a sample of employed men for selected years between 1968 and 1983.[20] If the demographic composition of the employed had remained constant at its 1980 distribution, the arithmetic average of individual replacement rates would have fallen over the period. Dilnot and Morris find, for example, that in 1968, 87 percent of net earnings were replaced by jobless benefits during the first thirteen weeks of unemployment. By 1980 the percentage replaced had dropped to 73. After the 1982 reforms the replacement rate in the first thirteen weeks of unemployment fell to 60 percent. Interestingly, Dilnot and Morris find that the net replacement rate at the start of the second year of unemployment was unaffected by the 1982 reforms, confirming the CERC calculations in table 1. (The replacement rate in

20. A. W. Dilnot and C. N. Morris, "Private Costs and Benefits of Unemployment: Measuring Replacement Rates," *Oxford Economic Papers*, vol. 34 (November 1983), pp. 321–40.

the fifty-third week of unemployment was 50 percent both before and after the 1982 reforms.)[21]

Dilnot and Morris's findings cast strong doubt on the proposition that rising replacement rates are an important explanation for the growth of joblessness in Britain, particularly in the late 1970s and early 1980s. Several other authors have performed crude calculations of the replacement rate over time. Three of these sets of computations are shown in columns 7, 8, and 9 of table 2. (Details are spelled out in the data appendix.) None of the analysts finds evidence of an upward drift in replacement rates from the late 1960s to the early or mid-1980s; Smee and I find evidence that replacement rates have declined.

The remaining columns in table 2 provide additional details about jobless benefits and unemployment in Britain. Column 1 shows the trend in total U.K. unemployment, where unemployment is measured under U.S. Bureau of Labor Statistics concepts. The BLS definition is used here as elsewhere in the paper for the sake of consistency. Column 2 shows the number of recipients of the non-means-tested insurance benefit, and column 3, of the means-tested supplementary benefit.[22]

Column 4 gives my estimate of the fraction of all unemployed covered by either UB or SB for the unemployed. Unlike the replacement rate, the fraction of unemployed covered by UB or SB payments has shown a marked upward trend over the past twenty years.[23] The British

21. Ibid., p. 332.

22. Some recipients of UB also collect ERS or SB payments or both. These recipients are included in the totals reported in column 2. People who simultaneously collect UB and SB are excluded from the totals reported in column 3. The totals reported in columns 2 and 3 represent the averages of monthly counts of recipients in one, two, or three months of the year, depending on the number of counts reported in my statistical sources. In 1967–75 and again in 1984 the totals are based on reported counts for Great Britain only. These totals were inflated by 4 percent to account for the exclusion of beneficiaries in Northern Ireland. For these reasons the figures should be viewed as imperfect estimates of the average number of insured unemployed over the year.

23. Some of the increase after the mid-1970s can be explained by a change in the insurance contribution requirements for married women. Working wives could formerly elect to make lower weekly contributions than other workers, but in exchange they forfeited their right to collect unemployment insurance when laid off. Under these circumstances, many women failed to collect insurance upon losing their jobs. When working wives were forced to make the same insurance contributions as other workers, their take-up of benefits increased. This change in behavior cannot explain much of the trend in coverage, however, because the fraction of unemployed covered by UB has actually fallen quite markedly. Most of the rise in the combined UB and SB coverage ratio is due to a rapid increase in unemployed SB recipients. These recipients have either exhausted UB or have too little recent work experience to qualify for UB.

Table 2. *Unemployment Coverage and Outlays in the United Kingdom, 1966–85*

Year	Unemployment (thousands)[a] (1)	Recipients of UB (thousands) (2)	Recipients of SB (thousands)[b] (3)	Coverage ratio[c] (4)	Expenditure per recipient[d] (5)	Expenditure per person unemployed[d] (6)	Replacement rate (percent) Smee (7)	Nickell/ Layard (8)	Burtless (9)
1966	570	*	*	*	*	690	42	48	*
1967	830	360	108	0.56	1,738	980	48	53	*
1968	810	330	139	0.58	1,864	1,080	48	52	*
1969	770	307	139	0.58	1,778	1,030	46	51	*
1970	770	326	149	0.62	1,835	1,130	46	51	*
1971	980	473	206	0.69	1,715	1,189	47	51	*
1972	1,070	453	263	0.67	1,975	1,323	42	47	47
1973	820	258	230	0.59	1,767	1,051	45	47	41
1974	790	264	202	0.59	2,256	1,330	43	47	57
1975	1,180	453	298	0.64	1,908	1,216	44	49	47
1976	1,540	617	434	0.68	1,871	1,277	44	50	48
1977	1,660	578	545	0.68	1,786	1,208	44	51	*
1978	1,650	537	546	0.66	1,743	1,144	40	50	43
1979	1,420	486	502	0.70	1,650	1,148	38	46	40
1980	1,850	804	614	0.77	1,489	1,141	39	46	33
1981	2,790	*	*	*	*	1,066	42	50	*
1982	3,030	1,016	1,385	0.79	1,773	1,410	39	54	*
1983	3,190	970	1,649	0.82	1,419	1,166	*	54	37
1984	3,180	1,013	1,851	0.90	1,329	1,200	*	*	34
1985	3,070	*	*	*	*	*	*	*	*

Sources: See text and data appendix.
* Not ascertained.
a. Number of persons unemployed, under U.S. definition.
b. Unemployed recipients of supplementary benefit, excluding those also in receipt of UB.
c. Recipients of UB and unemployed recipients of SB divided by number of persons unemployed.
d. Per capita outlays on UB, ERS, and SB for the unemployed in constant 1980 pounds.

government now provides subsistence incomes to a high percentage of jobless workers.

Column 5 in table 2 shows the trend in real outlays on UB, ERS, and SB per recipient of these benefits. (Outlays are measured in 1980 pounds.) After showing no clear trend from 1966 to 1976, per capita outlays fell sharply through 1980, partly because of the erosion in the value of ERS benefits. Outlays per unemployed person, shown in column 6, do not follow the same pattern. The growth in the fraction of unemployed workers collecting benefits has tended to offset the decline in benefits paid out to each recipient. The picture of jobless benefits shown in table 2 is one of stable or declining replacement rates among those receiving benefits but rising recipiency rates among the unemployed as a whole.

France

The French unemployment insurance system was established under a collective bargaining agreement in 1958. Until 1979 this system was run in tandem with a separate program of public assistance for the unemployed, many of whom simultaneously received benefits under the unemployment insurance scheme. In recent years the combined system of insurance and assistance has been repeatedly and significantly over-hauled, and it would be difficult to give an entirely accurate description of the system that covered more than two or three years. (A more detailed account of the main reforms can be found in the sources mentioned in the data appendix.) Here I will simply describe some of the prominent features of the current system and note several of the more important recent reforms.

Eligible unemployed workers can receive one of two different kinds of payments. The basic benefit is *allocation de base,* which is a daily payment keyed to average wages earned during a base period. An unemployed worker can draw basic benefits for between three and forty-two months, depending on his or her recent work experience. (Younger workers and workers with little experience receive benefits for shorter periods.) Workers who exhaust the basic benefit are usually eligible for an "end-of-entitlement benefit" (*allocation de fin de droits*), a flat daily benefit that can continue for six to thirty months depending on age and recent work experience. The insurance system also imposes a cap on the combined duration of payments under the basic and end-of-entitle-

Table 3. *Percentage of Previous Household Income Maintained during First and Second Years of Unemployment, France, 1980, 1982*[a]

Earnings level and family situation	October 1980				December 1982			
	First year		Second year		First year		Second year	
	Economic[c]	Noneconomic[c]	Minimum[d]	Maximum[d]	Economic[c]	Noneconomic[c]	Minimum[d]	Maximum[d]
Two-thirds average earnings[b]								
Single	97	78	43	82	82	78	43	78
Married, 0 children	97	77	43	79	81	76	43	76
Married, 2 children	98	82	54	82	85	81	54	81
Average earnings[b]								
Single	83	68	35	71	76	67	35	67
Married, 0 children	83	67	33	70	76	66	33	66
Married, 2 children	84	70	48	72	78	69	48	69
Twice average earnings[b]								
Single	76	59	26	62	69	59	26	59
Married, 0 children	74	58	24	60	67	57	24	57
Married, 2 children	80	64	31	63	75	64	31	64

Source: See table 1.
a. It is assumed that the breadwinner is the sole earner in the household and is fully insured for unemployment benefits.
b. Average earnings of an adult full-time production worker in manufacturing.
c. Reason for unemployment; "economic" reflects mass layoffs.
d. Minimum is computed as three months' receipt of basic benefit (*allocation de base*) and twelve months' receipt of end-of-entitlement benefit (*allocation de fin de droits*); maximum is computed as twelve months' basic benefit, usually available to older dismissed workers with one year or more of recent employment experience.

ment programs. This cap ranges from three to sixty months, and for a typical unemployed worker under age 50 would be thirty months.

Besides these two main forms of insurance for laid-off workers, flat-rate unemployment benefits (*allocations d'insertion*) are also available to young school leavers and other categories of job seekers who have little or no previous work experience.

Several features of the French system are notable. First, daily benefits for experienced unemployed workers are always related to past earnings, at least during the initial period of unemployment. In addition, the ceiling on benefits is high. This makes it possible for unemployed workers to enjoy reasonably high replacement rates even if their previous earnings were well above average. Second, benefits are reduced as the spell of unemployment lengthens. Third, older workers are permitted to draw benefits much longer than workers under age 50. In fact, workers over 60 can draw benefits until they reach the normal pension age. A fourth distinctive feature of the French system has gradually been eliminated. Formerly, French workers dismissed "for economic reasons" (that is, in mass layoffs) were treated much more generously than other laid-off workers. Reforms after 1981 first reduced and then eliminated this advantage over other classes of the unemployed.

CERC's calculations of French replacement rates in 1980 and late 1982 are shown in table 3. The figures reflect the situation of workers who had good employment histories before their layoff (workers with less than six months' employment in the twelve months leading up to unemployment would not have qualified for these benefit levels, especially after the 1982 reforms). On the whole the CERC calculations show a pattern of generous treatment of laid-off workers, especially those dismissed for economic reasons and those older than 50. Replacement rates were high even in the second year of unemployment, particularly for workers paid average or below-average wages. Benefits have been trimmed since 1982, but replacement rates remain relatively high.

Little historical information exists with which to calculate the trend in French replacement rates over time. Columns 8 and 9 in table 4 show two sets of estimates for limited time intervals. Claassen and Lane attempt to estimate the ratio of average benefit paid to all insurance and assistance recipients to average French earnings.[24] As one analyst has

24. Emil-Maria Claassen and Georges Lane, "The Effects of Unemployment Benefits on the Unemployment Rate in France," in H. G. Grubel and M. A. Walker, eds.,

Table 4. Unemployment Coverage and Outlays in France, 1966–85

Year	Unemployment (thousands)[a] (1)	Recipients of insurance (thousands)[b] (2)	Recipients of assistance (thousands)[c] (3)	Count of recipients (thousands)[d] (4)	Coverage ratio[e] (5)	Expenditure per recipient[f] (6)	Expenditure per person unemployed[f] (7)	Replacement rate (percent) Claassen/Lane (8)	Replacement rate (percent) Burtless (9)
1966	350	51	36	*	*	*	2,550	*	*
1967	370	75	54	*	*	*	3,580	56	*
1968	490	107	112	*	*	*	5,150	62	*
1969	460	89	104	*	*	*	5,570	72	*
1970	510	98	110	*	*	*	5,200	60	*
1971	570	125	128	*	*	*	5,670	57	*
1972	590	135	144	248	0.42	15,900	6,680	59	43
1973	570	128	136	226	0.40	20,180	8,000	61	53
1974	610	152	161	264	0.43	22,370	9,680	62	57
1975	900	297	325	494	0.55	25,980	14,260	73	66
1976	990	364	433	621	0.63	26,320	16,510	*	65
1977	1,070	436	526	747	0.70	26,170	18,270	*	*
1978	1,180	518	617	887	0.75	28,170	21,170	*	66
1979	1,360	*	*	*	*	*	23,740	*	*
1980	1,450	727	93	945	0.65	34,710	22,620	*	86
1981	1,690	1,004	143	1,267	0.75	*	*	*	*
1982	1,920	*	*	*	*	*	*	*	*
1983	1,960	*	*	*	*	*	*	*	*
1984	2,310	*	*	*	*	*	*	*	*
1985	2,410	1,321	403	1,724	0.72	*	*	*	*

Sources: See data appendix.
* Not ascertained.
a. Number of persons unemployed, under U.S. definition.
b. Number of recipients of ASSEDIC insurance benefits. In 1980–81 the September totals of recipients of *allocations de base* and *allocations spéciales*.
c. Number of unemployed recipients of unemployment assistance. Until 1978 assistance recipients might also receive insurance benefits. In 1980–81 the September totals of recipients of *allocations forfaitaires*; in 1985, recipients of *allocations de solidarité spécifique* and flat-rate unemployment benefits (*allocations d'insertion*).
d. Unduplicated count of insurance and assistance recipients.
e. Unduplicated count divided by number of persons unemployed.
f. Per capita outlays on unemployment insurance and assistance, in constant 1980 French francs.

pointed out, this calculation may be marred by an incorrect estimate of the number of recipients.[25] My own estimate shows the trend in expenditures per recipient divided by the net earnings of an average production worker in manufacturing. This calculation may be no more reliable than the earlier one of Claassen and Lane. Both sets of estimates, however, show a general upward drift in replacement rates from the late 1960s through the early 1980s. The trend was probably reversed by the legislative reforms of 1982 and 1984.

Table 4 also contains some additional data on French jobless benefits similar to those reported earlier on the British system. Column 5 shows the ratio of recipients of insurance and assistance to all unemployed. The coverage ratio has risen strongly since the early 1970s, nearly doubling between 1972–73 and 1981. The combined effect of the growing coverage ratio and rising replacement rate is shown in column 7, which gives the amount of insurance and assistance spending per unemployed worker. Per capita real expenditures rose at an astonishing pace over the period, increasing nearly ninefold between 1966 and 1980. Because unemployment more than quadrupled between those years, the fiscal effect was enormous. France is the only country of the five examined where increased generosity in jobless benefits might have contributed substantially to rising unemployment.

West Germany

Unlike France, Germany has a long-established and fairly stable system of jobless pay. The German system includes two separate programs, unemployment insurance (*Arbeitslosengeld*) for experienced unemployed workers and unemployment assistance (*Arbeitslosenhilfe*) for other categories of the unemployed (primarily, unemployed workers who have exhausted insurance). Insurance benefits are not subject to a means test and are financed through a payroll tax imposed on employers and workers. Assistance payments are means-tested and financed out of general revenues.

An unemployed worker is eligible to receive insurance if he or she

Unemployment Insurance: Global Evidence of Its Effects on Unemployment (Vancouver: Fraser Institute, 1978), pp. 204–33.

25. See Roger T. Kaufman, "An Analysis of the Secular Increase in Unemployment in France and Great Britain" (Northampton, Mass.: Smith College Department of Economics, 1983), pp. 35–37.

has satisfied the contribution requirement. This requirement has varied over the past fifteen years. In the mid-1970s an unemployed person was required to have made contributions for at least six months during the three-year period before registration for benefits. Since 1981 this contribution requirement has been stiffened. The duration of benefits is linked to the duration of contributions in the worker's base period, with a maximum duration of twelve months' benefits. Reforms in the 1980s have effectively reduced the duration of benefits for workers with limited work experience during the base period. But starting in 1985 unemployed workers over 50 were permitted to draw more than twelve months' benefits if they had worked steadily during the base period. Workers over 55 can now draw up to two years' insurance benefits.

In recent years the method of determining weekly benefits has also varied. Until 1975 the benefit was 62.5 percent of the worker's earnings, net of social security contributions and income taxes, in the weeks immediately preceding layoff. In 1975 the benefit, which is tax free, was raised to 68 percent of previous net earnings. The calculation of the base wage was modified during the early 1980s to reduce the replacement rate, and benefits were further reduced in 1984 when the replacement rate for childless unemployed workers was lowered from 68 to 63 percent.

The qualifying requirements for unemployment assistance are more lenient than for insurance, but benefits are lower and are subject to a means test. To be eligible for assistance the applicant must have been an employee for five months in the year preceding registration in unemployment. Most recipients of assistance are people who have exhausted their regular insurance benefits. The assistance benefit is determined as a percentage of a worker's wages in employment, less income tax and social security contribution. This percentage was set at 52.5 percent until 1975, when it was raised to 58 percent. In 1984 the replacement rate was reduced to 56 percent for jobless workers without dependent children. In principle, unemployment assistance is granted without any time limit.

Like the French system, the German system became more liberal in the mid-1970s when unemployment began to rise after the first oil shock. Benefits were liberalized in Germany by increasing the replacement rate in both the insurance and assistance programs. Eligibility criteria were tightened and benefit levels reduced in the 1980s, however, after the second oil shock and another round of rising unemployment.[26] In both

26. Note, however, that the system is now somewhat more generous to older

France and Germany the primary motivation for cutting benefits in the 1980s was a desire for fiscal balance, not concern over microeconomic work incentives.

German jobless pay offers moderately high but not excessive replacement rates to experienced laid-off workers. The CERC study of European unemployment programs shows that breadwinners who had earned the average wage or two-thirds the average wage received a 66 percent replacement rate in their first year of unemployment and a 56 percent replacement rate in their second. By contrast, breadwinners who had earned twice the average wage received 51 percent and 44 percent, respectively.[27] The lower replacement rate for better-paid workers is due to a cap on wages that are subject to replacement. The CERC computations were made on the basis of laws in effect in 1980. Since that year, replacement rates for breadwinners have fallen somewhat.

The trend in German replacement rates is shown in columns 7 and 8 of table 5. Bruche and Reissert have computed the ratio of the average monthly unemployment insurance benefit to the average net wage per employee.[28] This ratio, shown as column 7, was stable until 1982 and has fallen slightly since that year. My own calculation appears in column 8. I have computed the average insurance and assistance payment per recipient and then divided this figure by the OECD estimate of the net wage of an average production worker in manufacturing. My estimates show a trend that is similar to the one found by Bruche and Reissert— stability through the early 1980s and a slight decline since then. Much of this trend may simply be attributable to the changing composition of the unemployed receiving insurance and assistance.

Columns 2 and 3 in table 5 show the number of insurance and assistance recipients, respectively. As in Britain, the number of people receiving assistance has risen faster than the number receiving insurance, largely because the fraction of unemployed who have exhausted their insurance benefits has grown enormously. The proportion of unemployed who receive either insurance or assistance, shown in column 4, has declined in the past decade. This trend is a natural consequence of the rising duration of average spells of unemployment in Germany. Although a

experienced workers, inasmuch as they are eligible to draw insurance for up to two years.

27. See CERC, *L'Indemnisation du Chômage*, p. 85.

28. Gert Bruche and Bernd Reissert, "The Financing of Labor Market Policy in the Federal Republic of Germany," draft translation of *Die Finanzierung der Arbeitsmarktpolitik: System, Effektivität, Reformansätze* (Frankfurt and New York: Campus, 1985).

Table 5. *Unemployment Coverage and Outlays in West Germany, 1967–85*

Year	Unemploy- ment (thousands)[a] (1)	Recipients of insurance (thousands)[b] (2)	Recipients of assis- tance (thousands)[c] (3)	Coverage ratio[d] (4)	Expenditure per recipient[e] (5)	Expenditure per person unemployed[e] (6)	Replacement rate (percent) Bruchel Reissert (7)	Burtless (8)
1967	340	320	36	1.05	7,370	7,720	*	*
1968	290	192	53	0.84	8,240	6,960	*	*
1969	170	105	28	0.78	8,420	6,580	*	*
1970	140	96	17	0.81	8,770	7,080	*	*
1971	160	120	15	0.84	9,130	7,700	*	*
1972	190	157	20	0.93	9,760	9,100	*	50
1973	190	154	23	0.93	10,000	9,320	*	51
1974	420	352	40	0.93	10,370	9,680	*	53
1975	890	707	110	0.92	10,310	9,470	54	52
1976	890	615	165	0.88	9,680	8,480	51	48
1977	900	557	163	0.80	9,440	7,550	49	*
1978	870	516	157	0.77	9,860	7,630	49	45
1979	780	448	134	0.74	10,110	7,530	50	47
1980	770	454	122	0.75	10,190	7,630	50	46
1981	1,090	698	170	0.80	10,540	8,390	52	50
1982	1,580	926	291	0.77	10,010	7,710	52	*
1983	1,990	1,014	485	0.75	9,440	7,110	49	47
1984	2,090	859	598	0.70	8,950	6,240	48	44
1985	2,130	836	617	0.68	8,810	6,010	48	*

Sources: See data appendix.
* Not ascertained.
a. Number of persons unemployed, under U.S. definition.
b. Number of recipients of unemployment insurance (*Arbeitslosengeld*).
c. Number of recipients of unemployment assistance (*Arbeitslosenhilfe*).
d. Number of recipients of unemployment insurance and assistance divided by the total number of persons unemployed.
e. Per capita outlays on unemployment insurance and assistance, in constant 1980 deutsche marks.

high fraction of job losers initially qualifies for insurance, only a smaller fraction qualifies for unemployment assistance, because of the means test. As more and more people exhaust their insurance benefits, the number of unemployed failing to qualify for either insurance or assistance is rising. By tightening eligibility conditions during the first half of the 1980s, the German government further reduced the fraction of unemployed qualifying for insurance or assistance.

Columns 5 and 6 in table 5 show the trends in jobless outlays per recipient and per unemployed worker, respectively. Real benefits per recipient generally rose through 1981, but with cyclical swings in the trend. Part of the trend and a great deal of the cyclical swings were caused by shifts in the composition of unemployment over time. Since 1981, real benefits per recipient and per unemployed worker have fallen rather substantially.

Sweden

Unemployment insurance societies associated with labor unions provide most insurance coverage in Sweden. Membership in such societies is voluntary, but the great majority of the labor force belongs (with 72 percent coverage in 1980).[29] Besides the insurance societies, the government offers unemployment assistance under a cash benefit (KAS) program, introduced in 1974. This program gives income protection to workers who are not members of insurance societies or who are members but have not yet become eligible for benefits, to new labor market entrants, and to unemployed workers more than 60 years old who have exhausted benefits. KAS benefits are substantially lower than insurance benefits. Unlike assistance payments in Britain and Germany, they are not subject to a means test.

To be eligible for regular insurance benefits, a worker must have paid dues to an insurance society for at least twelve months before the claim and worked for five of the twelve months preceding unemployment. Workers are required to register as job seekers with the employment office. Since 1974 unemployed workers qualifying for insurance have been eligible to draw benefits for sixty weeks, or ninety weeks in the case of workers aged 55 and older. The amount of the benefit, which is

29. Anders Björklund and Bertil Holmlund, "The Economics of Unemployment Insurance: The Case of Sweden," Working Paper 167 (Stockholm: Industrial Institute for Economic and Social Research, October 1984), p. 15.

Table 6. *Percentage of Previous Household Income Maintained during First and Second Years of Unemployment, Sweden, 1980*

Earnings level and family situation	First year[a]		Second year[b] Insurance and KAS
	Insurance	KAS	
Two-thirds average earnings[c]			
Single	90	25	39
Married, 0 children	91	29	42
Married, 2 children	92	40	50
Average earnings[c]			
Single	63	18	28
Married, 0 children	65	21	30
Married, 2 children	69	29	37
Twice average earnings[c]			
Single	40	11	17
Married, 0 children	41	13	19
Married, 2 children	45	19	24

Source: See table 1.

a. The two columns reflect the situation of a worker who is fully entitled to insurance society benefits, on the one hand, or KAS assistance benefits only, on the other.

b. Replacement rate for a worker under 55 who was entitled to full insurance benefits during the initial year of unemployment.

c. Average earnings of an adult full-time production worker in manufacturing.

taxable, depends on several factors, but most payments fall within a narrow range. CERC reports that in 1980, 95 percent of all payments were between 180 and 195 kronor a day, or about 76 percent of the salary of an average employee.[30] Sweden's payment scheme, like Britain's, yields extremely high replacement rates for low-wage workers.

The eligibility criteria for KAS assistance are somewhat more lenient than those for regular insurance. School leavers can receive KAS payments, but only after they have been unemployed for three months. Daily benefits are a flat payment equal in 1980 to about 28 percent of the salary of an average worker. KAS payments can be received for up to thirty weeks by unemployed workers under age 55, for up to sixty weeks by unemployed workers between 55 and 59, and for ninety weeks by workers over 60.

Swedish replacement rates for 1980 are shown in table 6. The replacement rates for insured unemployed workers are quite generous for workers whose previous earnings were below average, but fall sharply at higher wage levels. Replacement rates are much lower for workers

30. CERC, *L'Indemnisation du Chômage*, p. 23.

who are eligible only for KAS payments. The replacement rate in the second year of joblessness is therefore sharply below the rate during the first year, even among workers entitled to full insurance benefits upon layoff. Björklund and Holmlund have computed the trend in replacement rates for men unemployed three months.[31] Their estimates are shown in column 7 of table 7. Björklund and Holmlund find a gradual upward drift in replacement rates over the past two decades, but with substantial year-to-year fluctuations. My own calculations (column 8), which show the ratio of the average insurance and KAS benefit to the net wage of an average production worker, demonstrate an erratic rise in benefits relative to net income in employment.

Over the past two decades the most important development in the Swedish system has been the growth in coverage of unemployed workers (see columns 3 and 4 of table 7). Column 3 shows the ratio of all unemployed workers covered by the regular unemployment insurance system. This ratio has risen because more and more employees have chosen to join insurance societies. Column 4 shows the fraction of all unemployment days during the year that were compensated by either regular insurance or KAS payments. This ratio has grown even more rapidly than the ratio of insured to total unemployed because of rising take-up of KAS benefits. As a result of this rising coverage, the benefit payments per unemployed person rose by nearly half between 1974 and 1981 (see column 6). The rapid growth in coverage and the upward drift in insurance replacement rates have not been accompanied by an explosion in the rate of unemployment. Although Swedish unemployment rose over the late 1970s and early 1980s, the increase was much more moderate than in other OECD countries, particularly OECD countries in Europe.

United States

Established under the Social Security Act of 1935, the U.S. unemployment insurance system assumed its current shape and size shortly after World War II, and it has not been modified in any important way since then, except for changes covering new categories of workers. Virtually all paid employment in the United States has been covered by

---

31. Björklund and Holmlund, "Economics of Unemployment Insurance," p. 40.

Table 7. *Unemployment Coverage and Outlays in Sweden, 1966–85*

Year	Unemployment (thousands)[a] (1)	Insured unemployment (thousands)[b] (2)	Insurance coverage ratio[c] (3)	Overall coverage ratio[d] (4)	Expenditure per recipient[e] (5)	Expenditure per person unemployed[e] (6)	Replacement rate (percent) Björklund/ Holmlund (7)	Replacement rate (percent) Burtless (8)
1966	59	22	0.37	*	*	*	55	*
1967	80	29	0.36	*	*	*	58	*
1968	85	33	0.39	*	*	*	58	*
1969	73	30	0.41	*	*	*	67	*
1970	59	30	0.51	*	*	*	63	*
1971	101	45	0.45	*	*	*	55	*
1972	107	48	0.45	*	*	*	62	*
1973	98	46	0.47	0.51	*	*	59	*
1974	80	39	0.49	0.52	32,490	16,770	61	72
1975	67	37	0.55	0.64	27,780	17,770	63	58
1976	66	33	0.50	0.63	31,420	19,660	60	65
1977	75	34	0.45	0.60	35,470	21,380	67	*
1978	94	46	0.49	0.64	36,340	23,310	67	81
1979	88	45	0.51	0.68	37,720	25,510	68	82
1980	86	44	0.51	0.69	34,530	23,850	64	77
1981	108	59	0.55	0.74	33,750	24,810	62	77
1982	137	80	0.58	0.78	34,020	26,400	65	*
1983	151	92	0.61	0.83	36,800	30,590	73	86
1984	136	92	0.68	0.87	37,900	32,970	71	88
1985	125	85	0.68	0.86	39,190	33,580	67	*

Sources: See data appendix.

* Not ascertained.

a. Number of persons unemployed, under U.S. definition.

b. Insured unemployed under regular unemployment insurance funds.

c. Insured unemployment divided by total unemployment.

d. Fraction of all unemployed days for which a benefit was paid under unemployment insurance funds or the cash assistance program (KAS).

e. Per capita outlays on unemployment insurance and assistance (KAS), in constant 1980 Swedish kronor.

unemployment insurance since 1976. The American insurance system is not, strictly speaking, a single program at all, but a collection of fifty state-level systems, each with its own eligibility criteria and payment formula. The state programs are designed and administered under broad federal guidelines, however, and share common characteristics that distinguish them strongly from insurance programs in Europe.

To be eligible for insurance benefits, a new claimant in the United States must have a recent work history meeting certain minimum requirements. The detailed requirements vary considerably from state to state. In general, to be eligible workers must have had covered earnings in a minimum number of recent calendar quarters, or have attained a minimum level of total earnings, or both. Like Germany, but unlike Britain, France, and Sweden, the United States has no program providing insurance protection to new labor market entrants, reentrants without a recent work history, or job losers and job leavers with only brief recent histories of employment. The typical American recipient of unemployment insurance is on temporary or permanent layoff. Workers who voluntarily leave their last jobs or who are dismissed for misconduct are completely denied benefits in several states and are disqualified from receiving benefits for several weeks in others. To remain eligible for benefits, an unemployed worker must be available for work and register for employment at a job service office. (Workers on temporary layoff are exempt from the latter requirement.)

Typically, an eligible claimant for unemployment insurance is entitled to at most six months of benefits. The duration varies by state and depends on the specific work history of the claimant, but most new claimants are eligible for twenty-four to twenty-six weeks of payments. The maximum duration of an award can be extended to nine months in states with especially high insured unemployment rates, but nowadays such extensions are quite rare. In exceptional circumstances, the federal government has established programs for workers exhausting regular benefits. In 1975–77 the federal supplemental benefit program, combined with the regular unemployment insurance program, offered benefits for up to fifteen months. Between October 1982 and March 1985 the federal supplemental compensation program, combined with regular unemployment insurance, offered benefits for eight to thirteen months, depending on the state level of insured unemployment. As a general rule, however, newly unemployed workers can expect to exhaust insurance benefits if they are without a job longer than six months.

The United States offers no backup system of unemployment assistance to protect the incomes of people who exhaust insurance. All states offer means-tested public assistance to families with low income and few liquid assets, but in many states it is extremely difficult for single people, childless couples, or two-parent families to qualify for such assistance. The federal government provides food stamp benefits under more liberal criteria, but these benefits are intended to cover only the cost of food, not of other items in the family budget. Food stamp benefits are therefore quite low. A primary breadwinner who exhausts insurance benefits can expect to suffer a substantial income loss.

Weekly benefit levels in the U.S. insurance system vary widely, both among states and among workers. All states attempt to link a worker's payment to the level of earnings reported in the base period. The state formulas for determining benefits are too complicated (and numerous) to be explained here. I will consider instead the average relation between benefits and past earnings.

A number of economists analyzing the U.S. system have reported that benefits on average replace about 60 to 70 percent of the net earnings lost through unemployment.[32] These estimates appear to be based on a comparison of the potential benefit that would be received during an early week of insured unemployment and the weekly after-tax wage on a worker's most recent job. The estimates reflect an average of the replacement rates computed for a large sample of employed and unemployed workers, but they nonetheless can give a misleading impression of the average benefit received by a typical insurance claimant. Vroman has estimated that the average actual replacement rate ranged between 39 and 46 percent among 1980 unemployment insurance recipients.[33] The higher figure reflects the rate for weeks in which compensation was actually paid; the lower figure reflects the effect of waiting weeks and other periods during which compensation was not payable.

The OECD has estimated the net replacement rate of money wages

32. See Martin Feldstein, "Unemployment Compensation: Adverse Incentives and Distributional Anomalies," *National Tax Journal*, vol. 27 (June 1974), pp. 231–44; Kim B. Clark and Lawrence H. Summers, "Unemployment Insurance and Labor Market Transitions," in Martin Neil Baily, ed., *Workers, Jobs, and Inflation* (Brookings, 1982), pp. 279–324; and Robert Topel, "Unemployment and Unemployment Insurance," in Ronald G. Ehrenberg, ed., *Research in Labor Economics*, vol. 7 (Greenwich, Conn.: JAI Press, 1985), pp. 91–136.

33. Vroman, "State Replacement Rates in 1980," p. 176.

for a fully insured American breadwinner.[34] Its calculations are virtually identical to the earlier ones performed by CERC. OECD analysts estimated the fraction of net income in 1980 that would be replaced if an insured breadwinner were unemployed one year. The estimates for the United States show replacement rates among average production workers ranging between 35 and 41 percent, depending on a worker's family situation. The replacement rate in the first half year is approximately 50 percent, but then falls to around 25 percent after insurance benefits are exhausted. This rate of replacement is well below the rate for a comparable production worker in France, Germany, or Sweden. It is similar to the rate for a single worker in Britain, but below the rate for married British workers. The difference in replacement rates largely stems from the shorter duration of U.S. payments. The average weekly benefit level in the United States is not far below levels in Europe, but insurance benefits last only half as long.

Table 8 contains descriptive information about the U.S. insurance system over the past two decades. Column 3 gives information on the trend in the coverage ratio, that is, the fraction of all unemployed who are covered by some form of insurance payment. This ratio has displayed wide variation, ranging from a low of 0.34 in 1984–85 to a high of 0.77 in 1975. Some of the variation is attributable to cyclical changes in the composition of unemployment. During recessions a larger fraction of the unemployed are on temporary or permanent layoff. Since job losers are far more likely to be eligible for benefits than job leavers, new entrants, and reentrants, the share of unemployed who receive benefits expands. With the decline in the number of job losers during a cyclical recovery, the fraction of unemployed collecting benefits shrinks. The extraordinary ballooning of the proportion receiving benefits in 1975–76 was due to temporary federal programs for the long-term jobless and certain other classes of unemployed. The overall trend in the coverage ratio, controlling for the state of the economy, is downward. Because eligibility criteria for insurance have been tightened, a smaller fraction of new job losers now collects benefits.[35]

The fourth and fifth columns in table 8 show the trend in real insurance expenditures per recipient and per unemployed person. There is no evidence in column 4 that the real insurance benefit per recipient has

---

34. *OECD Employment Outlook* (Paris: OECD, 1984), pp. 94–95.
35. Gary Burtless, "Why Is Insured Unemployment So Low?" *Brookings Papers on Economic Activity, 1:1983*, pp. 225–49.

Table 8. *Unemployment Coverage and Outlays in the United States, 1966–85*

Year	Unemploy- ment (thousands)[a] (1)	Insured unemploy- ment (thousands)[b] (2)	Coverage ratio[c] (3)	Expenditure per recipient[d] (4)	Expenditure per person unemployed[d] (5)	Replacement rate (percent)		
						Ashenfelter/ Card (6)	Topel (7)	Burtless (8)
1966	2,875	1,129	0.39	4,290	1,690	50	*	*
1967	2,975	1,270	0.43	4,360	1,860	50	*	*
1968	2,817	1,187	0.42	4,410	1,860	50	*	*
1969	2,832	1,177	0.42	4,450	1,850	50	*	*
1970	4,093	2,070	0.51	4,300	2,170	50	*	*
1971	5,016	2,608	0.52	4,810	2,500	53	*	45
1972	4,882	2,192	0.45	5,430	2,440	54	*	40
1973	4,365	1,793	0.41	4,750	1,950	51	*	41
1974	5,156	2,558	0.50	4,600	2,280	51	*	41
1975	7,929	6,110	0.77	4,560	3,510	51	*	41
1976	7,406	4,998	0.67	4,790	3,230	54	*	41
1977	6,991	3,880	0.55	4,650	2,580	54	62	*
1978	6,202	2,645	0.43	4,900	2,090	53	60	40
1979	6,137	2,619	0.43	4,480	1,910	51	58	39
1980	7,637	3,837	0.50	4,860	2,440	53	58	45
1981	8,273	3,410	0.41	4,450	1,840	53	58	43
1982	10,678	4,795	0.45	4,490	2,020	56	*	*
1983	10,717	4,660	0.43	4,690	2,040	55	*	44
1984	8,539	2,920	0.34	4,350	1,490	53	*	40
1985	8,312	2,785	0.34	4,350	1,460	53	*	*

Sources: See data appendix.
* Not ascertained.
a. Number of persons unemployed, under U.S. definition.
b. Insured unemployment under all state, federal, extended, and special unemployment insurance programs, including federal supplemental benefits and compensation.
c. Insured unemployment divided by total unemployment.
d. Per capita outlays on all unemployment insurance benefits, in constant 1980 dollars.

risen in the past twenty years. Because of the secular decline in the coverage ratio, however, there has been a marked reduction in real outlays per unemployed worker, especially since the mid-1970s. Columns 6, 7, and 8 contain alternative estimates of the average replacement rate in the U.S. insurance system. These figures show little or no trend in the replacement rate over time. Weekly benefits have risen roughly in line with net wages. The main changes in the U.S. program during this period were two temporary extensions in the duration of benefits (in 1975–77 and 1982–85) and reduced liberality in granting benefits to new job losers, beginning in 1980.

Effect of Jobless Pay on Unemployment Differences

Table 9 summarizes some of the main differences in national unemployment insurance systems described in the previous section. Information in the table refers to features of the programs in 1979–80 unless otherwise noted. Column 1 shows the percentage of unemployed covered by insurance or assistance benefits in the five countries.[36] Britain and Germany had the highest coverage ratios, while the United States, by a wide margin, had the lowest. Columns 2 and 3 show the net replacement rates in the first and second years of joblessness for a fully insured average-wage worker with a dependent spouse but no children. The calculations are those described above and reported by CERC and OECD. Jobless pay in France, Germany, and Sweden replaced about two-thirds of lost net earnings during the first year of unemployment, while the British system replaced about half and the American system a bit more than a third. The replacement rate in France could be much higher—up to 83 percent—in the case of workers laid off "for economic reasons." The low replacement rate in the United States is due largely to the limited duration of benefits. If insurance payments lasted a full year, the U.S. replacement rate would be higher than the rate shown for Britain. Figures in the third column indicate a considerable amount of variability in replacement rates during the second year of unemployment. While Germany offers moderately generous benefits to unemployed

36. Strictly speaking, the coverage ratio is defined as the average number of unemployed workers covered by insurance or assistance payments divided by the average total number of unemployed under the BLS definition. Some people collecting benefits do not meet the BLS definition of unemployment.

Table 9. Differences in Jobless Benefits and Unemployment in Five Countries, 1979–80

| Country | Coverage ratio^a (1) | Replacement rate (percent)^b | | Benefit related to past weekly earnings? (4) | Duration of benefits (months)^c (5) | New entrants covered? (6) | Source of financing (7) | Percentage of long-term unemployment^d | |
		Year 1 (2)	Year 2 (3)					More than 6 months (8)	More than 12 months (9)
United Kingdom	0.70–0.77	48	40	No	12 or indefinite	Yes	Payroll tax; general revenues	40	25
France	0.65–0.75	67	33–70^e	Yes	21–45^e	Yes	Payroll tax; general revenues	55	30
Germany	0.74–0.80	66	56	Yes	12 or indefinite	No	Payroll tax; general revenues	40	20
Sweden	0.68–0.74	65	30	No^f	14 or 21	Yes	Contributions; general revenues	20	7
United States	0.41–0.50	37	g	Yes	6 or 9^h	No	Experience-rated payroll tax	9	4

Sources: See data appendix.

a. Average number of recipients of unemployment insurance or unemployment assistance divided by the total number of persons unemployed in 1979–81.
b. Net replacement rate in first and second years of unemployment for average-wage worker who is married to dependent spouse and has no dependent children.
c. Potential duration of unemployment insurance and follow-on unemployment assistance for fully insured workers; "indefinite" implies that follow-on benefits can last indefinitely for workers who pass a means test.
d. Percentage of all 1979 unemployment that lasts longer than six or twelve months, respectively.
e. Replacement rate and duration depend on age and discretionary extension of allocation de base (see text).
f. Although benefits are in principle related to past earnings, most benefit amounts in fact fall within an extremely narrow range because of a ceiling on benefits.
g. There is no follow-on program of unemployment insurance or assistance in the second year.
h. Six months is the usual maximum duration of benefits. Workers in states with exceptionally high insured unemployment are entitled to nine months of benefits.

workers who meet a means test, replacement rates in Sweden and Britain are considerably lower. The second-year replacement rate in France is highly variable and depends on the age of the worker and the discretion of the benefit authorities in granting individual extensions in basic benefits. Unemployed workers in the United States are not eligible to receive regular or follow-on insurance payments in the second year of unemployment.

Column 4 contains an indicator of the relation between weekly benefit payments and the worker's earnings before unemployment. If payments are closely tied to wages, the replacement rate will remain more or less constant over a wide range of previous weekly earnings.[37] On the other hand, if payments are essentially independent of previous earnings, the replacement rate for poorly paid workers will be well above the rate for average-wage workers. This fact can have important implications for the distribution of unemployment across workers, because the largest work disincentives will be strongly concentrated on the lowest earners.

The most significant difference between unemployment insurance in Europe and the United States is the maximum permitted duration of insurance and follow-on assistance payments. Insurance payments usually stop after just six months in the United States, while they can continue at least a year in the four European countries. Less generous follow-on assistance is available for seven additional months in Sweden, nine months in France, and indefinitely in Britain and Germany. The United States offers no equivalent income protection to the long-term unemployed.

The difference in average unemployment duration between Europe and the United States can also influence the way in which one interprets coverage ratios on the two sides of the Atlantic. Typically, spells of unemployment in Europe are much longer than they are in the United States. The percentage of all unemployed who have been jobless at least six and twelve months is shown in the last two columns of table 9. Note that the percentage of long-term unemployment is four times higher in Britain and Germany than in the United States. If the incidence of long-term unemployment were as high in the United States as it is in Europe, the fraction of American unemployed collecting jobless benefits would

---

37. This will be true up to a maximum weekly level of previous wages. France, Germany, and the United States only insure wages below a fixed amount. In Germany and the United States, this amount is not far above the average weekly wage; in France, it is well above the average weekly wage.

Table 10. *Civilian Unemployment Rates in Five Countries, 1967–85*[a]

Percent

Country	1967–73	1975–76	1979	1982	1985
France	2.4	4.4	6.0	8.3	10.4
Germany	0.8	3.4	3.0	5.9	7.9
Sweden	2.2	1.6	2.1	3.1	2.8
United Kingdom	3.4	5.2	5.4	11.4	11.3
United States	4.6	8.1	5.8	9.7	7.2

Source: See data appendix.
a. Civilian unemployment rate according to definition of U.S. Bureau of Labor Statistics.

be even smaller than indicated in column 1. For example, if the distribution of unemployment durations were the same in the United States
as the average for Britain, France, and Germany, the coverage ratio in
1979–81 would have been in the range of 0.23–0.32 rather than 0.41–
0.50. This constructed rate is dramatically lower than the indicated rates
for any of the European countries. Of course, the short average duration
of American unemployment implies that the U.S. replacement rate
reported in table 9 is somewhat misleading. Because very few insured
unemployed workers experience a full year's unemployment, the typical
insured worker in the United States actually receives a much higher net
replacement rate for those months in which he is unemployed.[38]

Can differences in jobless pay explain differences in the levels or
trends in unemployment among countries? Civilian unemployment rates
in the five countries are displayed in table 10. Figures in the first two
columns demonstrate the well-known fact that Europe traditionally
enjoyed much lower joblessness than the United States. In the seven
years before the first oil shock, the U.S. unemployment rate was 1.4
times the rate in Britain, about 2 times the rate in France and Sweden,
and nearly 6 times the rate in Germany. This baseline pattern is difficult
to explain by reference to differences in jobless pay. Since the United
States has historically offered the least generous benefits, it should have
enjoyed the lowest, not the highest, rate of joblessness.

Unemployment rose in all five countries between the late 1960s and
the mid-1980s. The rise was greatest—both absolutely and as a proportion
of initial unemployment—in Britain, France, and Germany. Joblessness
in those countries is now more severe than in the United States, where
the trend growth in unemployment has been much more moderate. The

38. For consistency, I am defining the net replacement rate as it is measured by
CERC and OECD, not by Wayne Vroman.

trend growth in measured unemployment in Sweden has been quite slow. Again, this pattern is not easy to explain solely by reference to differences in jobless pay. Although the slow growth in U.S. unemployment might be explained, in part, by the low level of benefits available to jobless Americans, it is difficult to explain why unemployment has grown even more slowly in Sweden, notwithstanding the high and rising level of Swedish benefits.

Even if Sweden is excluded from the comparison, there are problems with the naive hypothesis that higher jobless pay is associated with greater joblessness. Unemployment has risen sharply in Britain despite falling real expenditures per recipient and a probable decline in the average replacement rate since the mid-1970s. Similarly, unemployment shot up in Germany after 1979, though the system of unemployment pay has remained almost unchanged for two decades. Even if replacement rates for the newly unemployed are somewhat higher today than they were in the late 1960s, it is implausible that the modest change in benefits induced such a disproportionate rise in joblessness. Finally, U.S. joblessness has risen, not fallen, over a ten-year period in which the insurance coverage rate of newly unemployed workers has plunged.[39]

I have argued that neither the differences between countries in unemployment level nor the differences in trend unemployment can be principally explained by differences in jobless pay. This conclusion is hardly surprising. For three of the countries examined—Britain, Germany, and the United States—there was little liberalization in jobless benefits after the 1967–73 period. Even if *all* unemployment in the early 1970s was caused by excessive jobless pay, one would still have to explain why unemployment has jumped by 10 percentage points in Britain, 7 points in Germany, and 2½ points in the United States. On the other hand, this evidence does not demonstrate that unemployment benefits played no role in the rise of unemployment. But it clearly was not the sole or even main cause.

A more meaningful question is how do different systems of unemployment pay contribute to high joblessness when the economy is affected by a demand- or supply-side shock. One example of a demand-side shock is a sudden reduction in domestic or foreign demand for

39. Gary Burtless and Wayne Vroman, "The Performance of Unemployment Insurance since 1979," in Barbara D. Dennis, ed., *Proceedings of the 37th Annual Meeting of the Industrial Relations Research Association* (Madison, Wisc.: IRRA, 1985), pp. 138–46.

domestically produced output. A supply-side shock might be a radical improvement in technology that suddenly reduces demand for labor at the prevailing wage. Both types of shock can cause a temporary spurt in joblessness, irrespective of the generosity of unemployment benefits. Either the layoff rate will rise or the new hire rate will decline, depending on the employer response.

Baily and Feldstein have suggested that incomplete experience rating of the employer-employee premium payments for unemployment insurance can cause employers to prefer temporary layoffs to other possible responses to a demand shock. As noted earlier, this hypothesis has been examined with U.S. data. Rather strikingly, it is now claimed that incomplete experience rating is the *main* reason that unemployment insurance contributes to higher U.S. unemployment.[40] In one of the first empirical studies of financing effects, Feldstein found evidence that half of all temporary layoff unemployment (or 12–13 percent of 1971 unemployment) was due to the financing structure of insurance.[41] Topel estimated that incomplete experience rating was responsible for 40–90 percent of the overall effect of unemployment insurance on adult male unemployment. He estimated the overall effect to be in the range of 1.6 to 2.8 percentage points, or between 30 and 55 percent of all unemployment among American adult men over the period 1977–81.[42]

The Baily-Feldstein hypothesis provides an explanation of why employers would respond differently to a shock depending on the financing of the unemployment insurance system, but it does not go very far toward explaining the different unemployment patterns displayed in table 10. Column 7 in table 9 describes the financing method for insurance in the five countries. Only the United States has a financing mechanism that penalizes individual employers (and, implicitly, their employees) for above-average utilization of insurance benefits. The other four countries finance insurance benefits with a payroll tax that does not vary to reflect previous claims experience. (Britain, however, requires employers to pay allowances for the first five days of temporary unemployment, and Sweden requires employers to pay for a large share of the

40. See Robert Topel and Finis Welch, "Unemployment Insurance: Survey and Extensions," *Economica*, vol. 47 (August 1980), pp. 351–79; and Robert Topel, "Unemployment and Unemployment Insurance," pp. 128–29.

41. Martin Feldstein, "The Effect of Unemployment Insurance on Temporary Layoff Unemployment," *American Economic Review*, vol. 68 (December 1978), pp. 834–46.

42. Topel, "Unemployment and Unemployment Insurance," pp. 129–30.

benefits paid out to workers on temporary as opposed to permanent layoff.) Most European countries require employers to make severance payments to certain *permanently* laid off employees, but this restriction should only encourage the use of temporary layoffs.

Contrary to the Baily-Feldstein hypothesis, European employers appear to use temporary layoffs far less often than employers in the United States.[43] The main reasons seem to be legal and institutional differences in European and American labor-management relations. Moy and Sorrentino make the point, for example, that hours reductions and work sharing are more attractive options in Europe than in the United States.[44] For example, short-time working is totally subsidized by public funds in Germany, making short hours an attractive alternative to layoffs. Moreover, European workers appear to enjoy much stronger legal protections against layoff than those available in the United States. Though these legal restraints usually do not specifically prohibit temporary layoffs, employers may nonetheless treat layoffs of any kind—including temporary layoffs—as a strategy of last resort.[45]

The propensity of American employers to use temporary layoffs is indirectly shown in table 10. The cyclical variability of U.S. unemployment is far greater than the variability in Europe. Part of this extra variability is caused by temporary-layoff unemployment; U.S. employers appear in general far more willing to vary employment levels in response to a shock in demand.[46] As just noted, however, this attitude

43. See Felix R. FitzRoy and Robert A. Hart, "Hours, Layoffs and Unemployment Insurance Funding: Theory and Practice in an International Perspective," *Economic Journal,* vol. 95 (September 1985), pp. 700–13.

44. Joyanna Moy and Constance Sorrentino, "Unemployment, Labor Force Trends, and Layoff Practices in Ten Countries," *Monthly Labor Review,* vol. 104 (December 1981), pp. 3–13. FitzRoy and Hart, in "Hours, Layoffs and Unemployment Insurance Funding," argue that the financing mechanism for unemployment insurance in the United States makes temporary layoffs more attractive than shorter hours in that country. The hypothesis rests on the argument that the U.S. insurance tax is closer to a head tax on laborers than a payroll tax on wages. This gives employers an incentive to economize on laborers rather than on hours per week during a downturn. The argument appears to ignore the fact that the "head tax" in the United States is determined on the basis of the employer's past unemployment insurance claims experience, whereas in Europe the payroll tax is independent of individual claims experience. This difference would appear to give U.S. employers a much more powerful incentive to avoid layoffs than is present in Europe.

45. For a more complete discussion of the comparison between U.S. and European job protection laws and regulations, see the paper in this volume by Robert J. Flanagan.

46. Robert A. Hart, "Working Time and Employment within an International

cannot be explained by adverse incentives arising from unemployment insurance, since the financial incentives to respond to temporary downward shocks with layoffs appear even stronger in most European countries.

The adverse incentives of the unemployment insurance system on individual job search behavior can, however, explain why shock-induced unemployment persists longer in Europe than in the United States. Jobless pay raises the stock of European unemployed because it makes the unemployed "choosy" and hence lowers the rate of reemployment, not because it raises the flow from employment to unemployment. The effect of insurance on the unemployment duration of insured workers has been more intensively studied than almost any topic in empirical labor economics.[47] Almost without exception, the published studies have found a statistically significant relationship between the duration of a completed spell of unemployment and the level of benefits available to the unemployed worker. In summarizing the early U.S. studies, Hamermesh concluded that a 10 percentage point rise in the gross replacement rate leads to an increase in the average insured spell of unemployment of about one-half week. If an average completed spell of insured unemployment is thirteen weeks, a 50 percent gross replacement rate would account for approximately a fifth (2.5/13) of the average completed spell.[48] In a later survey, Welch estimated that the effect of insurance on the total unemployment duration—including the uninsured portion after benefit exhaustion—is about one and a half weeks for every $10 rise in the weekly benefit amount (benefits were measured in 1970 dollars).[49] Since the average weekly benefit in the early 1970s was about $50, this implies that recipients of benefits spent approximately seven and a half additional weeks in unemployment. Classen has performed

Perspective," Discussion Paper 85-34 (Berlin: International Institute of Management, 1985).

47. For partial surveys, see Daniel S. Hamermesh, *Jobless Pay and the Economy* (Johns Hopkins University Press, 1977); Finis Welch, "What Have We Learned from Empirical Studies of Unemployment Insurance?" *Industrial and Labor Relations Review*, vol. 30 (July 1977), pp. 451–61; Topel and Welch, "Unemployment Insurance: Survey and Extensions"; and A. B. Atkinson, "Income Maintenance and Social Insurance: A Survey," in Alan Auerbach and Martin Feldstein, *Handbook of Public Economics*, vol. 2 (Amsterdam: North-Holland, forthcoming).

48. The estimate of the average completed spell is taken from Robert A. Moffitt, "Unemployment Insurance and the Distribution of Unemployment Spells," *Journal of Econometrics*, vol. 28 (1985), p. 89.

49. Welch, "What Have We Learned?" p. 460.

some of the most careful studies in this area based on U.S. administrative records.[50] Her estimates suggest that the elasticity of insured unemployment duration with respect to changes in the insurance replacement rate is about 0.6 to 1.0 for average workers. Several British economists have obtained virtually identical elasticity estimates for the unemployment insurance program in Britain, though Atkinson and others warn that the elasticity estimate is not well determined in the data.[51]

In comparing insurance incentives in the United States and Europe, however, the effect of potential benefit *duration* on completed unemployment spells is more important than the size of the *replacement rate*. Insurance payments can continue at least twice as long in Europe as they can in the United States, and European assistance payments can make the difference in potential duration far greater. Moffitt and Nicholson, and Moffitt, have provided the best estimates of the effect of insurance duration on the reemployment rate or unemployment duration of insured workers.[52] In both studies the authors found statistically significant responses to variations in the potential benefit duration. A one-week increase in the potential duration of jobless pay was predicted to cause an increase in the duration of joblessness of about 0.10 to 0.15 week. The two studies also found a statistically significant effect of benefit amount on unemployment duration.

With some effort, the Moffitt and Nicholson, and Moffitt, estimates can be used to assess the likely range of effect of more generous jobless benefits in Europe compared with the United States. If workers expect to be limited to only insurance benefits, British and German workers can

50. Kathleen P. Classen, "The Effect of Unemployment Insurance," and "Unemployment Insurance and Job Search," in Steven A. Lippman and John J. McCall, eds., *Studies in the Economics of Search* (Amsterdam: North-Holland, 1979), pp. 191–219.

51. Tony Lancaster, "Econometric Methods for the Duration of Unemployment," *Econometrica*, vol. 47 (July 1979), pp. 939–56; Stephen Nickell, "Estimating the Probability of Leaving Unemployment," *Econometrica*, vol. 47 (September 1979), pp. 1249–66; Nickell, "Effect of Unemployment and Related Benefits"; and A. B. Atkinson, J. Gomulka, and J. Micklewright, "Unemployment Benefit, Duration and Incentives in Britain: How Robust Is the Evidence?" *Journal of Public Economics*, vol. 23 (February–March 1984), pp. 3–26. Atkinson and others point out that the estimated elasticity is sensitive to seemingly trivial changes in the statistical specification and to alternative methods of representing the benefit level. They note that under plausible specifications the best estimate of effect is zero.

52. Robert A. Moffitt and Walter Nicholson, "The Effect of Unemployment Insurance on Unemployment: The Case of Federal Supplemental Benefits," *Review of Economics and Statistics*, vol. 64 (February 1982), pp. 1–11; and Moffitt, "Unemployment Insurance and the Distribution of Unemployment Spells."

expect twenty-six weeks of benefits beyond the twenty-six weeks potentially available to Americans; Swedish workers can expect thirty-four weeks additional benefits; and an average French worker might expect fifty additional weeks. These longer durations of potential benefits could add two and a half to four weeks to the average completed spell of unemployment in Britain and Germany, three and a half to five weeks to an average spell in Sweden, and five to seven and a half weeks to an average spell in France. To these estimates must be added the effect of higher weekly replacement rates often available in Europe, but this addition is probably fairly small—no more than two weeks of added unemployment in France, Germany, and Sweden, and less than that in Britain. If workers also respond to the availability of assistance or flat-rate follow-on insurance after the exhaustion of regular insurance benefits, the potential effect of benefit duration on unemployment spells could be significantly greater than these estimates. For example, low-income unemployed workers in Britain and Germany are entitled to benefits of indefinite duration.

Evidence on the duration of average unemployment spells in Europe and the United States in fact *supports* the hypothesis that durations were longer in European countries, even before joblessness soared in the late 1970s. For example, the average uncompleted duration of spells of unemployment among British men was about thirty-three weeks in the period 1965–74. The average duration among all unemployed in the United States was only ten weeks. As a proportion of average U.S. unemployment duration in 1973, the average duration in Sweden was 1.7 times greater, the duration in Germany was 2.1 times greater, the duration in Britain was 3.8 times greater, and the duration in France was 4.0 times greater.[53]

Conceivably, insurance benefits had an important effect on the duration of joblessness of European workers who became unemployed, but the overall effect on unemployment was modest because so few workers were exposed to adverse insurance incentives. In France and Germany, for example, less than 1 percent of the labor force was typically in receipt of jobless benefits between 1967 and 1973. The comparable figure in the United States was more than 2 percent. Even though the less generous U.S. system may have caused fewer adverse incentives among the workers who were exposed to it, the layoff policies of

---

53. *OECD Employment Outlook* (Paris: OECD, 1983), p. 58.

American employers caused a larger share of workers to be exposed to adverse incentives. In other words, in the late 1960s and early 1970s generous European uncmployment benefits did not do very much to raise unemployment. Those workers who were laid off were able to search longer for a suitable job but compared with the United States there were so few layoffs that the overall European unemployment rate was much lower. In view of the fundamental difference between layoff policies in Europe and the United States, there is no reason to believe that the total effect of jobless pay would be greater in Europe than in the United States under conditions approaching full employment, notwithstanding the greater generosity of jobless benefits in Europe.

This conclusion is reinforced by one additional consideration. As noted earlier, the adverse incentive effects on job search can be greatly reduced if there are effective methods to monitor the search and job acceptance behavior of insured workers. In this respect the U.S. system provides weaker safeguards against malingering than those available to systems in Europe. Compared with government employment services in Europe, the U.S. Employment Service is relatively ineffective in aiding and monitoring the search for jobs. The Swedish government, for example, requires employers to register all job vacancies with the state employment service. Hence it is quite simple to refer insured job seekers to suitable jobs and penalize workers who refuse to search for or accept suitable work. The U.S. Employment Service is unaware of most available vacancies and therefore finds it much more difficult to enforce the search requirement.

The relative effects of the U.S. and European systems might be quite different, however, after a severe demand- or supply-side shock. Should large numbers of experienced European workers actually be exposed to jobless pay by being laid off, the more generous payment schemes could have much greater consequences than they did in the early 1970s. Not only would the overall effect of benefits be increased by the growth in the number of workers exposed to adverse incentives, but the effect per jobless worker might rise. First, the adverse influence of benefits on job search could grow if the stigma of receiving benefits declined. Such a decline might occur as a natural result of swelling benefit rolls. If a greater fraction of one's peers were receiving benefits, the stigma attached to remaining on the rolls could fall. This change could cause an increase in reservation wages or a decline in search efforts. Second, the rise in the number of unemployed workers relative to job vacancies would make it more difficult for the insurance authorities to enforce regulations requiring the serious search for and acceptance of suitable job offers. Recall that these regulations can reduce the adverse effects of high replacement rates. If enforcement of the regulations were to decline, an unchanged replacement rate could have a larger effect on job-seeking activities.[54]

But there is an important reason to think an adverse shock might actually reduce the impact of jobless pay on the duration of unemployment. Earlier I described two models of labor-market response. When the labor market is characterized by a high ratio of vacancies to unemployed workers, jobless pay clearly can raise the average duration and level of unemployment. On the other hand, when unemployed workers greatly outnumber job vacancies, there is no strong reason to believe that the disincentive effects of jobless pay on *insured* workers will raise the average unemployment duration experienced by *all* job seekers, including both the insured and uninsured. Uninsured and poorly insured job seekers, who are in competition with well-insured workers for a limited number of vacancies, must enjoy much shorter spells of unemployment than they would in a world without insurance. Between the early and late 1970s, European labor markets moved from a world in which vacancies were plentiful relative to job seekers to one in which vacancies were very scarce.

There is little empirical evidence with which to judge whether a particular unemployment insurance system would affect unemployment duration more when joblessness is high than when it is low. Using microeconomic evidence about the effects of British replacement rates on individual probabilities of escape from unemployment, Atkinson and Micklewright find that the effect was no larger during a period of high unemployment (1975–77) than during a period of low unemployment (1972–75).[55] This casts doubt on the idea that reduced stigma from receipt of benefits or slack enforcement of search regulations causes insured workers to be more adversely affected by the same replacement rate.

Under the assumption that the effect of benefits on individual workers has not grown simply because unemployment has risen, one must

54. This consideration is likely to be more important in Europe than in the United States. Because of weaknesses in the U.S. Employment Service, American search requirements are difficult to enforce even at full employment. Hence the effect of high unemployment on enforcement efforts is likely to be smaller in the United States than in Europe.

55. The effect may in fact have been somewhat smaller. See Atkinson and Micklewright, *Unemployment Benefits and Unemployment Duration*, p. 221.

conclude that the contribution of jobless pay to the recent high rate of European unemployment is modest. The microeconomic evidence on the relation between unemployment benefits and unemployment durations implies that only a small fraction of current durations can be attributable to benefits. For purposes of comparison, the Moffitt and Nicholson estimates suggest that completed unemployment durations in Britain might be four to nine weeks longer than in the United States as a result of more generous benefits.[56] The size of this differential effect can have risen by no more than two or three weeks as a result of changes in the U.S. and British systems over the period 1970–86. (It could even be argued that the effect has gone in the opposite direction in light of the curtailment and eventual abandonment of the earnings related benefit in Britain.) These effects on unemployment duration should be put in perspective with the actual increases in duration observed in Britain. In 1965–69 the average interrupted spell of British unemployment lasted thirty-one weeks. By 1984 the average interrupted spell was nearly sixty-nine weeks, or thirty-eight weeks longer.[57] The average *completed* spell of British unemployment obviously rose by far more than thirty-eight weeks. Given the microeconomic evidence, the increase in the length of British unemployment spells is many times greater than any increase that could be reasonably attributed to jobless benefits.

The situation in Germany is similar to that in Britain. Only in France and Sweden were jobless benefits substantially raised in the 1970s and early 1980s, and in Sweden the rise in unemployment over the period was modest. For France it is reasonable to argue that broader coverage and increased benefit levels served to reduce reemployment incentives among unemployed workers. Because the number of workers experiencing unemployment shot up, the number affected by jobless pay also rose. It is thus plausible to suggest that the French insurance system, by creating adverse incentives for unemployed workers, has significantly raised French unemployment above what it would be under a less-generous system. Yet even in France the overwhelming share of higher joblessness must be attributable to other factors.

I suggested earlier that generous jobless pay could also raise unem-

56. Moffitt and Nicholson, "Effect of Unemployment Insurance on Unemployment," p. 10.

57. These durations were measured for registered unemployed men with spells of unemployment currently in progress. See Richard Layard and Stephen Nickell, "Unemployment in Britain," Discussion Paper 240 (London School of Economics, Centre for Labour Economics, January 1986), p. 54.

ployment by changing the wage-bargaining stance of unions or increasing the payroll tax burden imposed on employers. The latter effect is discussed more extensively in other papers in this volume and will not be addressed here. The effect of jobless pay on union wage-setting behavior deserves closer attention. The central argument is that high jobless pay encourages unions to demand excessive real wages. As I showed earlier, the differential between unemployment benefit levels in Europe and the United States existed well before the recent surge in European joblessness. There has been no rise in jobless pay in either Britain or Germany that would explain why British or German unions are any more greedy today than they were in the late 1960s or early 1970s. Nor can relative trends in insurance generosity explain why European unions would suddenly have become much more greedy than unions in the United States. Hence it is hard to explain the relative trends in European and U.S. unemployment by reference to the effect of insurance generosity on wage bargaining.

One might argue that the effect of high jobless pay on union pay demands is more destabilizing when the economy has experienced adverse shocks. Unions are more inclined to make reckless demands in a declining economy when insurance protection is good than when it is poor. According to this line of reasoning, American wage bargains were more responsible than wage bargains in Europe after the two oil shocks, partly because American unions were constrained by poor unemployment insurance protection. Although this argument is internally consistent, there is no evidence to support or refute it. Until such evidence is found, the effect of unemployment insurance on wage bargaining must remain an open question.

Summary

In this survey I find little to support the view that differences in jobless pay can plausibly explain the differential trends in unemployment in Europe and the United States. The five countries I examine provide very different insurance schemes for their unemployed workers. All schemes are similar in offering limited-duration insurance benefits to experienced workers who lose their jobs. They differ in the generosity of the benefits offered, the relation between benefit levels and past earnings, the maximum duration of benefits, and the method of financing benefits. The several national systems also differ widely in the income protection they offer to job leavers, new labor market entrants, and long-term unemployed workers who exhaust regular insurance benefits. Moreover, the five countries differ with respect to trends over time in the generosity of their programs.

A simple model linking generous unemployment pay to high joblessness must clearly be rejected. For two decades jobless benefits have been less generous in the United States than in Europe, as measured by typical replacement rates and the percentage of unemployed receiving payments. Controlling for differences in the distribution of unemployment durations in the five countries, the United States appears to have an even less generous system than is indicated by simple measures of generosity, such as the weekly replacement rate and the proportion of unemployed covered by benefits. Yet for most of the past twenty years, unemployment has been higher in the United States than Europe. In more recent years, Sweden has enjoyed low unemployment despite offering very generous income support to the unemployed. Furthermore, the trends in joblessness within individual countries do not correspond well to trends in the generosity of benefits. Only in France has a significant rise in joblessness occurred at the same time as a major increase in the generosity of unemployment benefits.

Nor does the international evidence support the hypothesis that generous benefits financed through a non-experience-rated payroll tax are responsible for an increased probability of layoff unemployment. Among the five countries considered, the United Staes is unique in penalizing individual employers for a high layoff rate, but it is also the country in which employers are most inclined to use layoffs in response to fluctuations in demand. Hence it is hard to argue that jobless benefits figure prominently in explaining cross-country differences in entry into layoff unemployment.

The international evidence is more consistent with the proposition that generous benefits can lengthen the completed spell of unemployment by reducing the rate of job entry among the unemployed. Even when unemployment rates were much lower in Europe than in the United States, the average duration of unemployment spells was longer in Europe. The overall influence of unemployment benefits on the rate of unemployment was reduced, however, by the smaller number of workers entering unemployment and hence facing the adverse incentives created by insurance. When the number of affected unemployed workers rose after the oil shocks of the middle and late 1970s, the potential scope of the adverse effects increased dramatically.

High jobless benefits in Europe have certainly slowed down the entry into employment of some unemployed workers. But it is not clear why reemployment should be retarded any more when labor markets are slack than when they are tight. Arguably, the aggregate effect of jobless pay on average unemployment durations should be smaller in slack markets than in tight ones. If one uses the microeconomic estimates of the effect of jobless pay on individual reemployment gains, the predicted influence of European jobless benefits on unemployment durations appears small in comparison with the rise in duration that has actually occurred in recent years, except in the case of Sweden, where the rise in duration has been moderate.[58]

This analysis suggests that jobless pay cannot be responsible for higher equilibrium unemployment in Europe compared with the United States, although it can be responsible for a slower adjustment in employment and wages after the economy experiences a severe shock in demand for labor. By raising reservation wages in Europe vis-à-vis the United States, higher jobless benefits could have slowed the speed of adjustment of wages paid to newly employed European workers. If a sharply lower equilibrium wage is needed to restore the economy to full employment, generous jobless pay can reduce the pressure on unemployed workers to accept the reduced wage offers. It is hard to believe, however, that employers refrain from reducing their wage offers to new workers because of a fear that high jobless benefits will meaningfully affect the number or quality of job applicants. This argument is credible when unemployment is 2 percent, but not when the number of job seekers exceeds the number of vacancies by ten to one or more. (A related argument is that generous jobless benefits cause *employed* workers to be more resistant to necessary wage reductions. But assessing the evidence for this proposition is beyond the scope of this paper.)

The most plausible interpretation of the evidence presented here is that generous jobless benefits have slowed the reemployment of jobless

58. One reason for the slow rise in Swedish unemployment durations is the broad scope of public employment and training programs that remove jobless workers from unemployment. An average of about 165,000 workers and trainees participated in these programs during 1984–85, a number that is more than 25 percent above the average level of open unemployment in Sweden. None of the other four countries offers manpower programs on this scale.

workers in three of the four European countries examined—Britain, France, and Germany. But this effect of jobless pay is far too small to explain the large rise in unemployment durations in Europe or the enormous rise of unemployment levels in Britain, France, and Germany compared with those in Sweden and the United States.

Data Appendix

This appendix identifies the main and supplemental sources of information used in the text and tables of the paper. A Reference List of the works cited here appears at the end of the appendix.

United Kingdom

The primary source used as a basis for describing the British system of unemployment insurance is Atkinson and Micklewright, especially chapter 2. In addition, Kaufman; Grais; OECD, *Unemployment Compensation and Related Employment Policy Measures*; and Centre d'Etude des Revenus et des Coûts, *L'Indemnisation du Chômage en France et à l'Etranger,* and *Changements Intervenus depuis 1982 dans les Systèmes d'Indemnisation du Chômage en France et dans Quatre Pays Etrangers* provided useful supplementary information. The sources for the data in table 2 are:

Column 1: Unpublished data from U.S. Bureau of Labor Statistics.

Columns 2 and 3: Data for 1967–76 are from *British Labour Statistics Yearbook, 1976,* pp. 270–71, yearly average of monthly figures for February, May, and November (author's adjustments required to account for exclusion of Northern Ireland in published statistics); 1975–83 data are derived from United Kingdom, *Annual Abstract of Statistics, 1985,* p. 55 (1981 data are missing because of an industrial dispute).

Column 4: See sources for columns 1–3.

Columns 5 and 6: Current expenditures are derived from Varley, p. 43. Expenditures are deflated by a consumer price index taken from the International Monetary Fund's International Financial Statistics data tape. Unemployment data and recipient sources are the same as those described for columns 1–3.

Column 7: Source is Smee, p. 128. Smee computes the replacement rate by computing total outlays on unemployment benefit, supplementary benefit (for the unemployed), and earnings related supplement and then dividing this total by the average number of registered unemployed. To determine the actual replacement rate, he then divides this average benefit by "total net earnings," which is a weighted average of the estimated *net* earnings of the various age, sex, and family groups represented in the unemployment register.

Column 8: Source is Layard and Nickell, p. 101. The reported replacement rate is intended to measure the ratio of annual net income in unemployment to net income in work. The benefit in unemployment is computed by assuming that the demographic composition of the unemployed remains constant and suitably adjusting the benefit to reflect supplementary benefits and rent reimbursement in a single-earner family.

Column 9: My measure of the replacement rate is the gross expenditure per recipient (see column 5) divided by net earnings of an average U.K. production worker in manufacturing, as measured by the OECD in *The Tax/Benefit Position of Selected Income Groups in OECD Member Countries, 1972–76,* and *1974–78; The 1980 Tax/Benefit Position of a Typical Worker in OECD Member Countries;* and *The Tax/Benefit Position of Production Workers, 1979–84.* The tax situation of a single person is assumed in computing the net earnings of the average worker.

France

The primary sources for the description of the French unemployment system before 1979 are Kaufman and OECD, *Unemployment Compensation and Related Employment Measures.* The system after 1979 is described in CERC, *L'Indemnisation* and *Changements,* and Grais. The sources for the data in table 4 are:

Column 1: Unpublished data from U.S. Bureau of Labor Statistics.

Columns 2 and 3: Data for 1966–78 are from Kaufman, p. 36; 1980–81 data are monthly totals for September, from CERC, *L'Indemnisation,* p. 45; 1985 data are from Dupeyroux, p. 1086, and cover March 1985.

Column 4: OECD, *High Unemployment: A Challenge for Income Support Policies,* p. 245; and Dupeyroux, p. 1086.

Column 5: See sources for columns 1 and 4.

Columns 6 and 7: Current expenditures are derived from OECD, *High Unemployment,* p. 237. Expenditures are deflated using a consumer price index from the IMF International Financial Statistics data tape. Unemployment and recipient data are the same as for columns 1 and 4.

Column 8: Claassen and Lane's estimates as corrected are reported in Kaufman, p. 35. Claassen and Lane divided the total amount of benefit outlays by the total number of beneficiaries, and, in turn, divided this constructed "average benefit" by average earnings.

Column 9: My measure of replacement rate is the gross expenditure per recipient (see column 6) divided by net earnings of an average French production worker in manufacturing, as measured by the OECD in *Tax/ Benefit Position . . . , 1972–76*, and *1974–78, 1980 Tax/Benefit Position*, and *Tax/Benefit Position . . . , 1979–84*. The tax situation of a single person is assumed in computing the net earnings of the average worker.

Germany

The basic source for the description of German unemployment insurance and assistance in the early 1970s is OECD, *Unemployment Compensation*. Later information is derived from CERC, *L'Indemnisation* and *Changements,* and Bruche and Reissert. The sources for the data in table 5 are:

Column 1: Unpublished data from the U.S. Bureau of Labor Statistics.

Columns 2 and 3: Bundesminister für Arbeit und Sozialordnung, p. 8.14, and private communication from Bernd Reissert.

Column 4: See sources for columns 1–3.

Columns 5 and 6: Current expenditures are derived from OECD, *High Unemployment,* p. 238; Bruche and Reissert, table 2; and private communication from Bernd Reissert. Expenditures are deflated by a consumer price index from the IMF International Financial Statistics data tape. Expenditures exclude transfers from the unemployment funds to sickness insurance and pension funds.

These transfers were estimated by the author for the years 1967–72 as 16 percent of outlays on insurance and 19 percent of outlays on assistance—the same percentages reported for 1973 in Bruche and Reissert.

Column 7: Bruche and Reissert, table 31, and private communication from Bernd Reissert. Computed as the average monthly insurance payment (*Arbeitslosengeld*) divided by the average net monthly earnings of employees.

Column 8: My measure of replacement rate is the gross expenditure per recipient (see column 5) divided by net earnings of an average German production worker in manufacturing, as measured by OECD in

Tax/Benefit Position . . . , *1972–76,* and *1974–78, 1980 Tax/Benefit Position,* and *Tax/Benefit Position* . . . , *1979–84.* The tax situation of a single person is assumed in computing the net earnings of the average worker.

Sweden

The basic source of information for the Swedish unemployment system is Björklund and Holmlund. Supplemental information is available in OECD, *Unemployment Compensation,* CERC, *L'Indemnisation* and *Changements.* The sources for the data in table 7 are:

Column 1: Unpublished data from the U.S. Bureau of Labor Statistics.

Columns 2 and 3: OECD, *Main Economic Indicators,* various issues.

Column 4: Wadensjö, p. 16; and, for 1985, private communication from Bertil Holmlund.

Columns 5 and 6: Current expenditures on unemployment insurance are derived from Björklund and Holmlund, pp. 6 and 15. Expenditures are deflated by a consumer price index from the IMF International Financial Statistics data tape.

Column 7: Björklund and Holmlund, p. 40, show "average replacement rates among insured, male blue-collar workers" who experience an unemployment spell of exactly three months.

Column 8: My measure of the replacement rate is the gross expenditure per recipient (see column 5) divided by net earnings of an average Swedish production worker in manufacturing, as measured by the OECD in *Tax/Benefit Position* . . . , *1972–76,* and *1974–78, 1980 Tax/Benefit Position,* and *Tax/Benefit Position* . . . , *1979–84.* The tax situation of a single person is assumed in computing the net earnings of the average worker.

United States

This description of the U.S. unemployment system is based on Burtless and the sources cited therein. The sources for the data in table 8 are:

Column 1: Data from the U.S. Bureau of Labor Statistics.

Column 2: U.S. Office of Federal Statistical Policy and Standards, and others, *1980 Supplement to Economic Indicators,* p. 41; and U.S. Council of Economic Advisers, *Economic Indicators,* p. 13.

Column 3: See sources for columns 1 and 2.

Columns 4 and 5: Current expenditures are derived from OECD, *High Unemployment,* p. 242; Vroman, "The Reagan Administration and Unemployment Insurance," p. 16; *Survey of Current Business,* vol. 66 (July 1986), p. 48. Expenditures are deflated by a consumer price index taken from the IMF International Financial Statistics data tape.

Column 6: Ashenfelter and Card, table 9b, compute the ratio of the average weekly unemployment insurance benefit to the net weekly earnings of an average U.S. worker.

Column 7: Topel, p. 112. Topel uses a complicated computer algorithm to impute weekly benefit amounts for full-time employed and unemployed U.S. males who reside in twelve states. He then computes an individual's net replacement rate as the ratio of this imputed weekly benefit to the worker's weekly net wage and computes the arithmetic average of the resulting replacement rates for men in the twelve states. I have computed the weighted average of the twelve separate state estimates, weighting each state by the size of its labor force.

Column 8: My measure of replacement rate is the gross expenditure per recipient (see column 4) divided by net earnings of an average U.S. production worker in manufacturing, as measured by the OECD in *Tax/ Benefit Position . . . , 1972–76,* and *1974–78, 1980 Tax/Benefit Position,* and *Tax/Benefit Position . . . , 1979–84.* The tax situation of a single person is assumed in computing the net earnings of the average worker.

Table 9

Column 1: See coverage ratios reported in tables 2, 4, 5, 7, and 8.

Columns 2 and 3: Data for Britain, France, Germany, and Sweden are from CERC, *L'Indemnisation,* p. 63. Data for the United States are from *OECD Employment Outlook* (1984), p. 94.

Columns 4–7: See text and sources, listed above, for individual country descriptions of unemployment insurance systems.

Columns 8 and 9: *OECD Employment Outlook* (1985), p. 126.

Table 10

For all countries except Sweden, see *Economic Report of the President, January 1987,* p. 367; for Sweden, 1967–82, see OECD, *Historical*

Statistics, 1960–84, p. 41, and for 1985, see OECD, *Main Economic Indicators*, April 1987, p. 148.

Reference List

Ashenfelter, Orley, and David Card. "Why Have Unemployment Rates in Canada and the United States Diverged?" *Economica*, vol. 53 (1986, *Supplement*), pp. S171–96.

Atkinson, A. B., and John Micklewright. *Unemployment Benefits and Unemployment Duration*. London: Suntory-Toyota International Centre for Economics and Related Disciplines, 1985.

Björklund, Anders, and Bertil Holmlund. "The Economics of Unemployment Insurance: The Case of Sweden." Working Paper 167. Stockholm: Industrial Institute for Economic and Social Research, 1986.

British Central Statistical Office. *Annual Abstract of Statistics, 1985*. London: Her Majesty's Stationery Office, 1985.

———. *British Labour Statistics Yearbook, 1976*. London: HMSO, 1978.

Bruche, Gert, and Bernd Reissert. "The Financing of Labor Market Policy in the Federal Republic of Germany." Berlin: International Institute of Management, 1985. Draft translation of *Die Finanzierung der Arbeitsmarktpolitik: System, Effektivität, Reformansätze*. Frankfurt and New York: Campus, 1985.

Bundesminister für Arbeit und Sozialordnung. *Statistisches Taschenbuch 1985: Arbeits- und Sozialstatistik*. Bonn: Bundesminister für Arbeit und Sozialordnung, 1985.

Burtless, Gary. "Why Is Insured Unemployment So Low?" *Brookings Papers on Economic Activity, 1: 1983*, pp. 225–49.

Centre d'Etude des Revenus et des Coûts. *L'Indemnisation du Chômage en France et à l'Etranger*. Paris: CERC, 1982.

———. *Changements Intervenus depuis 1982 dans les Systèmes d'Indemnisation du Chômage en France et dans Quatre Pays Etrangers*. Paris: CERC, 1984.

Claassen, Emil-Maria, and Georges Lane. "The Effects of Unemployment Benefits on the Unemployment Rate in France," in H. G. Grubel and M. A. Walker, eds., *Unemployment Insurance: Global Evidence of Its Effects on Unemployment*. Vancouver: Fraser Institute, 1978.

Dupeyroux, Jean-Jacques. *Droit de la Sécurité Sociale*. Paris: Dalloz, 1986.

Economic Report of the President, January 1987.

Grais, Bernard. *Layoffs and Short-Time Working in Selected OECD Countries.* Paris: OECD, 1983.

Kaufman, Roger T. "An Analysis of the Secular Increase in Unemployment in France and Great Britain." Northamptom, Mass.: Smith College Department of Economics, 1983.

Layard, Richard, and Stephen Nickell. "Unemployment in Britain." Discussion Paper 240. London School of Economics, Centre for Labour Economics, January 1986.

Organization for Economic Cooperation and Development. *The Tax/ Benefit Position of Selected Income Groups in OECD Member Countries, 1972–76*; and *1974–78.* Paris: OECD, 1978, 1980.

———. *Unemployment Compensation and Related Employment Policy Measures.* Paris: OECD, 1979.

———. *The 1980 Tax/Benefit Position of a Typical Worker in OECD Member Countries.* Paris: OECD, 1981.

———. *Employment Outlook.* Paris: OECD, 1983, 1984, 1985.

———. *High Unemployment: A Challenge for Income Support Policies.* Paris: OECD, 1984.

———. *Historical Statistics, 1960–84.* Paris: OECD, 1986.

———. *The Tax/Benefit Position of Production Workers, 1979–84.* Paris: OECD, 1986.

———. *Main Economic Indicators.* Paris: OECD, 1987.

Smee, Clive H. "Unemployment Compensation Replacement Rates: A United Kingdom View," in Organization for Economic Cooperation and Development, *High Unemployment: A Challenge for Income Support Policies.* Paris: OECD, 1984.

Topel, Robert. "Unemployment and Unemployment Insurance," in Ronald G. Ehrenberg, ed., *Research in Labor Economics,* vol. 7. Greenwich, Conn.: JAI Press, 1985.

Topel, Robert, and Finis Welch. "Unemployment Insurance: Survey and Extensions," *Economica,* vol. 47 (August 1980), pp. 351–79.

U.S. Council of Economic Advisers. *Economic Indicators,* July 1986. Washington, D.C.: Government Printing Office, 1986.

U. S. Department of Commerce, Bureau of Economic Analysis. *Survey of Current Business,* vol. 66 (July 1986).

U.S. Office of Federal Statistical Policy and Standards, and others. *1980 Supplement to Economic Indicators: Historical and Descriptive Background.* Joint Committee Print. 96 Cong. 2 sess. Washington, D.C.: Government Printing Office, 1980.

Varley, Rita. "The Government Household Transfer Data Base, 1960–1984." Working Paper 36. Paris: OECD, Department of Economics and Statistics, September 1986.

Vroman, Wayne. "The Reagan Administration and Unemployment Insurance." Washington, D.C.: The Urban Institute, 1984.

Wadensjö, Eskil. *The Financial Effects of Unemployment and Labor Market Policy Programs for Public Authorities*. Stockholm: Swedish Institute for Social Research, 1985.

Comment by Stephen J. Nickell

Gary Burtless has written a comprehensive and informative paper on the relationship between unemployment insurance (UI) systems and the high rates of unemployment in Europe. His overall conclusion is that there seems little reason to believe that European UI systems have contributed greatly to the enormous increases in European unemployment experienced in the last decade. I certainly would not demur, simply because, as Burtless makes clear, the weight of the evidence is strongly against this hypothesis. This is probably the view of the vast majority of European economists, both academic and in government, although there is a minority who would disagree. Patrick Minford is a good representative of this minority, and it is worth looking more closely at his argument.[59]

The economy can be divided into two sectors, a highly unionized or "formal" sector and a competitive, nonunion or "informal" sector. Wages in the union sector are higher than in the competitive sector, and labor supply to the competitive sector is highly elastic at a wage closely related to the benefit level. Suppose that an increase in union pressure raises wages in the formal sector, thereby causing workers to enter the informal, competitive sector. Because supply to this sector is so elastic, this fresh influx of workers barely affects competitive wages and competitive-sector employment hardly moves. Consequently, most of the displaced workers become unemployed. It is this interaction between the benefit system, which pays out indefinitely, and increasing pressure on wages by trade unions that underlies the marked rise in unemployment in the recent past.

59. Patrick Minford, *Unemployment: Cause and Cure* (Oxford: Basil Blackwell, 1985).

The key to the argument is the notion that labor supply to the competitive sector is highly elastic at or around the unemployment benefit level. This view appears to be at variance with the cross-sectional estimates of a relatively low elasticity of unemployment duration with respect to benefits discussed by Burtless. Minford argues that these estimates do not reflect the true position, because most people have a threshold wage at or around the benefit level, and the competitive sector can generate a large number of jobs at a wage close to this level. Unemployed workers either take these jobs or remain unemployed for long periods. The implication of this picture for a cross section is that one would observe almost no effect of benefits on unemployment duration for those workers whose earnings-replacement rate is well below unity but an enormously large effect at replacement rates around one. The low empirical estimates arise as a result of averaging.

Two pieces of evidence argue against this view. First, benefit levels, tastes,[60] and wages in the competitive sector all exhibit a great deal of variation. This would tend to make the aggregate labor supply curve to the competitive sector much less elastic than is required for the above story. Second, Narendranathan, Stern, and I investigated the hypothesis that benefit effects on unemployment duration differ markedly with the level of individual replacement ratios and found little evidence to support this view.[61]

Having dealt with this question, I turn to my main theme: wage determination. If the UI system is to contribute to unemployment, it must have some effect on wages. This question is not really touched on by Burtless, so it seems worth expanding upon. The relationship among the UI system, wage determination, and unemployment has a long intellectual history for, as Pigou noted in 1927,

in the post-war period . . . there is strong reason to believe . . . that, partly through direct State action, and partly through the added strength given to work-people's organisations engaged in wage bargaining by the development of unemployment insurance, wage rates have, over a wide area, been set at a level which is too high . . . and that the very large percentage of unemployment which

---

60. An indication of the high variability of tastes for work and leisure is the fact that some 8 percent of employees (at least in 1972) had potential benefits that would have left them 90 percent as well off had they been unemployed. See Stephen J. Nickell, "A Picture of Male Unemployment in Britain," *Economic Journal*, vol. 90 (December 1980), p. 787.

61. See W. Narendranathan, Stephen J. Nickell, and J. Stern, "Unemployment Benefits Revisited," *Economic Journal*, vol. 95 (June 1985), pp. 307–29.

has prevailed during the whole of the last six years is due in considerable measure to this new factor in our economic life.[62]

Whatever theory of wage determination is espoused, it is generally the case that higher unemployment benefits will lead to higher wages and lower employment. This relationship is true in competitive models, efficiency wage models, or union-bargaining models, a comprehensive selection of which are set out by Johnson and Layard.[63] Here I present a rather general model of this relationship and discuss some of the evidence.

To describe this general model, one begins with the behavior of firms, in particular with regard to price setting. Operating in a value-added context, firms set (valued-added) prices (p) as a markup on hourly labor costs (w). This markup may be influenced by several factors. First, it may rise with the level of activity in the output market. However, since output is related to employment through the production function, one can translate output-market activity into labor market activity as measured by the level of unemployment, say. Second, the markup will tend to fall if inflation is rising,[64] both because prices will not be adjusted enough upward for higher wages, and because firms will tend to underestimate competitors' prices and keep their prices low to retain business. Finally, there may be other secular factors (Z_p), such as the degree of monopoly, that are relevant here.

Wages in turn are set as a markup on expected prices. This markup will tend to increase with the level of activity in the labor market and is also influenced by a host of other factors (z) reflecting wage pressure and real wage resistance, including the level of unemployment benefits. Furthermore, if inflation is rising, then prices turn out to be higher than expected, and the real wage outcome will be lower than that bargained for or originally set.

In the long run, trend productivity growth will, on the one hand, lower unit labor costs (at fixed wages) and thus lower the markup of prices on wages, and will, on the other hand, lead to wage setters or bargainers

62. A. C. Pigou, "Wage Policy and Unemployment," *Economic Journal*, vol. 37 (September 1927), p. 355.

63. G. E. Johnson, and Richard Layard, "The Natural Rate of Unemployment: Explanation and Policy," in Orley Ashenfelter and Richard Layard, eds., *Handbook of Labor Economics*, vol. 2 (Amsterdam: North-Holland, 1986), pp. 921–99.

64. More formally, one should say that the markup will tend to fall if prices turn out higher than expected. In what follows, positive price surprises are treated as synonymous with rising inflation.

generating a higher markup of wages on prices. So in static, long-linear form one has the following model:

(1) price setting: $p - w = \alpha_0 - \alpha_1 \Delta^2 p - \alpha_2 u - \alpha_3 x + Z_p,$

and

(2) wage setting: $w - p = \beta_0 - \beta_1 \Delta^2 p - \beta_2 u - \beta_3 x + z,$

where

w = hourly labor cost
p = value-added prices
u = employment
x = trend productivity
Z_p = exogenous secular factors influencing the price markup
z = exogenous wage-pressure factors including the effect of unemployment benefits.

All the parameters are nonnegative.

Two points are worth noting at this juncture. First, this is a very general framework subsuming the competitive labor-market model, for example, when $\alpha_1 = 0$, $\alpha_2 > 0$, or the pure markup or normal cost pricing model when $\alpha_2 = 0$. Second, one may complete the macroeconomic model with the following:

(3)   production function: $y = f(u,x),$

and

(4)   aggregate demand: $y = y^d(\phi),$

where y = value-added output and ϕ the exogenous determinants of real demand. So given the "resources" of the economy as specified by x, the model will, in the short run, yield w, p, u, y for any given level of demand factors (ϕ), wage pressure (z), and "price pressure" (Z_p). In the long run, the model reveals the given z, Z_p, the levels of y, u, $w - p$, and demand y^d, consistent with stable inflation ($\Delta^2 p = 0$). The level of u is, of course, the NAIRU.[65]

65. This is, apparently, a closed economy model. In an open economy there are real exchange rate effects in the demand factors, ϕ, and the wage pressure factors, z. In the short run, these may be thought of as effectively exogenous, pinned down by the monetary and fiscal policy mix. In the long run, the NAIRU is fixed by a trade balance condition or something related to it (for example, purchasing power parity). Full details may be found in Richard Layard and Stephen J. Nickell, "Unemployment in Britain," *Economica*, vol. 53 (1986, *Supplement*), pp. S121–69.

Figure 2. *A Rise in Unemployment Benefit*[a]

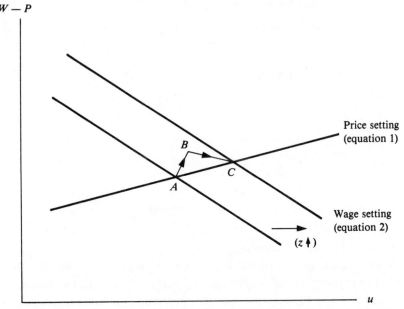

$W - P$

Price setting
(equation 1)

B

C

A

Wage setting
(equation 2)

$(z \uparrow)$

u

a. The price and wage lines are drawn at stable inflation ($\Delta^2 p = 0$). Rising or falling inflation generates a point off the lines.

It is clear that if one starts from long-run equilibrium, then other things being equal, a rise in benefits will raise wage pressure and cause both inflation and unemployment to increase. This is illustrated in figure 2, where the increase in wage pressure shifts the wage line to the right and one moves from *A* to a point such as *B*. Increasing inflation moves one above the price-setting line and below the wage-setting line. (Remember that increasing inflation reduces the price markup on wages and therefore *raises* the "price-determined" real wage.) Real wages also rise during this process. At a later stage, the continuous rise in inflation will, in one way or another, provoke a fall in real demand in order to stabilize inflation, and the economy moves to the new, higher level of equilibrium unemployment at *C*. The ultimate impact on real wages depends entirely on *price-setting behavior*. If prices are set on the basis of normal cost, the lower level of activity will have no long-run effect on the price markup wages, and real wages will revert to their original level (in the context of figure 2, the price-setting line is horizontal). So, in this case, although unemployment has risen because of the increase in wage pressure brought about by the rise in benefits, the real wage outcome is unaffected in the long run.[66] This framework, therefore, brings out two important points. First, increases in wage pressure can raise the NAIRU without any change in the real wage and hence the wage gap.[67] In other words, one can have supply-side-induced unemployment without real wages being too high. Second, the higher NAIRU comes about through a reduction in real demand, which is, of course, needed to stabilize inflation. So it is clearly pointless to blame the fall in demand for the rise in unemployment. Unemployment has risen because of the rise in wage pressure generated by higher benefits.

Having seen the mechanism by which higher benefit replacement rates lead to increases in unemployment (although not necessarily to increases in the real wage), one may ask what the evidence is on this issue. The key thing to look for is the presence of benefit or replacement ratio effects in wage equations, and it must be said that such evidence is rather feeble. First, most estimated wage equations contain no such effect, although it is probably also true that in the preponderance of such cases, the effect was not even sought. There is some evidence for the United Kingdom, however. Minford, Beenstock and others, and Layard and I all present wage equations in which unemployment benefit levels or replacement ratios play a significant role. Minford also produces some evidence for other countries.[68] The observed effects are not highly robust, essentially because it is difficult to produce an empirical counterpart to a wage equation, such as equation 2, that includes *all* relevant wage-pressure variables. The main problem is to produce time series for all the possible effects, some of which are hard even to quantify. Given the importance of the question, further research in this area is imperative, and simply omitting most relevant variables and hoping for the best, a commonplace approach, does not seem to be the best research strategy.

In conclusion, my view of the importance of the UI systems in explaining European unemployment essentially coincides with that of

66. This is not simply a fanciful theoretical exercise. In practice the vast majority of estimated price equations in macroeconometric models contain little or no demand effect.

67. This finding is yet another reason for skepticism about the use of wage gaps in macroeconomic analysis and may be added to the long list of such reasons presented by Charles L. Schultze in this volume.

68. See Patrick Minford, "Labour Market Equilibrium in An Open Economy," *Oxford Economic Papers*, vol. 35 (November 1983, *Supplement*), pp. 207–44; W. Beenstock and others, "A Medium Term Macroeconomic Model of the U.K. Economy, 1950–82" (London: City University Business School, 1985); Layard and Nickell, "Unemployment in Britain"; and Minford, *Unemployment: Cause and Cure*.

Burtless. Even if there are significant effects on wages, the fact that most systems have not improved in generosity in recent years is enough to rule them out as a salient factor in explaining the rise in European unemployment.

Comment by Jules Theeuwes

Burtless's paper makes two important points about the effects of the unemployment benefit schemes on the level of unemployment in Europe. First, the unemployment schemes differ in many respects among different countries. Eligibility criteria, levels and time schedules of benefit payments, and so forth are all specified very differently. Moreover, because these specifications change over time, it is hard to capture this diversity in a single number, such as an average aggregated replacement ratio. Therefore, aggregate econometric analysis and comparison over time and among countries that use this single indicator are not very reliable. Second, using microeconomic information is a more promising avenue to measure the potential impact of unemployment benefits on specific individuals or households. Although these micro studies are not completely free from statistical and measurement problems, the positive effect of benefit levels on the duration of unemployment that they reveal is significant and can be more or less trusted, but is quantitatively too small to explain the unemployment growth in Europe in the 1970s and 1980s. Possibly the strongest effect is the tendency for unemployment spells to last longer in European countries than in the United States because of the markedly greater length of most European benefit schemes.

These points are clearly presented in this paper, they are well documented, and I completely agree with them. Hence the comments that I offer are intended more to supplement and to elaborate these points than to take issue with them.

When discussing the expected effect of insurance on unemployment, Burtless questions the direct link made between the positive effect of unemployment benefits on unemployment duration on the one hand and a higher aggregate level of unemployment on the other. He qualifies this by pointing out that the ultimate effect also depends on the nature of the labor market and the extent of eligibility benefits.

If there are both insured and uninsured workers and the labor market is tight, implying many unemployed and few vacancies, then whatever job opportunities are not taken by the insured unemployed will be taken by the uninsured. As a consequence, the level of aggregate unemployment will not be influenced. In a labor market in which both unemployment and vacancies are high, however, the greater search intensity of the insured unemployed will increase the level of unemployment. Although I agree with this reasoning, I would like to take it a bit further and relate it to possible shifts in the Beveridge curves (UV curves).[69] Points on the Beveridge curve describe different UV combinations and hence different labor market situations. According to Burtless's reasoning, an increase in the generosity of benefits would shift the Beveridge curve out, but in a tilted way. The effect would be larger the greater was the number of unemployed relative to the number of vacancies. It would be interesting to test this hypothesis.

The paper contains a fairly detailed description of unemployment benefit schemes and changes in those schemes in Germany, France, Sweden, the United Kingdom, and the United States. Burtless calculates the net after-tax income level of the unemployed, which varies substantially depending on household situation and previous earnings. What one learns is that the effect on net disposable income of being unemployed depends not only on the unemployment schemes alone but also on the whole taxation system that translates gross earned or unearned income into net disposable income. This translation gets even more complicated if one also takes income-related subsidies into account. Examples of these are rent subsidies or schooling subsidies that come into effect when net income dips below a certain level. The point I want to make is that even with an unchanged structure of unemployment benefits, a changing income tax and subsidy structure might cause large differences in the net replacement ratios over time. It cannot be stressed enough that the net disposable income of an unemployed person is a highly nonlinear function of his or her previous income, household characteristics, and duration of unemployment. Average aggregate replacement rates hide more than they reveal. These rates will change with the composition of the unemployment and employment stock, with changes in taxes and subsidies, and with changes in the benefit structure. Hence they are noninformative about the latter. One should avoid drawing conclusions from them.

69. A discussion of possible shifts in the Beveridge curves of European countries can be found in Robert J. Flanagan's paper in this volume.

After having described the ins and outs of the unemployment benefit schemes in the five countries under consideration, Burtless spends some time rejecting what he calls the "naive hypothesis" that higher jobless pay is associated with higher unemployment rates. Looking at the trends in both unemployment and unemployment benefits for various countries, he rejects this hypothesis. Obviously, nobody would expect otherwise. But economists know that neither significant bivariate correlation nor the lack of it tells them anything about the strength of a causal relation. One should not bother correlating two variables that belong to a larger causal system. Hence one should not bother about "naive hypotheses."[70]

The unemployment level is a stock variable. The stock changes if the inflow into it differs from the outflow. Hence one could research the effect of the unemployment benefit system on the rate of inflow and outflow to and from unemployment. Assume, to keep things simple, that there are only three states (or stocks) that a person can be in: employment (E), unemployment (U), and out of the labor force (O). Inflow into and outflow from unemployment can be either from or to employment ($E - U$ and $U - O$) or from or to out-of-the-labor-force status ($O - U$ and $U - O$). Empirical studies usually concentrate on the depressing influence unemployment benefits might have on the rate of transition from unemployment to employment ($U - E$). As Burtless correctly stresses, that is where most of the action is. But to be complete one should study the effects on all flows in and out of unemployment. These certainly exist. The Baily-Feldstein hypothesis on the use of temporary layoffs in the United States can be seen as a hypothesis about increasing transitions from employment into unemployment ($E - U$). In Europe the favorable treatment of elderly unemployed (in Holland unemployed aged 57.5 years and older are not required to search for a job and can stay unemployed till early retirement) might increase layoffs of older workers (possibly with their consent). If unemployment benefits are provided for new labor market entrants (for example, school-leavers), transitions from out of the labor force into unemployment ($O - U$) might

---

70. The evidence of a "simple" aggregate relationship between unemployment rates (or changes in these rates) and replacement rates in OECD countries in either 1972 or 1981 is rejected on the basis of both diffuse scatter diagrams and low correlation coefficients. The same point could be made here. See Peter Saunders and Friedrich Klau, *OECD Economic Studies: The Role of the Public Sector*, no. 4 (Spring 1985, *Special Issue*), pp. 149–51.

increase. In Holland registered unemployment soars every year in the summer as school-leavers register to get unemployment benefits. Also the transition from unemployment to out of the labor force ($U - O$) might be influenced by the unemployment benefits structure. If a woman planning to leave the labor force finds herself unemployed, she might just as well stay unemployed until the benefit stream stops. I do not think that in the aggregate these effects are large, but they might be important for certain groups and influence the composition of unemployment.

The Burtless paper concentrates on unemployment benefits, and that is what its title promises. But in a welfare state unemployment benefits are part of a whole income-guarantee system. One might even define a welfare state as a state that provides a person with a decent income no matter what the person does. A possible effect of these other benefit schemes, such as early retirement, is to reduce labor supply and reduce the unemployment statistics. Another example from the Dutch welfare state is the disability allowance scheme, which provides higher net benefit levels than the unemployment scheme. The disability program contains a lot of hidden unemployment. A person applying for a disability allowance might be judged to be 100 percent economically handicapped, even if his or her physical handicap was much less, because an administrative determination was made that as a result of diminished skills he or she would not be able to find a job. A person who is declared 100 percent economically handicapped gets the full disability benefit. The number of people on the disability scheme grew tremendously in the 1970s. Currently, there are as many people receiving disability benefits in Holland as are receiving unemployment benefits. One could safely argue that if this disability scheme had not existed, measured unemployment would have been much higher. In general, the number of inactive people (between 15 and 65 years old) has been constantly growing in the past decades. In 1984, 54 percent of the population in that age category was "jobless" in the Netherlands.[71]

Finally, the financing of the welfare state must be examined as a possible source of unemployment. The founding fathers of the welfare state did not know what they were doing. At least they did not (or could not have been expected to) predict the tremendous financial burden of the generous schemes that they enacted to attain a more just and equal income distribution. In Holland the disability scheme was introduced in

71. See *OECD Employment Outlook* (Paris: OECD, September 1986), p. 142.

1967.[72] At that time the expectation was that at most 150,000 persons would claim it in any given year. In 1985 more than 750,000 people were on the scheme. Another example to illustrate the same point is the unemployment benefit scheme for new labor force entrants or reentrants. When this scheme was introduced in 1965, the maximum number of recipients expected was 3,000. In 1975 almost 175,000 people were on it. This welfare state has to be financed somehow; for a large part it is done through social security taxes on labor income. But that does not mean that labor income is where the burden rests. In Holland the incidence of the social security premiums is a hotly debated issue. Dutch wage equations all contain variables to measure the degree to which the burden of social security payments has been shifted from workers to employers. The consensus is that workers have succeeded in shifting the burden of the welfare state to employers.[73] This change has meant smaller profits, higher labor costs, higher prices, and of course increases in the level of unemployment. These effects might even be larger (in absolute value) than the unemployment-raising consequences of the benefits themselves.

General Discussion

One participant argued that Gary Burtless's paper should have focused more on the effects unemployment benefits have on the level of real wages. He offered two observations: first, that to be unemployed in the United States is far more frightening than to be unemployed in Europe; and second, that although employment has grown much faster in the United States than in Europe since the early 1970s, per capital real income has risen much more slowly. One interpretation of these facts is that America has produced a remarkably efficient form of market-driven work-sharing by keeping wages down to levels at which those seeking work can be employed. Europe has tried to promote work-sharing in the opposite manner and has not progressed very far. In the United States

72. See Netherlands Scientific Council for Government Policy, *Do We Make Work Our Business?* Report 13-1978 (The Hague: Wetenschappelijke Raad veer het Regeringsbeleid, 1977), p. 46.

73. For some insights into the effect of shifting forward social security contributions (and direct taxes) into higher wages in various countries, see Anthonie Knoester, "Stagnation and the Inverted Haavelmo Effect: Some International Evidence," *De Economist*, vol. 131, no. 4 (1983), pp. 548–84.

an unemployed person will, in the end, go out and sell his services at whatever price he can get. This is generally not the case in Europe. In Germany, there is very little downward pressure on wage levels because a firm cannot offer a job below the collectively bargained rate, and a person receiving unemployment benefits is not required to take a job at or below his or her previous skill level. In the United Kingdom, employers are unlikely to offer wages lower than those of the currently employed because they are not prepared to put up with the disruption resulting from the complaints of those already employed. These microeconomic differences, it was argued, explain the slow response of real wages to various shocks in Europe as compared with the United States.

Another discussant took issue with Burtless's arguments on two grounds. First, unemployment insurance and other kinds of tax transfer schemes—of which there are many in Europe—not only affect the job search behavior of the unemployed but may also reduce the costs of being out of work so much that they raise real wages. Thus these schemes can affect unemployment indirectly through their effect on wage bargaining. Second, individual workers do not normally see any coupling between the size of their projected social security benefits and the taxes or premiums their employers pay, and therefore do not consider those employer taxes part of their wages. As social security taxes rise, pressure for wage increases does not ease. Again, real wages end up higher and employment lower.

Temporary layoff occurs less often in Europe than in the United States. One suggested explanation was that some European countries such as Germany and France integrate programs for short-time working with the unemployment insurance schemes. It was also pointed out that one or two European countries do in fact have relatively high levels of temporary unemployment. Unemployed workers in Denmark experienced many more spells of unemployment than either American workers or other European workers. In effect, the Danish system seems to encourage temporary unemployment because it mandates that a worker who has more than two hours of unemployment during any week receives benefits. This prompts employers to lay off workers on a Friday if there is a slight downturn.

It was suggested that Burtless's description of French unemployment compensation is outdated. The French system has become significantly less generous than it was in the mid-1970s. Hence, while it may have been true that the system's relative generosity contributed to the rise in unemployment in the 1970s, the same could certainly not be said for the increase in French unemployment since 1982–83.

The discussion at this point once more turned to the questions raised earlier about whether Europe's problem was principally one of slow growth or of high unemployment. One discussant asked whether the generosity of unemployment benefits and the apparent lack of political concern about high unemployment meant that growth not unemployment was the central problem. Another participant responded that the very high rates of youth unemployment characterizing Europe (outside of Germany) were the real problem. How does one go about getting on with the business of establishing oneself and raising a family with no products of employment? Still another participant suggested that whatever the problem of unemployment, manufacturing industries were experiencing severe challenges arising from the dramatic post-1973 slowdown in the growth of capital stock and the huge absolute decline in labor inputs. There was also a discussion of the two ways in which growth is related to unemployment. From the demand side, higher output growth is required to absorb the unemployed, and the question is whether real wage aspirations allow this to be accomplished without an acceleration or large rise in inflation. From the supply side, substantial increases in unemployment may require Europe, as they did the United States, to put people to work on lower-productivity jobs, which in turn implies slower growth in output per worker.

Finally, one participant noted that most European policymakers do not adhere to the philosophy that growth must be increased to reduce unemployment. To avoid a slowdown in world growth, he asserted, someone must attempt to show policymakers that if Europe continues on its present economic path, in the medium term there will be unfortunate repercussions.

ROBERT J. FLANAGAN

Labor Market Behavior and European Economic Growth

FOR ALMOST twenty-five years following 1950, American students of unemployment examined European labor markets for clues as to why European unemployment rates were consistently lower than those in North America. Relatively low European unemployment rates were one of the "stylized facts" of comparative macroeconomics. Since 1970, unemployment in Europe has grown relentlessly and with much less cyclical sensitivity than in North America. By the 1980s the stylized fact was reversed, with the double-digit unemployment rates in many European countries significantly higher than North American rates. Students of unemployment began examining European labor markets for features that would explain comparatively high and persistent unemployment.

This paper examines the growth of European unemployment and the reversal of comparative unemployment experience in Europe and the United States. The first section narrows down the nature of the unemployment increase descriptively to a list of key features to be explained, and the last two sections consider alternative explanations. It now seems well accepted in the research community that both low aggregate demand and high real wages explain some of the growth in European unemployment. A rise in the unemployment rate associated with either of these causes is accompanied by a fall in the vacancy rate. But most countries have also experienced higher unemployment at any given job vacancy rate for reasons that are not well understood.

This paper has benefited from the research assistance of Lori Wilson and the comments of participants in the CEPS Macroeconomic Workshop and the Brookings Conference on Impediments to European Growth. The help of Werner Sengenberger and Jacques Rojot is also appreciated. Portions of the paper were prepared while I was a guest of the FIEF Institute (Trade Union Institute for Economic Research) in Stockholm.

The role of institutionally induced reductions in labor mobility on economic growth and unemployment is considered, but it rapidly becomes clear that traditional supply-side hypotheses make little progress in explaining the list of real and stylized facts developed in the first section. The end of the paper addresses the demand side of the labor market and the effects of increased pay compression in Europe on the behavior of employers concerned with internal performance efficiency in a world in which the true quality of workers is imperfectly known at the time of hire and continual monitoring of performance is difficult.

The Growth of European Unemployment

Between 1969 and 1985 the unemployment rate in the European Community increased from 2.0 percent to 12 percent. There were only two years in which unemployment did not increase. Unemployment in the United States rose from 3.5 to 9.7 percent in 1982 before declining to 7.3 percent in 1985. In Europe, however, the growth of unemployment accelerated in the 1980s, and no similar increase in unemployment can be found during the postwar period. These figures incorporate common concepts and definitions over the entire period, so technical issues of measurement cannot be invoked to account for comparative differences in either the change or the relative levels of observed unemployment. If anything, increasing short-time work, enrollments in labor market programs, remigration of foreign workers, and overmanning in nationalized industries have reduced effective labor input without registering in the official unemployment statistics.[1] The difference in the growth of unemployment between Europe and the United States is therefore undoubtedly understated.

Two general sources of aggregate unemployment change and comparative differences in aggregate unemployment are generally recognized: change (differences) attributable to macroeconomic policy and

1. For selected estimates of the understatement of unemployment attributable to some of these factors, see Wolfgang Franz and Heinz Konig, "The Nature and Causes of Unemployment in the Federal Republic of Germany since the Seventies: An Empirical Investigation," *Economica*, vol. 53 (1986, *Supplement*) pp. S219–44; Jeffrey Sachs and Charles Wyplosz, "The Economic Consequences of President Mitterrand," *Economic Policy*, no. 2 (April 1986), pp. 261–322; and Frank P. Stafford, "Unemployment and Labor Market Policy in Sweden and the United States," in Gunnar Eliasson, Bertil Holmlund, and Frank P. Stafford, eds., *Studies in Labor Market Behavior: Sweden and the United States* (Stockholm: Almqvist and Wiksell, 1981), pp. 21–66.

Table 1. *Nonaccelerating Inflation Rate of Unemployment, Four European Countries, Japan, and the United States, 1971–87*

Country	Period[a]	Average un-employment rate	NAIRU estimates[b]
France	1971–76	2.5	0.0
	1977–82	6.3	4.3
	1983–87	10.1	6.0
Germany	1971–76	2.1	1.1
	1977–82	4.2	3.1
	1983–87	8.0	6.0
United Kingdom	1971–75	3.0	4.2
	1976–80	5.4	7.6
	1981–83	10.6	9.4
Italy	1971–76	5.9	7.6
	1977–82	7.8	7.0
	1983–87	10.7	7.3
Japan	1971–76	1.5	1.3
	1977–82	2.2	2.5
	1983–87	2.8	2.5
United States	1971–76	6.3	5.4
	1977–82	7.2	5.7
	1983–87	7.6	6.0

Sources: *OECD Economic Outlook,* no. 40 (December 1986), p. 30. Data for the United Kingdom are from David Coe and F. Gagliardi, "Nominal Wage Determination in Ten OECD Countries," Working Paper 19 (Paris: OECD, Department of Economics and Statistics, March 1985), p. 30.

a. 1986–87 data are OECD projections.

b. The NAIRU estimates use the average rate of growth of import prices over the complete estimation period of the aggregate wage equations.

change (differences) attributable to structural characteristics of labor markets. Although these are not mutually exclusive, the hypothesis that changes in European unemployment reflect differences in the balance between aggregate demand and supply provides a useful point of departure.

This simple hypothesis is not sufficient, for there is considerable evidence that the equilibrium or nonaccelerating inflation rate of unemployment (NAIRU) has shifted up during the late 1970s and early 1980s. Estimates of the NAIRU are presented in table 1 along with actual unemployment rates. Three features of the data are notable. First, the growth of observed unemployment has been accompanied by a growth in the NAIRU. Cyclical adjustments are not the only factors at work. Second, the growth of unemployment exceeds the rise in the NAIRU in all countries. One cannot absolve aggregate demand from contributory negligence. Third, the NAIRU has increased more in most of Europe than in North America. Indeed, the post-1970 reversal in the stylized facts concerning comparative unemployment rates can be seen in the NAIRU estimates and therefore can be traced to factors underlying its determination.

The growth of real wages relative to the levels merited by productivity trends since the 1973–74 and 1979 oil crises is a second commonly advanced explanation for shifts in the NAIRU. The extensive research on this hypothesis generally finds a negative relationship between employment and real wages in all countries except the United States,[2] but is unclear about why real wages have risen to levels that produce unemployment. Studies also find, however, that declining demand and increased "structural" unemployment contribute importantly. The rest of this section explores this last phenomenon.

Shifting Beveridge Curve

Many explanations for shifts in the NAIRU assign some responsibility to increasing difficulties in the adjustment of existing labor resources to changes in labor demand. Conceptually, there are two possible causes of these increased difficulties. First, the pace of structural change may have increased so that even if labor mobility had remained unchanged there would have been an increased maladjustment between labor demands and the availability of labor supplies. Second, the mobility of labor may have decreased so that a steady pace of structural change may nevertheless have produced a growing maladjustment. A standard approach to testing for maladjustment in the labor market is to test for a shift in the *Beveridge curve,* the relationship between the aggregate unemployment and job vacancy rates. For a given labor market structure, the unemployment-vacancy (UV) curve describes the negative cyclical relationship between the two rates; as demand declines, vacancies decrease and unemployment increases. The curve is generally convex to the origin, reflecting frictional minima in unemployment and vacancy rates during periods of very high and low demand, respectively.

Changes in structural and frictional unemployment are reflected in shifts in the Beveridge curve. In particular, changes that impede the adjustment of labor supply to labor demand increase the amount of unemployment associated with a given vacancy rate. Many European

2. C. R. Bean, P. R. G. Layard, and S. J. Nickell, "The Rise in Unemployment: A Multi-Country Study," *Economica,* vol. 53 (1986, *Supplement*), pp. S1–S22; and P. R. G. Layard and S. J. Nickell, "Unemployment in Britain," ibid., pp. S121–69.

countries have experienced an adverse shift in the UV relation over the period in which the NAIRU has increased. For the United Kingdom, the UV curve has shifted outward more or less continually since the mid-1960s.[3] In Germany, outward shifts in the curve seem to have occurred in the mid-1970s and again in the mid-1980s. The shift is larger when the analysis is conducted on vacancy data adjusted for the fraction of new hires resulting from the intervention of the labor office and on unemployment data adjusted for discouraged workers, persons in training programs, involuntary remigration of non–European Community workers, and short-time workers.[4]

In France, the only outward shift (in the early 1970s) that can be identified from the data may be an artifact of a change in the procedures for reporting job vacancies.[5] In Sweden, the curve, based on vacancy duration, appears to have shifted out since the 1960s.[6] Shifts in the UV relationship are not restricted to Europe, however. Although the United States has no official job vacancy series, an index of help-wanted ads in newspapers is sometimes used in its stead. The relationship between this index and unemployment appears to have shifted out between the 1960s and the 1970s[7] and thus preceded the sharp divergence in U.S. and European unemployment experience.

The Pace of Structural Change

Even a rudimentary review of labor force data for European countries shows large regional and industrial differences in unemployment rates. Moreover, employment flourishes in the service sector, while the man-

3. For an analysis of data for the United Kingdom, see Richard Jackman, Richard Layard, and Christopher Pissarides, "On Vacancies," Discussion Paper 165 (London School of Economics, Centre for Labour Economics, 1985).

4. The German data are analyzed in Wolfgang Franz, "Match or Mismatch? The Anatomy of Structural/Frictional Unemployment in Germany: A Theoretical and Empirical Investigation" (University of Stuttgart, January 5, 1986).

5. Claude Thélot, "La Croissance du Chômage depuis Vingt Ans: Interprétations Macroéconomiques," *Economie et Statistique,* no. 183 (December 1985), p. 71.

6. For an analysis of Swedish data substituting the duration of job vacancies for the vacancy rate, see Nils Henrik Schager, "The Replacement of the UV-Curve with a New Measure of Hiring Efficiency," Working Paper 149 (Stockholm: Industrial Institute for Economic and Social Research, 1985).

7. James L. Medoff and Katharine G. Abraham, "Unemployment, Unsatisfied Demand for Labor, and Compensation Growth, 1956–80," in Martin Neil Baily, ed., *Workers, Jobs, and Inflation* (Brookings, 1982), pp. 49–88.

ufacturing sector stagnates. Regional and industrial variations in unemployment have been persistent features of all economies, including the U.S. economy, but by themselves do not explain comparative differences in unemployment growth. *Increasing* "mismatch" or structural maladjustment of labor supply to labor demand is needed to make a case that structural change is behind the outward shift in the Beveridge (UV) curve.

The argument that structural unemployment rose in the late 1970s and early 1980s rests on two propositions. The first is that a one-time structural shift in the economy, on top of the ongoing pace of economic change, would generate only a transitory rise in unemployment. After initially increasing, unemployment would fall back as market adjustment mechanisms eventually allocated the work force to the new structure of demand. But a permanent increase in the pace of structural change would tend to raise the long-term level of frictional unemployment; there would be a larger flow of people both into and out of unemployment, and the pool of those unemployed between jobs would be larger. But if the labor market were highly flexible, the rise in unemployment accompanying a change in the pace of structural change would not be very large.

Therefore, the second element of the increasing structural imbalance argument is a denial that these traditional labor market adjustment mechanisms work sufficiently well to cope with the pace of structural change. Traditional mechanisms of labor allocation can fail when relative wages are not sufficiently flexible to provide adequate market signals of where additional labor input will be valued most or when labor is immobile—workers do not respond to even valid market signals in their allocational choices. The mismatch hypothesis would attribute the relative growth of European unemployment to greater structural change or relatively inflexible adjustment mechanisms in Europe. Moreover, since unemployment in Europe did not simply rise to a new plateau but kept on growing for some fifteen years, it is often argued not only that adjustment mechanisms are relatively inflexible but also that their inflexibility has gotten worse over time.

The two aspects of the mismatch hypothesis are initially examined in summary fashion by reviewing the behavior of an index of the sectoral dispersion in employment growth and an index of structural imbalance. The first index captures industrial variations in employment growth.[8] The index, *IE*, of structural change in employment is defined as

8. The index was apparently developed in David Lilien, "Sectoral Shifts and Cyclical Unemployment," *Journal of Political Economy*, vol. 90 (August 1982), pp. 777–93.

Table 2. *Interindustry Dispersion of Employment Growth Rates, Four European Countries, Japan, and the United States, 1960–83*
Annual average of index[a]

Years	France	Germany	Sweden	United Kingdom	Japan	United States
1960–64	2.29	2.64	n.a.	1.93	3.62	2.43
1965–69	2.76	3.21	4.61	2.21	3.21	2.08
1970–74	2.84	3.21	4.32	2.47	3.68	2.33
1976	2.28	2.28	3.66	2.06	1.79	1.49
1977	1.99	2.16	3.19	1.23	1.95	1.43
1978	2.16	1.56	3.31	0.94	2.40	1.92
1979	1.67	1.76	3.22	1.49	3.38	1.33
1980	1.37	1.43	1.75	2.34	2.65	2.37
1981	1.85	1.94	2.53	5.20	2.04	1.95
1982	1.81	2.31	2.62	2.80	1.79	3.94
1983	n.a.	1.71	2.01	3.07	2.13	3.30

Sources: For the United States, Japan, Sweden, author's computations based on OECD, *Labor Force Statistics* (Paris: OECD, various years); for the United Kingdom, France, and Germany, R. Jackman and S. Roper, "Structural Unemployment," Discussion Paper 233 (London School of Economics, Centre for Labour Economics, October 1985), table 8.
n.a. Not available.
a. The index is defined in equation 1 in the text.

(1) $$IE = [\Sigma e_{it} (d \log E_{it} - d \log E_t)^2]^{\frac{1}{2}},$$

in which e_{it} is the share of sector i in total employment in year t, E_{it} is employment in sector i in period t, and E_t is aggregate employment in year t. Increases in the index signal increasing sectoral dispersion of employment growth rates, and conversely. Data for six countries are reported in table 2. The first three rows of the table contain annual averages of *IE* for five-year periods beginning in 1960. These are followed by values of the index for individual years beginning in 1976.

In Europe, the dispersion of employment growth rates increased during the 1960s and early 1970s, while in the United States and Japan, structural change did not accelerate until the mid-1970s. During the last half of the 1970s, however, structural change was less than in any of the earlier periods in Europe and the United States. For France, Germany, and Sweden, this remained true into the 1980s, although the pace of structural change in the United Kingdom increased considerably at this time. In general, the data indicate that growth of structural change preceded by many years the sustained growth in European unemployment. At least with respect to the nine broad industrial sectors used for the computations in table 2, the pace of structural change in the United States and Japan between 1976 and 1981 falls within the range experienced in Europe. Unemployment stories based on international differences in structural change are not supported by these data.

The data reviewed in table 2 refer to structural change that is accomplished. Behind assertions of inflexible labor market adjustments is the implication that the failure of labor supply to adjust to new patterns of labor demand stifled potential structural change. (Some potential structural change may not be registered in an index based on dispersion of realized employment growth rates.) This failure would produce a growing imbalance in the pattern of unemployment and vacancies across sectors. Sectors in which new demand emerges would have increasing job vacancies, while declining sectors in which labor is unwilling to leave would have increasing unemployment.

A straightforward approach to measuring structural imbalances in labor markets is to assume that structural unemployment exists if total unemployment could be reduced by the movement of a worker or a job from one sector to another. Most recent analyses of mismatch in labor markets have taken this approach and used data on unemployment and job vacancies to compute the index

(2) $$IU = \tfrac{1}{2}\Sigma \, |u_i - v_i|$$

in which u_i is the share of unemployment and v_i is the share of job vacancies in sector i.[9] Obviously, v_i is more than u_i in sectors with excess demand and less in sectors with excess supply. Intuitively, the index shows the proportion of the unemployed who would have to change sectors to remove unemployment associated with structural imbalances. (Note, however, that unemployment is not zero when $IU = 0$. Even at full employment in a cyclical sense, some frictional unemployment would remain.) The index, IU, will rise when labor remains "trapped" in traditional sectors, while labor demand expands in new sectors, or when labor supply or demand fails to respond to market signals during periods of structural change. If labor market mechanisms are working well, however, structural change will occur without an increase in IU.

Estimates of IU by region, industry, and occupation are reported for several European countries in table 3.[10] Since the index is sensitive to

9. The properties of this and several other measures of structural imbalance are discussed in R. Jackman and S. Roper, "Structural Unemployment," Discussion Paper 233 (London School of Economics, Centre for Labour Economics, October 1985).

10. Values are not provided for the United States because the country lacks reliable job vacancy data.

Table 3. *Index of Mismatch between Unemployment and Vacancies by Region and Industry, Four European Countries, 1970–83*[a]

Years	France		Germany		Sweden		Great Britain	
	Region	Industry	Region	Industry	Region	Industry	Region	Industry
1970–74	.24	.31[b]	.15	.13[c]	.26	.19	.30	.25
1975	.12	.24	.09	.18	.24	.14	.20	.26
1976	.12	.24	.10	.11	.23	.14	.17	.23
1977	.13	.24	.13	.08	.26	.25	.20	.21
1978	.15	.22	.16	.11	.25	.28	.25	.21
1979	.14	.26	.17	.11	.28	.21	.26	.21
1980	.16	.29	.16	.09	.25	.17	.27	.27
1981	.15	.26	.17	.13	.29	.32	.19	.35
1982	.15	.31	.18	.16	.24	.34	.20	.33
1983	n.a.	n.a.	.18	n.a.	n.a.	n.a.	.14	n.a.

Source: Jackman and Roper, "Structural Unemployment," tables 1, 5, 6.
n.a. Not available.
a. The index is defined in equation 2 of the text.
b. 1973–74.
c. 1974.

the number (narrowness of definition) of sectors, little should be made of cross-country comparisons. The first row of the table presents annual averages of the index for the first half of the 1970s. Subsequent rows provide annual values of the index beginning in 1975. For France and the United Kingdom, the data indicate that mismatch by region was generally lower in the last half of the 1970s than in the first half. There has been a more pronounced increase in Germany since the mid-1970s, but it has not risen much above the level of the early 1970s. There was little change in the Swedish index. According to these data, increasing regional mismatch of labor resources is not the main source of shifting Beveridge curves.[11]

The industrial mismatch data tell a similar story for the late 1970s— the indexes for each country but Sweden are below the average value for the first half of the 1970s—but show increasing industrial mismatch in the early 1980s.[12] By the early 1980s the indexes for Great Britain and Sweden exceeded their values for the early 1970s, consistent with the evidence on the changing structure of employment growth in table 2. During the same period, the industrial mismatch indexes for France and Germany rose to about the level of the early 1970s, despite the absence

11. Similar findings have been reported in Jackman and others, "On Vacancies"; Franz, "Match or Mismatch?" and Thélot, "La Croissance du Chômage."
12. Since cyclical swings in aggregate output and employment fall with differential impact on different industries, both the *IE* and the industry *IU* indexes may be procyclical. Some of the increase after 1980 may be due to an increase in cyclical slack.

of a parallel rise in the industrial index of structural change in table 2. In these countries, some potential employment growth may have been hindered by the lack of adjustment of labor supply to industries of expanding demand.

In summary, while employment growth indexes provide some indication of increased structural change in many European economies, the increase occurs *after* the growth of unemployment and is not accompanied by a parallel growth in structural imbalances, as measured by sectoral patterns of job vacancy and unemployment rates. Clearly, the central task is to explain why the Beveridge curve for individual sectors has shifted out—that is, why a given job vacancy rate was associated with so much more unemployment in virtually all sectors by the early 1980s.

Unemployment Flows

Changes in the stock of unemployment observed at a given job vacancy rate equal the difference between flows into and out of unemployment. Flow data are more easily connected to explicit labor market behavior, so that the analysis of flows may narrow the range of admissible hypotheses concerning the growth of European unemployment. Flows into unemployment come from layoffs, quits, and labor force entry or reentry from school or housework, for example. Outflows from unemployment, which control the duration of an unemployment spell, result from hiring (job acceptance) activity or withdrawal from the labor force. Analyses of the behavior of these flows in the three largest European economies yield a common conclusion: secular European unemployment growth is almost entirely the result of a decline in the likelihood of leaving unemployment.

Changes in British unemployment mainly reflect changes in the rate at which the unemployed move into employment, and to a very large extent changes in this rate have been driven by changes in labor demand. Nevertheless, there has also been a downward drift in the likelihood that an unemployed person will become employed for a given job vacancy rate. This drift cannot be explained by changes in structural mismatch indexes, such as those reviewed in table 3.[13] The growth of unemploy-

13. Christopher Pissarides, "Unemployment and Vacancies in Britain," *Economic Policy*, no. 3 (October 1986), pp. 500–59.

ment in France also appears to reflect a substantial decline in the probability of moving from unemployment to employment. The French data for all workers also indicate a modest upward drift in the odds that an employed person will incur unemployment, but this appears to be mainly the result of a very sharp increase in this probability for young workers.[14]

Similar results emerge from an analysis of unemployment and labor force flows for the Federal Republic of Germany for 1973–84.[15] These data have been used to construct the probabilities that an employed person becomes unemployed (flow from employment to unemployment during the period divided by employment at the beginning of the period) and that an unemployed person finds and accepts a job (flow from unemployment to employment divided by unemployment level at beginning of period). The regression analysis reported in table 4 displays the cyclical and secular variation in these probabilities. Flows into and out of unemployment are related to the German vacancy rate, which captures cyclical influences, and a time trend. Flows from employment to unemployment, from unemployment to employment, and from unemployment to out of the labor force are analyzed. The German unemployment flows appear to follow the same general pattern observed in the British and French data. There is cyclical variation in both flows, so that as the German job vacancy rate falls, the flow into unemployment increases and the flow out of unemployment declines. In addition, the probability that an employed person will incur unemployment has been declining (for a given vacancy rate), so that the increase in German structural unemployment cannot be attributed to a secular increase in the likelihood of losing a job. Indeed, between 1973 and 1984, flows from employment declined from 84 percent to 72 percent of total inflows to unemployment.[16] (Inflows from the marginally attached labor force have increased by a similar amount.) Interestingly, only males have experienced a statistically significant declining likelihood of moving from employment to unemployment. Over the same period, the likelihood that an unemployed person will find a job declined. Unemployment duration increased. But

14. Michel Barge and Robert Salais, "The Situation of Young People on the Labor Market, 1973–1980: The Case of France," in John P. Martin, ed., *The Nature of Youth Unemployment: An Analysis for Policy-Makers* (Paris: OECD, 1984), pp. 90–96.

15. Hans-Uwe Bach and Lutz Reyher, *Arbeitskrafte—Gesamtrechnung* [Labor Force—Overall Figures] (Nuremberg: Institut für Arbeitsmarkt und Berufsforschung, 1985).

16. Ibid.

Table 4. *Unemployment Flows in Germany, 1973–84*

Dependent variable	Regression coefficients			Summary statistics	
	Constant	Vacancy rate	Time trend	Durbin-Watson	$\bar{R}^2$
Employment to unemployment					
All workers	0.16	−0.038	−0.0019	2.25	0.91
	(18.02)	(8.40)	(2.65)		
Men	0.10	−0.25	−0.0017	1.62	0.85
	(14.09)	(6.81)	(2.77)		
Women	0.06	−0.013	−0.0003	1.02	0.83
	(11.58)	(5.05)	(0.66)		
Unemployment to employment					
All workers	1.53	1.38	−0.11	1.02	0.88
	(2.25)	(4.08)	(2.00)		
Men	1.29	1.71	−0.08	1.34	0.92
	(2.09)	(5.56)	(1.66)		
Women	1.63	1.06	−0.12	0.92	0.85
	(2.34)	(3.05)	(2.18)		
Unemployment to nonparticipation					
All workers	0.27	0.60	0.027	1.52	0.73
	(0.96)	(4.33)	(1.19)		
Men	0.51	0.27	0.00008	1.60	0.57
	(2.40)	(2.55)	(0.005)		
Women	0.77	0.08	−0.022	1.64	0.59
	(4.94)	(1.02)	(1.76)		

Source: Hans-Uwe Bach and Lutz Reyher, *Arbeitskrafte—Gesamtrechnung* [Labor Force—Overall Figures] (Nuremberg: Institut für Arbeitsmarkt und Berufsforschung, 1985). The numbers in parentheses are *t*-statistics (absolute values).

this result is statistically significant only for women. There is no significant trend in exits from unemployment to other destinations.

The finding that women are likely to incur spells of unemployment that are more and more difficult to terminate by finding a new job is consistent with a world in which men are increasingly valued insiders, while women (who are more likely to be new employment applicants) are often relegated to temporary work with greater unemployment exposure. Conceivably, men gain more job security than women from employment protection legislation, although this possibility is supported only by the findings concerning flows from employment to unemployment. Some other grounds for leaning toward the first of these hypotheses are discussed later in the paper.

Lengthening unemployment spells are a central feature of the growth of European unemployment, but the collapse of labor demand can explain only part of rising unemployment durations. The comparatively long duration of European unemployment is not a new phenomenon.[17] The differences with the United States, however, have become more extreme. In 1985 the proportion of the unemployed who had been jobless twelve months or more was about 9.5 percent in the United States, 47 percent in France, 31 percent in Germany, and 41 percent in the United Kingdom.[18] Relative to the 1970s, long duration is more often concentrated among youth and women in most European countries. There appears to be a growing schism in European labor markets between those with stable employment—"insiders" with substantial prior work experience—and relatively inexperienced "outsiders" who increasingly resemble a class of unemployed or intermittently employed workers. (In contrast, the variations in unemployment in the United States mainly reflect changes in inflows.)[19]

Therefore, explanations of the growing structural component of European unemployment must center on why workers are more reluctant to accept jobs or why employers are more reluctant to hire workers. The former hypothesis has received the most attention to date, particularly with regard to the effects of the unemployment insurance (UI) system. Theoretical research on labor market search has stressed the potential influence of unemployment insurance systems on unemployment duration. During the period under consideration, however, there has not been enough change (or even change in the right direction) in the generosity of UI systems to account for longer periods of unemployment.[20] The next section pursues the worker search intensity idea further by examining sectoral labor mobility. Employer hiring policy is addressed in the third section.

Labor Mobility

Despite the small increase in measured structural mismatch, political discussions of unemployment in Europe have accorded responsibility

17. Even when the European NAIRU was comparatively low, unemployment duration was comparatively high. See Robert J. Flanagan, "The U.S. Phillips Curve and International Unemployment Rate Differentials," *American Economic Review*, vol. 63 (March 1973), pp. 114–31.

18. *OECD Employment Outlook* (Paris: OECD, September 1986), p. 142.

19. Michael R. Darby, John C. Haltiwanger, and Mark W. Plant, "The Ins and Outs of Unemployment: The Ins Wins," Working Paper 1997 (Cambridge, Mass.: National Bureau of Economic Research, August 1986).

20. Layard and Nickell, "Unemployment in Britain"; Pissarides, "Unemployment and Vacancies"; and Franz, "Match or Mismatch?" The paper by Gary Burtless in this volume reaches the same conclusion.

Table 5. *Mobility Matrices: Distribution of Employed in 1977 by Labor Force Status One Year Earlier, Three European Countries*
Percent

1977 sector of employment	1976 labor force status						
	Employed					Nonactive	
	Agriculture	Industry	Services	Unemployed	Total	Housewives	Students
France							
Agriculture	88.8	1.1	1.7	0.5	7.3	3.4	1.7
Industry	0.5	89.2	3.4	1.9	4.0	1.0	2.5
Services	0.4	2.4	88.2	1.9	6.4	2.3	3.2
Germany							
Agriculture	83.8	1.7	2.8	0.6	10.9	5.3	1.4
Industry	0.2	86.7	6.3	1.5	3.9	1.1	2.1
Services	0.4	5.1	86.1	1.3	6.1	2.3	2.8
United Kingdom							
Agriculture	90.6	1.3	2.0	**	4.5	**	3.4
Industry	0.1	89.7	3.1	2.2	4.3	1.3	2.4
Services	0.1	2.1	89.0	1.5	6.7	2.9	3.3

Source: Eurostat, *Labor Force Sample Survey, 1973–1975–1977* (Luxembourg: Statistical Office of the European Communities, 1980), tables VI/3, VI/4, VI/5. Figures are rounded.
** Unreliable data because of the small size of the sample.

for unemployment to a lack of *flexibility* in European labor markets. The term is used in many ways, but one prominent version holds that a myriad of regulations established by laws and collective bargaining thwart the normal allocational mechanisms to the point where employers are reluctant to expand demand for fear of encountering labor bottlenecks. Constraints on external mobility—the reallocation of labor across firms and sectors—are seen as a source of reduced demand and of unemployment. (The internal allocation of labor resources and effort within firms, the focus of the next section, is largely ignored.) Two general kinds of restrictions on labor mobility are alleged: direct restrictions on labor turnover, such as employment protection laws, and distortions of the wage structure so that relative wages no longer provide accurate signals of where labor resources are valued most. Changes in the extent of mobility and the effects of unemployment protection laws on turnover and unemployment are discussed in this section.

Mobility patterns between the agriculture, industry, and service sectors present a rather traditional, but nonetheless instructive, introduction to basic descriptive features of the mobility process. This picture is seen in the interindustry mobility matrices for Germany, France, and the United Kingdom in table 5. These matrices show the employment situation in 1977 of workers employed in each of the major industrial sectors one year earlier. Over a period of one year, transfers of labor from agriculture have ceased to be a consequential source of employment expansion in either the industrial or service sectors. The unemployed and particularly new labor-force entrants are a greater source of employment growth. Students play a particularly important role in the employment growth of industry and services. (Housewives play a proportionately more important role in the small agriculture sectors.)

In contrast to labor supplied by new entrants and the unemployed, interindustry mobility is slight at this level of aggregation. Of those employed both years, at least 93 percent remained in the same industrial sector. This underscores the fact that much of the flexibility in external labor force allocation comes from its most recent entrants and from the unemployed. Moreover, the basic precepts of human capital theory as well as empirical evidence on migration suggest that this lesson is largely independent of the institutional structures of labor markets. It is the youngest workers who have the strongest incentives to make the investments that the allocation of labor resources typically requires. The fact that major external reallocations of labor resources occur through the choices made by new labor-force entrants emphasizes the importance of the wage incentives facing students making career choices over the wage incentives facing labor generally in guiding labor mobility.

Job Changing Among the Employed

The longer average job tenure in Europe compared with that in the United States is standard evidence of lower labor mobility in Europe.[21] Attempts to interpret this fact confront a fundamental conflict between textbook and modern theories of wage determination over the efficiency aspects of labor mobility. Under traditional neoclassical theory, which provides no rationale for a long-term nexus between employee and employer, labor mobility is a "good" to the extent that it results in the movement of labor resources from low-productivity to high-productivity employment. Modern theories have focused on efficiency considerations that result in wage policies designed to bind workers to firms in career employment relationships. In some modern efficiency wage theories,

21. *OECD Employment Outlook* (Paris: OECD, September 1984), chap. 4.

Table 6. *Measures of Labor Mobility, Three European Countries and the United States, 1968–84*

Annual average percentage

Country and measure	Sex of worker	1968–70	1971–73	1974–77	1978–80	1981–84
France[a]						
Percent of workers changing sector of employment	Male	6.6[b]	6.2	5.2[c]	4.8	3.4[d]
	Female	5.0[b]	4.6	3.7[c]	3.4	2.6[d]
Percent of workers changing establishments	Male	4.0[b]	3.6	2.8[c]	2.8	2.6[d]
	Female	3.4[b]	3.5	2.6[c]	2.5	2.7[d]
Percent of workers changing firms	Male	6.3[b]	6.1	3.8[c]	3.7	2.8[d]
	Female	5.1[b]	5.5	3.0[c]	3.0	2.5[d]
Sweden						
Quit rate	...	2.7	1.9	1.8	1.6	1.3
Separations rate	...	3.0	2.3	2.0	1.7	1.6
United Kingdom						
Percent of full-time workers changing employer	Male	n.a.	14[e]	10.8[f]	10[g]	6.0[h]
	Female	n.a.	18[e]	13.5[f]	13[g]	9.0[h]
Separations rate	...	2.9	2.5	2.4	2.0	1.7
United States						
Quit rate	...	2.4	2.3	1.8	1.9	1.3[i]
Separations rate	...	4.8	4.4	4.2	4.0	3.6[i]

Sources: For France, Michel Cézard and Daniel Rault, "La Crise a Freiné la Mobilité Sectorielle," *Economie et Statistique*, no. 184 (January 1986), p. 42; for the United Kingdom, U.K. Office of Population Censuses and Surveys, *Labour Force Survey 1983*, and U.K. Department of Employment, *Employment Gazette*, various issues; for Sweden, Sveriges officiella statistik, *Statistiska Meddelanden, Am 1978:32; 1970–80* (Stockholm: Statistiska centralbyrån), and "Am 1981–84" (manuscript); and for the United States, U.S. Department of Labor, Bureau of Labor Statistics, *Handbook of Labor Statistics* (GPO, 1983), table 77.

n.a. Not available.

a. Fiscal years (March–March). Changes in definition between 1974 and 1975 and between 1981 and 1982 produced some of the decline in the French mobility series.
b. Averages for 1969 and 1970.
c. 1975–77.
d. 1982–84.
e. 1973 only.
f. 1975 and 1976.
g. 1979 and 1980.
h. 1981–83.
i. 1981 only.

workers' interests in job security are matched by employers' interest in low turnover.[22]

The tension between these views and resulting confusion over the role of labor mobility are seen in the popular tendency to compare European labor markets unfavorably with both North American (greater external mobility) and Japanese (less external mobility) markets. The two views need not be mutually exclusive. New cohorts may provide most of the external mobility, while experienced workers may be mainly found in career relationships, consistent with the pattern observed in table 5. The challenge is to differentiate long job tenure resulting from mutually agreeable career employment relationships from that resulting from institutional restrictions. For purposes of addressing the increase in European unemployment during the 1970s, however, the question is whether there has been a change in the extent of labor mobility in Europe and whether that change can be explained by changes in institutional restrictions on labor markets.

By all indications, labor mobility in Europe declined during the 1970s. Several measures of job changing or quitting are reported in table 6. The eclectic array of measures reflects the absence of comparable data on turnover and mobility for all European countries, a fact that also limits the possibilities for extensive comparative analysis. Within these limits, the data indicate higher labor turnover in the United States than in Europe. However, much of the difference appears to be attributable to higher layoff rates in the United States. (Compare U.S. and Swedish data.) These measures also document the decline in mobility in Europe, but indicate falling turnover in the United States as well! This does not accord well with popular descriptions (for example, Eurosclerosis and its "progeny"), which emphasize uniquely European labor-market institutions as barriers to labor mobility. Influences common to all countries appear more important. Finally, the general decline in mobility (particularly total separations rates) supports the conclusions of the

22. The relationship between a firm's training policy and labor turnover is developed in Gary Becker, *Human Capital* (New York: National Bureau of Economic Research, 1964), chap. 2. For a discussion of the various contractual considerations fostering career employment relationships, see Robert J. Flanagan, "Implicit Contracts, Explicit Contracts, and Wages," *American Economic Review*, vol. 74 (May 1984, *Papers and Proceedings, 1983*), pp. 345–49, and the papers cited therein. Employer motivations for paying noncompetitive wages in order to reduce turnover are reviewed in Janet Yellen, "Efficiency Wage Models of Unemployment," in ibid., pp. 200–05, and papers cited therein.

analysis of unemployment flows: the growth of European unemployment has been less the result of job loss than of failure to be hired. The reduced likelihood of leaving unemployment—failure to be hired or to accept a job—is the central difficulty.

Job changing in real labor markets rarely matches the frictionless model found in most textbooks. In markets with wage distortions and other market imperfections, quantity rationing is important, and both job availability and pay differentials enter the rational calculus of job changing. Indeed, relative vacancy rates are less rigid than relative wages and are at least as important in the allocation of labor across industrial sectors.[23] General declines in job availability should therefore reduce job changing. Inverting the Eurosclerosis discussion, demand influences mobility.

It is therefore important to control for the effect of declining job availability on mobility during the 1970s before examining the scope for direct institutional impacts on labor allocation or indirect effects through institutional impacts on the wage structure. Insofar as such analyses are possible in European labor markets, they substantially reduce the scope for general institutional restrictions on the decline in labor mobility reported earlier. For example, the decrease in the Swedish quit rate appears to be almost entirely the result of a decline in job vacancies (a lower probability of receiving a job offer), longer average job tenure (especially among women), and a gradual increase in plant size.[24] The vacancy rate has also declined in the United Kingdom over the period covered by table 6, but a formal analysis of the effects of job availability is precluded by the limited number of observations on the extent of job changing.

A regression analysis of the French data on job changes between 1969 and 1981 appears in table 7. The percentage of male and female workers changing their sector of employment was regressed on the job vacancy rate (a measure of job availability), the coefficient of variation of industry hourly wages (a proxy for potential wage gains), and a time trend. (In trial regressions, a dummy variable to check for potential effects of

23. Christopher Pissarides, "The Role of Relative Wages and Excess Demand in the Sectoral Flow of Labour," *Review of Economic Studies,* vol. 45 (October 1978), pp. 453–67.

24. Bertil Holmlund, *Labor Mobility: Studies of Labor Turnover and Migration in the Swedish Labor Market* (Stockholm: Industrial Institute for Economic and Social Research, 1984), chap. 4.

Table 7. *Changes in Economic Sector, France, 1969–81*[a]

Dependent variable	Regression coefficients				Summary statistics	
	Constant	Vacancy rate	Wage dispersion	Time trend	Durbin-Watson	R^2
MCHANGE[b]	−2.08	0.097	1.47	−0.013	3.32	0.96
	(2.29)	(3.43)	(4.46)	(2.25)		
FCHANGE[c]	−1.91	0.127	1.32	−0.023	1.60	0.89
	(1.08)	(2.31)	(2.06)	(1.98)		

Sources: For MCHANGE and FCHANGE, Cézard and Rault, "La Crise a Freiné la Mobilité Sectorielle," pp. 42–62; for the vacancy rate, OECD, *Main Economic Indicators* (various issues), and *Labor Force Statistics, 1964–84* (Paris: OECD, 1986); and for wage dispersion, F. Klau and A. Mittelstädt, "Labour Market Flexibility and External Price Shocks," Working Paper 24 (Paris: OECD, Department of Economics and Statistics, September 1985), p. 27.

a. All variables except the time trend are in natural logarithms. The numbers in parentheses are *t*-statistics.
b. Proportion of men changing industrial sector of employment during year.
c. Proportion of women changing industrial sector of employment during year.

changes in the statistical definition of job mobility was included but was not statistically significant. This variable has been omitted from the reported regressions.) Both the vacancy rate and the wage dispersion have a significant positive relationship to intersectoral job changes, with the elasticity with respect to wage incentives larger than the elasticity with respect to job availability. Not unexpectedly, much of the observed decline in mobility reflects the decline of demand. Institutional arrangements that narrow the industrial wage structure also reduce the interindustry mobility of French workers. Within the confines of annual data, these two effects explain much of the variation in intersectoral job changes. Nevertheless, the significant time trend indicates that there is room for direct institutional influences on labor mobility. This is consistent with the analysis of job protection legislation that follows.

Employment Protection Legislation

Europe and the United States starkly differ in the treatment of dismissals under statutory law. Throughout Europe, legislation and collective bargaining long ago displaced the common law presumption that a worker may be terminated at the will of the employer. Although employment protection policies vary considerably across European countries, all address the concept of just cause for dismissal, the procedures to be followed in dismissing workers, and the remedies applied for unjust dismissals.[25] Legislative protections against dismissal

25. For detailed discussions of the employment protection policies of individual

were extended in most countries during the 1970s and then partially relaxed during the 1980s following a substantial increase in employer opposition to the laws. No such legislation exists in the United States, where a "just cause" standard for dismissals is limited to the public sector and collective bargaining agreements in the private sector. Although many state courts have found very significant exceptions to the traditional "at will" doctrine since the late 1970s, the United States still does not have a comprehensive national policy toward dismissals.

The inferences that are frequently drawn from these differences in the statutory treatment of dismissals are not supported by experience on either continent. Both the constraints imposed on European employers by employment protection legislation and the flexibility of American employers regarding dismissals are overstated. Given the general concerns of this paper, the focus is on economic layoffs rather than disciplinary dismissals.

Central to most European laws is the notion that the employment relationship is permanent. Short-term fractures in the relationship, such as temporary layoffs, are virtually unknown. Nonetheless, economic pressures are recognized in varying degrees as a justification for dismissals in all countries, although substantial periods of advance notice are generally required. In countries with relatively stringent laws (for example, France and Germany), employers must show that adjustment methods that would avoid layoffs (such as short-time work and retraining) have been exhausted before dismissals can be approved. In Germany, lack of profitability is not in itself a sufficient justification; authorities must be convinced that dismissals are a last resort. In other countries, the laws provide more flexibility. Under the British Employment Protection Acts, employers charged with an unfair dismissal need demonstrate only that the dismissal fell under an approved category (such as lack of qualifications, employee conduct, or economic layoff) and that the dismissal was a reasonable response to the cause. In Sweden,

---

countries, see John Gennard and C. J. Lockyer (Strathclyde University, Glascow), "Job Security: United Kingdom," paper prepared for the OECD, June 1985; Patrick Minford, *Unemployment: Cause and Cure,* 2d ed. (Oxford: Basil Blackwell, 1985), app. B; Werner Sengenberger (Institut für Sozialwissenschaftliche Forschung, Munich), "Job Security: Germany," paper prepared for the OECD, June 1985; Ann Henning, *Tidsbegränsad anställning* [Temporary Employment] (Lund: Wallin and Dalholm, 1984), chaps. 2, 3; Reinhold Fahlbeck, "Interests: A Union Battle for Survival," *Stanford Journal of International Law,* vol. 20 (Fall 1984), pp. 295–327; and Michael J. Piore, "Perspectives on Labor Market Flexibility," *Industrial Relations,* vol. 25 (Spring 1986), pp. 146–66.

economic considerations, including shortage of work, constitute a just cause for dismissal, and the Labor Court usually cannot examine an employer's judgment that business conditions warrant dismissals.[26] Moreover, official procedures in all countries may be avoided by negotiating a severance pay agreement with workers who are to be dismissed. Finally, none of the statutes provides universal coverage of the work force. Qualifying periods ranging from six months to two years of employment with a firm are typical. Most laws exempt temporary workers (fixed-term contracts), part-time workers, and workers in small firms.

Charges arising under the legislation are typically adjudicated outside of the normal court system, by special labor courts or industrial tribunals. Two features of the remedial actions of these bodies are notable. First, reinstatement is rare. Second, monetary compensation for unfair dismissals is comparatively low. In 1983 about 30,000 unfair dismissal claims reached industrial tribunals in the United Kingdom, of which about two-thirds were settled or withdrawn. About 3,300 claims (11 percent of the total) were upheld with an average award of around $2,000. (The maximum permissible award was about $7,900.)[27] Over 80 percent of those plaintiffs seeking compensation rather than reinstatement received awards in accord with their preferences at the time of a hearing. In Germany, labor courts can order either reinstatement or compensation when a remedy is warranted. Compensation is determined by these courts but is limited to a maximum of twelve months' normal earnings (somewhat more for workers over fifty years of age). Not surprisingly, a 1981 survey showed that compensation was the remedy in the majority of dismissal cases brought in Germany during that year.[28] In Sweden, a successful claimant receives 15,000 kronor (about $2,200) plus wages lost during the period of litigation. The Swedish Labor Court, which

26. On the other hand, it is very difficult to fire an individual employee for poor performance. Under Swedish employment policy "displeasing employees enjoy considerable protection, whereas redundant employees enjoy virtually none." Fahlbeck, "Interests," p. 307.

27. According to a survey done on the 350 "successful" cases heard in the Northern Tribunal Region between June 1976 and June 1978. Gennard and Lockyer, "Job Security," p. 16.

28. Paul Lewis, "An Analysis of Why Legislation Has Failed to Provide Employment Protection for Unfairly Dismissed Employees," *British Journal of Industrial Relations,* vol. 19 (November 1981), pp. 316–26; and Linda Dickens and others, "Why Legislation Has Failed to Provide Employment Protection: A Note," *British Journal of Industrial Relations,* vol. 20 (July 1982), pp. 257–58.

Table 8. *Percent of Unemployment Resulting from Dismissal, Three European Countries and the United States, Selected Years, 1973–81*

Country	1973	1975	1977	1979	1981	Average
France	38	43	41	44	41	41
Germany	28	62	42	32	42	41
United Kingdom	44	35	32	38	56	41
United States	39	55	45	43	52	47

Sources: For France, Germany, and the United Kingdom, Eurostat, *Labour Force Sample Survey, 1973–1975–1977* (Luxembourg: Statistical Office of the European Communities, October 1980), table V/8; *1979* (SOEC, February 1981), table 52; *1981* (SOEC, July 1983), table 53; and for the United States, *Economic Report of the President, February 1985*, table B-31.

hears claims of unjust dismissal, can also award reinstatement to successful claimants, and if the employer refuses reinstatement, the claimant is entitled to severance pay ranging from sixteen months' wages for workers with less than five years of work experience with a firm to thirty-two months' wages for workers with ten or more years of experience.

Clearly, European employment protection laws do not provide anything approaching lifetime job rights. Layoffs can and do occur. Even in France, where employers must apply to national labor inspectors for permission to dismiss workers and may encounter significant administrative delays in obtaining approval, about 90 percent of the layoff requests are eventually approved. Reinstatement is rare, even when a dismissal is not for just cause. Moreover, layoffs continue to constitute an important source of European unemployment. During the 1970s and early 1980s, for example, the similarity between Europe and the United States in the share of unemployment accounted for by dismissals was remarkable given the effects that are attributed to the presence of employment protection statutes in Europe (table 8). Consistent with this is the fact that European employers (outside of Greece, Italy, and France) rank levels of demand as a stronger barrier to employment than employment protection laws.[29]

The monetary remedies for unjust discharges in Europe are weaker than in the United States. Although punitive damages are often possible in principle under European employment protection statutes, they are almost never assessed. Monetary damages are almost exclusively compensatory and in some cases are capped. This starkly contrasts with the

29. Gernot Nerb, "Employment Problems: Views of Businessmen and the Workforce," *European Economy*, no. 27 (March 1986), pp. 71–72.

situation in the United States. Although there is no national dismissal statute, many state courts have increasingly recognized important exceptions to the doctrine of employment at will, including some that can be invoked in situations of economic layoffs. Since many of the admissible actions constitute torts, punitive as well as compensatory damages can be claimed. Few cases brought in the United States fail to claim a cause of action justifying punitive damages. In a sample of 102 trials of wrongful discharge cases in California between January 1982 and February 1986, for example, jury awards for general damages ranged from no money to $6 million and averaged $344,069. Punitive damage awards ranged from nothing to $ 4.5 million and averaged $557,355. Plaintiffs prevailed in three-quarters of the verdicts.[30] The size of monetary awards under European employment protection statutes seems minuscule compared with the results of the leave-it-to-the-courts approach to dismissal policy in the United States. Layoffs in the United States are also relatively costly to most firms because the unemployment insurance taxes paid by employers are more experience-related than in Europe. American employers in most states would seem to have comparatively strong incentives to consider their dismissal policy carefully.

Effects of Dismissal Legislation

The greater similarity between the dismissal incentives in the United States and Europe than one might infer from the presence or absence of legislation does not mean that the European statutes have no economic effects. Procedural delays, severance payments, and compensatory awards all raise the labor cost per employee. This will reduce the volume of layoffs, even though layoffs are technically feasible. It will also create incentives for employers to substitute capital for labor and uncovered workers for covered workers. Both effects have been visible in France, which has a relatively stringent policy. Layoffs were virtually stable between 1977 and 1982, while unemployment almost doubled. The use of temporary workers doubled between 1974 and 1979, and the proportion of advertised vacancies for temporary workers has increased. With a relaxation in the legislation this group declined from 4.6 percent in 1980

30. Data are from issues of *Jury Verdicts Weekly*, January 1982–Febuary 1986. Some awards are eventually reduced by judges if they determine that the evidence does not support the conclusions reached by the jury.

to 3.6 percent in 1983.[31] An increase in temporary workers has been seen in other European countries.

It is much less obvious that the structure of incentives established by employment protection legislation can materially affect the level of unemployment. Employers face fluctuations of uncertain duration in the conditions determining the demand for labor. To the extent that protection legislation is effective in raising the cost of job separations, employers may delay layoffs and hoard more labor during such fluctuations than they would otherwise. But counterbalancing this effect, which tends to reduce unemployment, will be two forces working in the other direction. First, employers will have an incentive to be more careful in their hiring decisions. Any given stock of desired employment will now be associated with smaller outflows (fewer dismissals) and also smaller inflows (fewer new hires). The reduced inflow to unemployment resulting from protection legislation will be balanced by a smaller outflow, as the unemployed find it harder to obtain jobs. Moreover, since the protection legislation will impose additional labor hoarding and raise hiring costs, it will increase the cost of labor, induce a substitution of capital for labor, and at any given real interest rate tend to lower the stock of desired employment. On balance, therefore, to the extent such legislation is effective in raising the cost of dismissals, it may increase the average unemployment rate. The earlier discussion of the specifics of such legislation, however, suggests that the "bite" of the legislation is probably not sufficiently strong to raise the cost of labor enough to have a very large depressing effect on the stock of unemployment.[32]

On the other hand, employment protection legislation may affect the concentration, if not the total volume, of unemployment. Existing employees may have more job security, but job seekers will have a longer period of job search or repeated unemployment spells associated with temporary work. Thus employment protection legislation may be one source of insider-outsider relationships in labor markets.

How does the development of these relationships affect the future adjustment of labor supply to labor demand? Aside from the evidence reviewed in the first section, which showed little increase in mismatch

31. *OECD Economic Surveys, 1984–1985: France* (Paris: OECD, July 1985), pp. 42–43.

32. This is consistent with findings of Pissarides, "Unemployment and Vacancies in Britain"; and Stephen Nickell, "The Determinants of Equilibrium Unemployment in Britain," *Economic Journal,* vol. 92 (September 1982), pp. 555–75.

during a period of growing statutory employment protection in Europe, it appears that the development of insider-outsider relationships would leave the burden of external labor force adjustments exactly where it has always been—on the young and the newest labor-force entrants, those who have the strongest incentives to make the training and mobility investments that are part of all intersectoral labor supply adjustments.

In summary, there is limited evidence of barriers to growth on the supply side of European labor markets. The much-remarked decline of labor mobility in Europe during the 1970s and early 1980s appears in large measure to reflect the decline in labor demand. While there is scope for direct constraints on personnel decisions—notably dismissal legislation—to reduce turnover flows, the effect on layoff and hiring flows should be similar, and the long-term effect on the desired stock of employment is not likely to be large. The evidence also indicates that institutional compression of the external wage structure will reduce mobility in good times or in bad. Although it has been suggested that narrowing the interindustry wage structure may mean that employment losses in low-wage industries are offset in the long run by employment gains in high-wage industries,[33] this view seems to overlook the fact that equilibrium industrial wage differentials are determined in part by interindustry differences in occupational structure and nonpecuniary employment conditions. Wage compression at the top would therefore tend to reduce incentives for investment in education and training. Nevertheless, the narrowing of industrial wage structures in Europe has not been associated with the growing sectoral mismatch of labor resources predicted by theories of external labor mobility. Constraints on the wage structure constitute a source of unemployment and a barrier to growth in Europe only moderately through traditionally emphasized effects on external labor mobility. The more important effects are likely to be on screening and internal pay structures, a topic addressed next.

European Employment as a Hiring Problem

The previous sections have considered the nature of the growth of European unemployment and the deficiencies of some supply-side

33. Olivier Blanchard and others, "Employment and Growth in Europe: A Two-Handed Approach," in Blanchard, Rudiger Dornbusch, and Richard Layard, eds., *Restoring Europe's Prosperity: Macroeconomic Papers from the Centre for European Policy Studies* (MIT Press, 1986), p. 108.

explanations of this development. It is now apparent that what is needed is a coherent explanation for a rather diverse set of facts. (1) European unemployment growth cannot be entirely explained by deficient demand or by real wage growth. (2) For a given job vacancy rate, the unemployment rate has increased in virtually all sectors. (Increased structural imbalance explains little of the unemployment growth.) (3) The probability that an employed person will incur unemployment has changed little, although there has been an increase in the probability that new entrants and groups with marginal labor force attachments will incur unemployment. (4) The decreased probability of leaving unemployment has become the main source of increased joblessness, so that increased duration of unemployment accounts for most of European unemployment growth. (5) The rise in unemployment falls disproportionately on relatively inexperienced workers. (6) Hire rates have fallen dramatically. (7) The decline in external labor mobility is more the result of the decline in labor demand than a source of it. (8) Long job tenure is seen as a "bad" in discussions of European labor markets, but a "good" in discussions of Japanese labor markets. (9) Employer opposition to employment protection laws grew significantly in the late 1970s and early 1980s. Not all of these facts apply with equal force in each European country, but they appear to be sufficiently common to serve as the core set of labor market features that a successful hypothesis should explain.

Lengthening unemployment of the type described in facts (2) through (4) can occur because workers are choosier about the jobs they accept or because employers are choosier about the workers they accept. Prior empirical analyses of European unemployment have focused on the hypothesis that search intensity has declined in response to more generous unemployment benefits. But, as noted earlier, this hypothesis has not proved very fruitful for the period under study. The more appropriate question is why European employers are more reluctant to hire at any given vacancy rate. Questions concerning employers' hiring policy redirect attention away from issues in external mobility that have dominated the European discussion to date and focus instead on issues raised by employers' concerns about internal performance efficiency.

Shifting the focus to internal performance efficiency raises the issue of performance incentives and introduces the structure of compensation within organizations into the discussion of unemployment. However, the relationship between pay structure and unemployment is now framed quite differently than in traditional analyses of the wage structure and external allocation of labor. For most jobs, labor turnover is costly. Employers, therefore, have economic reasons for preferring a long-term employment relationship, quite apart from legal obligations. Yet employers may be unable to determine fully the quality of a new employee without a period of on-the-job observation, and continual monitoring of individual performance is often very costly.

In this environment, an employer may choose between three strategies. The first is the traditional "trial and error method" in which unsatisfactory employees are fired after an initial period of observation on the job. The second is a search-intensive strategy in which employers incur substantial screening costs in order to determine which of the applicants for employment are most suitable for the enterprise. The third is the establishment of compensation systems that will be accepted only by workers who intend to be stable, high-performance employees. By raising the costs of layoffs, the antidismissal laws reviewed in the previous section have reduced the applicability of the first strategy (except to exempted groups such as temporary or part-time workers). European employers have had to turn increasingly to the second and third alternatives for jobs where information on worker competence develops slowly.

Wage Compression and Labor Demand

One method of achieving the third alternative is through a compensation scheme in which pay increases with job tenure in an organization. Workers accept wages that are lower than their marginal product early in their career in exchange for wages that exceed their marginal product late in their career, so long as their performance merits retaining them. (Pay and marginal product are equal in an expected value sense.) The initial low wages are a kind of performance bond posted in the expectation that good performance will lead to continued employment, wage increases, and high relative wages late in the career. Workers who are unlikely to perform well or remain at the job long would not rationally accept employment at a firm offering such a compensation plan, and self-selection would substitute for costly employer screening. Those who accept employment under such compensation schemes effectively signal that they have the desired but unobservable performance characteristics. Steep pay-tenure profiles reflect efforts by firms to avoid the agency problems inherent in career employment relationships by "bonding" workers to firms. Some systems of deferred compensation are consistent with this idea. The firm's wage policy initiates self-selection mechanisms that reduce the need to incur screening costs.[34]

The mechanisms of reducing screening costs depend on the freedom to establish pay structures that set self-selection in motion. Institutional constraints on this freedom will force employers to shift to the strategy of substantial screening of applicants. In particular, reductions in pay inequality will tend to move employers toward search-intensive hiring strategies, which because of the costliness of a hiring mistake involve high screening costs and fewer hires. These costs are not reflected in common measures of fixed labor costs, which are usually restricted to charges required by law or collective agreement. That broad organizations for collective action, such as centralized trade union federations or governments, should pursue such a policy is not surprising. In a world of log-normal wage distributions, pay compression policies should command majority support. Formal modeling of union behavior to the contrary, wage equity should be and is a fundamental goal of large labor organizations.

The pay compression hypothesis makes real progress in explaining the basic facts about the growth of European unemployment listed at the beginning of this section. First, various dimensions of pay inequality have decreased in many countries over the period in which unemployment increased (fact 1).[35] Earnings profiles by age or job tenure have also flattened during the period, to such an extent in some countries that there is little difference between the pay of a youthful new hire and the pay of an experienced adult worker. In Sweden, for example, the wage premium for experienced adult workers has fallen from about 45 percent in the late 1960s to about 25 percent in the early 1980s.[36] Wage differentials between skills and within general skill categories have also narrowed in several countries. In France, where the narrowing was particularly rapid following the disruptions of 1968 and then again in the second half of the

34. Joanne Salop and Steven Salop, "Self-Selection and Turnover in the Labor Market," *Quarterly Journal of Economics,* vol. 90 (November 1976), pp. 619–27. For a related argument, see Edward Lazear, "Agency, Earnings Profiles, Productivity, and Hours Restrictions," *American Economic Review,* vol. 71 (September 1981), pp. 606–20.

35. *OECD Employment Outlook* (Paris: OECD, September 1985), chap. 5.

36. Anders Björklund, "Assessing the Decline of Wage Dispersion in Sweden," Working Paper 157 (Stockholm: Industrial Institute for Economic and Social Research, May 1986), p. 6.

Table 9. *Declining Relative Wages, France, Selected Years, 1965–83*

Item	Executive	Middle manager	Low level, white collar	Manual
A. *Occupational wage level*[a]				
1968	3.50	1.66	0.88	0.79
1973	3.25	1.56	0.87	0.81
1980	2.60	1.34	0.84	0.82
1983	2.53	1.31	0.82	0.80
B. *Within occupation wage dispersal*				
Decile 9/decile 5				
1965	n.a.	1.92	1.67	1.68
1970	n.a.	1.71	1.61	1.65
1973	1.50	1.72	1.65	1.69
1980	1.91	1.57	1.55	1.57
Decile 5/decile 1				
1965	n.a.	1.89	1.93	1.93
1970	n.a.	1.81	1.79	1.75
1973	1.97	1.94	1.76	1.78
1980	1.91	1.59	1.59	1.61

Source: Centre d'Etude des Revenues et des Coûts, *Les Revenues des Français: La Croissance et la Crise (1960–1983)*, no. 77 (Paris: CERC, 1985), pp. 83, 91.
n.a. Not available.
a. In each year, average wage for all workers equals 1.0.

1970s, the decline of interoccupational wages occurred mainly from compression at the top (table 9, panel A). Narrowing of within-occupation wage dispersion occurred from both falling wages (relative to the median) for the highest paid workers in each occupational category and, more notably, increasing relative wages for the lowest paid in each category (table 9, panel B).

The institutional mechanisms of pay compression in these countries are quite clear. In Sweden, the central federation of blue-collar workers, which conducts bargaining on a nationwide scale, actively pursued a "solidaristic wage policy" that produced extensive pay compression into the late 1970s. In France and Italy, a combination of union bargaining and politically determined indexation schemes narrowed pay structures. In France, where the extent of formal union membership is similar to that in the United States (about 20 percent of nonagricultural employment), the legal extension of collective bargaining settlements to unorganized firms significantly broadens union coverage. In 1972 about 75 percent of French workers had their (minimum) wages determined as a result of collective bargaining agreements, but coverage ranged from 85 percent in firms with more than 500 workers to about 55 percent in firms with fewer than 50 workers. By 1981 collective bargaining coverage had risen to 90 percent, largely as a result of the growing influence of collective bargaining on the wages of workers in small firms.[37]

Political action to narrow the wage structure in France is more far reaching. For example, the national minimum wage, *salaire minimum interprofessionnel de croissance* (SMIC), provides 100 percent compensation for price increases every two months if the rate of inflation is at least 2 percent. The SMIC applies to all workers and has had the effect of narrowing the dispersion of wages considerably. The average hourly earnings of French production workers was 70 percent higher than the SMIC in 1967. Following the widespread social disruptions in 1968, the SMIC began a sustained increase relative to average wages, with the result that in 1983 a French worker's average hourly earnings were only 26 percent above the SMIC.[38] (The comparable figure for U.S. workers is 100 percent immediately following amendment, which is increasingly rare, of the minimum wage legislation. Since the U.S. minimum wage is not indexed, this gap widens between legislative revisions.)

A similar sequence of developments occurred in Italy. During the late 1960s and early 1970s, Italian unions emphasized greater pay equality as a bargaining objective and raised the relative wage of unskilled workers by negotiating lump-sum wage increases. The more powerful effect on pay equality occurred with a revision in 1975 of the *scala mobile,* the nationwide automatic cost-of-living escalation. The revision established more frequent inflation adjustments and shifted from percentage to absolute indexation payments. By the late 1970s, *scala mobile* payments constituted two-thirds to three-quarters of the earnings increases of Italian workers and had drastically compressed both interindustry and interoccupational wage differentials. Between 1975 and the end of 1982, for example, the wage of all major occupation groups declined relative to the lowest paid manual workers in agriculture. In general, the wages of relatively skilled nonmanual workers declined relative to the wages of manual workers in all industries. In the trade and transport industries, the 25 percent wage premium of nonmanual workers in 1975 dropped to a 5 to 10 percent premium in 1982. In industry the relative wage of nonmanual workers fell from 1.5 to 1.2 over the same period.[39]

37. Centre d'Etude des Revenus et des Coûts, *Les Revenus des Français: La Croissance et la Crise (1960–1983),* no. 77 (Paris: CERC, 1985), p. 67.
    38. Ibid., p. 66.
    39. Paolo Garonna and Elena Pisani, ''Italian Unions in Transition: The Crisis of

Table 10. *Skill Differentials in Three Industries, United Kingdom, Selected Years, 1970–79*

Ratio of hourly earnings of skilled workers to hourly earnings of laborers

	Timeworkers			Pieceworkers		
Year	Engineering	Ship-building	Chemicals	Engineering	Ship-building	Chemicals
1970	144	126	109	148	147	111
1975	132	122	104	132	131	108
1979	130	125	107	131	118	107

Source: Ken Mayhew, "Incomes Policy and the Private Sector," in J. L. Fallick and R. F. Elliott, eds., *Incomes Policies, Inflation and Relative Pay* (London: Allen and Unwin, 1981), p. 87.

In the United Kingdom, collective bargaining and incomes policy rules regarding low-paid workers resulted in a compression of skill differentials (table 10). Further evaluation of the pay compression hypothesis requires elusive data on changes in internal pay structures over the past decade. Indeed, modern wage theories caution that easily observed average wages may not be the best measures of pay for many allocation decisions.

Second, the hypothesis explains why the growth of unemployment is mainly the result of increasing duration and why unemployment is increasingly concentrated in "outsiders"—new entrants and groups with marginal labor force attachment (facts 3 through 5). Employers know the performance characteristics of insiders. Their problem is to distinguish between good and bad performances among outsiders when institutional constraints on compensation structures preclude signaling by outsiders with desirable performance characteristics. As constraints on the development of internal performance incentives lead employers to more extensive screening of new hires, it will be more difficult for outsiders to become insiders. Unemployment duration will be longer as the probability of leaving unemployment declines.

This insider-outsider story rests on the effects of increasing equality on the employment policies of firms in which monitoring is imperfect and career employment relationships are important. It is not a substitute for deficient demand or real wage gap explanations of unemployment growth but extends the latter to incorporate the higher screening costs

Political Unionism," in Richard Edwards, Paolo Garonna, and Franz Tödtling, eds., *Unions in Crisis and Beyond: Perspectives from Six Countries* (Dover, Mass.: Auburn House, 1986), pp. 140–45; and Robert J. Flanagan, David W. Soskice, and Lloyd Ulman, *Unionism, Economic Stabilization, and Incomes Policies: European Experience* (Brookings, 1983), pp. 529–60.

faced by employers as a result of pay compression. Moreover, the argument here is not restricted to the standard point that policies which raise the relative wage of low-wage workers should reduce the relative employment of these workers. Although this has been a factor, particularly in countries like the United Kingdom and France where increased minimum wages for youth have reduced their relative employment,[40] the growth of European structural unemployment is not restricted to youth. Moreover, raising minimum wages does not by itself preclude reestablishing the pay structure. The argument here rests on the demonstrable pay *compression* in many countries. Equality will tend to raise unemployment among all inexperienced labor force groups (fact 2) in employment situations in which performance is difficult to monitor as a result of the increased importance of the screening function.

This interpretation also explains the paradox that long job tenure is perceived as a "good" in Japan but as a "bad" in Europe. In Japan, employers have considerable control over their wage structure, and in the largest firms—those that provide the most substantial career employment relationships—wage-tenure profiles are very steep. Indeed, profiles are considerably steeper in Japan than in the United States, where profiles are in turn steeper than in Europe.[41] Long job tenures in Japan are associated with considerable flexibility to establish compensation systems producing desired internal performance incentives.

Finally, this interpretation explains the increased furor over employment protection legislation in Europe and the increasingly successful efforts to have such legislation modified. In many countries, including some in which employers are known for the toughness of their collective organizations, controversy over the legislation was apparently less when it was passed than during the 1980s.[42] Modest resistance to institutional change often signals change whose main effect is to codify existing practices. This appears to have been the case with dismissal laws in

---

40. Williams Wells, "The Relative Pay and Employment of Young People," Research Paper 42 (London: U.K. Department of Employment, 1983); and Barge and Salais, "Situation of Young People."

41. Masanori Hashimoto and John Raisian, "Employment Tenure and Earnings Profiles in Japan and the United States," *American Economic Review*, vol. 75 (September 1985), pp. 721–35. For evidence on the flatness of age-earnings profiles in European countries, see Christopher Saunders and David Marsden, *Pay Inequalities in the European Communities* (London: Butterworths, 1981), p. 315.

42. See Sengenberger, "Job Security: Germany"; and Gennard and Lockyer, "Job Security: United Kingdom."

some countries. Existing practices rested on the availability of personnel strategies that limited the need to dismiss, however. Direct restrictions on dismissal are acceptable to employers who are able to maintain control over the internal wage structure. By adopting pay structures that result in the self-selection of desirable employees, employers lessen the importance of dismissal flexibility. When control over the establishment of internal pay structures is lost, however, employers must incur screening costs in order to select employees whose performance is likely to be consistent with the firm's objectives. To the extent that selection errors can be reduced only by incurring higher screening costs, there will be a greater incentive to use dismissals to eliminate such errors. Dismissal costs, such as those associated with employment protection legislation, now become more important and formerly acceptable policies become objectionable. Growing resistance to employment protection policy reflects an effort to reduce costs that attain importance when internal performance efficiency must be sought through a screening strategy rather than through internal pay structures.

While the pay compression hypothesis explains the facts of European unemployment rather well, compression of internal wage structures does not appear to be a feature of all European economies over the past fifteen years. Pay compression should have more serious employment consequences in countries where firms tend to have vertically structured internal labor markets and where employers make considerable investments in their workers. In countries with horizontally structured internal labor markets with standardized, general skills, such as are provided under the system of occupational training in Germany, the costs of turnover arguably are relatively low because individual skill differences are smaller. Not surprisingly, given intercountry variations in labor market institutions and internal labor markets, a single hypothesis is unlikely to explain the reluctance of employers to hire in all European economies.

Many of the facts listed at the beginning of this section could be explained by a model in which employers become increasingly careful about hiring for any given unemployment rate as uncertainty concerning the extent and sustainability of a future expansion increases. This is particularly true in a world of institutional rules governing dismissals and the internal allocation of labor. Arguably, longer screening periods are a reaction to a constraint that has become binding only in the past decade. As noted in the previous section, however, the net effect on unemployment should be small and of uncertain sign. The empirical side of this argument presents difficulties also. In most countries dismissal legislation has been relaxed somewhat during the 1980s, when unemployment rates (including NAIRUs) were increasing. But the central point that deserves more research attention is this: institutional rules developed by labor unions and governments can result in more extensive screening of prospective employees by employers—the empirical pattern observed in Europe in the past decade.

Institutional-Wage Push

Some recent discussions of the consequences of institutional behavior for unemployment have emphasized instead real-wage push by unions.[43] According to these arguments, union bargaining objectives are set according to the interests of employed union members (insiders), whose welfare is maximized subject to the constraint of the employer's labor demand function. When unemployment increases, wage objectives are traded against the job security interests of the diminishing number of employed union members and without regard to the interests of the unemployed members (outsiders). After an initiating shock, real wages and unemployment will continue to increase as a result of the policies of the wage-setting institutions.

Models in which unions routinely maximize utility subject to a labor demand curve present a rather austere view of collective bargaining. Indeed, a bargaining process does not exist in the monopoly union model in which the union chooses the wage and the employer chooses the profit-maximizing employment level given the wage. Without a bargaining process, considerations of bargaining power play no role. In particular, the effect of negotiations in one period on future bargaining power is ignored. In insider-outsider models of union-wage push, the union is as likely to achieve its objectives when it is small as when it is large: membership size is irrelevant to union power. The failure to consider intertemporal variations in bargaining power—in particular, how the consequences of today's negotiations influence tomorrow's bargaining power—seems odd and unpersuasive to anyone who has followed

43. Examples include Olivier J. Blanchard and Lawrence H. Summers, "Hysteresis and the European Unemployment Problem," in Stanley Fischer, ed., *NBER Macroeconomics Annual 1986* (Cambridge, Mass.: NBER, 1986), pp. 15–89; and Sachs and Wyplosz, "Economic Consequences of President Mitterrand."

changes in the fortunes of unions in the United States since the late 1970s.

A second consequence of abstracting from bargaining power is that the employer plays an extraordinarily passive role in the models underlying the union hysteresis models. The passivity is peculiar not only in terms of what seems to be observed in collective bargaining, but also from the perspective of many modern theories of real wages and unemployment. As noted earlier, efficiency wage theories and insider-outsider stories offer several reasons why employers may rationally choose to pay a wage above the market-clearing rate in nonunion settings.[44] The implicit contract literature describes why employers and nonunion workers might find it in their best interests to develop employment arrangements with relatively rigid wages. In each of these analyses, employer rather than union preferences could account for a failure of real wages to adjust downward in response to supply shocks.

If union considerations were paramount in the real wage increase, employer resistance would register as increasing strikes. Strike activity would not increase in an environment of employer acquiescence. Indeed, collective bargaining in this instance might be a veil over jointly held objectives. Strike activity in fact tapered off, while real wages grew in most major European countries in the late 1970s.[45]

Equity versus Unemployment

Pay compression appears to be a near-universal policy among trade unions and governments, but pay compression policies generally interfere with the efficiency of both the external allocation of labor and internal performance incentives. How much equity would be lost by abandoning pay compression policies? The general answer is that changing the distribution of wages is not a particularly powerful method of changing the distribution of income. Two arguments on this issue are

44. Yellen, "Efficiency Wage Models"; and Assar Lindbeck and Dennis J. Snower, "Wage Setting, Unemployment, and Insider-Outsider Relations," *American Economic Review*, vol. 76 (May 1986, *Papers and Proceedings, 1985*), pp. 235–39, and papers cited therein.

45. The notable exception is Sweden, where conflicts between major blocs of blue-collar, white-collar, and public-sector workers increasingly disrupted Sweden's placid, corporatist, bargaining arrangements. See Robert J. Flanagan, "Efficiency and Equality in Swedish Labor Markets," in Barry P. Bosworth and Alice M. Rivlin, eds., *The Swedish Economy* (Brookings, 1987), pp. 125–74.

quite familiar. Every economics textbook demonstrates how institutional pay compression is generally accompanied by quantity adjustments that tend to offset the effect on income. In addition, much of the potential effect of wage inequality on income inequality is offset by political influences on the income distribution.[46]

Less well appreciated, however, is the fact that the effect of institutional pay compression policies on earnings inequality is undone to a considerable extent by the mobility of individuals through the earnings structure. Negotiated or legislated pay compression policies will lower individual inequality to the extent that individuals maintain their relative position in the earnings structure. In fact, the relative earnings position of a worker appears to be quite volatile. Interfirm mobility and internal changes in job status substantially rearrange the relative earnings positions of workers, even over periods as short as a year. In Sweden, for example, over half the workers remaining in the same plant between 1984 and 1985 changed their decile of the earnings structure.[47] While some of the changes observed for periods this short may be transitory, a picture of considerable mobility in both directions through the earnings distribution emerges when longer periods are used.[48] A similar picture may be inferred for Germany from data on the extent to which the unemployed find jobs in the same industry as their last job. Data for May and June 1981 indicate that a minority of workers end up in the same industry. This suggests a higher probability of change in relative earnings position than if workers were returning to the same industry.[49] Since often a minority of workers maintain their relative earnings position over even short periods of time, changes in pay structures resulting from pay compression policies are unlikely to be powerful influences on overall income equality.

46. For a detailed analysis of Swedish data on this point, see Assar Lindbeck, "Interpreting Income Distribution in a Welfare State: The Case of Sweden," *European Economic Review*, vol. 21 (1983), pp. 227–56.

47. Lennart A. Jonsson and Claes-Henric Siven, *Varför Löneskillnader?* (Stockholm: Svenska Arbetsgivareföreningen, 1986), p. 19.

48. Evidence is reviewed in Flanagan, "Efficiency and Equality," pp. 151–53.

49. Ulrich Brasche and others, *Auswirkungen des Strukturwandels auf den Arbeitsmarkt, Anforderungen des Struckturwandels und das Beschäftigungssystem* [Effects of Structural Change of the Labor Market, Demands of Structural Change and the Employment System] (Berlin: Deutsches Institut für Wirtschaftsforschung, 1983), p. 177.

Conclusions

Barriers to external mobility have not changed in ways that explain the growth of unemployment in Europe. Indeed, the decline in labor mobility in Europe is tied more closely to the collapse of labor demand. Moreover, the preceding analysis of dismissal restrictions indicates that the effect of the restrictions on unemployment is ambiguous and probably small. Differences in dismissal constraints between Europe and the United States tend to be overstated.

The problem instead is with hiring, and this problem is not solely the result of lower demand. Restrictions on the ability of firms to set internal performance incentives when workers' true abilities are not known at the time of hiring and when continuous monitoring of performance is very costly increase the importance of the screening function of firms and raise screening costs. This makes firms more cautious about hiring and makes it more difficult for workers whose performance is not already known from prior employment experience to obtain jobs. Further analysis of hiring decisions and the mechanisms leading to pay compression and other incentives for increased screening is obviously desirable, but the pay compression hypothesis appears to explain a wide array of European labor market facts. The policy implication of this diagnosis is that the mechanisms producing pay compression and increased screening should receive as much attention as those generating higher-than-warranted real wages.

Comment by Bertil Holmlund

This is a well-informed and interesting paper on European labor markets. As is usually the case, bold and provocative hypotheses will invite objections, and Robert Flanagan's essay is no exception to this rule.

His main focus is the outward shift of the Beveridge curve, or the UV curve; that is, the relationship between unemployment and vacancies. Flanagan offers a penetrating discussion of purported explanations of these shifts in UV curves that have taken place in many countries. The usual analysis argues that a rise in unemployment at given vacancy rates indicates increased maladjustment in the labor market. This may be due to reduced search intensities on the part of workers, to increased screening on the part of employers, or perhaps to a general fall in labor mobility. Flanagan rejects a number of popular views in this respect and offers instead his own ingenious interpretation—the pay compression hypothesis.

The Beveridge Curve

Let me first offer some comments regarding the Beveridge curve. Although the past few years have seen a rebirth of this tool, a very shaky understanding still exists of the purported relationship between unemployment and vacancies. The major reason is probably that neither a good theory nor many empirical studies of the determination of vacancies have been developed. This state of the art is in stark contrast to the conventional neoclassical theory of labor demand, where empirical studies abound. Unfortunately, there is no role for vacancies in the traditional theory of labor demand.

Empirical Beveridge curves may occasionally show rather erratic behavior. For example, the Swedish Beveridge curve shifted out in 1968 (for reasons that are somewhat mysterious), whereas it shifted back inward in the mid-1970s (for reasons that are better understood), and shifted out again in the early 1980s. It is hard to believe that all these shifts reflect changes in labor market mismatch in any meaningful sense. For example, the inward shift in the Swedish Beveridge curve was related to a fall in layoff rates and unemployment inflow, which in turn presumably was caused by a combination of employment protection legislation and labor market policies that discourage layoffs (such as subsidies to firms with excess labor).

Theory, as well as empirical observations, suggests some caution in using Beveridge curves as indicators of labor market performance and labor market flexibility. Unemployment and vacancies are interacting endogenous variables, determined by various exogenous variables on the supply side and the demand side of the labor market. There is no obvious reason to expect that movements in these exogenous variables should map out a stable relationship between the two endogenous variables.

It would be desirable to have the Beveridge curve embedded in a somewhat broader labor market model that explained both unemployment and vacancies. Without this framework it is difficult to interpret shifts of the Beveridge curve and to draw policy conclusions. The usual supply-side variables (unemployment benefits, for example) have a role to play here, but there is certainly also a role for the usual demand-side variables, such as relative factor prices.

A more or less explicit assumption in Flanagan's discussion is that changes in aggregate demand or real wages influence labor demand through the number of vacancies. Unemployment increases that have occurred at a *given* number of vacancies are therefore attributed to various maladjustment phenomena, including reduction in search intensities and labor mobility. But the traditional theory of labor demand states that firms' employment decisions depend on output and input prices, and there is no particularly strong reason to ignore a possible link between factor prices and hiring rates, even at a given number of vacancies.

The recommendation of cautiousness is reinforced by the data problems involved. Statistics on vacancies are collected by different methods in different countries, and administrative changes in these countries occur frequently. One would like to see some efforts to produce vacancy statistics with the same quality as unemployment data in labor force surveys. Regular surveys to employers would presumably be necessary, although the conceptual problems should be recognized.

In conclusion, the lack of a good theoretical and empirical knowledge of how vacancies are determined, or even what vacancies really stand for, seriously hampers understanding of shifts of the Beveridge curve.

Employment Protection

Consider now Flanagan's very informative discussion of employment protection in Europe and the United States. He adopts the view that employment protection should reduce unemployment inflow and increase unemployment duration, probably with negligible impact on the size of the stock of unemployment. However, to the extent that employment protection raises fixed labor costs, some reduction in the level of employment desired by firms is likely, and employment protection from that perspective is similar to increases in the real wage. The same holds for legislation that raises the cost to the firm of *changing* the size of the work force; that will also on average reduce the demand for labor.

One aspect of employment protection mentioned by Flanagan is

advance notification, an important part of at least the Swedish employment protection legislation from the mid-1970s. In Sweden the employer
must notify workers before any planned layoff; the advance notice
required ranges between one month for young workers to six months for
workers above age 45. This period should facilitate their job search; in
fact, Swedish law explicitly gives the layoff-notified workers the right to
visit employment exchange offices and prospective new employers.
There is every reason to expect that these rules will facilitate job-to-job
transitions without intervening unemployment, although some costs in
terms of productivity reductions may be involved.

The effect of employment protection on unemployment duration is
typically seen in firms' screening behavior. Presumably, the difficulties
in firing will produce more careful screening of job applicants; a rise in
unemployment duration is therefore to be expected. But there may also
be effects on the supply side. Standard job-search models show that job
searchers' behavior depends on vacancies and wage offers in the labor
market. Their behavior also depends, however, on the prospective layoff
risks. Higher layoff risks associated with job offers tend to induce
workers to search less hard to find jobs. To the extent that employment
protection raises the value of employment relative to unemployment,
unemployed workers may become more eager to find a job.

Pay Compression

Now if employment protection or lower mobility does not explain the
rise in European unemployment, what does explain it? Here comes the
most interesting, but in my view also the least persuasive, part of the
paper—namely, the pay compression hypothesis. Flanagan argues that
restrictions on firms' freedom to choose upward sloping wage profiles
as a self-selection device will induce more screening of job applicants,
and this, in turn, will raise unemployment duration. I agree that this
hypothesis is plausible, but it seems unlikely that it will stand up as a
coherent explanation of the diverse facts of European unemployment in
an unregulated labor market.

The paper is written as if outside intervention in firms' wage-setting
rules is bound to increase unemployment. I do not think that a strong
theoretical case can be made for such a general claim. In fact, one theory
used as an example by Flanagan—the efficiency wage theory—attempts
to explain the possibility of involuntary unemployment. For example, if

workers' ability is positively correlated with reservation wages, an unemployed worker may well be unwilling to underbid his or her employed colleagues because this would function as an adverse signal about the worker's quality. Because of the signal of low ability that is involved, workers may fear that firms would turn away job applicants wanting to work for less than the going efficiency wage.

Some versions of efficiency wage models also entail wage dispersion for homogenous workers, which in turn may induce excessive search and an associated excessive level of frictional unemployment. In general, it is not obvious how intervention in such markets will affect unemployment. It is easy to see circumstances under which pay compression could actually reduce unemployment, whereas unemployment might increase under other conditions. From our rather limited knowledge in this area, strong conclusions do not seem to be warranted.

The empirical side of the pay compression hypothesis appears even more problematic. If the pay compression is a major explanation of the rise in unemployment, unemployment should increase more in countries where pay compression has been most pronounced. I have taken a very preliminary look at this, using data on unemployment and interindustry wage dispersion from fourteen OECD countries (table 11). I have no direct data on intrafirm wage dispersion, the relevant variable for Flanagan's hypothesis, but I assume the same forces that produce low *intrafirm* wage dispersion (like solidaristic wage policies) also tend to produce low *intraindustry* dispersion. Granted this assumption, suppose that changes in unemployment during the 1970s are related to changes in interindustry wage dispersion during the same period. No correlation at all is found between unemployment increases and pay compression. And if the level of unemployment is related to the degree of wage dispersion, a positive relationship is found in the early 1970s as well as in the early 1980s. These observations do not constitute strong tests. But the very clear absence of any association in the expected direction indicates that pay compression is probably not a major explanation of the rise in European unemployment.

Flanagan tries to make too much out of the bonding versus screening idea. Screening can also take place on the job through temporary employment contracts—employment for a trial period—and perhaps by hiring part-timers. If firms are restricted in their use of bonding arrangements, they may prefer temporary employment contracts instead of screening before hiring. Of course, employment protection may preclude

Table 11. *Unemployment Rate and Interindustry Wage Dispersion in Selected OECD Countries, 1967–74, 1980–83*[a]

Percent

Country	Unemployment rate, 1967–74 (period average) (1)	Unemployment rate, 1980–83 (period average) (2)	Wage dispersion, 1972 (3)	Wage dispersion, 1982 (4)	Change in unemployment rate (2−1)	Change in wage dispersion (4−3)
Austria	1.5	3.0	14.3	18.9	1.5	4.6
Belgium	2.6	11.5	16.6	16.1	8.9	−0.5
Canada	5.2	9.4	23.2	25.5	4.2	2.3
Denmark	1.3	9.9	12.8	14.9	8.6	2.1
Finland	2.5	5.4	16.6	15.4	2.9	−1.2
France	2.5	7.5	14.6	12.3	5.0	−2.3
Germany	1.1	5.4	12.8	12.8	4.3	0.0
Italy	5.6	8.6	18.3	10.5	3.0	−7.8
Japan	1.3	2.3	23.1	26.4	1.0	3.3
Norway	1.7	2.4	14.4	14.7	0.7	0.3
Sweden	2.2	2.8	11.2	10.0	0.6	−1.2
Switzerland	0.0	0.5	11.5	13.7	0.5	2.2
United Kingdom	3.4	10.9	14.7	17.1	7.5	2.4
United States	4.6	8.4	23.9	25.2	3.8	1.3

Sources: For unemployment: C. R. Bean, P. R. G. Layard, and S. J. Nickell, "The Rise in Unemployment: A Multi-Country Study," *Economica*, vol. 53 (1986, *Supplement*), p. S1; for wage dispersion: data supplied by the Swedish Employers' Federation.

a. Wage dispersion refers to the coefficient of variation for interindustry wage differences (blue-collar workers).

such temporary employment arrangements, but at least in Sweden this option is open to firms, and Flanagan reports that fixed-term contracts are feasible in other countries as well. The effects of pay compression may then show up in unemployment inflow, and the structure of unemployment inflow, rather than in unemployment duration. Indeed, the Swedish labor market has seen some increase in separations from temporary jobs. The basic bonding-screening hypothesis would gain in crediblity if cross-country comparisons indicate that pay compression goes hand in hand with a growth of temporary jobs.

Is there any independent evidence on the bonding-screening hypothesis? For example, are the flatter wage profiles in unionized U.S. firms—compared with the nonunionized firms—accompanied by more elaborate screening arrangements? Are vacancy durations longer in sectors where firms face constraints in their choice of wage profiles? The data needed for careful studies of these questions may not be easily available, but in principle such tests could be done.

Having expressed my skepticism regarding Flanagan's pay compression story, I should add that wage equalization may influence the structure, and perhaps the level, of unemployment through other routes. Legislated or negotiated minimum wages may explain part of the relative increase in youth unemployment.

Concluding Remarks

The reasons for the outward shifts of the Beveridge curve and for the apparent rise in the NAIRU are little understood. I am afraid that this conference has not made significant progress in reducing our confusion in this respect, although we may be confused at a higher level, to quote Erik Lundberg.

As noted earlier, one problem with the Beveridge curve is the limited knowledge of the determinants of vacancies. Numerous models purport to explain workers' job search behavior, but theoretical and empirical work dealing with firms' search and recruitment decisions are rare. It is not surprising, therefore, that the interpretations of shifting Beveridge curves become difficult. There are thus good reasons to put more research effort into understanding firms' hiring decisions, and Flanagan's suggestions in this respect are well taken.

A second point is related to supply-side explanations of unemployment increases and outward shifting Beveridge curves. It may well be that country differences in unemployment benefits are unable to explain diverging trends in unemployment. But as far as I know, there is not much information on how the work test is enforced in different countries. Adverse incentive effects of high benefits may be offset by stringent rules for work acceptance. A centralized employment exchange system, including training programs and perhaps temporary public jobs, may be a useful device here. Institutional differences regarding labor market policies deserve serious consideration among the potential explanations of intercountry differences in unemployment.

Comment by John P. Martin

This paper analyzes the reversal of unemployment experience between the United States and Europe since 1970. It begins by accepting the conventional view that "too high" real wages and low aggregate demand are both partly responsible for some, but not all, of the rise in

European unemployment. It then offers other explanations, from a labor economist's standpoint, that could account for higher European unemployment.

The search for alternative explanations begins with the hypothesis of growing mismatches. A variety of studies have shown that the Beveridge (UV) curve has shifted adversely in many European countries over the past two decades. However, it also appears that there has been a similar adverse shift in the United States.

What factors might account for this adverse shift in the Beveridge curve? One common argument, widely voiced in the media and in political debate, is that it is due to structural change. The paper points out that this hypothesis rests on two empirical assertions: (1) European labor markets have undergone more rapid structural change than the U.S. labor market; and (2) the traditional labor market adjustment mechanisms have become less flexible in Europe.

These two elements of the mismatch story are tested by means of aggregate indexes of structural change in employment and mismatches on a regional and industrial basis. While the aggregate indexes are not ideal measures for the exercise at hand, they do point to a very clear conclusion: stories based on a speedup in the pace of structural change get little or no support from the data. The Organization for Economic Cooperation and Development has done some similar exercises and come to the same conclusion.

The paper then examines gross flows data. I agree with Flanagan that flows data could be very useful in studying the issues he addresses. Unfortunately, such data are not available for most European countries.[50] Outside Sweden, to the best of my knowledge, no other European country makes regular flows data available on the monthly or quarterly transitions between employment, unemployment, and not in the labor force, such as one can obtain from the U.S. Census Bureau's current population surveys or the monthly household surveys in Canada, Australia, and Japan.

Consequently, Flanagan is forced to rely on a few scattered studies of gross flows in France, the United Kingdom, and Germany. He argues that these studies all come to the same conclusion: most of the rise in

50. Flows data are available for members of the European Community from the EC's annual *Labour Force Survey,* but they clearly understate the dynamics of unemployment since they refer to a comparison of *current* labor force status with the person's reported status one year earlier.

Table 12. *Distribution and Average Length of Current Job Tenure, United States and Four European Countries, 1978, 1983, 1984*
Percent unless otherwise specified

| Country and year | Under 2 years | | 2–9 years | 10 years or more | | Total | Average job tenure (years)[a] |
	All	Under 1 year		All	20 years or more		
France (1978)	17.8	...	47.0	35.2	13.2	100	9.5
Germany (1978)	18.6	...	43.7	37.7	15.1	100	10.0
Italy (1978)	12.9	...	50.4	36.7	9.1	100	9.4
United Kingdom (1984)	27.5	18.5	43.1	29.4	10.0	100	8.5
United States (1983)	38.5	27.3	34.2	27.3	10.0	100	7.2

Sources: Data for France, Germany, Italy are from Eurostat, *Structure of Earnings, 1978–79* (Luxembourg: Statistical Office of the European Communities, various issues), in industry, wholesale and retail distribution, banking, and insurance, and are collected from establishments with ten or more employees; data for the United Kingdom are from U.K. Office of Population Censuses and Surveys, *Labour Force Survey* (London: Her Majesty's Stationery Office, various issues); data for the United States are from the supplementary survey to the U.S. Census Bureau's current population survey and refer to all employed persons in the month of January.
a. Average job tenure was calculated by using the mid-points of closed job intervals. For the group aged 20 and over, a mid-point of 27.5 years was used.

unemployment is accounted for by a secular decline in the probability of an unemployed person exiting from unemployment to employment.

The net result, according to Flanagan, is a growing segmentation of European labor markets between "insiders," who enjoy long-term job attachment together with rising real wages, and an increasing number of "outsiders," who are either locked into low-wage, unstable employment or drifting into longer and longer spells of unemployment. Such segmentation is less marked in the U.S. labor market.

What does the evidence on mobility patterns in Europe and the United States show about the relative sizes of the insider and outsider groups? One partial measure of mobility is the average tenure of a spell of employment for those *currently* employed.[51] Average job tenure in the four major European countries is typically about two years longer than it is in the United States (see table 12). Much of this difference is accounted for by the greater share of short-duration jobs in the United States: almost 40 percent of those employed in 1983 were in their current job for less than two years compared with under 20 percent in France, Germany, and Italy and under 30 percent in the United Kingdom. Thus if insiders were approximated as the group of workers with stable employment, it seems that this group would account for a larger fraction of the European work force.

51. For a detailed description of the job tenure data, see *OECD Employment Outlook* (Paris: OECD, September 1984), pp. 113–14.

Table 13. *Short- and Long-Tenure Jobs, United States and Four European Countries, Selected Years, 1972–79*

Country and year	Proportion of persons currently employed with job tenure	
	Under 2 years	10 years or more
France		
1972	26.3	30.7
1978	17.8	35.2
Germany		
1972	25.0	33.5
1978	18.6	37.7
Italy		
1972	20.0	28.0
1978	12.9	36.7
United Kingdom		
1975	24.0	33.4
1979	24.4	30.5
United States		
1973	37.0	25.4
1978	39.9	23.2

Sources: Data for France, Germany, and Italy are from Eurostat, *Structure of Earnings in Industry, 1972,* and *Structure of Earnings,* 1978–79 (Luxembourg: SOEC, various issues). Unlike the data for 1978, the service sector is excluded from coverage in 1972. However, this should not bias the results greatly. For example, data for France for 1978 on the same basis as in 1972 show proportions of 16.8 and 36.7 percent, respectively, for those with tenure less than two years and those with tenure of ten years or more. Data for the United Kingdom are from U.K. Department of Employment, *New Earnings Survey* (London: HMSO, various issues) and refer to Great Britain only. The coverage relates to full-time men aged 21 and over and full-time women aged 18 and over. Manual and nonmanual workers are covered. Data are based on a 1 percent sample of Inland Revenue records relating to employees covered by PAYE (pay-as-you-earn) schemes. The basic list of employees in the sample excludes employees whose employment commenced only a month or two before the survey reference date. Thus persons with tenure of less than one year are not adequately represented in the sample. For source of U.S. data, see table 12.

The relevant question for the purposes of this paper, however, is, has the size of the insiders' group increased relatively more in Europe than in the United States since 1970? The available data on job tenure do not give an unambiguous answer. Nevertheless, the proportion of workers in long-duration jobs (defined as current job tenure of ten years or more)—taken as a rough proxy for insiders—increased in three of the four largest European countries between 1972 and 1978, whereas it fell slightly in the United Kingdom and the United States (see table 13). Over the same period, the proportion of workers in short-duration jobs in Germany, France, and Italy fell, remained stable in the United Kingdom, but rose slightly in the United States. Unfortunately, job tenure data for most of the European countries after 1978 are not available so the extent to which the apparent increase in the relative size of the insiders' group has continued in recent years cannot be checked.

Data on job tenure need to be complemented by data on labor turnover to get a fuller picture of mobility patterns. While the data on labor turnover summarized in the paper are neither very comprehensive nor comparable across countries, they do show a clear message—namely, there has been a secular decline in European labor mobility.

One candidate to explain the secular decline in European labor mobility is employment protection legislation. This explanation has been much favored by employer organizations in Europe and, *prima facie*, they appear to have a case. Many European countries extended employment protection in the 1970s, although the period since OPEC II has seen a reversal of this trend in countries such as France, Germany, and the United Kingdom. Needless to say, no such increase in statutory employment security occurred in the United States.

Flanagan is rightly cautious about drawing too hasty conclusions from this for a comparison of European-U.S. unemployment performance. Even if legislation and collective bargaining practices on job security have not prevented layoffs in European countries, they have affected the structure of employment and unemployment by raising total labor costs and by changing the ratio of fixed to variable labor costs (one important factor not mentioned in the paper). They have created incentives for employers to substitute capital for labor and uncovered workers for covered workers.

In addition, as Flanagan points out, the impact of employment protection on the *level* of unemployment is theoretically ambiguous. For increased employment protection to result in higher unemployment, the effect on the outflow from unemployment to employment must exceed the effect on the outflow from employment to unemployment. This is an empirical question upon which there is almost no evidence. There is some partial evidence in two papers by Stephen Nickell in which he tried to investigate these effects using U.K. data on unemployment flows.[52] Unfortunately, his two papers come to contradictory conclusions on this point: his 1979 results suggested that the increase in employment

52. Stephen Nickell, "Unemployment and the Structure of Labor Costs," in Karl Brunner and Allan H. Meltzer, eds., *Policies for Employment, Prices, and Exchange Rates,* Carnegie-Rochester Conference Series on Public Policy, vol. 11 (Amsterdam: North-Holland, 1979), pp. 187–222; and S. J. Nickell, "The Determinants of Equilibrium Unemployment in Britain," *Economic Journal,* vol. 92 (September 1982), pp. 555–75.

protection in the United Kingdom had raised the equilibrium unemployment rate, whereas his 1982 paper came to the opposite conclusion!

Having discussed various supply-side explanations for European
unemployment and dismissed them as either not matching the stylized
facts or as being of second order of importance, Flanagan turns in the
third section to the heart of the paper. He seeks to relate the compression
of wage structures to the shift in hiring behavior of European employers.
In particular, he wishes to shift the focus of the debate away from
external mobility—although he recognizes that this has been influenced
by the decline in wage dispersion—to internal mobility and the costs of
screening workers and monitoring their performance. In this, he is
clearly influenced by efficiency wage theories as well as by agency
models à la Ed Lazear. To the degree that institutional forces served to
compress pay differentials within European firms, Flanagan argues that
employers were forced to be more careful in their hiring decisions.

I find the pay compression hypothesis in a world where monitoring is
costly and long-term attachments are common to be a novel and
stimulating way of thinking about the European unemployment problems. At first sight it does seem to answer many of the stylized facts
listed in the paper.

I have, however, some questions about this story. First, as Flanagan
acknowledges, there are several competing hypotheses—insider-outsider hysteresis, aided and abetted by union power, and growing employer uncertainty about future demand prospects to name but two—
and he provides no evidence that would permit a choice between them.

Second, insufficient evidence supports the pay compression story.
Flanagan presents a variety of evidence on interindustry and occupational wage differentials for France, Italy, Sweden, and the United
Kingdom. Even for these four countries, the evidence is not entirely
clear cut, especially for the United Kingdom, where evidence in favor
of pay compression is weak. It is also unclear, as Flanagan admits,
whether data on average earnings by industry or broad occupational
groups are ideal measures to test the pay compression hypothesis. It
seems to me that one would want earnings data disaggregated by age,
occupation, and firm size at a minimum, complemented by microeconomic studies of how internal pay structures within firms have evolved.
The only possible source of such comparative earnings data is the
European Community's *Structure of Earnings Survey*. This is extremely
difficult to use and has the added drawback that the latest year available
is 1978.

Third, even if better evidence could be found to support the hypothesis of pay compression, the paper never really addresses the question of why this occurred. The reader is given some references to "institutional forces" but little else. Flanagan's silence on this key point for policy-makers is disappointing.

Fourth, the role of unions in the pay compression story is not entirely clear to me. Suppose pay compression arises from unions pursuing equal pay strategies. This would produce relatively flat tenure-wage profiles. But unions have other effects as well. They may reduce quits, which presumably affects hiring and monitoring costs. Is there any evidence that in Europe the duration of job vacancies is longer in union firms relative to nonunion firms than it is in the United States?

Fifth, one of the stylized facts cited in the paper is that unemployment is increasingly concentrated among new entrants and people with mar-ginal labor force attachment—essentially youths and women. As table 14 shows, this is correct if data on the demographic composition of the long-term unemployment in 1973 is compared with 1985 data. However, the composition of the long-term unemployed since 1979 has shifted: prime-aged adults now account for a growing proportion of the long-term unemployed. This partly reflects the severity of the last recession. For young people the pattern is more mixed since 1979. In those countries where unemployment has tended to decline during the upswing, the proportion of young people in long-term unemployment has fallen. Where unemployment is increasing, the share of young people in long-term unemployment has also tended to rise. Finally, the share of women in long-term unemployment has declined almost everywhere since 1979.

Sixth, the paper neglects an important dimension to the hiring deci-sion: the increasing propensity of European employers to hire part-timers instead of full-timers.[53] Part-time employment has risen as a proportion of total employment since 1973 in many European countries, whereas such a trend is not apparent for the United States, once the involuntary element in part-time employment is taken into account.[54]

---

53. For evidence on the growth of part-time employment, see *OECD Employment Outlook* (Paris: OECD, September 1985), pp. 26–29; the available evidence on temporary work is analyzed in the forthcoming 1987 *OECD Employment Outlook*.

54. Over the 1973–84 period, there is a positive trend in total U.S. part-time employment, after controlling for the effects of the cycle. But this trend arises from an increase in involuntary part-time employment, not from an increase in voluntary part-time employment. See R. G. Ehrenberg, P. Rosenberg, and J. Li, "Part-Time Employ-ment in the United States," paper presented to the Conference on Employment, Unemployment and Hours of Work in Berlin, September 1986.

Table 14. *Composition of Long-Term Unemployment by Age and Sex, United States and Six European Countries, Selected Years, 1973–85*[a]

Percent

| Country and year | Decomposition by age[b] | | | Decomposition by sex | | Total long-term unemployment (thousands) |
	Youths	Prime-aged adults	Older workers	Males	Females	
Austria						
1973	14.9	34.8	50.3	43.6	56.4	2.0
1975	14.2	39.6	46.2	45.4	54.6	2.3
1979	12.8	40.9	46.3	52.3	47.7	2.8
1982	13.4	43.8	42.8	58.8	41.2	4.0
1985	17.9	53.5	28.5	63.8	36.3	12.9
Belgium						
1973	5.2	22.3	72.5	58.7	41.3	42.0
1975	11.1	28.7	60.2	46.2	53.8	58.1
1979	21.0	46.9	32.1	29.3	70.7	160.2
1982	23.0	49.6	27.3	37.9	62.1	263.3
1985	21.7	55.8	22.5	39.8	60.2	311.1
France						
1973	17.9	37.9	44.3	54.2	45.8	75.9
1975	25.8	44.5	29.7	36.5	63.5	129.3
1979	28.1	46.2	25.7	37.5	62.5	371.4
1982	31.2	45.3	23.5	38.3	61.7	629.0
1985	30.9	50.4	18.7	42.9	57.1	1,030.3
Germany						
1973	3.4	23.8	72.8	73.8	26.2	18.4
1975	12.8	43.3	43.9	62.3	37.7	96.7
1979	9.0	35.1	55.9	48.1	51.9	146.3
1982	14.8	44.6	40.6	53.1	46.9	386.1
1985	10.7	43.3	46.0	54.6	45.4	665.8

Information on trends in temporary work across countries is much more sparse than the data on part-time employment. However, the EC's annual *Labour Force Survey* does identify temporary workers since 1983; such jobs cover a wide range of work arrangements including seasonal and casual work and fixed-term contracts. The use of temporary workers rose in most EC countries between 1983 and 1985, but the phenomenon still remains rather marginal, typically accounting for less than 7 percent of total employment in 1985.[55]

The rise of part-time employment and temporary work is partly a supply-driven phenomenon, but it is also influenced by relative price

55. Eurostat, *Labour Force Survey: Results, 1985,* Series 3c (Luxembourg: Statistical Office of the European Communities, forthcoming).

Table 14 *(continued)*

Country and year	Decomposition by age[b]			Decomposition by sex		Total long-term unemployment (thousands)
	Youths	Prime-aged adults	Older workers	Males	Females	
Netherlands						
1973	8.4	49.2	42.4	84.8	15.2	12.1
1975	11.6	54.3	34.1	82.4	17.6	19.5
1979	23.7	52.2	24.1	69.0	31.0	51.0
1982	32.9	54.5	12.6	69.3	30.7	153.6
1985	28.0	61.5	10.4	67.5	32.5	407.2
United Kingdom[c]						
1973	6.3	23.7	70.0	91.0	9.0	150.9
1975	8.4	25.1	66.5	90.3	9.7	143.0
1980	17.1	32.2	50.7	78.5	21.5	364.1
1982	26.0	37.4	36.5	79.2	20.8	1,070.5
1985	26.4	41.1	32.5	76.6	23.4	1,326.8
United States						
1973	26.1	35.9	38.0	64.1	35.9	142.0
1975	26.1	36.3	37.5	64.6	35.4	421.0
1979	27.8	39.4	32.8	60.2	39.8	259.0
1982	28.5	49.8	21.7	68.7	31.3	824.0
1985	20.6	51.5	27.9	67.2	32.8	786.0

Sources: Author's calculations based on sources cited in "Statistical Annex," *OECD Employment Outlook* (Paris: OECD, September 1986), table k.

a. The long-term unemployed are defined as those continuously unemployed for one year or more.

b. *Youths* generally refers to the age group 15 to 24 with the following exceptions: the age group is 16 to 24 in the United Kingdom and the United States and 17 to 24 in Austria. *Prime-aged adults* refers to the age group 25 to 44 with the following exceptions: 25 to 49 in Austria, France, and the Netherlands. *Older workers* refers to the age group 45 and over with the following exceptions: 50 and over for Austria, France, and the Netherlands.

c. Data for 1973 and 1975 refer to Great Britain only.

and output developments. To the extent that the relative costs of hiring a part-timer or a temporary worker have fallen, employers should be led to substitute part-time or temporary workers for full-time workers. Since most part-timers in Europe are adult women and most temporary workers are under 25,[56] much of these inflows to employment bypass the pool of the unemployed, most of whom state that they are looking for full-time work. Greater recourse to part-time and temporary workers also permits on-the-job screening at lower cost to employers.

Have the relative costs fallen for part-timers and temporary workers relative to full-timers in Europe? Unfortunately, hard data are not easy to come by on this issue, but the indications are that the answer is yes. Part-timers in many European countries have much poorer access to fringe benefits such as paid vacations, sick pay, and occupational pension

56. *OECD Employment Outlook* (September 1985), pp. 26–29.

schemes.[57] When this is combined with greater employer uncertainty about future demand and profitability, it produces a convincing explanation of the shift in hiring patterns.

Finally, I would like to return to the macroeconomic debate about "too high" real wages and employment performance. Bean, Layard, and Nickell show that the degree of centralization in collective bargaining—what they call corporatism—is an important element in this story.[58] Labor market adjustment appears to have been faster in the more corporatist economies. Work that two colleagues at the OECD and I are carrying out on trends in interindustry wage dispersion across OECD countries shows that more corporatist economies, not surprisingly, have also witnessed declining wage differentials. This suggests that there could be some trade-off between microeconomic efficiency and macroeconomic performance.

To conclude, I enjoyed this stimulating and readable paper. I think Flanagan is right to focus on the apparent shift in hiring behavior of European employers. They, not the workers, appear to have become "choosier." In this he has drawn attention to the role of relative wages as a signaling device and argued strongly that the compression of wage structures is a source of European unemployment. Even if the old Scottish verdict of "not proven" applies at this stage, Flanagan's hypothesis presents a fascinating new agenda for research and policy analysis.

General Discussion

The absence of an explicit model of unemployment and job vacancies in Robert Flanagan's paper was noted. Participants felt some formal discussion of the relationship between unemployment and vacancies might be helpful for sorting out what is going on in European labor markets. In particular, they thought it would be beneficial to study how much of the increase in European unemployment reflects a movement along a Beveridge curve and how much reflects an outward shift in the curve.

57. In the United Kingdom, for example, employers do not have to pay payroll taxes for many part-time workers because of the minimum earnings threshold in the social security system.
58. See Bean and others, "The Rise in Unemployment."

There are three classes of explanations offered for such outward shifts. First, there could be an increased mismatch between the unemployed and the job vacancies in terms of skills and locations. Second, employees might have become more choosy in accepting jobs. Third, employers could have become choosier in selecting workers. Flanagan implicitly ruled out employee choosiness, whereas Jackman, Layard, and Pissarides had come down firmly on the side of it in their explanation. Data from Jackman, Layard, and Pissarides suggest that the dispersion of employment growth rates may have increased among regions in the United Kingdom after 1979.[59]

Skepticism concerning the accuracy of mismatch indexes based on the composition of statistics on registered unemployed workers and job vacancies was also expressed. Such measures may be distorted because employers may decide not to register some vacancies or because there may be changes over time in the types of jobs being registered. Moreover, the indicators are based upon rather crude breakdowns—for example, the classification of both nurses and nuclear physicists as professionals.

If increased employer choosiness was the reason for the shift in the Beveridge curve, the cyclically adjusted duration of vacancies should have risen. Calculations by Jackman, Layard, and Pissarides suggest, however, that the duration of vacancies in the United Kingdom between 1967 and 1983 fell slightly, whereas the average duration of unemployment rose considerably. Although these figures are not cyclically adjusted, they do seem to raise some questions about the validity of the employer choosiness explanation.

If a narrowing of intrafirm wage differentials was a major cause of the shift in the Beveridge curve, unemployment should be concentrated on new and inexperienced labor market entrants. But it was pointed out that in the United Kingdom, where wage compression does not appear to be a major trend, youth unemployment has risen more than in most countries. In Germany, however, unemployment is not concentrated among the young. In Sweden, where wage compression has been pronounced, youth unemployment has risen, but slowly. While special factors in each of these countries can help explain the trends, the evidence supporting Flanagan's hypothesis would not seem to be compelling.

59. Jackman and others, "On Vacancies," pp. 15–16.

Participants also contended that wage compression alone would not produce the observations discussed. In addition to steep wage profiles, two other methods could help firms obtain the best workers: screening all incoming employees intensively or hiring without screening, identifying the good workers, and firing the bad. Yet there has been very little acceleration in turnover; in fact, the data seem to indicate the opposite. This suggests the wage compression hypothesis cannot stand on its own; it must be combined with an increase in institutional constraints on firing if it is to explain the observations. In effect, firms are using neither a steep wage profile nor trial and error to match incoming employees with their requirements. They are therefore left with large increases in the nonwage costs of labor, which leads to more unemployment.

It was also noted that the compression of wages would cause workers to be less motivated to remain with an employer. Hence at the same time that there is a slowdown in hiring, there may also be an increase in the exit rate from employment. If wages were compressed, workers would not only be more willing to leave their jobs but also more willing to accept new jobs. The gains from searching are limited. Indeed, Lawrence Summers has argued that the rise in wage dispersion in the United States caused unemployment to increase because it increased the duration of job search.[60]

It was pointed out that while lifetime employment is an important institution in Japan, most of the firms involved are huge and produce a wide variety of products. Workers within those firms can thus be reassigned quickly and easily. Job mobility in terms of task mobility is thus high in Japan, whereas it is relatively low in Europe.

One participant cited two further reasons, beyond those discussed by Flanagan, why dismissal costs in the United States are high. First, in the United States, unlike Europe, unemployment insurance is experience rated, so firms that lay off workers will eventually have to bear the costs associated with such action. Second, equal employment legislation is far more pervasive in the United States than it is in Europe. But it was noted that in Germany firms must make so-called social plans for any group of employees they lay off. Hence, many financially strapped firms, which cannot afford these high dismissal costs, refrain from firing workers. In many cases these firms end up bankrupt, and all—not just

60. Lawrence H. Summers, "Why Is the Unemployment Rate So Very High near Full Employment?" BPEA, 2:1986, pp. 339–83.

some—of the workers are laid off. Thus high, not low, dismissal costs may lead to unemployment.

The paper was criticized for not providing a detailed analysis of important cross-national institutional differences with respect to labor markets. In particular, it was noted that corporatist economies have experienced better economic performance than others since 1973. Another comment indicated that corporatist economies did not necessarily have a better experience with respect to unemployment, but such economies did have more efficient labor markets.

CHARLES L. SCHULTZE

Real Wages, Real Wage Aspirations, and Unemployment in Europe

THE FACT of the steadily rising level of European unemployment after 1973, and its contrast with that of the United States, especially since 1982, needs no elaboration here. The use of labor in Europe has fallen by even more than the unemployment data indicate (see table 1). Since 1970 total labor input has fallen by 13 percent in Europe while rising by 27 percent in the United States. Male participation rates fell among all wage groups but sharply in workers over age fifty-five. Average hours worked per year declined steadily. Part of the decline in labor input undoubtedly reflected a greater than unitary income elasticity of leisure. Average weekly hours declined no faster after 1975 than before. But it is hard to escape the conclusion that most of the decline in labor input was associated with a fall in the demand for labor, especially when comparison is made with the data for the United States and Japan, countries on either side of Europe with respect to the levels of real income prevailing in the 1970s.

Explanations for Rising European Unemployment

Viewed from the perspective of labor markets, there are three broad classes of explanation for the rise in unemployment. The Keynesian explanation names as the villain a deficient demand for goods and services with its resulting shortfall in the derived demand for labor. By implication, macroeconomic policies have been excessively cautious,

Carl L. Liederman provided valuable research assistance for this paper. I am grateful to my Brookings colleague Barry P. Bosworth and the participants in the Brookings Conference on Impediments to European Economic Growth for helpful comments and advice.

230

Table 1. *Some Indicators of Labor Input, 1970, 1984*[a]

Country or region	Total labor input (index)[b]		Male partici- pation rates (percent)[c]		Average weekly hours of work (index)[d]		Standardized unemployment rates (percent)[e]	
	1970	1984	1970	1984	1970	1984	1970	1984
United States	100	127	87	85	100	102	4.8	7.4
Japan[f]	100	117	89	88	100	95	1.1	2.7
Europe	100	87	91	81	100	88	2.6	11.7

a. Private business economy for total labor input and average weekly hours of work; total economy for participation and unemployment rates.

b. Commission of the European Communities unpublished data; Europe is average of "Big Four": United Kingdom, France, Germany, Italy.

c. *OECD Employment Outlook* (Paris: OECD, September 1985 and 1986), pp. 40, 140, respectively; Europe is OECD Europe excluding Greece and the Netherlands.

d. Commission and BLS unpublished data (based on manufacturing only); Europe is "Big Four."

e. *OECD Historical Statistics: 1960–1984* (Paris: OECD, 1986), p. 41; Europe is "Big Four" plus Belgium and the Netherlands.

f. 1983 data for total labor input and average weekly hours of work.

and unemployment could be substantially reduced through stimulative monetary and fiscal policies with only modest cost in higher inflation. The neoclassical, excess real wage explanation holds that workers have successfully won wage increases that, in real terms, are in excess of what the economic system could pay a fully employed labor force.[1] Part of the labor force has been priced out of the market as employers reduced output and increased the substitution of capital for labor in response to the excessive wages. The excess wages may have resulted from an upward shift in wage aspirations or from failure of wage aspirations to adjust downward in the face of unfavorable supply shocks. According to this view, the excessive growth of real wages in European countries has increased the nonaccelerating inflation rate of unemployment (NAIRU)—that is, the rate below which unemployment can only temporarily be pushed, and even then only at the expense of continually rising inflation.

The third explanation concentrates on the supply side of the labor market. Several alternative possibilities have been put forward. One possibility is that a growing regional, occupational, or industrial mismatch between job vacancies and the unemployed has occurred. The

1. Real wages are not the result of wage bargains but are a joint product of wage bargains, aggregate demand, and other economic variables. Even if wage bargains have been excessive and a cause of higher unemployment, the ex post course of real wages is a poor indicator of the problem. Hence one should talk about excess real wage aspirations, not about excess real wages. For purposes of an introductory explanation of the excess real wage hypothesis I have ignored this point here but will take it up later in the paper.

mismatch may have arisen because of a stepped-up pace of industrial change or because of increased rigidities in the labor market itself. A rise in the reservation price of labor due to more generous eligibility rules and replacement ratios in unemployment insurance and related social benefits has also been cited as a possible reason for a downward shift in the European labor supply.[2]

The Keynesian and excess real wage explanation for the rise in unemployment share a common feature: they represent a movement *along* a given Beveridge curve, relating unemployment to vacancy rates. The other explanations involve an *upward shift* in the Beveridge curve. These alternative views need not, of course, be exclusive. The increase in European unemployment may have stemmed from a combination of some or all of the factors already cited.[3]

Recently another hypothesis has been advanced to explain the persistence of high unemployment in Europe—hysteresis.[4] According to this view, a rise in unemployment, after a time, loses some or all of its force to moderate wage increases. This phenomenon, labeled hysteresis, may arise from the fact that members of formal (union) and informal bargaining groups who lose their jobs also lose their influence over wage bargaining strategy. The "insiders," who have retained their jobs, do not take into account the benefits of wage moderation in giving employ-

---

2. This question is the principal subject of the paper in this volume by Gary Burtless.

3. Jeffrey D. Sachs, "Real Wages and Unemployment in the OECD Countries," *Brookings Papers on Economic Activity*, 1:1983, pp. 255–89, argues that the rise in unemployment in Germany and the United Kingdom until 1979 was largely due to excess real wages, but that the increase over the next two years was the result of the tightening of monetary policy. Similarly, Richard Layard and various of his colleagues have attributed the rise in unemployment to varying combinations of deficient aggregate demand, excess real wage aspirations, and an upward shift in the Beveridge curve. The importance of these different factors varies among countries. See, for example, P. R. G. Layard and S. J. Nickell, "Unemployment, Real Wages and Aggregate Demand in Europe, Japan, and the U.S.," Discussion Paper 214 (London School of Economics, Centre for Labour Economics, March 1985); and D. Grubb, R. Layard, and J. Symons, "Wages, Unemployment, and Incomes Policies," in Michael Emerson, ed., *Europe's Stagflation* (Oxford: Clarendon Press, 1984), pp. 57–88.

4. See, for example, Olivier J. Blanchard and Lawrence H. Summers, "Hysteresis and the European Unemployment Problem," in Stanley Fischer, ed., *NBER Macro-Economics Annual 1986* (MIT Press, 1986), pp. 15–78; and Assar Lindbeck and Dennis J. Snower, "Wage Setting, Unemployment, and Insider-Outsider Relations," *American Economic Review*, vol. 76 (May 1986, *Papers and Proceedings, 1985*), pp. 235–39, and "Efficiency Wages versus Insiders and Outsiders," Seminar Paper 362 (University of Stockholm, Institute for International Economic Studies, September 9, 1986).

ment to the "outsiders," those who are no longer working or new entrants into the labor force. Alternatively, hysteresis may arise from the effect of persistent unemployment on the unemployed who gradually lose their skills and motivation. The result is that unemployment feeds on itself. The longer it lasts the less it leads to the wage moderation that would cure it.

The Excess Real Wage Hypothesis

The most prominent single diagnosis of Europe's unemployment problem and more generally its weak demand for labor has been the excess real wage hypothesis.[5] This interpretation of economic developments has been widely accepted not only by professional economists but also by the political leaders of many European countries.[6] It has provided an important intellectual underpinning for the continuation in Europe of very cautious and conservative macroeconomic policies in the past several years, even after inflation had been pushed to relatively low levels.

There are two closely related components of the excess real wage hypothesis. First, the wage bargaining institutions of Europe, unlike those of the United States, produce wage outcomes that are characterized by downward *real wage rigidity*: when a slowdown in productivity growth, a fall in the terms of trade, or a rise in social security–related payroll taxes calls for a reduced rate of growth in real wages, European workers successfully resist accepting the lower real wage growth. They get money wage increases large enough to offset the higher inflation

5. By this time the literature is voluminous. Among the most frequently cited works are Herbert Giersch, "Aspects of Growth, Structural Change, and Employment—A Schumpeterian Perspective," *Weltwirtschaftliches Archiv,* vol. 115, no. 4 (1979), pp. 629–52; Jeffrey D. Sachs, "Wages, Profits, and Macroeconomic Adjustment: A Comparative Study," *BPEA, 2:1979,* pp. 269–319, and "Real Wages and Unemployment in the OECD Countries"; Michael Bruno, "Aggregate Supply and Demand Factors in OECD Unemployment: An Update," *Economica,* vol. 53 (1986, *Supplement*), pp. S35–52; Michael Bruno and Jeffrey D. Sachs, *Economics of Worldwide Stagflation* (Harvard University Press, 1985); William H. Branson and Julio J. Rotemberg, "International Adjustment with Wage Rigidity," *European Economic Review,* vol. 13 (May 1980), pp. 309–32; and David T. Coe, "Nominal Wages, the NAIRU and Wage Flexibility," *OECD Economic Studies,* no. 5 (Autumn 1985), pp. 87–126.

6. The emphasis on excess real wages in the semiannual issues of *OECD Economic Outlook* from 1981 through 1985 was probably quite representative of thinking in the economic and finance ministries of many European governments.

generated by slower productivity growth, falling terms of trade, or higher oil prices. Moreover, it takes relatively large doses of unemployment to eliminate the excessively ambitious real wage increases. The evidence cited for this interpretation of European wage behavior is twofold: (1) in Phillips-curve wage equations the coefficient of wage inflation on immediately preceding price inflation is close to unity in Europe but much less than unity in the United States; (2) the coefficient of wages on unemployment is low (in both areas).[7] The staff of the Organization for Economic Cooperation and Development (OECD) has accordingly estimated indexes of real wage rigidity as the ratio of the coefficient of wages on immediately prior price inflation to the coefficient on unemployment in augmented Phillips-curve equations.[8] They find this index for most European countries to be much higher than that for the United States.

The second aspect of the excess real wage explanation for Europe's troubles is that Europe's downward real wage rigidity in the 1970s came face to face with several unfavorable supply shocks. These shocks reduced the growth in real wages payable without a large profit squeeze. The growth of productivity declined sharply after 1973, and the price of imported oil rose substantially, first in 1974 and again in 1979–80. Moreover, in the late 1960s, just before these developments began, an explosion of wages in Europe had given an upward fillip to real wages. For all of these reasons the 1970s saw a sizable rise in actual real wages relative to the real wage that was consistent with maintaining high employment. One measure of the resulting excess is usually taken to be the rise in labor's share of value added, matched by a corresponding fall in the share going to capital. The increase in labor's share—the excess

7. See, for example, Sachs, "Wages, Profits, and Macroeconomic Adjustment," and "Real Wages and Unemployment"; Branson and Rotemberg, "International Adjustment with Wage Rigidity"; Grubb and others, "Wages, Unemployment, and Income Policies"; and Coe, "Nominal Wages, the NAIRU and Wage Flexibility."

8. *OECD Economic Outlook*, no. 37 (June 1985), p. 30. In a typical augmented Phillips curve equation, even if the coefficients on lagged price inflation sum to unity, a long lag structure on the price inflation term implies that the *level* of real wage aspirations will decline in the face of a price-raising supply shock. Hence the slower are nominal wages in adjusting to increases in consumer price inflation, the quicker will be the downward adjustment of the level of real wages to one-time supply shocks. But if the supply shock is a continuing one (for example, a permanent fall in the rate of growth of productivity), a lag in the response of wages to prices will not suffice to produce the required downward adjustment in the *rate of growth* of real wage aspirations. The NAIRU will rise.

of real product wages over what is warranted by economic conditions—is usually labeled the real wage gap.[9]

The OECD has postulated three unemployment-raising consequences of the increase in the real wage gap during the 1970s.[10] First, employers found it unprofitable to continue operating, or to bring back into operation, the older and less efficient parts of their plants. Workers associated with those operations became unemployed. This has been labeled labor shedding. Second, in producing the reduced level of output, firms substituted more capital for labor in order to minimize the cost-increasing effects of the excessive real wages. This has been called labor displacement. Third, because of squeezed profit margins the attractiveness of building new capacity declined, and investment for such purposes fell off. After a time, even if real wages were to moderate, the rate at which output could rise and unemployment fall would be limited by incipient capacity shortages.

To the extent the rise in European unemployment since the early 1970s has been the result of an increased real wage gap, and to the extent that wage bargains continue to reflect downward real wage rigidity, efforts to lower unemployment by expanding aggregate demand faster than potential output would be frustrated by workers' efforts to maintain real wages at excessive levels. The demand stimulus would produce only temporary gains in output and would ultimately be dissipated in higher inflation. The widespread acceptance of this view of Europe's economic situation has been an important element in explaining the very cautious macroeconomic policies pursued by European governments in recent years.

Evaluating the Excess Real Wage Hypothesis: A Preliminary Overview

Excessive wage settlements have been instrumental in raising unemployment in a number of European countries during the past ten years. But the actual course of real wages is not a reliable indicator of either the existence or the magnitude of the excess wage pressure. There are

9. Real product wages are nominal wages divided by the price of value added. The rate of productivity growth must be measured at high employment levels of activity, and the labor share adjusted accordingly, if it is to serve as a measure of the wage gap. This is a difficult task; see note 20.

10. *OECD Economic Outlook*, no. 37 (June 1985), p. 30.

circumstances under which real product wages can rise faster than productivity without indicating any excess wage pressures. Conversely, there are circumstances under which excess wage pressures can lead to a rise in unemployment without resulting in any increase in the wage gap. From the standpoint of the decisions of individual monopolistically competitive firms, real wages are not an exogenous but a choice variable.[11] From the standpoint of the economy as a whole, real wages are not a product of the wage-setting process alone, but are jointly determined by the interaction among that process, firms' pricing practices, the path of aggregate demand, and real exchange rates.

In the short and medium run, nominal wage-setting behavior on the part of firms and workers may fail to adjust to changes in supply conditions and produce accelerating inflation if aggregate demand is kept on a path that induces firms to maintain employment unchanged.[12] The "excessive" wage behavior may, for example, be the failure of nominal wage increases to fall sufficiently relative to the existing rate of inflation when unfavorable supply shocks occur. The unemployment rate that is required to keep inflation from accelerating then rises. The actual outcome, in terms of real wages, employment, and inflation, will depend upon what happens to aggregate demand.

As was the case in Europe in the 1970s, economic policy may initially, but will not ultimately, tolerate rising inflation. The combined thrust of monetary and fiscal policy will eventually turn restrictive, to reduce aggregate demand enough to halt the acceleration of inflation. Indeed, since the initial impact of the excess wage aspirations will have raised inflation, policy will usually go beyond stopping an acceleration of inflation—it will seek to reduce it. Actual unemployment rises to and beyond the new higher NAIRU. Once inflation has been reduced, the question then becomes whether ex ante wage goals or norms remain excessive relative to what is warranted by supply conditions so as to

11. Robert M. Solow, "Unemployment: Getting the Questions Right," *Economica*, vol. 53 (1986, *Supplement*), pp. S23–34, stresses this point.

12. If wage behavior is such that nominal wage increases do not respond one to one with increases in past (or expected) inflation, the excessive nominal wage bargains will produce a rise but not a continuing acceleration in inflation. Higher inflation becomes one mechanism to adjust real wages downward in line with adverse supply shocks. The wage equations developed later in this paper suggest that such behavior is characteristic of some European countries. But for ease of exposition, I assume at this point that nominal wage behavior is accelerationist in character, generating a specific value for the NAIRU.

keep the NAIRU at its new higher level. As long as the factors producing the excessive wage behavior are unchanged, unemployment cannot be reduced below the higher NAIRU without reinstating the tendency toward rising inflation. To the extent that in the short run firms set prices by a constant markup over labor costs, real wages will not change.[13] Excess real wage goals will have increased unemployment, but actual real wages will not have risen. On the other hand, as both Bean and Nickell point out in their comments in this volume, if firms equate prices to marginal costs along an upwardly sloping marginal cost curve, then as the monetary authorities pursue the restrictive policy necessary to halt the acceleration of inflation, markups will be squeezed and real wages will rise.[14] And if constant markups gradually give way to more flexible pricing in the face of persistent change in demand conditions, then real wages over time will follow a path determined by the interaction of these pricing practices and aggregate demand.

Thus what happened to real wages in Europe and their relationship to the rise of unemployment cannot be considered separately from the varying pattern of macroeconomic policies put in place to deal with the combined increases in inflation and unemployment that were generated by the combination of supply shocks and wage-setting practices. Although the pattern varied from country to country, its stark outlines are as follows. During the late 1960s in all the major European countries, a widely documented wage "explosion" took place.[15] Nominal wages began to rise faster than could be explained either by what was happening to prices or by demand-supply conditions in the labor market. A few years later, the combination of the 1973–74 oil shock, a fall in productivity growth, and the failure of wage aspirations to adjust downward simultaneously raised the aggregate supply curve and depressed aggregate demand. Both unemployment and inflation rose.

In the second half of the 1970s, European budgets moved strongly into structural deficits as new employment-supporting programs were introduced and as ambitious social programs, already in place, came

13. The relevant prices for this discussion are value-added prices.

14. Both Charles R. Bean and Stephen Nickell in their comments in this volume provide a further exposition of the argument given here, which is closely based on their published work and that of their colleague Richard Layard.

15. See George L. Perry, "Determinants of Wage Inflation around the World," *BPEA, 2:1975,* pp. 403–35; and Sachs, "Wages, Profits, and Macroeconomic Adjustment." The wage equations reported in this paper confirm the occurrence of an exogenous upward shift in nominal wages.

face to face with a structural decline in revenue growth. Unemployment rose, but not by enough to halt a rise in the inflation rate of value-added prices. After the second oil shock that itself reduced aggregate demand, most governments reversed course. They moved aggressively in a restrictive direction (France later than the others) to reduce or eliminate their growing structural budget deficits, to halt the new rise in inflation, and subsequently to reduce it. The result was an acceleration in the growth of unemployment and a strong decline in inflation. A critical issue now at stake is the extent to which the NAIRU remains substantially higher (or the unemployment-inflation trade-off remains substantially worse). That could have occurred either because ex ante real wage aspirations (that is, the wage demands that would be forthcoming at higher levels of employment) have not moderated sufficiently or because various supply-side factors have raised the Beveridge curve and kept it up.

For purposes of analyzing long-run developments, it is convenient to assume that aggregate demand is ultimately kept at the point where inflation does not accelerate. Actual unemployment then approximates the NAIRU, and aggregate demand drops out as one of the factors determining employment and real wages, leaving the neoclassical factors—labor supply functions, production functions, and the competitive environment—to determine real wages and employment. But even in the long run the relationship between excessive real wage aspirations and actual real wages is a complex one that depends importantly upon two factors—the elasticity of substitution between capital and labor in the production function and the factors determining the competitive environment (principally the real exchange rate). Some of the long-run changes in real wage outcomes and in profitability in European countries over the past two decades may have been driven not by excess real wage aspirations but by changes in capital intensity (most of which would have occurred at full employment) and by changes in real exchange rates. This is not to suggest that excess real wage aspirations have had no role in Europe's rising unemployment. During the 1970s in the European countries covered by this paper, ex ante wage norms did become excessive relative to what those economies could pay at high levels of employment without large rises in inflation. But the behavior of actual real wages (relative to productivity) is not a reliable measure of the existence or magnitude of the wage problem.

The Evolution of Real Wages and Profitability in Europe and the United States, 1960–85

This section examines the long-run behavior of real wages and profitability, as they were affected by the nature of production functions, the rate of technical progress, capital investment, and other "real" variables, as well as by the movements in real exchange rates. It concludes that the course of actual real wages over time is not a useful measure of the extent to which excessive wage aspirations have been responsible for the rise in European unemployment.

The Conceptual Basis of the Real Wage Gap

The real wage gap is conventionally measured as the rise in labor's income share from some base period, adjusted to exclude the effects of cyclical changes in productivity. It is also indexed by the excess of the rise in real product wages over the rise in average labor productivity cyclically adjusted, or by the excess of the rise in real purchasing power wages over the rise in productivity adjusted both for cyclical fluctuations and for changes in the terms of trade (or any other factors causing the path of consumer prices to diverge from the path of value-added prices in the relevant sector).[16]

The real wage gap can be expressed as

$$(1) \qquad s_1 = s_{10} + (\dot{w} - \dot{p}_v - \dot{x})$$

or

$$(2) \qquad s_1 = s_{10} + [(\dot{w} - \dot{p}_e) - (\dot{p}_c - \dot{p}_v) - \dot{x}],$$

where

s_1 = log of the labor share of income

$\dot{w}, \dot{p}_v, \dot{p}_c, \dot{x}$ = change in the log of nominal wages, value-added prices, consumer prices, and average labor productivity, respectively.

(Throughout this paper upper-case letters represent the level of a variable, lower-case letters represent logarithms, and lower-case letters

16. See Sachs, "Real Wages and Unemployment," p. 260.

with a dot (for example, $\dot{w}$) represent annual changes in logs.) According to Sachs and others who use the wage gap measure, equations 1 and 2, after the substitution of a cyclically corrected—that is, high-employ-ment—measure of productivity growth $\dot{x}^f$ for $\dot{x}$ will produce a reliable index of the downward pressure of excess real wage growth on unem-ployment:

$$\text{(1a)} \qquad s_1^f = s_{1_0} + (\dot{w} - \dot{p}_v - \dot{x}^f)$$

$$\text{(2a)} \qquad s_1^f = s_{1_0} [(\dot{w} - \dot{p}_c) - (\dot{p}_c - \dot{p}_v) - \dot{x}^f].$$

As equations 1a and 2a make clear, there are three completely equivalent ways in which the wage gap can be measured.

1. $S_1^f - S_{1_0}$: the change in the log of the adjusted labor share over some base period (chosen as a period in which actual employment and full employment are assumed to have coincided);

2. $\dot{w} - \dot{p}_v - \dot{x}^f$: the excess of *real product* wage increases over increases in trend productivity growth; and

3. $(\dot{w} - \dot{p}_c) - (\dot{p}_c - \dot{p}_v) - \dot{x}^f$: the excess of *real purchasing power* wage growth over trend productivity growth after adjustment for changes in terms of trade (or any other factors that cause consumer price inflation to differ from inflation in domestic value-added prices).

There are alternative interpretations of the wage gap. I follow the one elaborated by Krugman.[17] Excess real wages did not at first lead to reduced unemployment. Firms, confronted with plant redundancy laws or other governmental or union-imposed constraints on firing, tempo-rarily kept employment high in the face of excessive real wages, causing a rise in labor's share of income. After a while, however, employers reduced employment, moving up their short-run labor demand functions, thereby raising productivity.

Figure 1 illustrates the postulated relationship between the real wage gap and employment.[18] *MPL* is the demand for labor curve (in logs) for a given capital stock. LnN^* is the employment demand associated with full employment; ln$(W/P)^*$ is the warranted real wage—that is, the real wage that will induce employers to produce an output level and to choose a capital intensity of production consistent with the full employment of

17. Paul Krugman, "The Real Wage Gap and Employment," in Jacques Melitz and Charles Wyplosz, eds., *The French Economy: Theory and Policy* (Boulder, Colo.: Westview Press, 1985), pp. 51–69.

18. This figure is only an illustration. Neither the slope of the mpl and apl nor the size of the labor share is meant to portray reality.

Figure 1. *Derivation of the Real Wage Gap*

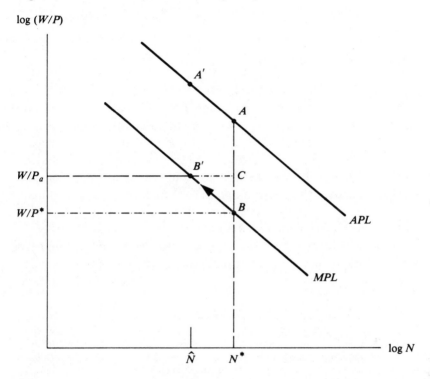

log (W/P)

the labor force. If the long-run production function is Cobb-Douglas, the log of the warranted labor share is $-AB$. If real wages are higher than this, say at $\ln(W/P)_a$, then during the disequilibrium period, before employers make an adjustment, employment remains at N^*, the log of the labor share is now higher, at $-AC$, and the wage gap is CB. Gradually, however, employers substitute capital for labor along their long-run production functions, moving from B to B'; employment falls from N^* to $\hat{N}$. In a Cobb-Douglas production function the wage gap, CB, bears a simple log-linear relationship to the ultimate employment decline CB' and is therefore said to be a good index of the downward pressure of excess real wages on employment.[19] Notice that in the long run, given a Cobb-Douglas production function, the excess rise in real wages is

19. See pp. 246–48 for a discussion of the difficulties of relating observed data to this construct.

matched by a proportionate increase in average (and marginal) productivity. The wage share falls back to its original level.[20]

Measures of the Wage Gap

The Commission of the European Communities has recently made
available a set of consistent data on income shares, output, capital and
labor inputs, and related variables for the nonfarm business sector
(excluding housing) and for manufacturing in the United States, Japan,
and the four large European countries (Germany, France, Italy, and the
United Kingdom). The labor share was adjusted by the Commission to
include the imputed labor income of the self-employed. The U.S. Bureau
of Labor Statistics regularly publishes similar data on the manufacturing
sector of twelve major industrial countries, including those listed here.[21]

From the Commission data, the share of labor S_1 and the adjusted
share S_1^t (assuming trend, not actual, productivity growth) were calculated for the total business sector. From the BLS data, similar calcula-

---

20. In the Bruno and Sachs version of the wage gap (*Economics of Worldwide
Stagflation*), wages are compared not to the current level of productivity (adjusted to
remove purely cyclical fluctuations) but to the presumably lower level of productivity
that is estimated to be consistent with full employment. That is, given a Cobb-Douglas
production function and competitive pricing, and assuming firms are currently operating
on or near their labor demand curves, the only way to raise employment to full-
employment levels is to lower real wages proportionally with the fall in marginal and
average productivity that would accompany the rise in employment. This approach is
almost impossible to make operational. First, one must assume what is the full-
employment level of employment. And then the productivity associated with that level
of employment must be estimated. To do so, Bruno and Sachs fit a productivity equation
with unemployment as one of its arguments and then calculate what productivity would
be at 1965–69 unemployment rates. The problem is that in only two of the five countries
they investigated (Germany and Canada) was there a significant positive coefficient of
productivity on unemployment, as the theory requires. Moreover, as best I was able to
calculate from the Bruno-Sachs text, in Germany only about 4 to 5 percentage points
of the 18 percent 1981 real wage gap was due to the difference between actual productivity
and full-employment productivity—most of the gap was attributable to an unexplained
excess of real wages over actual productivity. But under the Cobb-Douglas and the
competitive pricing assumption, actual real wages should not get very far out of line
with actual productivity. In the case of German manufacturing, for example, the puzzle
is not why real wages got so far out of line with some hypothetical full-employment
productivity, but why they got so far out of line with actual productivity. (This note
was added in response to a point made by Charles Bean in his discussion of an earlier
version of this paper.)

21. See the data appendix to this paper for a description of the series.

tions were made for the manufacturing sector.[22] To estimate the "adjusted" labor share, trend productivity was derived from an equation that allows for two kinds of cyclical influences: changes in the rate of growth of output, and the level of output relative to capacity.[23] Thus

$$(3) \qquad H^* = (Q/X_o e^{rt}) \left(\frac{Q}{Q^*} \right)^b$$

$$(4) \qquad \Delta H^* = \gamma(H^* - H_{-1}),$$

where

H^* = employers' desired hours of employment
H = actual hours of employment
Q = output
Q^* = potential or capacity output
X_o = average labor productivity in the base period
$r = \dot{x}^f$ = trend rate of growth of productivity.

The derivation of potential or capacity output Q^* is described in the second part of this paper. Through 1976 it is based on an estimate of potential output that is a centered nine-year geometric moving average of actual output. After 1976 potential was extrapolated on the basis of the change in the capital stock adjusted to trends in the output-capital ratio. The ratio Q/Q^*, in its log form $\hat{q}$, will subsequently be referred to as *the gap*.

In combination, equations 3 and 4 allow productivity to differ from trend both because of lags in adjusting actual to desired employment (the rate of change effect) and because of deviations of output from potential (the level effect).

By converting to logs and substituting equation 3 into equation 4, an equation can be fit to the time series, allowing for several breaks in the trend and the level of productivity as indicated by the data:

$$(5) \qquad \Delta h = \gamma[(q - h_{-1}) - x_o - r_i t - b\hat{q}].$$

22. The Commission also made available similar data on manufacturing. But I chose to use the BLS data for all the manufacturing calculations, since they are available on a more timely basis. The one exception was the manufacturing capital stock data, which are available from the Commission but not the BLS.

23. See Peter K. Clark, "Productivity and Profits in the 1980's: Are They Really Improving?" *BPEA*, 1:1984, pp. 133–67.

Figure 2. *Real Wage Gaps in Nonfarm Business and Manufacturing Sectors, Germany, France, and Italy, 1964–85*

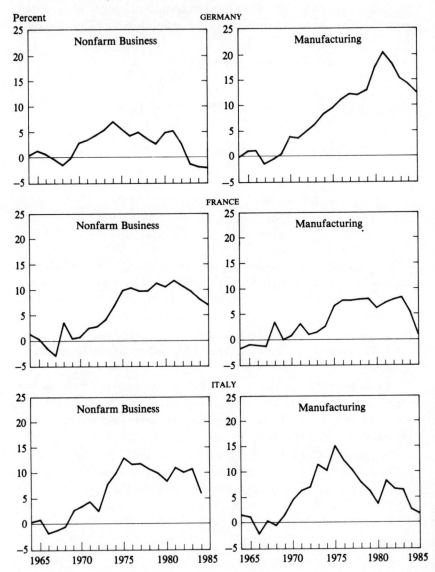

Figure 3. *Real Wage Gaps in Nonfarm Business and Manufacturing Sectors, United Kingdom and United States, 1964–85*

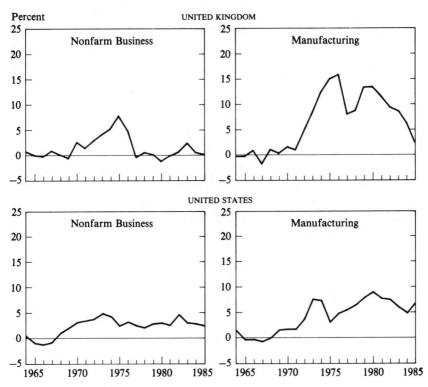

The r_i can be identified and used to generate the log of the cyclically adjusted labor share s_t^f, which, when compared with the base period share s_{1_o}, provides a measure of the wage gap.[24]

Figures 2 and 3 show the movement in wage gaps from an assumed zero level in 1965–69 for the total nonfarm business sector and for manufacturing. Except for France and Italy, the wage gap was principally a phenomenon of the manufacturing sector, not of the total business economy. In Germany, the United Kingdom, and the United States, wage gaps did appear in the total business economy in the 1970s, but they were relatively modest and have subsequently disappeared or (in

24. In Germany, France, and the United Kingdom some of the post-1980 changes in productivity can be explained by a shift in levels, captured by a shift in the constant of the equation.

the case of the United States remained quite low). In France and Italy, on the other hand, a sizable wage gap did open up in the total business sector. The gap diminished in recent years but remains substantial in France. In manufacturing, wage gaps opened up in all countries during the 1970s. Except in Germany, and to a lesser extent in the United States, they also have disappeared in recent years. In Germany the rise in the wage gap was quite substantial, and a large part of it still apparently remains.[25]

The path of unemployment in European countries does not follow closely that of the wage gap. In particular, the steepest rise in unemployment comes after 1980 as wage gaps are beginning to decline. It is implicit in at least some versions of the wage gap concept, however, that firms at first operate off their long-run notional labor demand curves, and only after a lag do they reduce employment by substituting capital for labor along their long-run labor demand curves (see figure 4).[26] Thus, it is argued, the initial rise in the real wage gap generated a disequilibrium response followed by a period of accelerated capital-labor substitution and faster productivity growth, explaining much of the very large increase in European unemployment after 1980.[27] Moreover, rising unemployment itself reduces wage demands, even if the pattern of wage aspirations has not fundamentally changed. Thus wage aspirations at high levels of employment may still be greater than what is warranted by supply conditions. And so, it has been argued, the partial reversal of the manufacturing real wage gaps over the past three to four years is not an indication that Europe has put the problem of excessive real wages behind it.

The Wage Gap with a Cobb-Douglas Production Function

As already noted, if the production function is Cobb-Douglas, only in the initial disequilibrium stages will excess real wages produce a real

25. In reading the charts, remember that the gap is equal to the cumulative *percent* changes in the adjusted labor share; the *percentage point* change in the shares is, of course, less than this.

26. If employers had continued to operate along their Cobb-Douglas generated labor demand curves, no ex post difference between the growth of real wages and productivity would ever have been observed.

27. The OECD in *OECD Economic Outlook,* no. 37 (June 1985), p. 30, explicitly suggested this explanation.

Figure 4. *Time Path of the Wage Gap*

Labor share, wage gap

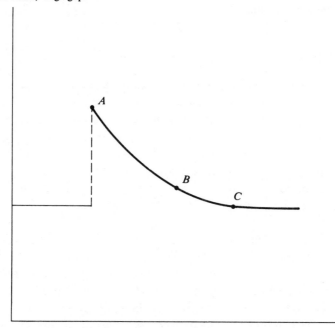

wage gap, and only then will the size of the real wage gap bear an unambiguous relationship to the magnitude of the unemployment it generates. Assume for the sake of argument an exogenous upward shift in real wages relative to their warranted level. Following Krugman, the subsequent trend path of the labor share is illustrated in figure 4. Point *A* is the wage gap immediately after the disturbance, point *B* represents a point at which employers have partially but not fully adjusted by cutting employment, and at point *C* the real wage gap has disappeared through a reduction in employment and an increase in productivity. The size of the wage gap itself will thus bear no unique relationship to the unemployment it generates.

The extent to which recent changes in wage shares in European countries represented movements along long-run production functions, along short-run (putty-clay) functions, or, as a third possibility, resulted from disequilibrium changes that departed from both curves remains uncertain. This inherent uncertainty poses insuperable problems for the use of wage gap data as the principal instrument to assess the presence or absence of excess wage aspirations and to evaluate their role in explaining unemployment.

The Wage Gap with a CES Production Function

The standard discussion of the real wage gap starts by assuming that the observed change in labor shares is a disequilibrium phenomenon. What happens if one starts from the other end? Surely over the period since the wage explosion took place, the productivity slowdown began, and the oil shocks occurred, employers must have gone a long way toward adjusting their labor inputs. Suppose, then, that the observed movements in the cyclically adjusted income share were principally an equilibrium response along long-run production functions. What does this imply?

If the production function is not Cobb-Douglas, and the elasticity of factor substitution is less than unity, increases in the capital-labor ratio will raise the labor share and produce a rising wage "gap." In the normal course of economic development, with a positive rate of technical progress, capital intensity will increase, the marginal product of labor will rise faster than the average product, and the labor share will grow along the *warranted* growth path.[28]

I have used the Commission and BLS data to infer from first-order conditions some parameters of a CES (constant elasticity of substitutions) production function. To assess the magnitude of the warranted change in the wage share, let

(6) $$Q = Ae^{\lambda t}[\delta K^{-\beta} + (1 - \delta)N^{-\beta}]^{-1/\beta},$$

the standard CES production function with Hicks's neutral technical process.

A widely used linear approximation to this function (with lower-case letters representing logs) is[29]

28. Along the warranted growth path, real wages are such that the substitution of capital for labor is consistent with the maintenance of high employment.

29. See, for example, John McCallum, "Wage Gaps, Factor Shares and Real Wages," *Scandinavian Journal of Economics,* vol. 87, no. 2 (1985), pp. 436–59; and Jacques R. Artus, "The Disequilibrium Real Wage Rate Hypothesis: An Empirical Evaluation," *International Monetary Fund Staff Papers,* vol. 31 (June 1984), pp. 249–302. The argument in the next several pages closely follows that of McCallum.

Table 2. *Elasticities of Factor Substitution*

	Value of σ		t-statistic on difference of σ from 1	
Country	Business sector	Manufacturing	Business sector	Manufacturing
Germany	1.00[a]	0.63	[a]	4.7
France	0.72	0.76	4.6	2.1
Italy	0.66	2.00	3.1	1.0
United Kingdom	1.00[a]	0.88	[a]	0.5
United States	0.73	0.68	2.3	3.1

Source: Author's calculations.
a. The coefficients on $(k - n)$ were virtually zero.

$$(7) \qquad q = a + \lambda t + \delta K + (1 - \delta) N - \frac{1}{2} \beta\, d(1 - d)(k - n)^2$$

$$(7a) \qquad \sigma \text{ (the elasticity of factor substitution)} = \frac{1}{1 + \beta}.$$

As McCallum shows, the capital income share S_k will then equal[30]

$$(8) \qquad S_k = \delta - \beta\delta(1 - \delta)(k - n).$$

Here δ is the "base-period" capital income share—that is, the share for the period in which the index of the capital-labor ratio is set at 1.0. A cyclically adjusted S_k, estimated as $1 - S_l^f$, was fit to the log of the capital-labor ratio for the period 1964–84. Before the capital-labor ratio was calculated, the capital stock was adjusted to reflect changing capacity utilization, that is, $k_{adj} = k + \hat{q}$. Thus the capital-labor ratio is the ratio between the utilized capital stock and the employed labor force. On the assumption that over the past two decades most of the changes in adjusted S_k arose from equilibrium movements along firms' notional labor demand curves, σ (the elasticity of factor substitution) can be extracted from the regression equation.[31] This was done for the total business and manufacturing sectors for the period 1964–84, with the results shown in table 2.

McCallum, using a different data base but the same approach, finds

30. See McCallum, "Wage Gaps, Factor Shares and Real Wages," p. 438.
31. In other words, S_k can be fit against $k - n$, and β and therefore σ can be extracted from equation 7.

elasticities of substitution in the manufacturing sector ranging from 0.56 for the United Kingdom to 0.83 for France. (The assumption of a Harrod neutral technology generated still lower values for σ in most European countries, according to McCallum.)[32] For the total business sector, the results reported in table 2 suggest German and United Kingdom elasticities insignificantly different from 1.0, while elasticities in France, Italy, and the United States are in the neighborhood of 0.7. For manufacturing, all countries but Italy and the United Kingdom have elasticities in the 0.60 to 0.75 range.

It is worth duplicating an exercise carried out by McCallum.[33] Assuming full adjustment of prices and capital-labor substitution along neoclassical labor demand curves, he writes

$$(9) \qquad S_k = \delta - \delta(1 - \delta)\beta[(k - n^*) + (n^* - n)],$$

where

$(n^* - n) =$ the shortfall of employment below its full employment level

$(k - n^*) =$ the warranted growth in the capital-labor ratio (that is, the capital-labor ratio consistent with full employment).

In manufacturing industries, the value of δ (the base-period capital income share) ranges between 0.25 and 0.30 for the various countries. With σ of 0.63 and 0.76 (the substitution elasticities for Germany and France), the value of the coefficient on $(k - n^*)$ and $(n^* - n)$ is about 0.10. From its 1965–69 base, the adjusted capital income share in German manufacturing fell by 13 percentage points to its trough in 1981 and by 6 percentage points in France to its trough in 1982. Even if exogenous excess real wage growth had been responsible for a 10 percentage point reduction in employment in each of these countries, the total effect would only have been to lower the profit share by 1½ percentage points in Germany and by ½ percentage point in France.

Thus one can assume that by about 1980 firms had more or less adjusted their employment to the higher real wages. The major factor driving income shares appears to have been the increase in capital intensity that would have occurred even at full employment. Again, using the 10 percent employment shortfall assumption, the *warranted*

32. McCallum, "Wage Gaps, Factor Shares and Real Wages," pp. 443–46.
33. Ibid., pp. 451–52.

capital-labor ratio grew by 63 percent in Germany and 70 percent in France.

The preceding conclusions suffer from a large element of question begging—but no more than bedevils the standard discussion of the real wage gap. The conclusions of the prior paragraph assume that observed real wage outcomes represent an *equilibrium* phenomenon and that the slope of the labor demand curve and the elasticity of factor substitution can be inferred from first-order conditions; any rise in the wage gap is associated with a change in capital intensity. In those countries where real wage gaps rose during the period of analysis, this necessarily implies an elasticity of factor substitution less than 1.0. And since capital-labor intensities would have risen very sharply over the period even if employment had been full, the arithmetic necessarily assigns only a small portion of the rise in the real wage gap to the increases in intensity associated with the shortfall from full employment. Alternatively, one could make the opposite assumption—namely, that the real wage gaps that opened up in the 1970s were principally the result of a disequilibrium response and were not due to the rise in capital intensities. All of the increase in the wage gap is, therefore, interpreted as unemployment waiting to happen, ultimately along a long-run labor demand curve with an elasticity of −2.0 or more.

The Role of Exchange Rates

In a small country operating in competitive world markets, prices of tradable goods produced domestically would be set by the domestic currency value of international prices. In the larger countries of Western Europe, and even more so in the United States, manufacturing firms operating in an environment of competition mixed with oligopoly, and influenced by customer market considerations, have some room to vary the prices they charge relative to international price levels. Changes in foreign prices affect markups but do not control them absolutely, as domestic manufacturers in a less than complete but still substantial way compete for exports in world markets and against imports in home markets.

It is not unreasonable to think of changes in real exchange rates as equivalent to an increase in the competitiveness of the market environment. As the real exchange rate rises, given enough time the number of actual and potential competitors and the intensity of competition increases. If so, a large rise in the real exchange rate—a relative fall in foreign competitors' prices expressed in home-country currency—increases the elasticity of demand facing the monopolistically competitive domestic producer of tradable goods. And this change in elasticity, in turn, shifts up the notional labor demand curve; *at any given level of aggregate demand*, firms, after an increase in the real exchange rate, will offer the same output and demand the same amount of labor at lower prices relative to wages—that is, at a higher real wage. The notional labor demand curve will be derived from the relationship

$$(10) \qquad \frac{W}{P} = \frac{1}{V} MPL,$$

where
   V = the monopolistic competitors' markup on marginal costs, and

$$(11) \qquad V = \frac{\eta}{\eta - 1,}$$

where
   η = the elasticity of the monopolistic competitors' product demand
         curve, which I assume to move inversely with the real exchange
         rate.[34]
   From the log-linear approximation to the CES production function in equation 8, it will hold, up to a constant, that

$$(12) \qquad n^d = \frac{\sigma}{S_k}\left(\lambda - \frac{w}{p} - v\right) + k.$$

An increase in the real exchange rate will lower v and raise the demand for labor, n^d, at a given level of aggregate demand for tradables and a given capital stock.[35] Similarly, it can be shown that the capital income share (and, therefore, the wage gap) depends not only on the elasticity

34. I also assume, for the usual reasons, that η is always equal to or larger than unity.
35. All of the preceding derivations assume a constant capital stock. To the extent the monopolistically competitive firms were initially earning only normal profits, the exchange rate increase would drive their profits down below normal and eventually force marginal operations out of business. But in the short and intermediate run, the results would be as given.

Table 3. *Regression Explaining the Margins of Prices over Standard Unit Labor Costs, Manufacturing Sector, Germany, France, Italy, and the United Kingdom, 1964–85*

Item	Germany	France	Italy	United Kingdom
Dependent variable, p^v				
Sum of coefficients on				
$sulc^a$	0.92 (16.3)	0.98 (84.3)	1.03 (112.1)	0.99 (67.7)
$p_{for}{}^b$	0.17 (1.8)	0.28 (2.0)	0.48 (3.1)	0.14 (1.8)
Standard error	0.011	0.014	0.016	0.02
ρ	0.70	0.43	0.11	0^c

Source: Author's calculations.
a. Standard unit labor costs. Sum of coefficients on single order three-term Almon lag starting with the current year.
b. Price of foreign manufactured goods relative to *sulc*. Sum of coefficients on single order three-term Almon lag starting in $t-1$.
c. Durbin-Watson = 1.97.

of substitution and the capital-labor ratio but also on the size of v and hence on the exchange rate.[36]

I constructed a measure of the inverse of the real exchange rate as the price of foreign manufactured goods (expressed in home-country currency relative to domestic standard unit labor costs).[37] That variable (p_{for}) was then entered, with a relatively long distributed lag, on an equation explaining the margin of prices over standard unit labor costs in the manufacturing sector. In the European countries, that variable helped explain margins, as shown in table 3. A rise in the domestic price of foreign tradable goods relative to domestic unit labor costs tended to raise domestic margins. The coefficients on unit labor costs are roughly consistent with the earlier findings about the possible magnitude of the elasticities of substitution in manufacturing: substantially less than 1 in Germany, modestly less than 1 in France and the United Kingdom, and higher than 1 in Italy.

36.
$$S_1 = \frac{N}{Q}(MPL)\left(\frac{1}{V}\right) = \frac{dq}{dn}\left(\frac{1}{V}\right) = 1 - S_k.$$

From equation 8,

$$S_k = 1 - \frac{(1 - \delta)}{V} - \frac{\beta(\delta)(1 - \delta)}{V}(k-n); \frac{dS_k}{dV} > 0.$$

37. With all variables in logs, $p_{for} = (ep^*_{for}) - sulc$; where p^* is a weighted average of foreign manufactured prices, e is the exchange rate, and *sulc* is domestic standard unit labor costs (log compensation per hour less log trend productivity). The variable p^*_{for} was derived by dividing the IMF relative value-added deflator (series 99 by 110) by the price of domestic manufacturing value added and inverting the result.

In Germany, where the movements of the real exchange rate have been very large over the past two decades, its (lagged) impact on manufacturing profit margins and the real wage gap could have been quite substantial, as seen in the following table:[38]

	Wage gap	Index of p_{for}, lagged
1964	− 0.4	100
1974	8.0	75
1979	12.7	65
1981	20.2	62
1985	12.3	66

The sharp rise in the German manufacturing wage gap between 1979 and 1981 is associated with a sudden virtual cessation of productivity growth for about three years. Before, and after, the association of the German wage gap with the real exchange rate resumed.

On the other hand, the coefficients on the exchange rate variable have low t-statistics and are not stable over the period. Fit for the subperiod 1973–85, the coefficients (and t-statistics) for France and Germany both become much larger than the ones shown above.[39] On balance, evidence about the effect of real exchange rates on the wage gap tends to be consistent with the hypothesis laid out earlier but is far from conclusive.

In summary, there is a compelling list of reasons why the real wage gap is not a useful measure of downward pressures on employment:

—Even in a highly simplified closed-economy model, with Cobb-Douglas production functions and exogenous real wages, there is no fixed relationship between the size of an actually observed wage gap and the unemployment rate. The observed real wage gaps will vary relative to actual and threatened unemployment proportionately as employers have or have not yet made their employment adjustments.

—Given the very large increases in the capital-labor ratio that have characterized all European countries over the past twenty-five years, it takes only a modest shortfall of the elasticity of substitution below unity to produce substantial increases in labor's share of income even when real wages are consistent with full employment. If, for example, the

38. The variable p_{for} was lagged with the weights from the equation in table 3.

39. If a dummy variable is entered reflecting the downshift of the German productivity path between 1980 and 1982, the coefficient and t-statistic on the p_{for} variable improve substantially. But truncating the German and French equations by one year substantially lowers the coefficients and t-statistics on p_{for}.

elasticity of substitution in manufacturing is taken at 0.7, most of the observed rise in the labor share would have occurred even if employment were 10 percent higher and the capital-labor ratio 10 percent lower than is actually the case.

—In the European countries, some evidence suggests that the labor share was influenced by changes in exchange rates. For any given level of aggregate demand, changes in the labor share arising from exchange rate movement need not produce a lower demand for labor. (In the long run, however, the resulting reduction in profitability may lead to lower investment in capacity in the tradable goods industries.)

As noted earlier, these findings in no sense exonerate excessive wage pressures as the villain insofar as rising unemployment in Europe is concerned. But they do cast doubt on the usefulness of the real wage gap as an index of the existence, magnitude, or timing of the problem.

The Determinants of Wages and Prices

This section of the paper develops alternative equations explaining nominal wage inflation in the nonfarm business sector. Using those equations, in conjunction with estimates of the trend growth in average and marginal labor productivity, I attempt to infer something about sources of the rise in European unemployment. In Germany, France, and Italy each of the three broad explanations of unemployment has some validity—deficient aggregate demand, excess wage aspirations relative to the economy's supply potential, and unfavorable labor market developments that have shifted the Beveridge curve up. In the United Kingdom, and possibly in the other countries, the data do suggest the pressure of hysteresis. The paper also cautions, however, that there are some severe limitations on the ability of aggregate time-series analysis to produce a reliable quantitative assessment of the components of the unemployment increase.

I use, with some modifications, a basic approach to the derivation of a wage equation developed by Robert Gordon.[40] From three equations determining three unknowns—employment, wages, and prices—a particular dynamic adjustment process is specified in which wages are the

40. Robert J. Gordon, "Wage-Price Dynamics and the Manufacturing Output Gap in Europe, Japan, and North America," paper prepared for the Conference on Unemployment in Yxtaholm, Sweden, September 26–27, 1985.

sticky variable. Given aggregate demand and sticky money wages, monopolistically competitive price-setting firms simultaneously determine employment and prices. The results, in terms of employment and real wages, then confront the labor supply schedule, and the level of excess labor demand or supply is thereby determined. In a Phillips curve framework, money wages are assumed to change in the direction of market clearing at a rate proportional to the excess supply or demand. This feeds back on prices and employment. Depending on the reactions of the policy authorities, the change in prices may or may not also feed back on the level of aggregate demand.[41]

Price Determination and Labor Demand

Given money wages, firms jointly solve the output (employment) and price decision. Prices are a function of wages, aggregate demand, and the average size of the monopolistic competitors' markup. The variables can be expressed in the level of logs as

$$(13) \qquad p = \phi(v, w, y),$$

where

y = an index of aggregate demand

w = money wages

v = the monopolistic competitors' markup of price on marginal costs

and the shape of ϕ is given by the production function. With profit maximization, output and price decisions are made so as to keep real wages proportional to the marginal product of labor with the proportionality given by v:

$$(14) \qquad (w - p_v^e) = z - v + \lambda^t + \frac{S_k}{\sigma}(k - n),$$

where

z = a constant

p_v^e = expected value-added prices

---

41. Thus in the long run if it is assumed that the authorities ultimately set aggregate demand to prevent an acceleration or deceleration of inflation, aggregate demand drops out, and one is back again to the neoclassical solution in two variables: real wages and employment.

and the other variables and coefficients have already been defined. By inverting equation 14, one gets the labor demand equation, given wages

(14a)
$$n^d = k - \frac{\sigma}{S_k}(w - p_v^e) + \frac{\sigma}{S_k}(z - v + \lambda).$$

Labor Supply

I assume labor supply to be given by the following set of relationships:

(15)
$$N^s = \left(\frac{W}{P_c^e}/H\right)^b N_o e^{st},$$

where

P_c^e = expected consumer prices (or the price level consistent with the Okun-Perry concept of a norm rate of inflation)

$H = (W/P_c^e)^*$ = the real wage target or norm that is compared with the expected real wage in making labor supply decisions[42]

$N_o e^{st}$ = the path of "high employment" employment

s = the growth rate of employment along that path.

Thus the supply function is written as deviations around a high employment path. Those deviations are themselves a function of deviations expected from target real wages. With the use of this term it is possible to investigate the characteristics of a warranted real wage growth that keeps the economy along the high-employment path, given the proposition that economic policy will not in the long run tolerate continually rising inflation.

Firms care about the price of the product or value-added prices. Workers care about consumer prices. Hence the price term entering the labor supply function P_c^e is different from the price entering the labor demand function P_v^e.

N^s is *effective* labor supply. I will interpret this equation not as a neoclassical supply function in the usual sense. First, it incorporates the concept of efficiency wages; labor morale, efficiency, and performance are influenced by the wage level. Second, it is realistic to think of it as the inverse of a wage-setting process that incorporates many of the elements set forth in the implicit contract literature. In particular, it

---

42. Gordon, from whom this form of the supply function is taken, uses the expression *wage aspirations* for this term. See ibid.

incorporates employers' assessments of the long-run consequences of making a change in wages relative to the target or norm wage. Thus the supply curve reflects not only the motivations and interests of workers but also the motivations and interests of employers who are concerned about labor efficiency and long-term labor relationships.

While at first blush it may seem strange to put employer motivations into the labor supply curve, doing so is a natural outcome of the microeconomic reasoning underlying the concepts of efficiency wages and implicit contracts. One of the chief reasons for wage stickiness is that employers have to worry about their long-term labor relations and their effective labor supply. Employers believe that the long-run effectiveness of their supply of labor is substantially affected by wage changes that are out of line with the norm, or expected, or going rate. Hence the elasticity of "labor supply" against real wages that is implicit in the function can be quite large without implying a highly elastic long-run labor supply function in the neoclassical sense of the term. The implications of this will become clear below.

Expressed in logs, equation 15 becomes

(15a) $\qquad n^s = b(w - p_v^e) - b(p_c^e - p_v^e) - bh + n_o + st.$

The $p_c^e - p_v^e$ term is the difference between consumer prices and manufacturing value-added prices and is most easily defined in its rate of change variant: the difference between the rate of change in consumer prices and the GNP deflator, principally reflecting change in the terms of trade. The h term is the log of the norm or aspiration real wage.

As noted earlier, firms are assumed to determine employment (output) and prices as joint decision variables, given wages and aggregate demand. I now make two key assumptions. First,

(16) $\qquad\qquad\qquad x_t = (n^d - n^s)$

and

(16a) $\qquad\qquad \dot{x} = -gx_t;$ that is, $-gx_t = \dot{n}^d - \dot{n}^s.$

In other words, when labor supply exceeds demand (or vice versa) wages change relative to expected prices, so as to eliminate a given fraction, g, of the excess labor supply (or demand) during a given time period.[43]

The second assumption is that the same economic slack variable that

43. Ibid., pp. 17–18.

indexes the strength of aggregate demand also indexes x_t. Alternative empirical versions of this variable are described at a later point in the paper. This assumption implies acceptance of the validity of a relatively stable Okun's law relationship. It also incorporates a major shortcut by ignoring any contemporaneous feedback between p_v and x_t. But since, in the equations to follow, it is the lagged value of the slack variable that carries the major part of the action, the shortcut may be acceptable.

It is now possible to specify an equation in nominal wage inflation by assuming that the starting value of x_t has been already determined by prior developments. By taking time derivatives of equations 14a and 15a and then substituting into equation 16, one gets

(17)
$$\dot{w} = \frac{1}{a+b}(\dot{k} + a\lambda - \dot{s}) + \frac{b}{a+b}(\dot{h} - \lambda)$$
$$+ \frac{b}{a+b}(\dot{p}_c^e - \dot{p}_v^e) + \dot{p}_v^e + gx_t,$$

where

$a = \sigma/S_k$
$b = $ the real wage labor supply elasticity
$\dot{k} = $ the rate of change in the capital stock
$\lambda = $ the rate of technical change
$\dot{h} = $ the change in workers' real wage aspirations
$(\dot{p}_c^e - \dot{p}_v^e) = $ the difference in the rate of growth of consumer and value-added prices
$x_t = $ the index of the level of excess demand (that is, the slack variable, yet to be defined).[44]

In addition to the usual elements of an augmented Phillips curve, wage inflation depends on the relationship between target wage inflation, $\dot{h}$, on the one hand, and the determinants of productivity growth, λ and $\dot{k} - \dot{s}$, on the other. If, as I believe is true, b is large—that is, if nominal wage bargains are very sticky, reflecting employers' reluctance to cut wages because of long-run supply-side reasons—then the coefficient on the first term $\dot{k} + a\lambda - s$ will be small and the coefficient on the second term incorporating $\dot{h}$ will be large. Unless changes in productivity growth are accompanied by changes in $\dot{h}$, money wage growth will not respond

---

44. The formulation used here assumes a path of the capital stock that is based on output growth and the cost of capital and is exogenous to wage outcomes.

very much. On the other hand, a large value for b means that the coefficient on $\dot{p}_c^e - \dot{p}_v^e$ is large, though less than 1.0, so that price-raising supply shocks will increase money wages relative to expected value-added prices. Only as employers and workers come to accept that the "aspiration" or "norm" wage increase, h, is no longer appropriate to the new conditions will nominal wage bargains subside toward this new and lower warranted level.

All of the variables in the first two terms are bundled together in the single constant term of the usual augmented Phillips curve. Thus when combined with a typical markup equation for prices, such equations imply that a decline in productivity growth will raise the NAIRU.[45]

From equations 14a, 15a, and 16, one can express the growth in the wage norm, h, that is consistent with an equilibrium which maintains employment along the high-employment path. To maintain employment along the high-employment path, h must be such as to produce a wage that keeps $\dot{n}^d = \dot{s}$, when expected and actual inflation are equal. From equation 14, taking time derivatives, the warranted wage growth can be expressed

$$(18) \qquad (\dot{w} - \dot{p}_v) = \lambda + \frac{S_k}{\sigma}(\dot{k} - \dot{s}).$$

To produce such a wage,

$$(19) \qquad h = \lambda + \frac{S_k}{\sigma}(\dot{k} - \dot{s}).$$

When that value is substituted for h, in the wage inflation equation 17, and $\dot{p}^e$ is set equal to $\dot{p}$, the warranted real wage can be obtained:

$$(19a) \qquad \dot{w}^* = \lambda + \dot{p}_v + \frac{(\dot{k} - \dot{s})}{a}.$$

Since $a = \dfrac{\sigma}{S_k}$, one gets the warranted wage growth (equation 18):

$$(19b) \qquad (\dot{w}^* - \dot{p}_v) = \lambda + \frac{S_k}{\sigma}(\dot{k} - \dot{s}).$$

If σ is less than 1.0, the warranted h can grow faster than average

45. That result also assumes adaptive expectations with a coefficient of unity relating $\dot{p}_v^e$ to $\dot{p}_v$, $\dot{p}_{v-1}$, and so on.

productivity since the marginal product will be growing faster than the average product. The $\dot{k}$ and λ that are relevant in determining the warranted real wage growth are, I assume, trend values; price decisions are not made on the basis of short-run fluctuations in productivity. As noted earlier, if wages are sticky for supply-side reasons, and supply shocks change the warranted path of wages, actual wages will begin to rise faster than warranted. Depending on the nature of the shock (for example, one time or continuing) and employers' pricing practices, the rate of inflation associated with a zero value of x_t will rise (and will begin to accelerate if the expected inflation rate is marked up one for one with actual inflation).

The literature on career labor markets and implicit contracts suggests that it is not easy to change h. Following the line of reasoning set forth by Arthur Okun, h can be thought of as an ongoing norm rate of wage increase (which may be different for different submarkets), generally accepted by employers and employees as the neutral benchmark around which bargaining takes place.[46] Maintenance of important and mutually profitable long-term associations between employers and specific groups of employees dictates that, even from the employers' standpoint, the norm is not likely to be changed easily and flexibly. When the warranted wage growth changes, the norm wage may not alter for some time.[47] But the wage norm is not set in concrete. Ultimately, sustained experience with altered conditions—long periods of higher unemployment or real wages rising less than the norm—will lead to an adjustment in the norm. Indeed, as George Perry has proposed, and I have suggested, nominal wage norms may be relatively sluggish to adjust to changes in inflation, ignoring relatively modest fluctuations but shifting discretely to reflect larger and more persistent changes in inflation.[48]

In essence, this formulation of the wage-setting process envisages two ways in which nominal wages adjust to economic changes: short-

46. Arthur M. Okun, *Prices and Quantities: A Macroeconomic Analysis* (Brookings, 1981), chaps. 2, 3. See also Charles L. Schultze, "Microeconomic Efficiency and Nominal Wage Stickiness," *American Economic Review*, vol. 75 (March 1985), pp. 1–15.

47. The results of the wage equation fitted below suggest that in most countries the wage norm is not fully indexed; that is, the wage norm is, in part at least, formulated in nominal terms.

48. George L. Perry, "Inflation in Theory and Practice," *BPEA, 1: 1980*, pp. 207–41; and Charles L. Schultze, "Some Macro Foundations for Micro Theory," *BPEA, 2:1981*, pp. 521–76, and *Other Times, Other Places: Macroeconomic Lessons from U.S. and European History* (Brookings, 1986).

term adjustments to movements in unemployment and inflation as represented by the coefficients on x, $\hat{p}_v^e$ and $p_c^e - p_v^e$; and longer term adjustments modeled as discrete shifts in the norm h.

The consequences for both inflation and unemployment of a sticky h combined with a sharp fall in productivity growth were severe. The annual percent drop in trend productivity growth between the pre–1973 period and the early 1980s was as follows:[49]

	Business sector	Manufacturing
Germany	− 3.3	− 1.8
France	− 3.1	− 3.1
Italy	− 2.6	− 2.8
United Kingdom	− 1.7	− 3.2
United States	− 1.2	− 0.6

Thus if wage growth were approximately at the warranted level before 1973, and h did not adjust when productivity dropped after 1973, the resulting excess wage pressures were substantial. Moreover, the drop in trend productivity growth and the consequent problem of ex ante excess wage aspirations were more severe in Europe than in the United States.

Measuring Excess Labor Demand or Supply

Conceptually, in the formulation I have outlined, two kinds of changes in the natural rate of unemployment can take place. First, there are those that involve movements *along* a given Beveridge curve and come about when wage norms get out of line with supply conditions. At any given initial excess demand for labor, a rise in the growth of wage norms or a deterioration in supply conditions—caused by a change in λ, $\dot{k} - \dot{s}$, or $\dot{p}_c^e - \dot{p}_v^e$—will set up an incipient rise in or an acceleration of inflation, the prevention of which requires an increase in unemployment relative to its earlier value. If and when the monetary authorities apply the necessary restrictive medicine, the actual unemployment rate will rise to match the increase in the natural rate. The second type of shift in the

49. In the United States, Germany, and the United Kingdom there is some evidence that the productivity trend in manufacturing (and in Germany for the total business sector) has recently risen back toward its pre-1973 rate (and in the case of the United States manufacturing possibly beyond). The measures of the productivity slowdown in the text table do not reflect this recent pickup.

natural rate of unemployment comes about through a *shift* in the Beveridge curve. An increasing mismatch between the distribution of job vacancies and the distribution of unemployment along occupational, regional, or industrial lines is one possibility. A deterioration in the mobility of labor is another possibility. A rise in the reservation price of labor, because of more generous unemployment compensation, is still a third. After a shift in the Beveridge curve, any given unemployment rate will imply a different degree of excess labor demand than previously. Even without a change in the growth of wage norms, in productivity growth, or in terms of trade, the natural rate of unemployment will change.[50] The two components to any change in the natural rate can be seen from a simple two-equation model. Let $U^*(B_0)$ equal the natural rate of unemployment in some base period, given a particular Beveridge curve (B_0):

$$(20) \qquad \dot{w}_t = a_1(U - U^*(B))_t + a_2\dot{p}_{-1} + a_3Z,$$

where

Z = all other elements of the wage equation, and

$$(21) \qquad \dot{p}_t = \dot{w}_t - \dot{x}_t,$$

where

$\dot{x}_t$ = trend productivity growth.

The natural rate, $\tilde{U}$, is that value of U, which when substituted in equation 20 keeps inflation from rising (or accelerating if $a_2 = 1.0$). A change in $\tilde{U}$ may occur either because of the interaction between wage aspirations and supply conditions, with a stable $U^*(B_0)$, or because $U^*(B)$ itself shifts.

If all changes in the natural rate of unemployment were of the first type—shifts along a given Beveridge curve—equation 20 could be translated into empirical form with the use of the following assumptions.

—In the short run, at least, changes in trend productivity growth are not matched by changes in wage norms.

—Expected inflation in both components of consumer prices, $\dot{p}_v$ and $(\dot{p}_c - \dot{p}_v)$, is based on some form of adaptive expectations.

—In the long run, value-added prices will have to rise proportionately

50. The term *natural rate* is used loosely here. If the coefficient of nominal wages on inflation in the wage equation is less than 1.0 and if unemployment is maintained at its previous level, the appearance of excess wage aspirations or any upward shift in the Beveridge curve will lead to a rise in but not an acceleration of inflation.

with standard unit labor costs (adjusted where appropriate to reflect the fact that if the elasticity of factor substitution is less than 1.0, prices will rise with the *marginal* unit labor costs that will increase at a slightly slower rate than average unit labor costs). A standard augmented Phillips curve could then be used with unemployment as the "slack" variable. Changes in the constant, as evidenced by coefficients on dummy variables, could be interpreted as changes in the growth of wage norms or aspirations. Using the third assumption about price formation, it would be possible to identify changes in the rate of unemployment that would be needed to keep inflation constant, given the actually experienced changes in the growth of productivity, in terms of trade, and in wage norms. Even if the natural rate was changing over time, as wage aspirations changed relative to productivity growth, the actual unemployment rate would still be the appropriate variable for measuring the excess demand for labor, x_t.

In fact, the assumption that reported unemployment rates have remained a good measure of excess labor demand is unwarranted. There is widespread evidence that Beveridge curves have shifted up in Europe (and the United States) over the past several decades.[51] A central problem in formulating empirical wage equations, therefore, is how to measure the slack variable—the excess demand for labor, x_t. In what follows I estimate wage equations based on several alternative measures of x_t and compare results.

Measuring the Slack Variable: The Gap

In the past Robert Gordon and I have used the ratio of actual output to trend output ($Q/Q^* = \hat{q}$) as a measure.[52] The conceptual justification for this measure is that over long periods of time actual output will gravitate toward a level consistent with the natural rate, while in the short and medium run, cyclical deviations can and will occur. Thus as a measure of labor market slack, the output ratio has the advantage that it takes into account shifts in the Beveridge curve; it does not treat as an increase in excess labor supply a rise in unemployment that matches a rise in the Beveridge curve. On the other hand, to the extent output ultimately gravitates to its "natural" level, the output ratio has the

51. See the evidence cited in the paper by Robert Flanagan in this volume.
52. Gordon, "Wage-Price Dynamics and the Manufacturing Output Gap"; and Schultze, "Microeconomic Efficiency and Nominal Wage Stickiness."

disadvantage that it also tends to filter out from the slack variable other changes in $\tilde{U}$ beyond those associated with changes in $U^*(B)$. Yet those changes should be allowed to remain in the slack variable and to influence wages. A rise in this component of the natural rate occurs precisely because of the necessity to create additional labor market slack in order to moderate the inflationary effect of any increase in the growth of wage aspirations relative to supply conditions in the economy. As will be shown, the advantages of using $\hat{q}$ appear to outweigh its disadvantages.

For the 1960s and 1970s the trend output required to measure the gap ($\hat{q}$) can be approximated by running a trend through actual GNP at points of high employment (Gordon) or, almost equivalently, by using a long-term centered moving average of the logarithms of actual GNP (Schultze).

The problem is what to do after 1979 or 1980. Gordon and I, in our earlier works, extrapolated the trend of the 1970s. But by 1985 this generates very large negative "gaps" in all the European countries.[53] It assumes that none of the slowdown in output growth since 1979, relative to the 1970s, incorporated a slowdown in the growth rate of potential GNP. This is an excessively strong assumption on which to base a measure of economic slack. I have, therefore, constructed an alternative and more conservative measure of the gap. It is based on the assumption that over longer periods of time business firms will tend to adjust their capital stock to their own assessment of the sustainable or natural output level. In the absence of direct evidence on the time path of the natural unemployment rate or the natural output level, this assumption—imperfect as it is—seemed preferable to any other alternative. Starting from this point, a measure of potential or natural output for the nonfarm business sector (excluding housing) was constructed as follows.

—Through 1976 potential output was measured by a nine-year centered moving average of the natural logs of actual output.

—Trend movements through 1980 in the capital-output ratio were identified from a regression (which allowed for a break in the trend in the mid-1970s, so as to pick up the decline in capital productivity then appearing in many countries).[54]

—Natural output was extrapolated from 1976 to 1985 on the basis of

53. For GDP originating in the nonfarm business sector, the extrapolated measures of potential imply, for example, that in 1985 Germany and France were operating at a gap of 8 and 10 percent, respectively (with the gap set equal to zero in 1965 to 1979).

54. The regression also included a cyclical term, based on capacity utilization surveys, to try to keep the trend coefficient free of cyclical influence.

Table 4. *Output Ratio,* $\hat{q}$, *for Nonfarm Business Sector (Excluding Housing), Selected Years, 1978–85*[a]
Percent

Country	1978	1980	1982	1983	1984	1985
Germany	−0.6	0.3	−6.5	−7.2	−6.0	−4.2
France	−0.4	−1.0	−3.5	−4.0	−4.0	−4.2
Italy	−2.0	2.7	−3.1	−6.9	−5.8	−5.3
United Kingdom	1.4	−4.9	−6.0	−2.8	−1.7	1.2
United States	1.8	−3.6	−9.9	−8.2	−3.4	−3.2

Source: Author's calculations.
a. $\hat{q}$ is expressed as $100(Q/Q^* - 1)$.

movements in the business capital stock adjusted for the pre-1980 trend in the capital-output ratio.[55]

The resulting measures of the gap, $\hat{q}$ (expressed as percentage deviations from a 1965–79 average, adjusted to exclude the deep recession year 1975), are given in table 4. Since the growth of the capital stock slowed significantly in all countries, especially after 1980 or 1981, these measures show a substantially smaller negative gap in recent years than do those based on an extrapolation of pre-1980 trends in potential output.

In all four European countries a logarithmic version of $\hat{q}$ gave results in wage equations that were superior to the linear versions in terms of goodness of fit. The log version of $\hat{q}$ was constructed to have the same characteristic as an unemployment rate: high levels of activity are represented by low values of the variable. It was defined as ln $(-\hat{q} + Z)$, where Z was chosen to make the lowest historical value of the variable $(-\hat{q} + Z)$ equal to 2.0, and is labeled ln $F(\hat{q})$.

THE UNEMPLOYMENT RATE. Two equations were developed with unemployment as the slack variable. The first simply uses the unemployment rate itself as a measure of labor market conditions.[56] For the reasons indicated earlier, however, the raw unemployment rate will not be the appropriate measure of labor market slack if the Beveridge curve has

55. A relatively small adjustment was also made to take account of changes in the trend of average weekly working hours. It was assumed that 25 percent of any such changes also appeared as changes in average hours of capital utilization. This adjustment slightly raised the growth of German potential through 1984 and then lowered it in 1985 to reflect the reduction in hours obtained after the 1984 German metal workers' strike. In France the adjustment slightly lowered potential output to reflect the 1981–82 "Auroux" laws that shortened the work week. See Jeffrey Sachs and Charles Wyplosz, "The Economic Consequences of President Mitterrand," *Economic Policy*, no. 2 (April 1986), pp. 271–72.

56. The unemployment rate used in this equation was the OECD standardized rate. See *OECD Economic Outlook*, no. 40 (December 1986), p. 167, and earlier issues.

shifted significantly over time. A second alternative, therefore, adds a time trend to the equation with unemployment, as a means of picking up a tendency for the excess demand for labor to increase at any given unemployment rate. Since there is little evidence that the Beveridge curve was shifting outward in the 1960s, the time trend began in 1970.

HYSTERESIS VARIABLES. Hysteresis occurs if the downward effect of unemployment on wages dissipates as the unemployment persists.[57] If the authorities misdiagnose hysteresis as a rise in the natural rate, and if they keep subjecting the economy to downward nominal pressure, the unemployment rate will rise over time in response to a one-time downward shock.

In measuring the hysteresis component of a wage equation, start with the standard formulation:

$$(22) \qquad \dot{w} = a_0 + a_1(U - U^*) + a_2 Z,$$

where

U^* = the level of unemployment, deviations from which generate downward pressure on wages

Z = all the other elements in the equation.

Following Gordon, suppose U^* itself is a weighted average of some natural rate, U^N (invariant to the actual level of unemployment), and $\widetilde{U}$ a moving average of recent past unemployment.[58] Then

$$(23) \qquad U^* = (1 - b)U^N + b\widetilde{U}$$

and

$$\dot{w} = (a_0 + (1 - b)U^N) + a_1 U - a_1 b\widetilde{U}$$

$$\dot{w} = \alpha + a_1 U - a_1 b\widetilde{U} + a_2 Z,$$

---

57. Hysteresis could occur for several reasons. One arises from the insider-outsider phenomenon analyzed by Lindbeck and Snower, "Wage Setting, Unemployment, and Insider-Outsider Relations," and "Efficiency Wages versus Insiders and Outsiders"; and by Blanchard and Summers, "Hysteresis and the European Unemployment Problem." "Inside" employed members of a union (or other work group with implicit bargaining power) do not take into account the welfare of the "outside" unemployed. As unemployment increases, the outsiders lose influence, and the fact of their unemployment and their willingness to work at reduced wages has no effect (or an attenuated one) on explicit or implicit wage bargaining. Alternatively, hysteresis might arise because the matrix of worker skills and work habits deteriorate. See Richard Layard and Stephen Nickell, "The Performance of the British Labour Market," paper presented at the Conference on the British Economy, Sussex, May 18–21, 1986.

58. This is the formulation used by Robert J. Gordon, "Productivity, Wages, and

where α includes the stable U^N and b is the hysteresis coefficient. If b_1 equals 1.0, there is perfect hysteresis. Initially an unemployment-raising shock will moderate wage demands, but as the moving average $\widetilde{U}$ catches up to the actual level of U, the new level of unemployment has no greater downward force on wages than the initial lower level of unemployment. To capture the hysteresis phenomenon, a three-year moving average of past unemployment, $U3_{-1}$, was entered into the equation. If the coefficients are of opposite signs (and they are), their ratio determines the size of the hysteresis coefficient.

Four basic formulations of the slack variable, x_t, were thus employed in the empirical work:

—$\hat{q}$: the gap (extrapolated from 1976 with changes in the business capital stock, adjusted for the trend in the capital-output rate);

—U: unemployment;

—U, $TIME70$: unemployment plus a time trend beginning in 1970; and

—U, $U3_{-1}$: unemployment plus a lagged three-term moving average of unemployment.

Empirical Formulation

As noted earlier in connection with the discussion of the wage gap, the Commission of the European Communities has developed a series of input, output, and factor share data for the nonfarm business sector in four European countries, the United States, and Japan. Those data were the basis for most of the time series used here. Average effective wages for the total nonfarm business sector were derived by dividing employee compensation by total employee hours worked.[59] The price of value added (p_v) is the implicit deflator for the GDP originating in the nonfarm business sector, derived by the Commission from national accounts data. It was necessary to update the Commission estimates for 1985, and in some cases for earlier years, with sources and methods outlined in the data appendix. Consumer prices (P_c) are taken from the

---

Prices Inside and Outside of Manufacturing in the U.S., Japan, and Europe,'' Working Paper 2070 (Cambridge, Mass: NBER, November 1986). Gordon applies this approach to $\hat{q}$ instead of U.

59. The Commission used the U.S. Bureau of Labor Statistics series of average hours worked in manufacturing in each of the four countries and applied it to the total business economy.

national account consumption deflators. The unemployment rates, as noted earlier, are the OECD standardized rates.

The wage equations incorporate a simple relationship between wage inflation and past price inflation. In addition, a set of dummies is used, specific to each country, to capture changes in wage norms. As will be shown, the coefficients of wages on past price inflation did not equal unity. Changes in the growth rate of wage norms, therefore, may also capture any discrete shifts that occur in response to large and sustained changes in inflation.

The final form of regression equations for the first alternative (using $\hat{q}$ or its log transformation) is

$$(24) \qquad \dot{w} = a_0 + a_{11}F(\hat{q}) + a_{12}F(\hat{q})_{(-1)} + a_2 \dot{p}_{v(-1)}$$
$$+ a_3(\dot{p}_c - \dot{p}_v) + \Sigma a_{4i}D_i + u_t.$$

The results are shown in table 5. Only in Germany was the coefficient on the unlagged value of $F(\hat{q})$ significant; except in Germany, therefore, the variable was dropped in fitting the regressions. In the United Kingdom both $F(\hat{q})_{-1}$ and $F(\hat{q})_{-2}$ were highly significant, and in table 5 the sum of these two coefficients is shown. The dummy variables are denoted by descriptive numerals that indicate the period over which they take on the value of 1.0. Thus $D6785$ takes on the value of zero through 1966 and 1.0 thereafter.[60] Regressions were fit over the years 1965–85.

Some Characteristics of the Wage Equations

In Germany, the United Kingdom, Italy, and the United States the coefficients on prior inflation in the value-added price index are significantly less than 1.0. In the United Kingdom the coefficient was effectively zero, and in Italy it was small. In contrast to these results, a number of other studies have found that nominal wages in Europe adjust relatively

---

60. In addition, a dummy, $D77$, was included for the United Kingdom to take into account the effect of that year's successful incomes policy, and a dummy, $D82$, was added to the French equation to reflect the effect of the very large increase in minimum wages enacted in the first year of the Mitterrand presidency. These dummies are not shown separately. There was a very large positive error in the Italian wage equation in 1973. This outlying observation clearly affected the values assigned to the coefficients. In fitting this and other versions of the Italian wage equation, I therefore excluded the year 1973.

Table 5. Regressions Explaining Nominal Wage Increases, Total Nonfarm Business Sector, 1965–85[a]

Item	Germany (log of $\hat{q}$)		France (log of $\hat{q}$)		Italy (log of $\hat{q}$)		United Kingdom (log of $\hat{q}$)		United States ($\hat{q}$)	
Coefficients on										
$F(\hat{q})$[b]	-4.4	(7.9)	-6.7	(10.8)	-6.1	(5.8)	-12.9	(10.8)	0.29	(6.0)
$\dot{p}_v(-1)$	0.53	(3.0)	0.69	(7.8)	0.39	(4.2)		c	0.60	(13.7)
$(\dot{p}_c - \dot{p}_v)_{-1}$	0.24	(1.1)	0.58	(3.2)	0.62	(2.2)	0.39	(2.0)	0.65	(4.2)
Dummies[d]	7.5	(6.3) D6970	10.9	(9.7) D68	4.1	(2.7) D7085	8.3	(11.9) D7085	1.95	(5.1) D6785
	-1.2	(2.2) D7985	3.9	(5.0) D6985	-4.2	(2.5) D8485	-5.6	(5.1) D8485	-1.73	(3.5) D8385
			-2.1	(2.6) D8485						
$\bar{R}^2$	0.91		0.95		0.92		0.95		0.94	
Standard error	1.07		0.95		1.82		1.31		0.56	
ρ	⋯		⋯		⋯		⋯		-0.54	
Durbin-Watson	2.05		1.87		2.31		1.93		⋯	

Source: Author's calculations.

a. Dependent variable: $\dot{w}$ (percent); annual change in compensation per hour. The numbers in parentheses are t-statistics.

b. Sum of coefficients on $F(\hat{q})$ and $F(\hat{q})_{-1}$ for Germany, and for $F(\hat{q})_{-1}$ in the United Kingdom. For other countries, the value shown is the coefficient on $F(\hat{q})_{-1}$.

c. Coefficient insignificant; the regression was refit without the variable.

d. Numerals after dummies denote year in which dummy is 1.0; otherwise zero. The D6970 dummy (for Germany) takes on the value of 0.5 in 1969 and 1.0 in 1970; additional dummies: D82 in France to take account of the large legislated rise in 1981; D77 in the United Kingdom to take account of that year's successful incomes policy. In the case of Italy, the year 1973 was excluded from the regression.

quickly and fully to prior inflation,[61] substantially faster than is the case in the United States. Indeed, this finding gave rise to the now conventional proposition that real wages are more rigid in Europe than they are in the United States. Some of the work that shows very high wage indexing in Europe enters the current period's inflation (alone or together with lagged inflation) as a variable in the wage equation.[62] However, in an earlier study that covered manufacturing wages in Germany, Italy, Sweden, the United Kingdom, and the United States, I found that a large fraction of current year wage increases is passed through into current year prices, and this fraction is larger in Europe than in the United States. As a consequence, entering current year inflation as a dependent variable into a wage equation will substantially bias up the coefficient on that variable since it will reflect a large current feedback of wages on prices. This bias will be larger in the European countries.

To investigate whether the formulation used in equation 24 might have biased downward the coefficient on value-added inflation, I tried a number of experiments. I added $\dot{p}_{v(-2)}$ to the equation. I also instrumented $\dot{p}_v$ and entered it without a lag in a two-stage least squares (TSLS) regression.[63] The results are shown in table 6. In Germany, France, and Italy, the coefficients on unlagged inflation are higher, but except in Italy only modestly so. And even in Italy the coefficient remains well below 1.0.

For Germany, Italy, and the United Kingdom, the TSLS equations with the unlagged value of $\dot{p}_v$ gave higher $\bar{R}^2$; for France and the United States, the $\bar{R}^2$ was lower. (Appendix table A-1 shows some main features of the TSLS equations.) On the other hand, except for Italy the stability of the TSLS coefficients tended to be somewhat inferior to that of the original OLS (ordinary least squares) equation.

---

61. Examples are Branson and Rotemberg, "International Adjustment with Wage Rigidity"; Sachs, "Real Wages and Unemployment"; Grubb and others, "Wages, Unemployment, and Incomes Policies"; and Coe, "Nominal Wages, the NAIRU and Wage Flexibility." In "Wage-Price Dynamics and the Manufacturing Output Gap," Gordon found widely differing coefficients on lagged $\dot{p}_v$ in eleven European countries, but a coefficient of close to 1.0 when, in that paper and a more recent one, he uses average data for all European countries.

62. Examples are Sachs, "Real Wages and Unemployment"; Grubb and others, "Wages, Unemployment, and Incomes Policies"; and Coe, "Nominal Wages, the NAIRU and Wage Flexibility."

63. The instruments were value-added inflation lagged once and twice, the lagged change in the real exchange rate, and all the other variables in the wage equations.

Table 6. *Coefficients on Inflation in Alternative Wage Equations*[a]

Country	Inflation term		
	$\dot{p}_{v\,(-1)}$	$[\dot{p}_{v\,(-1)}, \dot{p}_{(v\,(-2)}]^{b}$	$\dot{p}_{v(TSLS)}{}^{c}$
Germany	0.53	0.56	0.61
France	0.69	0.65	0.79
Italy	0.39	0.38	0.57
United Kingdom	. . .	0.04	0.12
United States	0.60	0.66	0.61

Source: Author's calculations.
a. The equations were the same as shown in table 5 except for the inflation term.
b. Values in the column are the sums of coefficients on $\dot{p}_{v(-1)}$ and $\dot{p}_{v(-2)}$.
c. An equation with both $\dot{p}_v$ and $\dot{p}_{v(-1)}$ performed no better, and showed a sum of coefficients no higher than those shown here.

In the case of Italy the existence of the *scala mobile* indexing system suggests that the TSLS equation, with contemporaneous values of $\dot{p}_v$, is the preferred version. And the goodness of fit of that version is substantially better in Italy. I use it later in estimating the natural rate of output and unemployment.

With respect to the terms of trade variables $(\dot{p}_c - \dot{p}_v)$, I reasoned that in Italy, given the scala mobile, it ought to be entered contemporaneously as an exogenous variable in the TSLS equations. In other countries, even in the TSLS equations, I continued to enter this variable with a lag on grounds that where no formal indexing exists the "surprise" component of inflation should not be entered contemporaneously, and that $\dot{p}_c - \dot{p}_v$ was unlikely to be well forecast in advance. In fact, however, in none of the TSLS equations does the $\dot{p}_c - \dot{p}_v$ term perform well.

The less than unitary elasticity of wage inflation on prior price inflation in the various equations does not imply that over long periods of time inflation erodes real wages. There is an allowance for "normal" inflation in the constant. Over the longer run a substantial and sustained increase in inflation will generate a new set of nominal wage norms captured in the equations by a shift in the constant.

As noted at the beginning of this paper, a widely documented wage explosion occurred in many European countries at the end of the 1960s. It shows up in the coefficients on the dummy variables in the equations. In Germany the explosion was a one-time phenomenon. There were extra-large wage increases in 1969 and 1970, but—measured in terms of rates of change—wage norms shifted back down again. In all other countries the growth rate of wage aspirations shifted up and stayed up during the 1970s. Moreover, the growth rate of wage aspirations did not quickly adjust downward in response to the fall in productivity growth that occurred in all countries after 1973. Beginning in 1979, however, first in Germany and later in other countries, norms shifted down again, presumably under the pressure of sustained unemployment and lower inflation.

Alternative Formulation of the Wage Equation

I compared the major features of the wage equations using $\hat{q}$ with the three formulations using unemployment, U. The first alternative simply repeats the earlier equations, substituting U for $\hat{q}$. The second adds a time trend to allow for an upwardly shifting Beveridge curve. The third is the hysteresis equation in which the unemployment variable takes the form:

$$(25) \qquad a_1 U - ba_1 U3_{-1},$$

where

$U3$ = a three-term moving average of past unemployment rates
b = the hysteresis coefficient.

As was the case with the $\hat{q}$ equation, the lags were longer in the United Kingdom, and the hysteresis regression was fitted with U_{-1} and $U3_{-2}$. The results are shown in table 7. For convenience the table repeats the key coefficients for the $\hat{q}$ form of the equation.[64]

The $\hat{q}$ version gives better regression statistics than does the alternative formulation. Outside of the United States the time trend takes on a significant positive value in all countries, suggesting an upward shifting of the Beveridge curve. As I pointed out earlier, one would expect—on conceptual grounds—that the $\hat{q}$ version would be superior to a formulation using unemployment, if a large part of the change in the natural rate of unemployment arose from shifts in the Beveridge curve. The superiority of the $\hat{q}$ formulation is at least weak evidence pointing toward the importance of such shifts.

64. Unemployment tends to lag behind $\hat{q}$ (see table 9 and the accompanying text). Thus U_t was substituted for $\hat{q}_{(-1)}$. In Germany, as noted earlier, the coefficients on both $F(\hat{q})$ and $F(\hat{q})_{(-1)}$ are significant and of the same sign. But if U_t and $U_{(-1)}$ are substituted for the $F(\hat{q})$ variable, the coefficient on $U_{(-1)}$ takes on the opposite sign to the coefficient on U_t. This could signal either hysteresis or a rising natural rate. In order to show the first two unemployment regressions clean of these phenomena, $U_{(-1)}$ was dropped. For the same reason, in the United Kingdom the first two unemployment equations contain only $U_{(-1)}$.

Table 7. *Comparison of Regression Equations with Alternative Measures of Labor Market Pressure, Total Nonfarm Business Sector, 1965–85*[a]

Item	Regression with $\hat{q}$	Regression with unemployment — Unemployment only	Regression with unemployment — Unemployment and time	Regression with unemployment — Hysteresis equation
Germany				
Coefficients on				
$\dot{p}_{w(-1)}$	0.53 (3.0)	0.48 (1.4)	0.46 (1.4)	1.32 (4.9)
$(\dot{p}_c - \dot{p}_v)_{-1}$	0.24 (1.1)	0.24 (0.6)	0.03 (0.1)	0.66 (2.0)
TIME	...	...	0.43 (1.6)	...
Hysteresis coefficient	...	...	...	0.87 (3.0)
Dummies	7.5 (6.3) D6970	7.5 (3.4) D6970	8.1 (3.8) D6970	9.0 (5.2) D6970
	−1.2 (2.2) D7985			
$\bar{R}^2$	0.91	0.71	0.73	0.78
Standard error	1.07	1.90	1.82	1.67
ρ	...	0.44	0.38	−0.11
Durbin-Watson	2.05	...	...	...
France				
Coefficients on				
$\dot{p}_{w(-1)}$	0.69 (7.8)	1.09 (3.8)	0.81 (3.3)	1.28 (3.9)
$(\dot{p}_c - \dot{p}_v)_{-1}$	0.58 (3.2)	1.14 (3.3)	1.25 (3.8)	1.40 (3.7)
TIME	...	...	1.76 (3.1)	...
Hysteresis coefficient[b]	...	...	...	0.83 (1.1)
Dummies	10.9 (9.7) D68	9.2 (4.4) D68	12.5 (5.5) D68	11.0 (4.4) D68
	3.9 (5.0) D6985		1.8 (1.0) D6985	
	−2.1 (2.6) D8485			
$\bar{R}^2$	0.95	0.73	0.82	0.73
Standard error	0.95	2.27	1.85	2.25
ρ	...	0.56	0.20	0.59
Durbin-Watson	1.87	...	...	...
Italy				
Coefficients on				
$\dot{p}_{w(-1)}$	0.39 (4.2)	0.40 (2.2)	[c]	0.49 (3.1)
$(\dot{p}_c - \dot{p}_v)_{-1}$	0.62 (2.2)	1.22 (2.8)	0.74 (1.6)	0.76 (1.8)
TIME	...	...	1.46 (2.4)	...

Item	(1)	(2)	(3)	(4)
Hysteresis coefficient	4.1 (2.7)	8.1 (3.6)	5.7 (2.1)	1.01 (2.4)
Dummies	−4.2 (2.5) D7085; … D8485	−4.8 (1.4) D7085; … D8485	… (2.1) (2.1)	5.1 (2.2) D7085; −7.5 (2.4) D8485
$\bar{R}^2$	0.92	0.77	0.78	0.83
Standard error	1.82	3.00	2.93	2.58
ρ	…	…	…	…
Durbin-Watson	2.31	1.90	1.90	2.16

United Kingdom

Item	(1)	(2)	(3)	(4)
Coefficients on				
$\dot{p}_{x(-1)}$	0.39 (2.0)	0.55 (4.9)	0.19 (2.1)	0.45 (4.5)
$(\dot{p}_c - \dot{p}_v)_{-1}$	c	1.74 (5.8)	1.57 (9.6)	1.83 (7.7)
TIME			1.01 (5.5)	
Hysteresis coefficient[b]	8.3 (11.9); −5.6 (5.1)	7.3 (5.3)	5.69 (7.3)	1.06 (3.1)
Dummies[b]	D7085 D8485	D7085	D7085	6.75 (6.2) D7085; −6.25 (2.1) D8485
$\bar{R}^2$	0.95	0.79	0.93	0.87
Standard error	1.31	2.78	1.62	2.23
ρ	…	−0.62	−0.81	−0.67
Durbin-Watson	1.93	…	…	…

United States

Item	Regression with $\hat{q}$	Unemployment only[d]
Coefficients on		
$\dot{p}_{x(-1)}$	0.60 (13.7)	0.85 (4.9)
$(\dot{p}_c - \dot{p}_v)_{-1}$	0.65 (4.2)	1.29 (6.1)
TIME	…	…
Dummies	1.95 (5.1) D6785; −1.73 (3.5) D8385	1.51 (2.2) D6785; −2.31 (2.4) D8385
$\bar{R}^2$	0.94	0.87
Standard error	0.56	0.86
ρ	−0.54	−0.31
Durbin-Watson	…	…

Source: Author's calculations.

a. The numbers in parentheses are t-statistics. Whenever a dummy variable had a t-statistic of less than 1.0, it was dropped and the equation refitted without it.

b. Additional dummies: D82 in France, D77 in the United Kingdom. See note 60 in text.

c. Insignificant; not used in regression.

d. In the United States neither the time trend nor the hysteresis coefficient was even close to significance.

In Germany, the United Kingdom, and Italy the hysteresis equation does much better than the "raw" unemployment equation, and the hysteresis coefficient is close to 1.0. But there is a major problem in determining the extent to which the results truly indicate the existence of hysteresis. The rise in European unemployment over the past fifteen years has been virtually monotonic. There have been very few years out of the past fifteen in which the unemployment rate has not risen in every European country. If, over the same period, the natural unemployment rate has also been rising more or less monotonically because of an upward shifting Beveridge curve, a moving average of past unemployment will pick up a substantial positive coefficient in a wage equation. The ratio of the coefficients on current and lagged unemployment would tend to be quite high, but this would not indicate the presence of hysteresis. If unemployment had fluctuated greatly over the period, it would be possible, with the test I have employed, to distinguish hysteresis from a rising natural rate. But under the conditions that have prevailed in Europe over the past fifteen years, such a distinction may be impossible to make.[65]

When a lagged moving average of the log of $\hat{q}$ was added to the $\hat{q}$ version of the equations, its coefficient did not provide any support for existence of hysteresis in three of the four European countries. In Germany there was only weak evidence for some hysteresis—a coefficient of 0.5 (with a t-statistic of 2.2).[66] This tends to strengthen the view that the hysteresis variable in the unemployment equations may be a proxy for a rising natural rate of unemployment. Nevertheless, indirect evidence presented later suggests the possibility of hysteresis in the United Kingdom.

In all but a few of the regressions using unemployment, a TSLS regression with an unlagged inflation term gave higher $\bar{R}^2$ than the OLS version with lagged inflation reported in table 7, in a number of cases substantially higher. But in no case is the goodness of fit superior to the regression with $\hat{q}$. Moreover, the coefficients on variables other than inflation are often erratic. With one exception, the $(\dot{p}_c - \dot{p}_v)$ terms became insignificant in all the European equations; all of the time

65. This point was originally made by Charles Bean in his discussion of a draft of this paper.
66. Gordon also finds that in equations using a gap variable the evidence for hysteresis in European wage determination is very weak. See "Productivity, Wages, and Prices."

variables become insignificant; and, except for Italy, the magnitude and significance of the hysteresis coefficient declined (see appendix table A-1).

Excess Wage Demands and the Natural Rate of Output

Using the coefficients from the $\hat{q}$ version of the wage equations, I have calculated the level of $\hat{q}$ at which wage inflation would equal the sum of the current trend increase in productivity, $\dot{x}$, and the 1985 rate of inflation in value-added prices. It is, therefore, the value of $\hat{q}$ that, when entered into the wage equation, satisfies the following conditions:

$$(26) \qquad \dot{w} - \dot{p}_{v1985} - \dot{x} = 0.$$

That value of $\hat{q}$ can be labeled the natural rate of output, $\hat{q}^N$. When $\hat{q}$ equals $\hat{q}^N$, there are no forces in the labor market tending to push inflation up or down. (Since the coefficient on $\dot{p}_v$ in the wage equation is less than 1.0 in all countries, the value of $\hat{q}^N$ varies positively with the rate of inflation.)

The determination of the current trend rate of productivity growth, $\dot{x}$, is critical in estimating the current value of the natural rates of output and unemployment. In France and Italy the recent trend is statistically easy to determine using equation 5. In Germany and the United Kingdom the problem is much more complicated. The recent course of German productivity growth in the nonfarm business sector is as follows (in percent a year): 1978, 4.4; 1979, 4.1; 1980, 1.5; 1981, 1.8; 1982, 1.2; 1983, 4.0; 1984, 3.0; 1985, 4.2; 1986, 2.4.[67]

Productivity growth declined sharply in 1980–82 and then rose again. In 1985 and 1986 average working hours fell as the agreement for shorter hours negotiated with the metal workers union in 1984 spread through the economy. Some of the rise in productivity in 1985 and 1986 may have been a one-time response to that development. To that extent the upward shift should not be included in estimating the trend.[68]

67. There is a statistically significant reduction in the trend growth of productivity in France after 1978 and a one-time upward shift in the level in 1982, perhaps an adjustment to the legislated reduction in average working hours. In Italy, after a reduction in the trend following 1973, there are no statistically discernible changes in trend or level.

68. For purposes of analyzing German productivity changes through 1986, the basic data set of the Commission of the European Communities was extended with the data on total GNP from *OECD Economic Outlook*, no. 41 (June 1987), pp. 27, 76 (on the

If the reduction in average working hours is ignored in calculating productivity in 1985 and 1986, the growth rates for those two years were 2.7 and 1.8, respectively. For purposes of the analysis I conservatively took account of only one-third of the 1985 and 1986 decline in average working hours in calculating productivity growth. I allow in the productivity equation for a decline in trend productivity growth after 1979 and a speedup after 1982 that is partly a one-time upward shift in the level of productivity and partly a recovery in the trend rate of growth. The resulting estimate of the current trend growth in hourly productivity is 2.8 percent a year.

There is a similar problem in the United Kingdom. Productivity growth rose sharply after 1980, dropped in 1984, and then partially recovered. In the United Kingdom, however, there is a substantial lag in adjusting labor input to changes in output. Inspection of the raw data can be misleading with respect to judging trends. On purely statistical grounds, a shift in the constant of the productivity equation after 1980, presumably reflecting the one-time effect of the closing of inefficient facilities, gives better results than the assumption of a change in trend. But this is slim grounds for choice, and accepting the one-time shift implied a very pessimistic value for the current trend of productivity growth in the United Kingdom. I chose to ignore the shift in the constant and kept a stable trend growth since 1974, at a 2.15 percent rate.

One final problem had to be handled before estimating the natural rate of output, $\hat{q}^N$. The German wage equation substantially underestimated the 1984 and 1985 wage increases. This may be partly due to the special nature of the metal workers' agreement of 1984, which reduced hours of work and raised hourly pay rates in 1985. Nevertheless, so as not to overestimate the value of $\hat{q}^N$, and the amount of slack in the German economy, I used the TSLS equation; it has a smaller underestimate in 1984 and 1985 and predicted a 1986 hourly compensation increase of 4.6 percent, which seems about right. As indicated earlier, the TSLS Italian equation, with the contemporaneous value of $\dot{p}_v$, is the preferred version, and it was used to estimate the Italian $\hat{q}^N$.[69]

---

basis of how changes in those data related to changes in the corresponding business sector data in recent years). Changes in aggregate hours worked in the business sector come from data furnished by the German Institut für Arbeitsmarkt und Berufsforschung and the staff of the OECD.

69. In both the German and Italian TSLS equations the coefficient on the $\dot{p}_c - \dot{p}_v$ variable was very small, insignificant, and in Germany had the "wrong" sign. The

On the basis of these judgments, the value of $\hat{q}^N$ was calculated. The resultant estimates (in percent) are the output analogs of the "natural rate" of unemployment, except that the coefficients of wage inflation on price inflation are less than 1.0. Consequently, when $\hat{q}$ exceeds $\hat{q}^N$ the level of inflation will rise but will not continually accelerate:[70]

	Germany	France	Italy	United Kingdom
$\hat{q}$, 1985	−4.2	−4.2	−5.3	1.2
$\hat{q}^N$, 1985, steady state	−2.3	−1.5	−2.4	−1.9
Difference	1.9	2.7	2.9	−3.1

According to these calculations there is some room in the three continental countries for expansion in demand and output relative to potential without running into an inflationary barrier.[71] In the United Kingdom, on the other hand, the equations suggest that at 1985 levels of the gap, wage aspirations are such as to lead to a rise in inflation or to an increase in real wages in excess of trend productivity growth.

It is hard to accept that the 13 percent unemployment rate in the United Kingdom is exerting no downward pressure on ex ante real wage bargains. Yet a similar calculation from the unemployment rate equation (including the time trend) gives approximately the same result. Moreover, in 1985 and 1986 wage inflation in the United Kingdom rose above the 1984 level.

The wage equation does not produce a reasonable result for the natural rate of output in the United States. It implies that at 1985 levels of $\hat{q}$ (and an unemployment rate of 7.1 percent), U.S. wage increases were somewhat excessive relative to 1985 price inflation and productivity growth, portending a rise in domestically generated inflation. But while the U.S. wage equation tracks wages quite well through 1984, it significantly overpredicts the rate of wage inflation in 1985 and 1986. And when fit through 1985 it forecasts a 0.8 percentage point rise in the 1986 rate of wage increase, whereas, in fact, the pace of wage increases moderated by almost 1 percentage point. The same pattern of overprediction occurs

---

equations were refit without it before estimating $\hat{q}^N$. The $\dot{p}_c - \dot{p}_v$ term was retained in the list of instruments for $\dot{p}_v$.

70. But as the earlier discussion made clear, persistent and sustained rises in inflation will eventually induce a rise in the growth rate of the nominal wage norm; utlimately, if $\hat{q}$ remains above $\hat{q}^N$, inflation will accelerate.

71. The estimated values of q^N from the OLS version of the German and Italian equations are −1.8 and −1.3, respectively. The estimated values of q^N for France and the United Kingdom in the TSLS version are −2.2 and −1.8, respectively.

Table 8. *Okun's Law Regressions, 1965–85*[a]

Item	Germany	France	Italy	United Kingdom
Independent variable: U(percent)				
Coefficients on				
$\hat{q}$, 1965–73	−0.26 (10.6)	−0.35 (6.1)	−0.19 (4.9)	−0.48 (7.4)
$\hat{q}$, 1974–85	−0.44 (4.0)	−0.35 ...	−0.19 ...	−0.48 ...
$\hat{q}$, 1981–85	−0.63 (6.0)	−0.51 (2.0)	−0.19 ...	−0.48 ...
TIME	0.26 (28.0)	0.40 (24.3)	0.16 (7.6)	b
D8185	...	...	1.22 (3.9)	...
$\bar{R}^2$	1.00	0.99	0.96	0.99
Standard error	0.17	0.22	0.33	0.40
ρ	−0.33	0.26	0.22	0.14

Source: Author's calculations.

a. Coefficients are the sum of terms in a three-period Almon lag beginning in the current period. The *t*-statistics (in parentheses) on the $\hat{q}$ term subsequent to 1973 give the significance of the difference between the coefficient for that period and the one for the prior period. For France the third $\hat{q}$ term is 1982–85.

b. Coefficients are *TIME* 1965–73, 0.15; *TIME* 1974–80, 0.36; *TIME* 1981–85, 1.31. The trend coefficients are dated from 1965 for Italy and from 1970 for Germany and France.

if the wage equation is refit with the U.S. Bureau of Labor Statistics series on compensation per hour in place of the wage index derived from the Commission data base. Approximately the same result emerges if unemployment is used as the slack variable instead of $\hat{q}$. Wage aspirations in the United States apparently continued to moderate in 1985 and 1986 in ways not captured by any of the formulations used thus far.

Unemployment

Through the use of Okun's law relating the unemployment rate to the gap between actual and potential GDP, it is possible to translate the "natural rate of output" $\hat{q}$ into an unemployment rate. Since the natural rate of unemployment has been rising, the equations relating U to $\hat{q}$ have a trend term in them. On the other hand, in Germany and France a given change in $\hat{q}$ now has a larger effect on U than it did in earlier years (see table 8). In estimating the unemployment that is implied by the "natural" output level, I have conservatively assumed that the trend rise in U relative to $\hat{q}$ continues for one more year after 1985. Actual and natural rates of unemployment for Germany, France, Italy, and the United Kingdom are then as follows:[72]

72. The relationship between the 1985 unemployment rate and the natural rate in each country is affected by the relatively long lag in the relationship between output

	Germany	France	Italy	United Kingdom
Actual rate				
1985	8.6	10.1	10.5	13.0
1986	8.3	10.3	n.a.	13.1
Natural rate	6.5	9.2	9.9	14.8

ACTUAL AND "NATURAL" UNEMPLOYMENT RATES: U.S. DEFINITIONS. The U.S. Bureau of Labor Statistics periodically publishes estimates of European unemployment rates adjusted to approximate U.S. definitions. Except for France, unemployment on U.S. concepts is lower than under the OECD "standardized" definition and dramatically so in Italy.[73] If it is assumed that the ratio between actual unemployment on OECD and U.S. definitions can be applied to estimates of natural unemployment, then the following can be derived (for 1985):

	Germany	France	Italy	United Kingdom
Actual unemployment rate				
OECD concept	8.6	10.1	10.5	13.0
U.S. concept	7.9	10.4	6.0	11.3
Natural unemployment rate				
U.S. concept	6.0	9.5	5.7	12.9

COMPONENTS OF THE RISE IN UNEMPLOYMENT SINCE 1968. Using the $\hat{q}$ equations, one can make a stab at estimating how much of the rise in the natural rate since the late 1960s represents a problem of excess wage aspirations. That part of the rise in the natural rate not attributable to excess wage aspirations presumably arose from changes in labor market conditions represented by an upward shift in the Beveridge curve.

On the assumption that in 1969 the growth of wage aspirations was in line with the growth of productivity and other supply conditions, I define

---

and unemployment. Thus, in Germany, $\hat{q}$ was improving between 1983 and 1985; if $\hat{q}$ stayed at its 1985 level, and one more year's updrift in U relative to $\hat{q}$ were allowed, the Okun's law equation would predict unemployment eventually falling to 7.8 percent (and by the second half of 1986 German unemployment was declining, only to have the decline interrupted by the growth slowdown in 1987).

73. See U.S. Bureau of Labor Statistics, *Monthly Labor Review*, vol. 110 (May 1987), p. 92; and *OECD Economic Outlook*, no. 40 (December 1986), p. 167. Starting in 1977, the Italian labor force survey included large numbers of persons enumerated as unemployed who reported that they had not sought work in the past thirty days. Under U.S. concepts these people would not be counted as unemployed. This may reflect a large number of people working irregularly in the "second economy" who previously held jobs in the primary economy.

excess wage aspirations to be the net balance of the shifts in the constant in the wage equations since that date (upward in the late 1960s, downward in the early 1980s)[74] plus the decline in productivity growth after 1973 (with sign reversed). Applying the coefficients on $\hat{q}$ from the wage equations, it is then possible to ask by how much $\hat{q}$ would have had to be lowered in 1985 to eliminate the net excess. The Okun's law equations are used to translate the required changes in $\hat{q}$ into unemployment rates. Since the coefficients on the inflation term in the wage equation are less than unity (very much so in the United Kingdom and Italy), some part of the shifts in the constant may reflect discrete adjustments of nominal norms to persistent changes in the rate of inflation. Fortunately, however, in all of the countries except Italy, the inflation rate in 1969—the base chosen for comparison—was not very different from inflation at the end point, 1985.

When this procedure is applied, the following results appear:

	Germany	France	Italy	United Kingdom
Total change in unemployment, 1969–85 (OECD definition)	7.7	7.8	4.9	9.9
Cyclical	2.1	0.9	0.6	0.0
Excess wage aspirations, net	0.7	1.7	0.6	0.9
Other (shifts in the Beveridge curve)	4.9	5.2	3.7	9.0

It appears that the largest part of the rise in European unemployment has been associated with upward shifting Beveridge curves. (If a negative cyclical component had been entered for the U.K. natural rate calculations, the shift in the U.K. Beveridge curve would have been even larger.)

If it is again assumed that a simple proportional adjustment can be applied, it is possible to estimate the level of unemployment, on U.S. concepts, that would prevail in Europe in 1985 in the absence of cyclical and excess wage components. Once again the actual rate of unemployment (shown in percent) is assumed to approximate the natural rate in 1969:

---

74. The one-time shifts in aspirations in Germany (1969–70) and France (1968) are not included, since my definition of excess wage norms relates to rates of growth in wages relative to rates of growth in prices and productivity.

	Germany	France	Italy	United Kingdom
Actual 1969	0.8	2.4	3.2	3.0
Natural rate 1985 (excluding excess wage components)	5.3	7.7	5.3	12.1

In the three continental countries the real puzzle may be not only why the outward shift of the Beveridge curve has been so large in the past fifteen years or so, but also why unemployment was so low in the 1960s and early 1970s.

For Germany, France, and the United Kingdom vacancy data are available from which a Beveridge curve can be directly fitted, with time trends or dummy variables to pick up shifts in the relationship between unemployment and vacancies. If the unemployment rate is directly fit against the inverse of the vacancy rate for 1970 to 1984, the vertical upward shift in the curves between 1970 and 1985, in terms of percentage points of unemployment, are Germany, 3.2, and United Kingdom, 9.8.[75] The directly estimated upward shift in the U.K. Beveridge curve is close to that estimated indirectly from the $\hat{q}$ variant of the wage equations, and the German direct estimate is 60 percent of the indirect.

In the case of France, changes in procedures for reporting job vacancies occurred in the early 1970s.[76] In any event, once a time trend or several dummy variables are introduced into the French equation, no significant relationship remains between vacancies and unemployment. For Italy data on vacancies were not available.

None of the research on unemployment-vacancy relationships in the United Kingdom suggests identifiable causes of a deterioration in labor market conditions that would produce anything like a 9 to 10 percentage point upward shift in the unemployment-vacancy curve.[77] In his paper in this volume, Robert Flanagan reviews the evidence for increasing

75. The equations were $U = f(1/V, 1/V_{-1}, TIME, DUMMIES)$, where U and V are the unemployment and vacancy rates, in percent. The period of fit was 1964–84. For the United Kingdom the time and dummy coefficients (and t-statistics) were: $TIME75$, 0.28 (5.0); $TIME81$, 1.35 (10.4); $S.E.E.$,0.30. For Germany the coefficients were; $D7584$, 1.60 (6.7); $TIME80$, 0.27 (1.9); $S.E.E.$,0.28.

76. Claude Thélot, "La Croissance du Chômage depuis Vingt Ans: Interprétations Macroéconomiques," Economie et Statistique, no. 183 (December 1985), p. 71.

77. See also Layard and Nickell, "Unemployment, Real Wages and Aggregate Demand," for further evidence on an increased mismatch in the United Kingdom and its absence elsewhere.

industrial and regional mismatches of unemployment and vacancies. He finds some evidence of an increased industrial mismatch in the United Kingdom in 1981 and 1982 and a rise in the interindustry dispersion of employment growth rates from 1979 to 1983. But the magnitudes of these changes do not seem nearly large enough to explain the steep rise in the U.K. Beveridge curve after 1980 and cannot at all explain its slower rise in the prior five or six years. In his paper Gary Burtless argues that a decreased search intensity, due to more generous unemployment benefits, cannot explain any substantial part of the rise in U.K. unemployment. Thus a major explanation of the U.K. unemployment phenomenon appears to be, by an elimination process, the phenomenon of hysteresis.

COMPARISONS WITH OTHER UNEMPLOYMENT ESTIMATES. In recent years a number of articles have tried to pin down the extent to which the natural unemployment rate has risen in European countries. Except for Germany, the estimates in this paper tend to be more "conservative" than those in most of the other studies (see table 9). Some of the differences may arise because of my relatively conservative estimates of the slack variable $\hat{q}$. Robert Gordon, for example, uses a conceptually similar variable, but one that takes on much larger negative values in recent years. He estimates a 1984 natural unemployment rate for an average of eleven European countries of 6.4 percent compared with an actual unemployment rate of 9.6 percent.[78] Differences may also stem from errors in the equations used in this paper to translate the gap, $\hat{q}$, into unemployment.

Use of wage equations and auxiliary relationships to infer something about the causes of the rise in unemployment can provide important insights into the problem. But the specific numerical results must obviously be used with great caution. The estimates of $\hat{q}^N$ are very sensitive to the value used for trend productivity growth. Given the sharp recent changes in productivity growth, identifying the prevailing trend is an uncertain business. As the earlier comparisons of alternative wage equations showed, the various coefficients of wages on the independent variables are quite sensitive to the particular specification used; this is especially true of the coefficient of wages on lagged inflation. And, while the $\hat{q}$ version of the wage equations outperforms the alternatives with unemployment, theoretical considerations suggest that $\hat{q}$ is not itself the structural measure of economic slack that is required for

78. Gordon, "Productivity, Wages, and Prices," table 1 and p. 46.

Table 9. *Alternative Estimates of the "Natural" Rate of Unemployment, 1979–87*

Country and year	Source	Estimate (percent)[a]	This paper (percent)	Actual rate (percent)[b]
Germany				
1979–82	Layard and Nickell	3.1	4.3	4.2
1981–83	Layard and others	4.8	5.0	6.1
1981–83	Coe	4.8, 7.7	5.0	6.1
1983–87	OECD	6.0	6.5[c]	8.6[d]
France				
1979–82	Layard and Nickell	7.2	6.8	6.9
1981–83	Layard and others	7.5	7.5	7.9
1981–83	Coe	3.8, 7.6	7.5	7.9
1983–87	OECD	6.0	9.2[c]	10.1[d]
Italy				
1981–83	Layard and others	7.4	9.0	9.0
1981–83	Coe	5.6, 6.6	9.0	9.0
1983–87	OECD	7.3	9.9[c]	10.5[d]
United Kingdom				
1979–82	Layard and Nickell	7.5	7.2	8.1
1981–83	Layard and others	9.9	9.9	11.2
1981–83	Coe	6.4, 8.5	9.9	11.2

Sources: P. R. G. Layard and S. J. Nickell, "Unemployment, Real Wages and Aggregate Demand in Europe, Japan and the U.S.," Discussion Paper 214 (London School of Economics, Centre for Labour Economics, March 1985), p. 66; Richard Layard and others, "Europe: The Case for Unsustainable Growth," in Olivier Blanchard, Rudiger Dornbusch, and Richard Layard, eds., *Restoring Europe's Prosperity: Macroeconomic Papers from the Centre for European Policy Studies* (MIT Press, 1986), p. 47; David T. Coe, "Nominal Wages, the NAIRU and Wage Flexibility," *OECD Economic Studies*, no. 5 (Autumn 1985), p. 113; and *OECD Economic Outlook*, no. 40 (December 1986), p. 30.

a. The natural rate of unemployment estimates of Layard and Nickell, Layard and others, and Coe have been adjusted by simple ratio techniques to conform to the OECD standardized unemployment concept used by the *OECD Economic Outlook* and this author. In most cases the differences were relatively small. But for the United Kingdom Layard and Nickell estimate the natural rate for *male* unemployment, which is substantially different from total unemployment. The simple ratio adjustment used here may not be fully appropriate.

b. OECD standardized unemployment rate.

c. Based on the 1985 value of q^N.

d. 1985 value.

purposes of estimating the wage equations. Finally, it is important to remember that none of the numerical estimates of the natural rates of output and employment make any allowance for the presence of hysteresis effects. The data and the analysis will, I think, sustain the broad conclusions reached but not the specific quantitative estimates.

Conclusions

In Germany, France, and Italy each of the three major sources of increased unemployment shares some of the responsibility for unemployment's large rise over the past fifteen years. In the three continental European countries, the wage and productivity equations suggest that there is some cyclical or Keynesian component to the current unemployment rate. Over the past fifteen years excessive wage aspirations also played a role in raising unemployment. At about the end of the 1960s, an autonomous rise in the growth of wage aspirations occurred. Not long thereafter productivity growth slowed, but the growth of wage aspirations did not adjust downward. The initial consequence was higher inflation. Ultimately, to check rising inflation, aggregate demand had to be restricted to levels producing higher unemployment. Subsequently, demand was restricted still further to eliminate the inflation that had occurred. This source of unemployment has been partly offset by a subsequent downward adjustment in the growth of wage norms, starting around 1979 for Germany and some years later in other countries. Over the period as a whole, excess wage aspirations have contributed a rather modest amount to the rise in unemployment since the late 1960s. Finally, there appears to have been a substantial rise in unemployment due to deteriorating supply conditions in the labor market, the specific nature of which this paper has not identified. Independent analysis of the relationship between unemployment and job vacancies tends to confirm this finding for Germany and the United Kingdom. It is conceivable that some of the rise in unemployment in these countries, not attributable to deficient aggregate demand or to excess aspirations, may have arisen from hysteresis phenomena. But this paper provides no independent evidence on that point. The apparent levels of the natural unemployment rate were so low in the late 1960s in Europe that part of the puzzle may be not so much why natural rates rose, but why they were so low to begin with.

In the case of the United Kingdom, very high levels of unemployment in the past several years have not been producing any further moderation in ex ante real wage demands. I could find no cyclical component to the current level of unemployment in the United Kingdom. Moreover, after a sizable (and statistically robust) downward shift in wage aspirations several years ago, the net contribution of excess wage aspirations to the rise in the U.K. unemployment since 1969 is quite small. This leaves a huge 9 or 10 percentage point rise in U.K. unemployment attributable to an upwardly shifting Beveridge curve—a finding closely confirmed by a separate analysis of the unemployment-vacancy relationship. Yet the evidence also suggests that the standard sources for a rise in the unemployment-vacancy curve cannot explain the U.K. phenomenon. Hysteresis thus emerges as a prime explanation.

It is, in fact, very difficult to infer quantitative conclusions about the degree of economic slack from wage equations. Especially in the case of France and Italy, the estimates appear to be quite sensitive to the specifications of the equation. In Germany and the United Kingdom, interpretation of the recent behavior of productivity is both important to the result and difficult to make. The estimates presented here seem reasonable, indeed quite conservative compared with other results. But a substantial dose of humility is needed in evaluating their validity.

Data Source Appendix

This appendix identifies the main sources of data for the nonfarm business and manufacturing sectors.

Nonfarm Business Sector (Excluding Housing)

The basic data for this sector come from an unpublished series prepared by the Economic and Financial Affairs Office of the Commission of the European Communities (Brussels, June 6, 1986). All references to Commission data refer to that series, called "Indicators of Profitability, Capital, Labour and Output for the Non-Agricultural Business Sector." It is available for Japan, the United States, and four European countries (Germany, France, Italy, and the United Kingdom) and provides a consistent set of data on current and constant price value added (with the former given in both market prices and factor costs), employment, average hours worked, compensation of employees, and gross and net capital stock, as well as other variables. Compensation per hour was calculated by dividing total employee compensation by aggregate hours worked. The nonagricultural business sector includes fuel and fuel products, manufactured products, building and construction and market sevices (including those of the public sector); it excludes the estimated component relating to the renting of immovable goods (that is, rents on dwellings). The series was compiled in late 1985 and is based on complete data through 1983. The 1984 data were in some cases partly forecast. Sources and methods for updating the data through 1985 and some revisions to the earlier data for Germany are described below.

The Commission series is an updated elaboration of the data described in Jorgen Mortensen's article, "Profitability, Relative Factor Prices and Capital/Labour Substitution in the Community, the United States and Japan, 1960–1983," appearing in *European Economy*, no. 20 (July 1984) pp. 29–67.

In the context of this paper, there are three additional notes of importance.

1. The self-employed: the Commission imputes a wage income to the self-employed equal to the average wage. This adjustment is particularly important because without it the downtrend that has occurred in the ratio of self-employed to total employment, in all countries (but especially in Italy), would bias the wage share upward.

2. Average weekly hours: for all countries, the Commission applied to the nonfarm business sector the series on average weekly hours in manufacturing published by the U.S. Department of Labor, Bureau of Labor Statistics (see below). The author revised and updated this series, using BLS data published in December 1986.

3. Updating the data to 1985 and revisions for 1984:

—*Germany*. The Commission data for Germany for 1984 (which was partly forecast) clearly needed revision. Constant price value added for the nonfarm business sector was estimated for 1984 and 1985 from the OECD national income accounts and from data in table B, p. 76, of the OECD's *Economic Surveys, 1985–1986: Germany*. Changes in deflators for the nonfarm business sector for 1984 and 1985 were estimated on the basis of their relationship to the change in the total GDP deflators in recent years. Changes in compensation per hour for 1984 and 1985 were estimated from the changes in compensation per employee in the business sector (*OECD Economic Outlook*, no. 40 [(December 1986)], table 20, p. 44) and an estimate of the change in average annual hours worked furnished by the German Institut für Arbeitsmarkt und Berufsforschung. The German gross capital stock was reestimated from 1982 onward by using extrapolators based on national income accounts data for private nonresidential investment and the replacement ratios implicit in the Commission data.

—*France, Italy, United Kingdom*. The 1984–85 change in constant price value added and the price deflator for the nonfarm business sector were estimated on the basis of recent relationships between these variables and their counterparts for the total GDP (available in the December 1986 *OECD Economic Outlook*). The 1985 gross capital stock was updated in the same way as explained above for Germany. For France and the United Kingdom the 1985 change in compensation per hour was set equal to the change in compensation per employee in the business sector, from the December 1986 *OECD Economic Outlook*. (The BLS series on average weekly hours in manufacturing showed only a minimal change for these two countries in 1985.) The Italian change in compensation per hour for 1985 was set equal to the change shown by the BLS for the Italian manufacturing sector, since in recent years changes in manufacturing and total business sector compensation per hour have been very similar.

Manufacturing Sector

With one exception the basic data for the manufacturing sector, referred to in the text as BLS data, come from the Office of Productivity and Technology of the Bureau of Labor Statistics, U.S. Department of Labor. Data on output, employment, average hours of work, and compensation per hour are published twice yearly for twelve countries. In addition, unpublished data underlying the indexes are available from the BLS, through the use of which it was possible to calculate the implicit value-added deflator. The capital stock data come from the Commission of the European Communities, which made available the manufacturing counterpart of the nonfarm business sector's "Indicators of Profitability," described before. Industrial classifications are, for the most part, in accordance with the international standard industrial classification (industrial classifications vary among countries, and these classifications can vary over time; the United Kingdom, for example, has included mining—less energy-related products—in its manufacturing sector since 1971).

Each country's main statistical office provides the BLS with underlying data for the manufacturing sector. All BLS estimates or adjustments are based on data provided by individual countries. For a more detailed discussion on sources and methods see Office of Productivity and Technology, "Underlying Data for Indexes of Output per Hour, Hourly Compensation, and Unit Labor Costs in Manufacturing, Twelve Countries, 1950–85" (BLS, unpublished).

Table A-1. *Some Results of Two-Stage Least Squares Regressions with Unlagged Inflation Term* ($\dot{p}_v$)[a]

Item	Equation with $\hat{q}$			Regression with unemployment					
				Unemployment only		Unemployment and time		Hysteresis equation	
Germany									
Coefficients on									
$\dot{p}_{v(-1)}$	0.61	(3.2)		0.83	(3.9)	0.74	(3.0)	1.02	(5.4)
$(\dot{p}_c - \dot{p}_v)_{-1}$	−0.08	(0.5)		−0.16	(0.7)	−0.27	(1.1)	−0.14	(0.7)
TIME	...			...		0.21	(1.1)	...	
Hysteresis coefficient	...			...		...		0.68	(2.0)
Dummies	4.1	(3.7)	D6970	3.7	(2.6) D6970	4.4	(2.7) D6970	2.86	(2.2) D6970
	−1.7	(3.6)	D7985						
$\bar{R}^2$	0.94			0.84		0.84		0.88	
Standard error	0.86			1.40		1.41		1.24	
Durbin-Watson	1.34			0.98		0.93		1.08	
France[b]									
Coefficients on									
$\dot{p}_{v(-1)}$	0.79	(5.5)		1.29	(8.3)	1.45	(4.9)	1.39	(9.4)
$(\dot{p}_c - \dot{p}_v)_{-1}$	−0.10	(0.5)		−0.25	(1.0)	−0.43	(1.1)	−0.24	(0.9)
TIME	...			...		−0.43	(0.6)	...	
Hysteresis coefficient	...			...		...		0.29	(0.2)
Dummies[b]	10.3	(6.6)	D68	9.4	(5.7) D68	8.6	(4.0) D68	8.8	(4.6) D68
	2.7	(2.2)	D6985	1.5	(1.2) D6985	1.4	(1.1) D6985		
	−1.7	(1.5)	D8485						
$\bar{R}^2$	0.91			0.90		0.88		0.88	
Standard error	1.30			1.40		1.50		1.51	
Durbin-Watson	1.57			1.57		1.53		1.32	

Italy

Coefficients on				
$\dot{p}_{v(-1)}$	0.57 (6.5)	0.60 (2.6)	0.10 (0.1)	0.58 (3.3)
$(\dot{p}_c - \dot{p}_v)$	0.08 (0.3)	−0.39 (0.8)	−0.55 (0.9)	−0.28 (0.7)
TIME	⋯	⋯	1.65 (0.5)	⋯
Hysteresis coefficient	⋯	⋯	⋯	1.05 (2.1)
Dummies	2.0 (1.6) D7085	5.1 (1.8) D7085	4.1 (1.4) D7085	3.6 (1.6) D7085
	−2.4 (2.1) D8485	−3.5 (1.1) D8485	−5.8 (0.8) D8485	−6.0 (1.9) D8485
$\bar{R}^2$	0.96	0.83	0.76	0.86
Standard error	1.23	2.62	3.07	2.35
Durbin-Watson	2.61	1.93	1.66	2.28

United Kingdom

Coefficients on				
$\dot{p}_{v(-1)}$	0.12 (0.9)	0.55 (3.6)	0.67 (2.3)	0.55 (3.5)
$(\dot{p}_c - \dot{p}_v)_{-1}$	0.37 (2.2)	0.26 (2.5)	0.58 (1.7)	0.70 (2.6)
TIME	⋯	⋯	0.04 (0.1)	⋯
Hysteresis coefficient[b]	⋯	⋯	⋯	0.81 (0.9)
Dummies[b]	7.4 (6.4) D7085	5.7 (3.0) D7085	4.4 (2.6) D7085	5.0 (2.8) D7085
	−5.3 (5.2) D8485			−4.0 (1.2) D8485
$\bar{R}^2$	0.97	0.89	0.89	0.89
Standard error	1.13	2.03	2.06	2.03
Durbin-Watson	2.19	2.84	2.86	2.89

Source: Author's calculations.

a. These equations include the same independent variables as the OLS equations. The numbers in parentheses are *t*-statistics. Instruments used for inflation variable: inflation ($\dot{p}_v$) lagged one and two years, and change in real exchange rate and all other right-hand side variables of the wage equation lagged one year.

b. Additional dummies: *D82* France, *D77* United Kingdom.

Comment by Jacques R. Artus

Schultze's paper covers many different issues. For the sake of brevity, I will limit my comments to what I consider to be the central issue, namely, the validity of the excess real wage rate hypothesis. This hypothesis states that the increase in real wage rates in Europe in the 1970s and early 1980s was not fully warranted, because of changes in production techniques, in the relative availability of labor and capital, in the price of energy, or in any other such factors that may influence the marginal productivity of labor corresponding to the full-employment labor force. Therefore, the increase in real wage rates contributed to the surge in unemployment, as well as to the introduction of Malthusian measures, such as mandatory reductions in the retirement age and the duration of the work week, and the expansion of government adminis-tration in order to create jobs. This hypothesis, of course, does not preclude other contributing factors. However, it is fair to say that the main advocates of this hypothesis claim that it explains most of the rise in unemployment. I focus on the manufacturing sector because the disequilibrium real wage rate hypothesis seems less relevant and more difficult to test in the agricultural and service sectors, where self-employment accounts for a much larger proportion of the labor force than in the manufacturing sector.

In the first part of his paper, Schultze considers whether the excess real wage rate hypothesis provides a useful analytical and empirical framework to analyze the unemployment problems in Europe. He asserts that it does not, because it leads to an empirical analysis that is inconclusive. My view is that this assertion is not warranted; it results largely from problems with data and the empirical methodology being used.

If one is not very careful, there can be a problem with the data. Most authors do not go back to original sources but use the data banks of the U.S. Bureau of Labor Statistics (BLS) or various international organi-zations in order to save time. Unfortunately, these organizations are not necessarily interested in calculating labor shares and, therefore, do not always collect the data that are appropriate for that purpose. For example, the data collected by the BLS are not always at factor cost; for France and Germany, they are at market prices. Data at market prices differ substantially from data at factor cost, and their use by some authors introduces undue confusion. For his analyses Schultze is mainly using the data from the Commission of the European Communities that are all at factor costs; he should not be surprised to find that they are different from the BLS data used by Bruno.

That leaves a problem resulting from deficiencies in the national account statistics of some countries. The main deficiency is that the data on value added in manufacturing from France and Italy are not net of inventory appreciation. Since the data on labor costs are calculated separately, the increase in inventory appreciation that occurred during the 1970s and early 1980s because of the rise in inflation is allocated to capital income, resulting in a large upward bias in the capital share and a corresponding downward bias in the labor share during this period. In a 1984 article I concluded, after a rough correction for inventory appreciation, that there were large increases in the labor share in manufacturing in all four major European countries (France, Germany, Italy, and the United Kingdom) during the 1970s.[79] These increases were larger than the increase observed in the United States.

The methodological problems are more complex. The real issue is whether the increase in the labor share is warranted, that is, consistent with the maintenance of full employment. Of course, certain factors warrant a change in the labor share; the simple observation that the labor share has increased does not by itself imply anything as far as the long-run demand for labor is concerned. Whether the increase is warranted can be determined only from an analytical framework that at least potentially allows an identification of the warranted change. At a strict minimum, this rules out the use of the Cobb-Douglas production function, which is characterized by the assumption of a constant labor share. Therefore, I will skip the section of Schultze's paper that is based on this function and go directly to the section based on the CES function.

Schultze argues that because the increases in labor shares that occurred in European countries during the 1970s can be explained by changes in the capital-labor ratios at full employment and in the real exchange rates, these increases may be warranted. I do not find this point convincing. To begin with, Schultze states that with elasticities of substitution between capital and labor (σ) of 0.63 and 0.76, most of the increases in the labor share in Germany and France during the 1970s can

79. Jacques R. Artus, "The Disequilibrium Real Wage Rate Hypothesis: An Empirical Evaluation" *International Monetary Fund Staff Papers,* vol. 31 (June 1984), pp. 249–302.

be explained by the increases in the capital-labor ratios. The problem with this argument is that the rises in capital intensity were larger during the 1960s, when there were little changes in labor share, than during the 1970s, when the bulk of the rise in labor share took place. Moreover, as noted by Schultze, the rise in capital intensity continued during the mid-1980s, when there were declines in labor share. There is no reason to assume that the relative weight of capital (δ) in the CES production function is constant in the long run. In fact, this weight must have been changing over time because if it did not, then, even with a relatively small deviation of σ from one, the four- to six-fold increases in capital-labor ratios observed over the past thirty years would have pushed the labor share close to zero or one (depending on whether σ is smaller or greater than one). In my 1984 paper I found that during the second half of the 1950s and the 1960s the relative weight of capital was increasing at a significant rate.[80] If this tendency is extrapolated to the 1970s and early 1980s, the increase in the relative weight of capital during this period would more or less offset the effect of the increase in the capital-labor ratios on the warranted labor shares. More precisely, I found that the warranted labor share declined somewhat in Germany and rose somewhat in the United Kingdom.

The real exchange rate argument is even less convincing. Certainly, a sudden major change in the real exchange rate will, for some time, affect monopolistic profit margins over marginal labor costs in the tradable goods sector and, more particularly, the capital share in manufacturing. The relevant question, however, is whether real exchange rate changes can account for long-lasting changes in the warranted capital share, namely, changes lasting a decade. I doubt that they can because the average degree of monopolistic power of the whole group of manufacturing exporters of a major industrial country is not likely to be large in the long run. But, of course, it is an empirical issue. My point is that the empirical evidence does not support the real exchange rate argument if real exchange rate is defined, as I believe it should be, as the ratio of own to "partner countries' " prices adjusted for exchange rate changes. Data on real effective exchange rates defined in this manner can be found, for example, in the IMF's *International Financial Statistics*. For Germany, they indicated a close correspondence between the increase in the real exchange rate and the increase in the labor share

80. Ibid.

from 1968 to 1974. From 1974 to 1981 there was a further continuous rise in the labor share, while the real exchange rate fluctuated around a flat trend from 1974 to 1979, then fell sharply from 1979 to 1981. Moreover, in 1982–83 there was a marked decline in the labor share, while the real exchange rate was appreciating again. For France and Italy, the apparent relationship is perverse; that is, the labor share adjusted for inventory appreciation rose sharply from 1968 to 1974, exactly during the period of depreciating real exchange rates. For the United Kingdom, there is no apparent relationship. Only for Sweden is the relationship relatively close, but then the changes in the actual labor share and in the real exchange rate were quite soon reversed.

In my 1984 article, I looked at the whole list of factors that could warrant the observed rise in labor share, including the possible effect of the change in the price of energy. My conclusion was that it was not really possible to view all or even most of the rise as being warranted.[81] The original study stopped in 1982. Recently I have updated the results to 1986 by using the estimates of the parameters obtained in the original study. The results suggest that the amount of excess real wage was substantially reduced from 1982 to 1986. Indeed, given the substantial margin for error in such estimates, rightly stressed by Paul Krugman in his paper, one can reasonably doubt that there is still a serious real wage problem in Europe, except possibly in the United Kingdom.

Comment by Charles R. Bean

The first part of this paper discusses movements in factors shares and the real wage gap. Schultze concludes that the real wage gap is not a very reliable diagnostic tool, essentially because the ex post real wage gap that is actually observed may have very little to do with the ex ante wage aspirations of wage bargainers. I think this view is correct, although I am not sure that Schultze makes the point as convincingly as he could.

Part of the problem is his use of what seems to be an unorthodox definition of the wage gap, which Schultze indexes by movements in labor's income share. By contrast, Bruno and Sachs, and others who have calculated wage gaps, define it as the difference between the actual

---

81. Ibid.

and the full-employment wage.[82] Assuming (a) competitive conditions and (b) a Cobb-Douglas technology, the latter is proportional to the full-employment average product of labor. Hence the wage gap may be indexed by a *cyclically corrected* labor income share using full employment rather than actual labor productivity. Thus Schultze's theoretical discussion seems somewhat beside the point, since it concerns the actual rather than the cyclically corrected labor share.

In fact, in calculating his wage gap series, Schultze uses the Bruno-Sachs definition. However, I am not sure that the cyclical correction has been calculated correctly. This relies on an equation relating labor input to output and capacity utilization. The discussion suggests that full-employment productivity is computed by setting capacity utilization to 100 percent, but surely output also needs to be returned to its full-employment level.

The wage gap is frequently used to allocate the blame for an increase in unemployment between classical (that is, supply) and Keynesian (that is, deficient demand) factors. If unemployment persists in spite of a zero wage gap, then the implication is often drawn that expansionary demand management policies are called for. Just how misleading his conclusion may be can be demonstrated in the context of the simple macroeconomic model developed by Layard and Nickell in a series of papers.[83] In this model the usual assumption of perfect competition is replaced by one of monopolistic competition. As a consequence, the ex post real wage is determined not only by the behavior of wage bargainers but also by the pricing policy of firms. In the limiting case of "normal cost" pricing, the ex post real wage is determined exclusively by pricing behavior.

This is demonstrated in figure 5. The positively sloped line is a labor supply curve and incorporates efficiency wage considerations. The negatively sloped line is a labor demand schedule, and the horizontal line is a pricing schedule. The variable σ is an index of real demand relative to potential demand. Under perfect competition, or a constant elasticity of product demand, the markup over marginal cost is invariant to the state of the cycle, and the markup over wages increases with activity (because of increasing marginal cost). Hence an increase in σ leaves the labor demand schedule unchanged but shifts the pricing

82. Michael Bruno and Jeffrey D. Sachs, *Economics of Worldwide Stagflation* (Harvard University Press, 1985).

83. See Richard Layard and Stephen Nickell, "Unemployment in Britain," *Economica*, vol. 53 (1986, *Supplement*), pp. S121–69 for the most complete exposition.

Figure 5. *Alternative Relationship between Real Wages and Unemployment*

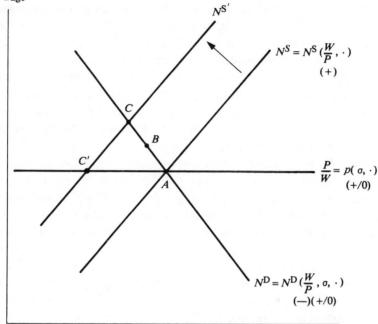

schedule down. By contrast, under normal cost pricing the markup of prices over wages does not vary with demand, which implies that the markup over marginal cost falls and so the labor demand is increasing in σ. An increase in σ shifts the labor demand curve up and leaves the pricing schedule unchanged.

Now consider what happens if there is some exogenous upward shift in the labor supply schedule (for example, because of a failure of wage aspirations to adjust to a fall in productivity growth). In the short run, because of sluggish nominal wages and prices, the economy would go to a point like *B*, where there is unanticipated inflation and, assuming a simple quantity theory for determining demand, an unanticipated fall in real demand. Over time, as nominal wages and prices continue to adjust upward, real demand falls further. In the competitive case the final equilibrium will be a point like *C*, where there is an observable wage gap. On the other hand, in the normal cost pricing case the final equilibrium is at C'. There is no wage gap, yet the increase in unemployment is entirely due to supply rather than demand factors and cannot be ameliorated by expansionary demand management policies.

Both Schultze and Bruno suggest that wage gaps have been falling recently, at a time when unemployment has been rising.[84] Schultze regards this as a bit of a puzzle, but it accords very well with the normal cost pricing story and suggests a path like ABC'.

In the second part of his paper, Schultze goes behind movements in observed wages and factor shares and tries to identify the exogenous factors at work shifting the "labor supply" schedule. I agree with this approach. However, I do not find his estimates of the Phillips curve entirely convincing for several reasons.

First, I am concerned about the low inflation coefficients in a number of countries. I am also concerned that the equations do not solve for a long-run value of the real wage. Growing evidence suggests that the Phillips curve should contain such a level effect,[85] and since Schultze does not allow for it, his wage equations may be seriously misspecified.

Second, it would be nice to go beyond constraints and ad hoc dummies in picking up movements in the warranted wage as a result of capital accumulation and other shifts (for example, because of changes in unemployment benefit levels). This is difficult to do, but absolutely necessary if one is to discriminate between competing theories. Changes in income taxes should also figure in the analysis.

Finally, there is the question of the appropriate activity term. Unemployment is a trended variable, but downward wage pressure does not appear to have increased. Thus, as Schultze notes, unemployment alone is not likely to be a good pressure-of-demand indicator unless there is something else trended in the equation to pick up the trend shift in the NAIRU. It is not really surprising that the output gap works better because trend changes in the natural rate have already been controlled for. However, despite some efforts, Schultze essentially leaves the reasons for these changes unexplained. As for hysteresis effects, the change in unemployment and the deviation of unemployment from a trend look pretty similar and are virtually indistinguishable on macro

84. Michael Bruno, "Aggregate Supply and Demand Factors in OECD Unemployment: An Update," *Economica*, vol. 53 (1986, *Supplement*), pp. S35–52.

85. C. R. Bean, P. R. G. Layard, and S. J. Nickell, "The Rise in Unemployment: A Multi-country Study," *Economica*, vol. 53 (1986, *Supplement*), pp. S1–22.

data. Those who get strong evidence of hysteresis effects invariably do not give the alternative hypothesis a run for its money. This is not to say that there are no hysteresis effects, rather that the evidence for them from macroeconomic time series is at best inconclusive.[86]

In conclusion, let me say that there are wide-ranging explanations for the rise in the NAIRU. They include simple sluggish adjustment of wage aspirations, efficiency wage and implicit contract theories, "insider-outsider" and other hysteresis models, as well as those explanations that focus on the effects of changes in unemployment benefits and the like. Many of these theories have similar implications for the comovements of aggregate time series, but very different policy implications. From a scientific point of view I am skeptical of the extent to which more can be learned from aggregate time-series exercises. Rather, microeconomic evidence of the determinants of wage-bargaining, and so on, is the best way to sort out the various competing hypotheses.

General Discussion

One participant noted that if European productivity growth is countercyclical, a great deal of the growth since 1979 was caused by output slack or unemployment rather than underlying technical progress. Accordingly, Europe's growth prospects are better if productivity growth is cyclical. He commented that Robert Gordon had found that only the United Kingdom had strong evidence of countercyclical productivity growth. But Charles Schultze had found such behavior in other countries. He suggested that Schultze's specification, which used the level rather than the change in labor inputs, might have influenced his results.

It was pointed out that the major source of the decline in the U.S. profit rate has been the enormous increase in the relative price of capital in the United States, a change not observed in Europe. It was suggested, however, that an appropriate correction of U.S. durable goods prices for changes in quality would indicate no decline in U.S. rates of profit.

Keynesian policies of demand stimulus were discussed. One partici-

86. Editors' note: The paper by Schultze now incorporates, with some modifications, the substance of the points made in this paragraph. They were not included in the original version of this paper presented at the October 1986 conference. Schultze thanks Professor Bean for pointing the way toward a major improvement in the analysis of the paper.

pant argued that the key issue was not whether but how much output slack was available. According to him, the current 9 percent unemployment rate in Europe is well above the NAIRU rate, which he estimated to be about 6 percent. There is, therefore, significant room for demand to expand.

Demand expansion is inappropriate, however, according to another discussant. If a problem remains a problem for a decade or so, he pointed out, then an explanation in terms of aggregate demand becomes less plausible. It is unlikely that the recent higher rates of inflation (as compared with the 1950s and 1960s) and the relatively higher unemployment rates in Europe compared with the United States can be explained by aggregate demand fluctuations. Secular changes might have been behind these changes. He endorsed the view that collective action has increased, blocking transactions that would yield full employment. But he noted that while this argument is consistent with the behavior of employment in continental countries, it does not appear to be consistent with the different behavior in the United Kingdom and the United States. The reasons for this divergence, he argued, center upon regional differences in the United States. Differences among states and regions in the United States are far greater than the differences within the European countries. In the United States, unemployment is strongly correlated with institutional differences among states; moreover, the pattern of labor migration since the 1960s shows a net migration from high-wage areas toward low-wage areas. This phenomenon strongly suggests that in parts of the United States monopoly wages block some people from getting employment. But since there is more or less free mobility of capital and labor, displaced labor goes to other (low-wage) areas. In the United Kingdom such mechanisms fail to operate.

There was a substantial discussion of hysteresis. One discussant noted that because of the strong trend in the actual unemployment rate, it makes a big difference in estimating hysteresis whether one employs the unemployment rate or the gap between the NAIRU and the actual unemployment rate. When the gap is used to estimate wage equations, the hysteresis hypothesis performs poorly. A hysteresis measure of the output gap does not seem to provide a satisfactory explanation of why the rise in European unit labor costs has slowed. He also stressed that those who recommend demand expansion in Europe do not claim there would be no acceleration in inflation; rather they claim that a decrease in unemployment can be achieved at the cost of a one-time increase in inflation. Inflation would rise but not accelerate.

Another participant argued along similar lines that a believer in hysteresis would think of the economy as behaving like the old-fashioned Phillips curve without expectations, that more output could always be achieved at the expense of permanently higher inflation. Thus a specification of wage equations implying the NAIRU as an exogenous number is inconsistent with the hysteresis view.

Another discussant reported that, considering the relationship between wages and unemployment of long duration, he could find no real evidence of hysteresis except, perhaps, in the United Kingdom. He added that while it seems reasonable the long-term unemployed may be outsiders, it is not realistic to argue that all the employed and all the short-term unemployed should be regarded as insiders. Testing this insider-outsider hypothesis more successfully would require a closer examination of the stock of the employed by length of job tenure and of the inflows to unemployment by length of job tenure.

The discussion turned to the role of pricing behavior in determining real wages. It was agreed that the markup in many European nations has been a function of the real exchange rate. But one participant argued that the real exchange rate should be defined as the ratio of traded to nontraded goods rather than the ratio used by Schultze in which the denominator was standard unit labor costs.

Another participant added that pricing behavior fundamentally determines how real wages move over the cycle. What caused price-setters to accept lower and lower margins after 1973? A constant-markup price model, such as that described by Charles Bean, or the suggestion of a sudden breakdown in monopolistic competition did not seem satisfactory to one participant. He suggested that changes in the international economy may have been the cause. In effect, the nature of the cost shock that hit people in 1973 was a reversal of the previous favorable terms of trade. These changes inevitably led to a fairly drastic change in expectations about the future path of demand; price-setters became much less sure of their ability to pass on costs and to induce demand by expanding capacity.

But the markup model was defended. Rising inflation is associated with a real wage gap within a setting of monopolistic competition. Constant markup pricing implies that if real wage aspirations rise, then in the long run the outcome will be higher unemployment but an unchanged real wage. Hence such pricing behavior ensures that real wage aspirations are in no sense fulfilled but rather are essentially killed off by the rise in unemployment needed to quell the inflation. One cannot look to real wage outcomes to determine the extent to which excessive real wage aspirations have been responsible for the rise in unemployment.

Other discussants countered, however, that the markup hypothesis was not supported by the facts. If it were valid, the operating surplus of individual corporations should not fluctuate more than the level of their sales. But prices fluctuate more than normal costs, corporations' net operating income is extremely volatile, and the markup of the product price over normal cost actually changes from year to year and even period to period.

Policy options were discussed. Many stressed that even after a lot of research a great deal of uncertainty exists about what went wrong and how much things may have improved in the past two or three years. Some participants felt that the only real option is to raise demand and wait. After nearly fifteen years—more than half a generation—of disappointed aspirations, no one can confidently predict just how quickly real wage aspirations would rise if somewhat faster growth were achieved. The only way to resolve the analytical debate being waged at this conference is to implement some program.

Another discussant agreed with this call for action but asked exactly what type of program should be implemented. He suggested that labor unions would react more favorably to an expansion if supply-side incentives were offered; hence he called for tax reforms that would reduce labor costs but not the disposable income of workers.

The discussion turned to capacity constraints on growth. European capital-output ratios have increased dramatically. Studies using recent observations suggest that to get 1 percent faster growth in Europe the share of investment in GNP would have to be increased by 3 percentage points. This result is generally used to assert the existence of an almost unbreakable capacity constraint. But one participant suggested this might be a cyclical rather than long-run phenomenon and that capital-output ratios would fall in the face of increased demand.

ROBERT Z. LAWRENCE

Trade Performance as a Constraint on European Growth

THE EARLY 1980s marked the nadir of European industrial performance. Throughout European industry, stagnant output, major plant closures, and massive layoffs created crisis conditions. Regardless of their ideological beliefs, governments were compelled to subsidize declining sectors such as steel and shipbuilding, to bail out firms threatened with bankruptcy in established industries such as automobiles (Peugeot and BL Ltd.—formerly British Leyland) and consumer electronics (AEG-Telefunken), and to embark on new initiatives to improve performance in technology-intensive sectors such as computers, semiconductors, and biotechnology. To be sure, some of the problems were associated with the recession engendered by the second oil crisis in 1979 and by overvalued currencies, but according to many observers, they also reflected deeply rooted structural causes.[1]

The problems facing many European industries dated to at least 1973. Their difficulties reflected an inability of political, labor, and capital market institutions to adjust to the new global environment. Over the postwar period European governments had vastly increased their commitments to their citizens not simply to maintain full employment, but to maintain employment in specific regions, firms, and even jobs. These commitments remained feasible as long as growth followed predictable

Gregory I. Hume provided excellent assistance.
1. The currencies of the four countries in our sample appeared overvalued. In Sweden the coalition government found it difficult to devalue adequately to reflect differences in inflation between Sweden and the rest of the members of the Organization for Economic Cooperation and Development. In France membership in the European monetary system and a strong franc were deliberately used to reduce inflation. In the United Kingdom tight monetary policy and a surge in the price of oil strengthened the pound. The shift by international investors away from the U.S. dollar in the late 1970s added to the secular rise in the deutsche mark.

and stable patterns, but when structural change after 1973 required a shift of resources from declining but politically powerful industries such as shipbuilding and steel, the commitments became extremely expensive and impeded change. Government spending on unemployment, early retirement benefits, social services, and industrial subsidies increased rapidly. Additional costs were hidden by the expansion of new forms of protectionism such as voluntary export restraints, orderly market agreements, selective government procurement, and cartel arrangements. Such protection also restricted the potential benefits from European integration.

Before 1973 governments also assumed major responsibilities in allocating credit, encouraging mergers, and nurturing "national champion" firms. Such measures created sluggish giants unable to respond flexibly to the new environment.[2] Capital markets in Europe appear to have been slow to recognize the areas of new growth: in France because allocation was heavily influenced by the state; in Germany because long-term relationships between banks and industry imparted a conservative bias to investment decisions; and in Sweden because profits were locked up in particular firms by tax laws. The structural changes in the 1970s (the slowdown in productivity growth, deterioration in the terms of trade, and perhaps the loss of competitiveness to Far Eastern nations) required lower growth in real wages. However, boosted by institutional arrangements such as indexation, job security regulations, and growing union power, wages failed to adjust. The resulting profits squeeze induced a slump in investment.

The implications of these problems were seen as particularly serious for European external competitiveness. These countries are open economies in which exports account for about 30 percent of manufacturing production. Trade is thus a critical determinant of industrial demand, and industry is in turn a crucial engine of growth for the rest of the economy.[3] For a while the expansion of the public sector was able to partially compensate for weak investment and a lack of external competitiveness. But by 1980 (with the exception of France) it was widely believed that fiscal deficits prohibited further stimulus from government

2. For an elaboration of this hypothesis see, for example, Paul A. Geroski and Alexis Jacquemin, "Industrial Change, Barriers to Mobility and European Industrial Policy," *Economic Policy*, no. 1 (November 1985), pp. 170–218.

3. In 1985 exports were 33.7 percent of production in Germany, 29.6 percent in France, and 27.9 percent in the United Kingdom. See *European Economy*, no. 25 (September 1985), p. 119.

spending, while monetary policy could not be used without unacceptably high inflation. Improving competitiveness was crucial for growth.

The competitive difficulties facing their industrial sectors were vividly depicted in the comments of several distinguished European authors at the time. About France, Jacques Delors wrote,

> The risk of a shrinking of the industrial base is also a worrying one, both as regards the economy's sensitivity to imports and the weakness of our investment in production. . . . Demand is shared out to the advantage of imports and to the detriment of internal production. This evolution results from the unfavorable specialization in French industry and the relative tightness in output capacities but most of all from insufficient competitiveness.[4]

According to Otmar Emminger,

> West Germany's international competitiveness at the end of the seventies was clearly weakened. Her exporters had been losing foreign market shares since 1978; greater still had been her market-share loss to foreign competitors at home. The mark's over-valuation as a result of the weakness of the dollar, excessive increases in West German labour costs and the growing challenge by Japan and the newly industrializing countries were responsible for both. . . .
>
> Since 1973, there has been a widespread fear that West Germany's economy is subject to a process of deindustrialization.[5]

About Sweden, Erik Lundberg wrote,

> The industrial sector has become too small due to the decline in employment and investment during the 1970s. The main problem is that this sector cannot generate the extra volume of goods needed to solve the balance of payments problem.[6]

Finally, on the United Kingdom, Samuel Brittan wrote,

> Bottlenecks on the supply-side—even when the unemployment statistics have been high—have limited the response of British industry to increases in overseas demand.[7]

Since the early 1980s the macroeconomic environment has improved considerably. The rise of the U.S. dollar has allowed European industry to become more competitive internationally. Profit shares have increased noticeably while wages have remained relatively restrained. There have

4. Jacques Delors, "France: Between Reform and Counter-Reform" in Ralf Dahrendorf, ed., *Europe's Economy in Crisis* (Holmes and Meier, 1982), p. 64.

5. Otmar Emminger, "West Germany: Europe's Driving Force?" in ibid., pp. 38–40.

6. Erik Lundberg, "The Rise and Fall of the Swedish Economic Model," in ibid., p. 209.

7. Samuel Brittan, "A Transformation of the English Sickness?" in ibid., p. 76.

also been major structural adjustments. Employment in shipbuilding, steel, textiles, and coal mining has been reduced. Subsidies have been cut back. Companies such as British Steel, Hoechst, and Thyssen have in some years actually turned a profit. A much greater awareness of the futility of maintaining outmoded operations has prevailed, even among French Socialists, whose slogan was once "there are no outmoded industries, only outmoded technologies." In addition, new European initiatives emphasizing the integration of the European common market and cooperation in such high-technology projects as Esprit have been launched.

Nonetheless, many Europeans remain pessimistic about the future of their manufacturing sector and call for a variety of policy responses to deal with competitive problems. They see an era of a weaker U.S. dollar as fraught with competitive difficulties. Some argue that Europe is now caught between emerging developing countries, which compete in traditional standardized products on the basis of cheap labor, and the United States and Japan, which dominate the markets for most high-technology products. Ultimately, they argue, Europe must compete in high-technology sectors, but to do so it must provide temporary "infant industry" protection at the European level.[8] Others, particularly in the United Kingdom and France, argue that their economies show a serious mismatch between domestic demand and supply, giving rise to extremely high import propensities in the course of expansion. They therefore advocate retreat behind national barriers to ensure that demand stimulus does not spill abroad.[9]

A third view rejects the protectionist argument but nonetheless argues that before governments act to stimulate domestic demand, an improvement in industrial competitiveness is required. Some advocate active industrial policies of various types. Others favor a cautious aggregate demand policy and a period of slow growth until industry itself restructures sufficiently to generate an export-led expansion. This view, typically German, sees export stimulus as necessary for expansion.

This paper considers whether medium-term growth in four European

8. Wolfgang Hager, "Protectionism and Autonomy: How to Preserve Free Trade in Europe," *International Affairs*, vol. 58 (Summer 1982), pp. 413–28; and Michel Richonnier, "Europe's Decline Is Not Irreversible," *Journal of Common Market Studies*, vol. 22 (March 1984), pp. 227–44.

9. Wynne Godley and Robert M. May, "The Macroeconomic Implications of Devaluation and Import Restriction," *Economic Policy Review*, no. 3 (March 1977), pp. 32–42.

countries is in fact threatened by their inability to compete in world markets. The first section examines the medium-term trade performance of the economics to evaluate the case that structural changes have inhibited European competitiveness enough to seriously constrain growth. The second section examines whether trade performance has indeed been the major source of the deindustrialization observed in some of the nations. The third section looks more closely at the nature of structural change within each manufacturing sector. Has trade played a major role in the shifts in the industrial composition of output? Is an improvement in European performance in high-technology trade a prerequisite for growth over the medium term?

Some prefatory remarks are called for here. First, the perspective for this analysis is the medium-term of four or five years. We are concerned, therefore, principally with the issue of long-term potential growth rather than the better utilization of existing resources. As Richard Cooper has shown elsewhere in this volume, most European economies could finance a trade deficit associated with a short-run cyclical expansion.[10] Over the medium term, however, trade flows must adjust to finance or offset such imbalances. A country seeking to grow faster than its trading partners may have to lower its terms of trade. If factor markets clear over the medium term, problems of external competitiveness should not impede the achievement of potential output measured in terms of domestic goods. In the short run, domestic expansion could indeed result in a trade deficit. But if such a deficit should exceed levels that can be financed, it should induce an adjustment in relative prices of products and productive factors that would restore full employment. Similarly, in the short run the loss of comparative advantage in a specific product may lead to a trade deficit. But with appropriate reallocations of production and demand, and perhaps a shift in real exchange rates, economies cannot lose comparative advantage in all products. Over the medium term, therefore, the external balance constraint should show up not as a gap between imports and exports but as a shift in the real exchange rate required to induce a resource shift compatible with full employment.[11] Those who see protection as a precondition for sustaining long-term European growth have more than just a pessimistic view of

10. At worst, expanding output to full-employment levels in the short run might require a one-time devaluation.

11. See for example, John Williamson, "Is There an External Constraint?" *National Institute Economic Review*, no. 109 (August 1984), pp. 73–77.

potential European trade performance; they also have a pessimistic view of market equilibrating mechanisms—even over the medium and long run.

Of course, trade performance problems could lead in the short run to the underutilization of resources. Deteriorating terms of trade will mean slower growth for real incomes even if not for real output. As such, like a productivity slowdown, in the short run deteriorating terms of trade could lead to problems in adjusting real wage growth to its appropriate levels without inflation or unemployment. In addition, the pace of change could be so rapid that a higher permanent level of transitional (frictional) unemployment is required. In *combination* therefore with imperfections in European factor markets, a loss in competitiveness in the sense of requiring lower real wages could increase unemployment. But the best solution to such problems is to improve the functioning of the factor markets. Policies that inefficiently bolster production in the existing industrial structure by intervening in trade are palliatives not cures. Policies that improve trade performance by enhancing innovation and raising efficiency may be able to offset the need for poorer terms of trade, but if factor markets function poorly, the economy will remain vulnerable to disturbances from other sources.

My focus here is therefore on trade performance as a constraint on long-run real output and income growth. Can the economies in the sample grow at rates similar to those of other OECD members without requiring continuous deterioration of their terms of trade? This vantage point is quite different from studies that try to assess the competitiveness of European industry more broadly. In particular, my concerns are aggregative. If, for example, at current exchange rates, firms in the electronics sector of a European economy were unable to earn a profit, they would have competitive problems. But if the economy as a whole could grow at potential without changing its terms of trade by specializing in other products, I would conclude it did not have a trade performance problem.

My focus is also different from the focus of those who compare European performance in particular industries (such as high technology) with that of the United States and Japan. Indeed, while improved performance in high-technology trade or any other type will raise welfare in the economies studied here, for three of the four economies it is not essential to match OECD growth at constant terms of trade.

Determinants of Aggregate Trade Performance:
A Medium-Term Perspective

The key issue is whether historically each of the four economies could have grown at its long-run potential rate, and, in the absence of exogenous shocks such as the price of oil, could have maintained a constant trade balance as a share of GDP without the need to devalue its real exchange rate. To resolve the issue requires regression analysis, and a word of caution on methodology is in order.

The typical function explaining import and export behavior is based on the assumption of imperfect substitution and infinite supply elasticities at home and abroad. While a cyclical variable or capacity utilization is sometimes introduced to capture non-price-rationing effects such as changes in delivery times, as well as the particular composition of demand, the most common specification makes the demand for imports or exports a function of their relative price and an activity variable. Although such equations have been fit to historical data with differing degrees of success, there are sound reasons to be suspicious of interpreting them as rigidly structural relationships. In particular, if a country should change its spending patterns, that is, the relationship between absorption and income or the composition of its absorption, this could affect its trade flows. If, for instance, long-run investment fell relative to savings and the long-run current account thus rose, ceteris paribus domestic demand for tradables would shift. These are not explicitly modeled in the regression. Nonetheless the regressions do provide a statistical summary of the historical relationship between trade flows, activity, and relative prices that may be useful if interpreted with caution.

West Germany: Structural Stability

When the German current account declined from a surplus of 1.4 percent of GNP in 1978 to a deficit of 2.0 percent in 1980, questions were raised in the minds of many Germans about the fundamental competitiveness of their economy. Indeed, concerns about competitiveness and the view that a domestically driven expansion would result in unacceptable balance of payments problems were a reason for the reluctance of German policymakers to stimulate their economy after 1981. It is

Figure 1. *Performance of Components of the West German Current Account, 1965–86*

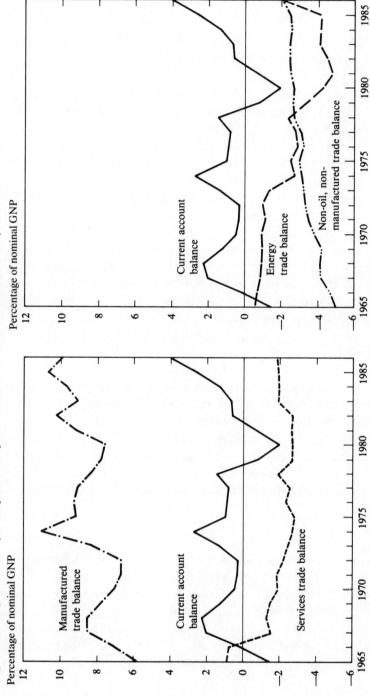

Sources: International Monetary Fund, *International Financial Statistics*; and Organization for Economic Cooperation and Development, *Monthly Statistics of Foreign Trade*, series A.

important, however, to distinguish the sources of the current account decline over that period to evaluate these concerns. Figure 1 depicts the component balances of the German current account as a share of nominal GNP and illustrates the crucial role played by manufacturing trade. A nation relatively poor in natural resources and tourist attractions, Germany is forced to compensate with an extraordinary performance in manufactured goods trade. Indeed, the unusually high share of manufacturing in its GNP can be accounted for by the composition of its international trade. The 25.3 percent of GDP absorbed by domestic German use of manufactured goods in 1985 is remarkably similar to the 23.1 percent for France and 23.5 percent for the United Kingdom.[12]

Given German dependence on foreign energy, it was quite natural for the trade balance to slump in response to the second oil price rise in 1979 (figure 1). Indeed, a first-cut analysis of German trade between 1978 and 1980 suggests that the oil price hike provides a sufficient explanation for the current account deficit. In particular, between 1978 and 1980 the $19 billion decline in oil trade was greater than the drop in the trade balance overall. The rise in total German export volumes of 6.6 percent and German manufactured export volumes of 11.1 percent was identical to the corresponding increases in the exports of all market economies.

In addition, German trade performance in the 1970s as a whole was satisfactory in comparison with the performances of trading partners. The volume of exports and imports grew at similar rates, and the terms of trade in manufacturing were unchanged. As a percent of GNP the trade balance fell by 2 percent over the decade, a decline that can be fully ascribed to the deterioration in the nonmanufacturing terms of trade. The manufacturing trade surplus in both 1970 and 1980 was about 7 percent of GNP.

But there are two reasons why the deficit caused great concern. First, Germany had not experienced a current account deficit in response to the first oil price shock. Indeed, its merchandise trade surplus actually increased between 1973 and 1974. The relationship between the growth rates of Germany and its trading partners was fundamentally different in the two oil-induced adjustments. In 1973 and 1974 Germany grew 1.4 and 0.3 percentage points more slowly than the total OECD; in 1979 and 1980 it grew 1.0 and 0.5 percentage points more rapidly. Second, the trends leading up to the second oil shock were different. While manufac-

---

12. The estimates are derived in table 13.

Table 1. West German Trade Equations, Selected Periods 1965–85[a]

Dependent variable	Period	Equation number	log QXW	log QXMW	T	log GNP80	log RPX[b]	log RPM[b]	$\bar{R}^2$	Standard error	Durbin-Watson statistic
log QX	1965–85	G1	1.25 (11.9)	...	−0.001 (0.22)	...	−0.55 (4.1)	...	0.997	0.023	2.0
	1965–85	G2	1.22 (69.2)	...	...	...	−0.53 (6.5)	...	0.997	0.023	2.1
	1965–74	G3	1.25 (30.8)	...	...	...	−0.49 (3.01)	...	0.998	0.017	2.2
	1975–85	G4	1.17 (11.6)	...	...	...	−0.66 (5.0)	...	0.983	0.024	1.4
log QM	1965–85	G5	...	...	−0.005 (0.88)	2.24 (12.5)	...	−0.42 (4.0)	0.997	0.020	1.7
	1965–74	G6	...	...	...	2.01 (18.6)	...	−0.59 (3.0)	0.992	0.028	1.2
	1975–85	G7	...	...	...	2.02 (18.7)	...	−0.49 (4.45)	0.986	0.015	2.4
	1965–85	G8	...	...	...	2.09 (71.8)	...	−0.49 (7.4)	0.997	0.021	1.3
log QXM	1965–85	G9	...	1.16 (12.9)	−0.014 (2.5)	...	−0.59 (4.9)	...	0.997	0.023	2.3
	1965–74	G10	...	1.17 (4.4)	−0.012 (0.45)	...	−0.55 (3.5)	...	0.998	0.017	2.4
	1975–85	G11	...	...	−0.02 (1.2)	2.70 (3.7)	−1.1 (2.6)	...	0.990	0.020	2.6
log QMM	1965–85	G12	...	...	...	2.32 (29.4)	...	−1.2 (1.8)	0.990	0.047	0.8

Source: International Monetary Fund, International Financial Statistics tape.
a. Annual data; t-statistics are in parentheses. QX is the volume of merchandise exports; QXM is the volume of manufactured exports; QMM is the volume of manufactured imports; QXW is the volume of world trade; QXMW is the volume of world manufactures trade; T is a time trend; GNP80 is GNP in 1980 dollars; RPX is the IMF relative manufacturing price series (current and two-year lags); and RPM is the ratio of manufacturing import unit values to domestic manufactures wholesale prices (current and one-year lag).
b. Current and one-year lag.

turing and raw materials balances were improving before the first oil shock, both were falling fairly steadily as a share of GNP before the second.

But was this evidence of a fundamental erosion in competitiveness? To answer this question, I have estimated a set of simple, demand-oriented equations explaining the volume of German merchandise exports and imports from 1965 to 1985. Equations for manufactured goods trade are also reported. The equations, with all variables expressed in logarithms so that the coefficients may be interpreted as elasticities, explain trade volumes in terms of activity and relative price variables. Exports are explained by the volume of world trade (QXW) as measured by the United Nations and two-year lags on the ratio of German to foreign export prices (RPX) as estimated by the International Monetary Fund. Imports are a function of German GNP and three-year lags on the ratio of German import prices to German wholesale prices.[13]

The equations, reported in table 1, do well in tracking German trade behavior and also reveal some interesting properties of trade performance. First, at constant relative prices, German export volumes grow 22 percent faster than world trade (equation G2). But German imports grow about twice as fast as German GNP. The import elasticity is 2.09 (equation G8). These relationships hold over the long run (note the lack of significance in the time trends in equations G1 and G5).

A third equation, which relates world export growth to growth in the OECD, has also been estimated, from 1970–85 annual data:

$$PQXW = -1.9 + 2.16\,POECD,$$
$$(1.9 \quad (7.42)$$

Standard error = 2.3; Durbin-Watson = 2.26; R^2 = 0.80

where $PQXW$ is the percentage change in world exports as measured by

13. The model underlying this specification assumes German and foreign products are imperfect substitutes and that German producers determine prices as a markup over unit costs. The heavy weight given to domestic costs in German price-setting is indicated in the following regression estimated using annual data from 1970 to 1985:

$$\log PMX = 0.11 \log PXManun + 0.80\,ULC + 0.06\,D74ON,$$
$$(2.5) \quad\quad\quad (20.0) \quad\quad\quad (3.8)$$

Standard error = 0.013; Durbin-Watson = 1.9

where log PMX is the log of German manufactured goods export prices, log $PXManun$ is the log of United Nations manufactured goods export unit values for developed countries, ULC is German unit labor costs, and $D74ON$ is a dummy variable equal to 1 after 1974. All variables are expressed in U.S. dollars.

the United Nations and *POECD* is the OECD percentage growth in GDP.[14] The three equations can be solved for the German GDP growth rate "warranted" in the past by any given growth rate in GDP for the OECD, the warranted rate being the growth rate at which imports rise as rapidly as exports at constant terms of trade, assuming of course historic absorption behavior.

This exercise yields the following relationships in percentages:

OECD growth	World exports	German exports	Warranted German growth
0	−1.9	−2.3	−1.1
2	2.4	3.0	1.4
3	4.6	5.7	2.7
5	8.9	10.9	5.1
6	11.1	13.7	6.4

The calculations indicate the sensitivity of the warranted German growth rate to growth in the OECD. At OECD growth rates lower than 5 percent Germany had to grow more slowly than the OECD to maintain its coverage ratio (the ratio of exports to imports); at rates about 5 percent, however, the warranted German rate exceeds that of the OECD.

While the demand for both exports and imports is inelastic (price elasticities of 0.55 and 0.49 for exports and imports, respectively), their sum is greater than unity, indicating that real exchange rate depreciation from initially balanced trade will improve the trade balance, and appreciation will worsen it. But the overall impact is not very large.[15] The low price elasticities for German products help explain the relatively strong trade performance despite the considerable real appreciation in the mark in the early 1970s. They also suggest, ironically, that Germany could afford to run a somewhat faster inflation rate than its trading partners— a real appreciation—without a major impact on its trade performance.

Splitting the sample period into two reveals a stable structural

14. Sources: United Nations, *Monthly Bulletin of Statistics,* various issues, and OECD, *Economic Outlook,* various issues.

15. Efforts to incorporate supply-side variables were not successful, nor were time trends that could capture cyclicality. These results are qualitatively similar to those obtained by the Commission of the European Communities. For the full period 1964 to 1981 their overall equations are very similar to those given here. Their export income elasticity was 1.31 and import income elasticity 1.95. Price elasticity was −0.99 for exports and −0.23 for imports. See "The External Constraint and the Operation of the Price and Income Elasticities of External Trade in the Community Countries, the United States of America and Japan," *European Economy,* no. 16 (July 1983), p. 133.

relationship between German trade and the volumes of world trade and German GNP. Tests (not reported) using a multiplicative dummy on the activity variable after 1974 confirm the stability of these income elasticities. Indeed, on the export side the equation fitted using data from 1965 to 1974 (table 1, G3) is virtually identical to that fitted over the entire sample period (G2).[16]

The results on the import side are similar. The equations fitted for 1965–74 and for the full period (G6 and G8) are very similar. In both exports and imports small declines in activity elasticities are evident in the equations fitted over 1975–85, but the German growth rate warranted by this system of equations fitted between 1975 and 1985 is virtually identical to that fitted for the earlier period. The equation for manufactured exports indicates that, ceteris paribus, German export volumes will grow as rapidly as world trade in manufactured goods and indicates no shift in the relationship between the growth of global markets and German manufactured exports when the sample period is split.

In sum, these equations do not indicate a marked deterioration in German trade performance after 1973. Nor do they indicate anything particularly unusual about German trade behavior from 1978 through 1981, given the underlying determinants of that behavior. When dummy variables equal to unity in these years are inserted into equations G2 and G8, the coefficients on the remaining variables are not significantly affected, and the errors in explaining these years are not significantly larger than those in the rest of the sample.

Equations G2 and G8 can be used to decompose the behavior of the German coverage ratio, the ratio of export values (VX) to import values (VM), over time. Since $VX = PXQX$ and $VM = PMQM$, where P denotes the price and Q the quantity of exports (X) and imports (M),

(1) $\log VX - \log VM = \log PX - \log PM + \log QX - \log QM.$

But since I have estimated

---

16. The estimates reported by the Commission of the European Communities are similar. They show income elasticities of German exports with respect to world demand of 0.99 between 1964 and 1973 and 1.25 between 1973 and 1981. For manufactured goods they show corresponding estimates of 0.89 and 0.87 respectively. Income elasticities of imports are 2.10 between 1964 and 1973 and 1.84 between 1973 and 1981, while for manufactured goods the estimates are 2.56 and 2.48, respectively. See "The External Constraint and the Operation of the Price and Income Elasticities," pp. 140–45.

Figure 2. *Performance of Components of the West German Coverage Ratio, 1966–86*

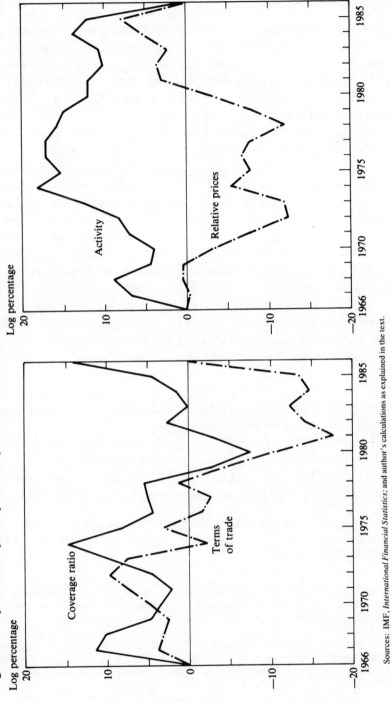

Sources: IMF, *International Financial Statistics;* and author's calculations as explained in the text.

(2) $$\log QX = \alpha \log QXW - \alpha \log RPX + EX$$

(3) $$\log QM = \beta \log \text{GDP} - \beta \log RPM + EM,$$

equations 2 and 3 can be substituted into equation 1 to yield

(4)
$$\log VX - \log VM = \underbrace{\alpha \log QXW - \beta \log GDP}_{\text{activity effect}}$$
$$\underbrace{- \alpha \log RPX + \beta \log RPM}_{\text{price effect}}$$
$$\underbrace{+ \log PX - \log PM}_{\text{terms of trade effect}} + \underbrace{EX - EM.}_{\text{residual}}$$

The results of such a decomposition, based so that 1966 is zero are reported in figure 2, which shows that through 1975 the activity effect imparted a strong upward bias to the coverage ratio. Between 1965 and 1973, given the growth in world trade volumes, German GDP could have increased at 5.0 percent a year at constant relative prices with little change in the coverage ratio. In fact, growth averaged 4.0 percent, with the result that the mark appreciated, providing a relative price effect that offset the tendency toward surplus.

The equation system explains the unexpected behavior of German trade between 1973 and 1974—indeed, it tracks the shift in the coverage ratio with an error of just 1.54 percentage points. Between 1973 and 1974, despite the oil shock, the German coverage ratio improved by 4.8 percent. The marginal impact of the rapid surge in world trade coupled with a decline in German growth raised the coverage ratio by 5.5 percent, and slower inflation in German products added another 7 percent, so that the terms of trade deterioration of 9.7 percent was more than offset.

From 1973 to 1980, Germany actually grew at the 2.5 real average annual percent growth rate that was warranted to maintain the coverage ratio. Between 1980 and 1985 real GNP growth of 1.3 percent was slightly below the warranted rate of 1.6 percent annually. The 12.0 percent improvement in the coverage ratio due to the improvement in relative German price competitiveness more than offset the 2.5 percent decline attributable to the deterioration of the terms of trade.

Thus by 1986 the German current account balance appeared unusually strong: the trade and current account surpluses were 5.8 and 4.0 percent of GNP, respectively.[17] By contrast, from 1970 to 1985 the average trade balance was 3.3 percent of GNP and the current account balance equal to 0.7 percent. The economy therefore had a trade surplus about 2.5

17. *OECD Economic Outlook*, no. 41 (June 1987), pp. 76–81.

Figure 3. *Performance of Components of the French Current Account, 1965–86*

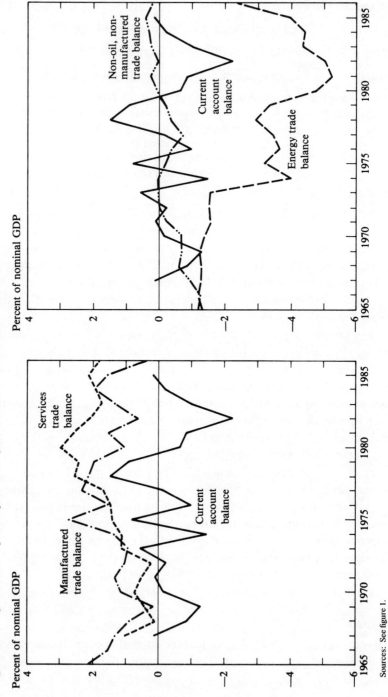

Percent of nominal GDP

Percent of nominal GDP

percent of GNP higher than its long-run average. However, two factors boosting the German current account, the strong dollar and low oil prices, did not persist through 1987. Assuming a real exchange rate 7 percent higher than in 1986 and oil prices 43 percent higher in dollars, and substituting them into equations G2 and G8 yields, after allowing for lags, a trade balance adjusted for these factors of 4.4 percent of GNP and a current account of about 2.4 percent. Equations G2 and G8 indicate that at constant relative prices, if activity and trade flows are related in the same way they have been over the past twenty years, German GNP could grow at 4 percent a year for two years in the face of a 3 percent growth in the GDP of the OECD without reducing Germany's current account balances below its long-run average. A third year of such relatively more rapid growth would bring the trade account to 1.8 percent of GNP (and the current account close to zero).

In sum, in the short term the German economy has considerable room to expand. Over the medium term, however, unless it adopts policies that change its absorption behavior at full employment, Germany is fairly tightly constrained by global economic growth. As an open economy Germany has difficulties expanding much more rapidly than the rest of the OECD for an extended period of time. In the past, at 3 percent OECD growth the German economy would have had to grow at 2.62 percent annually to maintain its coverage ratio at constant terms of trade. At 5 percent growth in the OECD, however, a 5 percent rise in German growth would be warranted.

This analysis does not suggest that competitiveness, in the sense of requiring a depreciation to maintain external balance, was actually a major constraint on the German economy in the 1970s. In fact, through the mid-1970s German growth was slower than warranted by global conditions.

France: Recent Problems

As shown in figure 3, the French current account has remained in rough balance for most of the past two decades. Consider in particular the changes in French trade and the activity variables that influence trade reported in table 2.

Between 1965–73 and 1973–80 a stable French trade performance is evident. While import volumes (QM) grew somewhat faster than export volumes (QX) in both periods, total French export volumes rose more

Table 2. *Total Changes in French Trade and Activity Variables,*
Selected Period, 1965–85
Changes in logarithms

Period	QX	QM	QXM	GDP	QXW	QXMW	COV	TOT
1965–73	82	91	82	42	69	80	−1.1	8.1
1973–80	38	39	42	19	26	38	−15.2	−14.0
1980–85	11	4.5	9	6	10	22	9.8	3.2

Sources: IMF, International Financial Statistics tape; and United Nations, *Monthly Bulletin of Trade Statistics* (various issues).

rapidly than world trade (QXW) and slightly faster than world exports of manufactured goods ($QXMW$). In both periods import volumes grew about twice as fast as French GDP. In 1965–73 an improvement in the terms of trade (TOT) of 8.1 percent kept the coverage ratio (COV) almost constant. In 1973–80 a deterioration of 14.0 percent constituted the major source of the 15.2 percent slump in the coverage ratio. The data suggest a relatively stable structure in French performance relative to foreign and domestic economic activity.

Between 1980 and 1985, however, trade behavior was noticeably different. The growth of French exports, particularly of manufactured goods, was unusually slow. Manufactured export volumes actually grew more slowly than total exports and at just below half the rate of world manufactured exports. While the French share in world manufactured export values had increased from 7.4 percent in 1970 to 8.0 percent in 1980, it declined to 6.6 percent in 1984. Imports, however, increased by less than GDP—roughly half their previous elasticity. In the regression analysis that follows I will confirm the relatively satisfactory and stable French trade performance through 1980 and the particularly poor performance of French manufactured exports thereafter.

Consider the regressions reported in table 3, in which total exports and imports are a function of relative French prices and foreign and domestic economic activity.[18] Export equation F1, fitted over the period 1965–85, confirms the elasticity of French exports with respect to world export volumes. Ceteris paribus, each 1 percent rise in world exports induces a 1.25 percent increase in French merchandise exports. Moreover, splitting the sample period into two (equations F2 and F3) indicates the stability of this relationship in both subperiods. On the import side, for the full sample period the GDP elasticity is estimated at 2.03. Taken

18. Considerable effort using two-stage least squares techniques to control for simultaneous equation estimation biases failed to provide superior equations.

Table 3. French Trade Equations, Selected Periods, 1965–85[a]

Dependent variable	Period	Equation number	log QXW	log GDP80	log RPX	log RPM	D74ON × log RPM	$\bar{R}^2$	Standard error	Durbin-Watson statistic
log QX	1965–85	F1	1.25 (43.6)	...	−0.82 (2.8)	...	...	0.998	0.023	1.8[b]
	1965–74	F2	1.21 (23.5)	...	−1.09[c] (1.8)	...	...	0.997	0.025	1.7[b]
	1975–85	F3	1.13 (10.9)	...	−0.72 (2.2)	...	...	0.980	0.022	1.1[b]
	1965–80	F4	1.27 (43.1)	...	−0.73 (1.72)	...	...	0.998	0.026	1.7[b]
log QM	1965–85	F5	...	2.03 (39.1)	...	−0.25 (2.2)	...	0.995	0.033	1.8
	1965–74	F6	...	1.99 (16.43)	...	−0.78 (1.03)	...	0.995	0.030	1.8
	1975–85	F7	...	2.25 (8.4)	...	−0.20 (0.74)	...	0.967	0.031	2.3
	1965–80	F8	...	2.05 (35.4)	...	−0.30 (1.7)	...	0.994	0.036	1.9
	1965–85	F9	...	2.09 (38.7)	...	−0.41 (3.2)	0.32 (2.1)	0.996	0.030	2.1

Source: International Monetary Fund, International Financial Statistics tape.
a. Annual data; *t*-statistics are in parentheses. *QM* is the volume of merchandise imports; *QXW* is the volume of world trade; *GDP80* is GDP in 1980 dollars; *QX* is the volume of merchandise exports; *RPM* is the ratio of manufacturing import unit values to domestic manufactures wholesale prices (current and one-year lag); *RPX* is the IMF relative manufacturing price series (current and two-year lags); *D74ON × RPM* is a dummy variable equal to 1 for all years after 1974 multiplied by *RPM*.
b. Corrected for first-order serial correlation.
c. Current and one-year lag.

Figure 4. *Performance of Components of the French Coverage Ratio, 1966–85*

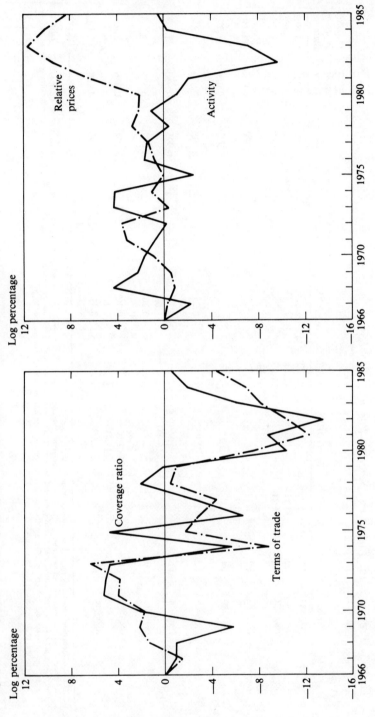

together with the regression relating OECD growth to world exports reported above, these equations suggest that a 3 percent increase in the GNP of the OECD yields a warranted growth rate of similar magnitudes for French GDP (2.8 percent). The warranted rate, is, however, particularly sensitive to OECD cyclical behavior. A 1 percent decline in the OECD growth rate yields a warranted rate of -2.6 percent for France. OECD growth at 5 percent would be compatible with a 5.7 percent increase for France.

Aggregate French trade does not appear very responsive to relative price shifts: the equations for the full sample period have elasticities for exports and imports that sum only to 1.07. Splitting the sample period indicates a significant decline in import price sensitivity after 1974. Estimated over the period 1965–74, equations F2 and F6 together yield coefficients that add to 1.87.[19] While the export price coefficient remains fairly stable, near 0.70 through 1980, the import price coefficient declines in absolute value. A multiplicative dummy variable used with the relative price term indicates that the decline in import price elasticity (equation F9) is statistically significant. It seems reasonable to hypothesize that the declining import price elasticity reflects the different composition of price changes in the two periods—in particular the dominant role of oil import prices, for which demand is highly inelastic, after 1973. Thus the import relative price coefficient should not be interpreted as the impact of a real devaluation due to a uniform change in relative French prices of all imported commodities. Indeed, a regression for French manufactured imports between 1973 and 1985 indicates an import price elasticity of -1.10. The post-1980 fall in the export price coefficient is attributable to the unusual behavior in manufactured exports explored below.

Equations F1 (estimated without correction for serial correlation) and F5 have been used to decompose shifts in the French coverage ratio into its components. These are illustrated in figure 4. In 1968–69, as might be expected, the system errs because of the impact of the strikes in that period on French production. Between 1966 and 1973 the coverage ratio was almost unchanged because of activity effects. The 5.45 percent average annual growth rate of the French economy was slightly below the warranted rate of 5.64 percent. Its rise reflected improvements in French terms of trade that offset the decline caused by the rise in relative prices.

19. Equation F2 has been estimated after dropping the unusual years of 1968 and 1969 from the sample.

Between 1973 and 1980 France grew more rapidly than its warranted rate—3.1 percent versus 2.4 percent. But this effect was countered by an improvement in relative prices. Between 1979 and 1980 an 8.5 percent downward shift in the coverage ratio resulted from deteriorating terms of trade and a 2.1 percent fall from relatively faster growth. Thus the decline of 10.6 percent in the coverage ratio is almost fully predicted by the equation system.

In 1981 France began to benefit from the impact of its devaluation; the relative price impact improved the coverage ratio by 4.5 percent. However, a 4.8 percent deterioration in the terms of trade nullified this effect. In 1982 the full impact of François Mitterrand's decision to grow rapidly in the face of slow OECD growth was felt: the coverage ratio fell 7.1 percent as a result. Despite some improvement in performance because of the weaker franc, the trade deficit reached its lowest point for the sample period. Thereafter, relatively slower growth and improvements in the terms of trade more than offset some of the erosion in France's relative price competitiveness between 1983 and 1985. Overall, the analysis points to terms of trade shocks as the dominant sources of French trade balance variance, with relative price effects and activity effects tending to be negatively correlated.

In sum, the regression analysis for aggregate French net exports performs fairly satisfactorily and suggests that through 1980 a relatively favorable impression of French competitiveness is warranted. At constant terms of trade France can match a growth rate of 3 percent in the OECD without a deterioration in its coverage ratio. The overall import income elasticity is typical of the countries in our sample and was stable through 1979.[20]

Estimates including the 1980s and out-of-sample forecasts for the 1980s do, however, paint a more disquieting picture: in 1981 an out-of-sample forecast using equation F4 indicates French exports were 4.6 percent higher than might have been expected. By 1985 exports were 2

20. These results hinge on the use of the relative export price series estimated by the International Monetary Fund. While this series conforms closely to those available from the OECD and the United Nations, it does not match the behavior of the relative price series as reported by the Institut National de la Statistique et des Etudes Economiques, *Le Mouvement Economique en France, 1949–1979* (May 1981), pp. 189–90. In particular, the INSEE series shows a substantial decline in the relative prices of French manufactured goods both between 1965 and 1973 and between 1973 and 1980. The INSEE series implies lower French manufactured unit value growth and thus faster volume growth.

Table 4. *French Manufactured Goods Trade Equations,*
Selected Periods, 1965–85[a]

Period	Equation number	log QXWM	log RPX	log CU	log PROF	$\bar{R}^2$	Standard error	Durbin-Watson statistic
1966–85	F10	1.13 (44.9)	0.79 (1.8)	0.55 (1.6)	. . .	0.994	0.039	1.5
1966–74[b]	F11	1.24 (14.2)	−1.64 (2.5)	−1.26 (1.4)	. . .	0.998	0.026	3.3
1975–85	F12	0.71 (6.3)	−0.64 (1.2)	1.07 (1.7)	. . .	0.973	0.026	1.6
1965–80	F13	1.19 (44.7)	−1.29 (2.5)	−0.72 (2.0)	. . .	0.997	0.030	1.5
1965–85	F14	1.13 (49.3)	−0.28 (0.92)	0.37 (1.3)	−0.46 (2.1)	0.996	0.035	1.6
1966–80	F15	1.17 (50.0)	. . .	−0.31 (0.97)	0.82 (2.14)	0.997	0.027	1.9

Sources: See table 1.

a. Annual data, *t*-statistics in parentheses. *QXWM* is the value of world manufactured goods trade manufacturing; *RPX* is the IMF relative manufacturing price series (current and two-year lags); *CU* is capacity utilization; and *PROF* is the ratio of export prices to unit labor costs in manufacturing (jointly estimated current and lagged one year).

b. Estimated with dummy variable for 1968 (not reported).

percent lower than expected. Equation F4 thus overpredicts the change of export volumes over the period by 6.6 percent. Imports, however, were higher than predicted by 6.3 percent in 1981 but on track by 1985. By making offsetting errors, the system predicts trade behavior with relative accuracy, but the prediction disguises an important shift in behavior. The French Socialists set out to "reconquer the domestic market." The equation system suggests they succeeded to some extent, although their policies may also have had a negative impact on French export performance.

The picture of unusually weak manufactured goods export performance between 1982 and 1985 is confirmed by a detailed analysis of behavior over this period. Consider the regressions explaining French manufactured export trade reported in table 4. Note first how poorly the regression (F14) fitted over the period 1965–85 performs. The coefficient on relative prices profitability and capacity utilization both have the wrong signs. Consider by contrast the reasonable behavior of equation F13 fitted from 1965 to 1980.[21] The demand for French manufactured

21. For estimates of French trade behavior in the 1970s, see Gilles Oudiz and Henri Sterdyniak, "Inflation, Employment and External Constraints: An Overview of the French Economy during the Seventies," in Jacques Melitz and Charles Wyplosz, eds., *The French Economy: Theory and Policy* (Boulder, Colo.: Westview Press, 1985), p. 40.

Table 5. *Indicators of French Manufacturing Competitiveness*
1980 = 100

Period	SQXM	SVXM	RPX	CU	PROF
1981	100	94	94	96	101
1982	100	91	93	96	105
1983	100	90	92	96	107
1984	95	87	95	97	117
1985[a]	92	86	97	98	121

Source: IFS tape.
a. Data are for first three quarters only.

exports is elastic (1.29), the price coefficient significant and appropriately signed. In addition, the capacity variable indicates a significant role for capacity constraints on French competitiveness. But as the dramatic differences in the coefficients between equations F13 and F10 might lead one to expect, F13 fitted from 1965 to 1980 does very poorly in explaining French manufactured trade from 1981 to 1985. In 1985, for example, the volume of French manufactured exports was 18 percent lower than the F13 equation would predict.

A second specification assumes French manufacturers are price-takers in world markets.[22] Thus their responses occur along a supply curve, expressed as the ratio of export prices to domestic unit labor costs. This variable, which is highly collinear with relative manufactured export unit value (*RPX*), also produces a reasonable equation fitted between 1965 and 1980, but it too goes awry in an out-of-sample forecast, indicating export volumes that are too low in 1985 by 25 percent. In sum, French manufacturing export behavior has been particularly mysterious in the 1980s. Despite the improvement in profitability and price competitiveness and the apparent increase in available production capacity shown in table 5, manufactured goods export volumes grew more slowly than world trade.

Between 1980 and 1983, as measured by the IMF, *RPX* declined by 8 percent; capacity utilization (*CU*), as reported by the Commission of the European Communities, fell by 4 percent; while between 1980 and 1985 the ratio of manufactured export prices to unit labor costs increased 21 percent. Yet between 1980 and 1985 the French share in developed-

22. A regression of French manufactured export prices on unit labor costs and the United Nations manufactured goods unit value index suggests about half of French export behavior matches the price-taker model, about half the price-setter: $\log PX = 0.52PW + 0.47ULC$.

country manufactured goods exports fell 8 percent in volume and 14 percent in value. When these variables are included in the sample, the regression (F14) finds the best way to fit the data is to give their coefficients the wrong sign.

One explanation for all this is that French manufactured exports have had a particularly unfavorable geographic composition over the past few years, given their emphasis on OPEC and Eastern European nations. But OECD estimates indicate an erosion in French market shares even when their particular geographic distribution is more precisely tracked.[23] A second hypothesis, favored by some French observers, is the long-run impact of declining industry profitability.[24] But it may also be the case that the industrial policies of the Mitterrand government have inhibited French manufacturing performance. An equation explaining French export prices on the basis of competitors' prices and domestic unit labor costs suggests French exporters preferred to enjoy higher profit margins rather than increased market shares, particularly in 1983 and 1984. In light of the weak response to their lower prices in 1982 and 1983, this behavior is perhaps explainable. But it does indicate a structural change in the behavior of French manufacturers that could have serious long-term implications.

Between 1983 and 1986, the relative price competitiveness of French manufactured goods exports, as measured by the International Monetary Fund, declined by 8 percent. In 1986 the ratio of the trade balance in manufactured products to GNP was lower than in any year since 1965. Nonetheless, the French current account was almost balanced, primarily because of low energy prices. Reflecting the rise in net foreign borrowing in the 1980s and declining revenue from major foreign works projects, the balance in services and net investment income, while substantial (1.8 percent of GNP), was about 1 percent lower than its 1980 peak level. Unlike Germany, therefore, France does not have much scope for

23. A constant-market-shares analysis undertaken by the OECD indicates that between 1978–79 and 1983–84 the geographical and product mix effects together can account for only 5.3 of the 21.0 percent fall in the French market share. See *OECD Economic Surveys, 1986–87: France* (Paris: OECD, 1987), p. 21.

24. As Edmond Malinvaud has noted, "the inability of French firms to benefit much up to now from the recent favourable shift of labour costs and production prices in international currency is worth noting; in 1982–3 it could be attributed to the fact that demand was more depressed abroad than in France, but that explanation can no longer hold in 1984. The present mediocre performance of the French market share may be related to the pronounced decline in profitability in the early 1980s." "The Rise of Unemployment in France," *Economica*, no. 53 (1986, *Supplement*), p. S203.

Figure 5. *Performance of Components of the Swedish Current Account, 1965–86*

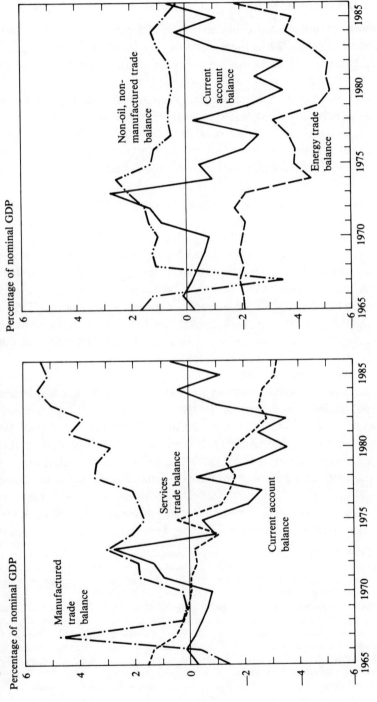

Sources: See figure 1.

exceeding its warranted growth without moving into current account deficit or sustaining a real devaluation.

Sweden: Trade Effects of Macroeconomic Imbalances

Since 1973 the international competitiveness of the Swedish economy has been a constant source of concern for Swedish policymakers.[25] There are two major lines of explanation for Sweden's balance of payments problems since that year. One emphasizes microeconomic and structural factors, the other macroeconomic imbalances. The structural argument is that Swedish industry was poorly equipped to cope with the post-1973 international environment. Sweden's industrial composition was too heavily weighted with declining sectors and its exports were too concentrated in slow-growing markets. Moreover, rigidities in domestic labor and capital markets coupled with inappropriate industrial policies inhibited the adjustment from declining to expanding sectors.

The second line of argument emphasizes the external consequences of macroeconomic imbalances. Swedish budgetary policies failed to adjust to an era of slower growth. The government financed its deficits by borrowing from abroad. This slump in the national savings rate was reflected in current account deficits and growing international indebtedness. In addition, wages failed to adjust to the lower real growth forecasts warranted by the decline in productivity growth after 1973. Wages squeezed the profits of industries, which were unable to pass such increases on in higher prices. The slump in the profitability of price-taking industries discouraged supply and hurt performance in international markets.

My evidence here indicates this latter interpretation provides most of the explanation.

Figure 5 shows the trends in the major components of the Swedish current account. The balance of trade in manufactured goods has sustained a continuous upward improvement since 1965. The balance in petroleum products eroded through 1982 and improved thereafter. The balance in agricultural, forestry, and non-oil minerals experienced a major slump in 1976 and some recovery after 1982. The balance in

25. This section updates the study of Robert Z. Lawrence and Barry P. Bosworth, "Adjusting to Slower Economic Growth: The External Sector," in Barry P. Bosworth and Alice M. Rivlin, eds., *The Swedish Economy* (Brookings, 1987), pp. 60–69.

services, transfers, and factor payments showed a continuous downward trend.

The slumps in the oil and services balances are easily explained. The deterioration of the balance on net factor income is a straightforward consequence of the buildup of foreign debt. The balance in nonmanufactured goods primarily reflects changes in world demand for raw materials. The key questions about the rest of trade relate both to historical interpretation and to the future. Was a real devaluation required in the 1970s not simply to offset deterioration in the external balance because of higher oil prices and growing international indebtedness but also to offset a deterioration that would otherwise have occurred in the rest of the trade balance? And in the future, if the Swedish terms of trade remain constant and Sweden and the rest of the world grow at long-run trend rates, would the trade balance tend to erode?

The *1984 Medium Term Survey of the Swedish Economy* provides pessimistic answers to both questions: "terms of trade have deteriorated because relative prices in the exposed sector have had to be lowered continuously in order to contain the loss of shares for Swedish producers at home as well as abroad." It also suggests that to achieve a current account surplus of 1 percent of GDP in 1990, relative price declines of about 18 percent need to be achieved over the 1980s.[26]

If such an analysis is accurate, its implications are serious both for living standards and for the choice of inflation objectives. Since non-oil imports amounted to 22.3 percent of Swedish GNP in 1984, a deterioration in the terms of trade of almost 2.0 percent a year would be a significant drag on improvements in economic welfare. In addition, even the rather ambitious objective of holding the rate of increase in unit costs to that of Sweden's major trading partners would be incompatible with external balance. For the exchange rate to remain fixed, costs would have to rise less than those of its trading partners.

Among the factors believed to have detracted from Swedish competitiveness in the 1970s are a poor mix of products and markets, the profits squeeze in Swedish industry, and the impact of expanding public-sector spending and policies in crowding out industrial capacity.

According to several studies, among them the *1984 Medium Term Survey,* Sweden has an unfavorable mix of exports in terms of commodity

---

26. Swedish Ministry of Finance, *The 1984 Medium Term Survey of the Swedish Economy* (Stockholm, 1984), p. 58. About 10 percentage points of this had been achieved by 1984.

composition and geographic concentration. In particular, dependence on exports of iron ore, steel, forest products, metal products, and power machinery is seen as especially disadvantageous in the global environment of the 1970s. Similarly, a concentration on slow-growing European markets has hurt.[27] The survey ascribes about a third of the fall in Swedish market share to an unfavorable commodity mix. Similarly, using constant market shares analysis, Eva Horwitz concluded that between 1970 and 1980 these factors together could account for almost 70 percent of the shrinkage in Swedish market shares.[28]

Many Swedish firms are price-takers in global markets. Thus an increase in unit labor costs exceeding that of competitors will squeeze profit margins. Between 1969 and 1978 the share of profits in value added in Swedish manufacturing declined from 30 percent to 15.2 percent.[29] In goods production (agriculture, mining, and manufacturing) the slump was 10 percentage points. By the late 1970s the solvency of many firms was seriously in question. Government subsidies for capital-intensive sectors such as shipbuilding, steel, and mining exploded; poor profitability retarded capacity growth and reduced the supply of manufactured goods in export and import-competing industries.

A major devaluation of the kronar in 1981–82 translated into large gains in profitability. Indeed, in 1984 the profit share amounted to 33 percent of value added in manufacturing, a share higher than at any time since the 1960s.[30] Accordingly, if poor profitability explained the weak performance in the late 1970s, it ought not to have been a significant

27. MOF, *1984 Medium Term Survey*, pp. 58–59. The survey reports that while world trade grew at an annual rate of 6.1 percent in the 1970s, Swedish exports increased at only 3.3 percent. It ascribes an annual rate of −0.9 percent to unfavorable commodity composition and −1.7 percent to factors such as unfavorable relative price and profitability conditions (p. 214).

28. Eva Christina Horwitz, "Export Performance of the Nordic Countries, 1965–82—A Constant-Market-Shares Analysis," in Det Økonomiske Rad (Danish Economic Council) and others, *Economic Growth in a Nordic Perspective* (Finland: DOR, 1984), pp. 259–84. This is updated in Horwitz, "Marknadsandelar för Svensk Export, 1978–1984" (Stockholm: Kommerskollegium [Swedish Board of Commerce], February 25, 1986).

29. Organization for Economic Cooperation and Development, *National Accounts, 1971–1983*, vol. 2: *Detailed Tables* (Paris: OECD, 1985), pp. 49, 453; and Sveriges officiella statistik, *Nationalräkenskaper, 1970–1984* (Stockholm: Statistiska centralbyrån, 1985) [Official Statistics of Sweden, *National Accounts Annual Report, 1970–1984* (Stockholm: Statistics Sweden, 1985)].

30. For an analysis, see Swedish National Industrial Board (SIND) "Productivity and Gross Profits 1985: Toward Industrial Renewal?" (Stockholm: SIND, 1985).

factor by the mid-1980s. But the adjustment in profitability levels since 1978 is unlikely to be repeated.

The exploding relative share of the government sector is also widely believed to have had a retarding effect on Swedish competitiveness. The effect could have operated both directly and indirectly. First, the government competes with industry for worker talent. Second, the expansion in government demand will switch the attention of firms away from producing tradables and toward nontradables. Third, several government programs ostensibly designed to aid industry may actually have increased tax burdens, reduced work incentives, and undermined the work ethic; and by keeping assets and labor in slow-growing sectors, they may have delayed the reallocation of resources to high-growth activities.

While the arguments that these factors have reduced the Swedish share in world trade may be valid, they do not answer the key question of concern here. An improvement in the overall trade balance is quite compatible with a declining share in foreign markets, provided imports expand more slowly than exports. To explain what happened, one needs estimates of the income elasticities of both imports and exports that can be applied to the trend rate of economic growth in Sweden and abroad. In what follows, I obtain such estimates using variables reflecting costs, profits, capacity utilization, and the share of government in total GDP to explain the volumes of Swedish exports and non-oil imports. Estimates for both manufacturing and overall trade are provided.

In estimating the equations, I assume that Swedish firms can be grouped into two polar types—price-takers and price-setters. Price-takers are concerned with the relationship between the world price and domestic costs, and an equation relating the quantity of exports to these variables will be a supply curve. I have attempted to capture this relationship by relating exports of price-takers (Q_1) to the share of labor costs in domestic production (SVA), a measure of profitability: $Q_1 = f(SVA)$. But for price-setters, with constant markups over standard unit labor costs, exports depend on the relationship between their prices (Pm) and those of foreign exporters (P_w), and the equation provides an estimate of the demand elasticity.[31] In addition, other factors such as world income and capacity utilization (designed to reflect delivery speed)

31. The assumption of infinitely elastic supply curves for price-setters allows an equation relating the quantity of exports to the relative price of domestic and foreign products to be interpreted as a demand curve.

might be included in such a system: thus $Q_2 = F(Pm/Pw, Cu, Y)$. The overall equation for total exports is a weighted average of Q_1 and Q_2, where the weight is the share of each in total exports. Thus the coefficients on export prices and standard unit labor costs should not be taken to be the overall price and supply elasticities for price-setters and -takers, respectively, but rather those elasticities multiplied by the appropriate share in total trade.

I obtained a measure of the relative importance of price-takers in Swedish exports by estimating an equation identical to that reported earlier for German and French export prices. The equation indicated that about 60 percent of Swedish export firms are price-takers and 40 percent are price-setters.[32]

Tables 6 and 7 show equations for both manufacturing and overall trade that reflect these formulations. Equation S1 reports a conventional demand specification in which the quantity of manufactured exports is explained by the volume of world exports (QXW) and the relative export price of Swedish manufactured goods (RP) as measured by the International Monetary Fund. Since the variables are expressed in logarithms, the coefficients can be interpreted as elasticities. The equation has a standard error of 2.1 percent and a Durbin-Watson statistic that strongly suggests omitted variables (table 6).

The substantial contribution to the equation's explanatory power made by the inclusion of variables capturing the supply side is shown in equation S2. The complete specification tracks the volume of manufactured exports with a standard error of less than 0.9 percent, less than half that of the simple demand-side specification. The equation suggests that the demand for the products of Swedish price-setters has an elasticity of 1.8 (0.75/0.42). That estimate may be somewhat high because I was forced to use the overall unit value index instead of the prices of just the price-setters. Similarly, the estimate suggests that in price-taking sectors, supply has an elasticity of about 0.33. The supply-side variables are each statistically significant and point to the significant contributions of domestic economic factors in determining export performances.

Equations S3 and S4 repeat the exercise with the total volume of Swedish exports (QX). As might be expected, when the agricultural and minerals sectors are included—sectors that contain a greater share of

32. The specific equation was
$$\log PX = -0.69 + 0.61 \log PW + 0.42 \log ULC.$$
$$(4.1) \quad (6.8) \quad \quad (4.3)$$

Table 6. *Swedish Export Equations*[a]

Dependent variable	Equation number	log QXW	log RP	log SVA	log CU	log G/GDP	$\bar{R}^2$	Standard error	Durbin-Watson statistic
log QXM	S1	0.94 (27.5)	-0.75 (8.2)	...	...	...	0.990	0.021	1.3
log QXM	S2	0.99 (19.4)	-0.75 (10.7)	-0.21 (3.0)	-0.095 (6.5)	-0.22 (2.1)	0.999	0.009	2.8
log QX	S3	0.90 (12.7)	-0.73 (3.9)	...	...	...	0.951	0.045	0.8
log QX	S4	1.16 (16.1)	-0.46 (4.9)	-0.55 (6.2)	-0.047 (2.2)	-0.56 (3.8)	0.997	0.013	2.3

Sources: Based on annual data for 1970–84. See Sveriges officiella statistik, *Allmän Månadsstatistik* (Statistiska centralbyrån, various issues) [Official Statistics of Sweden, *Monthly Digest of Swedish Statistics* (Stockholm: Statistics Sweden, various issues)]; Sveriges officiella statistik, *Nationalräkenskaper, 1970–84* (Stockholm: Statistiska centralbyrån, 1985) [Official Statistics of Sweden, *National Accounts Annual Report, 1970–1984* (Stockholm: Statistics Sweden, 1985)]; and data from Swedish National Institute of Economic Research.

a. The numbers in parentheses are *t*-statistics. *QXM* is the volume of manufactured exports; *QX* is the volume of merchandise exports; *QXW* is the volume of world trade as measured by the United Nations; *RP* is the ratio of Swedish export prices to those of its competitors as measured by the IMF (the reported coefficient is the sum of the current and lagged price terms); *SVA* is the share of labor compensation in value added; *CU* is the index of capacity utilization; and *G/GDP* is the ratio of government spending to GNP.

Table 7. *Swedish Import Equations*[a]

Dependent variable	Equation number	log IMWD	T	log RPM	log G/GDP	$\bar{R}^2$	Standard error	Durbin-Watson statistic
log QMM	S1	0.93 (6.7)	...	0.71 (2.8)	...	0.887	0.028	1.2
log QMM	S2	1.05 (6.5)	...	1.17 (2.8)	0.19 (1.3)	0.906	0.027	1.5
log QM	S3	1.17 (10.3)	...	0.01 (0.003)	0.25 (2.5)	0.987	0.019	1.9
log QM	S4	1.31 (7.6)	-0.494×10^{-2} (1.03)	0.01 (0.04)	0.35 (2.5)	0.989	0.019	2.2

Sources: Based on annual data for 1972–85; see notes to table 6.
a. The numbers in parentheses are *t*-statistics. *QMM* is the volume of manufactured imports; *QM* is the volume of merchandise imports; *IMWD* is the weighted average of demand components; *T* is a time trend; *RPM* is the ratio of domestic manufactured goods wholesale prices to the import price index for manufactured goods (reported coefficient is the sum of the coefficients on the current and lagged price terms); and *G/GDP* is the ratio of government spending to GDP.

price-takers—the importance of profitability increases. At the level of aggregate exports, the price elasticities and supply elasticities both seem to be fairly close to unity.

How well does an equation such as S4, estimated from a sample period of 1970–81, work in tracking Swedish export performance after devaluation? An out-of-sample forecast provides errors of 1.3 percent in 1982, 0.95 percent in 1983, and −4.8 percent in 1984, thus suggesting a relatively high degree of structural stability.

Equations for imports are reported in table 7. To measure the demand for imports, I have used a data series of the Swedish National Institute of Economic Research that weighs the components of GDP by their import intensity on the basis of an input-output table. I was unable to find a role for profit shares and capacity utilization in explaining import demand. There is some evidence that a growing government sector increases manufacturing imports and stronger evidence that it increases imports of total merchandise. While the aggregate import equation has a positive time trend, the addition of the government share of GDP to the equation eliminates the significance of the coefficient on the time trend and *G/GDP* is positive and statistically significant. This result is particularly striking. Under normal circumstances, one would expect to see a negative coefficient on the *G/GDP* variable since government spending on services is relatively less import-intensive than other components of GDP. The positive coefficient strongly suggests a crowding-out effect of an expanding government sector on the domestic supply of tradables. However, the inclusion of nonmanufactured imports in the

Table 8. *Decomposition of the Swedish Manufactured Goods Trade Balance, 1972–84*

Percentage points of actual change unless otherwise indicated

Manufactured goods	Actual change (percent)	Contributors to change					
		Market growth	Capacity utilization	Relative prices	Profits share	Government expansion	Error
1972–78							
Exports	25.5	31.3	4.1	−5.0	−2.1	−4.4	1.6
Imports	7.4	13.5	. . .	−11.2	. . .	4.0	1.1
Net Balance	18.1	17.8	4.1	6.2	−2.1	−8.4	0.5
1978–84							
Exports	26.1	13.7	−4.0	10.2	4.6	0.0	1.6
Imports	13.0	22.3	. . .	−8.3	. . .	0.0	−1.0
Net Balance	13.1	−8.6	−4.0	18.5	4.6	0.0	2.6

Source: Author's calculations as explained in text.

definition of the dependent variable eliminates the prior incidence of a significant influence of relative prices. The out-of-sample forecast errors using the import equation are 0.04 percent for 1982, 2.6 percent for 1983, and − 2.4 percent for 1984.

I have used equations S2 from table 6 and S2 from table 7 to decompose changes in the volume of manufacturing trade into their underlying components, and the results are shown in table 8. It is convenient to split the sample period into two periods, 1972–78 and 1978–84. And it is striking how different are the forces driving the manufacturing trade balances between the two.

In both periods the volume of Swedish manufactured exports increased by similar percentages, 25.5 and 26.1. Yet the composition of that growth was very different. In 1972–78 Sweden benefited from a relatively strong expansion of the world economy that increased its exports by 31.3 percent. However, exports were 11.5 percent less than what they might have been—5 percent of the shortfall was caused by a rise in relative prices, 2.1 percent by squeezed profit margins in manufacturing, and 4.4 percent by the crowding out of exports due to the expansion in the government sector. Only the low level of capacity utilization in industry added to export growth. At the same time imports were held down by the recession in Sweden. Essentially, macroeconomic developments disguised a deteriorating structural position.

In 1978–84 foreign economic growth was much slower; exports increased only 13.7 percent while domestic activity expanded more rapidly than before. However, the relative size of the government sector did not increase, the decline in the relative price of Swedish products boosted exports by 10.2 percent, and the improvement in profit margins added an additional 4.6 percent.

In figure 6 equations S2 from table 6 and S2 from table 7 are combined to show the determinants of the net change in the coverage ratio. In turn, the shift of the trade balance can be decomposed into its underlying components. First, differences in the rates of growth of the foreign and domestic markets held down the trade balance between 1972 and 1975; Sweden's relatively slower growth was a strong positive force from 1975 to 1978, but its expansion in the early 1980s was a factor reducing its trade balance. Over the period as a whole the growth of markets made a net positive contribution to the Swedish trade balance. Second, noncompetitive prices hurt the trade balance before 1977 but have improved and helped restore the balance since then. The major source of secular decline in the trade balance during the period as a whole is the growth of government in the domestic economy.

This analysis suggests that Swedish manufacturing does not suffer from a secular decline in its competitiveness. Rather, higher oil prices and increased indebtedness necessitated a growing manufacturing trade surplus and that surplus had to be supplied by real exchange rate devaluations. The major lasting negative influence on competitiveness would seem to have been a crowding-out effect resulting from growing government demand for services. In the absence of major shifts in its external terms of trade and in its national savings rate, Sweden should in the future be able to maintain external balance without real exchange rate depreciation. Combining the Swedish export elasticity on world trade of 1.16 with estimates of an import elasticity of 1.64 (derived from the elasticity of the import demand variable with respect to GDP) indicates that a 3.2 percent rise in Swedish growth is the warranted response to a 3 percent growth rate in the OECD.[33]

United Kingdom

The structure of the British current account has been dramatically transformed since 1973 (figure 7). Between 1965 and 1973, on average the United Kingdom had deficits in energy trade of 1.6 percent of GDP and in other primary commodities of 5.4 percent that were offset by surpluses in services (2.9 percent of GDP) and manufactured goods (4.2

---

33. For a more extensive discussion of Swedish competitiveness see Barry P. Bosworth and Alice M. Rivlin, eds., *The Swedish Economy* (Brookings, 1987).

Figure 6. *Performance of Components of the Swedish Coverage Ratio, 1972–85*

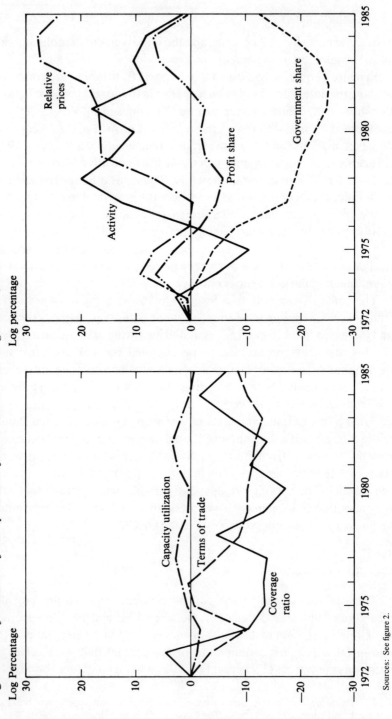

Log Percentage

Log percentage

Sources: See figure 2.

Figure 7. *Performance of Components of the British Current Account, 1965–86*

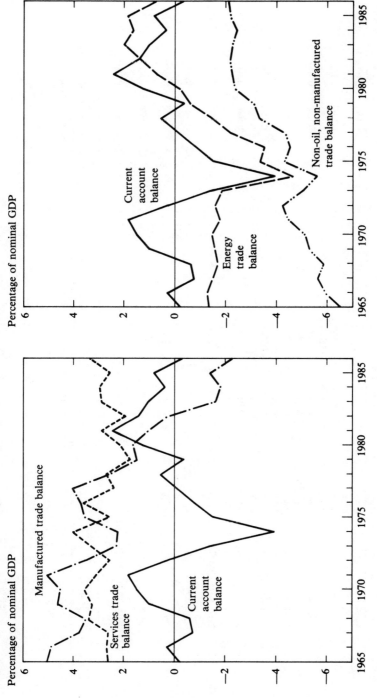

Sources: See figure 1.

Table 9. U.K. Trade Equations, Selected Periods, 1964–85[a]

Dependent variable	Period[b]	Equation number[b]	log QXW	T	DT74ON	log PROF(−1)	log RPX	log GDP80	log RPM	$\bar{R}^2$	Standard error	Durbin-Watson statistic
log QX	1965–85	U1	0.45 (6.2)	0.023 (5.2)	…	…	−0.20 (2.0)	…	…	0.995	0.022	2.23
	1964–85	U2	0.70 (39.3)	…	0.014 (9.2)	0.53 (3.7)	…	…	…	0.997	0.017	2.1
	1964–85	U3	0.69 (33.9)	…	0.017 (6.8)	0.41 (1.8)	−0.13 (1.2)	…	…	0.998	0.017	2.3
	1964–74	U4	0.69 (25.8)	…	0.02 (0.9)	0.83 (2.3)	…	…	…	0.993	0.020	2.1
	1975–85	U5	0.65 (5.2)	…	0.015 (3.7)	0.44 (2.7)	…	…	…	0.985	0.016	2.3
	1964–78	U6	0.69 (31.2)	…	0.016 (3.7)	0.61 (2.3)	…	…	…	0.996	0.019	2.2
log QM	1965–85	U7	…	−0.005 (0.11)	…	…	…	2.17 (10.5)	−0.31 (3.9)	0.995	0.019	2.2
	1965–85	U8	…	…	…	…	…	2.15 (42.8)	−0.30 (4.5)	0.995	0.011	2.4
	1965–75	U9	…	…	…	…	…	2.13 (18.6)	−0.30 (1.3)	0.994	0.019	3.3
	1975–85	U10	…	…	…	…	…	2.46 (16.4)	−0.11 (0.95)	0.988	0.017	2.0
	1965–78	U11	…	…	…	…	…	2.09 (24.8)	−0.27 (3.4)	0.995	0.016	3.1

Out of sample	Equation U6	Equation U11
1979	−0.03	0.02
1980	−0.01	0.01
1981	−0.01	−0.01
1982	0.02	−0.01
1983	−0.02	−0.01
1984	−0.03	0.04
1985	−0.02	0.04

Source: IFS tape and Bureau of Labor Statistics

a. Annual data; t-statistics are in parentheses. QX is the volume of merchandise exports; QM is the volume of merchandise imports; QXW is the volume of world trade; T is the time trend; $DT74ON$ is a time trend after 1973; $PROF$ is the ratio of export prices to unit labor costs in manufacturing; RPX is the IMF relative manufacturing price series (current and one-year lag); $GDP80$ is GDP in 1980 dollars; and RPM is the ratio of manufacturing import unit values to domestic manufactures wholesale prices (current, and one- and two-year lags).

b.

percent). From 1974 to 1984 the increases in the balances in energy (up 3.5 percent of GDP) and primary commodities (up 2.7 percent) were countered by a decline in the balance of trade in manufactured goods (down 4.1 percent) and services (down 0.5 percent).

Britain has become an energy-rich creditor nation with a growing dependence on the rest of the world for manufactured goods. Between 1972 and 1985 the share of manufactured goods in its goods exports declined from 88 to 70 percent while the share of manufactured goods in its goods imports increased from 56 to 71 percent.[34] Over the same period manufactured imports doubled their share in domestic consumption (up from 18 to 33 percent) while exports increased from 19 to 28 percent of production.[35] Despite its plummeting trade balance in manufactured goods Britain improved its current account from a deficit of 4.0 percent of GDP in 1974 to a peak surplus of 2.6 percent of GDP in 1981 and a surplus of 1.2 percent in 1985. As figure 7 indicates, these shifts have mainly reflected developments in merchandise trade.

U.K. trade behavior can be explained with the aid of the regressions in tables 9 and 10. The export equations in table 9 imply disappointing British export behavior since 1974, except for oil exports. Equation U2 explains U.K. exports on the basis of world export volumes (QXW), a time trend after 1973 ($DT74ON$), and the ratio of U.K. export prices to unit labor costs in manufacturing ($PROF$). Overall the equation tracks exports precisely (a standard error of 1.7 percent) with variables that are statistically significant. Each 1 percent rise in world exports is associated with a 0.7 percent rise in U.K. export volumes. This elasticity appears to have remained fairly constant and is virtually identical over the periods 1964–74 (equation U4) and 1975–85 (equation U5).[36] Since U.K. exporters, particularly of nonmanufactured goods, tend to be price-takers, the supply-side formulation appears suitable for simulation purposes. As equation U3 indicates, there is collinearity between the profitability and relative price variables, but the coefficient of profits is more significant and higher in absolute value. As equation U1 indicates, the use of only the relative price variable results in an extremely low export price elasticity of 0.2.

The supply elasticity deteriorated between the sample periods (compare equations U4 and U5), although the difference is not statistically

34. Imports measured c.i.f. from IMF.
35. *European Economy*, no. 25 (September 1985), Statistical Annex, p. 117.
36. When a time trend is used for the entire period together with *DT74ON*, it is not significant.

significant. Equation U6 fitted through 1978 does extremely well when used to forecast out of sample: it tracks U.K. exports over the turbulent 1979–85 period with errors similar to the 1.9 percent standard error of the equation. Except for a positive trend after 1974, therefore, U.K. exports have been related in a stable fashion to world market growth and domestic costs.

Imports reveal a similar stability. Each 1 percent increase in U.K. growth gives rise to a 2.15 percent increase in imports. Equation U9, fitted between 1965 and 1975, is almost identical to U8, which fitted over the entire sample period. As might be expected, U9 tracks U.K. 1976–85 imports precisely. There is some indication of an increase in the import income elasticity and a decline in the price elasticity, but it is not statistically significant.

Taken together, the equations strongly suggest that oil exports have played a crucial role in the British external balance. Without the 1.4 percent a year exogenous growth in exports, the United Kingdom would have an extremely low warranted growth rate. According to this system of equations, a 3 percent growth rate in the OECD entails a warranted growth rate for Britain of just 1.5 percent. With an additional 1.5 percent exogenous rise in U.K. exports, however, growth of 2.2 percent would be warranted.

What if Britain sought to grow more rapidly? What would be the terms of trade cost of an additional 1 percent increase in real GDP? Taking even the highest estimate of the supply-price elasticity for exports (0.83 in equation U4) together with the 0.30 price elasticity estimated in the import equation yields the pessimistic conclusion that, starting from an initially balanced position, the Marshall-Lerner conditions are barely satisfied. A devaluation would therefore provide little scope to grow more rapidly.

But are these estimated elasticities for costs and prices unusually low? The literature is divided. John Williamson cites estimates of -2.0 for U.K. exports and -1.0 for imports as the "typical" price elasticities in the survey by Stern and Schumaker published in 1976.[37] He also reports that the Liverpool model for the United Kingdom has price elasticities that sum to -1.7. But estimates by the Commission of the European Communities for 1964–81 give export and import elasticities of -0.29 and -0.24, respectively.[38]

37. Williamson, "Is There an External Constraint?"
38. "The External Constraint and the Operation of the Price and Income Elasticities

Williamson's elasticity optimism is not supported, by U.K. behavior in the face of the massive sterling appreciation between 1977 and 1980, as an inspection of the export data (in logs with 1980 equaling 0) from that period reveals.

	QXNO	QX	QXW	RPX
1977	-0.03	-0.07	-0.11	-0.23
1978	-0.01	-0.05	-0.06	-0.17
1979	-0.01	-0.01	0.00	-0.11
1981	-0.04	-0.01	0.00	-0.01

Between 1977 and 1981 the relative price of U.K. exports (RPX) increased by 22 percent. If the price elasticity had been unity, exports would have fallen by 22 percent because of the price effects. World exports increased 11 percent. Assuming a unitary activity elasticity for the United Kingdom (my estimates suggest 0.7 is more reasonable), U.K. exports would have increased 11 percent because of activity. All told, U.K. exports would have therefore declined by 12 percent. In fact, the volume of U.K. non-oil exports increased by 1 percent. This implies that relative U.K. prices reduced exports by just 10 percent, an elasticity much closer to 0.35 than to unity.[39]

But even with more elastic price assumptions, offsetting faster growth with real depreciation could be costly. If the price elasticities of U.K. imports and exports are both unity, starting from balanced trade, a 1 percent real devaluation will improve the trade balance by 1 percent of the value of imports. Given an import-GDP elasticity of 2, therefore, each 1 percent rise in GDP would require a real depreciation of 2 percent to preserve balance. Thus given unitary export and import price elasticities, without the exogenous trend growth in oil exports, Britain could match a 3 percent OECD growth rate with an annual real devaluation of 3 percent a year. In 1984 U.K. merchandise imports were equal to 23.3 percent of GDP. A 3 percent deterioration in the real terms of trade

---

of External Trade in the Community Countries, the United States of America and Japan," *European Economy*, no. 16 (July 1983), pp. 140–45.

39. The use of a constant elasticity assumption may not be warranted for large changes in the exchange rate. In the recent appreciation of the U.S. dollar there was a noteworthy decline in U.S. manufactured export price elasticities, as might be expected. As the currency appreciates, the export mix becomes more heavily concentrated with products that have relatively inelastic demands, which may call into question the standard practice of imposing a constant elasticity over the sample period. This suggests a relatively limited potential range for offsetting faster growth by small devaluations when the currency is initially highly overvalued.

Figure 8. *Performance of Components of the British Coverage Ratio, 1966–86*

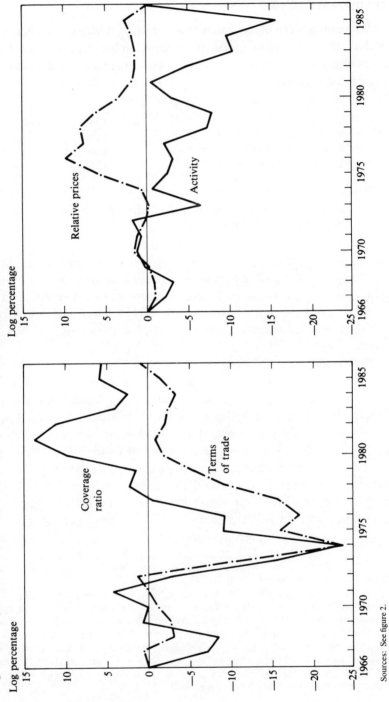

Sources: See figure 2.

would reduce real incomes by 0.7 percent. Thus while Britain might be able to match the OECD rate of output growth of 3 percent with devaluation, real incomes would only rise 2.3 percent. Roughly half the gains in output would be offset by the deterioration in the terms of trade. With an exogenous trend rise in exports of 1.5 percent a year, a depreciation of 1.5 percent would be required to achieve the requisite 3 percent growth in output. But again, half the output gain from devaluation would be offset by the deteriorating terms of trade.

Based on equations U2 and U8, figure 8 shows the determinants of the U.K. coverage ratio between 1966 and 1986. Terms of trade fluctuations strongly influenced the coverage ratio through 1974. In particular, between 1966 and 1974 Britain grew at an annual rate of 2.72 percent, roughly the 2.9 percent rate warranted by the rise in world trade. And relative import and export prices had little overall impact. Terms of trade have also been important since 1974. As a result of the real appreciation of the pound and oil price increases, the U.K. terms of trade in the 1980s are similar to their levels before 1973. In addition, slower-than-warranted growth through 1978, particularly in light of oil exports and improvements in relative prices, helped restore the coverage ratio to just above its 1966 level (the current accounts in both 1966 and 1978 were close to balance). Thereafter, however, price and activity effects were offsetting. Through 1981 the deep slump in Britain counteracted the impact of the strong pound on costs and prices. Since 1981, growth has exceeded the warranted rate while relative prices have improved.

The picture of British trade performance would not be complete without some attention to the performance of manufacturing. The regressions on manufactured goods trade reinforce the pessimistic implications of those for aggregate trade (see table 10). On the export side, pricing behavior suggests British manufacturers are, like those in Sweden, fairly evenly divided between price-setters and price-takers. Consider this regression of U.K. manufactured goods prices (log $PXMAN$) against current and two-year lags on foreign manufactured goods prices as measured by the United Nations (log $PXMW$) and unit labor costs for the United Kingdom (ULC) from 1966 to 1985:

$$\log PXMAN = -0.62 + 0.49 \log ULC + 0.56 \log PXMW.$$
$$(11.8) \quad (7.9) \quad\quad\quad (7.7)$$

Standard error = 0.023; Durbin-Watson = 1.2[40]

40. The same specification fitted through 1978 has coefficients of 0.57 on ULC and

Table 10. U.K. Manufactured Goods Exports and Imports, Selected Periods, 1964–85[a]

Dependent variable	Period	Equation number	log QXMW	log RPX(−1)	log PROF(−1)	T	log GDP80	log RPMM	$\bar{R}^2$	Standard error	Durbin-Watson statistic
log QXM	1964–82	U1	0.70 (5.8)	−0.33 (1.9)	0.65 (1.8)	−0.006 (0.69)	...	...	0.992	0.026	2.1
	1964–82	U2	0.61 (39.1)	−0.42 (3.3)	0.61 (1.7)	...	...	...	0.991	0.026	2.2
	1964–74	U3	0.63 (19.4)	−0.03 (0.03)	0.50 (0.82)	...	...	...	0.991	0.024	2.7
	1964–80	U4	0.63 (45.0)	−0.18 (1.4)	0.40 (1.3)	...	...	...	0.995	0.021	2.6
	1972–82	U5	0.61 (7.0)	−0.39 (1.7)	0.78 (1.3)	...	...	...	0.918	0.033	2.2
	1970–82	U6	0.62 (13.2)	−0.42 (2.4)	0.66 (1.3)	...	...	...	0.956	0.030	2.2
log QMM	1972–82	U7	...	...	...	0.024 (3.1)	2.69 (6.2)	−0.55 (3.1)	0.994	0.024	3.15
	1972–85	U8	...	...	...	0.028 (3.9)	2.41 (6.2)	−0.45 (2.9)	0.996	0.023	2.35
	1974–82	U9	...	...	...	0.009 (0.66)	3.35 (9.8)	−0.87 (2.8)	0.998	0.013	2.28

Sources: See table 9.

a. Annual data; t-statistics are in parentheses. QXM is manufactured export volumes; QMM is manufactured import volumes; $QXMW$ is the United Nations volume of world manufactured goods trade; RPX is the IMF ratio of export unit values in manufacturing; $PROF$ is the ratio of export prices to unit labor costs; $GDP80$ is GDP in 1980 dollars; and $RPMM$ is the ratio of import unit values for manufactured goods to the domestic wholesale price index (coefficient is the sum of current, one-year and two-year lags).

Accordingly, both cost and price variables should help explain trade behavior.[41] Equation U1 in table 10 indicates an elasticity of 0.7 for U.K. exports with respect to world manufactured export volumes, but a negative, albeit insignificant, time trend. Equation U2 drops the time trend, providing an elasticity of 0.61 that appears to remain constant over various sample periods.[42] The equation indicates that both price-taking and price setting behavior is significant. Each 1 percent increase in relative U.K. prices leads to a 0.42 percent loss of exports on the part of price-setters. Each 1 percent rise in prices relative to unit labor costs induces a 0.61 percent rise in exports of price-takers.[43]

The import equation is particularly striking. It captures the trend penetration of the U.K. market, which occurs apparently regardless of the overall U.K. growth rate at about 3 percent a year. The specific meaning of this trend term has been a matter of contention. In particular, there is a debate about whether it results from a decline in the non-price competitiveness of U.K. products or is simply the consequence of increased international specialization in production caused by the removal of trade barriers, lower transportation costs, and so forth.[44] In addition, with an elasticity of about 2.5, British manufactured imports are highly responsive to GDP.

Together these equations form a system that, if interpreted structur-

---

0.45 on *PXMW*, suggesting a shift toward greater price-taking behavior in recent periods. Nonetheless, the regression tracks U.K manufactured goods export prices, out of sample through 1985 wth a mean absolute error of 0.025, quite in line with the standard error of the within-sample estimates.

41. Unfortunately, data availability was limited. Import data were only available from 1970, while both export and import series are, according to the NIESR, discontinuous after 1982. Therefore I concentrate on the period 1970 to 1982.

42. This elasticity is very similar to that of the export equations surveyed in R. Anderton and A. Dunnett, "Modelling the Behavior of Export Volumes of Manufactures: An Evaluation of the Performance of Different Measures of International Competitiveness," Discussion Paper 126 (London: National Institute of Economic and Social Research, May 1987).

43. Together the coefficients sum to around unity. Capacity utilization was also used, without significant results. In addition, two-stage least-squares formulations were experimented with. These did not change the equation markedly or improve its performance.

44. For further discussion, see Keith Cuthbertson, "The Behaviour of U.K. Imports of Manufactured Goods," *National Institute Economic Review*, vol. 3 (August 1985), pp. 31–38. Cuthbertson finds a positive import trend of 3.3 percent a year or an impact of specialization of 3.0 percent over the period 1967–83. His price elasticity over three years is 0.78, very similar to mine.

ally, has extremely pessimistic implications for the future of U.K. manufactured goods trade. At a 3 percent growth rate in the OECD, for example, U.K. manufacturing exports would increase by 0.6 × 6.0, or 3.6 percent.[45] However, after offsetting the voracious appetite for import growth of 3 percent, GDP could rise just 0.33 percent before absorbing the export revenue. Manufactured goods trade is more price elastic than trade overall, so there might be some potential for offsetting the deterioration in the manufacturing balance by real depreciation. The price and cost elasticities in the equations sum to about 1.4.

Caution should be used in interpreting the implications of these equations. While they are generally used to build structural models, they may be far more useful if regarded as statistical summaries of past relationships between certain endogenous variables. As history this system depicts the strength of the competitive problems facing British industry. For prognosis the system should only be used with great care. This is particularly the case when an unexplained time trend term plays such an important role.

Despite its poor manufacturing performance, the United Kingdom has managed to maintain external balance by generating surpluses in services trade and in interest, profits, and dividends. The change in the net services balance as a percent of GNP in the 1980s was small. The dominant source of strength in the British current account was the rise in the balance on net earnings in the form of interest, profits, and dividends by 1.1 percent of GNP. However, this improvement should not be extrapolated. It reflected the cumulative impact of the current account surpluses in the 1980s (making the United Kingdom a substantial net creditor internationally) and the effects of sterling depreciation on the translation of foreign profits into domestic currency. With its current account more closely in balance, Britain will no longer be expanding its net creditor position. In the absence of further sterling depreciation, its net foreign earnings will be dependent on net foreign profits. Accordingly, in the absence of higher oil prices, trade could become a constraint on U.K. growth in the late 1980s.

45. From 1970 to 1985, using annual data,
$$\%QXMW = -0.23 \times 1.94\%OECD,$$
$$(0.14) \quad (4.4)$$
Standard error = 3.3; Durbin-Watson = 2.38.

where $\%QXMW$ is the percentage growth in developed country manufactured goods exports and $\%OECD$ the percentage growth in the OECD.

Is Trade Deindustrializing Europe?

A fear of deindustrialization and its consequences haunts the policy discussion in almost every European country. The industrial base is seen as having shrunk excessively, and a loss of international competitiveness is frequently fingered as the major culprit.

It is important to distinguish between the concepts of deindustrialization and their causes.[46] First, what is industry? For the purposes of this analysis, I define it narrowly, referring only to the manufacturing sector and excluding mining and construction. Second, does deindustrialization refer to inputs (employment and capital—the "manufacturing base") or to outputs (nominal sales, output volumes)? Concerns about the dislocation of production factors and their adjustment costs suggest examining inputs; concerns about the ability to satisfy needs, the nation's role as an "industrial power," suggest examining output. Third, is deindustrialization to be measured in absolute terms or relative to the rest of the economy? Absolute declines in employment, for example, at rates faster than voluntary attrition may be more costly than growth rates for manufacturing employment that are positive athough lower than rates elsewhere. Finally, it is important to recognize that factors other than international competitiveness, such as secular and cyclical domestic demand shifts and productivity growth, may be important in determining the size of the manufacturing sector. Indeed, I will demonstrate here that these factors rather than trade have been the major sources of the falling employment observed in Sweden, Germany, and France. Only in the United Kingdom has trade been a dominant source of deindustrialization.

Table 11 depicts the importance of manufacturing in the four economies. Each has experienced a major decline in manufacturing employment. Between 1973 and 1985 manufacturing employment fell 17.2 percent in France, 17.2 percent in Germany, 11.5 percent in Sweden, and 30.6 percent in the United Kingdom. Manufacturing employment has also fallen considerably as a share of total employment. Overall, the capital stock in manufacturing has grown more rapidly than output in France, Germany, and the United Kingdom, although in each economy,

---

46. For a more detailed discussion see Alec Cairncross, "What Is De-industrialization?" in Frank Blackaby, ed., *De-industrialization* (London: Heinemann Educational, 1979), pp. 5-17.

Table 11. *Manufacturing Sector Size and Share of the Economy in France, Germany, United Kingdom, and Sweden, Selected Years, 1960–85*
Billions of 1980 francs, deutsche marks, pounds, or kronor, as relevant, unless otherwise specified

Year	GDP[a]	Manufacturing value added	Manufacturing employment (millions)	Manufacturing gross capital	Manufacturing share (percent)			
					Real GDP[a]	Nominal GDP[a]	Total employment	Business (nonfarm) capital
France								
1960	1,122	232	4.93	565	20.7	27.4	31.5	33.7
1965	1,492	330	5.11	726	22.2	27.4	30.9	34.4
1970	1,939	480	5.11	953	24.8	26.8	30.8	33.9
1973	2,280	580	5.41	1,140	25.5	26.6	31.0	33.7
1975	2,358	590	5.33	1,243	25.1	26.2	30.3	32.9
1979	2,741	695	5.08	1,411	25.2	25.3	28.1	30.8
1980	2,769	698	5.06	1,456	25.1	25.2	27.7	30.3
1981	2,782	693	4.89	1,493	24.7	24.7	26.9	29.9
1982	2,832	694	4.82	1,524	24.3	24.3	26.4	29.3
1983	2,853	703	4.71	1,555	24.5	24.1	25.9	29.0
1984	2,896	710	4.58	1,587	24.6	24.0	25.3	28.7
1985	2,938	711	4.48	1,622[b]	24.3	23.9	24.7	28.4[b]
Germany								
1960	732	226	8.62	328	30.9	37.5	40.3	39.5
1965	923	302	9.23	483	32.8	37.6	41.8	39.8
1970	1,134	393	9.58	640	34.6	38.4	43.3	39.0
1973	1,274	436	9.37	746	34.2	36.3	41.0	37.4
1975	1,258	412	8.65	783	32.8	34.4	39.4	35.9
1979	1,464	483	8.53	855	33.0	33.7	37.7	33.0
1980	1,485	483	8.57	877	32.5	32.5	37.4	32.3
1981	1,485	476	8.37	894	32.0	31.7	36.7	31.7
1982	1,471	464	8.06	905	31.6	31.5	36.0	31.1
1983	1,498	469	7.73	915	31.3	31.3	35.2	30.3

Year								
1984	1,543	482	7.65	924	31.3	31.0	34.8	29.7
1985	1,581	506	7.76	936[b]	32.0	32.1	33.0	29.1[b]
United Kingdom								
1960	144	42	8.23	103	31.2	32.9	33.7	36.1
1965	168	49	8.40	126	31.1	30.7	32.9	35.5
1970	190	56	8.29	151	31.5	28.8	33.3	34.0
1973	215	61	7.79	165	30.7	27.8	33.9	32.9
1975	212	56	7.47	175	28.8	26.0	32.4	32.2
1979	236	59	7.20	194	26.9	25.1	30.7	30.6
1980	230	54	6.89	198	25.2	23.4	29.6	30.2
1981	228	51	6.17	200	23.9	21.7	27.8	29.6
1982	230	51	5.85	201	23.6	21.5	27.0	29.0
1983	239	52	5.56	203	23.3	21.1	26.0	28.4
1984	244	54	5.48	205	23.7	21.8	25.5	27.9
1985	253	56	5.41	207[b]	23.6	21.9	24.9	27.3[b]
Sweden								
1960	...	...	...	...	...	...	...	...
1965	351	80	1.03	225.7	22.5	27.6	30.8	35.2
1970	433	101	1.00	284.1	22.8	24.9	28.8	35.6
1973	465	109	0.973	322.3	23.1	23.6	27.4	35.6
1975	492	115	1.01	354.1	23.0	25.9	27.0	35.8
1979	517	113	0.944	395.1	21.4	21.8	24.7	35.5
1980	525	113	0.943	404.8	21.1	21.5	24.3	35.3
1981	524	109	0.914	413.0	20.5	20.4	23.6	35.1
1982	528	109	0.876	418.9	20.2	20.1	22.8	34.8
1983	541	114	0.853	424.5	20.8	20.6	22.2	34.3
1984	562	121	0.855	432.4	21.2	22.0	22.0	34.0
1985	574	124	0.861	...	21.2	21.9	21.9	...

Sources: Data on GDP (GNP for West Germany) are from IMF, *International Financial Statistics*; data on manufacturing employment and on manufacturing share of real GDP and nominal GNP for West Germany) and total employment are from OECD, *Main Economic Indicators*; data on manufacturing gross capital are from Commission of the European Communities, "Indicators of Profitability," table 11; and data on manufacturing share of business (nonfarm) capital are from CEC, "Indicators of Manufacturing," table 15.

a. Figures on West Germany are for GNP.

b. Forecast.

Table 12. *Relationship between Manufacturing Output and GDP for Germany, France, United Kingdom, and Sweden, 1960–73*[a]

Dependent variable	T	GDP	Standard error	$\bar{R}^2$	Durbin-Watson statistic	Out-of-sample forecast, 1974–85		
						Error 1980	Error 1985	Mean absolute error
Germany	−0.024	1.76	0.014	0.996	0.80	−0.012	0.046	0.012
log QMAN	(2.1)	(6.5)						
France[b]	0.03	0.75	0.01	0.999	2.4	−0.18	−0.36	0.183
log QMAN	(1.1)	(1.44)						
France[b,c]		1.32	0.01	0.999	2.1	−0.07	−0.13	0.07
log QMAN		(89.7)						
United Kingdom	−0.03	2.21	0.018	0.984	1.4	−0.13	−0.08	0.073
log QMAN	(2.1)	(3.8)						
Sweden	−0.017	1.59	0.019	0.993	1.2	−0.045	−0.015	0.032
log QMAN	(1.3)	(5.3)						

Sources: Data on GDP are from IMF, *International Financial Statistics;* data on manufacturing output are from Bureau of Labor Statistics.

a. The numbers in parentheses are *t*-statistics. QMAN is the volume of real manufacturing.

b. Estimated with dummies for 1968 and 1969.

c. Estimated using current and one-period lag for GDP.

capital has also shifted away from manufacturing, particularly in recent years.[47]

On the output side, deindustrialization is less apparent. In France real value added in manufacturing increased almost as rapidly as real GDP between 1973 and 1985; in Germany and Sweden growth was less rapid, the manufacturing share in output declining by about 2 percentage points. In the United Kingdom, however, absolute deindustrialization is evident, not just in employment but also in output. In 1985 U.K. manufacturing output was actually 8.2 percent lower than in 1973. In all countries manufacturing has fallen considerably as a share of nominal GDP. This mainly reflects declining relative prices caused by faster productivity growth.

Is the declining share of manufacturing accounted for by deviations of GDP from trend or by a structural shift in the relationship between GDP and manufacturing output? One test is to estimate the sensitivity of manufacturing output to GDP growth between 1960 and 1973 and, given the actual changes in GDP, to forecast out-of-sample manufacturing growth in 1980 and 1985.

Table 12 shows the results of such an exercise. The equations, fitted

47. Charles Schultze's "Real Wages" paper in this volume deals with this in greater detail.

through 1973, confirm the sensitivity of manufacturing value added to overall GDP growth. In Germany, for example, the elasticity is 1.8; the negative time trend implies that it takes a growth rate of at least 1.4 percent for manufacturing output not to fall, and a rate of 3.16 percent for manufacturing to remain a constant share of German GDP.

Seven years out of sample, the equation does well for Germany. In 1980 German output is closely predicted (an error of just over 1 percent), suggesting that the historical sensitivity of manufacturing output to deviations of GDP from trend suffices to account for the slow manufacturing growth until 1980. In 1985 actual German output was 4.6 percent higher than predicted.

In the remaining economies, large negative errors in 1980 do suggest a departure from previous trends. In France, manufacturing output increased almost as rapidly as GDP from 1973 to 1985. While this marked a shift from manufacturing's rising share before 1973, in terms of output it does not indicate a path of deindustrialization. In the United Kingdom and Sweden, manufacturing was 13 percent and 4.5 percent below forecast, respectively, in 1980, but just 8 percent and 1.5 percent below in 1985. This suggests some return to previous relationships to GDP in these economies since 1980. Between 1980 and 1985, in fact, manufacturing output in these economies was actually stronger than would have been expected, given GDP growth.[48] In sum, with the exception of Germany, between 1973 and 1980 manufacturing growth expanded considerably less than might have been expected. Thereafter, however, it has grown faster than predicted, given GDP growth in three of the four countries.

What role did trade play in this result? A rough estimate can be obtained using the definition that production, P, must equal the trade balance, $X - M$, plus net domestic use, U: $P \equiv X - M + U$. In the short run, in which the ratio of actual to potential output can fluctuate, it is generally unwarranted to use the net trade balance as a measure of the contribution of trade to employment growth.[49] A given level of

48. A similar analysis of manufacturing employment, given output, is again able to track German and British manufacturing through 1980 with reasonable accuracy. After that, however, German employment is about 4.4 percent higher while that in the United Kingdom is 14.5 percent lower than would have been expected.

49. In a simple Keynesian multiplier model, for example, if the only leakage were imports, in equilibrium a rise in exports would induce a rise in imports of equal size. The growth of domestic absorption would be entirely due to exports, yet our methodology would ascribe the growth as due to domestic use.

resource utilization is, however, an assumption appropriate for the medium-term analysis used here. Nonetheless, it should be stressed that this is obviously an exercise using ex post data rather than a simulation with a behavioral model.[50]

While estimates of value added in manufacturing are readily obtained, estimates of the value added by trade require some restrictive assumptions. Ideally, this analysis would use input-output analysis to take into account both direct and indirect effects due to trade. Unfortunately, the scope of this study prevents such an exercise. Instead, I have obtained an estimate of the impact of a dollar's worth of manufactured goods exports on domestic value-added using regression analysis. I assume that if a product were not imported, it would be produced at home and would contribute to value added in manufacturing by the same proportion. In addition, I assume that in the absence of imports, demand would switch to home goods with a unitary elasticity and that domestic value added and exports were perfect substitutes. This allows deflation of an estimate of the net value-added trade balance by the value-added deflator for manufacturing.

The results of this exercise indicate that with the exception of the United Kingdom domestic use rather than international trade performance accounts for the weakness of manufacturing output in the sample countries, particularly from 1980 through 1985. In table 13 the German trade balance, in 1980 dollars, was about the same share of manufactured output in 1973 and 1980. Thus trade had very little impact on the share of aggregate manufacturing output in GDP over the period. Between 1980 and 1985 trade boosted output by 7.4 percent of its 1980 level. Indeed, while domestic German use of manufacturing was 6.5 percent lower in 1985 than in 1980, output was up by 4.9 percent. Total German employment in manufacturing between 1980 and 1985 fell by 9.5 percent. However, trade actually increased employment in manufacturing by 4.3 percent so that *slow domestic use* was the reason for the slump in German manufacturing. This result is very different from the conclusions in a study by Donges, Klodt, and Schmidt.[51] They note that domestic final

50. For a more complete discussion and references to methodological questions, see Robert Z. Lawrence, *Can America Compete?* (Brookings, 1984), and the references cited there.

51. Juergen B. Donges, Henning Klodt, and Klaus-Dieter Schmidt, "The West German Economy Towards the Year 2000: An Analysis of Structural Change," Working Paper 268 (Kiel Institute of World Economics, September 1986).

Table 13. *Share of Trade and Domestic Use in Manufacturing Output and Employment, by Country, Selected Years, 1965–85*

	Output share (percent)[a]			Employment (millions)		
Year	Total	Due to trade[b]	Due to domestic use	Total	Due to trade	Due to domestic use
			France			
1965	22.1	1.2	20.9	5.10	0.28	4.82
1970	24.8	0.8	24.0	5.11	0.15	4.96
1973	25.5	0.7	24.8	5.41	0.13	5.28
1975	25.0	1.8	23.2	5.33	0.40	4.93
1979	25.4	1.4	24.0	5.08	0.28	4.80
1980	25.2	0.7	24.5	5.06	0.15	4.91
1981	24.9	1.1	23.8	4.89	0.22	4.67
1982	24.5	0.4	24.1	4.82	0.09	4.73
1983	24.7	1.0	23.7	4.71	0.18	4.53
1984	24.5	1.4	23.1	4.58	0.26	4.32
1985	24.2	1.1	23.1	4.44	0.20	4.24
			Germany			
1965	32.8	3.3	29.5	9.23	0.91	8.32
1970	34.6	4.0	30.6	9.58	1.11	8.47
1973	34.2	4.9	29.3	9.37	1.35	8.02
1975	32.8	5.6	27.2	8.65	1.46	7.19
1979	33.0	4.8	28.2	8.54	1.24	7.30
1980	32.5	4.8	27.7	8.57	1.27	7.30
1981	32.0	5.8	26.2	8.37	1.52	6.85
1982	31.6	6.5	25.1	8.06	1.65	6.41
1983	31.3	5.7	25.6	7.73	1.41	6.32
1984	31.3	6.2	25.1	7.65	1.51	6.14
1985	32.0	6.7	25.3	7.76	1.64	6.12

consumption of goods in Germany did not decline as a share of GDP between 1970 and 1984 and argue that the relative decline of manufacturing in Germany is explained by the loss of market shares in world trade and in domestic markets. However, export and import shares are not the relevant indicators of the net contribution of trade, and these authors ignore the effects of the dramatic fall in investment, particularly in *structures* (which embody goods) that occurred in Germany between 1973 and 1984. By contrast, my results are more closely in line with the estimates using input-output analysis reported in Buigues and Goybet.[52]

In Sweden, trade made a small, positive contribution to manufacturing

52. Pierre Buigues and Phillipe Goybet, "Competitiveness of European Industry: Situation to Date," *European Economy*, no. 25 (September 1985), p. 32.

Table 13 (continued)

	Output share (percent)[a]			Employment (millions)		
Year	Total	Due to trade[b]	Due to domestic use	Total	Due to trade	Due to domestic use
			United Kingdom			
1965	29.0	0.9	28.1	8.40	0.26	8.14
1970	29.3	0.9	28.4	8.29	0.26	8.03
1973	28.5	0.5	28.0	7.79	0.14	7.65
1975	26.7	1.2	25.5	7.47	0.36	7.11
1979	25.0	0.8	24.2	7.20	0.24	6.96
1980	23.4	1.2	22.2	6.89	0.36	6.53
1981	22.2	0.9	21.3	6.17	0.25	5.92
1982	22.1	0.3	21.8	5.85	0.06	5.79
1983	21.9	−1.6	23.5	5.56	−0.40	5.96
1984	22.3	−1.7	24.0	5.48	−0.44	5.92
1985	22.1	−1.4	23.5	5.41	−0.34	5.75
			Sweden			
1965	22.9	−0.8	23.7	1.03	−0.040	1.07
1970	23.2	0.1	23.1	1.00	0.007	0.993
1973	23.5	2.0	21.5	0.973	0.081	0.892
1975	23.5	1.0	22.5	1.01	0.043	0.967
1979	21.8	2.2	19.6	0.944	0.096	0.848
1980	21.5	1.9	19.6	0.943	0.082	0.861
1981	20.9	2.9	18.0	0.914	0.127	0.787
1982	20.6	2.6	18.0	0.876	0.111	0.765
1983	21.2	3.4	17.8	0.853	0.136	0.717
1984	21.6	3.7	17.9	0.855	0.146	0.709
1985	21.5	3.5	18.0	0.866	0.141	0.725

Sources: OECD, *National Accounts;* OECD, *Monthly Trade Statistics,* series A; and author's calculations.
a. Share of real 1980 GDP accounted for by manufactured value added.
b. Adjusted ratio of the manufactured trade balance to real 1980 GDP. Trade balance deflated by the manufacturing GDP deflator and adjusted by the estimated manufacturing value-added content of trade.

employment until 1980, but thereafter its role was extremely important. From 1980 to 1985 employment due to domestic use fell by almost 136,000 while that due to trade increased by about 59,000. In France the trade balance in manufacturing was a slightly higher share of manufacturing output in 1980 than in 1973 (4.3 versus 3.4 percent), the same as it was in 1970. Thus in each of these countries, trade had little impact on overall employment between 1973 and 1980, but in varying degrees, its impact was positive thereafter.

This finding would have come as a great surprise to anyone following the debate on French economic policy in the early 1980s. The "conquest" of the domestic market was a matter of great concern, particularly for the French Socialist party. But the penetration of the French market by imports grew in a remarkably parallel fashion with the rise in exports as a share of overall production.[53] The net aggregate impact of trade on manufacturing output and employment was actually very small.

Other factors may explain the alarm. The first reflects a concern about the increased interdependence of French and foreign economies. Between 1970 and 1980 the ratios of exports to production and imports to consumption in French manufacturing virtually doubled. (It must be noted that France remains more closed than Germany.) The second is that for France 1963 to 1973 had been a period in which manufacturing's share in aggregate output was growing strongly. Between 1965 and 1973, for example, manufacturing increased as a share of real French GDP by 3 percentage points. It is also interesting, however, that this trend was associated with a deterioration in the French manufacturing trade balance, so that it was actually driven, on balance, by the strength of domestic use. In fact, the switch in domestic use away from manufacturing after 1973 was the reason for the unusually weak performance of French manufacturing output.

The United Kingdom is the only country in the sample in which trade exerted a substantial negative impact on both output and employment in manufacturing between 1973 and 1985. Between 1973 and 1980, 2.8 percentage points of the 11.6 percent drop in employment can be attributed to trade. Between 1980 and 1985 the negative impact of trade was massive: of the 21.5 percent decline in manufacturing employment about 11.3 percentage points were due to domestic use and 10.2 to trade. Overall, between 1973 and 1985, 6.2 points of the 30.6 percentage point decline in British manufacturing employment can be attributed to trade.

In each of the countries, slow domestic demand associated with slow overall growth has been the major reason for the fall in manufacturing employment. In Germany domestic demand behaved as it would have been expected to, given GNP growth, and was the source of the manufacturing slump. In fact, the fall was so large that by 1985, in contrast to 1970, German domestic use of manufactured products was roughly in line with that of other major industrial countries. In France after 1973, domestic use switched away from manufactured goods. Despite a small positive impact from trade after 1973, this development caused the sluggishness in aggregate French employment. In Sweden

53. See *OECD Economic Surveys, 1983–84: France* (Paris: OECD, 1984), pp. 32–36.

the story is similar. A massive expansion in government services expenditures, coupled with a switch in consumption away from durables, explains the contraction of manufacturing. In these nations, therefore, while trade may have exerted a negative impact on particular sectors, overall it was not responsible for deindustrialization defined either relative to overall output or to employment.

Industrial Structure, Structural Change, and Trade Performance

Many Europeans believe the massive dislocation of their economies since 1973 has been caused by an acceleration in the pace of structural change. While the two oil shocks and new technologies are often singled out as important sources of this turbulence, international competition is the most common explanation. Indeed the causal relationship between trade and economic structure is seen as strong and running in both directions. First, strong competition from the United States and Japan is blamed for European problems in high-technology industries, while strong competition from newly industrializing countries is blamed for European problems in other industries. Second, shifting toward an appropriate industrial structure is often the goal of industrial policy advocates who see such a structure as the key to strong performance of their economies. In this section, I examine some evidence relating to these issues.

The Pace of Change

One measure of structural change uses the sum of absolute differences in the values of shares in a given sector.[54] Surprisingly perhaps, this measure indicates that the amount of structural change in manufacturing employment in most countries was similar in the decades before and after 1973 (the exceptions are Japan, in which there was much less structural change after 1973, and the United Kingdom, in which there was 63 percent more change).[55] Structural shifts in value added were

54. $I = (0.5) \Sigma |ai1 - ai2|$, where I is the structural change index, $ai1$ and $ai2$ are the shares of sector i in periods 1 and 2.

55. Computed using data from the *United Nations Yearbook of Industrial Statistics*. For similar conclusions see United Nations, *Economic Survey of Europe* (New York: UN, 1981).

Table 14. *Correlation Coefficients for Production, Exports, and Imports for Six OECD Member Nations, 1983*[a]

Item	France	Germany	United Kingdom	Sweden	United States	Japan
Production						
France	1.00					
Germany	0.81	1.00				
United Kingdom	0.96	0.74	1.00			
Sweden	0.78	0.71	0.76	1.00		
United States	0.93	0.81	0.90	0.82	1.00	
Japan	0.88	0.91	0.81	0.79	0.89	1.00
Exports						
France	1.00					
Germany	0.88	1.00				
United Kingdom	0.85	0.82	1.00			
Sweden	0.44	0.65	0.39	1.00		
United States	0.74	0.80	0.89	0.47	1.00	
Japan	0.52	0.74	0.40	0.55	0.53	1.00
Imports						
France	1.00					
Germany	0.91	1.00				
United Kingdom	0.93	0.84	1.00			
Sweden	0.86	0.83	0.75	1.00		
United States	0.69	0.64	0.80	0.66	1.00	
Japan	0.71	0.81	0.61	0.64	0.31	1.00

Source: OECD Compatible Trade and Production Data Base.
a. Values of $R > 0.43$ are significant at 95 percent level.

also similar in the two decades, or slightly less in the decade after 1973, with the exception of the United Kingdom. Therefore, it is not the unusual pace of structural change that has provided difficulties (except for Britain), but the environment of slow growth in which change has been accomplished and the nature of the industries shrinking most rapidly. In particular, these industries have been capital-intensive, with large plants and highly unionized labor forces that often dominate the economies of the regions in which they are located.

The second concern is that Europe's industrial structure has been inapproprate for the new global environment and particularly sluggish in accommodating changes in global conditions. To test these arguments, I use a data base compiled by the OECD in which the value of industrial production and trade are classified into twenty-two sectors.

PRODUCTION. As table 14 shows, industrial structures are remarkably similar. In 1983, for example, the mean correlation between the six sample countries was .833. The correlation of France, the United

Table 15. *Structural Change Indexes for Manufacturing Value Added and Employment in Six OECD Member Nations, 1963–73, 1973–83*[a]

Country	Value added		Employment	
	1963–73	1973–83	1963–73	1973–83
France	18.67	12.62	10.62	11.31
Germany	10.47	8.13	7.01	8.52
United Kingdom	10.12	18.82	3.71	7.25
Sweden	10.83	8.06	8.44	8.30
United States	5.37	8.39	9.45	11.36
Japan	13.53	10.13	11.03	6.72

Sources: UN, *Yearbook of Industrial Statistics*, vol. 1 (various issues); *Swedish National Accounts*, app. 5; and author's calculations.

a. Since the number of sectors surveyed differs across countries, the data, while comparable across time, are not comparable across countries.

Kingdom, and Germany with the United States was .93, .90, and .81, respectively, and with Japan .88, .81, and .91. Structure is thus unlikely to explain the differences in industrial performance. Nor, for the most part, can the differences be seen in the amount of structural change across manufacturing sectors. As table 15 shows, the amount of structural change in value added between 1973 and 1983 was similar in Sweden, Germany, and the United States. Only the United Kingdom, in which the change was much greater, stands out as unusual. The average correlation in changes in shares between 1973 and 1983 was a statistically significant .47.

A difference in the nature of structural change emerges, however, when the sectors are grouped by technological intensity (table 16). In 1973 the shares of high-technology sectors in production were similar in Europe (where they averaged 11 percent in the four countries), the United States (13.3 percent), and Japan (13.9 percent). In 1983, however, the European shares averaged 12 percent, but high technology accounted for 16 percent of production in both Japan and the United States.[56] Europe has indeed been more sluggish in shifting toward high-technology production: only in France has the share increased.

The European economies have shifted production and employment out of major low-technology industries such as steel, shipbuilding, coal

56. The OECD defines high technology rather narrowly. The term encompasses aerospace, office equipment and machinery, electronic components, drugs and medicines, instruments, and electrical machinery. Sectors such as chemicals and nonelectrical machinery and (sometimes) automobiles included here under medium technology are often considered high technology in other classification systems. See Bureau of Labor Statistics, *Monthly Labor Review*, for alternative definitions.

Table 16. *Share of Production, Exports, and Imports by Level of Technology for Six OECD Member Nations, 1973, 1983*
Percent

Country and year	Production High tech	Medium tech	Low tech	Exports High tech	Medium tech	Low tech	Imports High tech	Medium tech	Low tech
France									
1973	10	29	61	13	40	47	15	39	37
1983	12	33	55	17	43	40	18	38	35
Germany									
1973	13	35	53	15	52	33	13	31	56
1983	13	40	48	17	53	30	19	32	49
United Kingdom									
1973	12	30	59	18	49	33	16	34	50
1983	11	27	62	25	44	31	22	39	39
Sweden									
1973	10	28	63	12	35	53	16	37	48
1983	10	29	62	15	38	48	19	39	42
United States									
1973	13	33	54	27	47	26	14	39	47
1983	16	30	54	34	42	24	20	40	39
Japan									
1973	14	31	55	21	36	43	14	33	53
1983	16	33	51	29	46	25	18	32	50

Source: OECD Compatible Trade and Production Data Base.

mining, and textiles. Table 17 shows the massive employment declines that have occurred, particularly over the past five years. While in the short run, therefore, the European approach was to try to prevent such change by the use of subsidies and protection, eventually budgetary realities compelled adjustment.[57]

BUSINESS FORMATION. A lack of entrepreneurship is sometimes blamed for the poor European performance, and the difficulty of opening and closing new small businesses has been the subject of much policy attention. In a path-breaking work, Catherine Armington and associates have measured entry and exit rates for firms in the United States and collected comparable data from other countries.[58] These data confirm

57. The lack of adjustment in French shipbuilding through 1984 is a conspicuous exception. Recent events suggest, however, that shrinkage is imminent. See Andrew Fisher, "A Question Now of Survival: European Shipbuilding," *Financial Times* (London), June 17, 1986.

58. "Entry and Exit of Firms: An International Comparison," paper presented at "A European Future in High-Tech," Centre for European Policy Studies Conference, Brussels, 1985.

Table 17. *Change in Employment in Declining Industries for Six OECD Member Nations, by Industry, Selected Periods, 1970–85*
Percent

Country and period	Manufacturing	Textiles	Iron and steel	Shipbuilding[a]	Coal mining
France					
1970–75	1.7	−11.7	2.6	8.0	−29.3
1975–80	−6.1	−20.2	−19.8	−3.0	−25.0
1980–85	−12.0	−20.0	−20.0	−1.0	...
Germany					
1970–75	−11.2	−28.9	−11.4	−2.6	−18.4
1975–80	−1.0	−11.2	−13.4	−25.0	−8.4
1980–85	−12.0	−24.0	−44.0	−22.0	...
United Kingdom					
1970–75	−6.6	−16.8	−13.4	−6.0	−11.0
1975–80	−12.6	−31.2	−18.1	−29.9	−6.3
1980–83	−21.5	−24.4	−41.5	−19.4	−16.4
Sweden					
1970–75	2.0	−23.2	2.8	34.4	−16.7[b]
1975–80	−7.8	−23.6	−12.2	−36.2	−14.0
1980–85	−11.0	−25.0	−22.0	−44.0	−18.6[c]
United States					
1970–75	−6.1	−10.5	−9.2	23.2	46.6
1975–80	12.3	−1.0	−4.3	8.4	15.0
1980–85	−8.0	−18.0	−37.0	−20.0	...
Japan					
1970–75	−3.3	−20.7	−8.4	23.7	...
1975–80	−3.0	−16.5	−14.9	−46.2	...
1980–85	5.0	−9.0	−11.0	−21.0	...

Sources: OECD, *National Accounts;* UN, *Indicators of Industrial Activity;* Bureau of Labor Statistics, *Employment and Earnings;* and *Swedish National Accounts Statistics,* app. 5.
a. Data for French shipbuilding in 1970–75 include all transportation.
b. Includes crude petroleum production and other mining.
c. Data are for 1980–84 only.

that rates of entry and exit by new businesses tend to be higher in the United States (7.6 and 9.2 percent, respectively) than in Germany (6.7 and 6.9), and France (3.9 and 5.0). They also show that the United Kingdom has the fastest business turnover (entry 12.5 and exit 9.6).

TRADE. Differences in trade structures are considerably greater than those of production. In 1983 the mean correlation in the industrial structure of manufactured exports for the six countries was .64 for exports and .73 for imports. But again, it would be hard to use structure as an explanation for performance. The poor export performance of manufactures in Britain, for example, occurred despite a .82 correlation with Germany and .89 with the United States in 1983 export shares.[59] Indeed, between 1973 and 1984 the market for British exports, as measured by OECD export growth weighted by British export shares in 1973, grew at the same rate as OECD manufactured exports overall. The Japanese had a 1973 export market structure that grew more rapidly than the OECD average between 1973 and 1984, but the 10 percent faster growth in its export markets can scarcely explain the 73 percent increase in its 1983 market share.

Viewed from another perspective, however, the export correlations may provide some insight into trade performance. Export correlations also indicate each nation's major competitors. German exports are highly correlated with those of France (.88), the United States (.80), and Japan (.74). The French structure resembles that of Germany (.88), Britain (.85), and the United States (.74); Britain's structure resembles that of the United States (.89). These correlations suggest strongly that the major European countries compete heavily with each other and the United States in global markets. The desire to retain such structures is an important problem preventing rationalization in the European market. Japan and Sweden have, by contrast, quite different export product structures, indicating they have had a greater ability to carve out market niches or drive out competitors.[60]

As has the composition of its output, the structure of German exports has remained markedly more stable than that of the other countries (table 18). The German economy has continued to export in its areas of traditional strength—mainly mechanical engineering products. The United Kingdom and Japan have made the largest shifts in the composition of both exports and imports.

In sum, structural change per se tells us very little. The best performer, Japan, and the worst, the United Kingdom, display the greatest changes, while Germany, with the least change in structure, performed better than other European countries.

TRADE AND INDUSTRIAL STRUCTURE. What role is trade playing in shifting

59. The similarity in industrial and trade structures of the United Kingdom and Germany is brought out well in Alan Peacock and others, *Structural Economic Policies in West Germany and the United Kingdom* (London: Anglo-German Foundation for the Study of Industrial Society, 1980), p. 18.

60. While in 1983 the correlation between Japanese and U.S. manufactured goods exports was low (.53), the correlation between Japanese exports and U.S. imports was much higher (.74), an increase from .40 in 1973.

Table 18. *Structural Indexes for Production, Exports, and Imports in Six OECD Member Nations, 1973–83*[a]

Country	Production	Exports	Imports
France	11.13	10.57	12.90
Germany	8.37	9.52	13.01
United Kingdom	17.32	14.15	16.14
Sweden	11.85	13.49	10.13
United States	11.83	11.01	11.55
Japan	11.68	21.14	17.73

Source: OECD Compatible Trade and Production Data Base (using 22 manufacturing industries).

a. The indexes are summations of the absolute changes in each industry's share of total production, exports, and imports between 1973 and 1983. $I = 100 \times 0.5 \Sigma|a_i^1 - a_i^2|$, where a_i^1 and a_i^2 are the shares of sector i in periods 1 and 2.

the structure of European industry? I have already argued that, with the exception of the United Kingdom, domestic use rather than trade is the driving factor behind industry's shrinking share of GNP in Germany and Sweden. Table 19 shows the results of a preliminary effort to gauge the relative impact of trade and domestic use on the shifting shares of high-, medium-, and low-technology products in manufacturing production. To do the exercise rigorously would require extensive manipulations of the input-output tables for each country, so a back-of-the envelope estimate is presented here. In addition to the assumptions elaborated in the previous section, I assume that exports (and imports if they were to be made domestically) would require 70 percent of their output in domestic manufacturing for each dollar of final sales. Thus the impact due to trade is $0.70 (X - M)$.

With the exception of Sweden, trade has caused the share of low-technology production to contract. But the decline in the low-technology share in industry is overwhelmingly a reflection of domestic use rather than competition from imports. In France and Germany trade constituted 6 percent and 20 percent, respectively, of the source of the declining share of low-technology products. In Sweden, because of a strong trade performance in wood and paper products, trade virtually offset the declining share due to domestic use. Since competition from low-technology imports has not been the overwhelming reason for the shrinkage of low-technology production, protecting these sectors would not have offset much of their declining shares in production.

Similarly, only in Japan was trade the dominant factor in the rising share of high-technology products. The major rise in the U.S. production share devoted to high technology reflects domestic use. With the exception of France, the reasons for the relatively slow shift toward high-technology production in Europe must again be found in domestic use. In France trade raised the share, but by just 0.2 percent, while in Germany it detracted by just −0.5 percent. The largest impact of trade came in the positive effect it had on the share of medium-technology products in Germany and Japan and the negative impact in medium-technology products in the United Kingdom.

HIGH-TECHNOLOGY TRADE. Japan and the United States have rapidly concentrated their exports in high-technology products. The share of these products in their manufacturing exports is almost double the share in production. With the exception of pharmaceuticals and aerospace, European performance in high-technology trade is generally considered weak.

This performance, particularly in electronics and computers, has become a matter of great concern. Many believe that unless Europe becomes more competitive in these sectors, its growth rate will stagnate. But this argument needs to be qualified. First, it is important to distinguish between the use of technology and its production. Undoubtedly, European productivity growth requires the application of new technologies. But is it necessary to become self-reliant in or a net exporter of these products for Europe to sustain its economic growth over the medium term? Is it not possible for Europe to continue to specialize in its traditional strengths, while meeting some of its needs for high-technology products by buying them from abroad?

This strategy has been successful in the past decade. Moreover, despite the panic evident in most European discussions of high technology, it is striking that, as classified by the OECD, Germany and France had trade surpluses of $5.3 billion and $0.53 billion, respectively, in high-technology products in 1983. The Swedish deficit was about the same in nominal dollars in 1983 (− $0.30 billion) as in 1974 (− $0.36 billion). Thus even viewed within the narrow category of high technology, three of the four countries in the sample have been able to pay their way. While the balance was negative in the United Kingdom in 1983, it was only 8 percent of the U.K. manufactures deficit (high-technology products accounted for 25 and 22 percent of manufactured exports and imports, respectively).

A more stringent consideration that captures trends in growth is to examine high-technology coverage rates. In Sweden and France these ratios have statistically significant upward trends between 1970 and 1983

Table 19. Share Changes in Manufacturing Production Due to Domestic Use and Trade Classified by Intensity of Technology for Six OECD Member Nations, 1973, 1983

Percent

Country and type of use	High technology			Medium technology			Low technology		
	1973	1983	Change	1973	1983	Change	1973	1983	Change
France									
Production	10.4	12.4	2.0	28.5	33.0	4.5	61.1	54.6	-6.5
Share due to domestic use[a]	10.5	12.3	1.8	28.0	31.8	3.8	59.4	53.3	-6.1
Share due to trade[b]	-0.1	0.1	0.2	0.5	1.2	0.7	1.7	1.3	-0.4
Germany									
Production	12.5	12.5	0.0	34.5	40.0	5.5	52.9	47.5	-5.4
Share due to domestic use[a]	11.0	11.5	0.5	27.6	31.1	3.5	53.5	49.2	-4.3
Share due to trade[b]	1.5	1.0	-0.5	6.9	8.9	2.0	-0.6	-1.7	-1.1
United Kingdom									
Production	11.7	11.1	-0.6	29.6	27.3	-2.3	58.6	61.6	3.0
Share due to domestic use[a]	11.4	11.4	0	27.8	27.7	-0.1	61.4	64.4	3.0
Share due to trade[b]	0.3	-0.3	-0.6	1.8	-0.4	-2.2	-2.8	-2.8	0
Sweden									
Production	9.6	9.6	0	27.7	28.5	0.8	62.6	61.8	-0.8
Share due to domestic use[a]	10.0	10.0	0	26.6	26.3	-0.3	59.3	57.0	-2.3
Share due to trade[b]	-0.4	-0.4	0	1.1	2.2	1.1	3.3	4.8	1.5
United States									
Production	13.2	16.3	3.1	32.7	30.2	-2.5	54.0	53.5	-0.5
Share due to domestic use[a]	12.7	15.9	3.2	32.6	30.8	-1.8	55.1	55.1	0.0
Share due to trade[b]	0.5	0.4	-0.1	0.1	-0.6	-0.7	-1.1	-1.6	-0.5
Japan									
Production	13.9	15.9	2.0	30.8	33.2	2.4	55.3	50.9	-4.4
Share due to domestic use[a]	12.9	13.6	0.7	29.4	29.6	0.2	54.1	50.0	-4.1
Share due to trade[b]	1.0	2.3	1.3	1.4	3.6	2.2	1.2	0.9	-0.3

Source: OECD Compatible Trade and Production Data Base (using 22 manufacturing industries).
a. Percentage points of total production.
b. Trade balance adjusted by assumed 70 percent manufacturing production content of trade.

Table 20. *High-Technology Coverage Ratios in Four OECD Member Nations, Selected Years, 1970–83*

Country	1970	1973	1980	1983
France	0.97	0.94	1.03	1.04
Germany	1.80	1.80	1.33	1.24
United Kingdom	1.41	1.10	1.15	0.94
Sweden	0.75	0.88	0.89	0.93

Source: Data supplied by OECD.

of about 1 percent a year (table 20). In the United Kingdom and Germany, however, negative and significant annual trends of 3.0 and 3.1 percent, respectively, are evident.

Germany and High-Technology Trade

The German economy has become increasingly specialized in medium-technology products. Although it still has a surplus in high-technology products (and a coverage ratio of 1.24 in 1983), the fact that German high-technology imports have increased more rapidly than exports has become a matter of great concern.

From 1973 to 1983 the value of German high-technology imports grew 46 percent faster than other manufactured goods imports, but exports of high technology grew 15 percent faster than other manufactured goods exports. Can Germany sustain such relative growth rates for a long period of time? Is a strategy of concentrating in medium-technology products viable?

A simple simulation suggests that it is. Assume that OECD nations were to grow at 3 percent a year between 1983 and 1993. On the basis of previous relationships, this would imply an annual increase in world manufactured trade of 5.6 percent. Assume that, as in the past decade, high-technology exports grow 3.1 percent a year more rapidly than the manufacturing average, raising their global share from their current 20 percent to 26 percent.[61] This would imply that non–high-technology trade would rise by 60 percent. Assume the Germans maintain their import and export shares in such trade, but also assume German high-technology exports and imports, respectively, rise 15 and 46 percent more rapidly than the rest of manufactured trade. Over the decade, German non–high-technology exports and imports would increase by 60

61. Estimated from 1983 import data from the OECD.

percent, while high-technology exports and imports would grow 75 and 106 percent, respectively.

By 1993, therefore, overall German manufactured exports would rise by 61.4 percent and manufactured imports by 66.9 percent. High-technology products would account for 18.0 percent of German manufactured exports and 22.6 percent of manufactured imports. However, in 1983 the value of German manufactured exports was 1.38 times greater than the value of imports. Under these assumptions, the manufactured goods trade surplus would have increased by 49 percent between 1983 and 1993. Assuming Germany grew at 3 percent a year over the period, its GDP would be 34.4 percent higher. Thus the manufactured goods trade balance would be a 42 percent higher share of GDP than it was in 1983.

In sum, therefore, the German surplus is currently so large that, provided Germany can maintain its coverage ratio in non–high-technology products, a feat it has accomplished in the past decade for all trade, it could readily afford the high-technology imports.

I am not suggesting Germany ought not to try to improve its trade performance in high-technology products, but simply that even in the absence of such improvements high-technology trade performance is not a major constraint on German growth.

Structural Issues: The Case of France

Of the nations in the sample, France has the most activist industrial policy, probably because the French are the most displeased with their industrial structure.

Problems relating to the patterns of output are often provided as explanations for the perception that the French economy has performed poorly. The output of French manufacturing is said to be inappropriately matched to domestic demand. As a result, foreign manufacturers have captured an increasing share of the domestic market. A second problem may be the composition of France's net exports. French trade is very closely balanced in virtually every major product category. Thus unlike the Japanese, who have tremendous strength in sectors such as automobiles and consumer electronics, or the United States in aerospace, computers, and chemicals, or Germany in automobiles and engineering products, France has no such dominant poles. In France, as Berthelot has written, "with the exception of aircraft and shipbuilding, no category

Table 21. *Correlation Coefficients for Production and Imports for Six OECD Member Nations, 1973, 1983*

Country and type of use	Domestic use[a] 1973	1983	Exports 1973	1983	Production 1973	1983
France						
Production	1.0	1.0	0.81	0.73	. . .	. . .
Imports	0.80	0.77	0.91	0.93	0.79	0.77
Germany						
Production	0.96	0.96	0.74	0.83	. . .	. . .
Imports	0.89	0.78	0.44	0.54	0.81	0.68
United Kingdom						
Production	0.99	1.0	0.45	0.51	. . .	. . .
Imports	0.79	0.65	0.57	0.78	0.77	0.63
Sweden						
Production	1.00	0.95	0.65	0.74	. . .	. . .
Imports	0.36	0.54	0.30	0.47	0.35	0.39
United States						
Production	1.00	1.0	0.60	0.49	. . .	. . .
Imports	0.81	0.64	0.53	0.48	0.80	0.60
Japan						
Production	0.99	0.98	0.43	0.49	. . .	. . .
Imports	0.56	0.55	−0.90	−0.19	0.50	0.46

Source: OECD Compatible Trade and Production Data Base.
a. Use = production − 0.7 (trade balance).

of products generates surpluses of comparable importance for external equilibrium, as found in Japan, the FRG or in Italy. . . . This situation reflects too much inter-sectorial specialisation, which makes these industries inadapted to their role in determining the overall industrial structure and in creating genuine poles of competitiveness.''[62] France, he argues, is more vulnerable to market losses in particular areas because of its particular structure. Indeed, the notion of developing *filières*, or structures of competitiveness, was a key feature—now abandoned—of the initial strategy of the Mitterrand government.

The correlations reported in table 21 do not support the idea that output is not matched to domestic demand but do lend credence to the observation that the French trade structure is unusually close to balance in most sectors.[63] Of the six major industrial countries considered here,

62. Y. Berthelot, "French Attitudes towards Foreign Trade Policy," paper presented at a conference at the American Enterprise Institute, March 2–3, 1984, p. 11. See also André Orléan "L'Insertion dans les Echanges Internationaux: Comparaison de Cinq Grands Pays Développés," *Economie et Statistique*, no. 184 (January 1986), pp. 25–39.

63. In fact, it is hard to see how these views coexist, given the relatively balanced position of French trade overall. Presumably, if imports grow rapidly in the face of inadequate domestic production, this would create a pole of uncompetitiveness. If

domestic use and production in France are the most highly correlated in the data for both 1973 and 1983. If imports respond to changes in overall demand more rapidly than production, there should presumably be a declining correlation between domestic production and imports. As table 21 shows, this drop is at best marginal. The data do, however, confirm the unusually balanced nature of French trade in manufactured goods. Overall exports and imports of manufactured goods were highly correlated (.91) in 1973 and even more so (.93) in 1983. In fact, French exports are more highly correlated with French imports than with domestic production, suggesting the dominance of intraindustry trade in particular sectors. By contrast, in 1983 the United Kingdom had the second highest correlation of manufactured exports and imports (.78); Sweden, Germany, and the United States had about .5; and the Japanese had − .19.

This lack of poles of competitiveness may offend those committed to a prestigious leadership role for the French in particular product categories, but it is not obvious that trade, evenly balanced by product category, is more vulnerable to sudden competitive losses. In fact, the reverse is more plausible: if French products are fairly close substitutes for those of competitors in many categories, in the aggregate trade should be more responsive to shifts in the real exchange rate. Thus losses in particular sectors should be more easily offset by broad improvements at the margin elsewhere than if trade were highly concentrated. To be sure, if elasticities are high, there may be relatively less room to live with an overvalued exchange rate without large negative impacts on the trade balance, but such deficits are easily offset with appropriate exchange rate shifts.[64] To an outside observer, however, it is ironic that a nation such as France, which is extremely committed to industrial policies, did not develop major poles of competitiveness. Some ascribe this to the highly targeted, project-oriented nature of French policies.[65] Rather than focus on the development of general competence and the diffusion of technology and skills, French policy has been devoted to grand projects, which, because of their objectives (prestige, military

overall trade were balanced, there would be an offsetting tendency for improvements elsewhere leading to further imbalances.

64. Indeed, my empirical estimates indicate that before the recent problems the relative price sensitivity for French manufactured exports was − 1.60 for 1966–74 and − 1.3 for 1966–80.

65. Henry Ergas, "Does Technology Policy Matter?" in Bruce G. Guile and Harvey Brooks, eds., *Technology and Global Industry: Companies and Nations in the World Economy* (National Academy Press, 1987), pp. 191–245.

security, and so forth) tend to have weak spillovers. It is ironic that the Germans and Swedes have adopted more diffusion-oriented, less targeted approaches and have developed particularly strong trade performance in certain sectors.

Summary and Conclusions

International trade performance constrains the growth of national real incomes if growth at long-run potential requires a deterioration in real terms of trade. The regression evidence presented here suggests that, of the four countries in the sample, France, Germany, and Sweden were able in the past to match OECD growth rates of 3 to 4 percent without requiring improvements in their terms of trade. In the absence of an exogenous boost from oil export revenues, however, the United Kingdom was only able to grow at about half the OECD rate.

The relationship between activity and trade performance in Germany has not shifted appreciably over the past two decades. Similarly, such relationships remained fairly constant in the United Kingdom (with the exception of oil exports) and in France through 1980. Thereafter, French export growth has been slower than expected, and offset in part by relatively slower import growth. French performance in manufactured goods trade has been exceptionally poor since 1981. Despite declines in prices relative to those of competitors, the availability of excess capacity, and widened profit margins, France has lost volume shares in global manufactured goods markets. By contrast, during the 1970s it retained such shares without a decline in relative export prices. The structural changes put into place since 1980 have hurt French trade performance.

The poor performance of Sweden between 1974 and 1980 reflected the failure to offset relatively rapid domestic inflation with appropriate exchange rate adjustments. The expansion of the government sector had a negative impact on trade performance, but restoration of profitability and an improvement in relative price competitiveness brought about by two major devaluations have raised the Swedish current account back to balance. The real terms of trade deteriorations in manufactured goods were required, not to offset a slump in manufacturing competitiveness, but to generate a surplus in manufacturing to offset the deterioration in the balances on energy trade and the rise in Swedish international indebtedness. In the absence of external shocks such as higher oil prices and internal shifts in the distribution of income between wages and profits, Sweden should be able to match an OECD growth rate of 3 percent a year without real devaluation.

With the exception of the United Kingdom, trade is not deindustrializing Europe. In the aggregate, the growth of manufactured goods exports since 1973 has more than matched the rapid penetration of domestic markets by foreign products. This performance has actually made a positive contribution to manufacturing employment. Although manufacturing value added failed to grow as rapidly as GDP in Germany and Sweden, the reason was a shift in domestic use brought about in Germany by the decline in investment as a share of GDP and in Sweden by the expansion of the public-sector share, the decline in investment share, and shifting patterns of private consumption. In Germany manufacturing output conformed to its historical relationship to GNP through 1980 and was stronger than might have been expected, given GNP growth thereafter. In France output increased as rapidly as GNP between 1973 and 1985. In Sweden manufacturing output grew more slowly through about 1980 but with the improvement in international competitiveness returned to its historic relationship with GNP by 1985.

Judged by almost all criteria, the United Kingdom has deindustrialized over the past two decades. Trade reinforced declining domestic use of manufactured goods, and losses due to trade accounted for almost half the 31 percent decline in manufacturing employment between 1973 and 1985. British trade performance can in part be explained by the effects of the strong pound, but other factors not captured by cost and price variables appear more important over the medium run. Historically, British manufactured goods exports rise only 0.6 percent for each 1 percent increase in world manufactured goods trade. By contrast, the observed short-run import income elasticity was 3 and was combined with a 3 percent trend in manufactured goods import growth.

With the exception of the United Kingdom, the pace of structural adjustment in the manufacturing sectors has not accelerated since 1973. The slow-growth environment and the nature and location of the industries adversely affected have made adjustment more difficult. While European subsidy policies have delayed adjustment, major downsizing has been accomplished in steel, shipping, and coal mining. Nonetheless, despite the European Community's policies, coal mining in Germany remains heavily subsidized, while steel and shipbuilding have not yet become self-financing.

Although foreign trade is frequently seen as the major source of structural change, it has been much less important than the slow growth of domestic use in shrinking the share of low-technology products in European production. With the exception of France, the share of high technology in manufacturing output has not increased from 1973 to 1983, but the overall impact of trade on the size of the high-technology sectors has been relatively minor.

There is no one-to-one relationship between structural flexibility and competitive performance. Germany, with the least structural change, has performed relatively well in international competition; the United Kingdom, with the most, has performed relatively poorly. Nor is there a strong relationship between a particular industrial structure and overall performance. Production structures across all European countries in this sample are similar to those in the United States and Japan. The poor U.K. trade performance cannot be ascribed to specialization in products with particularly slow growth of demand. Similarly, Japanese performance is much stronger than trade structure alone can explain.

This evidence suggests that appropriate adjustment processes rather than structures should be the goal of industrial policies. Policies should try to complement and reinforce market forces rather than determine particular outcomes. It is all too tempting for industrial policies to try to create structures, be they large firms, national champions, or production capacity in particular sectors such as high technology or integrated linkages. But such structures are not automatically linked to performance. Centralized government policies that aim at particular structures are unlikely to obtain strong performances that are precisely tailored to market forces.[66] In particular, the desire on the part of European governments to maintain a complete range of industrial activities is a major obstacle to improved competitiveness.

Over the medium term, policies that supplement and reinforce the operation of market forces can be an important stimulus to competition. In particular, the removal of barriers to integration at the European level would make an important contribution toward strengthening market

66. On the basis of an extensive comparative study of European industry, Sheperd and Duchêne conclude, "the evidence suggests that, from a national viewpoint, first-best policies tend to be those that combine competition with the 'right' environmental policies, while structural policies are second-best, resorted to in situations where strong firms are few on the ground." Geoffrey Shepherd, François Duchêne, and Christopher Saunders, eds., *Europe's Industries: Public and Private Strategies for Change* (Cornell University Press, 1983), p. 22.

structures. While this paper has concentrated on trade, what may be traded is heavily influenced by government regulation. In this regard, the removal of impediments to competition in services deserves major policy focus.

Many of the findings in this paper conflict with the ideas of those who have blamed trade performance for slow growth since 1973, particularly in the manufacturing sectors of Germany, France, and Sweden. Despite allegations that increased mismatches between domestic demand and supply have raised import propensities, the relationships between trade and economic activity have actually remained quite stable. And despite allegations that declining shares of home and foreign markets have reduced the manufacturing base, I have found that, again with the exception of the United Kingdom, trade actually added to output and employment. The major source of the declining share of manufacturing in some economies stems from changed patterns of domestic use. There is disquieting evidence on the trade performance of British manufacturing for the past fifteen years and French export performance since 1980. The source of this poor performance is not readily explained by the product composition of output. The solution lies not simply in ensuring the production of particular products but in reforming the structure of the manufacturing sector. In the case of France the relatively recent nature of the problems suggests industrial policies since 1980 may be the major culprit. In the United Kingdom the problems appear more endemic.

In the introduction I emphasized that the concern here was medium-term growth. Nonetheless, with the exception of the United Kingdom inadequate manufacturing trade performance should not be seen as a major obstacle to the more complete utilization of resources. While the evidence on France is more ambiguous, neither Sweden nor Germany would experience competitive difficulties in growing at their long-run potential, given a global environment in which growth was about 3 percent.

Comment by Alexis Jacquemin

Lawrence's paper attempts to assess the effect of international competitiveness on European growth. The substantive empirical findings quantifying the interdependences are among the highlights I find very useful for understanding some of the situations occurring between 1965 and 1985. Among them is the contrast between the United Kingdom, in which international trade depressed output and employment in manufacturing, and other European countries—West Germany, France, and Sweden—in which slow domestic demand associated with slow overall growth seems to have been the major reason for the slump in manufacturing and employment. The view that the United Kingdom has deindustrialized over the past two decades and that trade has reinforced declining domestic use of manufactured goods confirms the opinion that Kaldor defended for a long time.[67]

Another interesting finding of Lawrence is on the one hand the remarkable similarity between industrialized countries in the distribution of the shares of industrial sectors in their total manufacturing output, and on the other hand the differences in overall performance. This confirms results published ten years ago by the Economic Commission for Europe of the United Nations.[68] It was noticed that from the 1950s to the 1970s broad industrial structure was increasingly similar among industrial countries, despite rapid changes in the distribution of output and employment among industrial branches; and no overall relation was found between national growth rates and the amount of shift in broad industrial structure.

Finally, I agree with Lawrence that appropriate adjustments linked to the removal of barriers to European integration rather than attempts to implement the "right" industrial structure or to defend "national champions" should be the goal of industrial policies.

Because several of Lawrence's methodological choices are important and could limit the interest of his results, I should like to comment on the paper in two ways. First, I shall discuss some of these limits. Second, I shall suggest some complementary analyses.

Lawrence insists that his concerns are aggregative, based on medium-term average evolutions, and focus on the role of one possible factor, trade. These choices tend to conceal important phenomena and relationships. Let me illustrate this point. Clearly the various equations tested do not constitute the blocks of a macroeconomic model, even in a partial equilibrium setting. This does not suppress their interest. The problem, however, is that within this limited framework the results of the econo-

67. Nicholas Kaldor, "Comment" on Alex Cairncross, "What is De-Industrialization?" in Frank Blackaby, ed., De-Industrialization, pp. 18–25.

68. United Nations, Economic Commission for Europe, Structure and Change in European Industry (Geneva: UN, 1977).

metric estimation can lead to overly simple interpretations based on direct causal links between too few variables. There could be biases created by aggregation over markets and commodities.[69] Also, indirect relationships as well as feedback effects tend to be ignored.

In the case of West Germany, Lawrence's results lead him to conclude that although elasticities are relatively small, the Marshall-Lerner conditions are satisfied. This implies that real exchange rate appreciation will worsen the trade balance and that low price elasticities for German products explain the relatively strong trade performance despite the appreciation of the deutsche mark. More complete models incorporating elasticity, income, and wealth effects, and distinguishing between sectors according to the nature of the competitive process, can lead to a deeper analysis.[70] German industries can be classified on the basis of their pricing behavior on international markets as either price-setters (implying a substantial degree of product differentiation) or price-takers. Given this distinction, a decrease in the relative price between "competitive" and "noncompetitive" goods as a consequence of a revaluation of the real exchange rate does have important structural effects. Resources shift into the noncompetitive activities, which are more export intensive and correspond to fast-growing industries, and the trade surplus

69. A sectoral view of the economy suggests that there are discontinuous sector-specific responses to shocks, and these responses aggregate to give a nonlinear response of the economy as a whole. This is, for example, the point of view of Edmond Malinvaud, *Mass Unemployment* (New York: Blackwell, 1984), who stresses that different types of unemployment may be present in different sectors. The problem of aggregation bias defined by the deviation of the macroeconomic parameters from the average of the corresponding microeconomic parameters is well known. Equally important is the problem of predicting the variations in dependent variables by means of an aggregate model instead of a disaggregate one. See M. H. Pesaran, R. G. Pierse, and M. S. Kumar, "On the Problem of Aggregation in Econometrics," Banca D'Italia Temi di discussione del Servizio Studi, no. 67 (Rome, July 1986). For empirical analyses showing that different regimes characterize a given economy and that the structure of employment and layoff decisions will vary across industries and firms, see Robert H. Topel, "Inventories, Layoffs, and the Short-Run Demand for Labor," *American Economic Review*, vol. 72 (September 1982), pp. 769–87; and Henri R. Sneessens, "Investment and the Inflation-Unemployment Tradeoff in a Macroeconomic Rationing Model with Monopolistic Competition," *European Economic Review*, vol. 31 (April 1987), pp. 781–808.

70. Alfred Steinherr and Colette Morel, "The Reaction of Prices and of the Balance of Payments to Revaluation of the Deutsche Mark," *Weltwirtschaftliches Archiv*, vol. 115, no. 2 (1979) pp. 425–49; and Alfred Steinherr, "Effectiveness of Exchange Rate Policy for Trade Account Adjustment," *International Monetary Fund Staff Papers*, vol. 28 (March 1981), pp. 199–224.

tends to increase, at least for a substantial period. Furthermore, the decline in domestic investment as a share of GDP is not unrelated to trade. Comparing export unit values with domestic labor costs suggests that the appreciation of the deutsche mark in the 1970s combined with downward rigidity of nominal wages has been partly translated into an increasing loss of profitability. This has led to the slowdown of domestic investment, accompanied by a sharp rise in investment abroad, that has tended to reduce income growth and hence the growth of import demand.

The usefulness of disaggregation reappears when Lawrence compares the industrial structures of different countries. This usefulness does not require that the explanation of differences in national performance lies in differences of industry structure as a whole. Nor can one conclude from the contrast between similarity in national structure and disparity in national performance that specific industrial characteristics do not matter. Indeed, what matters is the structural analysis of and within a given industry, namely, the distribution of market shares and the existing degree of competition, the size and vintage of plants, the average age and structure of the capital stock, the R&D intensity, the institutional and economic conditions of entry and exit, and the degree of product differentiation.

More generally, given that usually over a long period fluctuations in exchange rates tend to compensate for a relative rise in domestic currency costs of production, and given that the broad manufacturing composition of domestic output of manufactures and of exports is more or less similar among European countries, the differences between their income elasticities of demand for manufactured imports, as well as the differences between the elasticities of foreign demand for their exports, could be partly explained by various specific characteristics in nonprice-competitive advantages: product quality, timely delivery, reliability, and after-sales services play a central role. For example, the fact that the shares of the textile industry in the manufacturing activities of countries A and B are more or less similar is compatible with different performances explained by different generic strategic dimensions characterizing the industry in the two countries: one could be mainly based on full line, low manufacturing cost, little service, and moderate quality; the other on narrow line, high price, high technology, and high quality.

European evidence based on case studies suggests that such differences indeed play an important role. Not only do different strategies appear to dominate a given industry in different countries, but also different countries pursue characteristic strategic themes across sectors. "One can note, for instance, the promptness of German firms to move into more specialized markets (e.g., in textile, steel, and cars)" or the ubiquity and past success of Italian public enterprises and the current success of small-scale, cooperative production in that country. These differences concern both national capacity (or incapacity) of reacting to opportunities for industrial change and the way in which these capacities are organized.[71] They are at the basis of the relationship between activity and trade performance but are ignored by purely aggregative concerns.

The possible blur created by excessive aggregation is increased by using average trends. As an illustration, one may look at the effect of an appreciation or depreciation of a given currency on industrial competitiveness. It is accepted that exchange rate adjustments have no real effect in the steady stream of an economy. However, in the medium term, a period adopted by Lawrence, the situation is different, and whole segments of industry can be definitely affected.

Lawrence's paper suggests that, on the average, periods of appreciation might be seen as being compensated by periods of depreciation, and structural stability of a country can be inferred from testing simple macroeconomics equations including a (not significant) time trend variable. However, one cannot neglect the role of asymmetric and noncompensating effects on industrial structure. Indeed, many choices of the firms can be influenced in a more or less irreversible way by the level as well as by the expected changes of the exchange rate. An example is the choice between exporting and direct investment. When the foreign currency depreciates, all other things equal, the domestic currency cost of producing in the foreign country decreases, barriers to entry fall, and direct investment is encouraged. But this rise of direct investment modifies in a durable way the characteristics and the competitiveness of the industrial structure at home and in the foreign country. The entry of U.S. multinationals' subsidiaries in Europe in 1958–65 and, in the 1970s, the outflow of direct investment from Europe to the United States at the expense of domestic investment have certainly had real and persistent consequences.

This argument could be linked to what is called the hysteresis view. In this case it is the view that external and temporary shocks can have

71. Geoffrey Shepherd, "Industrial Change in European Countries: The Experience of Six Sectors," in Alexis Jacquemin, ed., *European Industry: Public Policy and Corporate Strategy* (Oxford: Clarendon Press, 1984), p. 212.

long-run effects on capital stock and on portfolio industrial assets.[72] The cause of such a persistence could be that investments involve the commitment of sunk assets, among them information about the target markets.

At this stage, it may be useful to mention briefly some information on the evolution of European trade flows that could complement those provided by a global analysis. When studying trade performances of European countries, one should not simply look at them from a world trade point of view but distinguish between trade within the European Community and that between the EC and the rest of the world.

According to a study that I made with Sapir, there has been not only a general slowdown of European international trade (which reflects the slow growth of GNP), but also, between 1973 and 1983, a relative decline of intra-EC trade to the benefit of trade with the rest of the world.[73] More specifically, there has been a decline, characteristic of all the European countries, in the role of domestic manufacturing production in meeting domestic demand. This phenomenon of increased external dependence shows itself in a simultaneous increase in imports of EC and extra-EC origin. But unlike the development observed from 1960 to 1970, the dependence of the European countries has taken on less and less a European dimension, and more and more a worldwide one.

Furthermore, the overall evolution at the one- and two-digit level of the NACE classification has tended to conceal very different trends at the level of a more disaggregated classification. A limited number of industries have been identified at the three-digit level that, because of their relative importance in imports as a whole and the scale of the decline they are suffering, are the chief components of the aggregate changes.

It is striking that industries whose index has strongly fallen cover not only traditional products such as knitting, leather goods, and made-up textile goods but also growth and high-technology sectors such as office machinery and data processing equipment and telecommunications

---

72. In the case of unemployment, Sneessens shows, on the basis of a distinction between short-run and long-run monopolistic competition equilibriums, that the damages caused by an adverse supply shock should not be expected to be eliminated at once by a positive supply shock of similar importance occurring several years later. See "Investment and the Inflation-Unemployment Tradeoff."

73. Alexis Jacquemin and André Sapir, "Intra-EC Trade: A Sectoral Analysis," Economics Working Document 24 (Brussels: Centre for European Policy Studies, January 1987), pp. 5–68.

equipment. There is also a general tendency for industries that have undergone a relative decline of intra-EC imports to have also experienced a relative increase of intra-EC exports at the expense of exports to the rest of the world. The more imports from the rest of the world penetrate the common market, the less European producers are able to penetrate outside markets. I think that this is a problem of European competitiveness and a concern for potential European growth.

A regression analysis has been used to identify various factors that could influence the level and change in the share of intra-EC trade. Two types of variables have been distinguished. Some, such as intensity of research and development, and human capital, are conducive to intra-EC trade and enable a better resistance to imports of outside origin, on the basis of assets reflecting genuine competitive advantages and favoring trade creation. Others, such as the common external tariff and common agricultural policy, while also being conducive to intra-EC trade, probably promote it at the expense of greater integration into world competitiveness and induce trade diversion effects. Just as the influence of the first type of variable could well be strengthened through various EC policies such as cooperation in R&D and the accumulation of human capital, so the part played by the second type would be considered makeshift, having to be gradually phased out. In fact, the influence of these latter variables tends to decline over time, suggesting a declining protection.

To conclude, I think that to understand the complex mutual relations between trade performance and European growth, it is necessary to complement macroeconomic thinking by less aggregated analyses able to provide a better understanding of causal channels and of the direct and indirect effects at work. In terms of policy implication this also suggests that micro-oriented selective actions against well-identified sources of European barriers and rigidities in the markets and at the level of European corporations are useful. Many of these actions are described in one of the Commission's white papers and have nothing to do with industrial targeting.[74] They respond to the need to improve the diffusion and the incorporation of new technologies into processes and products, to convert technological potential into industrial and commercial success, and to extend the importance of spin-off effects. Actions must also be directed toward the service sector and could be one of the

74. Commission of the European Communities, "Completing the Internal Market," White Paper from the Commission to the European Council (Brussels, June 14, 1985).

greatest boosts to competitiveness, not only in the services themselves but also in all those industries that are inextricably linked to them.

General Discussion

Discussants took issue with the way Robert Lawrence specified the trade equations in his paper, in particular for his concentration on goods at the expense of services and for paying insufficient attention to Europe's emergence as a major agricultural exporter. In most of his equations Lawrence models trade as influenced by relative prices and demand. But, it was argued, in the longer run exports and imports are influenced by supply-side factors—namely, the growth of domestic capacity. With no variable to capture the rate of growth of potential output, Lawrence intertwines response of exports to short-run changes in foreign demand with the longer-run determinants of exports. Although it may be difficult to measure, an indicator of the rate of growth of potential output should be included in the model. It was observed that if such supply-side measures are included in the estimated import equations for the United Kingdom, the activity elasticities would be lower and the overall price elasticities higher. Even as modified, however, these equations would also give pessimistic results. It was argued that the supply side also had to be considered in explaining European agricultural exports. These are completely determined by supply because restitution payments are set at a level to move the products in world trade.

One participant pointed out that over the past three or four decades, after taking into consideration cyclical variations, trade has grown markedly faster than output in all the larger European countries. The methodology employed in Lawrence's paper seems to link trade and output in a manner that does not allow for these trends to taper off.

However, another participant countered that if the issue is how fast demand can be boosted without running into the need for a depreciating currency, then the elasticities from a model such as Lawrence's do in fact pick up the supply-side response on those occasions when demand is boosted. In effect, the model may be considered a type of crude reduced form.

It was observed that deindustrialization is a problem of greater concern to politicians than to economists. Lawrence's finding that international trade has not led to deindustrialization in Europe (except in the United

Kingdom) could be explained by the impact of higher oil prices. After the oil shocks, most European countries had to expand traditional exports to pay for higher energy bills. This provided a stimulus to manufacturing exports. But these effects worked in the opposite direction for the United Kingdom as it became an oil exporter. The recent declines in the price of oil in Europe, it was then conjectured, could now produce deindustrialization to the extent that countries no longer need to push their manufactured exports.

The discussion turned to the outlook for European trade performance. A participant suggested that most European countries will experience three sources of decline in manufacturing trade. First, lower oil and commodity prices in the third world mean Europe must now make room for the manufactured exports of developing countries. Second, Europe must adjust to the lower dollar. Third, it must adjust to the loss of markets in OPEC member nations. The external environment for European manufactured exports will be unfavorable.

It was argued that in recent years German technological performance has shown signs of improvement. The export successes certain German industries have had in the U.S. market, where they compete with both the Japanese and the Americans, has boosted their confidence and accelerated the incorporation of higher technologies in both products and production methods. The response of German firms of all sizes to slack domestic demand and low capacity utilization has been to export. If the domestic economy is squeezed enough, surprisingly positive boosts to German competitiveness may result as German industries search for additional geographic and commodity niches.

But another participant found sobering Lawrence's argument that even a strong European economy such as Germany's could not grow appreciably faster than permitted by the overall growth of the OECD.

Mention was made that a hysteresis problem could arise in the United Kingdom because of the recent decline in oil prices. As the appreciation of the pound levels off, the fear is that British producers, having lost export markets and domestic markets, will now find it extremely difficult to recover the market shares they had before the original sterling appreciation.

One participant observed that the notion of competitiveness is similar to the notion of solvency insofar as it is perfectly appropriate when applied to a particular firm or even an industry but is illegitimate and nonsensical when applied to an entire nation. Another participant raised some questions about how competitiveness should be measured. He pointed out that using some form of relative price term to measure it seems troublesome, yet economists seem unable to find any alternative.

One participant pointed out that studies of Europe's technology gap are highly sensitive to the commodity classification they use. In effect, with relatively small changes in classification, one could argue that Europe has been lagging behind or has been improving relative to the rest of the industrialized world in high-technology industries.

ROBERT Z. ALIBER

Financial Markets and the Growth of Europe

In the early 1980s the economy of Western Europe grew less rapidly than that of the United States. This paper examines whether the slower growth of Western Europe can be explained by financial market phenomena and especially whether the cost of capital to firms headquartered in the various countries in Western Europe is high relative to the anticipated profitability of new investments. At one time—the 1950s and the 1960s—production and employment in Western Europe increased more rapidly than in the United States; even then considerable attention was directed at the inadequacies of its financial system by the European Community, the OECD, and the Bank for International Settlements. The potency of these incentives may have diminished, and the question is whether particular institutional features of the European financial arrangements recently have been a significant deterrent to economic growth.

Table 1, rows (A), shows the growth in employment and industrial production in the United States and Western Europe in the 1980s. Had each country's trade and current account balance remained unchanged as a share of its gross national product, the growth of employment and industrial production in the United States would have been substantially more rapid than in most countries in Western Europe, as is evident in rows (B) in the table. Thus the increase in the U.S. trade deficit since 1980 has been associated with a decline in employment and industrial production in the U.S. tradable goods industries and in the firms that are suppliers to these industries, while the counterpart increases in the trade surpluses in various countries in Western Europe have been associated with the increase in employment and industrial production in their tradable goods industries. The adjusted values are estimated on the

Reid Click has provided extensive assistance in developing the data for this paper.

384

assumption that each country's trade surplus would have remained constant as a percentage of its gross domestic product at the value for 1980. The adjustments are based on two key assumptions: all of the observed changes in trade balances reflect changes in the volume of exports and imports of industrial products (hence changes in imports of primary products including petroleum are ignored); and changes in employment and industrial production are directly proportional to changes in the trade balance.[1] For several small countries—the Netherlands and Sweden—as well as for Germany, the increases in their trade surpluses have had dramatic implications for the observed increases in employment and industrial production. One inference from these data on national trade balances is that growth in demand has been relatively stronger in the United States than in most other countries; a second inference is that a significant part of the observed increases in output and employment in the various countries in Western Europe reflects the increase in net exports to the United States.

Changes in the pattern of direct foreign investment suggest developments consistent with those associated with changes in the trade balances. Thus over the past decade, firms headquartered in the various countries in Western Europe have increased their investments in the United States, while the foreign investments of U.S. firms have declined. In 1970 firms headquartered in the United States accounted for two-thirds of the total outflows of direct foreign investment of the eight industrial countries included in the data. A decade later they accounted for less than one-half of the total of direct foreign investment of these eight countries. In 1970 the United States accounted for one-fourth of the inflows; a decade later the United States accounted for more than one-half of the inflows.

Changes in the national pattern of direct foreign investment reflect changes in the relationship between the anticipated profitability on investments in plant and equipment in each country and the cost of capital to firms headquartered in different countries. An increase in investment in plant and equipment within a country indicates an increase in the anticipated profit rate. However, if the anticipated profitability on domestic investment has declined while the anticipated profitability on foreign investment has increased, firms—those headquartered both at

1. Many countries in Western Europe are more extensively import dependent for energy than the United States. The value of petroleum imports was unusually large in 1980 because of the surge in prices in the previous years.

Table 1. *Employment and Industrial Production in the United States and Selected OECD Countries, 1980–85*

1980 = 100; TB/GNP in percent

Country[a]		1980	1981	1982	1983	1984	1985
United States							
E	(A)	100	101	99	100	105	108
IP	(A)	100	102	95	101	112	115
TB/GNP	(A)	−0.9	−0.9	−1.2	−2.0	−3.0	−3.1
E	(B)	100	101	100	104	113	117
IP	(B)	100	102	96	105	120	124
Canada							
E	(A)	100	101	91	89	86	88
IP	(A)	100	101	90	95	104	108
TB/GNP	(A)	3.1	2.3	5.1	4.7	5.0	3.9
E	(B)	100	104	83	83	78	85
IP	(B)	100	104	82	89	96	105
Japan							
E	(A)	100	101	102	102	103	105
IP	(A)	100	101	101	105	117	122
TB/GNP	(A)	0.2	1.7	1.7	2.7	3.5	4.2
E	(B)	100	95	96	92	90	89
IP	(B)	100	95	95	95	104	106
Germany							
E	(A)	100	98	94	90	90	91
IP	(A)	100	98	95	95	98	103
TB/GNP	(A)	1.1	2.4	3.8	3.3	3.6	4.6
E	(B)	100	93	83	81	80	77
IP	(B)	100	93	84	86	88	89
France							
E	(A)	100	98	98	96	94	94
IP	(A)	100	99	97	98	99	101
TB/GNP	(A)	−2.0	−1.7	−2.9	n.a.	n.a.	n.a.
E	(B)	100	97	102	n.a.	n.a.	n.a.
IP	(B)	100	98	101	n.a.	n.a.	n.a.

home and in various foreign countries—might reduce their investments in the home economy and increase their investments in the foreign economy. Anticipated profitability is thus location specific. In contrast, the cost of capital is firm specific, or at least specific to firms headquartered in individual countries. If the cost of capital to firms headquartered in a particular country increases, the volume of both their domestic and foreign investments would decline. Hence changes in the levels of investment in particular countries reflect changes in anticipated profitability on these investments, while changes in the shares of these invest-

Table 1 *(continued)*

Country[a]		1980	1981	1982	1983	1984	1985
Great Britain							
E	(A)	100	96	94	95	96	94
IP	(A)	100	97	98	102	103	108
TB/GNP	(A)	0.6	1.4	0.8	−0.3	−1.4	−0.5
E	(B)	100	93	93	99	104	98
IP	(B)	100	94	97	106	111	112
Italy							
E	(A)	100	99	98	95	79	88
IP	(A)	100	99	95	92	95	97
TB/GNP	(A)	−4.1	−3.1	−2.6	−0.9	−1.7	n.a.
E	(B)	100	95	92	82	69	n.a.
IP	(B)	100	95	89	79	85	n.a.
Netherlands							
E	(A)	100	97	93	90	88	89
IP	(A)	100	98	94	97	101	105
TB/GNP	(A)	−0.8	2.8	3.4	3.2	4.4	4.3
E	(B)	100	83	76	74	67	69
IP	(B)	100	84	77	81	80	85
Sweden							
E	(A)	100	96	93	93	94	95
IP	(A)	100	98	97	101	109	111
TB/GNP	(A)	−1.8	0.1	−0.2	2.1	3.7	2.4
E	(B)	100	88	87	77	72	78
IP	(B)	100	90	91	85	87	94

Source: International Monetary Fund, *International Financial Statistics*, vol. 40 (May 1987).
n.a. Not available.
a.   E = employment
         IP = industrial production
TB/GNP = trade balance as a percentage of gross national product
         (A) = actual
         (B) = adjusted for a constant trade balance.

ments undertaken by U.S. firms and by foreign firms reflect changes in the relationship between their costs of capital.

The more rapid increase in employment and industrial production in the United States than in Western Europe is consistent with the hypothesis that the anticipated profit rate on new investments in the United States increased relative to the anticipated profit rate on new investments in Western Europe. Changes in the pattern of direct foreign investment shown in table 2 are consistent with the hypothesis that the cost of capital for U.S. firms has increased relative to the cost of capital for firms headquartered in Western Europe.

Both the trade balance data and the direct foreign investment data are the outputs or consequences of financial market phenomena. The objec-

Table 2. *Shares of Outflows and Inflows of Direct Foreign Investment, Selected OECD Countries, 1970, 1980, 1983*

Percent

	Outflows			Inflows		
Country	1970	1980	1983	1970	1980	1983
United States	66	44	22	26	57	53
Canada[a]	3	6	9	15	2	1
Japan	3	5	16	2	1	2
Germany	8	9	13	11	1	5
France	3	7	8	11	11	8
Great Britain	11[b]	18[b]	16[b]	15[c]	20[c]	22[c]
Italy[a]	1	2	10	11	2	6
Netherlands[a]	5	7	7	9	6	3
Total	100	100	100	100	100	100

Source: U.S. Department of Commerce, *International Economic Indicators*, vol. 11 (March 1985), pp. 54–55. Figures are rounded.

a. Excludes reinvested earnings.

b. Excludes oil companies' investment abroad.

c. Excludes overseas oil companies' investment in Great Britain.

tive of this paper is to determine whether the actual data support these observations on savings rates, interest rates, and costs of financial intermediation. In particular, are the relationships between anticipated profitability and the cost of capital consistent with national differences in the rates of economic growth?

In market economies like those in Western Europe and the United States, the rate of economic growth reflects the relation between the anticipated profitability on the new investments that firms might make in a wide variety of projects and the cost of capital that these same firms associate with each of these projects. Firms invest as long as the anticipated profitability on particular projects exceeds the cost of capital associated with these projects; such investments increase their anticipated profits and their market value. The level of investment in each country—and hence the rate of national economic growth—varies as the anticipated profitability on investment changes relative to the firms' cost of capital. The term *corporate borrowers* is used deliberately, for the assumption is that differences among industrial countries in the rates of economic growth largely reflect differences among them in levels of investment in plant and equipment and that most such investments are made by private firms. The growth in employment reflects the growth in demand for labor in the private sector; the public sector is the employer of last resort.

In a macro context, financial market phenomena involve the relationship between the levels of saving and investment at high or target levels of employment. The relationship between the level of national saving and the rate of economic growth in a country is double edged. On the one hand, a high level of saving facilitates a high rate of economic growth for a given level of demand both by increasing the supply of funds for new investment available and by reducing the cost of capital to firms. A high level of investment in turn means a more rapid growth of supply capabilities. On the other hand, if the level of national saving increases too rapidly or is too high relative to the attractive investment possibilities, the level of investment may decline because of sluggishness in the rate of growth of demand; in this case, the decline in anticipated profitability dominates the decline in the cost of capital.[2] A high level of saving is the necessary condition for a high rate of economic growth; the sufficient condition is that there is an abundant supply of attractive investment opportunities whose anticipated profitability is high relative to the cost of capital. If growth in production is sluggish, high levels of employment may be attained only if the savings rate falls; then higher levels of consumer expenditure lead to a return to high employment and effective utilization of capacity. But the economy would then grow less rapidly once at high employment because supply capabilities would increase at a less rapid rate. Hence the question about economic growth in Western Europe posed by the macro question is whether the slow growth in the early 1980s means that supply capabilities are growing less rapidly or whether instead demand is growing relative to supply capabilities.

Financial market phenomena might affect rates of economic growth in a micro context through a set of structural arguments that involve the savings rate, the costs of financial intermediation, and the cost of capital to firms. These variables influence both the level of the interest rate paid investors and the size of the wedge between the interest paid investors and the interest rate charged borrowers.

There are several stylized facts about European financial markets that may bear on this question. First, they lack liquidity; as a result, investors

2. The Japanese postwar experience illustrates this distinction between supply-constrained growth and demand-constrained growth. Until the late 1960s, domestic demand exceded supply capabilities, and the Japanese current account was usually in deficit. In the late 1960s, supply capabilities expanded by more than enough to satisfy domestic demand, and since then Japan usually has had current account surpluses—although these surpluses were obscured by the OPEC shocks.

demand higher interest rates to compensate for this feature. Second, information on firms is poor and unreliable, so that investors operate in a riskier financial environment and demand higher interest rates. Third, competition among banks is limited so that the spread between the interest rate paid investors and the interest rate paid by borrowers is larger than in the United States.[3] Fourth, the large number of national markets in Western Europe means that the potential economies of scale in financial markets are not fully realized. Hence each national financial market lacks the depth, breadth, and resiliency of the U.S. market—and even of the Japanese market. The absence of scale also means that the wedge between the savings function and the investment function is larger than in an integrated continental financial market. Fifth, European financial markets are segmented into twenty national markets by currency, taxes, exchange controls, national regulation, language, financial practices, and other distinctions identified with national boundaries. As a result of this segmentation, investment capital may be allocated less efficiently than in an integrated continental market; the volume of capital flows to those geographic regions where its marginal product is highest is smaller than if the capital market were fully integrated. Within Western Europe, the countries of more rapid growth have been importers of capital and exporters of labor; the countries of less rapid growth have been exporters of capital and importers of labor. The segmentation effect introduces a wedge that causes the interest rates paid by borrowers in the high interest rate countries to exceed the interest rates received by investors in the low interest rate countries by a substantial amount.

These institutional features and the traditional determinants of supply and demand in credit markets suggest several hypotheses about weak European investment. One possibility is that savings rates or savings levels in Western Europe are too low; investment in the various countries in Western Europe might then be constrained by inadequate saving, which could cause interest rates in the several countries in Western Europe to be higher than interest rates in the United States. A second

3. In the late 1960s the U.S. balance-of-payments deficit was attributable to the inadequacies in European financial markets; this conclusion was based on the observation that the United States "lent long and borrowed short" in its international financial transactions. See Emile Despres, Charles P. Kindleberger, and Walter S. Salant, "The Dollar and World Liquidity: A Minority View," *Economist,* February 5, 1986, pp. 526–29; and Charles P. Kindleberger, *Balance-of-Payments Deficits and the International Market for Liquidity,* Essays in International Finance 46 (Princeton University, Department of Economics, 1965).

possibility is that financial markets are inefficient, and because of the high cost of intermediation, the interest return to investors would be lower than in the United States, while the interest payments of borrowers would be higher. (This type of explanation could be consistent with either the slower growth of capacity or the low level of anticipated profitability.) The third possibility is that the anticipated profitability on new investments in Western Europe is too low relative to the cost of capital to firms headquartered in various countries in Western Europe, and more so than in the United States. The lower level of anticipated profitability may reflect relatively more excess capacity. Or profits on production in Western Europe may have been squeezed, perhaps because prices have been reduced on tradable goods in response to the real appreciation of the German mark, the Swiss franc, and other European currencies relative to the U.S. dollar.

Each of these factors—the high cost of capital, the high cost of financial intermediation, and the low level of anticipated profitability—could explain why rates of economic expansion in countries in Western Europe have been more sluggish than the rate of U.S. economic growth. The structural, scale, and segmentation effects might explain why the cost of capital to European firms might be high even though the savings rate in various countries in Western Europe is higher than in the United States. Alternatively, the cost of capital to firms headquartered in one of the countries in Western Europe might be below the cost of capital to U.S. firms; then the lower rate of economic growth in Western Europe might be explained by the level of anticipated profitability.

The remainder of this paper relates differences in rates of economic growth in the United States and in various countries in Western Europe to differences in the anticipated profitability on new investments and to the cost of capital to firms headquartered in the United States and in Western Europe. It examines a number of hypotheses associated with financial market phenomena that might explain more sluggish growth in the various countries in Western Europe, with the objective of demonstrating that the cost of capital to these firms is not higher than the cost of capital to U.S. firms. The logical inference is that the anticipated profitability on new investments in Western Europe must be below the anticipated profitability on new investments in the United States.

The paper is divided into three sections. The first section analyzes the data on savings in the United States and other OECD countries to determine whether the volume of saving in Western Europe or the price demanded by savers might explain the sluggishness of growth in Western Europe. The second section discusses the wedges in the banking system and in the financial markets between the interest rate paid investors and the interest rate charged borrowers; its purpose is to determine whether national differences in levels of investment might be explained by national differences in costs of financial intermediation. Finally, the cost of capital for firms headquartered in the United States and in the various countries in Western Europe is compared.

The Level of Savings and Economic Growth in Western Europe

One possible financial explanation for the sluggishness of European growth is that usually associated with many of the developing countries—namely, the level of savings is too low, which means the level of investment is also low. The popular view, however, is that the savings rate in the various countries in Western Europe is higher than the savings rate in the United States; the higher savings rate might reflect a higher return to savers or investors, with the consequence that the cost of capital to firms in Western Europe would be higher than the cost of capital to U.S. firms. The differences in savings rates can be tested indirectly by their implications for capital flows or the current account balance and directly by examining the level of savings in relation to GNP and the levels of real interest rates.

The current account balance as a ratio of GDP for the United States and other OECD countries is shown in table 3. Most of the countries in Western Europe have had current account surpluses; France is the principal exception. These current account data suggest that the domestic saving in most countries in Western Europe has been more than adequate to satisfy domestic investment requirements and that a nontrivial component of domestic saving has financed the import of foreign securities. In contrast, since 1982 the United States has incurred current account deficits.

The trade and current account surpluses generated by the countries in Western Europe are inconsistent with the view that the source of slow growth is the shortage of capital; if there were a shortage of capital in Western Europe, these countries almost certainly would have had

Table 3. *Current Account Balance as Percentage of Gross Domestic Product, Selected OECD Countries, 1979–85*

Country	1979	1980	1981	1982	1983	1984	1985
United States	0.1	0.4	0.3	0.0	-1.0	-2.4	-2.9
Canada	-2.0	-0.6	-2.0	0.4	0.2	0.3	-0.5
Japan	-0.9	-1.0	0.5	0.7	1.8	2.8	3.7
Germany	-0.8	-1.8	-0.8	0.5	0.6	1.0	2.2
France	0.0	-1.4	-1.4	-3.0	-1.7	-0.8	-0.8
Great Britain	0.0	1.5	2.3	1.2	0.7	-0.3	1.0
Italy	1.7	-2.5	-2.3	-1.6	0.2	-0.9	-1.2
Netherlands	-1.2	-1.5	2.2	3.2	3.1	4.1	4.3
Sweden	-2.2	-3.6	-2.5	-3.6	-1.0	0.4	-1.2
Switzerland	2.7	-0.5	2.9	4.1	4.0	4.8	5.6

Source: *OECD Economic Outlook*, no. 40 (December 1986), p. 160.

Table 4. *Gross Savings as Percentage of Gross Domestic Product, Selected OECD Countries, 1979–85*

Country	1979	1980	1981	1982	1983	1984	1985
United States	21.0	19.2	19.8	16.8	15.8	17.4	16.5
Canada	22.5	22.9	22.4	19.0	19.2	19.4	18.6
Japan	31.5	31.1	31.1	30.5	29.8	30.6	31.4
Germany	22.7	21.8	20.2	20.3	21.1	21.5	22.2
France	22.8	22.2	19.7	18.6	18.1	18.5	18.0
Great Britain	20.0	18.4	17.3	17.6	17.5	18.5	19.2
Italy	23.0	22.5	19.0	18.4	17.9	18.1	17.7
Netherlands	20.3	20.1	20.5	21.1	21.5	23.4	24.1
Sweden	17.8	17.7	15.7	14.2	16.4	18.0	17.8
Switzerland	26.6	26.7	28.4	28.1	27.9	28.9	30.0

Source: *OECD Economic Outlook*, no. 40 (December 1986), p. 159.

current account deficits and imported capital from abroad. The current account surpluses also suggest that the anticipated return on foreign securities and foreign investments exceeds that on domestic investments by more than enough to compensate for the various cross-border risks.

Table 4 presents the ratio of gross savings to gross domestic product for Western European countries and for the United States, Canada, and Japan from 1979 to 1985. The gross savings rate in virtually every country in Western Europe is consistently higher as a percentage of national income than in the United States. However, the excess of the savings rate in most of these countries over the savings rate in the United States is not especially large, and these observed differences might be small relative to the measurement error inherent in the development of the

Table 5. *Nominal and Real Money Market Rates, Selected OECD Countries, 1979–85*[a]

Percent

Country	1979	1980	1981	1982	1983	1984	1985
United States	11.20	13.36	16.38	12.26	9.09	10.23	8.10
	−0.10	−0.14	5.98	6.06	5.89	5.93	4.50
Canada	11.68	12.80	17.72	13.64	9.30	11.06	9.43
	2.58	2.60	5.32	2.84	3.50	6.76	5.43
Japan	n.a.	n.a.	7.69	7.12	6.72	6.32	6.70
	n.a.	n.a.	2.79	4.52	4.92	4.02	4.70
Germany	6.69	9.54	12.11	8.88	5.78	5.99	5.40
	2.59	4.14	5.81	3.58	2.48	3.59	3.20
France	9.48	12.20	15.26	14.73	12.63	11.88	10.08
	−1.32	−1.10	1.86	2.93	3.03	4.48	4.28
Great Britain	13.59	16.10	13.48	12.02	9.90	9.49	11.95
	0.19	−1.90	1.58	3.42	5.30	4.49	5.85
Italy	11.86	17.17	19.60	20.18	18.44	17.27	15.25
	−2.94	−4.03	1.80	3.68	3.74	6.47	6.05
Netherlands	9.03	10.13	11.01	8.06	5.28	5.78	6.30
	4.83	3.63	4.31	2.16	2.48	2.48	4.10
Sweden	8.19	12.17	14.35	13.29	10.85	11.17	13.85
	0.99	−1.53	2.25	4.69	1.95	3.17	6.45
Switzerland	n.a.	5.15	7.82	3.87	3.04	3.58	4.15
	n.a.	1.15	1.32	−1.83	0.04	0.68	0.75

Source: IMF, *International Financial Statistics, 1986 Yearbook.*

n.a. Not available.

a. Average of annual rates. For each country the top row presents the nominal interest rates and the bottom row the real interest rates.

savings data. Nevertheless, the implication of national differences in savings rates is that real interest rates in various countries in Western Europe would be lower than in the United States on the assumption that the investment demands are similar.

Cross-country comparisons of interest rates are complicated by national differences in the rates of inflation; the exception is that the nominal interest rates will tend to be higher in the countries with the higher rates of inflation. The nominal and inflation-adjusted money market interest rates and government bond interest rates are shown in tables 5 and 6; the adjustment involves subtracting the observed inflation rate from the nominal interest rate to obtain the real interest rate. Real interest rates on government bonds in most of the Western European countries shown have been substantially below real interest rates on U.S. government bonds from 1982 to 1985. The dispersion of real interest rates appears higher in recent years. In a certain world, real interest

Table 6. *Nominal and Real Government Bond Yields, Selected OECD Countries, 1979–85*[a]

Percent

Country	1979	1980	1981	1982	1983	1984	1985
United States	9.33	11.39	13.72	12.92	11.34	12.48	10.97
	−1.97	−2.11	3.32	6.72	8.14	8.18	7.37
Canada	10.21	12.48	15.22	14.26	11.79	12.75	11.04
	1.11	2.28	2.82	3.46	5.99	8.45	7.04
Japan	7.69	9.22	8.66	8.06	7.42	6.81	6.34
	4.09	1.22	3.76	5.46	5.62	4.51	4.34
Germany	7.40	8.50	10.38	8.95	7.89	7.78	6.87
	3.30	3.10	4.08	3.65	4.59	5.38	4.67
France	9.48	13.03	15.79	15.69	13.63	12.54	10.94
	−1.32	−0.27	2.39	3.89	4.03	5.14	5.14
Great Britain	12.99	13.79	14.74	12.88	10.81	10.69	10.62
	−0.41	−4.21	2.84	4.28	6.21	5.69	4.52
Italy	14.05	16.11	20.58	20.90	18.02	14.95	13.00
	−0.75	−5.09	2.78	4.40	3.32	4.15	3.80
Netherlands	8.78	10.21	11.55	10.10	8.61	8.33	7.34
	4.58	3.71	4.85	4.20	5.81	5.03	5.14
Sweden	10.47	11.74	13.49	13.04	12.30	12.28	13.09
	3.27	−1.96	1.39	4.44	3.40	4.28	5.69
Switzerland	3.45	4.77	5.57	4.83	4.52	4.70	4.78
	−0.15	0.77	−0.93	−0.87	1.52	1.80	1.38

Source: IMF, *International Financial Statistics, 1986 Yearbook*.

a. Average of annual rates. For each country the top row presents the nominal interest rates and the bottom row the real interest rates.

rates on comparable assets denominated in different currencies would not differ significantly after adjustment for anticipated—and subsequently observed—changes in exchange rates. In an uncertain world, however, an interest rate differential may remain even after this adjustment and might be construed to represent a payment to investors for incurring various cross-border risks.

Data on these three factors—the current account balance, gross savings, and the real interest rate—are consistent with one another and inconsistent with the hypothesis that the sluggishness in investment and employment in Western Europe reflects a savings constraint. But there is more to the story, since the cost of capital to firms headquartered in Western Europe has increased because the funds have flowed from Western Europe to the United States. And the counterfactual question is whether countries in Western Europe might have grown faster if European investors had not found foreign securities more attractive; this question translates into whether the positive impacts on European growth of a lower interest rate would have outweighed the negative impacts of a reduction in the current account surpluses.

The Costs of Financial Intermediation

One financial factor that might explain the sluggishness in growth and employment in Western Europe, despite the higher savings rate and the lower interest rate paid lenders, is that the costs of financial intermediation might be higher than in the United States. The costs of financial intermediation are a wedge between the returns paid to savers or investors and the interest rates charged borrowers. If this wedge is substantially larger in Western Europe than in the United States, then the European advantage in the form of a lower real rate of interest on benchmark government securities might be partially or fully negated. The costs of financial intermediation include the costs of reserve requirements, other indirect and direct taxes, and the costs of capital of financial intermediaries. Higher costs of financial intermediation in Western Europe than in the United States might reflect the scale effect, or the less extensive competition among banks in most countries in Western Europe, or both.

Financial transfers between investors and borrowers can be made directly or through financial intermediaries—by either market finance or bank finance. Both types of finance incur costs; both create wedges between the interest and dividend payments of the borrowers and the interest and dividend receipts of savers and investors. Borrowers and investors seek to minimize their share of these costs. They choose between market finance and bank finance on the basis of relative costs, risks, and any compensatory differences. Investors associate a number of advantages with bank finance, including lower transactions costs, professional risk appraisal, a capital cushion, and diversification. Borrowers choose between market finance and bank finance primarily on the basis of cost—if market finance is a viable option. Some borrowers may prefer market finance for its anonymous quality, but the market can be a fair-weather friend; in moments of distress, investors may be reluctant to supply more funds to the borrowers, while bank finance still might be available.

The cross-country comparison of the costs of financial intermediation involves the measurement of two wedges, one for bank finance and one for market finance. The magnitude of the wedge for market finance tends to be similar to the magnitude of the wedge for bank finance. However, countries differ in the ratio of bank finance to market finance; the stylized fact is that this ratio is lower for the United States than for most other countries. As firms increase in size, they "graduate" from bank finance to market finance. One key question is whether the costs of direct finance and of bank finance differ significantly among countries, and especially whether these costs are likely to be significantly higher in several of the countries in Western Europe than in the United States and by more than enough to dominate the advantage of lower interest rates paid investors. A derivative question is whether the profile of these costs for small savers and large savers, and for small borrowers and large borrowers, is likely to differ significantly between the United States and the various countries in Western Europe.

European banks compete directly with U.S. banks in Eurocurrency deposit and loan markets and in the Eurobond markets. When these banks compete in the same market, the interest rates paid investors differ only modestly, reflecting the risks specific to the financial intermediary.[4] The implication is that the wedges for firms headquartered in different countries that have access to the Eurocurrency and Eurobond markets do not differ significantly in size. Moreover, if the wedges for bank and market finance were significantly higher in various countries in Western Europe than in the United States, some of the borrowers and investors based in these countries would transact in the offshore financial markets rather than in their domestic markets—unless they were constrained by exchange controls or the cost of using offshore financial intermediaries was too high. Just as large investors and borrowers choose between bank and market finance on the basis of cost, so they choose between transactions in domestic, foreign, and offshore centers on the basis of cost. The size of the wedge between large borrowers and investors may be similar in most European countries and in the offshore market; however, the proportion of borrowers in different countries that have access to the Euromarkets may differ.[5] The consequences of a

4. Robert Z. Aliber, "External Shocks and U.S. Domestic Financial Stability," in Federal Reserve Bank of San Francisco, *The Search for Financial Stability: The Past Fifty Years* (San Francisco, 1985), pp. 87–111.

5. The wedges in Eurodeposit and Eurobond markets are not significantly different by currency. Thus the size of the wedge on a Eurodollar transactions and that on a Euromark or a EuroSwiss franc transaction of the same magnitude are comparable. Eurobanks charge the same wedge, independent of the currency.

Table 7. *Transaction Costs in Financial Markets,*
Selected OECD Countries[a]

Percent unless otherwise specified

| | Instrument[a] | |
Country	Corporate bonds	Equities
United States	Bid-ask spread; active market: ¼ to ⅜	Small transactions (fixed fees); large transactions (variable fees)
Japan	0.25 to 0.35	$850 + 0.60
Germany	2.65	6.00
France	1.65	2.15
Great Britain	0.30	0.50
Italy	0.70	0.70
Netherlands	0.23 to 0.70	0.23 to 0.70

Source: L. J. Kemp, *A Guide to World Money and Capital Markets* (London: McGraw-Hill, 1981).
a. For comparisons, the transactions are assumed to be the local currency equivalent of U.S. $1,000,000.

larger wedge in the various countries in Western Europe than in the United States attributable to the scale and structural effects would be relevant only for those investors and borrowers whose size precludes ready access to the offshore market.

Measuring the wedges involved in market and bank finance is comparable to measuring transactions costs in the foreign exchange market or the equities market or the real estate market. Occasionally transactions costs are stated explicitly, as in many real estate transactions. Frequently, however, part of transactions costs is buried in the price or in the interest rate, especially in market finance. Thus the magnitude of the wedges is likely to vary significantly by the size of the investors and the borrowers, much as in the foreign exchange market and in most security markets. Hence, insofar as the scale and structural effects differ significantly among countries, they are likely to affect the transactions of smaller borrowers and smaller investors more so than those of borrowers and investors that have access to the Euromarkets.

The estimates of wedges on market finance costs noted in table 7 are those transactions costs incurred on direct purchases of corporate bonds and shares on a transaction of $1 million or equivalent. Countries may differ significantly in the size of the wedges involved in market finance, which would primarily affect the loans of smaller borrowers and investors.

The ratios of gross earnings margins to total assets and the ratios of operating costs to total assets for the United States and a few countries

Table 8. *Ratios of Gross Earnings Margins and of Operating Costs to Total Assets, Selected OECD Countries, 1977–81*

Percent

Country[a]	1977	1978	1979	1980	1981
United States					
I	3.63	3.80	3.89	3.98	4.07
II	2.45	2.49	2.54	2.63	2.76
Germany					
I	2.81	2.72	2.55	2.58	2.91
II	2.18	2.10	2.06	2.14	2.20
France					
I	2.99	2.93	2.90	3.09	3.06
II	2.18	2.18	2.15	2.08	2.03
Italy					
I	3.86	3.56	3.34	4.03	4.33
II	2.43	2.30	2.22	2.45	2.41
Sweden					
I	3.34	3.48	3.25	2.71	2.76
II	1.97	1.90	1.79	1.65	1.50

Source: Roberto de Rezende Rocha, "The Costs of Intermediation in Developing Countries: A Preliminary Investigation," in James A. Hanson and Roberto de Rezende Rocha, *High Interest Rates, Spreads, and the Costs of Intermediation: Two Studies,* Industry and Finance Series, vol. 18 (Washington, D.C.: World Bank, 1986), pp. 24–25.

a. I = gross earnings margins as a percent of total assets
II = operating costs as a percent of total assets.

in Western Europe are summarized in table 8. The inference from these data is that the costs of intermediation on bank finance are not lower in the United States than in the other OECD countries.

Thus the differences among countries in the magnitude of the wedges relevant for smaller borrowers might be in the order of several tenths of 1 percent—perhaps forty or fifty basis points—and hence not likely to be large enough to offset the advantage of lower nominal and real interest rates.

The Cost of Capital to European Firms and the Profitability of Investments in Western Europe

Firms headquartered in various countries in Western Europe may be reluctant to increase their domestic investments at the pace necessary to achieve a more rapid increase in employment and industrial production because the anticipated profitability on new investments is too low relative to the cost of capital—or at least the anticipated profitability on various domestic projects is too low. The anticipated profitability and the cost of capital are analogous to the blades of the scissors: the volume of new investment depends on the relation between the cost of capital and anticipated profitability rather than on the absolute value of either the cost of capital or anticipated profitability.

In an ideal world, or at least a world with comprehensive data, the profitability of the investment projects in each country would be measured independently of the cost of capital. The profitability of the investments would be location specific; hence profitability data would be dimensionally equivalent to wage data. In contrast, the data on the cost of capital to firms headquartered in particular countries would reflect investors' estimates of the combined riskiness of the domestic projects of these firms and their projects in various foreign countries. Thus profitability is specific to the countries where the projects are located, while the cost of capital is a financial market phenomenon specific to the currency denomination of a firm's securities and especially of its equities; the cost of capital for each firm is relevant for its foreign investments as well as its domestic investments.

This section of the paper examines whether the sluggishness of the rate of economic growth in Western Europe relative to the United States can be better explained by the cost of capital or by anticipated profitability. The conclusion from the first section was that the real rate of interest was lower for countries in Western Europe than in the United States. The conclusion from the second section was that the costs of financial intermediation were probably not so much higher for the countries in Western Europe than in the United States, so that the cost of capital to firms in various countries in Western Europe was not likely to be higher than the cost of capital to U.S. firms.

According to finance theory, each project undertaken by a firm should have its own cost of capital that reflects both the risk of the project and the riskless rate of return. Each project has its own risk that measures the variance of the return on the project relative to the variance of return on the market. A firm must decide whether the addition of particular projects to its portfolio of projects will increase its return and reduce its risk. Finance theory provides no insight about which firm from a group of firms is most likely to undertake a particular project, except that some firms may not undertake a project if its inclusion in their family of projects does not reduce its risk because the anticipated return is below the firm's own cost of capital. Hence each firm may have its own cost of capital that reflects the riskiness of its portfolio of projects. In the international context, there may be significant differences in the cost of capital to firms headquartered in each country; thus there may be country-specific costs of capital that follow from the differences among countries in the real rate of interest.[6]

In market economies, firms mediate between the financial markets and the markets for projects. These firms obtain funds from investors under a variety of contractual arrangements when the incremental cost of capital is smaller than the anticipated return on the projects they might acquire. Investors can acquire riskless securities (those issued by the governments of the countries where they live or in which their consumption bundles are denominated) or risky securities (acquired only if the additional returns are sufficient to compensate for the incremental risks). The concern of investors with incremental risk means they will pay more for the debt and for the equities of a particular firm only if the additional anticipated return on these securities is deemed worthwhile in terms of the incremental risk. The incremental risks of corporate securities might be significantly higher in various countries in Western Europe than in the United States because of the structural factors or because of the segmentation effect. Thus each firm might be construed to be a mutual fund, constrained to acquire additional projects only when they increase the risk and reduce the return of the total portfolio.

The government bond in each national currency is identified as the riskless security, and the rates of return on government bonds are taken as the riskless rates of return; the rationale is that the government can never default because of its ability to repay with the funds obtained from money creation. National differences in the nominal-risk-free interest rates reflect anticipated changes in exchange rates and exchange controls and the risks associated with such changes. Moreover, investors may believe that bonds issued by some governments are less risky than those issued by other governments because governments differ in the likelihood that they will repudiate debt. Investors engage in arbitrage among national financial markets whenever the difference in anticipated returns is large relative to the differences in risks.

Differences among countries in their risk-free interest rate—the

6. Robert Z. Aliber, "The Equivalence of Real Interest Rates in a Multi-Currency World," in Peter Oppenheimer, ed., *Issues in International Economics* (Stocksfield, England: Oriel Press, 1980), pp. 273–97; and Frederic S. Mishkin, "The Real Interest Rate: An Empirical Investigation," in Karl Brunner and Allan H. Meltzer, eds., *The Costs and Consequences of Inflation*, Carnegie-Rochester Conference Series on Public Policy, vol. 15 (Amsterdam: North-Holland, 1981), pp. 151–200.

interest rate on government bonds—provide a benchmark for the returns on riskier securities denominated in the same currencies. The relationship between the risk-free rates on bonds denominated in particular currencies and those on other securities denominated in the same currencies, at least securities with the same name and presumed legal characteristics, may differ for several reasons. One is that these securities may differ in their risk attributes; the bonds and equities issued in some countries may be riskier than in others, either because of the greater risk of the underlying projects or because of the financial structure of the firm. Differences among countries in tax structures may explain why the returns on different securities differ; investors price securities to equalize after-tax returns on the margin. And the risk preferences of investors resident in particular countries may differ; there may be habitat effects.

Each firm's cost of capital is measured by the weighted average cost of its debt and of its equity. The weights reflect the prevailing market values of its debt and of its equity. The cost of debt is the market interest rate that the firm would have to pay if it were to issue an additional unit of debt. Similarly, the cost of equity is the return that holders of equity anticipate from the combination of dividends and anticipated change in the price of the firm's shares.

The cost of capital to firms headquartered in each country might be approximated by the interest rate on debt, on the presumption that the cost of equity to each firm increases as its leverage increases. According to this view, the cost of capital is not significantly affected by the relative importance of debt and equity in its capital structure. As the shares of debt and equity in the capital structure of the firm change, the cost of the debt component and the equity component of the capital structure change—but not the aggregate cost. Corporate bonds are a smaller part of the total capital of firms headquartered in Japan or in one of the Western European countries than of firms headquartered in the United States. To the extent that foreign firms rely more extensively on debt finance than U.S. firms do, the debt consists of bank loans. Because corporate bonds are such a small part of corporate capital, the cost of equity capital may be taken as a proxy for the aggregate cost of capital.

The cost of equity capital involves the anticipated returns on shares both in the form of dividends and price appreciation. If earnings are all paid out as dividends, then the cost of equity capital is approximated by the dividend-price ratio. But few firms pay out all their earnings in the form of dividends. An approximation to the cost of equity capital is

Table 9. *Valuation of National Equities, Selected OECD Countries, 1982–85*

Country[a]	1982	1983	1984	1985
United States				
P/BV	1.27	1.45	1.39	1.67
P/CE	5.5	6.4	5.6	6.9
P/E	10.1	12.2	9.9	13.7
Japan				
P/BV	1.97	2.18	2.60	2.71
P/CE	7.2	9.3	9.3	9.0
P/E	22.2	25.1	27.3	25.9
Germany				
P/BV	1.22	1.61	1.68	2.83
P/CE	3.3	4.4	4.3	6.0
P/E	11.2	15.0	13.5	16.7
France				
P/BV	0.62	1.03	1.20	1.59
P/CE	2.6	4.4	3.8	4.3
P/E	13.2	63.8	15.3	15.3
Great Britain				
P/BV	1.05	1.16	1.40	1.52
P/CE	5.4	5.7	6.4	6.8
P/E	9.8	10.4	11.1	12.1
Italy				
P/BV	1.02	0.96	0.94	1.75
P/CE	7.5	5.3	3.2	5.5
P/E	LOSS	LOSS	18.1	26.2
Netherlands				
P/BV	0.60	0.86	0.92	0.96
P/CE	2.7	3.3	3.1	3.3
P/E	5.9	6.4	6.2	8.2
Sweden				
P/BV	1.36	1.98	1.29	1.57
P/CE	5.9	7.9	4.6	6.0
P/E	13.3	15.2	7.4	10.0

Source: Morgan Stanley Capital International, *Perspective*, various monthly issues. Year-end valuations.
a. P/BV = ratio of price per share to book value per share
   P/CE = ratio of price to cash earnings (profits and depreciation)
   P/E = ratio of price to earnings.

provided by the price-earnings ratio or its reciprocal, the earnings-price ratio.

The price that investors will pay for equities denominated in each currency can be measured by several ratios (see table 9). The higher these ratios, the lower the cost of equity capital. Japan stands out in that

Table 10. *Change in Industrial Share Prices, Selected OECD Countries, 1980–85*
Percent change from previous year

Country	1981	1982	1983	1984	1985
United States	7.2	−7.4	35.1	0.4	14.7
Canada	−2.6	−21.1	45.1	−2.6	20.3
Japan	16.3	−0.4	17.9	26.1	22.1
Germany	0.4	−1.4	34.8	12.7	32.9
Great Britain	12.8	15.6	26.5	19.0	23.4
France	−11.9	−15.1	35.0	35.0	16.8
Italy	51.7	−18.9	24.4	12.3	66.8
Netherlands	5.6	1.6	44.4	27.0	29.4
Sweden	49.0	24.8	93.5	9.4	−6.9
Switzerland	−9.0	−1.4	29.2	13.7	30.3

Source: IMF, *International Financial Statistics, 1986 Yearbook.*

its ratios are significantly higher than for almost any other country; the cost of capital for firms headquartered in Japan is substantially smaller than for firms headquartered in the United States and various countries in Western Europe. The ratios for Germany and France are generally higher than those for the United States, while the ratios for the United States are similar to or higher than those for other European countries. By this measure, only firms headquartered in the Netherlands appear to have a consistently higher cost of capital than U.S. firms do.

Moreover, during the 1982–85 period, the increase in equity prices in most of the countries in Western Europe and in Japan was at least as large as the increase in equity prices in the United States. The implication is that during this period, the cost of capital to firms headquartered in these foreign countries declined relative to the cost of capital for U.S. firms.

Tables 9 and 10 suggest that the cost of capital to firms headquartered in Western Europe cannot explain the sluggishness of growth in employment and production. Indeed, for much of the 1980s the cost of capital for the firms headquartered in most of the countries in Western Europe was below the cost of capital for firms headquartered in the United States.

If firms headquartered in the various countries in Western Europe have a cost-of-capital advantage, and yet their rate of growth of output and employment is below that in the United States, anticipated profitability on new investment must be low. Anticipated profitability can be inferred from the current rate of return in manufacturing, which is shown

Table 11. *Rate of Return in Manufacturing, Selected OECD Countries, 1979–85*[a]

Percent

Country	1979	1980	1981	1982	1983	1984	1985
United States	15.2	12.3	12.6	10.6	13.6	17.5	18.3
Canada	13.1	12.8	11.7	7.0	8.1	10.2	10.5
Japan	21.7	21.1	19.9	19.7	19.3	20.3	20.2
Germany	14.4	12.2	11.2	11.7	13.2	14.1	16.3
France	14.3	13.4	12.5	12.2	12.4	12.4	13.5
Great Britain	6.5	5.7	5.3	6.1	6.9	7.9	8.2
Italy	16.4	18.2	15.3	14.9	13.6	15.1	14.6
Sweden	6.0	6.3	5.4	5.9	8.0	9.3	9.2

Source: Data supplied by OECD.
a. Gross operating surplus as percentage of gross capital stock.

in table 11. The rate of return on manufacturing dips in 1982 and then increases for all countries with the exception of Italy. In 1982 the rate of return on manufacturing in the United States was below that for most of the countries in Western Europe. By 1985, however, the rate of return on manufacturing in the United States was higher than the rate of return in any of the countries in Western Europe.

The rate of return can be construed to represent the product of a price term (profits per unit of sales) and a quantity term (the volume of sales). During the 1980–85 period of a sharply appreciating dollar, profits per unit of sales on manufacturing in the United States almost certainly declined because profits per unit of sales were squeezed between declining selling prices and modest increases in costs.[7] (This reflected the decline of effective U.S.-dollar selling prices of producers based in Western Europe and Japan as their currencies depreciated.) In Western Europe, in contrast, profits per unit of sales increased. However, the change in the quantity variable for the United States dominated the change in the unit profit variable. As a percent of value added, gross operating surplus increased in virtually every country with the recovery from the 1982 recession; Italy is the major exception (see table 12).

Although the percentage increase in operating profits for the United States is modestly larger than for most countries in Western Europe, the levels of operating profits in 1985 in the United States were remarkably

7. Richard Layard and others, "Europe: The Case for Unsustainable Growth," in Olivier Blanchard, Rudiger Dornbusch, and Richard Layard, eds., *Restoring Europe's Prosperity: Macroeconomic Papers from the Centre for European Policy Studies* (MIT Press, 1986), pp. 33–94.

Table 12. *Profits in Manufacturing, Selected OECD Countries,*
1979–85[a]

Percent

Country	1979	1980	1981	1982	1983	1984	1985
United States	24.2	21.8	22.7	21.2	25.9	30.0	30.9
Canada	33.8	34.6	32.9	24.7	27.5	32.2	32.9
Japan	43.4	43.7	42.0	42.0	41.3	42.1	42.1
Germany	28.8	25.6	24.5	26.1	28.8	30.2	32.8
France	30.3	29.2	28.4	28.1	28.6	28.6	31.1
Great Britain	22.4	21.0	21.3	23.9	26.2	28.2	28.6
Italy	35.5	37.8	34.5	34.6	33.2	36.5	36.3
Sweden	21.3	22.4	20.6	23.8	31.1	32.4	32.0

Source: Data supplied by the OECD.
a. Gross operating surplus as percentage of gross value added.

similar to the levels in most of the countries in Western Europe (Great
Britain is an outlier on the low side). The higher rate of return in
manufacturing in the United States (table 11) must be reconciled with
the similarities in the level of gross operating profits (table 12). Because
firms headquartered in one of the Western European countries have a
lower cost of capital than U.S. firms, gross operating profits exclusive
of the cost of capital are higher for those firms than for U.S. firms. The
contrast between the higher rate of return on U.S. manufacturing and
the lower ratio of gross operating profits to value added suggests that the
increase in output has been substantially larger in the United States than
in the countries in Western Europe. Profits per unit of sales in the various
countries in Western Europe are higher, in part or whole because of the
undervaluation of their currencies; however, the increase in output was
substantially greater in the United States. Financial factors did not
constrain the growth in industrial production and employment in Western
Europe. Indeed, these factors were a more positive influence on economic expansion in the various countries in Western Europe than in the
United States.

The fact that growth was more sluggish in Western Europe than in the
United States reflects a lower level of realized profitability—and presumably anticipated profitability. Firms headquartered in Western Europe
had a cost of capital advantage, and the anticipated profitability per unit
of sales was unusually high as a result of the undervaluation of their
currencies. Despite these advantages, the firms headquartered in the
several countries in Western Europe were reluctant to invest domestically at the rate necessary to reduce the unemployment rates. The

inference is that these firms could have invested more domestically if the domestic market had appeared more profitable, but they did not do so even though they had a cost-of-capital advantage.

Conclusions

Changes in employment and industrial production in the early 1980s partly reflect changes in the ratio of the trade surplus to gross domestic product for most countries since 1980. This ratio has declined for the United States, and the ratios for most countries in Western Europe have increased with the exception of Great Britain and France. Among the many factors contributing to changes in these ratios are changes in real exchange rates and in foreign and domestic demand. When the employment and industrial production in each country are adjusted as if each country's trade balance were a constant percentage of its gross domestic product, the United States' employment and industrial production increase more rapidly since 1980, and employment and growth in most countries in Western Europe increase less rapidly. The apparent declines in employment and industrial production when these adjustments are made for some of the smaller countries in Western Europe are dramatic.

Changes in the pattern of direct foreign investment result from the nexus between the anticipated profitability of new investments and the cost of capital associated with these investments. Increases in the level of investment in a particular country such as the United States may reflect increases in anticipated profitability of projects in that country. Changes in the share of investments in each country undertaken by firms headquartered there relative to firms headquartered in various foreign countries reflect changes in the relationship among the costs of capital of these different national firms. Two complementary inferences are based on the observed changes in the pattern of direct foreign investment. One is that the anticipated profitability of investments in the United States had increased significantly relative to investments in most countries in Western Europe, despite the increasing overvaluation of the U.S. dollar in the 1980–85 period. The other is that firms headquartered in Western Europe developed a significant cost-of-capital advantage. This explains the sharp increase in direct foreign investment by firms headquartered in various countries in Western Europe relative to firms headquartered in the United States and is consistent with the takeovers

of established U.S. firms by firms headquartered in various countries in
Western Europe (and Japan).

During the early 1980s, the savings rates in Western Europe were
higher than U.S. savings rates, while nominal and real interest rates
were lower. Firms headquartered in Western Europe would appear to
have a cost-of-capital advantage relative to U.S. firms, unless lower real
interest rates were dominated by higher costs of financial intermediation.
Several stylized facts suggest that the cost of bank and market finances—
loosely, the costs of financial intermediation—might be higher in various
countries in Western Europe than in the United States. European
markets are significantly smaller, and presumably the fewer players in
each market the less extensive the competition. In Eurodeposit and
Eurobond markets, however, the magnitude of the wedges associated
with financial institutions headquartered in various Western European
countries is not likely to differ significantly from that associated with
U.S. institutions operating in those markets. The implication is that
borrowers and investors based in the various European countries will
transact in the offshore market in their domestic currencies. Thus only
the smaller borrowers and investors are likely to incur the costs associated with the larger wedges in the various European countries. And even
then the higher costs associated with direct and indirect finances are not
likely to neutralize the cost-of-capital advantage of firms headquartered
in various countries in Western Europe because these cost differences
are likely to be in the order of several tenths of 1 percent.

Changes both in the growth of output and employment and in the
pattern of direct foreign investment could be explained by the national
differences in the cost of capital. The cost of capital for firms headquartered in each country would reflect the riskless rate of return on assets
denominated in that country's currency—in effect, the interest rate on
government bonds. The cost of capital to an individual firm would reflect
the risk that investors attach to its projects and activities and hence to
its securities. The smaller the risk, the higher the price that investors
would pay for the equities of the firm relative to the price they would
pay for the riskless security. The data on the ratio of equity prices to
book value and to cash earnings suggest that firms headquartered in
Germany and France (as well as in Japan) have had a cost-of-capital
advantage relative to firms headquartered in the United States. The data
do not suggest that firms headquartered in other Western European
countries (with the possible exception of the Netherlands) are at a cost-
of-capital disadvantage relative to U.S. firms. And so the slower rate of

growth of employment and of industrial production cannot be explained by financial market phenomena.

The profitability of investment—the rate of return in manufacturing—has increased in all industrial countries since 1982. The increase has been greatest for the United States. During this same period, firms producing in the United States were adversely affected by the sharp appreciation of the U.S. dollar, which greatly reduced U.S. competitiveness; by itself the stronger dollar should have squeezed the rate of return on manufacturing in the United States relative to the rates of return on manufacturing in those countries with the depreciating currencies. But the increase in demand in the United States was significantly more rapid than in Western Europe.

An extensive array of data—national savings rates, nominal and real interest rates, current account surpluses, direct foreign investment in the United States, the costs of intermediation for both bank finance and market finance, and the cost of equity capital—suggest that growth in industrial production and employment in Western Europe was not constrained by financial market phenomena. Instead the firms headquartered in most of the countries in Western Europe had a cost-of-capital advantage, which is the dominant and powerful explanation for the surge in their direct foreign investments in the United States.

The stylized facts about the comparative shortcomings of the financial markets in Western Europe—the lack of liquidity, the paucity of information, the small scale, the segmentation by twenty currencies—may well lead to higher interest rates in the various countries in Western Europe. But the empirical significance of these institutional arguments has been dominated by the lack of investment demand in the various countries in Western Europe and the low level of anticipated profitability on new investment in manufacturing compared with new investment in the United States. Conceivably, with superior institutional arrangements the level of interest rates in Western Europe could be so much lower that it could compensate for the lower rate of anticipated profitability. But the comparative data on the wedges in bank and market finance suggest that on average these institutional micro arguments are less significant than the macro considerations.

Comment by Hermann J. Dudler

In the second half of the 1960s, distinguished American economists examining the U.S. balance of payments identified a puzzling financial phenomenon: long-term financial capital "leaked" persistently into Europe, while European banks and central banks accumulated an excessive stock of short-term claims against the United States. They concluded that apparent imperfections constraining European financial markets forced the United States to assume the role of the world's financial intermediary. In contrast, conservative Europeans at that time felt that the U.S. dollar was stabilized at an overvalued level through official intervention and short-term interest rate policies, which produced a huge "dollar overhang." This dispute triggered a wealth of reports and studies on the functioning of European capital markets in the late 1960s that, no doubt, had beneficial side effects.

Twenty years later, some American economists looking at the U.S. national accounts discovered an equally embarrassing phenomenon: internal U.S. demand, badly needed at home, "leaks" into Europe, reflecting the weakening of the U.S. real foreign balance. At the same time, slowly growing European economies built up large savings surpluses. And there may again be a financial explanation: inefficient European intermediaries drive an excessive, deflationary wedge between the real rate of interest paid on savings instruments and the higher real cost of borrowing charged to investing corporations. The resulting weakness in European business capital spending has forced the United States to assume the role of the world's investment locomotive. In contrast, many unsophisticated Europeans argue that the U.S. economy and the world at large suffer from the aftermath of a severe Mundellian external crowding-out process initiated by U.S. fiscal and monetary policies. This conflict of views has prompted many studies on impediments to European growth and Europe's financial inefficiency, studies that, no doubt, will again yield beneficial side effects.

I am not suggesting that this caricature of a familiar U.S.-European debate on comparative efficiencies of financial systems has a direct bearing on Aliber's analysis. It would be unfair to visualize him walking in the footsteps of Charles P. Kindleberger, Walter S. Salant, and others who produced surprising pieces of international financial economics in an attempt to discuss away the overvaluation of the U.S. dollar in the latter half of the 1960s. On the contrary, his findings suggest that it would be difficult to attribute a significant part of the sluggishness of European business investment and industrial growth in the 1980s to imperfections in European financial markets. Nevertheless, the paper attempts to discuss this hypothesis quite explicitly in the context of the current growth debate.

To this end, the author develops a rudimentary analytical and statistical framework that clearly transcends the realm of economic variables ordinarily associated with the functioning of financial markets: domestic and foreign direct investment behavior in Europe and the United States is, as a first step, assessed on the basis of what I would regard as intermediate macroeconomic proxy variables. These represent the anticipated real rates of return on new capital investments in Europe and in the United States and the estimated real cost of placing risk-free debt instruments in national capital markets. The surprising results—investment returns seem to have been roughly equal on both sides of the Atlantic since the early 1980s, while European firms may have had a real cost-of-capital advantage—condemn the author to resort to intelligent armchair reasoning to solve the apparent statistical puzzle.

As a second step, Aliber develops various convincing arguments why the data presented may be misleading representations of the corresponding anticipated values. The stylized facts (that is, the relative weakness of corporate investment in Europe and a swing of direct investment flows toward the United States) seem to suggest that European investors have been at a comparative disadvantage with respect to risk-prone business capital spending undertaken in Europe since the early 1980s. However, the reader is finally left somewhat in the dark about what ultimately determined American and European investors' diverging perceptions of future real returns, entrepreneurial risk, and real borrowing costs. In other words, transatlantic growth differentials during the past few years remain largely unexplained, I suspect, because real rates of return, borrowing costs, investment, and output are all jointly determined in the economic system and cannot unequivocally be causally related in the global framework of the simple loanable funds model presented in the paper.

It seems intuitively obvious that, as Aliber explains, financial rigidities may not be at the heart of American-European growth differentials. After all, considered here is a macroeconomic development covering hardly more than a handful of years. Over such a time span, structural characteristics of money and capital markets are unlikely to undergo such a rapid change that relative investment and growth performances could be materially affected. Nevertheless, I find Aliber's attempt to discuss the real interest rate "wedge hypothesis" sensible for three reasons. First, a massive wave of financial deregulation and innovation has swept the U.S. financial system during the past five to seven years, while comparable developments in central Europe (excluding the United

Kingdom as a special case) have been less rapid or conspicuously absent. Second, with the European economy embarking on a steady, though somewhat hesitant, growth path, financial constraints, as indicated by Aliber, could carry an increasing weight. Finally, trade links and across-the-border investment and savings decisions have grown within Europe, while the formation of a common European capital market may now be seriously lagging because of many regulatory constraints.

To examine comparative efficiencies of U.S. and European financial markets empirically in a systematic manner, I suggest a less general approach than the ambitious quantitative framework proposed by Aliber. Nobody will seriously question the proposition that a hypothetical widening of a divergence in the relative performances of American and European financial systems is difficult to quantify in the short, intermediate, and possibly even long run. Given this restriction, how could one fruitfully proceed?

I think that the exercise could consist of two main stages. First, financial efficiency criteria would have to be selected under which longer-run developments of financial systems would be judged in the context of economic growth performance. Second, comparative financial market characteristics and their developments over the past five to seven years inside and outside the United States would have to be studied and evaluated in terms of the selected efficiency criteria.

The aims of such a study could be twofold. As in Aliber's paper, one could attempt, on the one hand, to find any evidence that the efficiency of European financial markets has deteriorated relative to that of the U.S. financial system and may thus contribute, however marginally, to Europe's comparatively weak growth performance. Irrespective of such findings, one could explore, on the other hand, the scope for improving the functioning of European financial markets to facilitate a lasting recovery of European corporate investment; that is, devise financial "supply-side" policies aimed at the removal of financial constraints on European growth.

The choice of appropriate and empirically applicable efficiency criteria is, of course, of crucial importance. Highly abstract concepts of market efficiency relating to optimal information processing or general equilibrium contracts of the Arrow-Debreu type may not be suitable for the purposes at hand. It could be useful, however, to pursue a concept that Tobin has referred to as the "functional efficiency" of financial sectors.[8]

8. James Tobin, "On the Efficiency of the Financial System," *Lloyds Bank Review*, no. 153 (July 1984), pp. 1–15.

Within this framework the human and capital resources devoted to the financial industries are related to the basic macroeconomic functions they perform. These include, according to Tobin, "the pooling of risks and their allocation to those most able and willing to bear them, a generalized insurance function . . . ; the facilitation of transactions by providing mechanisms and networks of payments; the mobilization of saving for investments in physical and human capital, domestic and foreign, private and public, and the allocation of saving to their more socially productive uses."[9]

Many empirical country and cross-country studies on the functioning of financial markets have implicitly or explicitly applied these criteria. The stylized facts on European financial markets that Aliber presents, in fact, draw heavily on historical studies of this type. Since he has put so much emphasis, however, on a loanable funds exposition of the problems and its attempted empirical verification, there was hardly enough room to elaborate the efficiency criteria applied, discuss the comparative features of U.S. and European financial markets, and evaluate the developments of these characteristics during the 1980s. To fully exploit the framework I have suggested, one individual academic author would certainly be overburdened unless he or she could draw heavily on empirical work done by qualified national and international research institutions and organizations. In a number of related areas, research projects and studies have indeed been taken in hand. What one misses, however, are sober and up-to-date assessments of the following aspects of the problem.

—A preliminary, unbiased evaluation of the economic costs and benefits of deregulation and financial innovation in the United States. Can the U.S. financial system at all serve as a model for Europe?

—Given a general trend toward abolition of administrative controls, the fostering of financial competition, and liberalization of capital movements in many European countries, the stylized facts on European financial rigidities have been changing over the past five to seven years. How serious are the remaining constraints in the context of recent economic growth performance?

—The rapid development of a largely unconstrained global market for "wholesale" financing services, in which both European and American nonbanks and financial institutions actively participate, may partly reduce the need for liberalization and deregulation policies at the national

9. Ibid., p. 3.

level. How important are the residual obstacles to smaller-sized economic operating units?

—From the viewpoint of functional efficiency, Europe's financial integration cannot be regarded as an aim in itself. Can an optimal area be determined for closer monetary and financial European integration including or excluding smaller Mediterranean countries or the United Kingdom?

These are, of course, partly secular issues, and I am not going to suggest any answer to the questions I raised.

Comment by Mario Monti

The paper by Aliber is interesting for three reasons. It addresses one of the key issues of the European economy, capital formation, and the role of financial markets. It does so by using a rather systematic framework. And it reaches an uncommon and somewhat provocative conclusion: financial markets probably have not been an impediment to European growth.

My comments address a few points in the paper that need some clarification or are not entirely convincing and issues that, though not included in Aliber's framework, are relevant and might alter his main conclusion. As to clarification, after Hermann J. Dudler's comments I shall confine myself to four observations.

—*Evidence on investment.* Investment is at the center of the stage—the key question in the paper is whether financial phenomena are responsible for the resistance of European firms to domestic investment—but virtually no data on investment are presented. A lot of evidence is produced on employment and industrial production, including their adjustment for a constant trade balance—an exercise that may be of interest but does not specifically concern investment or the financial markets.

If the behavior of investment were actually presented and discussed, it would become clear, for example, that since 1983 there has been a very substantial investment pickup in Europe (although it will have to continue at the present pace for several years to remove the capital constraint originated by the previous decline in investment).

—*Location and the cost of capital.* Aliber assumes that the profitability of investment is determined in the country where a plant is located, whereas the relevant cost of capital is the one prevailing in the country where the company has its headquarters. This assumption is crucial in drawing inferences—in terms of direct foreign investment across the Atlantic—that support his main conclusion.

However, the validity of the assumption is questionable because (1) for small firms, which do not normally invest abroad, the assumption is not relevant, and (2) for large firms the assumption is not very plausible, since such firms are increasingly able to also raise funds in countries other than those in which their headquarters are located.

—*Transaction costs.* The data given in table 7, "Transaction Costs in Financial Markets," are interesting. Yet for two reasons one should be cautious about taking them as an appropriate measure of the wedge in financial markets.

First, on a factual basis, it is puzzling to note, for example, that the commission for a transaction on equities in Germany is shown as 6 percent. If this is incorrect, the whole table should be further inspected with care. If it is correct, I would hesitate to interpret these figures as indicating any notion of market perfection or efficiency, particularly when one sees from the table that the transaction cost in the German stock market (6 percent) is nine times as large as that in the Italian stock market (0.7 percent).

Second, on a more conceptual basis, these may be measures of wedges on the mobility of financial instruments rather than wedges pertaining to the cost of financing. They have the same dimension as Tobin's proposed "sand" on foreign exchange transactions, rather than the dimension of interest rates or of a wedge between borrowing and lending rates. They represent a cost of brokerage rather than a cost of financial intermediation.

—*Cost-of-capital comparison.* The evidence does not seem to fully support the proposition that European firms have experienced a cost-of-capital advantage. That proposition rests mainly on two elements: the observation of capital flows and direct investment across the Atlantic (but this section, as already noted, relies on an assumption that raises perplexities); and a comparison of real interest rates (but this is done in terms of money market rates and government bonds rates, which are not those directly relevant for corporate finance). Even if the two problems could be overcome, one could not conclude that European financial markets are fundamentally well functioning. Finally, if there were some direct evidence of inefficiencies in European financial markets—limiting the volume of capital formation or its productivity—and if such inefficiencies could be removed, these improvements in Europe's financial system would help to achieve faster growth, irrespective of its performance relative to that of the U.S. financial system.

This leads to my comments concerning aspects that are not mentioned by Aliber but are relevant to the question whether financial markets in Europe are an impediment to growth. If these aspects are not taken into account, it is difficult to understand, among other things, why Europeans have recently given a great deal of attention to the issue of financial liberalization, both domestically and across national borders.

Particularly relevant to the efficiency of European investment are allocative constraints on financial flows, intensively used for a long time in several European countries. They may take many different forms, of which I shall mention three.

—*Administrative rationing of credit* (the scheme typically known in France as "encadrement du crédit"). Because it limits the admissible demand for credit by individual firms or sectors, its effects do not necessarily show up in interest rates and therefore in Aliber's measure of the cost of capital. Administrative rationing of capital tends nevertheless to compress the volume of investment and to distort its composition.

—*Ceilings on the supply of credit* that each bank may extend to the aggregate of its customers (the scheme typically known in Italy as "massimale sugli impieghi bancari"). This constraint freezes the loan market shares of individual banks, thereby reducing competition and generating X-inefficiencies. It also distorts the allocation of aggregate bank credit and tends to widen the wedge. (Interest rates on bank loans tend to increase and those of bank depositors to decrease, while the rates of return on government bonds tend to decline as the banking system increases its demand for bonds because of the supply constraint on commercial loans. The productive sector of the economy thus subsidizes the government sector.)

—*Restrictions on capital (out)flows* (observed in several European countries). These again have the financial side effect domestically of reducing the average level of interest rates on instruments available to domestic savers and of making it easier for the government sector— especially in combination with the credit ceiling mentioned earlier—to raise a larger volume of funds at a lower cost. These restrictions, therefore, effectively reduce the incentive to private saving and increase the portion of it absorbed by the government sector.

For these reasons, the steps toward financial liberalization observed in several European countries in the past few years, notably in France and Italy, should be regarded as important. As argued in greater detail elsewhere, allocative constraints have had an adverse effect on the process of capital formation in Europe and their phasing out is expected to contribute to a larger and more productive pattern of investment.[10]

Along with the improvement of domestic financial systems, a substantial role is to be played by the deeper integration among them. This aspect—which is also not considered in Aliber's analysis—is at the center of the current movement toward financial integration promoted by the Commission of the European Communities. As is well known, it takes the form of measures designed to achieve both the liberalization of capital movements and the liberalization of financial services among member countries. It is expected to be completed by 1992, according to EC plans.

The phasing out of domestic allocative constraints and of restrictions impeding financial integration in Europe should also help to create conditions more favorable to the establishment of effective financing systems for new firms, another traditional weakness of European financial systems. Since 1963 the second tier of exchange in the European Community has listed fewer than 600 companies, whereas during the decade 1974–84 the nationwide electronic dealing network in the United States created an active market of 5,000 listed equities with an annual trading volume of $153 billion—larger than the combined volume of business on the stock exchanges of the United Kingdom, Germany, France, Italy, and the Netherlands. Although the EC countries produce as many new start-ups in a year as the United States (about 600,000), there is no large-scale mechanism for trading the equity of those companies. Partly as a result of this situation, "European investors have provided American venture companies with a fifth of their capital in recent years. Last year [1985] alone, Europeans provided more than $600 million towards the $3.2 billion raised in venture capital in the United States."[11]

A final reflection may be appropriate at this point. When financial liberalization (domestic financial liberalization plus financial integration)

10. F. Modigliani and others, "Reducing Unemployment in Europe: The Role of Capital Formation," no. 28 (Brussels: Center for European Policy Studies, 1986).
11. "Bringing Europe's Small Companies to Market," *Euromoney*, February 1986, p. 18.

in Europe is advocated, does it not go against a new wave of financial reregulation, which may be building up recently? Is there a contrast of strategy between European financial liberalization and the concern expressed in recent reports by the Bank for International Settlements and other monetary or supervisory institutions—namely, that deregulation and innovation in the financial field may have proceeded too far?

I submit that there is no such contrast and that the two views are perfectly consistent as long as "financial liberalization" does not mean relaxing supervisory controls in fields such as the protection of depositors or the liquidity and solvency of banks. The kind of financial liberalization that is still needed in Europe means two precise elements, which are different from the ones that motivate the concern mentioned earlier. It means phasing out allocative constraints—mostly amounting to discriminations in favor of government financing—and phasing out restrictions on flows of capital and of financial services at least among the EC countries. Financial liberalization in this sense, far from bringing about more financial indiscipline as is sometimes feared, implies the reimposition of greater financial discipline where it is generally needed more, in the government sector.

Incidentally, the completion of this process of financial liberalization in Europe would establish in European financial markets conditions similar to those that—well before the deregulatory wave of the past few years—have traditionally been observed in the United States: the absence of substantial allocative constraints in favor of Treasury securities and the absence of restrictions on interstate capital flows.

General Discussion

The discussion considered the degree to which international capital markets have been liberalized in recent years and the effect such liberalization has had on the European economies. It was pointed out that the past two or three decades have seen a marked decrease both in the barriers among national capital markets and in the relative cost of communications and technology. While this liberalization has not progressed as far in Europe as in the United States, the impetus is toward reducing the financial impediments to European growth.

Another participant suggested that perceptions concerning the degree of integration of national financial markets and the mobility of capital depend greatly on what kind of capital flows are being measured. According to the Feldstein-Horioka theory based on the correlation of savings and investment, the mobility of real capital flows is low. But if one examines covered interest parity, financial markets are highly integrated; in countries without capital controls, domestic and offshore interest rate differentials are small. These facts suggest that real and financial rates of return may not be closely correlated; there may be perfect substitutability among financial assets but not among claims to real capital.

One participant felt that Aliber's discussion concentrated too much on the average spread that financial intermediaries charge when the quality of investment decisions made by financial markets was the important element in accounting for secular changes in growth rates. He questioned whether a fully liberalized equity market could allocate investment optimally, citing an article by Stiglitz and Grossman to support his argument that some bureaucratization of investment decisions is beneficial. Another discussant suggested that where banking institutions dominate financial intermediation (as in Germany) there is a tendency not only for rigidities in the availability of funds but also for perseverance in financial relationships. However, where financing is done primarily through equity markets (as in the United States and the United Kingdom) there is more flexibility but also more flightiness. Someone else argued, however, that British banks tend to require excessively quick payoffs on any investments made.

The impediments to financial intermediation posed by excessively stringent disclosure requirements within the United States were noted. It was pointed out that the only major capital market imperfection mentioned consistently by European industrialists is the shortage of venture capital.

The discussion also addressed several aspects of Aliber's methodology. Some reservations were voiced about his use of direct foreign investment data to draw conclusions about capital costs. An alternative explanation, noted by one participant, for the recent increase in direct foreign investment in the United States was the anticipation of new trade barriers. Another stressed that direct investments incorporate transfers of managerial and technical know-how to exploit niches in particular markets. European (and Japanese) companies with industry-specific innovations have managed to exploit profit possibilities in a number of areas within the U.S. economy. In effect, Euroinvestments, far from being a symptom of Eurosclerosis and U.S. technological superiority, have been a way of transferring European institutional, organizational, and technological achievements into the United States.

Aliber's treatment of the cost of capital was also questioned. According to the Modigliani-Miller investment theory, if stock exchanges are sufficiently related there should be no such thing as firm-specific or even country-specific financing. Given that, at least for major corporations, the arbitrage between different stock exchanges would appear to be perfect, the argument that firm-specific financial opportunities caused the influx of European direct investment into the United States seems misguided. Financing considerations, it was argued, are relatively unimportant in explaining a decision on whether to invest in the United States or in Europe. While the differential between interest rates reflects a forward premium or discount, this differential must be weighed against the exchange rate wedge reflecting expectations of future risks in the future exchange rate.

Another commentator questioned Aliber's estimates of what would have happened to employment and industrial production had countries run a constant trade balance in the early 1980s. He pointed out that monetary policy in the United States would most certainly have been much tighter had there been a constant trade balance and that the gains in employment suggested by Aliber would have been much lower.

Finally, it was suggested that taxes might play a crucial part in explaining Euroinvestment. While the effect of tax policy on aggregate investment may be ambiguous, its impact on smart people taking advantage of arbitrage opportunities is not. European tax codes have changed greatly since the 1970s, so a systematic examination of the various treatments of capital earned abroad versus capital earned at home and so forth might very well be in order.

Macroeconomic Constraints

PAUL N. COURANT

Fiscal Policy and European Economic Growth

FISCAL POLICY is nothing more nor less than policy regarding government budgets. Conventionally, a country's fiscal policy is described by the current level and composition of government spending and taxes. More properly, fiscal policy today also includes the government's plans for these variables—and therefore, implicitly, for money creation. Accounting identities ensure that the levels of taxes and spending determine whether the budget will be in deficit and therefore whether the nominal level of public debt will rise. Broadly viewed, the four countries considered in this paper—France, Germany, Sweden, and the United Kingdom—have pursued fiscal policies in the last fifteen years or so that have markedly raised government spending, taxes, deficits, and (except in the United Kingdom) debt as a fraction of gross domestic product. These developments are summarized in table 1.

The reduction in economic growth that has accompanied this rise in the government share in the economy has produced a shift in the terms

Without the kind help of dozens of people, both in the United States and Europe, this attempt to look at European fiscal policy would have been impossible. I am grateful to Deborah Laren for her usual exemplary research assistance and to Judith Jackson for helping put the manuscript together. I have benefited from discussions with Michael Emerson, Edward M. Gramlich, Val Koromzay, Odile Sallard, Michael McKee, Jean-Claude Chouraqui, Robert Bruce Montador, David Coe, Paul Champsaur, David Encaoua, Georges de Menil, Andrew Turnbull, Jurgen Mortenson, Villy Bergstrom, Hans Tson Söderström, Bertil Holmlund, Gunnar Eliasson, Bengt-Christian Ysander, John Oddling-Smee, John Kay, Mervyn A. King, Richard Layard, Andrea Boltho, Jacques Melitz, Gert Haller, Harald W. Rehm, Hans Kohler, Gerald Holtham, Willem H. Buiter, and, especially, Robert Z. Lawrence and Charles L. Schultze. Finally, Helene C. McCarren provided a wealth of information about her native continent and used her excellent command of the three relevant languages that I do not speak (French, British English, and German; the Swedes all speak American English) to help me arrange and decode my work on this project.

Table 1. *Government Expenditure, Revenue, and Saving, Four European Countries, Selected Years, 1971–84*

Percent of GDP

Account	1971	1975	1979	1981	1982	1983	1984
				France			
Expenditure							
Final consumption	13.4	14.4	14.9	15.8	16.2	16.4	16.4
Net capital accumulation[a]	3.2	3.3	2.1	2.1	2.3	2.1	1.8
Net interest	0.4	0.6	0.9	1.4	1.3	1.8	2.0
Current transfers to business	1.6	2.0	2.0	2.2	2.2	2.1	2.4
Social security	13.1	16.1	18.2	20.1	21.1	21.4	21.6
Current transfers to individuals excluding social security	4.0	4.4	4.5	4.5	4.6	4.6	4.7
Other current transfers	1.2	1.1	1.1	1.2	1.3	1.5	1.6
Total	36.9	41.9	43.8	47.2	49.0	49.9	50.4
Revenue							
Direct taxes	6.7	7.2	7.9	8.8	9.0	9.1	9.3
Indirect taxes	14.9	14.0	14.6	14.6	14.7	14.7	15.1
Social security contributions	13.1	15.3	17.5	18.3	18.9	19.6	19.7
Other receipts	3.0	3.1	3.1	3.7	3.6	3.5	3.5
Total	37.7	39.7	43.1	45.4	46.3	46.8	47.6
Saving[b]							
Revenues less expenditures	0.7	−2.2	−0.7	−1.8	−2.7	−3.1	−2.8
Government saving	3.9	1.1	1.4	0.3	−0.4	−1.0	−1.0
Primary surplus	1.2	−1.6	0.3	−0.4	−1.4	−1.3	−0.8
				Germany			
Expenditure							
Final consumption	16.9	20.5	19.6	20.6	20.3	20.0	20.1
Net capital accumulation[a]	5.7	5.0	4.8	4.3	3.9	3.5	3.3
Net interest	−0.3	0.4	0.6	0.9	0.9	1.2	1.2
Current transfers to business	1.7	2.0	2.2	1.9	1.8	1.8	2.1
Social security	8.9	12.2	11.7	12.2	12.7	12.4	12.1

Current transfers to individuals							
excluding social security	3.9	5.4	4.8	5.0	4.9	4.8	4.5
Other current transfers	1.5	2.0	2.3	2.4	2.4	2.4	2.5
Total	38.4	47.5	46.0	47.3	46.9	46.2	45.8
Revenue							
Direct taxes	11.3	12.1	12.6	12.2	12.1	12.0	12.2
Indirect taxes	13.1	12.7	13.1	12.8	12.6	12.8	13.0
Social security contributions	12.1	14.9	15.2	16.1	16.5	16.1	16.3
Other receipts	1.7	2.1	2.3	2.3	2.3	2.5	2.5
Total	38.3	41.8	43.3	43.4	43.5	43.5	43.9
Saving[b]							
Revenues less expenditures	-0.2	-5.7	-2.7	-3.9	-3.4	-2.7	-1.9
Government saving	5.6	-0.7	2.0	0.5	0.4	0.8	1.4
Primary surplus	-0.4	-5.3	-2.1	-2.9	-2.6	-1.5	-0.7
				Sweden			
Expenditure							
Final consumption	22.5	23.8	28.3	29.2	29.1	28.5	27.7
Net capital accumulation[a]	4.9	3.0	4.4	3.6	3.8	3.6	2.5
Net interest	-0.8	-1.1	-1.1	0.3	1.6	1.9	2.4
Current transfers to business	1.8	3.1	4.3	4.7	5.0	5.2	5.0
Social security	8.0	10.5	13.6	14.8	14.8	14.8	14.3
Current transfers to individuals							
excluding social security	4.0	3.7	3.9	3.6	3.8	3.7	3.5
Other current transfers	0.9	1.5	1.8	1.9	1.8	1.8	1.7
Total	41.3	44.4	55.2	58.1	59.8	59.5	57.0
Revenue							
Direct taxes	20.1	21.3	22.6	21.3	21.7	21.8	21.5
Indirect taxes	14.8	13.8	13.4	14.6	14.6	15.6	16.2
Social security contributions	8.2	8.6	13.5	15.0	13.8	13.6	13.2
Other receipts	3.4	3.5	2.7	2.3	3.3	3.7	3.8
Total	46.5	47.2	52.2	53.2	53.5	54.6	54.7

Table 1 (continued)

Account	1971	1975	1979	1981	1982	1983	1984
			United Kingdom				
Saving[b]							
Revenues less expenditures	5.2	2.8	-2.9	-4.9	-6.3	-4.9	-2.3
Government saving	10.1	5.8	1.4	-1.3	-2.5	-1.3	0.2
Primary surplus	4.4	1.6	-4.1	-4.6	-4.8	-3.0	0.1
Expenditure							
Final consumption	17.8	21.8	19.8	21.9	21.8	22.0	21.9
Net capital accumulation[a]	4.3	4.5	2.1	2.5	1.6	1.7	1.8
Net interest	1.9	2.1	2.9	3.6	3.4	3.3	3.4
Current transfers to business	1.6	3.5	2.3	2.3	2.0	2.0	2.5
Social security	5.1	6.1	6.1	6.8	6.8	6.7	6.8
Current transfers to individuals excluding social security	3.3	3.9	5.1	6.1	7.0	7.0	7.2
Other current transfers	1.0	1.0	1.6	1.3	1.3	1.4	1.4
Total	35.0	42.8	39.9	44.5	43.9	44.2	45.0
Revenue							
Direct taxes	14.8	16.6	13.4	14.8	15.3	15.1	15.4
Indirect taxes	14.7	12.9	14.9	16.3	16.6	16.2	16.1
Social security contributions	4.9	6.5	5.9	6.3	6.6	6.9	7.1
Other receipts	2.1	2.0	2.3	2.7	2.7	2.6	2.6
Total	36.4	38.0	36.6	40.0	41.2	40.7	41.2
Saving[b]							
Revenues less expenditures	1.4	-4.8	-3.3	-4.5	-2.7	-3.5	-3.9
Government saving	5.7	-0.3	-1.2	-2.0	-1.1	-1.8	-2.1
Primary surplus	3.3	-2.7	-0.4	-0.9	0.6	-0.2	-0.4

Sources: Organization for Economic Cooperation and Development, *National Accounts, 1971–83*, vol. 2: *Detailed Tables* (Paris: OECD, 1985), tables 1, 6; and OECD, *National Accounts, 1972–84*, vol. 2: *Detailed Tables* (Paris: OECD, 1986), tables 1, 6.
a. Includes net capital transfers.
b. Government saving is defined as revenues less expenditures plus net public capital formation. Primary surplus is defined as revenues less expenditures plus net interest.

of debate on fiscal policy. For half a century that debate had centered on the possibilities for achieving short-term stabilization through the proper setting of the fiscal policy variables. The recent years of persistent deficits and sluggish growth have focused the fiscal policy debate instead on the long-term effect of these variables on the structure of the economy. For example, it is striking that current stated goals for medium-term fiscal policy in all four of the countries are principally framed in terms of desired paths for deficits and debt (and monetary growth) rather than for real economic activity. Thus discussion of fiscal policy in Britain's medium-term financial strategy focuses on the public-sector borrowing requirement, which is taken (with little economic justification) as a measure of government crowding out of private financial capital.[1] Similarly, the thrust of a recent publication by the German Finance Ministry is accurately summarized in its title, *Tasks and Objectives of a New Fiscal Policy: The Limits to Public Indebtedness.* The Swedish budget stresses concerns with crowding out and argues that "it will not be sufficient to restore public sector financial equilibrium" in light of the needs for investment and a surplus on current account.[2] In France, the government's plan is to eliminate the primary deficit (the deficit excluding interest payments) over the next few years. Moreover, the policies themselves have largely followed the change in the terms of the discussion—sound finance has replaced functional finance in both rhetoric and practice.

Although most economists and policymakers agree that spending, taxes, deficits, and debt have effects on both the growth of potential output and the extent to which potential is realized, they do not agree on the nature of these effects nor on the relationships among them (save for the accounting identities that link them). I cannot settle these questions, but I propose to sort them out through an analytical discussion of the recent history and current prospects for fiscal policy in Germany, France, the United Kingdom, and Sweden. This introduction begins the sorting by describing the major channels through which fiscal policy might affect growth, thereby previewing the rest of the paper.

Whatever its longer run consequences, it is clear that fiscal policy, in conjunction with monetary policy, can have direct effects on short-run

1. Chancellor of the Exchequer, *Financial Statement and Budget Report, 1986–87* (London: Her Majesty's Stationery Office, 1986).
2. Swedish Ministry of Finance, *The Swedish Budget, 1986–87* (Stockholm, 1986), p. 33.

aggregate demand. The first section of this paper examines short-run policy as well as the constraints that concern over long-run effects may impose. Broadly, it is in the area of short-run effects that the record of the European economies is clearest—since the early 1980s all of the governments have tightened their budgets to a greater or lesser degree and all have seen unemployment rise and inflation fall. Moreover, discussions with officials and academic observers in all of the countries make it clear that both the budget tightening and its consequences have largely been intended. Inflation was the most important economic problem in 1980, and traditional Keynesian restraint has been part of the (generally successful) solution. The short-term trade-off between inflation and unemployment appears to be alive and well in Europe, and governments have allowed their economies to operate below their potential in return for downward pressure on inflation. Given that my assessment is roughly correct, that inflation is now generally quite low (except in Sweden), and that by almost any measure there is slack in at least two, and probably three, of the economies, the question is whether some combination of fiscal and monetary stimulus would be warranted.[3] The answer to this question, at least in the published statements of government officials, is "no." The most commonly given reason for this answer is that the longer term costs of deficits and debt outweigh any benefits that might be realized from economic stimulus and indeed may be so powerful as to prevent "Keynesian" reflationary policies from providing any stimulus at all.[4]

Several quite different phenomena are lumped together under the rubric of "longer term costs of deficits and debt." The clearest of these is "crowding out"—the depressing effect of public dissaving on long-term economic growth and wealth accumulation. In a closed economy at a given level of real GNP, national investment moves with national saving. Unless the "Ricardian equivalence theorem" holds, smaller deficits lead to more extensive capital accumulation and economic growth.[5] In an open economy, government saving is balanced either by domestic investment or by investment made abroad, but in any event it

3. Whether slack exists in Sweden depends upon how one measures it. And in the United Kingdom the existence of slack in the labor market depends importantly upon whether the hypothesis of hysteresis can explain recent wage behavior.

4. Another reason is that external constraints effectively prohibit unilateral policy. See Richard Cooper's paper in this volume for an assessment.

5. Robert Barro, "Are Government Bonds Net Wealth?" *Journal of Political Economy*, vol. 82 (November 1974), pp. 1095–1117.

increases the accumulation of wealth by nationals of the home economy. In either the closed or open economy, the logic of the saving-investment balance implies that if national wealth accumulation is a goal, then governments should engage in public saving.

This section of the paper also examines the growth-limiting effects of accumulated debt; although less easy to evaluate than those of deficits, these effects have been the subject of much attention lately.

The second and third sections of the paper discuss traditional issues of taxes and spending. The tax system and the content of public spending are the remaining major channels through which fiscal policy can influence economic growth. On the tax side, the subject of the third section, the route is clear: all major sources of government revenue distort private-sector decisions and reduce economic efficiency.[6] The excess burden of taxation belongs in any benefit-cost analysis of government spending; in general, the marginal excess burden is higher than the average excess burden, increasing roughly with the square of the wedge between price and marginal cost. Thus, reducing the overall level of taxation yields large marginal gains, and raising the level imposes large marginal costs. This argument, though a vague one, is the heart of the supply-side case for reducing taxation in general and, given the concern with deficits, for reducing the size of government spending. Between the 1970s and the early 1980s, marginal tax rates rose in the four economies, and the resulting tax wedges may indeed have affected the growth of economic welfare. However, income effects and substitution effects work in opposite directions for labor supply (and possibly for the supply of private savings), so the effect of the tax wedges on measured growth is likely to have been small and may have been positive.

A more precise and persuasive supply-side attack on tax distortions is made in King and Fullerton's work on capital taxation.[7] As documented there, the structure of capital taxation in many economies is such that the pretax rates of return (marginal products of capital) net of depreciation required to make a project profitable bear little relationship to after-tax rates of return. Many activities are, on balance, subsidized by the

6. What appears to be an interesting exception is the current proposal in the United Kingdom to institute a head tax to finance local government. This is discussed in detail later in the paper, and it remains to be seen whether the proposal is practical

7. Mervyn A. King and Don Fullerton, eds., *The Taxation of Income from Capital: A Comparative Study of the United States, the United Kingdom, Sweden, and West Germany* (University of Chicago Press, 1984).

tax system, while others are taxed quite heavily. With nonzero elasticities of substitution among different types of capital, such tax structures lower efficiency, and some of that cost is paid through lower economic growth.

The final major way in which fiscal policy can affect economic growth is through the content of public spending programs themselves. With tax-transfer programs discussed in another paper, I will focus here on government consumption and investment. All of the governments under study have targeted investment for a disproportionate amount of their recent spending reductions, which may affect long-term growth, and all have increased their shares of transfers and government consumption in GDP over the last fifteen years, suggesting that there may have been a reduction in (presumably more efficient) private-sector activity. Note, however, that much of the change predates, or is coincident with, the change in the growth of potential GDP, making it implausible that the cause of reduced growth in the past is primarily fiscal.[8]

The considerations previewed here fit together from a strategic policy point of view. Assume that fiscal and monetary policies can be coordinated for purposes of short-term stabilization among the major nations of Europe and that some slack exists in all of these economies except, perhaps, that of Sweden. If, at the same time, accumulating debt lowers potential growth through such channels as crowding out, then stabilization policy is to some extent constrained. The constraint can be relaxed, in principle, by changing the mix of fiscal and monetary policies—by moving toward budgets that are tighter over the business cycle in conjunction with monetary policy that is somewhat looser. Regardless of whether such a change is feasible, either separately or through coordination, the shift requires some combination of increased taxes and reduced government spending.[9] The ratio of government spending to GDP in the four economies under study here ranged from 0.450 to 0.570 in 1984, and the ratio of revenue to GDP ranged from 0.412 to 0.547. These amounts are substantial and suggest that any improvement in the efficiency of taxation and any possibilities for reducing the overall amount of expenditure to be financed are well worth examining: they may be efficiency enhancing in their own right and may facilitate the change in the policy mix. The result would be to give traditional

8. This does not mean, or course, that undoing these changes would not have salutary effects in the future.

9. See the paper by Richard Cooper in this volume.

stabilization policy some room for maneuver in the future; and the future, given the current amount of slack, may be now.

Fiscal Policy and Stabilization Problems

Most European economists and policymakers agree that the current stance of fiscal policy (and of aggregate-demand policy generally) is quite restrictive and that the European economies are operating below capacity. At the same time, few of them advocate fiscal stimulus (except for those outside of Germany who prescribe it for that country). The reasons most often given for rejecting stimulus are that (1) the continued accumulation of national debt is dangerous, (2) fiscal stimulus will crowd out investment and thus reduce long-term growth, and (3) it is simply ineffective. This section examines the proposition that recent fiscal policy in the four countries has been restrictive in the presence of unused productive capacity. Showing the proposition to be true, the section evaluates the various justifications for abjuring the traditional Keynesian prescription.

Measuring Fiscal Stance

To measure fiscal stance, I use the series on structural budget deficits, both adjusted and unadjusted for inflation, published by the Organization for Economic Cooperation and Development (OECD). The use of this imperfect measure requires some explanation.

The original argument favoring the "structural" (née full-employment) surplus as an indicator of the expansionary or contractionary stance of fiscal policy is that the effect of the level of economic activity on actual deficits does not influence it. Buiter (following Gramlich and Blinder and Solow) argues that structural surpluses should not be used in this way.[10] He notes that "there is no existing model of the economy that yields [any measure of government] deficit, the change in this deficit, its share in GDP or the change in its share in GDP as a measure of fiscal

10. Willem H. Buiter, "A Guide to Public Sector Debt and Deficits," *Economic Policy*, no. 1 (November 1985), pp. 14–79; Edward M. Gramlich, "Measures of the Aggregate Demand Impact of the Federal Budget," in Wilfred Lewis, Jr., ed., *Budget Concepts for Economic Analysis* (Brookings, 1968), pp. 110–44; and Alan S. Blinder and Robert M. Solow, "Analytical Foundations of Fiscal Policy," in Blinder and others, *The Economics of Public Finance* (Brookings, 1974), pp. 3–118.

impact on aggregate demand in any run."[11] This criticism of the various measures of fiscal stimulus is well founded; although one could write a model that would make Buiter's statement false, the model just would not be very good. However, Buiter draws a corollary from his conclusion: "shorthand" measures of fiscal impact should not be used at all, and fiscal impact can be assessed only in the context of explicit models that take intelligent account of expectations and the processing of information by private agents. The corollary does not follow.

As noted, high-employment or structural deficits highlight the effects of policy on deficits by excluding the effects of the level of economic activity. The exclusion is accomplished by selecting a reference level of economic activity such as full employment or "mid-cycle" employment and, given existing tax and spending rules, calculating the deficit at that reference level of activity. For most countries, the OECD calculates the reference level for GDP and employment by extrapolating potential GDP from a base year. If the extrapolated series is "too optimistic," structural deficits will be too low and the associated gaps between actual and potential GDP will be too high. If the extrapolation is "too pessimistic," the reverse will obtain. Given the manifest uncertainties about the behavior of potential GDP and economic capacity since 1973, the estimated GDP gaps and associated structural deficits cannot be taken as definitive. However, once an arbitrary path for potential is given, changes in the estimated structural deficit for a given country should be a reasonably good measure of changes in fiscal stance.

However, a good measure of change in fiscal stance is not necessarily a good measure of change in economic stimulus, in part because the various elements of the change (taxes, transfers, different types of government consumption and investment, interest) may all have different effects on aggregate demand. Yet, unless there are large year-to-year changes in the composition of taxes and spending, year-to-year changes in sensibly constructed measures of the structural deficit should at least show the direction of change in fiscal impact; the same logic applies to comparing the levels, for a given country, for any one consistently constructed series.[12] The problems of inflation adjustment and interest payments remain to be addressed.

11. Buiter, "Guide to Public Sector Debt," p. 54.
12. The structural deficit series used by Layard and others tells approximately the same story as does the OECD series. Richard Layard and others, "Europe: The Case for Unsustainable Growth," in Olivier Blanchard, Rudiger Dornbusch, and Richard

Two methods of adjusting structural deficits for inflation appear in the literature. In one, erosion of the value of outstanding debt is subtracted from the deficit. Thus if the inflation rate is p, and D is the value of outstanding debt, pD is treated as government revenue in calculating an "inflation-adjusted" budget. If the concern is to have the deficit measure be consistent with changes in the value of real debt, this procedure is always warranted.[13] A second procedure is to hypothesize a long-term real interest rate and to define the structural deficit as the structural primary deficit (government spending net of interest payments less revenues) plus hypothetical "real" interest payments on the debt.[14] The two methods are equivalent if real interest rates are constant, which is to say that they are not equivalent.

Assume that only real interest payments matter and that the multiplier on real interest payments is roughly the same as that for net taxes; then an inflation adjustment made directly to interest payments rather than to the existing volume of debt would yield an indicator no worse than the conventional structural deficit in a regime without inflation. Alternatively, if private consumption functions are based on Haig-Simons income, the inflation adjustment to existing net debt is preferred.[15] Finally, if nominal interest payments act like other sources of nominal income in consumption functions, no adjustment should be made when the structural deficit is used as a measure of fiscal stimulus.[16] In short, for assessing the effect of fiscal policy on demand, choosing the concept of structural deficit that works best is an empirical question, a fact that highlights Buiter's objection to any such concept that does not derive from an explicit model of the economy.

Both Eisner and Pieper and Muller and Price find that inflation-adjusted structural deficits are better indexes of fiscal stimulus (or, more

---

Layard, eds., *Restoring Europe's Prosperity: Macroeconomic Papers from the Centre for European Policy Studies* (MIT Press, 1986), pp. 33–94.

13. See Patrice Muller and Robert W. R. Price, "Structural Budget Deficits and Fiscal Stance," Working Paper 15 (OECD, Department of Economics and Statistics, July 1984), for a detailed discussion of inflation adjustments.

14. For an example of this procedure, see Layard and others, "Europe: The Case for Unsustainable Growth," pp. 54–55.

15. Strictly speaking, the adjustment should be made only to domestically held debt.

16. If, most plausibly, capital gains and losses on debt behave like other changes in wealth, then the inflation adjustment should be disaggregated from the rest of the structural deficit, because the marginal propensity to consume out of wealth is different from that out of income. But to make this adjustment would be modeling, in however rudimentary a way, and thus violating the "rules" of the structural surplus game.

properly, better predictors of short-run movements in real national income) than are unadjusted deficits.[17] The "models" used are quite different. Eisner and Pieper look at the effect of the level of various structural deficit measures on the change in gross national product (getting some very implausible steady-state results, which the authors explain should not be taken seriously). Muller and Price run changes in GNP and GDP against changes in the measures of deficit.[18]

Despite the conceptual difficulties, the evidence indicates that, for a number of economies, changes in the structural deficit consistently predict changes in measures of the level of economic activity, with the inflation-adjusted versions of the deficit doing better than the unadjusted versions (somewhat to my surprise, I confess, given the implication that changes in unrealized capital gains have nontrivial short-term multipliers). With this weakly comforting information in hand, I turn to a description and evaluation of the effects of recent fiscal policy on short-term economic activity.[19]

Recent Trends in Fiscal Policy

Following the logic of the preceding discussion and tempered with some skepticism about the relevance of inflation adjustment to a measure of fiscal stimulus, I use the OECD series for structural general-government deficits for each of the four economies from 1970 to 1986 to compare fiscal stimulus at different times for each country (table 2). (Using the

17. Robert Eisner and Paul J. Pieper, "A New View of the Federal Debt and Budget Deficits," *American Economic Review,* vol. 74 (March 1984), pp. 11–29; Muller and Price, "Structural Budget Deficits." Eisner and Pieper use a rather different procedure for making inflation adjustments, one in which they use a good series on net debt for the United States. Thus, their adjusted deficit is constructed so that the deficit in each year is the change in market value of net national debt. To get their structural deficit, they apply the same adjustments at the hypothetical full-employment level (5.1 percent unemployment), making use of the series on full-employment deficits from the Bureau of Economic Analysis. The OECD series used by Muller and Price is calculated at potential GDP, and the inflation adjustment is made on gross, rather than on net, public debt.

18. Their result is confirmed by simple regressions of the Muller and Price type using the OECD series on changes in structural surpluses for each of the four countries. The inflation-adjusted series perform somewhat better. Both series consistently have the right sign.

19. To put it another way, I am not enthusiastic about using structural deficits as measures of stimulus, for exactly the reasons that Buiter advances, but I find the OECD series to be usable for this purpose and to be the best available.

series to compare countries without deriving them from models of the individual countries would be pushing things a bit too far.) Both OECD series tell pretty much the same story, and that story is consistent with more detailed studies of countries for which such are available. The story is also consistent with the characterization by Layard and others of fiscal policy in Europe generally, data from which are shown in table 3.[20]

GERMANY. Under any definition of the structural deficit, Germany moved sharply into deficit after the first oil shock and moved sharply toward surplus after 1981. The "locomotive" exercise that followed the Bonn summit of 1978 appears in the data as a relatively small increase in the structural deficit in 1979 which stays roughly constant through 1981. After 1981 fiscal policy tightened in two big jumps (1981–82 and 1982–83) and has tightened gradually through 1985; it was expected to loosen slightly in 1986 (because of the scheduled tax reform that offsets recent fiscal drag) and to tighten again slightly in 1987. The tightening of fiscal policy in 1981–83 was a conscious effort on the part of the German government to reduce inflation and stem the increase in national debt. In this it has been successful, but (in conjunction with other demand-management policies) at the cost of raising the unemployment rate.

Budgetary "consolidation" in Germany has been achieved largely through reductions in spending (almost 3 percent of GNP between 1982 and 1985) rather than through changes in revenues, which have been roughly constant as a share of GNP throughout the recent period.[21] In 1986 the trend toward smaller deficits essentially will be halted by a tax reduction of 11 billion deutsche marks (DM), but it is forecast to resume in 1987 if the growth in public spending can be held, as planned, to 3 percent per year in nominal terms.[22] Neither the Deutsche Bundesbank nor the OECD expects the 3 percent target to be met, in large part

20. For a discussion of demand management policy from World War II to 1980, see John Bipsham and Andrea Boltho, "Demand Management," in Boltho, ed, *The European Economy: Growth and Crisis* (Oxford University Press, 1982), pp. 289–328. Writing in 1982, the authors were highly skeptical of the ability of macroeconomic policy to reduce inflation. The story they tell up to 1980 provides useful background to the discussion here and also to the discussion in the two reports of the CEPS macroeconomic policy group. Layard and others, "Europe: The Case for Unsustainable Growth"; and Oliver Blanchard and others, "Employment and Growth in Europe: A Two-Handed Approach," in Blanchard and others, eds., *Restoring Europe's Prosperity*, pp. 1–32.

21. *Report of the Deutsche Bundesbank for the Year 1985.*

22. Ibid., p. 21.

Table 2. *Measures of Fiscal Stimulus, Four European Countries, 1970–86*

Percent of GDP

Year	Conventional surplus or deficit (−)	OECD structural surplus or deficit (−)	OECD inflation-adjusted structural surplus or deficit (−)
		France	
1970	0.92	1.27	1.83
1971	0.74	1.04	1.60
1972	0.79	0.79	1.31
1973	0.95	0.75	1.28
1974	0.63	1.07	2.08
1975	− 2.23	− 0.02	0.98
1976	− 0.48	0.62	1.60
1977	− 0.83	0.17	1.05
1978	− 1.87	− 1.32	− 0.49
1979	− 0.68	− 0.39	0.57
1980	0.21	1.18	2.30
1981	− 1.79	− 0.02	1.05
1982	− 2.73	− 0.44	0.59
1983	− 3.07	− 0.49	0.52
1984	− 2.91	0.27	1.15
1985	− 2.58	1.02	1.78
1986	− 2.60	0.60	1.02
		Germany	
1970	0.20	0.00	− 0.31
1971	− 0.16	0.04	− 0.38
1972	− 0.53	− 0.38	− 0.75
1973	1.20	1.13	0.73
1974	− 1.30	− 0.55	− 0.94
1975	− 5.69	− 3.56	− 3.67
1976	− 3.43	− 2.54	− 2.43
1977	− 2.43	− 1.69	− 1.49
1978	− 2.43	− 1.99	− 1.77
1979	− 2.55	− 2.52	− 2.11
1980	− 2.89	− 2.39	− 1.70
1981	− 3.67	− 2.27	− 1.47
1982	− 3.29	− 0.77	− 0.08
1983	− 2.53	0.34	0.85
1984	− 1.92	0.32	0.76
1985	− 1.10	0.90	1.27
1986	− 0.83	0.73	0.73

Table 2 *(continued)*
Percent of GDP

Year	Conventional surplus or deficit (−)	OECD structural surplus or deficit (−)	OECD inflation-adjusted structural surplus or deficit (−)
Sweden			
1970	4.40	4.40	. . .
1971	5.18	5.81	3.89
1972	4.39	5.02	3.24
1973	4.07	3.86	1.61
1974	1.95	1.21	− 1.88
1975	2.74	1.79	− 1.31
1976	4.51	4.20	1.04
1977	1.66	3.71	0.55
1978	− 0.48	1.96	− 1.29
1979	− 2.95	− 1.54	− 3.52
1980	− 3.74	− 2.21	− 4.73
1981	− 4.91	− 1.92	− 3.91
1982	− 6.35	− 2.53	− 3.82
1983	− 4.98	− 1.49	− 2.38
1984	− 2.31	0.12	− 0.34
1985	− 2.30	− 0.09	− 0.38
1986	− 1.19	0.92	0.79
United Kingdom			
1970	2.45	2.45	6.10
1971	1.37	1.87	6.82
1972	− 1.83	− 1.45	2.07
1973	− 3.39	− 4.29	− 0.15
1974	− 3.77	− 3.56	3.98
1975	− 4.73	− 2.75	7.20
1976	− 4.91	− 2.67	4.38
1977	− 3.38	− 1.37	5.32
1978	− 4.23	− 3.08	1.03
1979	− 3.49	− 2.96	2.74
1980	− 3.52	− 1.97	4.39
1981	− 2.85	0.89	5.27
1982	− 2.34	2.42	5.62
1983	− 3.72	1.14	3.15
1984	− 3.89	0.66	2.48
1985	− 3.10	1.19	3.34
1986	− 3.24	0.82	2.40

Source: Data provided by the OECD.

Table 3. *Measures of Fiscal Stance for the European Community,*
1973–84

Percent of GDP except as noted

Year	Deficit (−) or surplus corrected for inflation and cycle		Index of fiscal stance (percent of trend GDP)c
	Measure 1a	Measure 2b	
1973	− 0.1	− 0.7	n.a.
1974	− 0.0	− 1.2	n.a.
1975	− 2.4	− 2.7	n.a.
1976	− 3.0	− 2.3	n.a.
1977	− 1.8	− 1.8	2.8
1978	− 3.3	− 2.7	3.9
1979	− 2.5	− 2.8	4.0
1980	− 1.5	− 1.9	4.0
1981	− 1.9	− 2.1	4.6
1982	− 1.4	− 0.8	3.3
1983	− 0.9	0.1	2.4
1984	− 0.4	1.5	1.5

Sources: Richard Layard and others, "Europe: The Case for Unsustainable Growth," in Olivier Blanchard, Rudiger Dornbusch, and Richard Layard, eds., *Restoring Europe's Prosperity: Macroeconomic Papers from the Centre for European Policy Studies* (MIT Press, 1986), tables 4, 6, and app. 3.
n.a. Not available.
a. Inflation correction is on net debt method.
b. Inflation correction is on real interest method.
c. The lower the index, the lower the stimulus.

because local governments will exceed it.[23] However, with revenues growing at about 4 percent per year,[24] the actual deficit will continue to fall. Consistent with the policy of fiscal consolidation, further tax reform is to some extent a hostage to slower expenditure growth—that is, although the government would like to reduce tax rates for supply-side reasons, it will not do so if this jeopardizes reductions in the deficit.[25] To some extent, and somewhat ironically, the requirement that tax reform be consistent with continued reduction in deficits may mean that a low rate of inflation in Germany (which, at zero, is lower than recently forecast) may slow tax reform. Germany has an unindexed and sharply progressive personal income tax system, and real receipts rise with

23. *OECD Economic Outlook,* no. 39 (May 1986), p. 97.
24. Ibid., p. 98.
25. *Report of the Deutsche Bundesbank,* p. 21; and German Ministry of Finance, *Tasks and Objectives of a New Fiscal Policy: The Limits to Public Indebtedness* (Bonn, 1985), p. 38.

inflation. Meanwhile, the nonautomatic spending components of budgets are planned in nominal terms. Thus unanticipated reductions in inflation (surely desirable in and of themselves) may cause deficits to be higher than planned. This possibility, although not found in the literature, was much on the minds of various commentators with whom I spoke in Europe.

Finally, it is worth noting here that implicit in current German fiscal policy is a model in which budgetary consolidation (that is, reduction of deficits) is, at least in the medium to long run, expansionary. This point is made prominently in the report of the Bundesbank and in the Finance Ministry's recently issued pamphlet on fiscal policy.[26] The essence of the argument is that budget consolidation increases business confidence in the prospects for long-term economic growth and therefore tends to raise investment. Thus Germany will continue to reject conventional reflationary fiscal policy as long as its policymakers believe that it will lead to more than 100 percent crowding out.

FRANCE. The story in France is somewhat different from Germany's. Fiscal policy responded less in France than in other countries to the first oil shock, although it clearly moved toward deficit after 1974. Fiscal policy moved sharply toward deficit in 1978; it jumped toward surplus in 1980 and then back again toward deficit in 1981 and 1982, the period of President Mitterrand's experiment with unilateral demand simulus. Although policy had tightened sharply in 1980, the Mitterrand deficits were smaller in magnitude than those of 1978–79. The government has run structural surpluses since 1984, although the surpluses for 1986 and 1987 were forecast to be somewhat lower than those for the years immediately preceding. The tightening of fiscal policy after 1982 was accomplished largely through increases in revenue rather than reductions in expenditure.

The expansionary policy of 1981 and 1982 is widely considered to have failed and, indeed, to have proved that unilateral reflationary action is not feasible for European economies. Yet, from the perspective of 1986, one can see that France had no recession in the early 1980s and that the increase in unemployment rates there from 1980 to 1985 was less than it was in the United Kingdom or in Germany.[27] To be sure, the

---

26. *Report of the Deutsche Bundesbank*, p. 20; and German Finance Ministry, *Tasks and Objectives of a New Fiscal Policy*.

27. See Jeffrey Sachs and Charles Wyplosz, "The Economic Consequences of

reduction in France's inflation has also been somewhat less. The French economy grew when others were declining (1981 and 1982), and then it grew more slowly than the others. But thus informed, it is hard to argue that the 1981–82 expansion has proved to be disastrous. Rather, the detailed timing of slow growth in France has been somewhat different from that of her neighbors.

THE UNITED KINGDOM. Changes in the inflation-adjusted and unadjusted measures in the United Kingdom have the lowest correlation (for levels or changes) of any of the four countries, a direct consequence of the fact that inflation has been more volatile in the United Kingdom than it has in the other countries. Under either measure, fiscal policy tightened following the first oil shock, then moved toward structural deficit in 1978.[28] The Thatcher government tightened budgets in 1980 and 1981; since then it has gradually loosened them, although fiscal and monetary policies remain much tighter than they were before 1981. Moreover, like France and unlike Sweden and Germany, Britain achieved most of the reduction in deficits through increased revenues, not lower spending.

Since 1980 the government in the United Kingdom has been more diligent than those in other countries in demonstrating to the private sector that it is unwilling to accommodate inflationary pressures. One element of this effort has been use of the public-sector borrowing requirement (PSBR) as a measure of fiscal stance. In each year since 1980, the government has published medium-term targets for the PSBR and has taken these seriously in planning budgets.

Broadly considered, the PSBR is merely the national accounts deficit less net sales of government assets. Because the government has been selling considerable quantitites of such assets in recent years as part of its "privatization" program, the PSBR consistently shows lower deficits than the national accounts do. The difference has permitted fiscal policy in the last few years to be somewhat less restrictive than would have been the case without the privatization program, given that the PSBR targets have not been adjusted to take account of privatization (which they have not).[29] However, there appears to be at least some slack in the

President Mitterrand," *Economic Policy,* no. 2 (April 1986), pp. 262–322, for an extended discussion.

28. David Begg, "U.K. Fiscal Policy since 1970," unpublished paper, May 1986, notes that the tightening was probably unintentional, but, in light of the supply consequences of the oil shock, not bad policy.

29. The amounts of money in question are nontrivial, amounting to more than £2

U.K. economy; given Layard and Nickell's evaluation that half or more of the increase in unemployment since 1979 is due to deficient demand, the downward bias of the PSBR as an indicator of the deficit may be a sheep in wolf's clothing.[30]

SWEDEN. Sweden has made much of her "third way" in macroeconomic policy. Under the third way, demand has been stimulated by a 16 percent devaluation in 1982 (following a 10 percent devaluation in 1981), while fiscal policy has been deliberately tightened to increase national saving.[31] The rest of the third way involves supply-side measures, including tax reduction, which are discussed later in this paper. The fiscal consequences of this strategy are plainly visible in the data, which show sharp increases in structural surpluses (reductions in deficits) in 1983 and a continued tightening of budgets thereafter.

The Swedish tightening of fiscal policy has consisted of reductions in the growth of spending (the 1986 share of spending in GDP is more than 3 percentage points lower than that in 1982) with ratios of revenues to GDP essentially unchanged. The stated goal of the government is to continue to reduce expenditures as a share of GDP while allowing the share of revenues to remain roughly constant.[32] The medium-term plan calls for the general government deficit to reach zero by 1990 (the 1986 level was 1.2 percent of GDP). The plausibility of reaching the 1990 target is difficult to assess, but based on the record so far, there is little doubt that the government in Sweden, like that in Germany, is committed to budgetary stringency. In view of the fact that fiscal policy in Sweden is explicitly directed at promoting national saving and that exchange rate policy has been the instrument for expanding the economy, there is little point in discussing fiscal policy under the rubric of stabilization policy. Rather, I will treat the Swedish case in more detail in the discussion of the effect of budget policy on national saving and investment.

GENERAL TRENDS. Although the story of how they got there varies country by country, the stance of fiscal policy in the most recent period shows a striking similarity. All of these economies have moved toward budgetary surplus in recent years, reducing fiscal stimulus (although the

---

billion in 1984–85 (⅔ percent of GDP) and forecast to rise to more than £4 billion (about 1½ percent of GDP) for the next few years.

30. R. Layard and S. Nickell, "The Causes of British Unemployment," *National Institute Economic Review*, no. 111 (February 1985), pp. 62–85.

31. See, for example, Swedish Ministry of Finance, *The Swedish Budget, 1985–86*, pp. 7–8.

32. Ibid., p. 25.

Table 4. *Selected Measures of Economic Slack, Four European Countries, 1980–86*
Percent

Country and year	Unemploy-ment rate[a] (1)	NAIRU Measure 1[b] (2)	NAIRU Measure 2 (3)	Inflation rate (4)	GDP or GNP gap Measure 1[c] (5)	GDP or GNP gap Measure 2[c] (6)
France						
1980	6.3	...	...	13.6	−1.0	...
1981	7.3	⎫	...	13.4	−3.3	...
1982	8.1	⎬ 4.0–8.0	6.9	11.8	−3.5	...
1983	8.3	⎭	...	9.6	−4.0	...
1984	9.7	...	...	7.4	−4.0	...
1985	10.1	...	...	5.8	−4.2	...
1986	10.0	...	...	...	...	−2.41
Germany						
1980	3.0	...	...	5.5	0.3	...
1981	4.4	⎫	...	6.3	−3.0	...
1982	6.1	⎬ 5.0–8.0	5.3	5.3	−6.5	...
1983	8.0	⎭	...	3.3	−7.2	...
1984	8.5	...	...	2.4	−6.0	...
1985	8.6	...	...	2.2	−4.2	...
1986	8.4	...	...	...	...	−0.83
Sweden						
1980	2.0	...	...	13.7	...	...
1981	2.5	...	...	12.1	...	...
1982	3.1	...	...	8.6	...	...
1983	3.5	...	...	8.9	...	...
1984	3.1	...	...	8.0	...	...
1985	2.8	...	...	7.4	...	...
1986	2.8	...	...	...	...	−1.23
United Kingdom						
1980	6.6	...	...	18.0	−4.9	...
1981	9.9	⎫	...	11.9	−7.2	...
1982	11.4	⎬ 6.0–8.0	9.5	8.6	−6.0	...
1983	12.6	⎭	...	4.6	−2.8	...
1984	13.0	...	...	5.0	−1.7	...
1985	13.2	...	...	6.1	1.2	...
1986	13.3	...	...	...	...	−0.73

Sources: Columns 1 and 4, from *OECD Economic Outlook*, no. 39 (May 1986), tables R12, R10; column 2, from David Coe, "Nominal Wages, the NAIRU, and Wage Flexibility," *OECD Economic Studies*, no. 5 (Autumn 1985), table 8; column 3, from Layard and others, "Europe: The Case for Unsustainable Growth," p. 47; column 5, data provided by Charles L. Schultze of Brookings; and column 6, from Jean-Claude Chouraqui, Brian Jones, and Robert Bruce Montador, "Public Debt in a Medium-Term Context and Its Implications for Fiscal Policy," Working Paper 30 (OECD, Department of Economics and Statistics, May 1986).
a. Rates for 1986 are for the first quarter.
b. Coe's range of estimates. See source.
c. Actual GDP less mid-cycle GDP.

inflation-adjusted measures "automatically" show an increase in stimulus as inflation has fallen). Broadly, all four economies are currently running fiscal policies that are quite contractionary relative to those of a few years ago, and they are doing so at a time when inflation is relatively low and unemployment (if one counts the roughly 4 percent of the Swedish labor force that participates in government employment programs of various kinds as unemployed) is high.

Table 4 presents six measures of economic slack for the period 1980 through 1986. With the exception of Schultze's measure of the GDP gap in the United Kingdom for 1985 (column 5), all of the measures tend to support the idea that there is some excess supply in these economies. Moreover, Schultze's finding that the United Kingdom is operating above potential with an unemployment rate of 13 percent is, to say the least, disturbing. This is not the place for an essay on the meaning of potential GDP (nor am I the person to write such an essay), but on the face of it an unemployment rate of 13 percent suggests that there is some potential (ambiguity intended) for increasing output through increasing labor input. Another piece of evidence supporting the notion that there is slack in the European economies comes from a recent survey done by the Commission of the European Communities, which found that the most important reason given by European firms for not increasing employment is inadequate demand.[33]

The Limits of Fiscal Policy: Solvency and National Debt

The ratio of national debt to GDP has been rising in three of the four economies in the recent period (the United Kingdom is the exception), although it is not high in any of them by historical standards, and it is much lower in all of them than in some other European countries, such as Italy. Much of the stated concern with deficits stems from traditional considerations of crowding out, which I discuss below. Some concern also attaches to the accumulation of debt as such, basically for two reasons. The first and, as will be seen for these economies, quite farfetched reason is the possibility that the government might become insolvent. The second and more realistic reason in current circumstances is the possibility that, by accumulating debt, government is committing itself to a future in which it uses a permanently higher share of distorting

33. *European Economy*, Supplement B (April 1986), p. 8.

taxes for debt service; it thereby reduces economic efficiency and increases the real resource cost of government-provided goods, services, and transfers.

Willem Buiter's recent analysis of the possibility that governments might become insolvent starts with the idea of a government balance sheet, and then goes well beyond the standard budget concepts to adopt broad definitions of government assets and liabilities.[34] Government assets include the value of natural resources, the present value of seigniorage, existing government financial assets, the net present value of current and future government-owned capital, and the present value of future tax revenues net of transfers; government liabilities include existing financial debt plus the present value of future government consumption. When the issue of solvency is framed in this way, it becomes apparent that the ultimate constraint on government solvency is national net worth, because governments can, at least in principle, adopt taxing and spending policies that appropriate as much national income and wealth as is desired.[35] In none of these countries is this constraint remotely binding.

It still makes sense, however, to consider the possibility that ratios of debt to GDP are growing at solvency-threatening rates. As the ratio of net government debt to GDP grows, simple arithmetic dictates that the primary surplus (taxes less noninterest spending) necessary to stop it also grows. This in turn implies, for a given level of real government activity, a higher (and hence more distorting) level of taxes than would otherwise be required. In short, even if solvency is not a constraint today, accumulation of debt may indeed lead to real problems tomorrow.

All this can be illustrated by a simple equation. If s^* is defined as the "permanent" (or average long-run) primary surplus divided by GDP, the condition for the ratio of net debt to GDP to be constant is that

$$(1) \qquad\qquad s^* = (i-g)\frac{D}{Y},$$

where i is the real interest rate, g is the growth rate of real GDP, D is net debt, and Y is real GDP. Ignoring seigniorage, any fiscal policy in which the right-hand side of this equation is greater than the left is not sustainable in the sense that at some time in the future primary surpluses

---

34. Buiter, "Guide to Public Sector Debt."
35. Of course, the supply-side consequences of extreme policies along these lines would greatly reduce the amounts available for appropriation.

must rise or debt must be repudiated. In the not-too-distant past, the constraint could be interpreted as nonbinding, because growth rates exceeded interest rates, but those days appear to be over.

Depending on the use to which equation 1 is put, s^* may be defined either as the primary budget surplus or the primary budget surplus net of government expenditures for public capital formation. If one is concerned mainly with potential increases in future tax rates, with their attendant excess burdens and distortions, the measure that includes all government spending is the appropriate one because government spending for capital formation, if financed by debt, must be covered by future revenues.[36] On the other hand, if one believes that government capital formation is efficient, in the sense of yielding benefits that cover opportunity costs including any excess tax burdens, then the latter definition makes more sense. The government can be assumed to be accumulating physical assets with a value at least as great as the present value of their financing, implying no change (or perhaps an improvement) in the comprehensive balance sheet. For most purposes, of course, it is the financial status of the government, and the future tax burden that it implies, which is of interest; thus the first definition of s^* (the entire primary surplus) should be used.

Table 5 shows critical values of s^*—these are the values that the average primary surplus must attain over the long term to maintain D/Y at its current level under the assumption that $i - g$ is 0.04 and 0.02. Table 5 also shows primary surpluses forecast for 1986, both on all expenditure and on current expenditure.[37] The message is straightforward: if the government's balance sheet is the object of interest, current primary surpluses as ratios to GDP in three of the four countries (France is the exception by 0.4 percentage point of GDP) exceed the critical value even if $i - g$ is as high as 0.04. When one looks at long-term financial health and counts government capital formation as part of the primary deficit,

36. This conclusion is mitigated to the extent that government capital formation increases future tax revenues or is financed by user charges; but it is in the nature of public goods that many public investments that increase national wealth have negligible first-order effects on public-sector revenue. In principle, of course, productive government investments should increase the rate of growth of real GDP, g, over at least some period.

37. Referring to the discussion immediately preceding, the primary surplus on current spending is the relevant item for evaluating whether government net worth is rising or falling, while the primary surplus on all noninterest expenditure is what matters for evaluating the financial condition of government. There is also a good deal of uncertainty about $i - g$, but it is arguably not less than 0.02 and not greater than 0.04.

Table 5. *Permanent Primary Surpluses Needed for "Solvency,"*
Four European Countries, 1986[a]

Percent of GDP

	To keep net debt/GDP constant		To keep net worth/GDP constant		Primary	Primary surplus on current	"Structural" primary
Country	*i−g=0.04*	*i−g=0.02*	*i−g=0.04*	*i−g=0.02*	*surplus*	*spending*[b]	*surplus*
France	0.7	0.4	−0.6	−0.3	−1.0	2.5	2.1
Germany	0.9	0.5	−1.9	−1.0	0.8	4.3	2.3
Sweden	0.6	0.4	. . .	. . .	0.4	3.9	2.5
United Kingdom	1.9	1.0	−0.8	−0.4	1.1	2.7	3.8

Sources: OECD, *National Accounts, 1971–83*, vol. 2: *Detailed Tables*, tables 6, 1; and Chouraqui and others, "Public Debt in a Medium-Term Context."

a. See text for calculations.

b. Estimated as the 1986 primary surplus plus 1983 outlays for net public capital formation (the latter includes net capital transfers).

then (again) only France's current surplus is below the critical value if $i−g$ is 0.02; all four countries are somewhat below the critical value if $i−g$ is 0.04 (although Germany and Sweden are still within 0.2 percentage point).[38]

In short, solvency does not seem to be a problem for any of these economies, especially when it is recalled that the surpluses used in table 5 were forecasts of actual 1986 primary surpluses. If GDP moved to mid-cycle levels, the surpluses would increase in all four countries.[39] More-over, it is important to stress that there is nothing magic about current ratios of net debt to GDP or of net worth to GDP. Increasing those ratios would require (in the steady state) some increase in s^*, but the effect of temporary expansionary fiscal programs on fiscal solvency is in general quite small. (Under the pessimistic assumption that $i−g$ is 0.04, an increase in the debt/GDP ratio of 10 percentage points requires an increase in s^* of 0.4 percentage point to maintain the new ratio.)

There is a cloud in this rosy picture, identified by Chouraqui and his

38. If the balance sheet approach is taken to its logical conclusion, and maintenance of the current ratio of government net worth (available only for Germany, France, and the United Kingdom) as distinct from net debt is taken as the desideratum of fiscal policy, even France is within 0.4 percentage point of the critical value for s^* under the least favorable set of assumptions.

39. I have no data on mid-cycle surpluses for these economies for 1986. Using structural surpluses defined as those that would obtain at potential GDP, all four economies are well above their threshold levels of s^* with current policy. Using mid-cycle surpluses for 1983 as calculated by Muller and Price, and subtracting net interest payments, only France is below the critical level if $i − g = 0.04$, and all four countries are "solvent" if $i − g = 0.02$.

colleagues at the OECD.[40] Demographic changes in Germany (but not in the other three countries) will, under current policy, greatly increase public pension spending relative to receipts and hence reduce primary surpluses. Assuming that Germany reaches mid-cycle GDP by 1989, Germany's net debt would rise to more than 80 percent of GDP by 2010 if there are no changes in tax or pension policy. France faces a somewhat weaker version of the same problem, with net debt rising to about 30 percent of GDP. England's net debt ratio would also rise sharply to about 135 percent of GDP, mostly because of the maturing of part of its social security system.[41] The effects of demographic change on pensions in Sweden go the other way—net debt would be negative by 2010.

These projections of net debt based on changes in social security systems demonstrate that the present values of government spending and taxing programs are the key to assessing solvency. The current primary surplus (even adjusted to mid-cycle levels of GDP) may not be a good predictor of the long-term primary surplus. Social security is not the only problem—another well-known example of a program whose fiscal content will not be constant is the United Kingdom's North Sea oil revenue. Before the decline in oil prices, North Sea oil revenues were 3.75 percent of GDP, and Oddling-Smee and Riley forecast them to decline to zero by 2020. As an alternative calculation, the authors estimated (again, at old oil prices) that with a 2.5 percent real discount rate, the permanent revenue from North Sea oil was about ¾ percent of GDP.[42] Both these views tell the same story: because of North Sea oil revenue, the actual primary surplus is an overestimate of the "permanent" primary surplus.[43]

Still, one must conclude that the "deficit problem" in these four

40. Jean-Claude Chouraqui, Brian Jones, and Robert Bruce Montador, "Public Debt in a Medium-Term Context and Its Implications for Fiscal Policy," Working Paper 30 (OECD, Department of Economics and Statistics, May 1986).

41. In all three countries, one would expect that the solution to this problem would be to reconfigure public pension systems so that that the problem does not materialize. Given the length of time involved, it should be possible to engineer "soft landings" in all three countries such that the value of claims to government pensions does not change abruptly.

42. John Oddling-Smee and Chris Riley, "Approaches to the PSBR," *National Institute Economic Review*, no. 113 (August 1985), pp. 65–80.

43. Another revenue source that may not be "permanent" is Bundesbank profits in Germany. Indeed, there is a running quarrel between the German Finance Ministry and the OECD regarding the extent to which these should be viewed as part of structural revenues. At stake are revenues of about 0.5 percent of GNP.

economies is, by and large, not one of long-term solvency.[44] Of course, debts and deficits can have less apocalyptic if still real effects on economic growth; growing ratios of debt to GDP, by raising the critical value of s^* in the future, imply that the excess burden of taxation will be greater, and the benefits deriving from government consumption smaller, in some combination, in the future. Finally, deficits and debt may lead to crowding out, to which I now turn.

The Limits of Fiscal Policy: Effects on National Saving and Investment

Ignoring foreign transfers, the conventional accounting identity for income in an open economy can be rewritten as

$$(2) \qquad\qquad I + I_g + X - M = S + T - C_g,$$

where I_g and C_g are government investment and consumption, respectively, and the other variables are the usual stand-ins for investment, exports, imports, saving, and taxes. Recalling that net exports are equal to the accumulation of wealth abroad, equation 2 says that national wealth accumulation is equal to national saving, both private and public. At a given level of national income, government can contribute more or less to national saving, and hence to wealth accumulation, by running larger or smaller surpluses (monetary policy is adjusted so that changes in surpluses do not change levels of real national income). This is just the old argument that a growth-oriented policy mix will involve budget surpluses and easy money, and the argument holds in open economies (where the growth of wealth is in the hands of nationals) as well as in closed economies (where the wealth is all in the form of domestically employed capital).[45]

---

44. This conclusion does not apply, of course, to all European economies. Italy, everyone's favorite example of a country with a debt problem, has a critical value of s^* of from 2 to 4 percent of GDP and a primary surplus of -3.6 percent of GDP. Apparently reflecting some concern with long-term solvency, long-term government bonds have a higher yield than corporate bonds in Italy, unlike the case in other countries. Even so, the market still exists and the interest rate on government bonds is finite.

45. For a ringing Keynesian endorsement of these old virtues, see Alan S. Blinder, "The Policy Mix: Lessons from the Recent Past," in The Economic Outlook for 1986 (University of Michigan, 1986), pp. 328–56. The case that government ought to be promoting growth is not an obvious one. Given that $i - g$ is positive, the golden rule

CROWDING OUT. In figure 1 (following Gramlich) I plot gross investment (private and public, domestic and foreign), net investment, and net wealth accumulation (net investment plus net lending abroad) against the government budget surplus plus net government capital formation.[46] Gramlich calls this last the "consolidated capital budget surplus," but the term "government saving" is equally appropriate and more convenient. Because inventory investment fluctuates so much, only fixed investment is included in the figure. Although figure 1 is not a "model" of capital formation, the figure itself is striking.[47] In all four countries, "net wealth accumulation" tracks government saving quite well. Private saving did not move so as to cancel the effects of changes in government saving. In Germany and France, where private saving (the residual in this chart) moves very little, the fit is strikingly good—one can account for a great deal of the change in net capital formation by looking at the change in the government's contribution. In Sweden and the United Kingdom the story has been somewhat different. Since the early seventies private saving has risen (especially in Sweden), but it has not been large enough to compensate for the decrease in the government saving.[48] Recent Swedish policy has been explicitly designed to solve the problem: the logic of the "third way" requires that public saving be used to finance domestic investment, which, through exports, is intended to lead to economic growth.

---

criterion is not being met, but meeting it necessarily implies some sacrifice from current generations, and no overwhelming ethical case exists for the golden rule, which is not an efficiency condition. If on some political or ethical criterion long-term growth is found to be adequate, concern with the government contribution to wealth accumulation vanishes.

46. Edward M. Gramlich, "Rethinking the Role of the Public Sector," in Barry P. Bosworth and Alice M. Rivlin, eds., *The Swedish Economy* (Brookings, 1987), pp. 250–86.

47. There are any number of reasons why one would not expect total fixed investment to track government saving perfectly. These include the "Ricardian equivalence theorem" (see Barro, "Are Government Bonds Net Wealth?") under which private saving would just offset changes in public saving; and feedback between public saving and private saving because changes in the former change interest rates. Social security accumulation on the part of government might also affect private saving, as in Martin Feldstein, "Social Security, Induced Retirement, and Aggregate Capital Accumulation," *Journal of Political Economy*, vol. 82 (September 1974), pp. 905–26. Also, there is plainly an element of simultaneity. For example, if investment declines, either autonomously or for cyclical reasons, automatic stabilizers will also reduce government saving.

48. In all four countries, some of the reduction in the consolidated surplus is due to a reduction in public capital formation. This issue is discussed in the last section of my paper.

Figure 1. *Savings, Wealth Accumulation, and Capital Formation,*
Four European Countries, 1971–84[a]

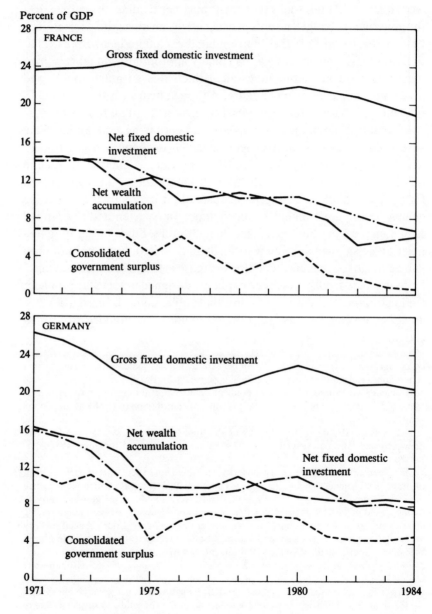

Percent of GDP

Figure 1 (*continued*)

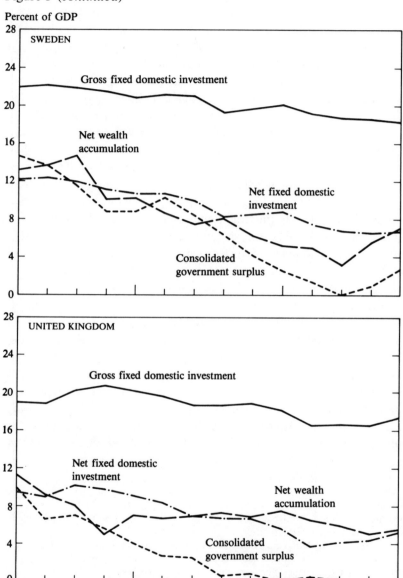

Percent of GDP

Sources: OECD, *National Accounts, 1971–83,* vol. 2: *Detailed Tables* (Paris: OECD, 1985), tables 1, 6, 10; and OECD, *National Accounts, 1972–84,* vol. 2: *Detailed Tables* (Paris: OECD, 1986), tables, 1, 6, 10.

a. *Consolidated government surplus* is general government saving plus net general government capital formation.

In Germany and France the fall in net wealth accumulation, which accompanies the fall in government saving, was closely matched by a fall in domestic investment. In the United Kingdom during the early 1970s and in Sweden from 1978 to 1982 foreign borrowing (negative net foreign investment) made it possible for a while to sustain domestic investment in the face of the decline in national saving. But over the last twenty-five years as a whole, the decline in national saving associated with the rising budget deficit was pretty closely matched by a decline in domestic investment. And so in all four countries, the natural interpretation of the data is that old-fashioned Keynesian crowding out is alive and well in Europe, and the lesson for economic growth is clear.

The crowding out of investment (or wealth accumulation) has a direct negative effect, over the long term, on the growth of potential income. Gramlich supplements this traditional argument with the observation that deficits, by leading to higher interest payments and hence larger future deficits, can lead to future crowding out as well: a given level of government saving will be harder to achieve by the amount of the increased interest payments.[49] At any time, the ratio of the government surplus to GDP is given by $s - iD/Y$, where s is the primary surplus divided by GDP; the higher is D/Y, for any primary surplus, the lower will be government saving. Moreover, although the condition for non-explosive growth in interest payments is just equation 1, the total surplus associated with s^* will be $-gD/Y$.[50] Thus, as accumulated debt rises, a solvent fiscal policy moves farther away from one that makes a positive contribution to national saving.[51]

Seen in this context, the increases in the debt to GDP ratios in Sweden and Germany during the past decade have made future public-sector

49. Gramlich, "Rethinking the Role of the Public Sector."

50. The arithmetic here is incorrect, but the basic logic is still correct if domestic economic policy has some effect on the domestic interest rate. In this case, lower government saving will raise domestic real interest rates and lead to still higher debt-service requirements in the future.

51. Here, the definition of s^* that makes the most sense is expenditures net of capital formation, as the latter does make a contribution to national saving. According to a recent paper by Aschauer, the immediate effect of public investment in the United States is to crowd out private investment by roughly three-quarters of the amount of the public investment. Over the longer run, however, public investment, by increasing the return to private investment, actually "crowds in" some private investment, making the size of both the public and private capital stocks greater than they would otherwise have been. See David Alan Aschauer, "Public Investment, Private Investment, and the Rate of Return," University of Michigan, August 1986.

contributions to long-term growth more difficult—politically, because spending must be reduced relative to trend (as has been done in both countries), or economically, because increased taxes generally imply increased distortions. (Public statements of both governments decry the fact that taxes cannot be reduced as much as the governments would like. Of course, it is hard to find any government at any time that does not make such statements.) This line of argument suggests that policies involving secular increases in debt relative to GDP may lead to long-term future crowding out, even if they are easily made consistent with solvency over the long haul. Thus to the extent that governments are concerned with the wealth accumulation of their citizens, the budgetary consequences of future interest payments are a valid reason for not accumulating debt, that is, for having a mid-cycle surplus at least as high as s^* in equation 1.

OTHER PROBLEMS WITH DEBT ACCUMULATION. There are at least two more arguments against debt accumulation that derive from the effect of interest payments on public budgets. One of these is directly related to the preceding discussion—to the extent that debt imposes a fixed charge on the budget, there is less room to do other things (or, more precisely, the marginal cost of doing other things is higher in a world of distorting taxes). The second argument is especially pertinent in light of the recent behavior of real interest rates. If real interest rates are at least partially determined on a world market and have some random component, then the existence of debt adds a *random* charge to the budget, which, ex ante, is also a random component of the income distribution. Thus not only is room for maneuver reduced the larger is the debt, but the government, in its planning, does not know how much the room will be reduced (or increased, should real interest rates fall), nor will it know the net distributional consequences of its budget. The smaller is the outstanding debt, the simpler will be fiscal planning and management, and, one hopes, the better will be the quality of public decisions regarding resource allocation and redistribution programs. Note, by the way, that on this argument the "right" concept of the primary surplus is the one that treats government capital formation as expenditure. The problem for the fiscal manager involves flows of money, and the fact that the government owns some roads and school buildings does not lighten the burden if the bonds used to finance them have to be rolled over at a new, higher interest rate.

Debt and deficits can lead to other kinds of crowding out, but most of these are hard to get at empirically, and the one that has been carefully studied (portfolio crowding out) does not seem to be important.[52] Finally, several arguments link the accumulation of national debt to risks of future inflation. One of these (the "unpleasant monetarist arithmetic" model of Sargent and Wallace) is technically correct but, as shown by Blanchard and others, unlikely to be of much practical significance.[53] To identify seigniorage as the ultimate mode of finance implies that governments cannot adjust their primary deficits to attain long-term solvency. Using plausible numbers, Blanchard and others show that the model of Sargent and Wallace implies an unlikely outcome, namely that governments would choose an extra 4 percent inflation over an extra 0.02 percent income tax rate.

A second class of arguments about inflation says that debt has negative effects that operate through expectations. In one variant of this claim, debt accumulation poses the risk of future repudiation, and the easiest mechanism for future repudiation of at least some debt is future inflation. Deficits today lead to inflation tomorrow, thus raising long interest rates (and thus short rates) today, which leads to crowding out. But the government would have no reason to use inflation as a means of reducing real debt, unless inflation is a cheaper means of "finance" than is meeting the condition for s^* in equation 1. Adding 1 percentage point or less to the "permanent" primary surplus will meet that condition for all of the economies looked at here, and it surely involves less political cost than deliberately re-inflating by amounts sufficient to substantially reduce the stock of real debt. Thus this argument makes sense only when economies are far from the critical value of s^*, which is not currently the case for the four under consideration here. In a second variant of the inflation argument, the "crowding out" is more than complete because business confidence is reduced by the fact of increased deficits themselves.[54] Thus not only does the interest rate rise, but the whole investment demand function shifts. This claim is extremely hard to evaluate, but it leads naturally to a discussion of the overall effectiveness of fiscal stimulus.

52. For an exhaustive catalogue of types of crowding out and an examination of the portfolio example, see Buiter, "A Guide to Public Sector Debt."

53. Thomas Sargent and Neil Wallace, "Some Unpleasant Monetarist Arithmetic," *Federal Reserve Bank of Minneapolis Quarterly Review*, vol. 5 (Fall 1981), pp. 1–17; and Olivier Blanchard, Rudiger Dornbusch, and Willem Buiter, "Public Debt and Fiscal Responsibility," in Blanchard and others, eds., *Restoring Europe's Prosperity*, pp. 125–53.

54. See German Finance Ministry, *Tasks and Objectives of a New Fiscal Policy*.

The Limits of Fiscal Policy: Would It Be Effective?

The preceding discussion leaves one in a quandary. On the one hand, the current high unemployment rates and the evidence of economic slack in Europe suggest that an increase in aggregrate demand could improve economic performance, at least in the short run. On the other hand, it is hard to argue that, after a decade of declining national savings, the long-run supply of ex ante savings exceeds investment demand. Moreover, even if it does, the costs associated with increasing deficits detailed above imply that the solution to the problem should not be a permanent increase in public-sector demand but primarily measures other than policies to increase profitability and investment. Thus the question arises whether an explicitly temporary increase in fiscal stimulus is warranted. That question divides, in turn, into two: (1) would a temporary stimulus work at all, and (2) would its effects vanish when it was withdrawn, leaving the economies with higher levels of debt following a "strawfire" of economic activity?

I find little evidence that fiscal policy is ineffective as a short-run stabilization tool. For one thing, the move toward fiscal stringency in the last five years in most of these economies seems to have worked in a quite conventional way—fiscal and monetary policies were tightened sharply, and both inflation and resource utilization (relative to trend) were reduced.[55] Moreover, the fiscal multipliers reported by Richard Cooper in this volume are all well above zero, again implying that were fiscal policy to become more stimulative, there would be an increase in the level of economic activity, at least in the short run. Cooper also reports that, in the INTERLINK model, coordinated fiscal stimulus would have no negative effects on current balances.

That a temporary stimulus would work for a time does not imply that it should be undertaken. Fiscal stimulus is not the only available form of expansionary policy. If societies are concerned with long-term growth, there is much to be said for the traditional preferred policy mix of tight budgets, to generate national savings, and loose money, to stimulate

---

55. The CEPS Macroeconomic Policy Group is careful to point out that although fiscal policy was almost certainly a major cause (with monetary policy) of slowed growth since 1980, stimulative fiscal policy alone might not be a powerful cure. Its argument against using fiscal stimulus alone is based on concerns with structural rigidities in European economies. Blanchard and others, "Employment and Growth in Europe."

investment demand that will soak up the savings and increase growth. Additionally, if one believes that macroeconomic equilibrium is achieved relatively quickly without government intervention, then fiscal stimulus makes little sense: if "full employment" will be achieved in a year or two anyhow, let nature take its course and maintain a lower level of debt, with its implication of a larger capital stock (or wealth stock), higher medium-term growth, and (to say the same thing another way) larger feasible permanent consumption in the future.[56]

The strongest argument for an explicitly temporary fiscal stimulus is one that is not yet formalized in the literature. A variant of the old pump-priming idea, it depends on the possibility that "hysteresis" in European labor markets exists and that a temporary increase in demand could thus lead to a permanent reduction in unemployment.[57] Hysteresis models imply that the long-term effects of economic slack can be very large indeed—a large fraction of the labor force may become essentially unemployable for a long period of time. Even if hysteresis is at work, however, it is not necessarily the case that a temporary fiscal stimulus would have permanent effects. The state of modeling on the subject is simply not sufficient to sort the question out, but the potential implications of a firm's finding that hysteresis can lead to a low-employment equilibrium trap are very large.

In the absence of such a finding, it is hard to make a case for fiscal stimulus in these economies. The relationships between government saving and national wealth accumulation on the one hand, and between government saving and national investment on the other, suggest that deficit finance reduces the growth of both wealth and the capital stock and thus lowers potential GNP and potential GDP. Traditional Keynesian fiscal stimulus is feasible, but it imposes real costs in the future. Unless the deficits are used to finance capital formation, or unless temporary deficits would reduce the nonaccelerating inflation rate of unemployment

56. If macroeconomic equilibrium is characterized as a situation in which resources are used to the fullest extent consistent with the avoidance of accelerating inflation, then anyone who believes that it is quickly achieved also presumably believes that structural unemployment accounts for most of Europe's twelve-year rise in joblessness, leaving little room for stimulus of any kind.

57. See Olivier J. Blanchard and Lawrence H. Summers, "Hysteresis and the European Unemployment Problem," in Stanley Fischer, ed., *NBER Macroeconomics Annual 1986* (MIT Press, 1986), pp. 15–78; and "Increasing Returns, Hysteresis, Real Wages, and Unemployment," unpublished paper, June 1986.

(NAIRU) because of hysteresis, there would be a transfer of consumption from the future to the present, but little else.[58]

Over the past five years or so, all of the governments under consideration have improved their budget balances by reducing the resources, relative to GDP, that they have devoted to public capital formation.[59] A strong argument can be made that the governments should improve the allocation of resources through increased public investment; moreover, it would be natural (and on traditional public finance criteria, warranted) to finance some of the increase through debt. Public investment programs are more likely to be credibly temporary than are many other types of government spending. This characteristic presents to governments the opportunity to engage in genuinely temporary fiscal stimulus when permanent fiscal stimulus is plainly unwarranted; it also offers the possibility of a "natural experiment" on the question of whether temporary stimulus can, as hysteresis models suggest it might, reduce the NAIRU and permanently increase the level of economic activity.

Taxation

Thus far the discussion has focused on the effects of deficits. The only role that taxes have played has been implicit—they raise revenue. Obviously, if deficits are a problem, increased taxes can be a solution, but it is a solution that raises problems of its own. In general, taxes are distorting, and the greater is the revenue raised by a given tax structure in an economy, the greater will be the loss of efficiency. Moreover, this loss will be greater on the margin than on average. The structure of taxation, for a given amount of revenue raised, will also affect resource allocation; in particular it will have an impact on saving and investment, precisely the issues that lead to concern about deficits.[60] Thus there is reason to examine both the level and structure of taxes, with particular emphasis on the effects of taxation on capital accumulation.

58. The CEPS Macroeconomic Policy Group characterizes the recent U.S. experience in this way. For another view, see Barry P. Bosworth, "Taxes and the Investment Recovery," *Brookings Papers on Economic Activity, 1:1985,* pp. 1–45.

59. This is treated in some detail in the last section of my paper.

60. Taxes also affect labor markets, and these effects are considered in Gary Burtless's paper in this volume.

The Structure and Level of Taxation since 1970

Both the structure and level of taxation vary greatly across the four countries.[61] In 1984, the last year for which comparable data are available, Sweden was the leader in tax revenue as a share of GDP (50.6 percent), and the United Kingdom had the lowest ratio of tax revenue to GDP (38.6 percent).[62] France and Germany were at 45.4 percent and 39.9 percent, respectively (table 6). Germany and the United Kingdom, with the lowest average tax rates, also show the lowest growth in tax revenue as share of GDP. Revenues as a share of GDP in Germany rose by 5.4 percentage points between 1970 and 1984, and by 1.4 points in the United Kingdom over the same period. In contrast, the corresponding figures were 10.4 percentage points for Sweden and 9.9 percentage points for France; in both cases, growth in social security contributions accounted for well more than half of the change. In France, most of the rest of the growth is accounted for by the personal income tax, receipts from which rose substantially, from 4.2 percent to 6.1 percent of GDP. In Sweden, "other" is the second leading source of growth.

The structure of taxation varies greatly among the four countries, but the structure in France approaches uniqueness. France relies far more heavily (43.4 percent of total tax revenue) on social security taxes and far less (13.5 percent) on personal income taxes than any of the other countries. The French personal income tax is especially striking because it combines a highly progressive rate structure (the top marginal bracket is 65 percent) with relatively low tax collections. This is surely a

61. The discussion here is just a brief overview. For details on the tax systems of the individual countries, see Krister Andersson, "The Swedish Tax System"; Annette Dengel, "The Tax System of the Federal Republic of Germany"; Jean-Louis Lienard, Kenneth C. Messere, and Jeffrey Owens, "The French Tax System"; and Nick Morris, "The United Kingdom Tax System"—all Brookings Discussion Papers dated April 1986. For a more complete treatment of the United Kingdom, see John Kay and Mervyn King, *The British Tax System*, 3d. ed. (Oxford University Press, 1983). For Germany, see German Ministry of Finance, *An ABC of Taxes in the Federal Republic of Germany* (Bonn, 1984).

62. Throughout this discussion, I use tax revenue rather than current receipts. For France, the United Kingdom, and Sweden, the difference, to a first approximation, is operating surplus, property income, fees, and so on, "other current transfers," and statistical discrepancy—lines 1, 2, 13, 14, and 20 in table 6 of the OECD *National Accounts*. For Germany, the OECD *Revenue Statistics* reports social security contributions much lower than those in the OECD *National Accounts*. Other sources, such as the Bundesbank, are closer to the *National Accounts*. In this discussion and in table 6, I use the *National Accounts* figures for German social security taxes.

prescription for a high ratio of excess burden to revenue raised. Sweden relies the most heavily on personal income taxes; in 1984 they were 38.5 percent of revenue, after fifteen years of trending downward from 49.8 percent in 1970. In Germany and the United Kingdom, 1984 personal income taxes accounted for 26.4 and 26.9 percent of revenue, respectively. Neither figure is very far from the corresponding 1970 values of 25.4 percent and 31.1 percent, but in the United Kingdom there was a major change in the intervening years—personal income taxes peaked at 38.2 percent of total revenue in 1976 and have been falling steadily ever since.

Indirect business taxes have fallen in relative importance in all of the countries except for the United Kingdom, where they have risen slightly (by 1.6 percent of revenue) over the period. Corporate income taxes have also fallen somewhat in relative importance in three of the countries, where they are no higher than 5.5 percent of total taxes; in the United Kingdom, they have not fallen in relative terms and in 1984 accounted for 11.2 percent of revenues.[63] Finally, only the United Kingdom relies in any substantial way on property taxes (10.8 percent of revenue in 1984, compared with 2.0 for France, the runner-up in this category).

Taxes and Capital Formation

The effect of the taxation of capital on investment (or, more properly, on the size and composition of the equilibrium capital stock) is a matter of substantial debate. There are two strands to the large amount of literature on the subject, which are related in principle but are rarely related in practice. Both strands derive from the Hall-Jorgenson model of investment, in which the rental price of capital determines the equilibrium capital stock.[64] The first strand looks at the effect of capital income taxation on aggregate investment. Essentially all modern macro models have investment equations in which the cost of capital plays a role, although it is fair to say that in most cases a simple accelerator model fits the data about as well.[65] As a stylized fact, cost of capital at

63. Effective corporate tax rates in the United Kingdom have increased substantially since 1984. This is discussed below in more detail.

64. Robert Hall and Dale W. Jorgensen, "Tax Policy and Investment Behavior," *American Economic Review*, vol. 59 (June 1969), pp. 388–401.

65. See, for example, Peter K. Clark, "Investment in the 1970s: Theory, Performance, and Prediction," *BPEA, 1:1979*, pp. 73–124.

Table 6. *Composition of General Government Taxes, Four European Countries, Selected Years, 1970–84*
Percent of total taxes

Taxes	1970	1975	1976	1977	1978	1979	1980	1981	1982	1983	1984
						France					
Personal income	11.8	12.2	12.7	13.2	13.1	12.5	12.9	13.2	12.9	13.4	13.5
Corporate income	6.3	5.3	5.8	5.6	4.7	4.7	5.0	5.1	5.1	4.3	4.0
Social security contributions	36.2	40.8	40.2	41.9	42.1	42.7	43.1	42.8	43.2	43.9	43.4
Recurring taxes on real property	1.5	1.4	1.9	1.6	1.6	1.7	1.7	1.7	1.7	1.8	2.0
Other property	2.0	2.0	1.8	1.7	1.8	1.9	1.9	2.0	2.0	2.0	2.4
Indirect business	37.7	32.9	32.4	30.5	31.2	31.3	30.1	29.7	29.6	29.0	28.8
Other	4.3	5.5	5.2	5.5	5.6	5.3	5.3	5.5	5.6	5.7	5.9
Total	100.0	100.0	100.0	100.0	100.0	100.0	100.0	100.0	100.0	100.0	100.0
Addendum:											
Total taxes as a percent of GDP	35.6	37.4	39.4	39.4	39.5	41.1	42.5	42.8	43.8	44.6	45.4
						Germany					
Personal income	25.4	27.9	28.0	29.0	28.0	27.1	27.8	26.9	26.6	26.3	26.4
Corporate income	5.4	4.1	4.3	5.1	5.4	5.7	5.1	4.7	4.7	4.8	5.1
Social security contributions[a]	33.5	38.6	39.1	37.9	37.8	37.9	38.3	39.9	40.8	40.2	39.9
Recurring taxes on real property	1.2	1.0	1.1	1.1	1.1	1.0	1.0	1.0	1.0	1.0	1.0
Other property	3.5	2.5	2.6	2.6	2.4	2.1	2.1	2.0	2.0	2.1	2.1
Indirect business	30.3	25.0	24.1	23.5	24.7	25.6	25.5	25.5	24.8	25.6	25.6
Other	0.6	0.8	0.8	0.7	0.7	0.6	0.2	0.0	0.0	0.0	0.0
Total	100.0	100.0	100.0	100.0	100.0	100.0	100.0	100.0	100.0	100.0	100.0
Addendum:											
Total taxes as a percent of GDP	34.5	38.7	39.7	40.8	40.4	40.1	40.4	40.3	40.4	40.2	39.9

Personal income	49.8	46.1	43.2	41.6	42.3	42.4	41.0	39.9	40.8	38.9	38.5
Corporate income	4.4	4.3	3.6	2.8	3.1	3.1	2.5	2.9	3.3	3.4	3.7
Social security contributions	14.9	19.5	23.3	25.5	26.9	27.3	28.8	29.4	27.7	26.9	26.2
Recurring taxes on real property	0.0	0.0	0.0	0.0	0.0	0.0	0.0	0.0	0.0	0.3	0.3
Other property	1.4	1.1	1.0	0.9	0.8	0.9	0.9	0.9	1.0	1.4	1.4
Indirect business	28.2	24.3	23.9	23.6	23.4	23.7	24.0	23.9	24.3	24.4	24.9
Other	1.2	4.5	5.0	5.5	3.5	2.6	2.8	3.1	2.9	4.7	5.0
Total	100.0	100.0	100.0	100.0	100.0	100.0	100.0	100.0	100.0	100.0	100.0
Addendum:											
Total taxes as a percent of GDP	40.2	43.9	48.2	50.5	50.9	49.5	49.4	51.1	49.9	50.5	50.6

United Kingdom

Personal income	31.1	38.2	38.2	35.1	32.9	31.3	30.0	29.5	28.4	27.7	26.9
Corporate income	9.3	6.2	5.2	6.6	7.6	7.6	7.8	9.2	9.6	10.8	11.2
Social security contributions	13.9	17.4	18.6	18.5	18.0	17.3	16.7	16.2	17.0	17.7	18.2
Recurring taxes on real property	9.7	11.1	10.6	10.5	10.5	10.7	10.7	11.5	11.4	11.1	10.8
Other property	2.8	1.5	1.5	1.5	1.5	1.6	1.4	1.4	1.3	1.5	1.4
Indirect business	28.8	25.4	25.8	26.2	26.6	27.0	29.2	28.2	28.9	29.8	30.4
Other	4.5	0.1	0.1	1.7	2.9	4.5	4.3	3.9	3.4	1.4	1.0
Total	100.0	100.0	100.0	100.0	100.0	100.0	100.0	100.0	100.0	100.0	100.0
Addendum:											
Total taxes as a percent of GDP	37.2	35.5	35.0	34.8	33.2	32.9	35.3	36.5	39.2	37.8	38.6

Sources: OECD, *Revenue Statistics of OECD Member Countries, 1965–1984* (Paris: OECD, 1985), tables 36, 44, 45, 56, 59, 111; and for social security contributions in Germany, OECD, *National Accounts, 1971–83*, vol. 2: *Detailed Tables*, table 6.4; and OECD, *National Accounts, 1972–84*, vol. 2: *Detailed Tables*, table 6.4.
a. For Germany only, social security contributions for 1984 were estimated as the 1984 value in *Revenue Statistics* multiplied by the average ratio of the *National Accounts* figure to the *Revenue Statistics* figure prevailing over the period 1980–84.

the level of gross fixed investment in equipment and structures is a significant but not especially powerful determinant of investment.[66]

The second strand in the literature involves an analysis of distortions in the composition and financing of the capital stock induced by a tax system in which capital income is taxed differently depending on the type of asset, the kind of owners, and the means of financing. In each of the four countries, these differences, as will be seen, are enormous, a fact that has been widely documented.[67]

King and Fullerton present detailed discussions of the tax systems of Germany, the United Kingdom, Sweden, and the United States. The taxation of capital income in all four of these countries is parameterized in a way that permits comparisons, both across countries and among assets of different kind, ownership and financing. Briefly, King, Fullerton, and their collaborators calculate the "tax wedge" between the net pretax rate of return on various stylized types of projects and the post-tax return received by various types of investors, and then use the calculated tax wedges to infer effective tax rates. The tax wedge includes both corporate and personal income taxes. In all, eighty-one types of projects are considered in terms of investments—in machinery, buildings, and inventories, in manufacturing, "other industry," and commerce; in terms of financing method—debt, new shares, and retained earnings; and in terms of ultimate ownership—by households, tax-exempt institutions, and insurance companies. Unfortunately, neither foreign owners nor investments in other countries by domestic owners are considered in this framework.

In the King-Fullerton framework, effective marginal tax rates are presented in two different but related ways. In the first, marginal tax rates are calculated under the assumption that the net real rate of return is equalized across types of investment projects. Following the King-

66. See Villy Bergstrom, *Studies in Swedish Post-War Industrial Investments* (Uppsala: Acta Universitatis Upsaliensis, 1982), for confirmation of this view for the Swedish case. In Sweden, however, there exists an "investment fund," held by the government, that is occasionally released. Releases do affect investment positively but also imply enormous changes in the cost of capital. More on this below. Many would argue that the stylized fact in the text is more stylized than fact. See, for example, Martin Feldstein and Joosung Jun, "The Effects of Tax Rules on Nonresidential Fixed Investment: Some Preliminary Evidence from the 1980s," in Feldstein, ed., *The Effects of Taxation on Capital Accumulation* (University of Chicago Press, 1987), pp. 101–56, and the references to papers by Feldstein and others cited therein.

67. King and Fullerton, eds., *The Taxation of Income from Capital,* is the most complete such study and will be drawn upon heavily below.

Fullerton notation, if the net pretax rate of return on a project is p and the net post-tax return to the saver is s, the tax wedge is $w = p - s$, and the tax rate is $t = (p - s)/p$. To compare countries, p is fixed at an arbitrary level (generally 10 percent in King-Fullerton) and the parameterization of the tax codes in the various countries is then used to generate the effective tax rates, t. These rates will vary both within countries (by type of project and owner) and across countries.

In general, one would expect that the assumption of constant real pretax rates of return on projects would not hold in practice. (If it did, the implication would be that the different tax wedges had no effect on the allocation of the capital stock.) Thus King and Fullerton also calculate effective tax rates under the assumption that arbitrage equalizes the after-corporate-tax rates of return on all projects at a constant real rate of return, r.[68]

The calculations for fixed r and for fixed p provide different but relevant information in assessing systems of capital taxation. The fixed r calculation is best interpreted as the marginal tax collections on an increase in the capital stock as allocated in practice, since it assumes that arbitrage opportunities have been undertaken and thus that p varies (it is highest for projects that have the highest tax rates). The fixed p calculation is a better "pure" measure of the effects of the tax system itself. Under a fixed p, differences in tax rates measure the potential distortions from a benchmark of no distortions—where the net pretax rate of return is equal on all projects. King and Fullerton present their results both ways, but unfortunately they did not study France, and the only calculations I have for France assume a fixed r.[69] Thus table 7 shows calculations with fixed p for Germany, the United Kingdom, and Sweden, and calculations with fixed r for France. The data for France are explicitly not comparable with those for the other countries in the table, although the pattern (but not the exact magnitudes) of differences in effective tax rates would hold if the calculations were made on the same basis as those for the other countries.

One potential problem with those calculations is that they implicitly

68. Note that this is not complete arbitrage. One could imagine reshuffling of portfolios to eliminate all arbitrage possibilities across investors with different personal marginal tax rates. That some of this goes on is certainly true, but it is also true that such arbitrage is not complete. I do not transfer all of my assets to my poorer neighbor, nor, alas, does my richer one transfer all of hers to me.

69. J. S. Alworth, "Taxation and the Cost of Capital: A Comparison of Six EC Countries," unpublished paper, December 1985.

Table 7. *Effective Rates of Tax on Investment, Four European Countries*

Percent

Investment category	Germany Inflation rate		Sweden Inflation rate		United Kingdom Inflation rate		Addendum: France[a] Inflation rate	
	0%	10%	0%	10%	0%	10%	0%	10%
Asset								
Machinery	38.1	46.6	−18.1	1.5	16	23	26.5	66.7
Buildings	42.7	31.2	28.9	37.3	58	59	55.1	69.1
Inventories	57.7	60.8	26.5	71.0	37	66	57.4	80.4
Industry								
Machinery	44.7	46.8	8.1	28.3	27	39	47.1	72.7
Other industry	50.8	57.9	29.6	62.6	34	44	47.5	71.5
Commerce	44.6	36.6	12.1	40.7	49	55	50.3	73.0
Source of finance								
Debt	12.1	−33.3	−12.9	6.4	22	23	32.7	53.4
New share issues	56.1	65.7	44.2	93.2	25	24	54.9	81.1
Retained earnings	72.0	111.5	40.9	69.5	38	50	53.2	77.9
Owner								
Households	59.7	82.0	57.1	108.0	35	45	68.1	102.4
Tax-exempt institutions	17.6	−17.9	−39.2	−52.8	28	38	21.1	35.6
Insurance companies	14.6	−38.9	−16.0	22.0	43	53	17.5	25.9
Overall	45.1	46.1	12.9	37.0	34	44	47.7	72.6

Sources: For Germany and Sweden, Mervyn A. King and Don Fullerton, eds., *The Taxation of Income from Capital* (University of Chicago Press, 1984), tables 4.20, 5.21; for the United Kingdom, Mervyn King, "Tax Reform in the UK and US," *Economic Policy*, no. 1 (November 1985), table 2; for France, J. S. Alworth, "Taxation and the Cost of Capital: A Comparison of Six EC Countries," unpublished paper, December 1985, tables 8, 9.

a. Numbers for France, which are on a "fixed *r*" basis (assumed to be 3 percent) are not comparable to those for the other countries, which are on a "fixed *p*" basis, with net pretax *p* assumed to be 10 percent.

assume that the "average" financing method and ultimate ownership of different kinds of assets are the same. In practice, structures tend to be much more highly levered than equipment;[70] in table 7 debt finance generally has a lower rate of effective tax than other forms of finance, while structures (under "average" finance) generally have higher rates than equipment. If one took account of the correlation between type of investment and type of finance, the tax rates on equipment would thus be somewhat higher and those on structures would be somewhat lower. Without taking into account the relationship between types of assets and means of finance, the King-Fullerton type of analysis is necessarily incomplete, and the measured distortions that are discussed in this section should be interpreted as being merely indicative of the potential for efficiency improvements.[71] Moreover, as King and Fullerton point out, implicit in their calculations is that finance of the marginal investment is the same as finance on average. If debt is the marginal financing instrument, all of the tax rates on different types of projects will be lower than reported in the table.

The four countries under examination here have quite different systems of capital taxation, and aspects of these will be compared below. But before turning to the comparisons, and notwithstanding the preceding paragraph, it is worth emphasizing the facts starkly brought out in table 7—each country has very large intra-economy distortions, by type of capital, by kind of owner, and by means of financing. It may be for good reasons that, say, Germany imposes tax rates on capital income that are higher than those in Sweden; but within Germany and within Sweden the dispersion of actual rates around the average is large and leads to real efficiency costs. Thus one should not focus too much on the mean marginal tax rates on capital income across countries; at least as important are the differences in marginal rates by type of project and investor within countries, as these are indicators of opportunities for efficiency-enhancing reform that are available to governments unilaterally. For Sweden and Germany, figure 2 shows histograms, taken from King and Fullerton, of the fraction of investment under 1980 law at actual 1980 inflation rates that is taxed at different marginal rates for the

70. Bosworth, "Taxes and the Investment Recovery."
71. What all of this implies is that eliminating distortions while maintaining a positive tax on the normal returns to capital is at best a tricky business. This is one of the arguments for a "cash flow" corporation tax, which is discussed in detail below.

Figure 2. *Proportion of Corporate Capital Taxed at Various Effective Tax Rates, Germany and Sweden, 1980*[a]

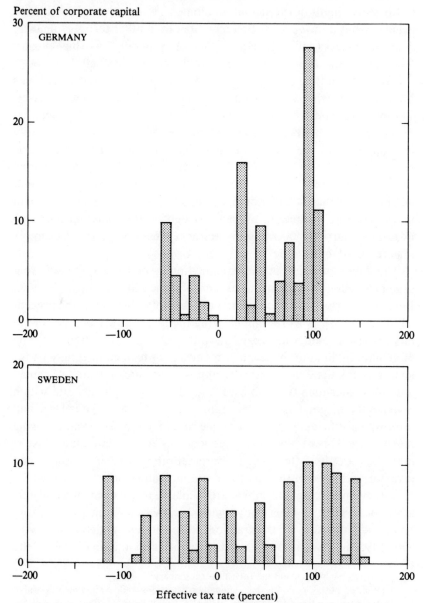

Percent of corporate capital

Effective tax rate (percent)

Source: Mervyn King and Don Fullerton, eds., *The Taxation of Income from Capital: A Comparative Study of the United States, the United Kingdom, Sweden, and West Germany* (University of Chicago Press, 1985), figs. 7.7, 7.8.
a. Fixed-*p* case.

fixed p case.[72] The distribution in Germany is much tighter than that in Sweden (although there is still a lot of variation), and the mean tax rate is also higher in Germany (48.1 percent compared with 35.6 percent in Sweden). But it is the variation that is most interesting, as it implies great scope for efficiency-enhancing and revenue-neutral (or revenue-increasing) changes in the structure of capital taxation.

It is worth noting here the main similarities and differences in the systems of capital taxation in the four countries. All four have both corporate and personal income taxes, and all four (unlike the United States) integrate the two at least partially. In Germany, the integration is essentially complete—dividends are effectively taxed only at the personal level.[73] In France, there is partial integration. A 50 percent credit on personal tax against corporate tax paid is given to individual taxpayers, leading to a 50 percent reduction in "double taxation" relative to systems in which there is no integration.[74] In addition, 3,000 francs (FF) of dividends are deductible from taxable income at the household level. With the recent reduction in the rate of corporate tax in the United Kingdom, the 30 percent credit for corporate taxes paid on dividends comes very close to full integration. This was not the case before 1986, when the 30 percent credit was considerably less than the marginal corporate rate (which was 52 percent before 1984 and has been falling, on a transition schedule, to the current rate of 35 percent). Sweden's system for providing partial integration is the weakest of the four. Under the "Annell legislation," firms may deduct dividends paid on newly issued shares for up to twenty years. Because the annual deduction is limited, the value of the Annell deductions depends on the nominal discount rate, and if this is positive, the present value of the deductions is necessarily less than unity, and thus integration is less than complete.

Studies by King and Fullerton and by others clearly show that in each country the effective tax rate on capital income in general is substantial and that there are huge differences in tax rates on capital of different types, ownership, and financing. But how important are these levels of

72. The United Kingdom is not shown because the tax law has changed greatly since 1980, and France is not shown because the analysis is not available.

73. King and Fullerton, eds., *Taxation of Income from Capital*, pp. 157–58.

74. Alworth, "Taxation and the Cost of Capital"; and Lienard and others, "French Tax System." Reduction of the corporate rate in France to 40 percent means that effective integration is now 61 percent.

taxation as determinants of aggregate investment, and how much loss of efficiency is caused by the internal distortions?

In a recent study Barry Bosworth disaggregates components of investment in more detail than do the macro models to analyze the U.S. Economic Recovery Tax Act of 1981 (ERTA). ERTA lowered the cost of capital on almost everything, although for some things much more than for others. Bosworth found that ERTA is not a good predictor of the growth of investment in disaggregated investment sectors, which suggests again that the effect of the cost of capital for both overall investment and its major components is quite weak.[75]

While the internal variations of effective tax rates are huge, the magnitude of the effects is less well established. For example, Gravelle estimates that if all capital in the United States were taxed at the same effective rate, then the resulting reallocations would increase the effective capital stock by about 2.5 percent.[76] This would translate into a one-time increase in GNP of about 0.7 percent, hardly the cure for any kind of sclerosis. Tax-induced distortions that might affect the allocation of capital in Europe do not look quantitatively dissimilar to those in the United States, so the scope for boosting growth by removing them is also probably not large. Even so, of course, removing them is a clear efficiency gain.

The case that capital taxation has large effects on the capital stock or on its allocation is not proved. But there are few other areas in which economists can be so certain about prescribing reforms that will enhance both efficiency and growth to some degree. Moreover, there are other sound public policy reasons for improving the taxation of income from capital, not the least of which is that the current systems in place lead to tax arbitrage, and that in itself is wasteful.[77] While empirical work to date does not support the proposition that reform of capital taxation will be a panacea for growth, there are no grounds, empirical or theoretical, for retaining a system that has high marginal rates on some enterprises, low and negative ones on others, and raises little revenue. Moreover,

75. Barry P. Bosworth, "Taxes and the Investment Recovery." See Feldstein and Jun, "Effects of Tax Rules," for both a rebuttal to Bosworth in particular and for strong support of the proposition that tax-induced changes in the cost of capital strongly influence investment behavior.

76. Jane G. Gravelle, "Capital Income Taxation and Efficiency in the Allocation of Investment," *National Tax Journal*, vol. 36 (September 1983), pp. 297–306.

77. C. Eugene Steuerle, *Taxes, Loans, and Inflation* (Brookings, 1985).

one problem endemic to all current tax systems (even after the latest reforms in the United Kingdom and the United States) is that the cost of capital is highly sensitive to the rate of inflation. To overhaul systems of capital taxation under the implicit assumption that inflation is going to be low and constant in the future suggests a confidence about future economic events that seems unwarranted by recent history.

SAVING AND INVESTMENT INCENTIVES. All four countries also have various schemes designed to promote specific kinds of saving and investment. As of 1986, the United Kingdom no longer offered any general investment credit, and depreciation allowed for tax purposes became much more like economic depreciation than it had been in the past. The United Kingdom thus has something quite close to a "pure" corporate income tax, although investment in machinery is still treated much better than that in inventories or structures. On the other hand, the United Kingdom retains a host of special savings provisions (termed "fiscal privilege" in the British literature) in its personal income tax code, so the return on investment varies a great deal according to who is doing the saving and in what form. To characterize fiscal privilege in the United Kingdom in any compact way is nigh to impossible, but the variation in effective tax rates paid as a function of the form of saving is enormous and leads Hills to conclude that "variations in fiscal privilege can be many times more important than the size of the underlying return on different assets."[78] After reading the Hills study, it is hard to believe that the savvy British taxpayer pays any tax on the returns to saving, although King's updating of the King-Fullerton analysis for the United Kingdom implies that at least some do.[79]

Germany, France, and Sweden have the "usual" array of special provisions designed to stimulate saving and investment—investment credits, accelerated depreciation, and so on. In this, Germany is the least distorting, with the lowest variation in effective tax rates across types of investment and investor. Fiscal privilege in France has not been studied (at least not in English) to the degree that it has in the United Kingdom, but there are schemes to encourage pension saving, life insurance coverage, homeownership, the purchase of equities in French

78. John Hills, *Savings and Fiscal Privilege,* rev. ed., Report Series no. 9 (London: Institute for Fiscal Studies, 1984), p. 9.
79. Mervyn King, "Tax Reform in the UK and US," *Economic Policy,* no. 1 (November 1985), p. 231.

firms, the ownership of rental property and of small business, and the like.[80] In Sweden, income tax returns distinguish capital income from other sources of income, and this disaggregation yields the remarkable result that at the personal level the capital tax base is negative, implying that if personal taxes on capital income were abolished, total revenues would rise. Moreover, the distributional impact of personal taxes on capital income in Sweden is regressive because higher income house-holds have the bulk of the losses, which offset income at higher tax rates.[81] One investment-enhancing scheme unique to Sweden is the system of "investment funds" under which corporations may set aside up to 50 percent of profits provided that they place half of the amount set aside in a special non-interest-bearing account in the central bank. With the statutory corporate rate at 52 percent, this scheme is always profitable for the firm. It is even more profitable on those occasions when the central bank periodically "releases" the funds back to the firms to finance new investment. Releases were used extensively as a counter-cyclical device during the 1970s and are now used almost continuously.[82]

As noted earlier, the literature on the relationship between capital taxation and investment is unsettled, with a great deal of evidence suggesting that tax policy is not very effective at inducing investment.[83] If economies are open to flows of financial capital, then even if such policies are effective, they may not meet a conventional benefit-cost test. For example, assume that all countries tax capital income at a zero rate and one country decides to implement a subsidy. If the world interest rate is approximately fixed, then such a policy will increase the equilib-rium capital stock in the subsidizing country, but given the declining marginal product of capital, the increased output will be less valuable than the amount of the subsidy. (There would also be a large transfer of rents from society as a whole to owners of capital.) This result need not hold for a tax reduction when the initial tax rate is positive—and I do not presume to say what the "optimal" tax rate on capital income might be.

80. France has a brochure outlining incentives to entrepreneurial activity that shows a pole vaulter in mid-vault, obviously moving upward at high speed. It is from the Minestère de L'Economie, des Finances, et du Budget, and is called "Loi sur le développement de l'initiative économique."

81. See Andersson, "Swedish Tax System," p. 45.

82. Bergstrom, *Studies in Swedish Post-War Industrial Investments*.

83. See Robert S. Chirinko, "Will 'The' Neoclassical Theory of Investment Please Rise? The General Structure of Investment Models and Their Implications for Tax Policy," University of Chicago, March 1986, for a recent review in support of this view.

But if such an "optimum" exists, reducing capital tax rates below it might indeed increase investment but would not, in general, be worth the cost.

Finally, none of the countries has indexed its corporate taxes for inflation, although the United Kingdom and France index their personal income taxes.[84] The importance of inflation to the cost of capital is one of the main themes of the King-Fullerton analysis and is documented in table 7. Strikingly, the recent U.K. reforms make the system of capital taxation much more vulnerable to inflation than it had been in the immediate past, when much investment was eligible for immediate write-off.

TAX REFORM. Table 7 makes it clear that room for reform exists in the systems of capital taxation in all four countries. One approach to reform, taken in the United Kingdom in 1984, is to move the system of capital income taxation toward a pure income tax by abolishing investment credits and allowing something close to economic depreciation for tax purposes. The consequence in the United Kingdom was that distortions declined but average marginal taxes on capital income rose. (The statutory rate dropped from 52 to 35 percent, but the elimination of various investment incentives far more than compensated for the lower rate.) The net effect of these changes on the equilibrium capital stock remains to be seen, and could constitute a very nice natural experiment (if tax reform can ever be said to be natural) that would shed some light on the importance of the cost of capital. Unfortunately, the natural experiment may not be allowed to run its course, as the transition rules for the recent British reform allowed the old incentives to remain in place while offering taxation at the new, lower statutory rate after April 1986. In consequence, the United Kingdom has had something of an investment boom, and it would not be surprising if it now had a period of slack in investment simply because of the timing of the rule changes. A period of slack, in turn, could lead to calls for reintroduction of special incentives, and if these are effective, the natural experiment will have implications more political than economic.[85]

In any event, the U.K. reforms are incomplete because a neutral corporate income tax would also require indexing depreciation allow-

84. Sweden indexed personal taxes from 1979 to 1985, at least in principle, but repealed the indexing law in 1985.

85. I would not be surprised if the current U.S. reform of corporate taxation meets the same fate that the U.K. reform may meet.

ances and interest deductions. Britain did not index, and none of the other countries in this study is contemplating doing so. Without indexing for inflation, effective rates of tax and their distribution across different types of investments and investors are sensitive to inflation rates, as seen in table 7. Rendering capital taxation neutral also requires that, at the household level, the taxation of the returns to saving be independent of the form of saving, a condition that does not hold now in any of the four countries.[86]

The other three countries have also "reformed" taxes to some extent in the last few years, but the reforms mostly have been straightforward reductions in rates. Germany is implementing the 1985 reform in two steps, one in 1986 and one in 1988; the major effect will be to undo recent bracket creep in the personal income tax. France widened personal income tax brackets in late 1985. Sweden has just completed a three-year "reform" (reduction) package that lowered marginal rates for most taxpayers. Gramlich reports that in 1982 almost half of Swedish taxpayers faced a marginal rate of 80 percent,[87] a rate now faced by only 10 percent of the taxpayers; however, about half still face marginal rates of 50 percent or more. In addition, Swedish corporations were exempted from local income taxes as of 1985. Proposals for tax reform abound in all four countries, but there are no significant governmental initiatives along the base-broadening, rate-reducing lines of recent U.K. (and U.S.) efforts.

Academic and policy discussions of comprehensive tax reform in recent decades have focused on two models—comprehensive income taxation and comprehensive consumption taxation. The former has the advantage of being more familiar and is the one toward which the United Kingdom has moved (for corporate taxation), and the United States has moved in general, in the last year. However, rules permitting a comprehensive income tax to be levied on real income are inevitably more complicated than those required to achieve a similar result with a comprehensive consumption tax. The reason is simple. In the consumption approach, investments (savings) are deducted from the tax base when undertaken, and returns, including principal, are taxed when realized, an expensing treatment that removes the need to index anything. Under an income tax, true economic depreciation should be

---

86. The recent U.S. reforms are incomplete in the same way—depreciation allowances are not indexed and some forms of saving, especially owner-occupied housing, continue to receive favorable treatment.

87. Gramlich, "Rethinking the Role of the Public Sector," p. 268.

deductible, as should real interest paid, while real interest received should be taxable. Also, real capital gains should be taxed on an accrual basis. At any constant rate of inflation, the income tax system can achieve a desired impact, but the impact will change when inflation does, and it is bizarre to assume that inflation will be constant in the future. Indexing is a potential solution (although it does not eliminate the difficulty of estimating true economic depreciation or of taxing capital gains on an accrual basis), but indexing of interest payments is difficult.[88] The second advantage to a consumption base is that it is automatically neutral across different types of investment. The tax base on investment is simply profits above a normal rate of return, or pure economic profits, and as every economist knows, such a tax is nondistorting. Overall, there is nothing in the European (or U.S.) experience in taxing capital income (as distinct from profits) to persuade me that the benefits from doing so outweigh the difficulties of doing so in an efficient and consistent way.

King and Aaron and Galper have shown that replacing corporate income taxes with cash flow taxes (effectively, consumption taxes on corporations) could raise current levels of revenue without raising the basic tax rate applying to corporations.[89] (In the United States, according to Aaron and Galper, the rate would be about the same as that applied to corporate income under the Tax Reform Act of 1986.) Similar results should be obtainable in Germany, France, and Sweden. The potential efficiency gains implicit in figure 2 and table 7, and the advantages of a cash flow corporate tax in a world with varying rates of inflation, make a strong argument for such reforms, although the trend in policy thinking seems to be in the other direction.[90]

The argument for personal cash flow (as distinct from income) taxes is much the same as the argument for corporate ones.[91] Again, my

88. The plan of the U.S. Treasury that came to be known as Treasury I made a proposal to do so, but it was never taken seriously by Congress.

89. King, "Tax Reform in the UK and US"; and Henry J. Aaron and Harvey Galper, *Assessing Tax Reform* (Brookings, 1985). The King calculations referred to here are for the United Kingdom; the Aaron and Galper work covers the U.S. system.

90. That the potential efficiency gains are large does not imply that the potential effect on measured economic growth would be large. Rather, there would be an unambiguous improvement in economic welfare.

91. Mervyn King, "The Cash Flow Corporation Tax," unpublished paper, February 1986, shows that the two reforms can be considered independently—integrating a personal income tax with a corporate cash flow tax is feasible and would reduce tax-induced distortions in rates of return on different types of investment.

sympathies are with the consumption base for personal taxation as well as corporate taxation, but in any event all four countries have substantial room to reduce tax expenditures and thus cut marginal tax rates without losing revenue.[92] Unless the tax expenditures are accomplishing some efficiency goal (and in general they are probably not doing so), there is an obvious efficiency gain from employing this strategy of cutting both tax expenditures and tax rates. The potential beneficial effects on growth arising from greater public-sector saving warrant the use of this strategy along with a subsequent increase in rates a bit above what is necessary to keep revenue constant—provided that aggregate demand can be maintained through monetary policy.

The effects of tax structure on economic growth are potentially significant, but the quantitative impacts of removing arbitrage opportunities across types of investment and of lowering the tax rate on capital are not known with any precision. Moreover, it seems unlikely that structural tax policy was the cause of the slow growth in Europe since 1973. Most of the bizarre (and by no means uniquely European) features of the tax systems that are in place today were in place then; if anything, the tax treatment of capital income in general has gotten lighter over the period (if also somewhat more capricious). Although taxes probably were not the basic cause of the problem, cleaning them up can be part of the solution, especially because more broadly based and less distorting tax structures could provide more room for fiscal maneuver and the possibility of increased public saving.

The Size and Composition of Public Expenditure

Much has been made in recent years of the growth of government, the causes of its growth, and the effects of increasingly large government on economic growth. The most popular indicator of the size of government is the share of public spending in GDP or GNP. But in a national accounts sense this share is a meaningless concept—it is like talking

92. See Paul N. Courant and Edward M. Gramlich, "The Expenditure Tax: Has the Idea's Time Finally Come?" in Joseph A. Pechman and others, *Tax Policy: New Directions and Possibilities* (Washington, D.C.: Center for National Policy, 1985). The answer to the question in the title of the paper is obviously "no."

about the share of transfer payments in final demand.[93] There is no exhaustive set of accounting categories that include public spending and that add up to GNP or GDP. Rather, $Y = C + I + G + X - M$, and G is government purchases of goods and services, which can be decomposed into consumption and investment. Taxes and transfers, of course, can have important effects on economic growth, but it is not the size of the tax-transfer system but the details of its rules that have these effects. Thus a tax-transfer system that consisted of large poll taxes and random redistribution of the proceeds would, in an economy closed to migration, probably have little effect on the level of economic activity, whereas an unemployment compensation scheme that had no experience rating, high replacement rates, and weak job-search requirements could have quite a large effect.[94] An evaluation of such rules is beyond the scope of this paper.

In the context of this paper, the reason for worrying about the level of transfers is that governments finance transfers partly by levying distorting taxes and partly by borrowing, and both of these financing mechanisms affect growth. Thus my concern with the size of transfer programs is motivated by the preceding two sections of the paper—their finance may lead to crowding out, or economic inefficiency, or both.

Like transfers, government consumption and investment also affect growth indirectly through their means of finance (although market-based user charges may have very little effect); but unlike transfers, they involve public use of real resources. If these resources have higher or lower value in private hands, the effect on growth is direct. Indeed,

93. While cognizant of these difficulties, a recent paper by Tullio uses expenditure shares as an index of the size of government and runs regressions in which economic growth over different periods is a function of the growth of government so measured. Tullio finds a significant relationship with the "right" sign—more growth in government leads to less growth in the economy—but the potential problem of reverse causation seems to me almost overwhelming. See Guiseppe Tullio, "Long Run Implications of the Increase in Taxation and Public Debt for Employment and Economic Growth in Europe," unpublished paper, May 1986. Mancur Olson's recent book, *The Rise and Decline of Nations* (Yale University Press, 1982), implies, that other things being equal, one of the ways in which interest groups may implement their growth-retarding agendas is through government programs. If so, this would imply that the growth of government can be interpreted as a partial instrument for the growth in rigidity that is at the heart of Olson's story and the motivation for many of the papers in the present volume.

94. For a discussion implying that the only meaningful way to look at the effect of fiscal policy is to look at the effect of government programs in individual lifetime budget constraints, see Laurence J. Kotlikoff, "Taxation and Savings: A Neoclassical Perspective," *Journal of Economic Literature*, vol. 22 (December 1984), pp. 1576–1629.

elevating the value of the resources involved is much of the stated motivation of the privatization program of the current U.K. government, although it is hard to see how selling off natural monopolies without improving the way that they are regulated will contribute much to growth.[95] Government investments in "infrastructure" may, of course, enhance growth. Here, too, it would be helpful to evaluate detailed content, but to do so would involve writing books rather than one paper.

In short, there is no good index of the size of government (consider, for a moment, regulation, which has not been touched upon here), so in the discussion below I consider overall spending (the motivation being fiscal), investment, and, in some detail, government consumption. I also discuss, where possible, the extent to which different fiscal federalism arrangements may have affected the general government totals, but this coverage is necessarily incomplete.

Growth of Expenditures

Of the four countries under review here, Sweden had the highest level of general government spending as a share of GDP in 1971, and the United Kingdom had the lowest. By 1984 Sweden and the United Kingdom still had the highest and lowest levels respectively, but they had moved farther apart (tables 1 and 8): whereas in 1971 the U.K. share was 85 percent of the Swedish share, in 1984 it was only 79 percent. However, the share in Britain grew much faster than that in Germany; indeed, general government spending in Germany as a share of GDP could go from being second highest in 1971 to the lowest if the 1971–84 growth rates were to persist. Nonetheless, the general pattern of a widening divergence between the top and bottom is consistent with the findings of a recent OECD study: the share of government spending in GDP in the initial period is positively correlated with the growth of that share.[96]

The timing of expenditure growth has been quite different in the four countries (table 1). In Germany essentially all of the 1971–83 growth had occurred by 1975. Indeed, the share of spending in GDP has fallen

95. For an illuminating discussion of this and other aspects of the U.K. privatization program, see George Yarrow, "Privatization in Theory and Practice," *Economic Policy,* no. 2 (April 1986), pp. 324–77.

96. Peter Saunders and Friedrich Klau, *OECD Economic Studies: The Role of the Public Sector,* no. 4 (Spring 1985, *Special Issue*), p. 118. The OECD study goes back to the early 1960s.

Table 8. *Growth of Government Spending, Four European Countries, 1971–84*

Percentage points of GDP

Spending category	Total	Central	Social security	State	Local
			Germany		
Final consumption	3.2	−0.3	2.1	0.9	0.5
Net capital accumulation	−2.4	−0.6	0.2	−0.5	−1.2
Net interest	1.5	0.5	0.2	0.7	0.1
Current transfers to business	0.4	0.3	0.0	0.0	0.1
Social security	3.2	0.0	3.2	0.0	0.0
Current transfers to individuals excluding social security	0.6	0.3	0.1	0.2	0.1
Other current transfers	1.0	0.7	0.2	0.0	0.1
Net intergovernmental expenditures	0.0	0.7	−0.5	0.1	−0.2
Total	7.4	1.6	5.2	1.3	−0.7
Addendum:					
Total spending, 1984	45.8	15.1	16.4	10.9	3.3

Spending category	Total	Central	Social security	Local
			France	
Final consumption	3.0	1.3	0.3	1.4
Net capital accumulation	−1.4	−0.8	−0.1	−0.6
Net interest	1.6	1.3	−0.1	0.4
Current transfers to business	0.8	0.7	0.0	0.1
Social security	8.5	0.0	8.5	0.0
Current transfers to individuals excluding social security	0.7	0.7	0.0	0.0
Other current transfers	0.4	0.0	0.1	0.3
Net intergovernmental expenditures	0.0	1.8	−1.5	−0.2
Total	13.5	5.0	7.1	1.4
Addendum:				
Total spending, 1984	50.4	26.4	19.5	4.7

somewhat since then. Growth in France was quite steady over the whole period. In the United Kingdom there was a sharp spurt of growth (similar to that in Germany) between 1971 and 1975, followed by some decline to 1979, and then sharp growth again to 1981, with little trend since then. A stated goal of the Thatcher government that it has not accomplished is reduction in the share of GDP accounted for either by general

Table 8 *(continued)*

Spending category	Total	Level of government		
		Central	Social security	Local
		Sweden		
Final consumption	5.2	−0.9	0.2	6.0
Net capital accumulation	−2.4	−0.5	0.0	−1.9
Net interest	3.2	5.3	−1.7	−0.4
Current transfers to business	3.2	2.4	0.3	0.3
Social security	6.3	1.2	5.1	0.0
Current transfers to individuals excluding social security	−0.5	−0.4	0.1	−0.1
Other current transfers	0.8	0.5	0.0	0.3
Net intergovernmental expenditures	0.0	2.8	−0.1	−2.7
Total	15.7	10.5	3.8	1.5
Addendum:				
Total spending, 1984	57.0	34.5	5.6	17.0
		United Kingdom		
Final consumption	4.1	2.7	0.0	1.3
Net capital accumulation	−2.5	−0.7	0.0	−1.8
Net interest	1.5	2.2	0.0	−0.7
Current transfers to business	0.9	0.6	0.0	0.2
Social security	1.7	0.0	1.7	0.0
Current transfers to individuals excluding social security	3.9	2.9	0.0	1.1
Other current transfers	0.4	0.4	0.0	0.0
Net intergovernmental expenditures	0.0	1.4	0.0	−1.3
Total	10.0	9.5	1.7	−1.1
Addendum:				
Total spending, 1984	45.0	33.3	6.1	5.7

Source: OECD, *National Accounts, 1971–83*, vol. 2: *Detailed Tables*, tables 1, 6, 6.1, 6.2, 6.3, 6.4; OECD, *National Accounts, 1972–84*, vol. 2: *Detailed Tables*, tables 1, 6, 6.1, 6.2, 6.3, 6.4.

government or by government consumption. In Sweden spending relative to GDP grew throughout the period until 1982, with the the biggest
increase (more than 10 percentage points of GDP) occurring between
1975 and 1979, before the discovery of the "third way."

Far from being a recent phenomenon, growth in government spending
as a share of GDP has been continuous since 1961 in these four countries.
Table 9 displays growth rates of real current public-sector disbursements
(total spending less public capital formation) and of real GDP for each
country over three periods: 1961 to 1973, 1973 to 1980 or 1981, and 1980

Table 9. *Average Annual Growth Rates of Current Public Disbursements and of Real GDP, Four European Countries, 1961–84*[a]

Percent

Country and category	1961–73	1973–80[b]	1980–84
France			
Real current public disbursements ($\dot{g}$)	6.4	6.1	3.8
Real GDP ($\dot{y}$)	5.4	2.5	1.3
"Excess" ($\dot{g}-\dot{y}$)	1.0	3.6	2.5
Germany			
Real current public disbursements ($\dot{g}$)	6.5	4.7	1.6
Real GDP ($\dot{y}$)	4.4	2.2	0.8
"Excess" ($\dot{g}-\dot{y}$)	2.1	2.5	0.8
Sweden			
Real current public disbursements ($\dot{g}$)	7.4	6.8	2.6
Real GDP ($\dot{y}$)	4.1	1.5	2.2
"Excess" ($\dot{g}-\dot{y}$)	3.3	5.3	0.4
United Kingdom			
Real current public disbursements ($\dot{g}$)	4.3	6.1	3.1
Real GDP ($\dot{y}$)	3.3	3.1	1.3
"Excess" ($\dot{g}-\dot{y}$)	1.0	3.0	1.8

Sources: OECD, *National Accounts, 1961–78*, vol. 2: *Detailed Tables* (Paris: OECD, 1980), tables 1, 9; OECD, *National Accounts, 1971–83* and *1972–84*, vol. 2: *Detailed Tables*, tables 1, 6.

a. Public disbursements are total government spending less public capital formation. The implicit GDP deflator is used for all calculations.

b. For France and Sweden, 1973–81.

(or 1981) to 1984. I used 1980 to define the end of the second period for Germany and the United Kingdom because that is when growth in spending dropped sharply; I used 1981 for France and Sweden for the same reason. For all of the countries other than the United Kingdom, the growth rate of real disbursements was most rapid from 1961 to 1973; GDP also grew rapidly during this period, but not as rapidly as spending. From 1973 to the beginning of the 1980s, GDP growth fell sharply (except in Britain), and the growth of government spending fell, but less sharply (except in Britain, where it rose sharply). In consequence, the rate of growth of spending as a share of GDP accelerated in all four countries in the second period. However, only in the United Kingdom can this change be interpreted as an acceleration of growth in the "welfare state." In the three other cases, lower GDP growth is the primary cause. Finally, in the most recent period, all four countries have greatly reduced the growth rates of real spending, but continued deterioration in the growth of GDP (except in Sweden) has meant continuing increases in current spending as a share of GDP, albeit at slower rates than in the 1970s. To the extent that there is some political inertia underlying the rate at which government expenditures grow, the causal relationship between the relative size of government and the pace of economic growth may have run in the reverse direction after 1973 (which is not to deny the possibility of a simultaneous chain of causation running the other way).

Data for the period since 1984 are not strictly comparable to the data shown in table 8, because detailed national accounts are not yet available. Nonetheless, judging from various sources, both Germany and Sweden clearly have reduced their spending shares since 1984, while France and the United Kingdom have not. Using the OECD definition of expenditure (which, unlike that in tables 1 and 8 is not net of transfers and interest), Germany reduced spending by 2.0 percent of GNP between 1983 and 1986.[97] Sweden's budget shows a reduction in outlays during 1983–85 of 2.6 percent of GDP.[98] By contrast, the share of spending in GDP in France in 1985 was 0.3 percent higher than in 1983.[99] The U.K. budget for 1986–87 shows a reduction in spending as a share of GDP of 2 percentage points between 1984–85 and 1985–86. This is an estimate, however, and should be evaluated with some caution.[100]

The components of growth also vary a good deal by country. Some of the differences are definitional (for example, in France, social security covers a multitude of transfers), but some obviously reflect real policy changes. Strikingly, all four countries show one negative element of growth—public-sector capital formation (including net capital transfers). This suggests that the 1984 figures relative to 1971 are more troublesome than they look (and here, the same basic pattern holds for 1986). If 1971 shares of GDP devoted to net public-sector capital formation had obtained in 1983, expenditures as shares of GDP would have been 2.4 percentage points higher in Germany, 1.4 in France, 2.5 in the United Kingdom, and 2.4 in Sweden. These numbers, which are noticeable fractions of total capital formation in these countries (or any other), imply that if there is less crowding out because of lower public spending, then the effect is overstated because direct public investment is also lower.

97. *OECD Economic Surveys, 1985–86: Germany* (Paris: OECD, 1986), p. 11.
98. *OECD Economic Surveys, 1984–85: Sweden* (Paris: OECD, 1985), p. 57.
99. *OECD Economic Surveys, 1984–85: France* (Paris: OECD, 1985), p. 15.
100. Chancellor of the Exchequer, *Financial Statement and Budget Report, 1986–87* (London: HMSO, 1986), p. 55.

Germany had the smallest growth in total expenditures over the period, a conclusion that would be strengthened were data through 1985 or 1986 available on a basis consistent with those in table 8. The bulk of the growth is from the social security system, whose share of GDP rose by 5.2 percentage points. The central government increased expenditures over the period by only 1.6 percent of GDP, with reductions in final consumption and net capital accumulation being overbalanced by increases in transfers and interest payments. State (Länder) and local governments also reduced capital formation over the period, while increasing consumption, net interest, and transfers. But the major action (except for the reduced capital formation at all levels of government) is the increase in both transfers and consumption by the social security system. Much of the increase in transfers can presumably be accounted for by increases in unemployment. Regarding social security, the leading cause of growth found by the OECD for 1960–75 was an increase in real benefits per recipient, with demographic changes a close second. For 1975–81 real benefits alone declined, but coverage and demography produced growth.[101] For 1990 and beyond, as discussed earlier, demography will tend to expand social security spending.

France, which in 1971 spent slightly less than Germany as a fraction of GDP, has long since overtaken its neighbor. General government consumption spending as a share of GDP increased less in France than in the other countries, with the bulk of the 3 percentage point increase shared by local and central government. France, like the other countries, also increased net interest paid, and the reduction in government capital formation was smaller for France than for any of the other countries. By far the largest share of increased government spending is social security transfers, which rose from 13.1 percent to 21.6 percent of GDP. Social security in France has unusually broad coverage; I think, but have not been able to verify, that it is especially affected by increased unemployment because the unemployment compensation system is folded into the social security system. France also reduced the retirement age in 1983, but the bulk of the growth took place before that. The same OECD study cited above in the discussion of Germany attributes over half of the real growth in pension benefits from 1975 to 1980 to increases in average real benefits per recipient.

In the United Kingdom, the expenditure item that grew the most was

101. OECD, *Social Expenditure, 1960–1990: Problems of Growth and Control* (Paris: OECD, 1985), p. 30.

government consumption, with two-thirds of the increase coming from the central government. The United Kingdom also had the largest decrease in capital formation, and four-fifths of this decrease was at the local level. The United Kingdom had an unusually small increase in social security spending and an unusually large increase in other transfers to persons, with the central government accounting for almost three-quarters of the increase. Presumably, unemployment insurance accounts for a good deal of this last category.

The central government in the United Kingdom recently has devoted much attention to the growth of spending by local government, an issue that is covered in a recent Green Paper.[102] Although it is not phrased this way in the paper, the heart of the government's concern is that the median (or decisive) local voter faces a tax price for additional local expenditures that is much lower than the potential benefit that voter would receive from those expenditures. Indeed, in some extreme cases, the median local voter may face a tax price of zero, for two reasons: (1) as in the United States, a large fraction of local expenditure is financed by taxes on business and through intergovernmental grants, and (2) as in the United States (but more so in the United Kingdom), a large fraction of local taxpayers either pay no property tax directly or receive full or partial rebates for property taxes (called "domestic rates") paid. In the government's view, efforts to use the grant system to change incentives at the margin have been unsuccessful; even though in many cases the cost to the local authority is more than a pound for a pound's worth of goods or services, the cost to the decisive voter is still well below the benefits received because that voter may not pay any tax and in any event does not pay business tax.

With the avowed purpose of improving accountability, the Green Paper proposes that business property taxes (nondomestic rates) be set at the national level and disbursed to the localities according to a "needs-based" formula that does not include any local decision variables, leaving localities essentially no discretion in taxing local business; it also proposes that domestic rates be abolished and replaced with a poll tax (for which the euphemism is "community charge"). In this way voters would be accountable at the margin—all voters would pay and all revenue at the margin would come from the community charge.

It is impossible to evaluate the scheme here, but two things are worth

---

102. Cmnd. 9714, *Paying for Local Government* (London: HMSO, January 1986).

noting.[103] First, the basic structures of local government support (and, for that matter, the functions performed by local government) are similar in the United Kingdom and the United States, yet the problem identified in the United Kingdom does not appear to be present here. Indeed, local government is viewed by the U.S. "conservative" movement as a model for the entire public sector, and to the extent that there is concern on efficiency grounds with local taxation of business, it is that business is taxed too lightly because communities are competing for employment. I do not presume that the British have analyzed their own circumstances incorrectly. Rather, I infer that the structure of the British housing market (renters must see no tax for the Green Paper to make sense) and the "entrepreneurial" character of local governments in the United Kingdom must be very different from the corresponding features in the United States. Indeed, the attitudes of local governments toward business may have as much to do with economic growth in the two countries as conventional fiscal policy does. Second, for all of the structural problems identified in the Green Paper, the bulk of the growth in government consumption since 1971 has been at the central government level; indeed, the share of spending in GDP at the local level has fallen slightly. In light of all of this, partisan politics may be one explanation for the Green Paper—the central government is Conservative and many of the local councils are Labour.

Sweden has exhibited the largest growth in spending of the four countries over the 1971–84 period; Sweden would hold its rank through 1986 even with the recent spending reductions. There were three main sources of growth. The share of public consumption in GDP rose by 5.1 percentage points (a 6.0 point increase among local and regional governments and a 0.9 point decrease by the central government). And the increase in social security transfers and central government business subsidies amounted to 5.1 and 2.4 percent of GDP, respectively. Over the same period, the fraction of GDP represented by net interest payments rose by 3.2 percentage points, while the share going to net government capital formation fell by 2.4 percentage points, leaving a small net effect on the budget but a larger net effect on long-term growth. Since 1983 local government consumption has fallen slightly as a share of GDP, as have transfers to business and central government transfers to persons, while social security has continued to grow.[104]

103. See S. R. Smith and D. L. Squire, "The Local Government Green Paper," *Fiscal Studies*, vol. 7 (May 1986), for a discussion of some of its aspects.
104. Gramlich, "Rethinking the Role of the Public Sector," table 7-3. Swedish

With subsidies getting under control and transfers dealt with elsewhere in this volume, the interesting item is local government consumption, and here it is difficult to tell a straightforward story. Sweden has two levels of local government: the 23 county governments provide health services and a few minor functions; the 280 municipalities pay for schools, police and fire services, sanitation, roads, and so on. Between them, the two levels of local government account for 74 percent of government consumption and 21 percent of GDP. But much of what the local governments do is mandated by the central government, and more than a quarter of their revenues come from central government grants. (Their tax revenue is also collected by the central government, on a base defined by the central government. The local governments have some choice of tax rate.) The bulk of the grants are closed-end special purpose grants, which may affect the content of local spending but which have no substitution effects at the margin. Thus the grants probably substitute fairly well for income, and with nearly uniform tax rates across localities, little opportunity exists for Swedes to vote with their feet. In short, Sweden may have the problem addressed in the U.K. Green Paper to a far worse degree than Britain. In Sweden, unlike the United Kingdom, local spending has been rising rapidly and is much greater than central government spending; and in Sweden, again unlike the United Kingdom, formulas for intergovernmental grants contain no incentives to curb spending at the margin.

Finally, along with the highest ratio of public consumption to GDP among the four economies, Sweden also has the highest ratio of public employment to total employment. In 1982, 31.8 percent of Swedish employment was in the public sector, compared with 15.6 percent in Germany, 16.1 percent in France, and 22.4 percent in the United Kingdom. Moreover, the share in Sweden grew by more than 11 percentage points between 1970 and 1982, while the share in the other countries grew by 4.4, 2.7, and 4.4 percentage points, respectively.[105] The rapid growth of government employment in Sweden may be due in part to the way in which people in labor market programs are counted. Nonetheless, it lends some support to the contention, voiced by many Swedish academics, that efficiency would improve if activities such as

---

industrial policy has changed recently to move away from the subsidy route, so at least this element of the budget should continue to fall. Indeed, Sweden is about to leave the shipbuilding business, the proximate cause being the disappearance of the subsidy.

105. Saunders and Klau, *OECD Economic Studies: The Role of the Public Sector*, p. 63.

health provision and day care were to some extent privatized, preferably through a voucher system of some kind.

The Content of Government Consumption and National Consumption

The growth and levels of government spending differ a good deal across the four countries, and to sort out the content of all of the expenditure programs and their effect on economic growth would require the efforts of four Congressional Budget Offices. More to raise questions than to answer them, I show in table 10 as much national accounts detail as is available on the content of government consumption and total (public plus private) final consumption for each of the four countries in 1982, the most recent year for which data are available for all four.

Because the countries report their data in different ways, some of the broad categories are low on intuitive content, to say the least, but the overall message of table 10 is that private decisions seem to some extent to unwind public ones—public plus private final consumption is a good deal more similar across the countries than is either public or private consumption. This shows most clearly in the aggregate. Although Germany was well below the other countries, spending only 75.2 percent of GDP on consumption in 1982, the other three countries are within 0.4 percent of GDP of each other, with France the highest at 80.9 percent. *Public* consumption, on the other hand, was lower in France than in any of the others.

The one category of consumption for which the disaggregation in the table is easy to interpret shows the same lack of relationship between public and total consumption. France pays for health care through social security, unlike the other countries, which provide health services directly; total expenditures for health care in France are 8.8 percent of GDP, a share very close to that in Sweden, slightly above that in Germany, and well above that in the United Kingdom, which finances a good fraction of its health care through queuing. To push the point further, the United States, with a smaller share of direct government spending on health than any of these countries, devotes a larger share of GNP to the sector than any of them. None of the other categories in which there are both public and private consumption are very easy to interpret, but it remains the case that the largest subaggregates (the first

Table 10. Public and Total Consumption, Four European Countries, 1982
Percent of GDP

Consumption category	France Public	France Total	Germany Public	Germany Total	Sweden Public	Sweden Total	United Kingdom Public	United Kingdom Total
Necessities, social security, and welfare	1.2	19.1	2.0	20.9	5.0	21.7	1.5	21.0
Food	0.0	13.7	0.0	14.0	0.0	12.9	0.0	15.6
Clothing	0.0	4.2	0.0	4.9	0.0	3.7	0.0	3.9
Social security and welfare	1.2	1.2	1.8	2.0	5.0	5.0	1.5	1.5
Housing, community development, fuel and energy, economic services	2.1	28.0	1.3	26.5	2.0	27.5	2.0	28.5
Housing, community development	n.a.	n.a.	0.3	13.9	0.5	14.7	0.7	14.0
Fuel and energy	n.a.	n.a.	0.0	3.0	n.a.	n.a.	0.1	3.2
Transportation and communication	0.4	9.5	0.6	9.2	n.a.	n.a.	0.6	10.6
Other economic services	n.a.	n.a.	0.3	0.3	n.a.	n.a.	0.7	0.7
Total less transportation and communication	1.6	18.6	...	...	...	...	...	...
Total less fuel and energy	...	...	...	...	1.5	12.8	...	...
Health and medical	0.5	8.8	6.2	7.5	7.5	8.7	4.8	5.4
Education, recreation and culture	5.9	10.2	4.6	8.9	7.6	12.7	4.8	10.3
Education	5.3	5.5	n.a.	n.a.	6.0	6.1	4.3	4.8
Recreation and culture	0.6	4.7	n.a.	n.a.	1.6	6.7	0.5	5.5
Public safety	0.9	0.9	1.6	1.6	0.0	0.0	1.6	1.6
Defense	3.5	3.5	2.8	2.8	3.0	3.0	5.2	5.2
General public services	2.1	2.1	2.1	2.1	3.8	3.8	1.1	1.1
Other government	0.1	0.1	0.0	0.0	0.2	0.2	0.0	0.0
Other private	0.0	8.1	0.0	4.8	0.0	3.2	0.0	7.3
Total	**16.2**	**80.9**	**20.4**	**75.2**	**29.1**	**80.8**	**21.0**	**80.5**

Sources: For France, Germany, and Sweden, OECD, *National Accounts, 1971–83*, vol. 2: *Detailed Tables*, tables 1, 2; and unpublished OECD data. For the United Kingdom, *United Kingdom National Accounts, 1985 Edition* (London: Her Majesty's Stationery Office, 1985), tables 9.4, 4.8.
n.a. Not available.

three categories in table 10) show essentially no relationship between public consumption and total consumption.

The tendency for broad categories of final consumption to be more similar to each other than public consumption in the four countries can be interpreted in a number of ways. It provides weak confirmation of the hypothesis that the private sector tends to compensate for what the public sector does. One could argue, then, that over the fairly large range of differences in public consumption shown in table 10, it simply does not make much difference whether consumption is private or public.[106] If this is so, most economists (and certainly all the Swedish economists with whom I have discussed the subject) would argue that consumption goods and services, especially potentially private ones such as health, day care, and (possibly) education, should be privately provided because markets are likely to lead to greater efficiency. Moreover, insofar as such goods are publicly provided, they should be financed at least in part through user fees. It is hard to quarrel with the argument, but it is also hard to see much obvious relationship between government consumption and final consumption, or between government consumption and economic growth.

Budget Reform?

I would like to end this discussion of public spending with a "hit list" of programs that could be reduced without much ill effect—programs that achieve little or are redundant. Unfortunately, I do not have enough information about program content in these countries to do so. I note that subsidies to industry and agriculture, some of which are undoubtedly in the form of capital transfers, are a likely target.[107] Although much of the attention to this subject has focused on Germany, the consensus is that Germany is not unusual relative to the European economies as a whole. Information on the quantity and effectiveness of subsidies is fragmentary and generally not comparable across countries. Moreover, many subsidies are in the form of tax expenditures, which are intrinsically difficult to define. Having said all this, I note that estimates by the European Community of the volume of subsidies in France, Germany,

---

106. Of course, it may matter a great deal in the distribution of consumer goods and service—who gets to consume how much.

107. *European Economy*, no. 22 (November 1984), pp. 44–51; and *OECD Economic Surveys, 1985–86: Germany*, p. 17, and table 4.

and the United Kingdom imply that the potential effect on budgets in all three countries is nontrivial. The estimates exclude agricultural subsidies and, given the nature of the exercise, they surely missed some nonagricultural subsidies; even so, the EC studies find that subsides in 1983 were about 1.4 percent of GDP in Germany, 2 percent in France, and 2.3 percent in the United Kingdom, with the last figure lower by now because of changes in corporate taxes.[108]

Another potential source of reductions in spending by central governments is aid to local governments. Gramlich's thesis, now standard in public finance discussions of fiscal federalism, is that efficiency theoretically would be enhanced if subsidies to local governments were restricted to cases in which there are benefit spillovers.[109] In Sweden, notes Gramlich, there is little justification for lump-sum grants to localities, since the public sector is already engaged in a wide variety of redistributive programs that act directly on individuals rather than on their local governments. Given the range of transfer programs that exist in all of these countries, the same general argument may apply and is obviously worth examining in detail. (It applies less to France than to the others, because there is so little local autonomy in French local government to begin with.) I do not know the mix of lump-sum and matching grants in the various countries, but I would be surprised to discover that the efficiency implications of grant programs in these countries were any more positive than they are in the United States, where most grants act like income transfers to local governments; such a policy is hard to justify in the United States and probably even harder to justify in Europe, where redistribution is one of the primary activities of the central government.

Identifying two broad program areas that should be examined for reduction is far short of producing a detailed list of the kind that the Congressional Budget Office produces for the United States every year. Moreover, the two areas I have identified here are high on (almost) any economist's list for the United States as well. Given their scope, transfer

108. Commission of the European Communities, Directorate-General for Economic and Financial Affairs, "Government Invervention in the Enterprise Sector (Industry and Services) in the Federal Republic of Germany," November 13, 1985; "Government Intervention in the Enterprise Sector in France," December 10, 1985; "Government Intervention in the Industry and Service Sector of the U.K. Economy," November 13, 1985. The Kiel Institute has much larger estimates for Germany, but also a much broader definition of subsidies. See OECD Economic Surveys, 1985–86: Germany, p. 24.

109. Gramlich, "Rethinking the Role of the Public Sector," p. 283.

programs in the European countries are presumably more redundant than those in the United States. If so, reducing the magnitude of such programs could increase efficiency with little consequence for equity and would also permit some combination of smaller structural deficits and lower marginal tax rates. Again, Gramlich has documented some of these possibilities for Sweden, and it is almost certain that similar opportunities exist for the other countries as well. It is much less clear, however, that the scope and content of public consumption makes much difference for economic growth. The relationship between public consumption and total consumption is hard to find (table 10), and although there are undoubtedly cases in which "privatization" would enhance efficiency, the magnitudes involved are simply unknown. Moreover, Sweden, which has by far the most developed public sector of any of these countries, does not have anything like the most advanced case of Eurosclerosis.

Writing about budget policy in this way reminds me of an experience that I had some years ago when I was on the staff of the Council of Economic Advisers. I was in charge of organizing a chapter of the *Economic Report of the President* on structural changes that could improve the performance of the economy, which was then in a state of stagflation. Although the chapter had a more respectable title when published, those of us who worked on it dubbed the piece "nickel and diming inflation to death." Identifying reforms of the public sectors in these four economies that are worth at least a careful look has much the same feel as the writing of that chapter. All of the reforms have the right sign, but even taken all together, they are unlikely to cause large improvements in growth in either the long or the short term.[110]

Conclusions

If Eurosclerosis is the problem that motivates this volume, the only way in which fiscal policy can be assigned a leading role as the cause of

---

110. This leads me to speculate on what might be decisive. In comparing the four countries through the informal sociological research method of riding subways and talking to people in bars, I found the person on the street in Stockholm was plainly much better educated and much more sympathetic to technical change than was the person on the street in London. Much of this paper has been about the effect of public-sector behavior on physical capital accumulation. I wonder, however, whether the real issue is not human capital accumulation.

the problem is through the mechanisms discussed in Mancur Olson's book: much of the growth in the size of government is associated with the ability of various interest groups to organize the economy in ways that protect their position, generally by making the system less responsive to innovation and change; this phenomenon makes fiscal policy both a cause and a symptom of the problem.[111] By the same token, restructuring of the "social contract" in ways that would leave markets more flexible would certainly involve reduction in the size of government, and this change in fiscal policy would be both a cause and a symptom of the cure. But the fundamental changes involved are political and social— changes in the size and content of government budgets would in some sense be going along for the ride.

Less speculatively, one notes that since 1980 fiscal policy has played a direct role in reducing short-term growth in these European countries (except in Sweden, where exchange rate policy has played an important role)—that is, in preventing the attainment of a growth path near to the growth path of potential GDP. Unless hysteresis is at work, however, this recent episode probably has only a relatively small effect on the growth of potential itself, and the budgetary consolidations in Germany and Sweden, which are both explicitly investment oriented, should have positive effects on future growth.[112] In any case, whether or not one is disposed to advocate fiscal stimulus in the current environment, stabilization policy of the last half-decade is not the primary cause of lower growth rates over the long haul, although it may be a major cause of recent poor performance.

If fiscal policy's role as part of the problem is uncertain, its potential role as part of the solution is clearer, and may be summarized as follows.

—National savings and investment rates have fallen in all four countries in the last fifteen years, and government has been a major cause, both directly (through public-sector accumulation) and indirectly (through public saving). Thus, in figure 1, the general downward slope of all the curves is as important as the relationships among them.[113] There

---

111. Olson, *Rise and Decline of Nations.*

112. The effects will be weaker than those associated with the increase in government net lending because in both countries some of the consolidation has been at the expense of public-sector capital accumulation.

113. Having made much of public-sector accumulation throughout this paper, I cannot resist telling a story that tends to leave one a little skeptical of its value. When in Stockholm, I visited the Wasa museum, which houses a warship that sank in the

is thus a strong argument for government to be a net contributor to capital formation; because of the arithmetic of national debt and interest payments, the longer this is postponed, the more difficult it will be.

—Therefore, any fiscal stimulus to demand should be explicitly temporary, and even the case for temporary stimulus is weak unless hysteresis in labor markets is important. The appropriate candidate for such stimulus is debt-financed public investment. Over the longer term, whether or not there is to be a short-term fiscal expansion, a shift in the policy mix toward tighter budgets and looser money would be the best means to improve longer term growth.

—Throughout the period under study, taxes on capital have been falling (this has just been reversed in the United Kingdom), suggesting that tax incentives to stimulate investment overall are not likely to be an effective means of raising investment in particular or demand in general.

—Quite independent of the appropriate macroeconomic stance of fiscal policy, there appears to be a good deal of potential for reform of both taxation and spending. The link between tax structure and growth is of uncertain strength, but there is room in all of these countries to lower tax rates while broadening the tax base, and there is room in all of them to remove tax-induced misallocations of capital while holding revenue from capital taxes constant. If overall revenue is held constant, there is simply an efficiency gain, no small thing in itself. Equally important, broader tax bases would allow all of these countries to increase the level of public saving at lower average and marginal efficiency costs than those that are imposed by the current systems. On the spending side, given the level of transfers in all of these economies, it seems likely that programs can be reconfigured in ways that would have approximately the same distributional effect as the current struc-tures (if that is what is desired) but involve fewer resources flowing through government. I do not know this to be true except for Sweden, for which Gramlich has documented the case, but the possibility is surely worth a careful look.

I offer all these conclusions with some trepidation. Traveling in

---

early seventeenth century. In a short film on the Wasa, the narrator explained that the monarchy at the time was worried about a potential shortage of wood for future warships and therefore had planted (circa 1625) a number of stands of the right kind of oak. These stands are now ready to harvest. The rate of return on this particular public investment, ex post, seems to have been a bit low, as oak is not used much for submarines. On the other hand, for all I know, the public investment portfolio of 1625 was well diversified, and other elements in it yielded very high returns.

Europe and discussing these issues with Europeans made it clear to me that the differences among societies and economies are enormous. I trust that anyone who reads this paper will try to take account of such differences among the social and political environments in interpreting my conclusions. At best, the discussion here provides a list of things to be looked at with care in the context of the individual countries.

Comment by Willem H. Buiter

Courant's interesting paper asks four broad questions. (1) Has fiscal policy contributed to the slowdown in growth in Europe? (2) Can reform of fiscal policy contribute to an improvement in growth? (3) Can fiscal policy be used for cyclical stabilization policy, should it be, and how does it affect growth? (4) Are European governments solvent or, more precisely, are their cyclically corrected tax and expenditure plans consistent with solvency?

While Courant makes no attempt to quantify the contribution (actual or potential) of fiscal policy to growth, he recognizes the many dimensions of fiscal policy and the many channels through which it can affect economic performance. Recapitulating and expanding his argument slightly, one can say that on the spending side both the volume and the structure or composition of "exhaustive" spending (spending on currently produced goods and services), now and expected in the future, are potentially important. The distinction between public consumption and public-sector capital formation, however difficult in practice (for example, in the case of education), matters for growth; so does the breakdown of current spending between wages and salaries on the one hand and the procurement of goods and services on the other. Much of what is classified as public consumption should, of course, not be counted as value added at all. Law and order, defense, and so on, are intermediate inputs into the production of private and public final goods and services. Their contribution is already counted in the value of these final goods and should not be counted again separately.

The level and structure of taxation, other revenues, subsidies, and transfer payments have important effects, as does the choice between borrowing and domestic credit expansion to finance the public-sector deficit.

The plan of this comment is as follows. In the first section I ask whether the European growth problem is unique (answer: no). The second section discusses the distinction between the effects of fiscal policy on the level of output and the effects on the growth rate of output. In the third section I point out that welfare-improving measures discussed by Courant need not raise growth. The fourth section considers some further issues concerning government solvency, and the fifth discusses how the concern for solvency limits the use of fiscal policy for stabilization.

Is There a Uniquely European Growth Problem?

Before turning to the issues raised by Courant's paper, I would like to dispute the view, apparently shared by the organizers of this conference, that European *growth* is in need of special attention and uniquely requires raising. A look at the data suggests that what singles out the European experience and differentiates it from the Japanese and U.S. experiences is the employment and unemployment record, not the growth record.

Since 1980, the average annual growth rate of real per capita GDP (as approximated by the annual growth differential between real GDP and population) has been equally miserable in the twelve-member European Community (just under 1.2 percent) and in the United States (just over 1.1 percent). The 3.3 percent average achieved by Japan since 1980 is, of course, considerably higher but constitutes a marked decline relative to its pre-OPEC growth rate. From 1961 to 1973 the average annual growth differential was 8.5 percent for Japan, 4.0 percent for Europe, and 2.8 percent for the United States.[114] Thus, as regards growth rate deceleration since those halcyon pre-1974 days, the problem is most severe for Japan, followed by Europe, with the United States experiencing the smallest decline. When the levels of the growth rates of the three areas are compared, the United States was at bottom in the past and is at bottom today, although the countries of the EC almost match its current dismal performance.

A strikingly different picture emerges when one considers the behavior of employment and unemployment. From 1980 to 1986 employment in

114. "Annual Economic Review, 1986–1987," *European Economy*, no. 29 (July 1986), pp. 141, 144.

Europe declined by 1.8 percent. In the United States it grew by 10.7 percent and in Japan by 6.3 percent. With due allowance for differences in population growth rates, participation rates, and so on, these differences in employment behavior are reflected in the differences in unemployment rates. Until 1981 the European unemployment rate was uniformly below that in the United States, sometimes quite significantly. Now the situation is reversed. The U.S. unemployment rate has come down significantly from its cyclical high in 1982 and 1983 and now appears stuck in the 6 to 7 percent region; in contrast, the European rate now stands at about 11 percent, with little prospect of a significant reduction in the near term. The low Japanese rate (despite some recent increases) reflects unique institutions and mechanisms for employment and work sharing and is not easily comparable with the U.S. and European rates as a measure of the underutilization of labor.

The major anomaly that needs to be explained is the difference between the European and U.S. employment records. There is also a severe European growth problem, but there is an even more severe growth problem in the United States and in Japan. It is the unemployment problem whose severity is uniquely European.

Level Effects versus Trend Rate Effects

In few if any conventional models dealing with long-run growth does fiscal policy have a permanent effect on the rate of growth of output. The trend rate of growth of potential output is constrained from above by the trend rate of growth of the nonreproducible factor of production with the lowest growth rate, when this trend rate of growth includes the trend rate of factor augmentation due to technical progress. In this framework, fiscal policy can influence the trend rate of growth of potential output only by influencing technical change or, if the labor force is the limiting factor of production, by influencing the trend growth rate of the labor force. Courant offers no evidence on this matter, so it seems safe to infer that he does not attribute to fiscal policy any significant effect on the trend growth rate of potential output.

Fiscal policy can, in the standard macroeconomic models, have an effect on the level of the path of potential output. In the simple, closed economy, two-factor growth models of Solow and Swan and in more recent optimizing versions of these models, fiscal policy influences saving and investment in the short run and wealth and the capital-labor ratio in the longer run.

Fiscal policy can affect private capital formation through a number of channels. There can be "direct" crowding out or crowding in of private capital formation by public capital formation, which can occur through the direct substitutability or complementarity of public- and private-sector capital in private production. Even without any direct complementarity or substitutability, fiscal policy actions may influence private behavior by changing prices or quantity constraints, or both, as they are perceived by private agents—"indirect" crowding out or crowding in. For example, even balanced-budget increases in public spending can, in a number of models, raise real interest rates. Distortionary taxes that raise the marginal cost of capital (at a given real interest rate) are another example. Finally, in models without debt neutrality, variations in the timing of lump-sum taxation and borrowing, for a given path of exhaustive public spending, will influence private saving and investment. Although Courant's paper recognizes most of these channels, it presents no empirical evidence, new or old, that allows one to assess their empirical significance.

These *level* effects will, in general, be spread out over time. During the transition from a low-level path to a high-level path, the rate of change or growth rate of real output must, by force of arithmetic, temporarily increase.

With finite samples and noisy data, the decomposition of time series behavior into level and change effects is a tricky and imprecise business. Twenty years of "temporarily" higher growth may well look like a permanent increase in the growth rate for most practical purposes. It is, however, good discipline and a useful safeguard against logical pitfalls to keep the two separate.

Measures That Improve Welfare Need Not Improve Growth (and Vice Versa)

The author presents an impressive (and depressing) array of evidence on distortions caused by the taxation and transfer-subsidy sides of European budgets. No doubt such distortions may affect the choices between labor and leisure, between consumption and saving, and between domestic capital formation and foreign investment; it may also affect the allocation of domestic capital formation between types of capital, sectors, regions, and so on.

As regards the normative implications of these distortions, the omnipresent swamp of "second best" prevents one from being confident about the consequences for welfare of reducing or eliminating them. As regards the positive economics, it is not at all clear whether their net result, relative to a nondistorted benchmark, is to reduce labor supply and saving or to bias the allocation of saving toward foreign investment. Reducing or eliminating these distortions might therefore not have the hoped-for effect of raising labor supply, saving, and domestic capital formation. Little is known, and the paper gives no evidence about the direction and magnitude of these effects in Europe. Any effects would, in all likelihood, be level effects rather than permanent growth rate effects.

GOVERNMENT SOLVENCY. The solvency constraint on the government's spending, taxation, and domestic credit expansion plans is a very weak one. In the simple closed economy of equation 3, let b be the government interest-bearing debt-GDP ratio, s the government's primary (non-interest) surplus as a percentage of GDP, m the high-powered money-GDP ratio, μ the proportional rate of growth of base money, i the real instantaneous interest rate, and g the growth rate of real GDP. The government's solvency constraint given in equation 4 is obtained from the government budget, provided the transversality condition in equation 5 is satisfied.

$$(3) \qquad\qquad \dot{b} \equiv -s + (i - g)b - \mu m$$

$$(4) \quad b(t) = \int_t^\infty s(v)e^{-\int_t^v [i(u) - g(u)]du}\, dv + \int_t^\infty \mu(v)m(v)e^{-\int_t^v [i(u) - g(u)]du}\, dv$$

$$(5) \qquad\qquad \lim_{\tau \to \infty} b(\tau)e^{-\int_t^\tau [i(u) - g(u)]du} = 0.$$

Equation 4 states that the outstanding debt equals the present value of future primary surpluses s and future seigniorage μm. Sooner or later the debt is serviced by running primary surpluses or by printing money. For this to hold, equation 5 must be satisfied. Equation 5 says that, *ultimately*, the growth rate of real debt must be smaller than the real interest rate or that the growth rate of the debt-GDP ratio must be less than the real interest rate minus the growth rate of real income. From equation 3 it follows that

(6)
$$\frac{\dot{b}}{b} = (i - g) - \frac{[s + \mu m]}{b}$$

Equation 5 means that ultimately $(\dot{b}/b) < (i - g)$; that is, there must be primary surpluses or monetization: $s + \mu m > 0$. Equations 5 and 4 do not by themselves imply that the debt-GDP ratio must remain bounded. In models by McCallum and Obstfeld the debt-output ratio could grow without bound while solvency is preserved.[115] This knife-edge case can occur if the entire amount of debt interest paid to government debt holders can be taxed away in a lump-sum manner. If only distortionary taxes exist or if other obstacles bar a forever-growing tax burden (such as rising collection costs or political limits on the tax burden), then equations 4 and 5 do indeed imply a finite upper bound on the debt-output ratio.

As I have shown in a number of places, planned public-sector capital formation will increase (reduce) public-sector net worth if the cash rate of return to the government on this investment exceeds (falls short of) the marginal cost of public-sector borrowing.[116] The relevant returns are direct and indirect cash returns to the government. The social rate of return per se is irrelevant for these solvency calculations if it is not reflected in an enhanced flow of resources to the government. Even worthwhile projects must be financed, and the cost-benefit analysis of any project should allow for the current or deferred cost of financing.

To evaluate the solvency of the European governments, Courant asks which value of the primary surplus will hold the debt-GDP ratio at its current level. From equation 3 this is easily seen to be

(7)
$$s^* = (i - g)b - \mu m.$$

For simplicity, seigniorage is omitted from Courant's calculations. In

115. Bennett T. McCallum, "Are Bond-Financed Deficits Inflationary? A Ricardian Analysis," *Journal of Political Economy*, vol. 92 (February 1984), pp. 123–35; and Maurice Obstfeld, "Speculative Attack and the External Constraint in a Maximizing Model of the Balance of Payments," *Canadian Journal of Economics*, vol. 19 (February 1986), pp. 1–22.

116. See, for example, Willem H. Buiter, "A Guide to Public Sector Debt and Deficits," *Economic Policy*, no. 1 (November 1985), pp. 14–79.

developed countries, this is unlikely to be misleading, as the velocity of circulation of high-powered money is very high (for example, in the United Kingdom, $m = 0.05$). Recently, the high-powered money growth rate in the United Kingdom has been between 5 and 6 percent a year, implying seigniorage equal to 0.25 or 0.30 percent of GDP only. Assuming values for $i - g$ of 0.02 and 0.04, Courant then calculates s^* for a number of European countries. These benchmark primary surpluses needed to keep the debt-GDP ratio constant are then compared with the current primary deficit and the current structural primary deficit. However, Courant's purposes require not the current primary deficit but the *permanent* primary deficit, s^p say; that is, that constant value of s whose present value (using $i - g$ as discount rates) equals the present value of the actual future planned or expected primary deficits. If $s^* > s^p$, then the government's fiscal plans are not consistent, and sooner or later measures will be required to adjust the primary surplus path upward. Cyclical corrections may offer a tentative first step in calculating the permanent deficit, but it is likely to be far too myopic: for example, demographic changes may cause predictable future changes in spending or receipts that are not at all captured by the usual structural deficit corrections.

Note that there is nothing uniquely interesting about the current debt-GDP ratio. One could use equation 7 for any constant debt-GDP ratio, above or below the current one. Indeed, while solvency in the presence of distortionary taxes sets a finite upper bound on the debt-GDP ratio, it does not require this ratio ever to become constant. Equation 7 is a restriction on equations 4 and 5 that is motivated by convenience but not dictated by the need for solvency.

Constraints on the Use of Fiscal Policy for Stabilization

What are the constraints on the use of fiscal policy for stabilization policy? I will restrict the analysis to possible obstacles to a fiscal stimulus. The first constraint could be a solvency constraint, which does not look like a very serious problem. European debt-GDP ratios have been rising through the 1980s, but the increase is slowing down and has indeed already been reversed in Germany and Denmark. The levels of the debt–annual GDP ratios at the end of 1985 were 31.8 percent for France, 42.7 percent for Germany, 103 percent for Italy, and 56.9 percent for the

United Kingdom.[117] While these ratios bear watching, especially in the case of Italy, they are hardly a paralyzing albatross around the neck of fiscal stabilization policy.

If any fiscal stimulus were to create a fear of government insolvency, one would be likely to see both an increase in the price of credit (reflecting default risk premiums) and a reduction in its availability through rationing. Severe financial crowding out would result. Such a fear would, however, be irrational, unless any fiscal stimulus and deficit increase are perceived as irreversible and therefore permanent. Recent experience alone in Europe gives the lie to this fear: spending has been cut and taxes have been raised. On many occasions in the postwar period, European countries have adopted contractionary fiscal policies for cyclical purposes.

True, the greater the credibility of the government's announcements about the reversibility of the countercyclical deficits, the less will be the upward pressure on long-term interest rates. Fiscally conservative governments will, therefore, be able to use countercyclical fiscal (and monetary) policy more effectively than governments with a reputation for paying less attention to longer-run solvency.

The second kind of constraints are international spillover constraints. Current account deficits tend to result from unilateral expansionary fiscal action. The solution to this problem is concerted fiscal action—macroeconomic policy coordination.

The third constraint is the presence of real resource constraints. Clearly, if the economy is at full employment or if all unemployment is frictional, structural, and classical, then fiscal policy is incapable of influencing the level of economic activity except through the real exchange rate and through the non-lump-sum character of actual taxes. However, fiscal policy can still affect the composition of demand and the current account.

It would be depressing to have to conclude that 11 percent unemployment is Europe's stabilization-policy-invariant natural rate. One challenge to this view is the hysteresis hypothesis, according to which there would be scope for an attack on the actual, history-dependent natural unemployment rate through expansionary policy, including fiscal policy. In some versions of this theory only unanticipated policy (or other shocks) can move the natural rate, but there is no logical necessity for

117. "Annual Economic Report, 1986–87," *European Economy*, no. 30 (November 1986), p. 53.

that. Even without subscribing to the hysteresis hypothesis in its extreme form, it seems likely that expansionary demand measures by themselves can achieve some durable gains in employment. This would call for a fiscal stimulus on top of the restructuring of public spending and taxation that is already under way—a busy fiscal agenda.

Conclusion

What has been the broad pattern of behavior of the important fiscal aggregates in Europe over the last twenty years and what have been its implications for the full-employment path of output? Exhaustive public consumption spending has increased somewhat as a percentage of GDP but not by much, and the upward trend has been reversed recently. Ignoring cyclical aspects, permanent, tax-financed increases in public consumption spending should not have any effect on the rate of capital accumulation and the growth rate.

Public-sector investment has declined as a proportion of GDP. If this had been reflected in a reduction in government borrowing, it would have made private investment higher and the current account deficit of the balance of payments lower than it would otherwise have been. In addition, there may have been adverse direct crowding out. Total national capital formation was reduced almost surely by these cuts in public-sector capital formation. The effect of this reduction on output depends on the relative rates of return of public and private capital formation. I know of no estimates of the marginal products of public and private capital for the European economies.

Transfers, tax expenditures, and subsidies grew rapidly. As a portion of GDP they now have stabilized or are subject to small cuts. No effect on the full-employment path of private investment should be expected from this change, except as it added to government deficits or influenced the cost of capital (at a given real interest rate) through the non-lump-sum nature of the taxes raised to finance the outlays.

Other useful measures of the size of government are lacking, including government employment and, perhaps most important, a measure of government "intrusiveness" through rules and regulations. A government could smother the private sector in red tape without being large as measured by spending share.

Economic theory and what little empirical evidence we have do not lead us to expect significant changes in capital formation and growth from the fiscal policy changes observed in Europe since the 1960s. Furthermore, the pictures presented by different European countries, both in terms of fiscal developments and growth, are distinct; this is clear in the paper and even more so when one considers some of the countries left out (such as Italy, the Netherlands, Belgium, Ireland, Switzerland, and Austria). There continue to be widely different levels and compositions of spending, widely different levels and structures of taxation, and widely different levels of public debt and deficits.

If there is such a thing as Eurosclerosis (and I don't subscribe to the naive "nothing moves in Europe" variant of this characterization of the current European experience), its roots are not in a common fiscal experience, nor is there likely to be a common fiscal cure.

Comment by Gerald Holtham

Paul Courant's statement about fiscal policy as a tool of macroeconomic stabilization needs underlining. He asserts that the strength of the case for some temporary fiscal stimulus in Europe depends on the extent to which there is "hysteresis" in European labor markets; that is, the extent to which a temporary demand stimulus could lead to a permanent reduction in unemployment. I agree with that so much that I am reminded of a remark by the late, great Bill Shankly, who was the manager of Liverpool, the most successful U.K. soccer team: "Some people say football is a matter of life and death, but I don't hold with that kind of talk. It's far more important than that."

The point needs to be made particularly in the United States. I had always thought of the United States as the home of the neoclassical synthesis, a place where the macroeconomic model of choice would be one in which the economy was assumed to have a long-run equilibrium path determined by the growth of the labor force and the growth of technically determined productivity. Such a model would also have a NAIRU determined by microeconomic factors. All of those things would be substantially invariant to what the government did with demand management policy. Yet because prices are sticky, the system would have Keynesian short-run dynamics. Imagine my surprise, then, on coming to the United States and finding graduates of the University of Chicago urging European economies to use fiscal stimulus to get rid of unemployment—unemployment that has persisted for five years and shows every indication of persisting for another five. If the standard model is right, how can such durable unemployment be a stabilization issue?

Consider the situation in Germany, for example. If you tell the Germans to stimulate their economy through demand management while you simultaneously believe that their economy has a unique and stable equilibrium, then you are asking them to engage in an astonishing piece of fine tuning. Just reflect on some numbers. Richard Layard, for example, estimates that the German NAIRU is some 1½ percentage points below actual unemployment.[118] We know that result is obtained by estimating a nominal wage equation. The standard errors on the estimated coefficients of such an equation are such that t-values never exceed 3. The NAIRU is a nonlinear combination of those coefficients so only heaven knows what the standard error on the estimated NAIRU is. It gets worse. What is trend labor productivity growth in Germany these days? And how fast will the economy grow next year? Not long ago it was fashionable to forecast 4 percent; the IMF was saying 3½ percent; now 2½ percent seems more like the consensus. What is the standard error on that forecast of 2½? From my experience at the OECD, where these things are done better, if anything, than average, I would guess the standard error was about 1½ percentage points. So how long will it take the German economy to reach an unknown NAIRU growing at an annual rate somewhere between 1 and 4 percent? No wonder the German government is nervous.

It seems to me that the Germans have every right to ask an American economist urging a fiscal stimulus, "Are you sure that the German economy has a unique equilibrium?" If the answer is yes, the next question is, "Are you sure it's stable?" If the answer is again yes, the only thing left to say is, "Close the door on your way out."

One can, of course, write down a model in which optimal policies are jumping around in response to stochastic shocks that hit the economy. But the real-world application of that is restricted to massive shocks like oil crises. Routine shocks do not move the major variables of the economy outside the limits of forecast error and uncertainty about the NAIRU— assuming it exists. Unless the economics profession has been talking nonsense about a vertical Phillips curve, it is difficult to make a cogent case against the current conduct of fiscal policy in Germany and some other European countries.

---

118. Layard and others, "Europe: The Case for Unsustainable Growth," p. 47.

Now suppose the economy is characterized by multiple equilibriums. It is then possible to be trapped at a level of output that is lower than necessary because of internally consistent expectations of output, a level at which the supposedly automatic mechanisms of stabilization working through real interest rates and real wages work slowly or not at all. Even then it is not clear that fiscal policy can effect the transition from the path of low output to that of high output, given all the difficulties with credibility and expectations of inflation to which Buiter referred. Nonetheless, perhaps it could succeed. Only if one is prepared to argue for such a characterization can a cogent case against current German fiscal policy be made.

I am not sure what I believe. I am sufficiently cautious to be nervous of the school that says "turn on the tap and hope." Yet it seems obvious that there are phases in business activity that are much more than brief stochastic disturbances to an immutable supply-drive path. And one need not spend a long time in Lorraine or South Wales to lose patience with talk of expectational errors or rigid real wages.

These reflections are rather inconclusive, but I hope they provoke people either to come out of the Keynesian closet or to shut up about fiscal stimulus. It is a vice for one to recommend to politicians policies that are incompatible with one's classroom teachings.

My other remark is on the topic of wage subsidies. In his comments on the Krugman paper, Armin Gutowski suggested that government taxes on wages, which have driven a wedge between take-home pay and wage costs to the employer, should be eased. I would go further. What is the shadow price for labor in an economy like the United Kingdom? Unemployment there would be around 15 percent if the definition had not been changed. The United Kingdom has had that kind of unemployment for a long time and will have something like it for a long time to come. I would argue that an estimate of the shadow price of nonspecialist labor over large areas of the country can be approximated by subtracting average unemployment benefits from the average wage and subtracting average income tax payments from what is left. The resulting shadow wage is about a third of what employers, including the government, are actually paying.

This means that if it were possible to pay a marginal employment subsidy, targeted at workers coming into employment from the unemployment register, it would be possible to subsidize some two-thirds of their wage costs with no real resource cost and no immediate budgetary cost either. Such a policy would, however, lessen the improvement in the government budget deficit as the economy moved toward full employment.

I am aware that precise targeting of marginal workers is impracticable. There is experience in some countries of paying wage subsidies—in Sweden and France, for example, where they are used as an instrument of regional policy. The conventional reading of that experience is that the net effects on output and employment are small because of associated labor churning and displacement as well as fiscal effects. There are large effects on the structure of employment, many of them benign, but little effect, it is said, on the level of employment.

However, if the shadow wage is only a third of the actual wage and unemployment is going to persist for five years—and I do not know anyone who thinks is is not—one could pay prospective employers a lump sum equal to half the present value of five years' wages when they hire someone from the unemployment register. I say one-half, not two-thirds, to make some allowance for churning and cheating. The French subsidies are on nothing like that scale. So despite the undramatic results of wage subsidies to date, I do not believe that all the possibilities have been exploited.

I had the experience of discussing this notion with policymakers from different European countries, and they were generally rather alarmed by it. Some began to ask why employers would take on even cheap labor if there were no more . . . they were about to say "demand" but realized that the statement would not be proper. Most of these policymakers settled for denouncing "artificial" employment. When asked for clarification, they would say, "Subsidies would stop the real wage from falling to the point where unemployment is genuinely reduced as the market clears."

That brings one right back to the position that if the problem is going to abolish itself, then, of course, one does not need to do anything. There is unquestionably a lingering feeling in Europe that the problem should abolish itself, and if it does not, perhaps it is not a problem. It is hard to refute such fatalism while promulgating theoretical models of a world where fatalism is the appropriate attitude. Which is where I came in.

General Discussion

The fundamental barrier to using fiscal policy in Europe, according to one participant, is that European economic officials believe such policies are ineffective, that, contrary to the Keynesian view, they change the composition but not the level of aggregate demand (except, perhaps, in the very short run). They lead not only to government borrowing that crowds out private investment but also to exchange rate crowding out, which occurs because fiscal expansion causes currency appreciation and a trade deficit.

Another commentator said that European policymakers perceive an external constraint imposed by attitudes in the financial markets: fiscal expansion, far from crowding out through exchange rate appreciation, leads to the opposite result—currency depreciation that ignites inflation. Moreover, this fear is much greater for a permanent fiscal expansion than for a temporary one. And so the problem is to convince the markets that any particular fiscal policy is going to be temporary, especially since some of the measures advocated (such as marginal employment subsidies) do not seem credible as temporary measures. The solution, therefore, is to use measures that are designed to work precisely because they are temporary, the classic example being temporary investment subsidies.

Other respondents reiterated that the existence of hysteresis is clearly the best justification for expanding demand. The hysteresis theory suggests that in Germany, with an unemployment rate above the NAIRU and low inflation, demand expansion would permanently lower the NAIRU and would cause not more inflation but less disinflation.

One discussant emphasized the importance of stable aggregate demand for investment decisions. He argued that monetary rather than fiscal policy should be used to guarantee investors a sufficient level of aggregate demand, pointing out that this goal lay behind the medium-term financial strategy in England. Others disagreed, stating that fiscal policy has to be the senior partner in supporting the desired path of aggregate demand. Monetary policy, while necessary, can only be used to tinker around at the margin; fiscal policy sets limits on what can be achieved with monetary policy in the first place. Coordinated fiscal policies among European nations to achieve a stable and somewhat expanded growth of aggregate demand is thus the best hope for spurring GNP growth.

German attitudes to fiscal expansion were also discussed. Germans have taken the experience of 1978–80 to indicate the failure of fiscal policies. They see increases in government spending as inefficient and counterproductive because economic agents realize such policies are temporary short-term measures and do not react with more investment. There has also been a revival in Germany of the neoclassical economic beliefs that as long as ideal clearing conditions are maintained within factor and financial markets, the economy will function appropriately; and that government intervention through monetary and fiscal policy is not necessary—and indeed is likely to be counterproductive. At the same time, however, the supply-side policies needed to permit market clearing are not considered politically feasible. The remarks made by Ralf Dahrendorf earlier reflected the perception that some minimum welfare state apparatus must be maintained. Thus there is an impasse in which the economists do not want to expand aggregate demand while others do not want to disband the welfare state. The policy of a one-time boost in fiscal demand to mop up unemployment is particularly unattractive to most Germans. It was suggested that a better approach would be a relatively ambitious long-term strategy with an announced schedule of structural reforms together with some fiscal stimulus.

One participant noted that the German impasse was evident in the positions of many Europeans at the conference. On the one hand, they seemed to be saying that interventionist policies should not be pursued because they will interfere with the natural adjustment process that will rectify the Eurosclerosis problem. On the other hand, they argue that any radical restructuring of the system is not warranted because there is a social consensus that the welfare state is all right. If there really is a belief that the institutional structure is here to stay, some nonneoclassical policies to correct the built-in distortions of the system would seem to make sense. In the face of the kinds of distortions said to exist within the European economy, there is a persuasive case for second-best policies such as wage subsidies. Europe could be fairly close to the favorable side of an interventionist Laffer curve, so that a little bit of spending on wage subsidies could generate more revenue than it costs. It is not necessarily fiscally irresponsible to experiment with such incentives.

One participant objected, however, that marginal employment subsidies were not desirable because evidence shows they achieve only small net increases in employment and output as a result of associated churning, displacement, and fiscal effects. Their major impact, he argued, is on the composition of employment rather than its level. But France was cited as an example of a nation in which marginal employment subsidies would be beneficial. The French government could subsidize two-thirds of the income of a low-paid worker who was coming off unemployment with no budgetary cost at all and without any real resource cost to the economy because the worker would not be receiving unemployment benefits. This assumes, of course, that the subsidy would be efficient in the sense of going only to those who would not, in its absence, have found a job.

Another participant argued that wage subsidies had other virtues. They may be targeted, as they were in the United Kingdom, to put pressure on youth wages, to reduce the power of the trade unions, and to dissuade the government from maintaining an inappropriate minimum wage.

It was pointed out that over the past fifteen to twenty years the tax on capital has been seriously eroded in Europe (as well as in the United States and Canada). This was accomplished by providing investment incentives through investment tax credits and accelerated depreciation allowances. Hence the taxation of capital would not seem to be one of the reasons that U.S. and European growth has slowed down. There is, however, heavy payroll taxation in all European countries. This suggests labor is the overtaxed factor.

If Europe desires lower unemployment, it was argued, it has only two choices: faster growth or work-sharing. Since there is not much support for work-sharing, faster growth seems essential. But another disagreed, arguing that a work-sharing policy could in fact be effective. He stressed, however, that it would not necessarily have to be a government-mediated process. Eradicating the barriers to entry into and mobility within the labor market would allow people to share the existing workload in a decentralized manner.

A participant noted the misleading nature of some measures of growth that included public-sector expansion. He considered the cause of hitherto unemployed mothers who, with the expansion of the welfare state, must now work to earn wages to pay taxes to cover the costs of looking after their children. In effect, the public sector has taken over functions that were previously performed by the family but were unrecorded and has turned them into welfare operations that must be paid for. The result is an increase of questionable merit in measured real GNP.

CHARLES L. SCHULTZE

Saving, Investment, and Profitability in Europe

OVER THE PAST two decades three common trends have characterized the economies of the major European countries in addition to a large rise in unemployment. First, national saving and investment have declined as a share of GNP. Second, a fall in saving by government has been a principal source of the national saving decline. And third, the profitability of private investment fell throughout most of the 1970s and the first several years of the 1980s, recovering only modestly thereafter, except in Germany, where the recovery was larger.

This paper briefly examines the behavior of saving and investment over the past two decades in Germany, France, Italy, and the United Kingdom. After presenting the basic data I explore whether structural changes in the aggregate supply of national saving or in the determinants of investment demand have become impediments to European growth. First, I look at business investment, concluding that the decline in the rate of growth of the business capital stock over the past fifteen years was closely linked to the fall in profitability that occurred during the same period, and explore some of the reasons for that fall in profitability. Evidence is offered that investment was further depressed after 1980 by the shortfall of national output below its potential. The paper then presents estimates, for each of the four countries, of the business investment share of GDP that would be needed to sustain a reasonable pace of long-term growth and concludes that current investment is somewhat below the levels required. I argue, however, that in Germany, France, and Italy, a feasible "catch-up" expansion of demand, sufficient

This chapter has benefited from the painstaking work of my research assistant Carl L. Liederman. I am grateful to my Brookings colleagues Barry P. Bosworth, Robert Z. Lawrence, and George L. Perry and participants in the Brookings Conference on Impediments to European Economic Growth for helpful comments and advice.

508

to raise output to its noninflationary potential (as estimated in my paper on real wages in this volume),[1] could directly and indirectly induce a recovery of investment demand to levels consistent, on the supply side, with long-term growth.

The concluding section deals with national saving rates. I argue that part of the decline in national saving rates in Europe has also been due to the shortfall of output below economic potential, especially but not solely through the effect of sluggish economic growth on government budget deficits. A catch-up increase in aggregate output and income would, it is argued, generate an increase in national saving large enough to match the rise in national investment required to sustain long-term growth at a reasonable pace. To say it another way, "high-employment" saving rates do appear sufficient in these countries to support the needed level of domestic investment. In the case of Germany, its export surplus and thus its net foreign investment have been declining. This leaves room for both the expansion in domestic business investment needed to sustain long-term growth *and* some deficit-creating fiscal stimulus. My essential conclusion, therefore, is that the underlying macroeconomic determinants of saving and investment are not themselves structural barriers to somewhat faster European growth.

Saving and Investment: The Historical Record

A nation's saving is the difference between its gross income and its consumption spending. Saving represents the national production (and income) that can be used for domestic investment or, through an export surplus, for investment abroad.

Table 1 sets forth the basic data on national saving for Germany, France, Italy, the United Kingdom, and, for comparison, the United States. National saving is the sum of saving by the private sector and by government. Government saving, in turn, is the difference between government revenues and government consumption outlays. It is thus equal to the sum of the government budget surplus (or, with a negative sign, the deficit) and government investment outlays.[2]

1. See Charles L. Schultze, "Real Wages, Real Wage Aspirations, and Unemployment in Europe" in this volume. (Hereafter Schultze, "Real Wages.")
2. The U.S. national income and product accounts do not separate government spending into consumption and investment. The U.S. data in table 1 came from the

Table 1. *Gross National Saving Rate and Components in Four European Countries and the United States, 1964–84*
Percent of GDP

Country	1964–68	1969–73	1974–78	1979–83	1984
Germany					
Private sector	21.7	21.0	20.2	19.5	19.8
Government	5.1	6.2	2.4	1.7	2.1
Total gross saving	26.8	27.2	22.5	21.2	21.9
France					
Private sector	20.3	20.8	20.3	18.6	18.2
Government	5.1	5.0	2.8	1.8	0.4
Total gross saving	25.4	25.8	23.1	20.3	18.6
Italy[a]					
Private sector	n.a.	25.4[a]	26.7	25.9	24.8
Government	n.a.	− 2.7[a]	− 4.9	− 5.7	− 7.1
Total gross saving	n.a.	22.7[a]	21.8	20.2	17.7
United Kingdom					
Private sector	15.3	15.0	16.7	18.7	19.9
Government	3.9	5.9	0.7	− 0.3	− 0.6
Total gross saving	19.3	20.9	17.4	18.4	19.3
United States					
Private sector	17.7	17.4	18.8	18.7	19.6
Government	2.3	1.7	− 0.1	− 1.0	− 3.1
Total gross saving	20.0	19.1	18.8	17.7	16.5

Source: Organization for Economic Cooperation and Development, *National Accounts*, various issues.
n.a. Not available.
a. No data available for Italy before 1970; used 1970–74, 1974–78 (overlap).

The data in table 1 are gross saving. They have not been adjusted to deduct the annual depreciation and obsolescence of the fixed capital stock. Thus the estimates measure the saving available for gross investment in each nation's stock of capital assets—investment made both to replace depreciating capital assets and to add to the stock of those assets. Broadly speaking, a country can invest its saving in two ways: it can add to its domestic stock of productive assets or, by running an export surplus, it can engage in foreign investment, acquiring ownership of foreign securities or other assets. (Foreign investment can be negative, reflecting an inflow of foreign saving; by running an import surplus, a country can borrow real resources from abroad and so invest domesti-

Organization for Economic Cooperation and Development, which does provide estimates for government investment, making it possible to calculate U.S. government saving as revenues less government consumption outlays. The 1984 estimate for U.S. government saving was calculated by the author.

Table 2. *Gross National Capital Formation in Four European Countries and the United States, 1964–84*
Percent of GDP

Country	1964–68	1969–73	1974–78	1979–83	1984
Germany					
Private domestic investment	22.0	22.2	17.6	18.6	18.6
Government investment	4.1	4.2	3.6	3.2	2.4
Foreign investment[a]	0.7	0.8	1.4	−0.4	1.0
Total	26.8	27.2	22.5	21.2	22.0
France					
Private domestic investment	21.2	22.1	20.7	18.8	16.2
Government investment	4.2	3.7	3.3	3.1	3.1
Foreign investment[a]	0.0	0.0	−0.8	−1.5	−0.6
Total	25.4	25.8	23.1	20.3	18.6
Italy					
Private domestic investment	n.a.	20.0[b]	19.1	17.4	14.5
Government investment	n.a.	3.1[b]	3.3	3.7	4.1
Foreign investment[a]	n.a.	−0.4[b]	−0.6	−0.9	−1.0
Total	n.a.	22.7[b]	21.8	20.2	17.7
United Kingdom					
Private domestic investment	15.4	15.3	16.0	14.9	15.3
Government investment	4.6	4.7	4.1	2.1	2.0
Foreign investment[a]	−0.7	0.3	−1.6	1.3	0.3
Total	19.3	20.3	18.5	18.2	17.6
United States					
Private domestic investment	16.5	16.7	16.8	16.4	17.7
Government investment	2.9	2.5	2.0	1.6	1.4
Foreign investment[a]	0.5	0.0	0.1	−0.2	−2.6
Total	20.0	19.2	18.9	17.8	16.5

Source: See table 1.
n.a. Not available.
a. Net foreign investment = −(net foreign borrowing).
b. No data available for Italy before 1970.

cally more than it saves. The United States has been doing this in a large way since 1982.)

The national income accounts are so defined and constructed that national saving is always equal to national capital formation, which is the sum of domestic and foreign investment.[3] Table 2 provides data on gross capital formation: gross domestic investment by government and by the private sector, plus foreign investment.

3. In the United States and the United Kingdom the income and production side of the national accounts are measured independently; there is always a small statistical discrepancy between the two measures, which shows up as a difference between national saving and investment.

Table 3. *Ratio of Net Capital Stock to Adjusted Output in Four European Countries and the United States, 1965–69, 1984*[a]

Year	Germany	France	Italy	United Kingdom	United States
1965–69	1.24	1.14	1.38	1.96	1.10
1984	1.55	1.41	1.43	2.69	1.19[b]

Source: Commission of the European Communities; see the data appendix to Charles L. Schultze, "Real Wages, Real Wage Aspirations, and Unemployment in Europe" in this volume.

a. Output was adjusted to "normal" capacity utilization levels using the estimated "gap" variable ($\hat{q}$) whose derivation is explained in my paper on real wages in this volume. The ratios shown in this table are based on data from the Commission covering the nonfarm business sector, excluding housing, while the data on private saving and investment in table 2 are for the whole economy. The Commission estimates are designed to show the changes in the capital stock within a given country but are not comparable across countries. That is, the fact that the German ratio of capital to output was higher in 1984 than it was in 1973 is significant, but that it was higher than in Italy is not significant.

b. 1983 for the United States.

In France, Germany, and Italy gross national saving rates have fallen substantially during the past two decades. In the mid-1960s national saving rates ranged from 19 to 27 percent; by 1984 the range was 18 to 22 percent. In all three countries most of the saving decline was the result of a sharp fall in government saving in the 1970s. Though national saving in the United Kingdom during the 1960s was much lower than in other European countries, the later saving decline was also smaller, so that by 1984 national saving rates in all four of the European countries were broadly in the same range. In the United States, the relatively low national saving rate of the 1960s fell even lower, all because of the decline in government saving, which became especially pronounced after 1981.

The decline in gross national investment as a share of GDP is clear from the data in table 2. In all countries but the United Kingdom the private investment share dropped. Business investment generally held up much better than government and housing investment. In Germany, France, and the United Kingdom and to a lesser extent in the United States and Italy a large and steady rise in the ratio of the capital stock to GNP lifted the ratio of depreciation to GNP over the period (see table 3). As a consequence *net* saving and investment rates—gross saving and investment less depreciation—fell even more than indicated by the data shown in tables 1 and 2. Because the capital stock has risen relative to GNP, it now requires a larger share of gross investment in GNP to produce a given rate of increase in the capital stock than was the case in earlier years. Thus not only have gross saving and investment rates declined, but a given gross saving rate yields a smaller rate of increase in the national stock of capital than it used to.

It is impossible, of course, to arrive at any conclusion about causality from tables 1 and 2. One cannot argue, for example, that the fall in the national saving rate caused the fall in investment. The causation could have run the other way: a fall in investment, for example, threatens a decline in aggregate demand and a rise in unemployment. Fear of these consequences may have been one of the considerations that induced European governments in the 1970s to pursue expansionary fiscal policies, which increased budget deficits and lowered national saving rates.[4]

The Determinants of Investment

It is the excess of the expected profitability of an investment relative to the cost of capital that motivates business firms to undertake new investments. If the profitability of new investment is high relative to the cost of capital, analysts usually conclude that a large backlog of unexploited investment opportunities exists and, hence, that the volume of new investment forthcoming will be high. Of course, there are no data on the *prospective* profitability of new investment. What is available are estimates of the after-the-fact profitability, or rate of return, on the existing business capital stock. Theoretically, the rate of return on the existing capital stock could diverge substantially from the profitability of new investment. For example, an unexpectedly large and widespread advance in cost-cutting methods that was tied to the installation of new machinery could, for a time, give rise to unusually large potential profits on new investment and simultaneously depress the profits on competing investments that had been made earlier. In fact, however, for the economy as a whole, as opposed to a narrow segment of it, a wide divergence is unlikely.

The normal expectation of business firms, when making an investment, is that technology will continue to advance, and an allowance for this is therefore incorporated in the estimate of future obsolescence that goes into calculating the expected profits from new investments. And so, unless the aggregate technological advance for the economy as a

4. Bosworth and Lawrence argue that this was precisely what happened in Sweden during the latter half of the 1970s. Barry P. Bosworth and Robert Z. Lawrence, "Adjusting to Slower Economic Growth: The Domestic Economy," in Bosworth and Alice M. Rivlin, eds., *The Swedish Economy* (Brookings, 1987), pp. 22–54.

Figure 1. *Neoclassical Investment Theory*

Rate of return (*r*)
and cost of capital (*C*)

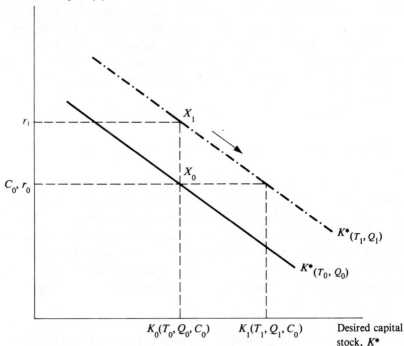

whole unexpectedly accelerates, the profitability of past investments now incorporated in the capital stock will not be pulled down below the profitability of new investment by continued technological advance. Though the pace of technological change historically has varied from period to period, a large surprise jump in technologial opportunities across many industries, wide and rapid enough to drive a large wedge between the profitability of new investment and the profitability of the existing capital stock, is unlikely. Thus, taken over long periods, the movement of actual rates of return may indeed serve as a rough index of the return to new investment.

Even granted the likelihood that the rate of return on the existing capital stock is a reasonably good index of the profitability of new investment, the usual empirical applications of neoclassical investment theory still do not incorporate the rate of return as an independent factor affecting investment. Figure 1 shows the bare bones of that neoclassical model. The desired capital stock (K^*) is an increasing function of desired output (Q) and technological opportunities (T) and a decreasing function of the cost of capital (C). Business firms will undertake additions to the stock of capital to the point where the rate of return (r) is equal to the cost of capital, adjusted for risk. Considering the economy as a whole, two chief factors operate to push K^* out to the right: rising demand for output and improving technology. As these two developments occur, the profit-maximizing stock of capital rises and net investment occurs. The higher the cost of capital, however, the smaller the gap between the actual and the desired stock of capital and the smaller the stimulus to net investment. The rate of return, at the existing size of the capital stock, rises from r_0 to r_1. The profit-maximizing stock of capital rises from K_0 to K_1, and investment occurs to expand the capital stock to that point. In that process r_1 is pushed down to r_0.

Most empirical applications of this approach assume that the pace of technological progress is relatively steady, and that business investment tends to keep the actual stock of capital close enough to the equilibrium or desired stock that the rate of return to the capital stock tends to track the cost of capital (r_1 is kept close to C_0). Thus the two principal determinants of investment are usually thought to be expected changes in the level of output and the cost of capital. The ex post rate of return itself is assigned no role.

In fact, however, the European data suggest that the rate of return has experienced serious changes not explainable by changes in the cost of capital. Table 4 presents estimates of the gross (before tax) return to capital as a percent of the gross capital stock at replacement cost.[5] In the second column the returns have also been adjusted to eliminate the effect of over- and underutilization of the capital stock—that is, the estimates in column 2 show what the rate of return would have been had the capital stock been utilized at the average 1965–79 level (assuming no change in the share of capital income in total income).[6] The table also gives estimates of real interest rates. The measures in table 4 provide a reasonably good index of the time path of the rate of return on invested

5. The rates of return have been adjusted to remove the influence on profits of merely cyclical changes in productivity growth. (These adjustments were seldom large.) Throughout the remainder of this paper references to the "rate of return" refer to these rates. It is widely accepted that purely cyclical changes in productivity growth are ignored in business decisions on pricing and investment.

6. The derivation of over- and underutilization, the "gap" ($\hat{q}$), is explained in Schultze, "Real Wages."

Table 4. *Gross Rates of Return and Real Interest Rates in Four European Countries and the United States, Selected Dates, 1962–84*
Percent

Country and period or year	Gross rate of return[a] (1)	Gross rate of return at "normal" capacity utilization[b] (2)	Real interest rate[c] (3)
Germany			
1962–65	16.7	16.6	2.7
1966–70	16.1	16.3	3.9
1971–75	13.6	13.5	2.3
1976–80	12.8	12.8	3.6
1981	11.3	11.7	6.1
1984	12.9	13.7	5.4
France			
1962–65	15.3	15.2	1.7
1966–70	16.9	17.1	3.8
1971–75	15.1	15.0	1.2
1976–80	12.1	12.2	1.2
1981	11.2	11.5	4.1
1984	11.8	12.3	5.2
Italy			
1962–65	13.7	13.6	1.1
1966–70	13.6	13.5	3.9
1971–75	9.7	9.7	−2.5
1976–80	7.9	7.9	−2.4
1981	7.6	7.6	2.8
1984	8.0	8.4	2.6
United Kingdom			
1962–65	10.2	10.4	2.9
1966–70	10.0	10.1	3.4
1971–75	8.0	8.0	0.4
1976–80	7.5	7.6	−2.1
1981	6.9	7.4	0.4
1984	7.0	7.1	6.4
United States			
1962–65	15.7	16.0	2.8
1966–70	14.9	14.9	1.4
1971–75	11.6	11.8	0.5
1976–80	11.2	11.3	0.9
1981	10.6	11.1	3.1
1984	11.3	11.7	9.1

Sources: Columns 1 and 2: author's calculations; column 3: IMF, *International Financial Statistics*, various issues.
a. Adjusted to eliminate the effect of cyclical changes in productivity.
b. Column 1 adjusted to eliminate the effect on profits of capacity utilization rates higher or lower than the 1965–79 average. The adjustment was done simply by multiplying the rate of return by the inverse of the output ratio, q.
c. Nominal rate on long-term government securities less the average of current and one-year lagged inflation rate in the deflator for private nonfarm business GDP (weights, $\frac{2}{3}$, $\frac{1}{3}$, respectively).

capital within each country. As noted earlier, however, comparisons cannot be made *across* countries, since the *levels* (as opposed to the time paths) of the capital stock are not comparable.

As the data in the table show, rates of return were substantially lower in the early 1980s than they had been in the 1960s. Yet real interest rates in the 1980s, after declining in the preceding decade, had, by 1984, generally returned to levels equal to or above those of the 1960s.

Changes in real interest rates may not be a reliable index of changes in the cost of capital. The after-tax cost of funds is probably more relevant for investment. Large reductions in the effective tax rate on income from investment would lower the cost of capital, presumably giving rise to an increased volume of additions to the capital stock that in turn would drive down the before-tax rate of return on the capital stock. There are only scattered data that allow comparison of effective marginal tax rates on income from capital. Fullerton and King's pathbreaking study did compare, for the United Kingdom, the United States, and Germany, marginal effective tax rates on investment in business capital for 1960, 1970, and 1980.[7] In the United Kingdom marginal effective rates dropped very sharply over the period. In the United States they were stable from 1960 to 1970 and then declined moderately, from 47 percent in 1970 to 37 percent in 1980. By contrast in Germany there was almost no decline from 1960 to 1970 or from 1970 to 1980. This fact is consistent with much cruder evidence that shows German corporate and local business taxes to have remained at about 3 percent of GDP between 1970 and 1980.[8] In France the ratio of corporate income taxes to GDP was the same low level in 1983 as in 1965 (2 percent).[9] Except for the United Kingdom, therefore, effective tax rates on capital do not appear to have fallen sharply.

In column 2 of table 4 the rates of return have been adjusted to reflect a "normal" utilization of the capital stock. By 1981 even these corrected rates of return had fallen below those of the 1960s and, usually by a smaller margin, below those of the early 1970s. Yet despite the much

7. Mervyn A. King and Don Fullerton, eds. *The Taxation of Income from Capital: A Comparative Study of the United States, the United Kingdom, Sweden, and West Germany* (University of Chicago Press, 1984), tables 3-23, 3-31, 3-32, 5-21, 5-24, 5-25, 6-20, 6-31, 6-32.

8. German business tax data from Joseph A. Pechman, ed., *Comparative Tax Systems: Europe, Canada, and Japan* (Arlington, Va.: Tax Analysts, 1987), pp. 290–91; GDP data from OECD, *National Accounts.*

9. Pechman, ed., *Comparative Tax Systems*, p. 195.

lower rate of return, the gross capital stock (in constant dollars) kept growing at 2.5 to 3.5 percent a year or more in all countries—a slower advance than in the 1960s but still a substantial rate of increase.

These facts suggest that contrary to the usual assumption, long periods of disequilibrium can occur, during which the rate of return diverges substantially from the cost of capital. The very high return to capital during the 1960s almost surely reflected a disequilibrium situation, a disequilibrium whose causes will be suggested in the next section of this paper. At the moment the important fact is that profitability was very high relative to the cost of capital.

In sum, the profitability of investment (the rate of return) may for lengthy periods diverge from long-run equilibrium. Other things being equal, the more the rate of profitability exceeds the cost of capital, the greater will be the incentives for investment. The rate of return on the existing capital stock, reflecting the extent of disequilibrium, thus played an independent role in determining the volume of investment during the 1960s and 1970s.

To the extent that lenders ration funds to business firms, profitability can influence the volume of investment in two other respects: first, directly, as a rough index of the flow of internally generated funds; and second, indirectly, because low profitability in a firm tends to worsen the lenders' evaluation of the quality of credit extended to that firm and to increase the stringency of credit rationing.[10]

Table 5 shows the results of some simple investment equations that highlight profitability. The dependent variable, k, is the rate of growth in the gross capital stock. All the independent variables were expressed as deviations from their means over the period of the regression.[11] Thus the constant in the equation is simply the mean rate of expansion of the capital stock over the period, which the equations do not attempt to explain. In all the European countries, the rate of return, lagged substantially, greatly influenced the growth of the stock of capital of private nonfarm business firms. Profitability affected capital growth most in Germany.[12] Among other European countries the influence of profits on

10. See *OECD Economic Surveys, 1985–86: Germany* (Paris: OECD, June 1986), pp. 57–66, for an application to Germany.

11. Except for the $\hat{q}$ variable, which has a mean of zero in the period 1965–79 (excluding the recession year 1975).

12. The OECD also reports this finding—changes in profitability had a larger effect on investment in Germany than in other European countries. *OECD Economic Surveys,*

Table 5. *Equations Explaining Fluctuations in Additions to the Gross Capital Stock in Four European Countries and the United States, 1964–84*[a]

Independent variable	Germany	France	Italy	United Kingdom	United States
Coefficients on					
π/K[b]	0.52	0.37	0.39	0.38	0.12
	(10.5)	(5.7)	(8.9)	(5.9)	(2.0)
$\hat{q}$	0.14	0.15	0.14	0.07	0.13
	(6.0)	(4.7)	(4.4)	(3.2)	(4.5)
i/r	−0.14	c	c	−0.03	c
	(3.0)	c	c	(1.8)	c
Summary statistic					
$\bar{R}^2$	0.97	0.95	0.95	0.90	0.78
Standard error	0.24	0.21	0.32	0.20	0.34
ρ	0.37	0.76	0.42	0.54	0.43

Sources: Author's calculations, and see Schultze, "Real Wages," data appendix.

a. Private nonfarm business, excluding housing. Dependent variable is the percent rate of growth per year in the gross capital stock. Independent variables are π/K, gross rate of return; $\hat{q}$, the gap, ratio of output to potential; and i/r, real interest rates. The numbers in parentheses are t-statistics. See note c to table 4.

b. Sum of coefficients on three-term Almon lag starting in t-1.

c. Insignificant; variable omitted from equation.

investment was also strong and statistically highly significant. In the United States the influence was much smaller than in Europe. Indeed, unlike the European situation, the rate of growth in the U.S. capital stock did not decline monotonically. It peaked in the late 1960s and in 1985 was about the same as in the early 1960s.

The level of output, relative to trend or potential, affected the growth of the capital stock similarly across all the continental European countries and the United States, but had somewhat less effect in the United Kingdom. Only in Germany was it possible to find a substantial effect of real interest rates.

Though the capital stock continued to grow in all the countries, that rate of growth fell sharply in Europe between the late 1960s and 1984 (see table 6). As is clear from table 6, much of that slide was associated with the decline in profitability, at least according to the results of the investment equations reported here.

Another look at table 4 reveals that by 1984 the profitability of business firms in Germany and to a lesser extent in France and Italy had partially recovered from the lows of 1981 or 1982. But the lags are quite long

1985–86: Germany, p. 57. According to the OECD this fact stems from the higher-than-average gearing ratios typical in German firms.

Table 6. *Growth Rate of the Gross Capital Stock in Four European Countries and the United States, 1970, 1984*
Percent unless otherwise specified

Item	Germany	France	Italy	United Kingdom	United States
1970	7.1	6.2	6.5	4.5	4.4
1984	3.3	3.0	2.5	2.8	3.6
Proportion of the decline attributable to lower profitability (from coefficients in table 5)	0.61	0.63	0.64	0.77	0.63

Source: Author's calculations based on regression results reported in table 5.

between a change in profits and its investment consequences—somewhere between two and two and a half years. Thus the increase in German and French profitability that began in 1983 did not show up in a strengthening of investment until 1984. In 1985 and 1986, however, business investment in Germany and France did rise markedly, growing by 5 to 6.5 percent and reflecting in part the earlier improvements in profitability. The United Kingdom was the exception: profitability did not strengthen substantially between 1981 and 1984, but gross fixed investment rose substantially in 1984 and 1985.

The Determinants of Profitability

In analyzing changes in the rate of return to capital it is usual to separate that variable into two main components:

$$(1) \qquad \Pi/PK = \frac{\Pi}{PQ} \cdot \frac{PQ}{PK}$$

$$(1a) \qquad \qquad = S_k \cdot \frac{PQ}{PK},$$

where Π = the gross operating surplus of business firms
PK = the gross capital stock valued at current prices
PQ = the value of output originating in business valued at current prices
S_k = the gross operating margin = capital share of income originating (the data are so defined that $S_k = 1 - S_l$, where S_l = is the labor share of income)

Q/K = the ratio of output to capital.

Equation 1a simply states that the return to capital is equal to the gross operating margin (the capital income share) times capital productivity—that is, output produced per unit of capital used.

Over the past several decades the decline in the rates of return in Europe and the United States has been affected by several elements that are not captured by the simple relationships shown in equations 1 and 1a. First, the price of capital goods has not moved completely in parallel with the overall price deflator for value added, as is implicitly assumed above: the price index in the numerator of the PQ/PK term has not been the same as the index in the denominator. Second, apparently there has been a long-term downtrend in the average weekly hours of capital use. Third, there have been important changes in the rate of capacity utilization, especially since 1980. The movements in the output-capital ratio, and in the rate of return, have thus been affected not only by such long-term developments as changes in technology and capital intensity but also by other factors whose influence should be taken into account.

Equation 2 provides a more complete decomposition of the elements affecting the rate of return.

| | | Ratio of output to the | Composite index of other factors: capital |
| Gross rate of return | Capital share of income | effective capital stock | hours trend, utilization rate, inverse of the relative price of capital goods |

$$(2) \quad (\Pi/P_kK) = (\Pi/PQ) \times (Q/KH_kU) \times (H_k) \times (U) \times (P/P_k)$$

Table 7 arranges the data for each of the major European countries and the United States in this form. The "effective" capital stock used in the denominator of the second column is derived through multiplying the constant-dollar capital stock by indexes of the trend of average weekly hours of capital use and of cyclical capacity utilization. In analyzing this table it is important to bear in mind that these are ex post data and cannot be used directly to assign causality. Thus, other things being equal, an increase in the relative price of capital goods or a trend decrease in weekly hours of capital use will reduce the return obtainable from an additional dollar of capital. That decline in potential profitability may reduce the pace of capital-labor substitution, which will in turn raise the output-capital ratio and restore the rate of return. Thus the rise in

Table 7. *Factors Influencing Rates of Return in Four European Countries and the United States, Selected Dates, 1961–85*[a]

Country and period or year	Gross rate of return[b] (Π/P_kK) (percent)	=	Capital share of income (Π/PQ) (percent)	×	Output/ effective capital stock (Q/KH_kU) (ratio)	×	Index of other factors[c] $(H_k) \times (U) \times (P/P_k)$
Germany							
1961–65	17.2		34.1		0.56		0.90
1966–73	15.4		32.9		0.50		0.93
1974–80	12.7		30.9		0.44		0.94
1981	11.3		31.2		0.41		0.89
1984	12.9		35.3		0.40		0.92
1985	13.0		35.4		0.39		0.94
France							
1961–65	15.1		34.9		0.46		0.93
1966–73	16.6		35.5		0.49		0.95
1974–80	12.5		30.0		0.46		0.90
1981	11.2		28.8		0.43		0.89
1984	11.8		31.1		0.43		0.91
1985	12.1		31.9		0.41		0.92
Italy							
1961–65	14.5		31.2		0.45		1.04
1966–73	12.6		26.6		0.46		1.04
1974–80	7.9		20.4		0.44		0.88
1981	7.6		20.2		0.43		0.87
1984	8.0		23.6		0.43		0.79
1985	n.a.		n.a.		0.42		0.79
United Kingdom							
1961–65	10.1		28.8		0.38		0.93
1966–73	9.5		29.0		0.34		0.96
1974–80	7.3		28.3		0.30		0.87
1981	6.9		30.1		0.28		0.90
1984	7.0		29.6		0.26		0.90
1985	7.0		30.0		0.26		0.92
United States							
1961–65	15.6		27.4		0.53		1.07
1966–73	13.9		25.8		0.52		1.04
1974–80	11.0		25.1		0.49		0.90
1981	10.6		25.4		0.48		0.87
1984	11.3		25.1		0.47		0.96
1985	11.7		25.4		0.46		0.96

Sources: Author's calculations from data furnished by the Commission of the European Communities. Estimates through 1984 from Commission data base. The 1985 estimates are very tentative. They were extrapolated from 1984 using principally OECD data on changes in output, wages, prices, and labor input; 1984–85 changes in capital stock were estimated from 1985 investment data. The 1985 rate of return estimates assume that the relative price of capital goods in that year moved at the average rate of change experienced between 1980 and 1984. Data cover the private nonfarm economy excluding housing.

n.a. Not available.

a. Profit share and rate of return include adjustment for factor cost versus market price.

b. Profit share and rate of return adjusted to eliminate effects of purely cyclical changes in productivity.

c. Product of indexes of hours trend; utilization rate; inverse of relative capital goods' prices; see text.

the relative price of capital goods or the fall in hours of capital use would show up ex post as a fall in investment, a rise in the effective output-capital ratio, and no change in the observed rate of return. In Italy, for example, where the relative price of capital goods behaved most unfavorably, the effective output-capital ratio fell least. Despite these interactions, the data in table 7 can provide some insights into why profitability has declined.

The first fact that emerges from table 7 is that in Germany, the United Kingdom, and the United States none of the decline in profitability between 1966–73 and 1984 stemmed from changes in gross margins, that is, in the capital income share (S_k). The stability of the capital income share for the total economy in these countries is noted in my paper on real wages. In Italy and France, the capital income share declined until 1981 and has only partially recovered since then. Nevertheless, even in those two countries most of the decline in profitability can be traced to other causes.

In Germany the modest fall in the capital income share during the 1970s and the healthy rise after 1981 were partly in response to the movements in the German real exchange rate. German manufacturing exports and imports are very large relative to business GDP. As a consequence, when the German real exchange rate rises so as to depress manufacturing profit margins, the effect shows up in the data for the total business sector. In the other European countries foreign trade is smaller relative to the economy, and real exchange rates do not show up as a principal factor moving the capital income share for the business sector as a whole (although they are important in the manufacturing sector of those countries).[13]

Germany, France, and the United Kingdom experienced large declines in the effective output-capital ratio. However, the other special factors (the relative price of capital goods, average weekly hours of capital use, and capacity utilization) in combination exerted only a mild influence on the rates of return. The declines in the effective output-capital ratio in these countries are consistent with the view expressed earlier that an important part of the decline in profitability reflected the movement from disequilibrium to equilibrium. (The special situations in Italy and the United States will be discussed later.) During the first decade and a half after the Second World War the technological frontier

13. See Schultze, "Real Wages," for a discussion of exchange rate effects in manufacturing.

was far out in front of the average technology incorporated in the capital stock of the major industrial nations. The low level of investment in the 1930s had been followed by a wartime period in which little investment was undertaken in civilian industries. But basic technological progress had continued, and in many areas had been stimulated by wartime requirements. The scarcity of capital in most industrial countries in those early postwar years generated abnormally high rates of return.

Incorporating technological advances into the capital stock tends to improve profitability by raising the output-capital ratio. But an increase in the stock of capital relative to labor tends to reduce profitability by driving down the output-capital ratio. In an equilibrium situation, with a constant cost of capital, the two opposing sets of forces tend to offset each other, and under a plausible set of assumptions keep the output-capital ratio unchanged.

In theory, a fall in the cost of capital could have induced the large volume of investment needed to produce the decline in the output-capital ratio that has occurred in Europe. As noted earlier, however, there has not been a drop in the cost of capital big enough and sustained enough to have produced this result. But it could have been produced in response to an initial disequilibrium characterized by capital scarcity and a high rate of return. The heavy investment in capital-labor substitution that was made in response to these initially high rates of return gradually drove down the output-capital ratio and reduced rates of return to and perhaps below long-run equilibrium levels. And, of course, as rates of return fell so did the volume of investment.

In all the European countries examined there has been a large downtrend in average weekly hours of work by the employed labor force. To the extent that average weekly hours of capital use also fall, then for any given technology and capital-labor ratio, the rate of return obtainable from a unit of capital input will decline. Direct data are not available on average hours of capital use, but it is possible to make some estimates. These are explained in my paper on real wages, where such estimates are developed to help translate data on the growth of the capital stock into measures of capacity output. The estimates assume that for the private nonfarm nonresidential capital stock, a reduction of 1 percent in average weekly hours of labor results in a 0.25 percent fall in average hours of capital use.[14] (For manufacturing each 1 percent

14. This result was obtained by conservatively assuming that changes in average

Table 8. *Relative Price of Capital Goods in Italy and the United States, Selected Years, 1960–84*[a]

Index (1960 = 100)

Year	Italy	United States[b]
1960	100	100
1970	103	105
1980	118	121
1984	125	110

Source: Commission of the European Communities data base, which covers private nonfarm economy including housing.

a. The price of capital goods is the deflator for the gross capital stock. (For all countries except the United States, this deflator is close to the deflator for nonresidential investment; but in the United States the Commission's capital stock deflator, through 1980, rises faster than the investment goods deflator.)

b. Part of the reversal in the uptrend of relative prices of capital goods in the United States can be explained by the growing importance of computers and related capital goods, whose quality-adjusted prices have been falling rapidly. For an analysis of these and other elements affecting the relative price of capital goods in the United States, see Barry P. Bosworth, "Taxes and the Investment Recovery," *BPEA, 1:1985*, pp. 16–17.

decline in average weekly labor hours was assumed to have a much larger effect on hours of capital use, perhaps on the order of 0.67 percent.)

By 1984 the decline in average hours of capital use in the European countries meant that for any given technology and capital-hour ratio, each unit of capital employed would generate 3 to 5 percent less output, and thus a rate of profitability that was 3 to 5 percent (or about 0.5 percentage point) less, than in the mid-1960s.

After 1980 lower capacity utilization, as captured by the "gap" measure I have been using, also reduced the output per unit of capital employed and so tended to lower profitability. Capacity utilization in the United Kingdom by 1985 had returned to normal levels, but in the continental countries was still below its average for the 1960s and 1970s.

During most of the period since 1960 a rise in the relative price of capital goods in Italy and the United States (see table 8) served to reduce the initially high levels of profitability. The large declines in the index of other factors for Italy, and in the United States until 1980, stem primarily from this source.

The effect of changes in the relative price of capital goods on the rate

weekly hours worked by labor do *not* affect hours of capital in trade, transportation, utilities, real estate, and most services. Moreover, they are assumed not to affect hours of capital use in the three big continuous process manufacturing industries—petroleum end products, chemicals, and primary metals. U.S. capital stock data for 1981 were used as weights to translate these assumptions into an estimated fraction of the private nonfarm nonresidential capital stock. Only the *trend* in the hours of capital utilization is relevant because *cyclical* changes in average hours of utilization are presumably captured in the capacity utilization index.

of return is a complex one. In all countries the price of producers' equipment rose more or less in parallel with the price of manufacturing output, which, because of differentially faster growth in productivity, rose much less than the price of value added for the business sector as a whole. Thus for all countries the relative price of producers' equipment has fallen over the past several decades and by about the same amount (20 to 25 percent from 1960 to 1984). But construction prices, as measured in the national accounts, rose much faster than output prices in all countries but Germany. For France and the United Kingdom the rises in the relative price of construction roughly cancelled the declines in relative equipment prices. But in Italy, and to a somewhat lesser extent in the United States, the reported increases in construction prices were so large as to raise the composite relative price of capital goods. For example, the deflator for nonresidential construction in Italy doubled relative to the deflator for producers' equipment during the period 1960–84. And it was in Italy and the United States where effective output-capital ratios fell the least.

Alternative explanations could link these phenomena. Construction price indexes may be biased upward to a particularly large degree, especially in Italy but also in the United States.[15] If this is indeed the correct explanation, it would align the behavior of Italy more closely with that of the other three European countries in terms of explaining the decline in profitability: an initial disequilibrium at very high profit rates led to heavy investment, pushing down the output-capital ratio and reducing profitability to or beyond an equilibrium level.

To sum up the argument to this point, business capital formation and the rate of profitability in the major European countries started from a very high level in the 1960s and trended downward thereafter. In Germany and the United Kingdom the decline in profitability was principally associated, not with a fall in capital's share of income, but with a fall in the output-capital ratio. In France the capital income share did fall and even after some recent recovery remains below earlier levels. But the French capital-output ratio also declined substantially. A feedback process was in operation: an initial disequilibrium period of capital

15. There is some evidence that the trend in the price indexes for nonresidential construction in the United States has an upward bias. See Paul Pieper, "Construction Price Statistics Revisited," paper prepared for the Conference on Technology and Capital Formation, Kennedy School of Government, Harvard University, November 7–9, 1985.

scarcity and very high rates of return induced heavy investment in capital-labor substitution, which in turn drove down the output-capital ratio and gradually depressed the initial, high rates of profitability. The declining profitability, after a lag, fed back on investment incentives and led to a fall in the growth rate of the capital stock. Given current high levels of real interest rates, the process may conceivably have pushed profitability down below long-run equilibrium levels. Only in Italy was the decline in the capital-output ratio a small one, and this result may be a statistical artifact stemming from an upward bias in the price index of nonresidential construction and a corresponding downward bias in the estimated capital stock.

The next step in the analysis is to ask whether the current levels of European national saving and domestic investment are sufficient, from a supply-side standpoint, to support reasonable economic growth over the next several years.

Investment Requirements for Medium-Term Growth

The scope for expansion of demand in the major European countries during the next several years depends on two elements: the growth of economic potential at a stable rate of resource use, and a temporary catch-up in demand and output large enough to absorb currently unused resources of labor and capital stock as far as this can be done without a renewal of significant inflationary pressures. My paper on real wages concludes that the binding constraint on the size of the catch-up is in labor markets rather than in shortages of capacity. Hence from a supply-side standpoint the investment share of GDP can be evaluated principally in terms of how well it supports the long-term growth of economic potential.

To illustrate the growth implications of recent trends in investment, I have calculated for each of the four European countries the business investment share of GDP that would be needed to support a reasonable growth of economic potential over the period 1985–90. The estimate of potential growth in the nonfarm business sector was based on the following assumptions.

—Growth in employment sufficient to absorb the expanding labor force at unchanged unemployment rates (assuming also that employment in nonfarm business grows at the same rate as aggregate employment and that recent trends in the average length of the work week continue).[16]

—A continuation of multifactor productivity growth at its most recent trend rate of growth.

—A rise in the capital stock consistent with projected movements in output and profitability (as explained in the next section of this paper).[17]

Thus,

$$(3) \qquad \dot{q}^* = \lambda + \dot{n}^* + S_k(\dot{k}^* - \dot{n}^*) + \dot{h},$$

where

$\dot{q}^*$ = projected rate of growth of economic potential
$\dot{n}^*$ = rate of growth in nonfarm business employment
λ = multifactor productivity growth
S_k = capital's share of income
$\dot{k}^*$ = growth of the capital stock
$\dot{h}$ = rate of change in average hours worked.

My labor force projections are based on, but are not in all cases the same as, projections of the population of working age and labor force participation rates furnished by member governments to the OECD and used by the OECD to make labor force projections. Two kinds of changes were made in the official projections. First, for Germany it appeared that the trends in participation rates by demographic groups for the period 1979–85 were more or less mechanically extrapolated to 1990. But participation rates in Germany respond quite sensitively to labor market conditions, and the period 1979–85 was one during which unemployment rose sharply. A regression of the German participation rate on a time trend and the German unemployment rate showed that almost all the decline in the participation rate from 1979 to 1985 (from 0.668 to 0.650) was accounted for by the rise in unemployment.[18] For purposes of projecting a neutral growth in the labor force under stable labor market conditions, simple extrapolation of the recent trends in participation

16. In Germany a small downward adjustment in business sector employment was made to allow for some growth outside that sector.

17. In the United Kingdom the capital stock was assumed to grow at the 1985 rate.

18. With GPR and GUN denoting the German participation rate and unemployment rate, respectively (in percentages), the regression was $GPR = 71.5 - 0.15TIME - 0.19TIME197484 + 0.27TIME197984 - 0.69GUN + 0.41GUN197484$; $\bar{R}^2 = 0.993$; standard error, 0.15; Durbin-Watson, 2.08; all coefficients significant at 1 percent confidence level. For each variable the coefficients with period designations are additive.

rates imparts a downward bias to the results.[19] To eliminate this bias, an alternative path of the future participation rate was forecast on the assumption of a constant unemployment rate. As a result, the 0.4 percent annual decline in the German labor force projected by the OECD was reduced to a 0.2 percent decline.

The second adjustment had to do with changes in the demographic composition of the labor force. In Germany and the United Kingdom the period ahead will witness absolute and relative decreases in the number of young people in the labor force and increases in the proportion of experienced prime-age workers, especially men. The demographic composition will move in the opposite direction in Italy. Young people have fewer annual working hours and lower productivity than prime-age workers. The demographic shifts will therefore affect potential output. The effect of these shifts could be captured by adjusting productivity growth; I chose to do it by weighting the employment data. George Perry constructed weights for major demographic groups in the United States, based on the annual hours of work and relative wages (presumed to reflect marginal productivity of each group).[20] In view of the narrower wage differentials in Europe, I compressed the weights to (an admittedly arbitrary) two-thirds of the dispersion shown in the Perry weights to arrive at a final estimate of "effective" labor force growth (see table 9). The projections of average working hours are a continuation of post-1980 trends. Since the large legislated reduction in French working hours in 1982, they have changed little. The 1982 reduction pushed French hours well below their close pre-1982 relationship with those of Germany. The projected trends gradually restore that relationship.[21]

Multifactor productivity growth for 1985–90 was projected by assuming that it continued at its most recent trend rate of growth.[22] (See table

---

19. Since I am projecting the growth in economic potential, with unemployment constant, I ignore any potential cyclical "snapback" of participation rates caused by catch-up growth in employment. That is subsumed later in the estimates of catch-up.

20. George L. Perry, "Changing Labor Markets and Inflation," *Brookings Papers on Economic Activity*, 3:1970, pp. 411–48.

21. The German downtrend in hours may be a little overstated, since it was influenced by the special union-negotiated reduction of 1985.

22. Multifactor productivity growth was calculated from the following relationship:

$$\lambda = r_t - S_k(\dot{k} - \dot{n})_t,$$

where

λ = multifactor productivity growth
S_k = the capital income share

Table 9. *Projected Labor Force Growth in Four European Countries, 1985–90*

Percent per year

Growth estimate	Germany	France	Italy	United Kingdom
Original OECD projection	−0.4	0.8	1.3	0.5
Adjustment to eliminate downward bias in participation rate	0.2	0.0	0.0	0.0
Adjustment for effect of changing demographic composition[a]	0.3	0.0	−0.4	0.2
Final estimate of effective labor force growth	0.1	0.8	0.9	0.7[a]

Sources: See text.
a. In the United Kingdom, but not in other countries, changes in demographic composition reduced the effective annual growth of employment by −0.3 percent in the 1979–85 period.

10.) The stock of business capital and thus the capital-labor ratio were then assumed to grow at a rate consistent with estimates of profitability and other determinants of investment projected later in this paper. The results show that compared with the recent trend, productivity growth speeds up a bit in Germany and Italy and falls slightly in France and the United Kingdom.

Table 10 sets forth the resulting projections of potential GDP growth in nonfarm business.[23] The numbers imply that to meet these projections for the growth of economic potential, the capital stock will have to rise fast enough to require, in the three continental countries, an increase in the share of nonfarm business investment in GDP relative to current levels.

The changes in the capital stock and the business-investment share of GDP that would be needed to yield the projected growth in the business capital stock are shown in table 11, together with historical compari-

---

r_t = the latest trend rate of growth in labor productivity estimated as described in Schultze, "Real Wages"

$(\dot{k} - \dot{n})$ = the trend rate of growth in the ratio of capital to employment.

As in the case of labor productivity, the trend in the adjusted capital-labor ratio was taken from an equation fitted with linear splines to pick up breaks in the trend. The trend equation also included $\hat{q}$, with lags as dictated by the data, to eliminate cyclical influences.

23. Since productivity in sectors outside of business is likely to grow more slowly, potential growth may be a little less for total than for business GDP.

Table 10. *Projected Growth of Potential GDP in the Nonfarm Business Sector and Its Components in Four European Countries, 1985–90, and Comparisons*[a]

Percent per year

Item	Germany	France	Italy	United Kingdom
Potential GDP	2.1	2.5	2.8	2.4
Average working hours	−0.6	−0.2	−0.5	−0.3
Adjusted employment[b]	−0.1	0.8	0.9	0.7
Multifactor productivity[c]	1.6	1.0	1.9	1.2
Capital-labor ratio				
1980–84[d]	3.6[e]	4.0	2.1	3.9
1985–90	3.8	2.9	2.3	2.7

Source: Author's calculations.

a. Nonfarm business sector excluding housing.

b. Adjusted for productivity effect of demographic shifts; see text. Except in Germany (see note 16) it was assumed that the rate of change of employment in the business sector matched that of the total economy.

c. 1985–90 assumed to equal 1979–84 trend for all countries but Germany, where trend is based on 1982–86; see Schultze, "Real Wages."

d. Trend growth in ratio of capital stock to employment.

e. Trend value, 1979–86.

sons.[24] In Germany the current investment share would have to increase by 0.5 percentage point and in other continental countries by about 1 percentage point, roughly back to the level of the early 1970s, to sustain the projected growth of economic potential.

The "required" increase in the investment share is more ambitious, compared with earlier periods, than is the increase in the growth of the capital stock because, as I have noted, the output-capital ratio has fallen substantially during the past twenty years.[25] Even though gross business investment fell only a little in most European countries, it supported a steadily smaller rate of growth in the capital stock. As the capital stock grew faster than output, it pushed the European countries onto a higher path of economic growth. Generally, the higher the path, the harder it is to maintain any given rate of growth because a larger share of the national income must go toward investment. Thus, merely to support a moderate growth of the capital stock, one well below that of the 1970s, requires a rise in the investment share to or above the level of the early 1970s.

24. To help later comparisons with the saving rate, the investment shares of GDP have been converted to a current-dollar basis on the assumption that relative prices for capital goods remain unchanged at 1984 levels. Business investment "requirements" were initially calculated as a ratio to GDP in the nonfarm business sector and then converted to a ratio to total GDP on the basis of the relationship between the two ratios in 1985.

25. The same phenomenon has been true for net investment.

Table 11. *Business Investment "Requirements" Compared with Actual Investment in Earlier Periods, Four European Countries, Selected Dates, 1961–90*[a]

Item	1961–73	1974–80	1983	1984	1985	Required 1985–90
Annual growth rate of business gross capital stock (percent per year)						
Germany	7.0	4.5	3.5	3.3	3.4	3.7
France	5.6	5.1	3.4	3.0	3.1	3.7
Italy	6.6	4.0	2.5	2.8	2.9	3.3
United Kingdom	4.4	3.9	2.8	3.1	3.4	3.4
Share of business investment in total GDP (percent)[b]						
Germany	13.0	11.9	12.1	11.9	12.2	12.7
France	12.3[c]	12.4	11.3	10.9	11.3	12.3
Italy	11.3[c]	11.6	10.3	11.1	n.a.	12.0
United Kingdom	11.8	13.1	11.3	12.6	13.4	13.4

Source: For 1961–85, growth of the business stock from Commission data base (see Schultze, "Real Wages," data appendix).
n.a. Not available.
a. Nonfarm business investment excluding housing; GDP refers to total GDP.
b. At current prices.
c. 1970–73 for France and Italy; earlier data not available.

The central message that emerges from this analysis of growth prospects is that some increase in investment above today's levels will be needed to satisfy, on the supply side, the requirements of potential growth shown in table 11. What are the prospects that the needed increases in investment can be secured, both from the standpoint of investment demand and from the standpoint of the supply of national saving?

The Effect of Catch-up in Demand on Profitability and Investment

In my paper on real wages the results of the wage equations are used to estimate how far demand and output in the European countries could rise relative to potential without generating excess wage pressure. (By "excess" is meant nominal wage increases large enough so as to threaten either an increase in the rate of inflation or an increase in real wages relative to productivity.) Table 12 repeats from that paper estimates of both the current gap between actual and potential output and the gap that would forestall any excess wage pressure.

Obviously the precision of the numbers in table 12 is spurious, but the

Table 12. *Gap between Actual and Potential 1985 Output and Gap Consistent with Zero Excess Wage Pressure, Four European Countries*

Item	Germany	France	Italy	United Kingdom
1985 gap (actual *less* potential GDP)	−4.2	−4.2	−5.3	1.2
Gap consistent with zero excess wage pressure	−2.3	−1.5	−2.4	−1.9

Source: See Schultze, "Real Wages."

broad results of the analysis suggest that aggregate demand and output could rise faster than potential for several years in France and Germany without untoward inflationary consequences.[26] In Italy inflation remains high, and maintaining some slack to reduce inflation further might be reasonable. But even there some catch-up would be possible. Spread over two years, a catch-up in business output relative to potential of 2, 2½, and 1½ percent, respectively, in Germany, France, and Italy seems clearly feasible, especially given the conservative nature of the estimates. In the United Kingdom, on the other hand, the estimates in my paper on real wages suggest that a large catch-up in output, though not in employment, has already occurred, and that wage increases have begun to rise even without further catch-up. Combining the potential annual growth in each nation with its possible two-year catch-up in output in the business sector relative to potential yields two-year expansions in aggregate demand and GDP (for nonfarm business) of 3 to 3¾ percent a year in the three continental countries. If these rates of growth were achieved in the nonfarm business sector, average GNP would grow a little slower, since the nonbusiness sectors have lower productivity growth and would probably not share fully in the catch-up expansion.

Before turning to the investment implications, I want to highlight an important aspect of these numbers. They remind us that improvements in productivity growth can have a twofold effect on the size of the achievable GNP growth. A rise in the rate of productivity growth directly adds to the growth rate of potential GNP. But as emphasized in my real

---

26. For the United Kingdom the analysis implies that current levels of demand are generating an escalation in wage increases. The OECD notes that real wages rose substantially more than productivity during the last several years in the United Kingdom. *OECD Economic Outlook*, no. 40 (December 1986), p. 92.

wage paper, for any given set of wage aspirations, it also raises the natural rate of output, $\hat{q}^N$—the output that can be achieved without reining inflationary pressures. Thus each rise of 0.1 percent in annual productivity growth increases the growth rate of potential by 0.1 percent and, in the four European countries studied here, also adds 0.1 to 0.2 percent to the noninflationary level of attainable output.

If a catch-up in output relative to potential along the lines suggested were in fact achieved, investment demand could be expected to improve in two ways:

—First, there would be a direct accelerator effect on investment from the rise in $\hat{q}$, as indicated by the investment-demand equation described earlier.

—Second, an increase in $\hat{q}$, by raising the ratio of output to the capital stock, will improve profitability. In turn, an improvement in profitability will improve investment demand.[27]

On the other hand, several factors would operate to depress profitability and investment. In Germany changes in the real exchange rate have significant but long-lagged effects on overall profitability in the business sector. Thus the recent rise in the German real exchange will lower German profitability.[28] In all four countries the projected growth of the capital stock is faster than the growth of economic potential itself. This rise in the capital-output ratio would tend to depress lower profitability and be a downward influence on investment demand.

All these effects of profitability were estimated, assuming a catch-up in aggregate demand of the postulated size.[29] These profitability estimates, together with the assumed rise in $\hat{q}$, were then inserted into the investment-demand equations to project investment. In table 13 the

27. Changes in profitability affect investment with a long lag. In some countries improvements in profitability have already occurred, which—if maintained—will show up in investment demand in the future.

28. The relation between the German capital-income share and the real exchange rate is discussed above under "The Determinants of Profitability." For each sustained 1 percent change in the real effective exchange rate (IMF series 99by 110), the German capital income share in the nonfarm business sector ultimately changes by about 0.2 percentage point. The IMF measure of the real effective exchange rate rose from an index value of 93 in 1984 to 98.7 in the third quarter of 1986 and for purposes of the estimate made in this section was assumed to rise further to 103 in 1987 and remain there.

29. In Germany the investment equation shows a significant effect of real interest rates (see table 5). These were assumed to remain at 4 percent, approximately the 1986 level.

Table 13. *Business Investment Share of GDP in Four European Countries, Required for Growth and Predicted, 1985*[a]

Percent

Share of GDP[b]	Germany	France	Italy	United Kingdom
Actual 1985	11.9	11.0	11.0[c]	13.4
Required to support potential growth	12.5	11.9	11.8	13.4
Predicted, given catch-up in output relative to potential	12.5	11.9	11.8	13.2

Sources: OECD, *National Accounts,* and author's calculations.

a. Private nonresidential investment as a share of total GDP. Both GDP and investment are measured in current prices.

b. For comparative purposes investment in all three rows has been expressed as a ratio to GDP *after* catch-up; these ratios are therefore slightly lower than those shown in table 10, which were expressed as shares of GDP *before* catch-up.

c. Actual investment ratio in 1984.

resulting investment shares are shown and compared with both the actual shares in 1985 and the shares "required" to achieve the projected growth of economic potential.

In Germany, France, and Italy the required investment share and the investment share predicted after catch-up are the same. This is no accident, since the estimates of potential GNP growth were themselves iterated until the required and predicted investment shares more or less matched. The result reflects an effort to determine what kind of long-term economic growth could be supported on the supply side under conditions of high employment. For the United Kingdom, where excess wage aspirations work against catch-up expansion in aggregate demand, the projected long-term growth—even though it implies a reduction in trend productivity growth—is still a little larger than can be supported by the structural level of profitability.

The Sufficiency of National Saving

This paper opened with a discussion of the decline in gross national saving rates in Europe. Between the late 1960s and 1984 the gross national saving rate in the three continental countries fell about 5 to 7 percentage points (see table 1). Most of the decline was in government

Table 14. *Regressions of Private and Government Saving Rates (Gross) against the Output Gap in Four European Countries, 1964–84*[a]

	Coefficient on $\hat{q}$			
Country	Total national saving rate		Government saving rate	
Germany	0.41	(5.6)	0.45	(6.6)
France	0.47	(6.7)	0.24	(2.8)
Italy[b]	0.29	(2.4)	0.23	(2.4)
United Kingdom	0.36	(2.5)	c	. . .

Sources: OECD, *National Accounts*, and author's calculations.
a. The numbers in parentheses are *t*-statistics.
b. 1970–84 for Italy; no earlier data available.
c. Coefficient on gap is insignificant.

saving, as both government investment fell and government financial surpluses turned into deficits.[30]

The decline in European national saving rates was to an important degree associated with the decline in output relative to potential. Table 14 shows regressions of the total gross private saving rate and the government saving rate against the gap ($\hat{q}$), plus a time trend.[31] When the regressions were fitted to 1964–80, the coefficients were not substantially altered, so the results do not arise simply from the large recent changes in $\hat{q}$.

In all four countries the total national saving rate was procyclical. In Germany and Italy all the procyclicality stemmed from the automatic stabilizing feature of the budget. Given the higher reliance of the German revenue system on income taxes, its greater cyclical sensitivity is not surprising. On the other hand, the lack of sensitivity in the British budget to cyclical swings in the economy is puzzling. The same lack of sensitivity was found when various cyclical indexes were used, and when the budget surplus was substituted for government saving.[32]

30. For Italy the existing budget deficits became larger. Between 1984, the last year of data in table 1, and 1986 the goverment financial deficit as a share of GDP declined in Germany, the United Kingdom, and Italy by 0.5 to 1 percentage point and remained constant in France. See *OECD Economic Outlook*, no. 40 (December 1986), p. 10. But the basic conclusion in the text still holds.

31. The trends were broken at several dates as dictated by the data; the sizes of coefficients on the gap were not very sensitive to the choice of dates.

32. The cyclical measures were the gap (the $\hat{q}$ used throughout this paper); an alternative measure of the gap based on a potential GDP extrapolated from 1979 at the

Table 15. *Change in National Saving Rates in Four European Countries, 1961–73 to 1984*
Percentage points

Rate	Germany	France	Italy[a]	United Kingdom
Unadjusted	−5.1	−6.7	−5.2	−0.2
Cyclically adjusted	−2.5	−4.8	−3.2	0.3

Source: Author's calculations.
a. Base period is 1970–73.

In the United Kingdom and France, but not in Germany and Italy, the private saving rate seems to respond to changes in the gap when the relationships reported above are used to adjust national saving rates to reflect a constant gap (see table 15). Lower output is responsible for roughly 60 percent of the decline in the gross saving rate in Germany, 40 percent of the decline in France, and 36 percent of the decline in Italy. A catch-up expansion of output in these three countries of the size suggested earlier would raise national saving rates by about 1.5 percentage points in Germany, 1.0 percentage point in France, and 0.5 percentage point in Italy above the 1984 levels reported in table 1.[33] For Germany and France, these increases in national saving rates from their 1984 levels should be enough to bring about the increases in investment shares needed to support the projected growth of potential GDP.

In the case of Germany, the national saving-investment balance is being sharply altered by the depreciating U.S. dollar and a widely expected decline in the German current account surplus. That surplus

---

1971–79 rate of change in output; a survey measure of capacity utilization in manufacturing; and the unemployment rate. (These equations, fit to 1970–84, included a time trend, broken in 1974, with a highly significant coefficient. When the time variable is removed, two of the four cyclical indicators—capacity utilization and the unemployment rate—take on a significant coefficient, but only for the government saving variable, not for the government financial budget balance.) On the other hand, Price and Muller report a very high sensitivity of the financial budget balance in the United Kingdom to a gap measure that appears to be derived in a way similar to the second alternative reported above. See Robert Price and Patrice Muller, "Structural Budget Indicators and the Interpretation of Fiscal Policy Stand in OECD Economies," *OECD Economic Studies*, no. 3 (Autumn 1984), p. 34. The semiannual *OECD Economic Outlook* also periodically publishes actual and cyclically adjusted budget balances, in which the United Kingdom budget does show cyclical sensitivity. I have not been able in the time available to resolve this inconsistency.

33. Some of that saving increase has already occurred. Between 1984 and 1986 the gap was reduced in Germany and the United Kingdom (but probably has risen again in Germany in 1987).

grew to 4.0 percent of GDP in 1986 from an average of 0.6 percent in the 1960s and 0.9 percent in the 1970s. Even if the German current account surplus does not fall below 1.5 percent of GDP, its decline to that level will free up for domestic investment an additional 2½ percentage points of national saving. That change, together with the effect on government saving of the catch-up in demand (beyond that which has occurred since 1984), would be significantly more than needed to accommodate the required increase in investment. Thus in Germany some degree of fiscal expansion could be undertaken without reducing the supply of national saving below the level needed to sustain the nation's longer-run requirements for business investment.

Conclusions

During the past several decades both the demand for investment goods and the supply of national saving have declined in the major countries of Europe. This paper has argued that an important part of the decline in the growth of the capital stock is the natural consequence of a movement toward equilibrium from an initial period of capital scarcity with rates of profitability and investment that were too high to be sustained. After 1980 investment also fell in response to the direct and indirect consequences of a drop in output relative to capacity.

Under conservative estimates, maintaining a reasonable growth of economic potential in the four large European countries would require some expansion in the shares of business investment in GDP. In Germany, France, and Italy an expansion of aggregate demand and output relative to potential, within limits set to avoid renewed inflationary pressure, could induce growth in investment demand large enough to meet those requirements. In the United Kingdom, on the other hand, excess wage pressure seems to rule out a significant further catch-up in demand, in the absence of which the U.K. investment share is unlikely to increase much above its current level (which is, however, well above its 1982 low point).

National saving rates have also fallen over the past two decades, largely because of declining government saving but also, especially in recent years, because of the slow growth in output relative to potential. In France fully and Italy partially, a noninflationary catch-up in demand would generate additions to the saving rate needed for expanded business investment. In Germany the current and prospective downturn in foreign investment, together with the rise in the national saving rate from a catch-up expansion, would not only bring about the requisite increase in business investment but leave some room for a fiscal stimulus. For these three important European nations, then, structural insufficiency of aggregate saving and investment does not appear to be a barrier to a sustained moderate growth in economic potential. However, barring a large speedup in the pace of technological advance (of which there are no signs at present), a return to the growth rate of the early 1970s is not feasible.

RICHARD N. COOPER

External Constraints on European Growth

THE TOPIC of this paper, external constraints on European growth, is of interest because all European economies are very open, engaging in extensive foreign trade and increasingly in international service and financial transactions. Therefore, the external economic environment strongly influences Europe's economic prospects and possibilities. European economies are not, taken one by one, as self-contained as the Soviet, Chinese, or even U.S. economy. Most European trade, however, is with other European countries, so that Europe as a whole is not notably more open than the United States, although it is rather more dependent on imports of raw materials and foodstuffs, and rather less dependent on imports of manufactured goods, than the United States is.

Definition of Terms

The openness of Europe subjects it to various external influences or *disturbances*—a term used here in a neutral way to include pleasant as well as unpleasant unforeseen developments. Examples of disturbances in the past fifteen years have been the two major oil shocks of 1974 and 1979–80, when the price of crude oil in world markets rose in the first shock by over a factor of 3 and in the second shock by a factor of about 2.5, cumulatively from about $3 a barrel in 1973 to about $33 a barrel in 1981. Both these increases in oil prices were associated with a general rise in commodity prices, especially dramatic in 1973–74. Less well known in the United States is the third oil shock, brought about when the dollar appreciated so strongly relative to European currencies that it raised oil prices in terms of German marks from 64 DM (deutsche marks) a barrel in January 1981 to 92 DM a barrel in March 1985. The

540

subsequent drop in oil prices was therefore much steeper in Europe than in the United States, as the dollar price of oil dropped from about $28 a barrel in the summer of 1985 to $15 a barrel a year later and the dollar depreciated against European currencies, so that, for example, the DM price of oil fell by over 60 percent.

The two world recessions of 1974–75 and 1981–82 were caused partly by the oil shocks themselves and partly by the policy reactions of major countries to the oil shocks and the consequent inflation. These recessions led to a drop in primary product prices, thus improving Europe's terms of trade, but also to a drop in demand for Europe's exports. The large increase in earnings of oil-exporting countries created new markets, but the effective demand occurred only with a lag. The recessions also led to a sharp drop in interest rates in 1975 and a more modest drop, with a lag, in late 1982. Both these developments affected European countries differently, depending on the extent to which they were net exporters of primary products and net external debtors, such as Sweden, or net importers of primary products and net creditors, such as West Germany.

In addition to these major global developments, Europe's economy has also been affected by two noteworthy developments in the United States: the decline in the value of the dollar in 1978 and the high U.S. interest rates in 1981–82. The former event was thought to place European exports under undue competitive pressure; the latter to prevent Europeans from easing monetary policy to combat the emerging recession. The high U.S. interest rates were also associated with a sharp rise in the value of the dollar, which, because world oil prices are set in terms of dollars, was said to be a source of inflation in Europe. That they also greatly stimulated European exports, the reverse of events in 1978, was downplayed by European observers.

There is no question, then, that European economies are subject to important external influences, but that is not the same as being subject to external constraints, unless the term *constraint* is defined so broadly as to encompass the whole of the external environment. The term *external constraint* has had a more restricted meaning in the context of framing national economic policy, dating from the Bretton Woods era of the 1950s and 1960s, a period of fixed exchange rates and low international mobility of capital. Under those circumstances any country that engaged in monetary or fiscal expansion relative to its trading partners would sooner or later be constrained by its inability to finance its growing import bill with finite foreign exchange reserves. As the economy expanded, imports would rise. They could be financed only so long as the country was willing to draw down its international reserves. To be sure, exchange rates could be changed in the event of "fundamental disequilibrium." But currency devaluation was considered a defeat, a political failure; in fact, there were virtually no European devaluations between the major realignment of 1949 and the late 1960s. France's devaluations of 1957–58 marked the only major exception. Europeans came to expect stability in exchange rates during this period.

This form of external constraint no doubt applies to many developing countries today, particularly since the debt crisis of 1982 and the virtual cessation of bank lending to these countries. But does it apply to Europe? There have been two important changes since the Bretton Woods period. First, changes in exchange rates have become much more acceptable, both internationally and within countries; indeed, many currencies are floating against other currencies. As recent experience indicates, changes in nominal exchange rates affect real exchange rates. The movement of exchange rates introduces an additional degree of freedom in the for- mulation of national economic policy, although not one that generally works quickly on the market for goods and services.

Second, a full-fledged international capital market has reemerged. It has been possible to get medium-term bank loans on a large scale since the early 1970s and to float long-term bonds on a large scale since the early 1980s. Now it is possible to issue marketable medium-term notes. The New York capital market was receptive to high-quality foreign bond issues even in the 1950s, but on a much smaller scale than today and only after compliance with U.S. registration requirements.

Under these altered circumstances, the external constraint on national macroeconomic management of the 1950s and 1960s is no longer opera- tive, at least for European countries with ready access to the international capital market. Any such country that wants to expand may do so; if it runs a current account deficit as a consequence, it can borrow abroad to cover the deficit, and it can allow its currency to depreciate in order to eliminate the deficit (which usually takes time, so it will still have to borrow or draw down its foreign assets for a while). By appropriate choice of policy mix, expanding fiscal policy and tightening monetary policy, it can increase economic activity without any depreciation of its currency; the monetary tightening will encourage domestic residents to borrow abroad to cover their credit needs. Indeed, expansion is possible even with *appreciation* of the currency, as the United States demon- strated in the period 1982–85, with sufficiently tight monetary policy to make the country an attractive place for financial investment by foreigners. Of course, such a policy will alter the mix of output away from the tradable goods sectors (generally factories and farms) to the nontradable sectors (such as defense contractors and health and other local services). This alteration of structure may be unwelcome in the long run. But the expansion need not be accompanied by such a change if the mix of monetary and fiscal measures is suitably chosen. The external constraint would then disappear.

If this is so, why have there been several instances in the past decade in which European countries seem to have operated under severe external constraints? Both Italy and Britain felt the need for International Monetary Fund (IMF) programs and loans in the mid-1970s, apparently a sign of some form of external constraint. France's new Socialist government launched an ambitious program of economic expansion in 1981–82 and then reversed course and curtailed demand in 1983, again under the apparent influence of external constraint. Denmark had an analogous problem and curtailed sharply its expansionist fiscal policy in 1983. And even Germany seemed to be experiencing external constraints when it ran current account deficits in 1980–81 and then became alarmed and took steps to move rapidly into surplus. This paper examines these various episodes to discover how the judgment of "no external constraint" may have to be qualified in the contemporary economic environment, and also examines the interesting case of Sweden in the early 1980s, where a sharp change of policy seemed to take advantage of opportunities offered by the country's openness, rather than being deterred by constraints.

The scope for successful and mutually beneficial coordination of policy among nations as a means for overcoming external constraints depends on exactly what those constraints are. If the constraint is difficulty in financing a balance-of-payments deficit, multilateral action can help by reducing the imbalance in payments. If the constraint is depreciation of the currency of an expanding country, multilateral action may help by reducing the extent of depreciation. Moreover, coordination may be mutually beneficial even in the absence of external constraints if it lowers some of the inevitable costs associated with any macroeconomic management, provided the costs of coordination are not higher than the benefits thus garnered. For instance, multilateral action may improve the "sacrifice ratio," the stimulus to inflation that results from reducing unemployment by a given amount.

What, then, might be the external constraints in today's world? First, the country might be unable, for reasons of domestic politics or institutions, to achieve the right mix of monetary and fiscal policy for expansion of domestic demand at a roughly unchanged rate; that is, it might be unable to attract just the right amount of funds from abroad to finance its expansion. This circumstance is most likely to arise if for some reason fiscal policy cannot be used as the main instrument of expansion, since reliance on monetary policy for expansion will lead to depreciation of the currency. Or it might arise if domestic entities have not established customer relations with the lenders of the international capital market, so some time may be required to negotiate new loans or bond issues; but this would be a transitory problem. Or it might arise if foreign lenders are uncomfortable with economic developments and prospects in the country. In these various cases the currency will depreciate, and the depreciation will increase the rate of inflation as measured by final prices. It will also increase the underlying rate of inflation insofar as increases in wages are triggered by a rise in the consumer price index. Since the currency depreciation will occur quickly following monetary expansion, the inflation will show up more quickly than would be the case in a closed economy or an economy operating with fixed exchange rates.

A second possible constraint is that general fiscal expansion will "leak" abroad through increased imports in an open economy, thereby diminishing the impact of a given fiscal stimulus on domestic output and employment. Because increases in government expenditure are typically made on nontradable goods, the first-round effects of such expenditure would remain, but the multiplier is diminished by a high marginal propensity to import. To the extent that fiscal action has undesired side effects, as it almost inevitably does in the form of hard-to-reverse expenditure increases or hard-to-reverse tax reductions, then the benefit cost calculus will turn against fiscal action the more open the economy is. And this may seem to be a constraint.

Economic openness may create new opportunities as well as impose constraints. In particular, for countries with a diverse range of imports, currency depreciation holds out the possibility of substituting domestic for foreign goods in the home market and for increasing exports. In short, competitive depreciation can stimulate domestic output and employment, albeit at the cost of some increase in the price level. Similarly, currency appreciation can be used to get virtually instant relief from inflationary pressures, albeit at some cost in loss of competitiveness of the country's products in world markets. Policymakers thus face a different set of policy options in a world of flexible exchange rates and high capital mobility, but it is not obviously a more constraining set of possible actions.

Finally, a country that elects to borrow abroad to finance expansion, even if it can achieve the right policy mix to avoid major movements in its exchange rate, may be concerned about the buildup of external debt and future debt-servicing obligations. Action in the present (perhaps including sound investment, perhaps not) is purchased by mortgaging some future income. Countries may rightly worry about the growth of the external debt that will also require a change in the structure of output (toward tradables) in order to service it. But is this properly considered an external constraint? The possibility of borrowing abroad also permits current consumption plus investment to exceed current output, and that should be seen as creating new opportunities, whether or not they are exercised in a particular period.

In this paper, I examine episodes in six European economies in which the external constraint allegedly inhibited independent economic policy. I then consider possible advantages of policies that are coordinated internationally.

United Kingdom, 1974–76

The United Kingdom went to the IMF for a $3.9 billion loan in late 1976. Why should that have been necessary if, as argued earlier, Britain had virtually unlimited access to international capital markets to finance any deficit that it was likely to run?

Britain had had a large economic boom in 1972–73, which is generally recognized to have been excessive. In 1973 real GNP grew 7.9 percent, and by the fourth quarter of 1973 unemployment had fallen to 2.2 percent, its lowest level in many years. In response, the government of Edward Heath moved to cut back the economy. To cool the economic boom, the minimum lending rate set by the Bank of England was raised in successive steps from 7.5 percent to 13 percent during 1973. As a result of increasing reliance on liability management and other institutional changes, however, this increase in interest rates did not have the same contractionary effect as it would have had in earlier periods. The Bank of England therefore introduced in December 1973 the supplementary special deposits scheme (which came to be known as "the corset"). Commercial

Table 1. *Macroeconomic Indicators for the United Kingdom,*
1973–78

Year	Real GDP (percent change)	GNP deflator (percent change)	Fiscal impulse (percent of GNP)[a]	Real effective exchange rate (1980–82 = 100)[b]	Pound/dollar (percent change)[c]	Current account (billions of dollars)	Change in reserves (billions of dollars)
1973	7.9	6.9	2.2	71	−1.1	−2.5	1.0
1974	−1.1	15.2	0.2	73	1.1	−7.7	0.5
1975	−0.7	27.1	2.4	76	−13.8	−3.5	−1.4
1976	3.9	14.9	−2.4	70	−15.9	−1.5	−3.2
1977	0.9	14.0	−2.6	74	12.0	0.1	14.7
1978	3.8	10.8	2.8	77	6.7	2.2	−2.3

Sources: International Monetary Fund, *International Financial Statistics, 1985 Yearbook;* IMF, *World Economic Outlook,* April 1982, app. B, table 50; and Morgan Guaranty Trust Company of New York, *World Financial Markets,* August 1983, p. 10.

a. Growth in central government expenditure (excluding unemployment compensation) in excess of growth of potential GNP, less growth in tax revenues in excess of growth in actual GNP.

b. Own-country trade-weighted index of fifteen other OECD currencies, deflated by wholesale price of nonfood manufactures.

c. From year end to year end; minus sign indicates a depreciation of the pound.

banks whose lending activity had expanded by more than 8 percent over the first six months the scheme was in effect were obliged to make special non-interest-bearing deposits in the Bank of England, the extent of which was related to the degree of excess over base period lending.[1] Fiscal action, however, remained expansionary through 1973; indeed, on one measure there was an expansionist swing in the structural budget position by almost 6 percent of GDP between 1970 and 1973, although the structural budget deficit leveled out in the latter year.[2]

As a consequence of the monetary actions and also of developments in the world economy, the British economy cooled off in 1974 and real GDP actually fell by 1.1 percent (see table 1). Britain went into recession sooner and more rapidly than other leading countries. Despite the slowing of the economy, the legacy of the boom, combined with the fourfold increase in oil prices in early 1974, produced a current account deficit of $7.7 billion in 1974, equal to 4 percent of GNP. This large deficit was financed in part by private capital inflows of $4.6 billion, including borrowing by local authorities and state enterprises such as the National

1. "The Supplementary Special Deposits Scheme," *Bank of England Quarterly Bulletin,* vol. 22 (March 1982), pp. 74–85.

2. C. J. Allsopp and D. G. Mayes, "Demand Management in Practice," in Derek Morris, ed., *The Economic System in the U.K.,* 3d ed. (Oxford University Press, 1985), p. 427.

Coal Board and the National Gas Board.[3] In addition, foreign monetary authorities—in large part the newly rich members of the Organization of Petroleum Exporting Countries (OPEC)—built up their balances in sterling by $3.2 billion between 1973 and 1974. The pound depreciated very little against the U.S. dollar between the end of 1972 and the end of 1974, despite Britain's huge current account deficit. The pound did depreciate somewhat against continental European currencies during 1973, as did the dollar. Indeed, British reserves actually grew by $950 million in 1973 and by a further $450 million in 1974.

Despite the recession and stability of the exchange rate, the rate of inflation soared. The strategy to combat inflation involved monetary (and belatedly fiscal) restraint, a strong emphasis on incomes policy to restrain wage increases, and (although it was unstated) a rise in unemployment. Unemployment had averaged 2.6 percent of the labor force in 1973 and 1974, but it was allowed or encouraged to rise to 5.3 percent by 1976 and 5.7 percent by 1977.

The dilemma of stagflation sharpened in 1975, when the rest of the world was clearly in recession and GDP declined further. The corset was removed in February 1975, the minimum lending rate was reduced to 9¾ percent in April 1975, and fiscal policy was eased. The current account deficit declined sharply, but capital inflows from the rest of the world fell even more, and Britain drew down its foreign exchange reserves by $1.4 billion. The pound depreciated markedly against the dollar and against other European currencies. But the 1975 depreciation was not sufficient to offset the relative inflation in Britain, and the British government became worried about the loss of competitiveness of British goods.

In 1975 Britain faced an unenviable mix of problems: high inflation and unemployment, declining foreign exchange reserves, and an erosion in international competitiveness. How were these problems to be tackled? Views on how best to manage the economy had altered since the late 1960s. First, the experience of 1970–71 suggested that the inflation rate had become less sensitive to unemployment—that is, the Phillips curve relationship was altering for the worse. Second, more attention had to be paid to monetary magnitudes than had been the practice up until then, especially in an inflationary environment and one in which institutional change was taking place rapidly. (Institutional change would

3. *Bank of England Quarterly Bulletin*, vol. 15 (March 1975), p. 6.

later plague the monetary magnitudes, too.) Third, there was growing sentiment that export-led growth was more sustainable than the traditional reliance on fiscally stimulated consumption. Export-led growth put a premium on enhanced competitiveness, on maintaining low unit-labor costs when measured in dollars or other foreign currencies. On this last count a depreciation of sterling would have been welcome. But since depreciation would also have increased prices, it had to be combined with an effective incomes policy, which had to be voluntary because of the extreme tensions that developed with organized labor during the Heath administration.

A mandatory limit on wages and salaries had been in effect since the pay freeze of November 1972. In November 1973 a limit on wage increases of 7 percent was established, with additional allowances for exceptional productivity increases and for increases in the retail price index of more than 7 percent above the October 1973 levels.[4] Wage indexation with this threshold was introduced as an anti-inflationary device, in the expectation that the wage limit would reduce inflation rates and the threshold would not be substantially breached. The scheme did not foresee the threefold increase in oil prices. In fact, wages (compensation per employee in the total economy) increased by 50 percent between 1973 and 1975.[5] Britain experienced a veritable wage explosion, as did Japan during this period. The mandatory incomes policy was converted into a voluntary scheme to be achieved by negotiation with the Trade Unions Council—the "social contract"— when the Labour government took over in 1974. Incomes policy continued in one form or another until the Thatcher government of 1979, when it was abandoned.

The current account continued to improve during 1976, but net capital inflows dropped sharply. In addition, foreign holders of sterling, who had built up their balances substantially in 1974, began drawing them down heavily in 1975. They fell by 1.5 billion pounds between March 1975 and September 1976, or by about $2.9 billion. The British authorities both borrowed abroad and sold reserves to break the fall in sterling. Reserves reached a low of $3.4 billion by the end of 1976, well below the comfort level. Could Britain have borrowed more than it did?

4. Cmnd. 5444, "The Price and Pay Code for Stage III, A Consultative Document," discussed in *OECD Economic Surveys, 1975: United Kingdom* (Paris: OECD, 1975), pp. 32–33.

5. "Annual Economic Review, 1985–86," in *European Economy*, no. 26 (November 1985), p. 171.

Politics help explain the evolution of Britain's economic policy at this time. The Heath government lost an election in early 1974, mainly over dissatisfaction with its handling of a serious and contentious miners' strike. The new Labour government under Harold Wilson lacked a reliable majority in Parliament, but that was rectified by new elections in the fall of 1974. Wilson announced his intention to retire in early 1976; there was much dissatisfaction with him, partly over his economic policy, since he was seen to preside over Britain's deepest postwar recession. A struggle over his successor developed within the Labour party. In the end, centrist James Callaghan won by a hair over Michael Foote of the left wing.

On the British views expressed above, Callaghan needed the cooperation of organized labor to restore sustainable growth, reduce inflation, and reduce unemployment. His economic problem was how to achieve and maintain international competitiveness. His political problem was how to do it and stay in office. This would require some currency depreciation, some wage moderation, and some promise to labor with respect to increases in their real incomes and reduction in unemployment. The government's answer was a straddle.

Chancellor of the Exchequer Denis Healey laid out the government's program in early 1976. It would involve no increase in government expenditure (apart from interest on the public debt), no change in the public-sector borrowing requirement (PSBR), which at 10.1 percent of GNP was already very high, and an agreement on wage restraint in order to improve international competitiveness. His budget in April 1976 called for *maximum* wage increases of 3 percent, which with wage drift would result in actual wage increases of 5 to 6 percent at a time when inflation in consumer prices was running at 17 percent.[6] Healey held out the possibility of a cut in the personal income tax that would preserve the real value of after-tax pay, as had been urged in February by the *Economist,* among others.[7]

The minimum lending rate had been at 10 percent during the middle of 1975, but was raised to 12 percent in October 1975 to inhibit outflows of capital during a period of political unsettlement. The rate was lowered again to 9 percent in March 1976. The rate on three-month Eurodollar deposits was then about 7 percent.[8] Inflation (on the retail price index)

6. *Economist,* April 10, 1976, pp. 81–82.

7. "We're Not Reflating—Much," *Economist,* February 7, 1976, p. 77.

8. Morgan Guaranty Trust Company of New York, "Statistical Appendix," *World Financial Markets,* May 20, 1975, p. 14.

in Britain was running at 17 percent, compared with 6 percent in the United States. Financial investment in Britain was attractive in early 1976 so long as the pound was not expected to depreciate by more than 3–4 percent at an annual rate.[9] But, as already noted, the British were ambivalent about currency depreciation. Some depreciation was considered desirable, so long as it could be made to stick. There was considerable uncertainty about where the pound would go, especially after the marked depreciation of 14 percent against the U.S. dollar in 1975. Local authorities and nationalized industries were reluctant to take the exchange risk associated with borrowing in foreign currencies. Her Majesty's Treasury obliged this concern by providing forward cover on such borrowings at a fee of one-eighth of 1 percent. As the amounts of such induced borrowing became large, it became clear that the British government was on line for the loans even though it was not borrowing directly abroad. At the prevailing interest rate differentials, foreigners were reluctant to buy sterling securities, and official holders of sterling balances were reducing them. (Net sales by foreigners of British government bonds were modest during 1975, but during 1976 there was a net purchase of 130 million pounds.)[10]

Chancellor Healey announced his intention to draw from the IMF oil facility in January 1976, but he wanted to put his program in place first. A sharp run on sterling began in the fall, said to have been prompted by an article in the *Observer* reporting that the IMF team would recommend an exchange rate of 1 pound to $1.50, as opposed to the prevailing rate of about $1.80. Britain sharply increased the minimum lending rate to 15 percent—a record up until that time—and reimposed the corset in November.

The British government signed a letter of intent with the IMF in

9. The differential on long-term government bond rates was substantially higher. During 1976 British long-term government bonds earned 14.4 percent, compared with 7.9 percent on long-term U.S. government bonds. Government bond rates in Britain were very much lower than the 24 percent inflation rate of the preceding year, which suggested that the British financial community did not expect inflation to continue at its recent high rates. On the other hand, at a 6.5 percent differential between British and American bonds, the pound would have had to depreciate to 1 U.S. dollar by 1986 for investment in British bonds not to have been superior (on the assumption of equal tax treatment) to investment in U.S. bonds. The fact that little foreign investment in British bonds took place during this period suggests that investors were still quite uncertain about the future prospects of inflation in Britain and of the exchange rate.

10. Bank of England, *The Development and Operation of Monetary Policy, 1960–1983* (Oxford: Clarendon Press, 1984), p. 86.

December 1976 which called for (1) limiting the PSBR to 8.7 billion pounds in fiscal 1977–78 (Britain's fiscal year runs from April through March); (2) limiting domestic credit expansion (DCE) to 9 billion pounds in 1976–77 and to 7.7 billion pounds in 1977–78; (3) reducing government expenditure by 1 billion pounds (on a base of about 60 billion pounds) in 1977–78; and (4) eschewing comprehensive controls on imports, as were then being recommended by the Cambridge Economic Policy Group.[11]

The letter of intent tracks well Healey's program announced eleven months earlier, plus his introduction in July 1976 of monetary targeting on M3.[12] One has the impression that Healey did not give away very much. There was some tightening in the PSBR and in government expenditure relative to his projections at the beginning of the year, but only for the subsequent fiscal year. The market reacted coolly to the content of the letter of intent—the pound dropped by 2 cents—but fortuitously there were excellent trade figures for December, and the whole situation turned around very quickly.

The current account was in small surplus for 1977, as against a Treasury forecast of a continuing deficit of about 1 billion pounds, and foreign capital flooded into Britain. The monetary authorities intervened heavily in the foreign exchange market to inhibit appreciation of the pound and added nearly $17 billion to their foreign exchange reserves. Wages increased by 10.6 percent in 1977 over 1976. This was much more than the 3 percent that Healey had asked for, but considerably lower than the wage increases of the previous four years, despite the steep depreciation of sterling during 1976. Interest rates were reduced sharply, with the minimum lending rate dropping from 15 percent in October 1976 to 5 percent in October 1977. The currency continued to appreciate despite this drop. Moreover, the growth in reserves was threatening the

11. *OECD Economic Surveys, 1977: United Kingdom* (Paris: OECD, 1977), pp. 57–58. The Cambridge Economic Policy Group based its recommendations for import controls on an econometric calculation that Britain needed 5 percent economic growth between 1975 and 1980 to reduce unemployment below 1 million, but that 5 percent growth would increase the imports of manufactured goods by more than 17½ percent annually. This would require a decline in British costs of 20 to 30 percent in relation to foreign costs in order to achieve a corresponding increase in British exports, which in turn would require a devaluation of nearly 40 percent, something that the British considered undesirable. See *Economist,* April 3, 1976, p. 12.

12. The relationship between M3 and domestic credit creation is the change in foreign exchange reserves. A DCE target is tighter than an M3 target so long as reserves are being lost. If, as actually happened in 1977, reserves increase, a DCE target is consistent with a more rapid increase in M3.

new monetary targets, so heavy intervention was abandoned in late 1977 and the pound was allowed to appreciate. It rose sharply against the dollar, to $1.91 as against $1.71 at the beginning of the year, but much more modestly against the other European currencies.

The current account continued to improve during 1978 as a result of world recovery, the lagged impact of improved British competitiveness, and the fact that Britain was substituting North Sea oil for imported oil at the rate of nearly 20 percent a year starting in 1976, a substitution that by itself improved the current account by 800 million pounds a year at the then prevailing oil prices.[13] This prospect was known in advance, however, so the only news was the fact that North Sea production was slightly ahead of schedule.

In summary, Britain faced something of a confidence crisis with some of the external holders of sterling and with other potential investors during 1976. It also faced a dilemma over monetary policy. On the one hand, concerns about unemployment and international competitiveness suggested an easing of monetary policy. On the other hand, anti-inflation objectives and external financial considerations suggested a tightening of monetary policy to draw in funds to cover the (declining) current account deficit, following the extensive external borrowing of 1974 and 1975. Early in 1976 monetary policy was eased. There was no indication from the market that Britain's creditworthiness was fundamentally impaired, only that yield differentials over the dollar and other currencies were not sufficient to cover the likely depreciation of the pound. In the end, one has the impression that Healey went to the IMF not so much because he needed the funds—although, as noted, external foreign exchange reserves dropped uncomfortably low—but to get external support and pressure for a policy that was controversial domestically, but necessary, Healey thought, to achieve Britain's economic objectives.

Italy, 1975–77

Italy had a booming economy in 1973–74 when it was hit by the sharp increase in oil prices. On both counts it experienced a large current account deficit of $8.1 billion during 1974, most of which was financed by official encouragement of Italian borrowing abroad, especially by the

13. *Bank of England Quarterly Bulletin*, vol. 16 (December 1976), p. 410.

Table 2. *Macroeconomic Indicators for Italy, 1973–78*

Year	Real GDP (percent change)	GNP deflator (percent change)	Fiscal impulse (percent of GNP)[a]	Real effective exchange rate (1980–82 = 100)[b]	Lira/special drawing rights (percent change)[c]	Balance of payments (billions of dollars)[d]	
						Current account	Capital account[e]
1973	7.0	11.5	1.5	109	−16.0	−2.5	2.4
1974	4.1	18.4	−0.8	114	−8.4	−8.1	6.9
1975	−3.6	17.6	1.3	107	−0.6	−0.6	−2.7
1976	5.9	17.9	−1.0	102	−27.0	−2.9	4.8
1977	1.9	19.2	−0.5	101	−4.1	2.4	3.4
1978	2.7	13.9	3.8	98	−2.1	6.2	−2.5

Sources: See table 1.
a. Growth in central government expenditure (excluding unemployment compensation) in excess of growth of potential GNP, less growth in tax revenues in excess of growth in actual GNP.
b. Own-country trade-weighted index of fifteen other OECD currencies, deflated by wholesale price of nonfood manufacturers.
c. From year end to year end; minus sign indicates a depreciation of the lira.
d. Sum of current and capital accounts equals change in net foreign reserves.
e. Including errors and omissions.

commercial banking system and by the state enterprises. These inflows financed most of the current account deficit (see table 2), leaving a drop in foreign exchange reserves of only $1 billion. External financing became more difficult to obtain as the year went by, and the Italian authorities tried to rein in the economy by a variety of means. Italy was also hit by the world recession of 1975, but the decline in Italian GNP was greater than that in its major foreign markets. The current account deficit dropped substantially, and Italy was able to repay some of the funds that it had borrowed during 1974.

As economic activity slumped and unemployment rose, the monetary authorities eased up in the second half of 1975 in order to stimulate domestic growth. Italy then experienced a foreign exchange crisis in the first quarter of 1976. As a result of a substantial private capital outflow as well as an inventory boom in imported goods, the lira depreciated by 13 percent on an Italian trade-weighted basis between 1975 and 1976 despite heavy intervention by the authorities, for which they borrowed funds from the Bundesbank, the Federal Reserve Bank, and the European Community.[14] The monetary authorities moved to tighten again, raising the discount rate to 12 percent in March (it had been 6 percent in the second half of 1975). They also tightened and enforced exchange controls, particularly on the export of currency by Italian residents, which had been taking place in great volume to Switzerland. The situation eased up for several months, but was followed by a second crisis in the

14. *Banca d'Italia Report for the Year 1977*, p. 66.

second half of September. In October the authorities raised the discount rate to 15 percent and moved to cut the budget, raise taxes, and limit the impact of the *scala mobile,* the system of wage indexation that prevailed in Italy. They also introduced a temporary 10 pecent import deposit requirement and imposed ceilings on bank loans made in lire. Required conversions of export earnings to lire were increased to 50 percent from the 30 percent that had been imposed earlier in the year. In March 1977 Italy obtained a loan of $530 million from the IMF and a further loan from the European Community.

The balance-of-payments situation turned around rapidly. Italy ran a large current account surplus of $2.4 billion during 1977, augmented by substantial capital inflows of over $3 billion. But economic growth, which had reached an unexpected rate of 5.9 percent during 1976 (2 percent had been forecast early in the year), dropped to 1.9 percent in 1977, not high enough to keep unemployment from rising. The large inflows of capital during 1976 were more than enough to finance the current account deficit of $2.9 billion in that year, but these came mostly toward the end of the year and mostly in the form of foreign financing for Italian exports and trade credits to finance Italian imports in response to the import deposit requirement.

The rapid turnaround in late 1976–77, satisfying in many respects, required tightened monetary and fiscal policy to bring about. Where were those hypothetical foreign funds available to European countries? The missing information in this brief story is that Italy's political crisis during this period led to a crisis in economic policy. The Communist party increased its share of the Italian vote sharply to 34 percent in the election of June 1975. The Socialists withdrew from Prime Minister Aldo Moro's cabinet in January 1976, leaving the Christian Democrats with a minority government. No party wanted an election, but given the political impasse one was held in June 1976. The impasse continued: the Communists held their vote at 34 percent, while the Christian Democrats held theirs at 39 percent. The Communist party wanted to form a grand coalition with the Christian Democrats, who refused. By mid-summer Giulio Andreotti had reached agreement with the Communists that they would not join the government, but that they also would not oppose the government's policies in Parliament. As prime minister, Andreotti promised to consult with the Communist leadership in framing government policies.

Throughout this period uncertainty about the political future of Italy

was great, and many Italians exported capital. There were rumors that
U.S. Secretary of State Henry Kissinger was extremely concerned about
the increasing encroachment of Italian Communists on the Italian
government and that the United States would not lend to Italy under
these circumstances. The *Economist* noted in 1976:

The foreign exchange market became convinced that the Americans were
under order not to lend any more to Italy because of the Communist threat, and
that the EEC would not help out. . . . The American banks were unable to lend,
not because of any Kissinger veto, but because in late 1974 the Comptroller of
the Currency gave all loans to Italy a special classification. He told banks that
he might decide in a year to make them start writing these loans off. He did not
do that, but is considering something equally unhelpful to Italy: Making the
banks lump all their loans to different state enterprises under one category as
loans to the Italian government, which has guaranteed them all. Since the banks
have a limit on lending to one client, this would effectively prevent the big banks
from lending more.[15]

In view of the political developments and concern about previous
lending to Italy, therefore, Italy did not face a "perfect" capital market
in early 1976. Even so, it was able later in the year to borrow extensively,
especially in the form of trade credits induced by the import deposit
requirement and export financing limitations.[16] The Banca d'Italia complained of foreign constraints on its actions. It also observed that
currency depreciation under the circumstances prevailing in Italy was
rapidly translated into price increases. This led the bank to intervene
heavily in the exchange market to limit the depreciation of currency in
early 1976. Nevertheless, there was a large real depreciation of the lira
at that time that contributed, along with world economic recovery, to
the substantial improvement in Italian exports during 1977.

The new agreement with the International Monetary Fund came in
March 1977, after Italy had already taken its monetary and fiscal
measures in the fall of 1976 and after signs of the turnaround were already
present. (Italy had borrowed from the IMF in 1974 up to its allowable
limit, but this limit was relaxed in January 1976, permitting Italy to
borrow the additional $530 million.) One reason for this late IMF
agreement was uncertainty about whether the program would work fully.
(The target current account of Italy for 1977 in its letter of intent to the
IMF was a deficit of about $567 million, in contrast to the actual surplus

15. "Wanted, a Government for Italy," *Economist*, February 7, 1976, pp. 71–72.
16. *Banca d'Italia Report for the Year 1976*, pp. 57–58.

of $2.4 billion.)[17] Another reason was the need to have external pressure in formulating difficult and politically contentious economic policies within Italy, especially regarding wage escalation. Italy agreed with the IMF to abolish seven public holidays, to relax the rules on overtime, and to suspend the scala mobile for middle- and upper-income workers, as well as to increase further the value-added tax and to impose a ceiling on central bank lending to the government. As the *Banker* put it, "With all its weakness, the government has achieved something that much stronger Italian governments of the last few years didn't even dare to dream of, by forcing the unions to eat humble pie and getting an unpopular piece of economic policy through Parliament, with the tacit approval of the Communists. . . . All the wrath was discharged on the IMF's broad shoulders."[18] By this time, Italy did not need the IMF's funds so much as it needed its disciplinary pressure.

Federal Republic of Germany, 1979–81

West Germany has developed a reputation for having a strong balance-of-payments position and a strong currency and for prudently managing fiscal and especially monetary policy. Yet German officials and other commentators have from time to time lamented the external constraints on German policy, even after the deutsche mark was allowed to float in the early 1970s. Often these constraints have taken the form of pressure from other countries, either the United States or other members of the European Community, to modify Germany's policies. But one development not involving such pressure stands out for its traumatic influence on German thinking about external constraints: the sharp tightening of monetary policy in early 1981 in response to a perceived crisis in Germany's balance-of-payments position. During 1980 Germany experienced a large current account deficit, an outflow of private capital, and despite substantial intervention in the foreign exchange market, a sharp depreciation of the mark. In the end, Germany skillfully altered its monetary policy to permit more of the deficit to be financed by private capital flows.[19]

17. Ibid., p. 76.
18. *Banker*, May 1977, p. 16.
19. Ulrich Camen, "FRG Monetary Policy Under External Constraints, 1979–84," Working Document 21 (Brussels: Centre for European Policy Studies, April 1986), p. 21.

This episode must be viewed in its historical context. From 1965 to 1979 Germany had not run a current account deficit; indeed, it had run few such deficits throughout its history. The nation rode through the first oil shock with a large surplus, although the surplus dropped from $10 billion in 1974 to only $4 billion during the world recession of 1975. Moreover, Germans had become accustomed to a steady appreciation of the mark since the onset of floating currencies (except for a modest depreciation in 1975), a factor they counted on to mitigate both internal and external inflationary pressures.

Germany's budget had been close to balance for many years. The first large budget deficit occurred in 1975, when it nearly equaled the cumulative deficits of the preceding twenty-five years. The deficit was clearly linked to the sharp recession of that year. Although the deficit declined in subsequent years, it remained large by German standards (around 2 percent of real GNP in 1978, for instance). A series of stimulative fiscal actions in 1977–79 reduced tax revenues (although with respect to the personal income tax, this just offset fiscal drag) and increased expenditures. In March 1977 the government undertook a four-year, 16 billion mark expenditure program on public works. In June of the same year it reduced taxes by over 11 billion marks. Following a commitment that was made at the July summit in Bonn, in November 1978 the Bundestag approved a 16.8 billion mark program of tax reduction and expenditure increases. Then in June 1980 there were tax reductions in excess of 15 billion marks. The total tax to GNP ratio declined only slightly, from 25 percent in 1977 to 24 percent in 1981. On balance, fiscal policy provided a stimulus of about 1 percent of GNP in 1978–79 and then turned modestly contractionary in 1980 (see table 3).

The recession of 1981 led to a substantial increase in the already large deficit. Federal government debt grew from 7 percent of GNP in 1974 (most of that debt was acquired, not through budget deficits, but as a result of postwar settlements on outstanding wartime debt) to nearly 20 percent at the end of 1982. The debt of all public authorities—including states and municipalities—came to about twice that. But government debt remained way below the debt of other major industrial countries, and both government and private sectors had large net external claims on the rest of the world. (*Gross* government debt to the rest of the world was 4.5 percent of GDP at the end of 1982.)

Organized labor had been very cooperative throughout the postwar period, reasonable in its wage demands, concerned with Germany's

Table 3. *Macroeconomic Indicators for West Germany, 1978–83*

Year	Real GDP (percent change)	GNP defla- tor (percent change)	Fiscal impulse (percent of GNP)[a]	Real effective exchange rate (1980–82 = 100)[b]	Deutsche mark/dollar (percent change)[c]	Current account (billions of dollars)	Change in reserves (billions of dollars)[d]
1978	3.5	4.2	0.4	106	13.2	9.2	13.5
1979	4.0	4.0	0.6	107	5.3	− 6.3	− 2.6
1980	1.9	4.5	− 0.4	104	− 13.1	− 16.0	− 11.4
1981	− 0.2	4.2	− 0.9	97	− 15.1	− 5.4	− 4.0
1982	− 1.0	4.6	− 2.1	100	− 5.4	3.1	2.3
1983	1.3	3.3	− 0.9	101	− 14.6	4.2	− 4.2

Sources: IMF, *International Financial Statistics, 1985 Yearbook;* IMF, *World Economic Outlook,* April 1986, table A17; and Morgan Guaranty, *World Financial Markets,* August 1983, p. 10, and April 1987, p. 14.

a. Growth in general government expenditure (excluding unemployment compensation) in excess of growth of potential GNP, less growth in tax revenues in excess of growth in actual GNP.

b. Own-country trade-weighted index of fifteen other OECD currencies, deflated by wholesale price of nonfood manufactures.

c. From year end to year end; minus sign indicates a depreciation of the deutsche mark.

d. Including valuation changes.

external position, and reluctant to strike. For a variety of reasons, labor became (by these standards) much more militant in the late 1970s. There was a severe strike by the large metal workers' union in 1978, and wage demands stiffened. Wages rose 7 to 8 percent in 1980 (including fringe benefits) compared with only 4 to 5 percent in the previous year.[20] There was also a marked drop in productivity growth, which rightly or wrongly was attributed to the decline in labor's apparent willingness to cooperate.

All these factors are background to the crisis of 1980–81. The deutsche mark had reached a peak of 1.71 to the U.S. dollar in early January 1980 and then began a long decline in both nominal and real terms.[21] A current account deficit emerged in 1979 when oil prices rose sharply; as oil prices continued to rise, it increased further in 1980, to $16 billion (see table 3). By mid-1980 foreigners and Germans alike were pronouncing an end to the "German miracle." A mood of malaise and even gloom set in.[22] Official spokesmen were still saying in June 1980 that the current account deficit "presents no special problems in the short run" in view of available means to finance it. Otmar Emminger, former president of the German Bundesbank and an astute analyst of the German economy,

20. *Report of the Deutsche Bundesbank for the Year 1980,* p. 5.

21. Morgan Guaranty, "Statistical Appendix," *World Financial Markets,* December 1980 and 1981 issues, pp. 14 and 17, respectively. On a German trade-weighted index of sixteen different currencies, the real effective exchange rate of the mark dropped by 7 percent between December 1979 and December 1980.

22. See, for example, John Dornberg, "Germany Faces a Troubled Decade," *Institutional Investor,* June 1980, pp. 169–74; and David Tinnin, "The Miracle Economy Hits the Skids," *Fortune,* April 20, 1981, pp. 137–38.

wrote early the next year, "Yet, within months, that allegedly harmless deficit was to become a millstone around the neck of German economic policy."[23]

The German government and Central Bank had been committed to a policy of restraint since 1979. Starting in that year, the Central Bank had adopted a target range for the growth in Central Bank money (as opposed to a point target, which had been in use since the early 1970s), and during 1979 and 1980 the growth in Central Bank money stayed at the lower end of the range. The Fiscal Planning Council, representing governments at the federal, state, and municipal levels, agreed at the end of 1979 that Germany should reverse the governments' expansionary budgetary policy and reduce their financial deficits below those of 1979.[24] In the event, the total public sector deficits increased sharply in 1980, to 59 billion DM as opposed to 47 billion DM in 1979. The Fiscal Planning Council resolved again at the end of 1980 that Germany should try not to exceed the level of new indebtedness recorded in 1980 "even if this results in a rise of less than 4 percent in public spending."[25] Once again, the deficits grew sharply, to about 80 billion DM in 1981, corresponding to over 5 percent of GNP. In both years, of course, the growth of the budget deficit reflected a marked weakening of the economy, such that revenues fell substantially below their estimated levels, and expenditures, especially those associated with higher unemployment, were above the budgeted levels. But these two factors alone, according to the Bundesbank, did not fully account for the growth in the deficit.[26]

Because the economy was weakening, the Bundesbank eased the growth of Central Bank money after mid-1980. The Lombard rate—the rate at which the Bundesbank buys eligible securities put to it by the commercial banks—was lowered one-half point to 9 percent in September, it having been raised in stages from 3.5 percent in early 1979.[27] At the time of this lowering, the U.S. discount rate was 11 percent, having recently been raised from 10 percent. Yield differentials in favor of U.S. investment were reinforced by German jitters over the political crisis in Poland. A large outflow of funds ensued at the turn of the year, putting

23. Otmar Emminger, "West Germany—Europe's Driving Force?" in Ralf Dahrendorf, ed., *Europe's Economy in Crisis* (New York: Holmes and Meier, 1982), p. 31.

24. *Report of the Deutsche Bundesbank for the Year 1980*, pp. 28–29, 13.

25. *Report of the Deutsche Bundesbank for the Year 1981*, pp. 31, 34.

26. Ibid., p. 31.

27. *Report of the Deutsche Bundesbank for the Year 1980*, pp. 28–34.

downward pressure on the German mark. The Bundesbank made large sales of dollars to support the mark in the foreign exchange market. In February 1981 the Bundesbank responded to the outflow by tightening its monetary stance and, more dramatically, by closing the Lombard window altogether so that commercial banks could no longer routinely meet their cash needs at the Bundesbank.[28] The German authorities had already removed controls in March 1980 and again in February 1981 on the inward movement of capital, most notably on securities with a maturity under one year. Finally, in December 1980 leading German banks were persuaded by the Bundesbank not to lend at long term to nonresidents for the period December 1980 to March 1981 and not to float new loans in Germany on behalf of foreigners.[29]

These actions together produced a sharp turnaround in private capital flows. The Bundesbank stated its objectives as follows: "Foreign confidence in the deutsche mark, which had been eroded by the massive deterioration in the German current account, had to be strengthened again. In these circumstances, monetary policy had no choice but to continue the strategy of tight and relatively expensive money and to create interest rate relationships vis-à-vis other countries which would cause the deutsche mark to remain an attractive investment currency." Later in the same report it added that "the fight against inflation and the prevention of an excessive depreciation had to be made the prime objectives of economic policy."[30]

Market interest rates rose sharply following this change in policy, the German government bond rate rising from 9.1 percent in January 1981 to 11.2 percent by August. The result was a major turnaround in the capital account. The German current account deficit dropped to $5.4 billion in 1981, fully covered by capital inflows, inclusive of direct government external borrowing of 21 billion German marks. Heavy foreign exchange market intervention continued with respect to the U.S. dollar, which was appreciating sharply during 1981, but the sales of dollars in the foreign exchange market were partially offset by interventions to prevent further appreciation of the German mark against other

28. The Bundesbank subsequently granted banks "special" Lombard loans at a rate of 12 percent. Ibid., p. 34; and *Report of the Deutsche Bundesbank for the Year 1981*, p. 5.

29. *Report of the Deutsche Bundesbank for the Year 1980*, p. 26.

30. Ibid., pp. 1, 28. This report was published a few months after the early 1981 change in policy. The Bundesbank has a statutory responsibility to stabilize the price level, so prevention of excessive depreciation is the important addition.

European currencies linked to the mark in the European monetary system (EMS). Consequently, German reserves declined much less in 1981 than they had in 1980. The German economy went into a slump in the second half of 1980, which continued through 1982 and from which in some respects it had not recovered fully even by 1985.

In early 1982 Otmar Emminger wrote that Germany's balance-of-payments deficit during this period imposed a "twofold limitation on its economic policies."[31] First, monetary policy was dominated by high U.S. interest rates, since Germany had to finance its current account deficit and so had to attract foreign capital and inhibit the outflow of domestic capital. Second, "all economic policies, in particular fiscal policy, had to be directed towards reducing the current account deficit."[32] In fact, the government did finally launch fiscal contraction in September 1981, when it cut expenditures for 1982 by 9.5 billion DM and raised taxes by 2.5 billion DM.[33]

The Council of Economic Experts, an official body of five independent academic economists, urged in the fall of 1981 a four-year "consolidation" of the budget. The council estimated the structural budget deficit at 40 billion DM, by which it meant the actual deficit corrected for the cyclical weaknesses of the economy and for the long-run deficit appropriate to a growing economy, which it reckoned to be about 1 percent of GDP at that time.[34] The September 1981 actions were considered a useful first step, and the council recommended further cuts by 8 to 10 billion DM per year for the period 1983–85 inclusive. It assumed that taxes were already high enough at 24 percent of GNP (40 percent of GNP if contributions to pensions and social insurance were included). The target should therefore be achieved by reducing government expenditures below what they would otherwise be, and this, the council reckoned, could be accomplished if government expenditures grew by only 3.5 percent a year while nominal GNP increased at 5.5 percent a year.[35]

The council's report provided the general framework for subsequent fiscal consolidation, and the structural deficit was reduced from 2.4

31. Emminger, "West Germany—Europe's Driving Force?" p. 31.

32. Ibid.

33. N. Kloten and K. H. Ketterer, "Fiscal Policy in West Germany: Anticyclical vs. Expenditure-Reducing Policies," in Stephen F. Frowen, ed., *Controlling Industrial Economics* (London: Macmillan, 1984), p. 304.

34. Ibid., p. 298.

35. Ibid., p. 303.

percent of GNP in 1981 to a surplus of 1.0 percent of GNP in 1985, based on OECD calculations.[36]

It is unclear to what extent fiscal consolidation was driven by external constraints. As noted, Emminger emphasized strongly the need to reduce the current account deficit. Why this was such an important objective he did not make clear, except to note that Germany had become a structural exporter of capital.[37] But that is circular reasoning, since whether a country is a structural capital exporter depends inter alia on its fiscal policy. Many other Germans—for example, Wilfried Guth, president of Deutschebank—found it abhorrent that Germany was "living beyond [its] means."[38] By this same balance-of-payments accounting standard, Canada has been living beyond its means in almost every year of its entire existence since 1867, yet it is unclear that Canadians or anyone else are the worse off for it. In fact, Canadians have invested much of their current account deficit. Emminger made the observation that Germany must run a large *trade* surplus to cover its extensive net expenditures on tourism and other imports of services as well as its exports of capital.[39] Some suggest that German tourism is excessive, and there was talk at the time that perhaps there should be special taxes or other limitations put on overseas spending by traveling Germans.

Emminger underlines the need for competitiveness for all of these reasons, but he is wary of achieving it through currency devaluation because of its inflationary impact.[40] Instead he advocates wage restraint and productivity growth. This is sound advice for every country, but not advice by which all countries can simultaneously improve their international competitiveness. If some countries are to run surpluses, others must run deficits. Not all countries can be sufficiently competitive to run surpluses. When the OPEC countries are in heavy surplus to the tune of over $100 billion, as they were in 1980, it is hardly surprising that even Germany ran a deficit. Yet this obvious point is virtually absent from Germans' discussion of their situation. Rather, German commentators adopt a small-country perspective: Germany is subject to external

36. Patrice Muller and Robert W. R. Price, "Structural Budget Deficits and Fiscal Stance," Working Paper 15 (Paris: OECD, Department of Economics and Statistics, July 1984), annex 1.

37. Emminger, "West Germany—Europe's Driving Force?" p. 39.

38. See Dornberg, "Germany Faces a Troubled Decade," p. 170.

39. Emminger, "West Germany—Europe's Driving Force?" p. 39.

40. Ibid.

influences, but the appropriate response is exclusively up to Germany, regardless of possible countervailing or counteracting responses elsewhere or of the pressure Germany's actions would put on other countries.

In contrast, Kloten and Ketterer, presumably in some sense representing the Council of Economic Experts, which Kloten chaired for many years, focus on *domestic* reasons for fiscal consolidation. They are concerned about the rapid growth of public debt, which some Germans remembered was repudiated in the aftermath of two world wars and inflated away in 1923. Their concerns relate to just how large the public debt could grow before public disaffection set in, as well as with the future tax burden required to service the debt. These arguments for fiscal consolidation were reinforced by doubts about the efficacy of fiscal stimulus under the circumstances prevailing in Germany in the early 1980s. As Kloten and Ketterer note:

> The very fact that the West German economy still moved into a deep recession [in 1981] proves that the conditions under which government expenditure financed by borrowing actually has an expansionary effect hardly exist any more, or perhaps do not exist at all. . . . Economic recovery is handicapped by growing doubts about the solidity of government finances. The extensive use of finance, as well as the expectation of future increases in taxes and painful stabilization measures have a depressing effect; these repercussions of fiscal policy reduced the expansionary effect and can even more than compensate for it.[41]

Kloten and Ketterer are impressed by Germany's exceptionally large fiscal stimulus in 1980–81, which they calculate to be about 3 percent of GNP, but the economy turned down nevertheless. In making this argument they ignore the influence of (1) the sharp increase in oil prices, (2) the worldwide economic slowdown, (3) the appreciation of the German mark until early 1980, whose effects on trade would be delayed until 1981 and even later, and (4) the tight monetary policy that had been maintained until September 1980. Indeed, a simulation by the Bundesbank suggested that the 1979–80 oil price increase alone reduced German real GNP by 1.8 percent in 1980, and it can hardly have done less in 1981 when on average oil prices were even higher.[42] Moreover, calculations by the IMF staff suggested that fiscal policy was contractionary, not expansionary, in 1980–81, by over 1 percent of GNP (table 3).[43] Provided

41. Kloten and Ketterer, "Fiscal Policy in West Germany," p. 300.
42. *Monthly Report of the Deutsche Bundesbank*, vol. 33 (April 1981), p. 17.
43. At a minimum, the discrepancy suggests the need for better international

that Germany was willing to pay appropriate interest rates, the absence of external financing was not considered to be a serious constraint.[44]

Except perhaps briefly in late 1980 and early 1981, monetary policy was not strongly influenced by external considerations, despite Germany's membership in the EMS after March 1979 (even though exchange market intervention was occasionally heavy). The Bundesbank stayed within its monetary range virtually thoughout the 1979–84 period. Camen showed that virtually 100 percent sterilization of any foreign exchange intervention occurred within two months of the intervention.[45] Within the target range of 3 percentage points, monetary policy could, by admission of the Bundesbank, be influenced by a desire to fine tune either the domestic economy or the exchange rate.[46] As the preceding history suggests, a conflict arose between the fall of 1980 and early 1981. For both years, the Bundesbank ended at the low end of its target range: 5 percent growth in Central Bank money for 1980, 4 percent for 1981.

Did external considerations influence the setting of the range? The range was lowered from 6-9 percent in 1979, to 5-8 percent in 1980, to 4-7 percent in 1981, where it remained in 1982 and 1983. This drop in range may have been part of the concerted anti-inflation program that the Bundesbank had been pursuing since 1979. Although the GNP deflator

---

agreement on what constitutes *fiscal stimulus*. Revised IMF estimates in 1987 reduce the contractionary impulse in 1980–81, but it remains contractionary.

44. The Bundesbank stated that financing the deficit is difficult, but it was then maintaining a monetary policy at marked variance with that obtaining outside Germany. *Report of the Deutsche Bundesbank for the Year 1980*, p. 25.

45. Camen's analysis showed a modest influence of contemporaneous exchange rate movement, as opposed to exchange market intervention, on the growth of central bank money over the whole floating rate period 1974–84, but not, curiously enough, during the 1979–84 period when the EMS prevailed (which includes the episode described here). Camen, "FRG Monetary Policy," p. 28. Hodgman and Resek find a strong influence of recent past movements in the deutsche mark–dollar rate on German interest rate policy, especially in quarters in which Germany runs a current account deficit. They do not find significant influence, however, if periods of deficit are not separated from periods of surplus. Their single equation reaction function is flawed by simultaneous equation bias, but removal of the bias would presumably reinforce this particular result. Incidentally, their significant monetary reaction function throws strong doubt on estimation of structural or reduced form equations that assume monetary policy is exogenous. Donald R. Hodgman and Robert W. Resek, "Determinants of Monetary Policy in France, the Federal Republic of Germany, Italy and the United Kingdom: A Comparative Analysis," in Hodgman, ed., *The Political Economy of Monetary Policy: National and International Aspects*, Proceedings of a Conference held in July 1983 (Federal Reserve Bank of Boston, 1983), pp. 156–57.

46. *Monthly Report of the Deutsche Bundesbank*, vol. 31 (December 1979), p. 10, and vol. 32 (February 1980), p. 9.

showed little change from around 4 percent over the period 1978–82, the consumer price index, influenced by oil prices, rose 2.7 percent in 1978, 4.2 percent in 1979, and 5.4 percent—a politically explosive rate for Germans—in 1980.

A basic lesson of the German experience is that in an open economy it is not possible to fix both the exchange rate and the interest rate unless the country is willing to draw down its reserves. Germany, in effect, did just this in 1980, but compromised in early 1981 by permitting some drop in the exchange rate and some rise in interest rates, so that the drawdown in reserves had virtually ceased by year end.

To sum up, Germans became greatly concerned with the buildup of total (not mainly external) debt. In this respect, Germany was like Denmark, but with a much lower ratio to GNP both of total government debt and of external debt. Germans were also deeply concerned about the weakness of exports and the loss of export competitiveness. Indeed, the absence of a current account surplus and vigorous exports in the Federal Republic apparently creates a serious malaise and loss of self-confidence, requiring immediate action to correct the situtation.

France, 1981–83

Under the anti-inflation program of Raymond Barre, the French economy slackened with a rise in unemployment in 1980. The new French government of President François Mitterrand, installed in June 1981, committed itself to reviving growth and reducing unemployment. Mitterrand was also committed to a Socialist program to nationalize banking and significant industry, strengthen the position of labor unions, change the distribution of income and wealth, and institute comprehensive economic planning. To these various ends, the new government nationalized all the major private banks, five major industrial groups, and several individual firms, bringing to 18 percent the share of nonagricultural output owned by the state.[47] It increased subsidies to state and private enterprises to help them grow or to keep them from declining (for example, coal and steel), and it also increased transfer payments to households, without corresponding increases in taxes. The general

47. Georges de Menil, "Discussion" of Jeffrey Sachs and Charles Wyplosz, "The Economic Consequences of President Mitterrand," *Economic Policy*, no. 2 (April 1986), p. 312.

Table 4. *Macroeconomic Indicators for France, 1979–85*

Year	Real GDP (percent change)	GNP deflator (percent change)	Fiscal impulse (percent of GNP)[a]	Real effective exchange rate (1980–82 = 100)[b]	French franc/special drawing rights (percent change)[c]	Current account (billions of dollars)	Change in reserves (billions of dollars)[d]
1979	3.3	10.4	−1.0	101	2.8	5.1	4.0
1980	1.1	12.2	−1.8	102	−8.8	−4.2	11.6
1981	0.5	11.8	0.6	100	−16.2	−4.8	−7.0
1982	1.8	12.6	0.3	97	−10.9	−12.1	−5.7
1983	0.7	9.5	−0.5	95	−17.8	−5.2	4.1
1984	1.5	7.3	−0.7	97	−7.6	−0.9	0.3
1985	1.3	5.9	−1.0	101	11.7	0.9	5.7

Sources: See table 3.

a. Growth in general government expenditure (excluding unemployment compensation) in excess of growth of potential GNP, less growth in tax revenues in excess of growth in actual GNP.

b. Own-country trade-weighted index of fifteen other OECD currencies, deflated by wholesale price of nonfood manufactures.

c. From year end to year end; minus sign indicates a depreciation of the French franc.

d. Including valuation changes.

budget went from a surplus of 0.3 percent of GDP in 1980 to a deficit of 1.6 percent of GDP in 1981 and then to a deficit of 2.9 percent of GDP in 1982.[48] Social charges were raised to cover part of the greater social payments. This increased the total tax wedge on wages, the ratio of wage cost to the firm and net pay (before income tax) to the worker, to 1.65 in 1983—up from 1.60 in 1980.[49] Structural social security expenditures reached 24 percent of potential GDP.[50] In addition, taxes on wealthy individuals were increased, bringing top marginal income tax rates to 75 percent and adding wealth taxes (since abandoned) of 2½ percent.[51] The overall fiscal impulse shifted toward expansion. Calculated to correct for cyclical variations in economic activity, it changed from −1.8 percent of GNP in 1980 to 0.6 percent in 1981 and to 0.3 percent in 1982 (table 4).

The minimum wage was increased 39 percent over 1981–82—an increase of 11.4 percent in real terms from the beginning of the Mitterrand government to July 1982. A fifth week of paid vacation was decreed. The normal work week was reduced from forty to thirty-nine hours. (Working hours per week were to decline to thirty-five, although further reductions were postponed in 1982.)[52] In February 1982, after a prolonged public

48. Morgan Guaranty, "The French Austerity Program," *World Financial Markets*, August 1983, p. 2.

49. Sachs and Wyplosz, "Economic Consequences of President Mitterrand," p. 302.

50. Ibid., p. 267.

51. De Menil, "Discussion," p. 312.

52. Sachs and Wyplosz, "Economic Consequences of President Mitterrand," p. 272.

debate, Mitterrand decreed that the reduction in the work week should take place without a reduction in pay. This decision was designated a "serious mistake" by Edmond Maire, secretary general of the major union favorable to the Socialist party.[53] Early retirement was made attractive by augmenting the pensions that early retirees would receive.

Mitterrand's entire program was predicated on consumer-led growth. The crucial importance of investment was recognized, but it was assumed that with an increase in public and private consumption, investment would soon follow. Insufficient allowance was made for the squeeze on profits resulting from the increased wages and other social expenditures, or for the loss of confidence that followed implementation of the Socialist program.

A currency devaluation was urged on the new government—the real effective exchange rate of the franc had been deteriorating slightly since 1977, and it was recognized that some of the new measures would increase costs. But the government rejected the advice at first, partly because a devaluation had been widely rumored. Exchange controls were tightened in May 1981 before the installation of the new government. The government changed its mind, however, and a devaluation within the European monetary system of 8.5 percent against the German mark took place in October 1981.

It was bad luck for the new French government that the world slipped into deep recession in 1982. Like governments around the world, it had not expected this development.[54] French exports declined by 3 percent in volume and by 9 percent in dollar value during 1982, after having already declined in 1981. Imports also declined in dollar value, by 3½ percent following a 9 percent decline in 1981, but imports rose 3½ percent in volume between 1981 and 1982. The French current account position worsened markedly from the second quarter of 1981 (when it ran a small but aberrant surplus) to the first quarter of 1983 (when the deficit reached about 1 percent of GDP). The current account deficit was $12.1 billion for all of 1982, up from $4.8 billion in 1981. Between 1980 and 1982

---

53. Bela Balassa, *Change and Challenge in the World Economy* (St. Martin's Press, 1985), p. 373.

54. For instance, the members of the Federal Open Market Committee of the U.S. Federal Reserve Board forecast in February 1982 a growth in nominal U.S. GNP of 8 to 10 percent for the coming year, fourth quarter to fourth quarter. In fact, nominal GNP grew by only 3.1 percent, with both real output and price increases being far less than were widely anticipated. "Record of Policy Actions of the Federal Open Market Committee," *Federal Reserve Bulletin,* vol. 68 (April 1982), p. 231.

inflation, as measured by the GDP deflator, remained about 12 percent. Inflation dropped somewhat more sharply in France's main trading partners (with the notable exception of Germany, where it remained between 4 and 5 percent). The worsening current account and relative price situation led to a second devaluation in June 1982, this time by 10 percent against the mark, and a declaratory change of policy toward less stimulus. However, the momentum from the actions of the first year continued, and the only *restrictive* measure that was added was to freeze all wages and prices for several months.[55] While French GDP rose throughout 1982, industrial production, influenced by the decline in exports, fell by 2 percent from 1981 and industrial employment remained unchanged. Unemployment continued to rise throughout 1982 and 1983.[56]

The Mitterrand government continued Barre's practice of setting monetary targets for M2, which is made up of currency, bank deposits, and Treasury bills in the hands of the public. Monetary control in France at this time operated mainly through limits on the loans each bank could make. (This practice has since been replaced by a system of marginal reserve requirements associated with increased bank lending.) Money market interest rates were manipulated by the Bank of France, which kept a watchful eye on the exchange rate. The sizable increase in government spending, largely financed through Treasury bills, tended to increase M2, so lending to private firms was sharply limited. Even so, the M2 target was exceeded in 1981, although it was met in 1982, thanks in some measure to the contractionary impact of the decline in foreign exchange reserves.[57]

A speculative run on the franc in the first quarter of 1983 prompted heated debate within the government over how to respond. Some argued for the imposition of extensive controls over imports, including goods coming from other members of the European common market. In the end, Mitterrand decided that the commitment to Europe was too impor-

55. Balassa, *Change and Challenge*, p. 378.
56. Total employment stabilized during 1982, but this overall development concealed the fact that employment in sheltered sectors of the economy—government and other sectors that were not subject to competition—rose, whereas employment in the sectors in competition with other countries declined substantially. See Sachs and Wyplosz, "Economic Consequences of President Mitterrand," p. 275.
57. See Florin Aftalion, "The Political Economy of French Monetary Policy," and Robert Raymond, "Discussion," in Hodgman, ed., *Political Economy of Monetary Policy*, pp. 7–25, 26–33.

tant for France, and that France should not drop out of the European monetary system or, de facto, out of the European Community. A third devaluation within the EMS was negotiated in March 1983, resulting in a devaluation of the franc by 8 percent against the German mark.[58] This devaluation was combined with an austerity program that involved consequential cuts in government spending and increases in taxes to hold the rising government budget deficit at 3 percent of GDP, as well as official restraints on wages and prices. A compulsory loan was instituted for a portion of 1982 tax bills. The target for M2 was reduced to 9 percent from an actual growth of 12 percent in 1982, and credit ceilings were lowered to 10 percent for 1983.[59]

Aided by world economic recovery, the situation turned around very quickly. Indeed, the turnaround in the current account was suspiciously quick, since it dropped from $4.8 billion in the first quarter of 1983 to $0.4 billion in the second quarter, and was in modest surplus by the fourth quarter of 1983. This suggests some speculative outflow through the current account, a possibility that is also implied by the fact that the government imposed tight restrictions on travel expenditures in cash by French residents and prohibited their use of credit cards abroad, so that travel had to be financed through a French travel agency.

This episode is frequently cited as one in which a national policy ran up against external constraints and had to be completely reversed. It must be closely examined to discover exactly the nature of the constraints.

Mitterrand came to power committed to a "radical break with capitalism."[60] His Socialist party was allied uneasily with the Communists and internally divided between the moderates and the left wing. There was talk of a "class front" in Parliament, as in society at large.[61] There was concern by the wealthy and even the middle classes about punitive taxation and even confiscation, concern that was reinforced by stories of French agents taking photographs of French residents entering or leaving Swiss banks. In short, Mitterrand did not come to power as a consensus leader, but as a leader for one segment of society. Those who did not identify with him and his views were frightened about the

58. Sachs and Wyplosz, "Economic Consequences of President Mitterrand," p. 276.
59. Morgan Guaranty, "The French Austerity Program," pp. 3–4.
60. Balassa, *Change and Challenge*, p. 363.
61. Ibid., p. 364.

consequences for their economic well-being. One manifestation of this concern was the sharp drop in stock prices during 1981 and early 1982 (a decline of 40 percent from 1980 in real terms), despite the government's assurances that the nationalizations were to be limited to those initially carried out, and despite the fact that even those nationalizations took place with compensation.[62]

Under the circumstances, it is not surprising that many French wanted to export their capital. The U.S. administration's trenchant talk with respect to Poland, the imposition of martial law in Poland, and the possibility that the Russians might feel obliged to move tanks and troops into that country were added incentives. Much capital fled the country, despite exchange controls. Errors and omissions in the balance-of-payments accounts, having been positive in 1980, were negative to the tune of $2.3 billion in 1981, $1 billion in 1982, and $0.9 billion in the first quarter of 1983 alone. The French monetary authorities moved to discourage outflows of capital by increasing interest rates in May 1981 to 19 percent, from which they declined slowly and erratically over the next eighteen months.[63] But the export of capital from France at this time was not motivated mainly by higher before-tax yields on foreign investments.

As a consequence of the outflow of capital, the French govenment faced financing requirements that involved the current account plus the outflow of resident capital. The government encouraged both the banks and the nationalized industries to borrow abroad, and together they did so to the extent of $14 billion in 1981 and again in 1982. In addition, the French government began direct borrowing abroad in late 1982. The experience was an unpleasant one. France considered drawing medium-term credit from the European Fund, but rejected the idea because that would entail economic conditions imposed by the European Community. Instead, it raised $4 billion from a consortium of commercial banks, an arrangement that was announced in mid-September 1982 and completed a month later. Many foreign banks were involved, and the terms were relatively good: 0.45 percent in up-front fees, plus 50 basis points over Libor. These terms were more favorable than those that Venezuela, which was still riding high on the oil boom at that time, had received the preceding month. However, French officials were deeply offended by

62. Sachs and Wyplosz, "Economic Consequences of President Mitterrand," p. 293.

63. Ibid., p. 270.

the question they were asked: who *exactly* was the guarantor of the loan, and what was the basis of the guarantee? They were also offended by the conditions of the loan: (1) that the debt would not be subordinated to any other official French debt; (2) that it include a cross-default clause against the outstanding debt of French government-owned enterprises; and (3) that dispute settlement take place in the courts of the lenders, not of France. Despite strong objections to these conditions, the French Treasury in the end agreed to them. The loan was oversubscribed by 50 percent, and in 1983 the commercial banks, having become disenchanted with Latin America, were eager to lend to France. However, the French government was reluctant to borrow further.

The reluctance did not stem so much from the unavailability of foreign funds as from the fact that the French program did not seem to be working. While GDP had risen, industrial production had not, and neither had employment beyond direct hires by the government itself. Investment did not pick up as expected, but, on the contrary, continued to decline. And inflation was greater than was expected or desired, especially given the declining inflation rates outside of France.

Why wasn't the program working? One theory, prevalent at the time, was that imports flooded in to satisfy increased French consumer demand, preventing an increase in French production and employment. This view led to a proposal to restrict imports, as had been urged in Britain by the Cambridge Economic Policy Group. But overall data do not show exceptional increases in imports. In volume terms they increased modestly more than real GDP, as had been the case for more than a decade. Rather, the explanation seems to be that there was much less slack in the French economy than French officials had believed.

Sachs and Wyplosz argue that the nonaccelerating inflation rate of unemployment (NAIRU) had risen steadily in France during the preceding two decades, largely because of the increase in real labor costs; that is, wages plus all of the social charges, paid vacations, and so on. They estimate that the NAIRU had reached 7.4 percent by 1981, roughly equal to the actual unemployment rate.[64] On this calculation, unemployment could not be reduced through increased consumer spending without stepping up the rate of inflation. In fact, as they point out, there was virtually no *net* stimulus to demand in France during 1981–82, since the increased fiscal thrust (at about 1.0 percent of GNP compared with 1980)

64. Ibid., p. 287.

was offset by the loss of exports (−0.9 percent of GDP) and the decline in investment induced by the sharp drop in the stock market (−0.7 percent of GDP).[65] France did not experience accelerating inflation because it did not experience much increase in demand relative to capacity, and indeed unemployment rose during 1982. But if there had been a net increase in demand, on this line of argument, France's inflation would have increased more rapidly. The increase in the NAIRU was influenced not only by steadily increasing social charges but also by increases in real take-home wages and by a slowdown in the growth of productivity, which in turn was influenced by weak investment during the preceding years.

Thus France might have been able to borrow more abroad to cover a current account deficit that arose, because France was out of phase with its major trading partners. Yet, if the interpretation above is correct, it might have been unwise to borrow in foreign currency in circumstances in which inflation was accelerating under the pressure of a policy of economic stimulus. It is perhaps more appropriate to consider a NAIRU equal to the observed unemployment rate as an internal constraint on national economic policy rather than as an external constraint.

What about the possibility of currency devaluation? In fact, France did improve its competitive position in fits and starts despite its somewhat greater inflation than that prevailing abroad. France's real effective exchange rate dropped by 1.5 percent between the second quarter of 1981 and the first quarter of 1983, before the third devaluation.[66] French competitiveness was improved further by the devaluation of March 1983. Devaluation, to the extent that it did not get passed fully into higher wages, could reduce the real wage to the firm and increase profit margins in those sectors of the economy that were open to foreign trade. Thus it would provide some incentive both to invest and to expand production and employment in those sectors, which seems to have been an important objective. But France was a charter member of the European monetary system. Currency devaluation—other than that taking place as a by-product of the sharp appreciation of the dollar in 1980 and 1981—required permission of France's EMS partners. The partners would probably not have agreed to any large change in the exchange rate. Indeed, each change was subject to intense negotiation over exactly which country

65. Ibid., p. 295.
66. Morgan Guaranty, "Effective Exchange Rates: Update and Refinement," *World Financial Markets*, August 1983, p. 10.

should move relative to the ecu baseline and by how much. The need for German permission to change France's exchange was a serious embarrassment to Mitterrand and to French dignity and independence. So the option of substituting external for internal sources of demand was limited, except insofar as it was brought about by wage moderation at home; that is, by a reversal of the policy that the Mitterrand government had launched.

There was, of course, the possibility of leaving the EMS altogether, as some French officials seriously urged in early 1983. But the EMS was associated with the European Community, and France's departure from it would have been interpreted as a de facto rejection of the European Community by the Socialist government, particularly if the departure had been accompanied by restrictions on imports. Other voices within the French government were concerned about a "vicious circle" of devaluation and inflation and welcomed the discipline that a more or less fixed exchange rate imposed. Indeed, in international forums France had long been an exponent of fixed exchange rates.

To summarize, the French program of the summer of 1981 was based on an incorrect assumption about the degree of slack then prevailing in the French economy. The overall program frightened French owners of capital; French officials were offended by inquiries and conditions on foreign loans; competitive devaluation was ruled out by commitment to the rules and procedures of the EMS. These factors taken together, as well as concern about the growth of external debt, persuaded French officials that they should reverse course in early 1983.[67]

Sweden, 1974–83

Sweden maintained extensive and apparently effective exchange controls and a "fixed" exchange rate from 1973 until 1985. Therefore,

---

67. The magnitude of debt in France was not large by international standards. Gross public debt as a percent of GDP grew from 15.1 percent at the end of 1980 to 21.4 percent at the end of 1984, a substantial increase, but even the latter figure left France toward the low end of industrial countries (calculated from International Monetary Fund, *International Financial Statistics*). Gross external indebtedness of France increased from $29.5 billion in May 1981 to $53.7 billion at the end of 1983, an increase of nearly $25 billion, most of which was by state-owned enterprises. See Balassa, *Change and Challenge,* p. 388. This was a large increase, but it still fell short of France's official claims on the rest of the world (including reserves), so that France's net official indebtedness to foreigners was negative.

the characterization of external constraints in the 1950s and 1960s seems to apply to Sweden right up to 1986, when exchange controls began to be gradually dismantled. This means that Sweden could suffer unacceptable reserve losses that would force some corrective monetary and fiscal action.

With this in mind, the broad course of Swedish economic developments since the first oil shock of 1974 can be described briefly as follows. Real growth in GDP over the 1974–85 period was 1.7 percent a year, an unspectacular performance compared with the 4.0 percent achieved from 1953 to 1974. But this modest growth conceals a dramatic change in economic structure. Industrial production stagnated during the decade between 1974 and 1985 (1974 was admittedly a peak year for industrial production), and manufacturing employment fell sharply. These declines were not compensated elsewhere in the private economy. Rather, the government sector grew from 49 percent of GDP in 1974 to 66 percent in 1984. Open unemployment remained virtually unchanged at around 2 percent throughout the 1970s, but then gradually rose in the 1980s to 3.1 percent in 1984. The sharp increase in government-sponsored labor market programs kept open unemployment down. If these programs are added, however, unemployment grew from 4.5 percent in 1974 to 7.7 percent in 1984.[68]

Tax revenues did not keep pace with the rapid growth of government expenditures. (Sweden was already the highest taxed OECD country.) Consequently, the central government deficit grew sharply after 1977, reaching 12 percent of GDP in 1982. The result was a substantial increase in public debt, from 21 percent of GDP in 1974 to 63 percent in 1984. This growth in government debt was not compensated by increases in private saving; rather, Sweden borrowed from the rest of the world. Its net asset position with respect to the rest of the world changed from a positive 6 percent of Sweden's GDP in 1974 to a net debit position of 24 percent of GDP by 1984.[69] The government deficit early in the period was financed by the Central Bank and the banking system, but in the early 1980s Sweden developed a local capital market for marketable government securities and increasingly financed the deficit without resort

68. Hans Tson Söderström, ed., *Sweden: The Road to Stability* (Stockholm: Studieförbundet Näringsliv och Samhälle [Business and Social Research Institute], 1985), p. 17.
69. Ibid.

to the banking system.[70] Inflation rates (consumer price index) reached 11.5 percent in 1977. By 1984 they had declined to 8 percent, averaging about 10 percent over the whole 1974–85 period.

These were the basic characteristics of the Swedish economy. What about economic policies? Sweden elected to ride out the first oil shock of 1974 without a decline in production or an increase in unemployment. It adopted the so-called overbridge policy, whereby increases in government spending, the release of investment allowances, and the stepping up of active labor market policies would cushion the domestic economy from the contractionary aspects of the oil shock and the subsequent world recession of 1974–75. The demand for Swedish exports fell sharply, and Sweden went into a current account deficit in 1974. The deficit was covered mainly by overseas borrowing by Swedish banks and firms. Then in 1975–76 Sweden experienced a "wage explosion." Wages are centrally bargained in Sweden between the leading labor organization, the Swedish Confederation of Trade Unions, or Landsorganisationen (LO), and the Swedish Employers' Confederation, or Svenska Arbetsgivareföreningen (SAF), under the so-called Swedish model. Wages rose 42 percent in two years. It is unclear to what extent this was an autonomous process, linked basically to pre-1974 developments, and to what extent it derived from the sharp increase in consumer prices that took place in 1974 in Sweden as in other OECD countries, combined with the active policy of maintaining high employment in Sweden. Whatever the cause, the consequence was a sharp decline in the cost competitiveness of Swedish goods in Sweden's major foreign markets, with a foreseeable further deterioration in the current account deficit. To correct for this, Sweden devalued the krona modestly in 1976 and more extensively (16 percent) in 1977 against the European snake to which the Swedish krona was tied until August 1977. This devaluation temporarily restored price competitiveness for manufactures and, combined with the general world boom of 1978–79, permitted a sharp increase in Swedish exports.[71]

70. Johan Myhrman and Jan Sundberg, "The Credit Market in Transformation," *Skandinaviska Enskilda Banken Quarterly Review*, no. 2 (1986), pp. 30–38.

71. Sweden did not allow the krona to float, however. It pegged the krona to a basket of currencies related to Sweden's trading partners. A disproportionate weight, over 20 percent, is given to the U.S. dollar because of the extent to which Swedish imports and some of Swedish exports, notably forest products, are quoted in dollar terms in world markets.

Then came the second oil shock and the second world recession starting in 1981. Sweden pursued a more restrained policy on this occasion, but it did not reverse its earlier policies and continued them to some extent. With a further loss of competitiveness, Sweden devalued by 10 percent in 1981. The recession deepened. The Swedish budget deficit and the current account deficit worsened in 1982 as Sweden went into a summer election campaign. During the campaign the ruling government composed of both conservatives and liberals was reluctant to devalue the currency or to tighten money. The conservative coalition, in power since 1976, had become associated with a willingness to devalue the currency, something that had been eschewed by the Socialists up until then. The substantial outflow of funds, despite capital controls, led to a loss of reserves and to a need to devalue after the election. The question was by how much. The Socialists won the election and decided to devalue by 20 percent to give Sweden a competitive edge for a longer period of time, or, to put the matter another way, to give Sweden some room for maneuver with respect to wage settlements in the next few years. It was implicit in this decision that money wages would not respond fully to the devaluation. Sweden consulted with the other Nordic countries, which were appalled by such a large devaluation, and out of deference to them Sweden scaled down the devaluation to 16 percent. Even so, Finland followed suit with a 6 percent devaluation, having devalued the Finmark by 4½ percent in just the preceding week. The devaluation left Sweden with a substantial improvement in competitiveness, and it was criticized abroad as a "competitive devaluation" of the type international rules are supposed to prevent.

The year 1982 marked a turning point in Swedish policy. The Swedish current account improved substantially in 1983 (table 5), and the Socialist government began to squeeze government spending to reduce the budget deficit. Open unemployment grew. By 1984 current balance had been restored for the first time in over a decade, and the budget deficit, including interest payments, had been reduced from 12 percent of GDP in 1982 to 5 percent in 1986. Wage settlements continued to be high compared with those of leading competitors, but not so high as to erode rapidly the competitive edge achieved by the 1982 devaluation. Swedish profits increased substantially, but private investment did not pick up until 1985. Wage pressures are still an important question in Sweden, especially public-sector wages, since public-sector employment has become the dominant component of the Swedish labor force. A show-

Table 5. *Macroeconomic Indicators for Sweden, 1979–85*

Year	Real GDP (percent change)	GNP defla-tor (percent change)	Fiscal impulse (percent of GNP)[a]	Real effective exchange rate (1980–82 = 100)[b]	Swedish krona/spe-cial draw-ing rights (percent change)[c]	Current account (billions of dollars)	Change in reserves (billions of dollars)[d]
1979	3.8	8.0	0.5	100	2.4	−2.4	−0.6
1980	1.7	11.7	2.3	101	−2.1	−4.4	−0.1
1981	−0.3	9.5	0.1	102	−16.3	−2.8	0.2
1982	0.8	8.6	1.0	96	−24.1	−3.5	−0.1
1983	2.4	9.8	n.a.	91	−4.1	−0.9	0.5
1984	3.4	7.9	n.a.	96	−5.2	0.4	−0.2
1985	2.3	6.8	n.a.	97	5.1	−1.0	1.9

Sources: See tables 1, 3.
n.a. Not available.
a. Growth in central government expenditure (excluding unemployment compensation) in excess of growth of potential GNP, less growth in tax revenues in excess of growth in actual GNP.
b. Own-country trade-weighted index of fifteen other OECD currencies, deflated by wholesale price of nonfood manufactures.
c. From year end to year end; minus sign indicates a depreciation of the krona.
d. Including valuation changes.

down between the Socialist government and government employees in 1986 was resolved inconclusively after a selective strike, and the issue remains contentious.

What does this story reveal about external constraints on Swedish economic policy? As noted earlier, Sweden had a fixed exchange rate and exchange controls throughout this period, so it was superficially like a country in the 1950s. However, when it pursued its overbridge strategy, being out of phase with its main trading partners, it was able to borrow as needed on the international capital market. Monetary policy was maintained to encourage firms and municipalities to use the freedom the exchange control authorities gave them to borrow abroad. The government bond yield rose successively to 8.8 percent in 1975, 10 percent in 1978, and 13.5 percent in 1981. Starting in 1977, the Swedish government began to borrow in scale directly abroad in order to prevent the depletion of its foreign exchange reserves, with exceptionally large borrowings in 1980.

The devaluation of 1976–77 did not represent a break with this policy; rather, it was designed merely to offset the loss of cost competitiveness arising from the 1975–76 wage explosion. In other words, Sweden was sensitive to the need to maintain international competitiveness, but apparently separated that issue from macroeconomic strategy. The same was roughly true of the 1981 devaluation.

Uneasiness developed after the second OPEC shock, as concern spread about the growth of Sweden's internal and external debt. In November 1982 Sweden changed its strategy to rely more on exports as a source of growth, to remove the guarantee on employment, and to reduce both the internal budget deficit and the external current account deficit. Calmfors suggests that in this year the government shifted its principal assignment from employment maintenance to maintenance of international competitiveness, reversing roles with the leading labor unions, which before then were relied on to preserve international competitiveness, supposedly through wage restraint, while the government maintained full employment.[72] Indeed, recent Swedish economic commentary seems preoccupied with international competitiveness, a preoccupation that is perhaps understandable in a country that exports 40 percent of its industrial production.[73] It is unclear whether this concern is with cost competitiveness per se or simply with a desire for strong export performance. Often the two go together, but the distinction becomes important in the context of a coordinated expansion by Sweden with its major trading partners. Would such an expansion alleviate Sweden's concerns about a deterioration in cost competitiveness or not? One cannot tell from the extant evidence.

To sum up, Sweden demonstrates that a country can swim against the prevailing macroeconomic tide by borrowing abroad, but that the price is a growth in external debt and future debt service. Swedes became concerned about these developments—net interest payments to foreigners reached 2.6 percent of GDP in 1982—and took steps to correct the situation while Sweden's credit rating was still excellent (that is, before foreigners began to worry seriously about the buildup of Swedish debt). Alternatively, a country such as Sweden can use currency devaluation to aid expansion, but the price is a decline in the terms of trade and inflationary pressures.

As this story shows, Sweden's economic prospects are strongly influenced by developments abroad: changes in the terms of trade and world booms and recessions. But despite these external influences, a single country has some scope for setting an independent course. This scope may diminish in the future, however, insofar as Sweden abandons its system of exchange control. Then it will experience both new sources

72. Lars Calmfors, "Sweden and Finland: A Comparison of Stabilisation Policy Strategies," *Skandinaviska Enskilda Banken Quarterly Review*, no. 4 (1984), p. 122.
73. See, for example, Det Økonomiske Råd [Danish Economic Council] and others, *Economic Growth in a Nordic Perspective* (Finland: DOR, 1984), chap. 6.

of disturbance and new constraints on its actions so long as it tries to maintain a fixed exchange rate.

Denmark, 1979–84

Denmark illustrates how policy such as that pursued by Sweden can be pushed to the point at which an external constraint emerges. Following the 1979 oil shock and subsequent recession, Denmark pursued a strategy basically similar to Sweden's: protect employment and ride out the world recession through macroeconomic management. (Unlike Sweden, Denmark had not pursued a strong expansionist policy after the first oil shock.) Denmark reflated in 1979, which, along with world recession and a rise in world interest rates, led to a large increase in budget deficits in 1981 and 1982. Deficits were aggravated by the growing unemployment and the generous unemployment benefits. Unlike Sweden, Denmark had run a current account deficit during the 1960s and early 1970s of 2 to 3 percent of GNP. This current account deficit jumped sharply in 1976 to 4 to 5 percent of GNP. Hence the rate of external borrowing accelerated. Denmark had currency devaluations in 1976 (4 percent), 1977 (two totaling 8 percent), 1979 (two totaling 8 percent), and 1982 (3 percent). An improvement in international competitiveness from 1979 to 1982 of nearly 20 percent measured in terms of unit labor costs was brought about by these devaluations and by substantial productivity growth, which together more than compensated for the 34 percent increase in wages over that period. Nonetheless, there was great public concern in Denmark about the growth in the budget deficit at interest rates that were way above the rate of growth of GNP. Questions were raised about the sustainability of Denmark's policy and the possibility of some ultimate confiscation of domestic bonds. Domestic interest rates were running at 20 percent, compared with an inflation rate of only 10 percent in 1982. The cumulative external debt reached 33 percent of GDP by the end of 1982, with net interest payments to foreigners amounting to 3.8 percent of GNP, making Denmark one of the most heavily indebted of the industrial countries. In September 1982 the Standard and Poor's rating agency put Danish securities on a credit watch, reducing its rating from AAA to AA + . This represented a small reduction, but when combined with market speculation about the possible need for a rescheduling of Danish external debt, it increased Danish concern about the debt.[74]

There were expectations of devaluation again in 1982. A new conservative government came to power in September 1982. It rejected devaluation on grounds that devaluation would aggravate inflation, in sharp contrast to the response of the new Socialist government in Sweden two months later. The new government froze prices, eliminated wage indexation, and committed itself to reduce the budget deficit. In the meantime, a new floating rate note issued by Denmark in the international market flopped. The yield on the note, taking front-end fees into account, was 0.53 percent above Libor, compared with 0.43 percent on a comparable note issued the previous February. Even so, the notes began trading at a heavy discount of 1.4 percent almost immediately. Thus the market signaled its concern about the Danish economy.[75] Feeling boxed in regarding its policy options, the Danish government moved sharply to restrain the budget deficit, with some measure of success since the deficit dropped from 40 billion kroner in 1982 to 26 billion kroner in 1984. Domestic interest rates on long-term bonds in response dropped from 22 percent in 1982 to 14 percent by the fall of 1983, and the AAA credit rating was restored.[76] Denmark's current account deficit declined from its peak of $3.0 billion in 1979 to $1.2 billion in 1983, rising again to $1.6 billion in 1984.

Summary and Observations on the Coordination of Policy

What can be learned from these episodes in recent European history in which external constraints seem to have been in operation? Signs of constraints on borrowing emerged in several countries, particularly Italy, France, and Denmark. But they were very weak signals, and in no case did they indicate that external credit had become unavailable. The countries could have borrowed much more. Italy represents the weakest case. Its problem was aggravated by the outflow of resident capital, but the current account deficit was declining rapidly and the problem was

---

74. See ibid., chap. 3 and statistical appendix.

75. Charles Grant, "Is Copenhagen Still as Wonderful?" *Euromoney*, January 1983, p. 17.

76. DOR and others, *Economic Growth in a Nordic Perspective*, pp. 81–82.

one of uncertainty over how the country would be governed rather than an unwillingness to lend to a government that could decide what it wanted to do and ran into an external constraint. As the experience of many developing countries since 1982 demonstrates, international sources of capital can effectively dry up, so that any current account deficit must be financed by drawing down claims on the rest of the world, and that is a process with distinct limits. But Canada has demonstrated that a country can borrow from the rest of the world year after year for decades without apparent difficulty, so long as the economy is doing well and is perceived to have good prospects. Western European countries are surely much closer to Canada on this spectrum of creditworthiness than they are to developing countries in Africa or Latin America.

In the end, changes in domestic policy occurred in all of the episodes discussed. But on close examination, it was not the external constraints that forced the change in policy, but discomfiture by domestic policy-makers with the consequences of their current line of policy. Both Britain and Italy called in the IMF in part to evoke some external discipline over domestic wage settlements—Britain to reinforce its incomes policy, Italy to back away from its strong wage indexation. In both cases the main objectives had been outlined by the government before the IMF was engaged. In both cases uncertainty about the government's ability to carry out its announced policy induced capital flight—mainly nonresident capital in Britain, mainly resident capital in Italy. Because of limited reserves, this capital flight compelled a policy reaction that obviously involved the balance of payments. Whether one wants to consider response to doubts about a country's ability to carry out its announced policies an "external constraint" is a question of semantic taste.

In all cases a major concern of policymakers was international competitiveness. Again, this is an external factor, but not obviously an external constraint. Indeed, explicitly in the case of Britain and Sweden, and implicitly in the case of Italy and Germany, selling abroad was seen to provide an important opportunity for pursuing employment and growth. Sweden quite deliberately switched toward major reliance on external demand in 1982. Concern with the buildup of debt, internal at least as much as external, was a major influence in leading Sweden, Denmark, and Germany to alter their policies. Rapid increases in domestic prices, quite apart from their implication for competitiveness, influenced decisionmakers in Britain, Germany, and probably France. France's announced policy, apart from contributing to higher inflation,

Table 6. Correlation Coefficients between Interest Rates in United States and Four European Countries, Selected Periods, 1960:1–1983:4

Country and period	Nominal interest rate				Real interest rate[a]			
	France	Germany	United Kingdom	United States	France	Germany	United Kingdom	United States
France								
1960:1–1972:1	...	0.64	0.73	0.92	...	0.65	0.25	0.20
1972:2–1979:1	...	0.49	0.52	0.58	...	0.71	0.51	0.64
1979:2–1983:4	...	0.57	0.04	0.44	...	0.06	0.73	0.75
Germany								
1960:1–1972:1	...	...	0.46	0.63	...	...	0.30	0.15
1972:2–1979:1	...	...	0.24	0.62	...	...	0.57	0.59
1979:2–1983:4	...	...	0.57	0.89	...	...	−0.27	0.31
Italy								
1960:1–1972:1	0.61	0.67	0.39	0.56	0.62	0.39	0.00	−0.18
1972:2–1979:1	0.08	−0.72	0.11	−0.21	−0.03	−0.29	0.35	0.43
1979:2–1983:4	0.88	0.41	−0.27	0.27	0.78	0.03	0.83	0.80
United Kingdom								
1960:1–1972:2	...	...	...	0.77	...	...	...	0.44
1972:2–1979:1	...	...	...	0.40	...	...	...	0.76
1979:2–1983:4	...	...	...	0.52	...	...	...	0.72

Source: Stefano Micossi and Tommaso Padoa-Schioppa, "Can Europeans Control Their Interest Rates?" no. 17 (Brussels: Centre for European Policy Studies, 1984), p.30.
a. Nominal interest rates deflated with the CPI growth rates in the four quarters up to the quarter of reference.

reducing competitiveness, and enlarging the national debt, seemed not to be working well in the sense that GNP was rising much less than its architects had hoped and planned. Fiscally led demand expansion seemed not to be effective.[77]

Like Britain, France, and Italy, Germany experienced an outflow of capital while it ran a current account deficit, and that fact forced a change in policy. To finance a current account deficit with foreign capital does require a willingness to pay an appropriate return, one obviously influenced by world market conditions. The return can be achieved through sufficiently high interest rates or through a drop in the value of the currency to the point at which expected currency appreciation is sufficient to compensate for a lower interest or dividend yield. What is not possible for an open economy is to determine, independently of world market conditions, the interest rate and the exchange rate. This the United States also learned during the 1981–84 period, when tight money and large budget deficits led to an unwelcome strong dollar.

This observation does not imply that domestic interest rates by themselves are determined by world market conditions or even that there is not some—albeit limited—scope for manipulating both interest rates and exchange rates. Table 6 shows the correlations between quarterly averages of short-term interest rates among five major countries over the period 1960 to 1983. These rates are broken into three subperiods to distinguish between fixed exchange rates (1960–72), floating exchange rates (1972–79), and floating exchange rates in the presence of the European monetary system (1979–83), when three of the countries listed had exchange rates that were constrained with respect to one another by the EMS. One might think that high capital mobility would lead to high correlations among short-term interest rates, especially between countries whose exchange rates are fixed to one another. Figure 1 does show a certain visual parallelism among interest rates, and the correlation coefficients of table 6 are generally positive. But they are remarkably low, with the notable exceptions of the correlation of 0.89 between U.S. and German short-term interest rates, and 0.88 between French and Italian, in the most recent period. Not surprisingly, the correlations are generally lower in the 1970s, the period of floating exchange rates, than during the 1960s, the Bretton Woods era.

With both higher and more varied inflation during the 1970s, and

77. In fact, this contemporary judgment was probably wrong. The world recession was unexpectedly deep, and France's 2 percent growth during 1982 was remarkable.

Figure 1. *Short-Term Interest Rates in the United States and Four European Countries, 1973–83*[a]

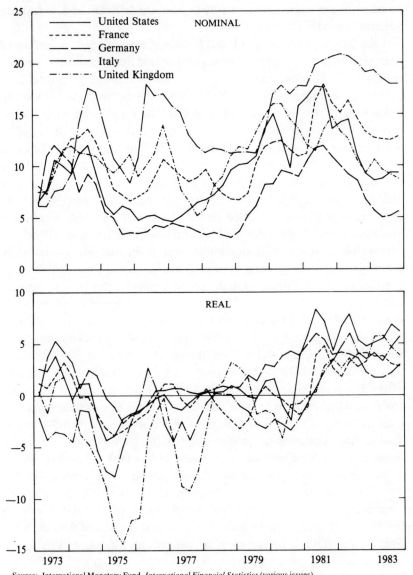

Source: International Monetary Fund, *International Financial Statistics* (various issues).
a. Real interest rates are obtained by deflating nominal interest rates with the (expost) CPI percentage changes in the four quarters up to and including the quarter of reference.

flexible exchange rates, it is perhaps not surprising that nominal interest rates were not highly correlated. The second panel of table 6 shows correlations among real short-term interest rates. These correlations are generally much higher in the most recent period—with the notable exception of Germany, which shows low correlations with all other countries and most remarkably with France and Italy, its EMS partners. Several factors may explain these low correlations. First, France and Italy still maintain exchange controls that are not entirely effective but that are known to bite at times of large incipient movements of capital.[78] Second, the EMS allows wide margins—4.5 percent for France and 12 percent for Italy—within which exchange rates are free to move. And third, the central rates of EMS were altered five times among these three currencies during the period 1979 to 1983.

A more formal vector autoregressive and multivariate analysis of weekly short-term nominal interest rates from 1979 to 1984 reveals that the U.S. federal funds rate had no significant influence on British or Italian interest rates and only modest influence on German and French short-term interest rates.[79]

With some qualification, then, a European country in today's world could pursue its own, independent macroeconomic policy. But that would require a willingness and an ability to fine tune the mix of monetary and fiscal policy to the external environment if a substantial change in the exchange rate is to be avoided. The need for internal coordination between a country's monetary and fiscal authorities may, of course, represent an insurmountable obstacle to independent national action. Moreover, this strategy involves a willingness to increase the country's external debt, hence foreign claims to future output. Under some circumstances, however, that would represent a sound investment.

The alternative is to allow or even encourage the currency to depre-

78. Sachs and Wyplosz, "Economic Consequences of President Mitterrand," p. 270.

79. The addition of U.S. interest rates to a vector autoregressive analysis of each country's weekly rate reduced the final prediction error by only 3½ percent for German interest rates, compared with an eighteen-week autoregression of the German interbank rate on its recent past values, and it reduced the final prediction error by only 2 percent in the similar analysis of the French call money rate. There was a statistically significant but small influence of German rates on French and Italian rates, as might be expected under a regime of fixed exchange rates, suggesting that the quarterly averages correlated in table 6 average out some of the association. Stefano Micossi and Tommaso Padoa-Schioppa, "Can Europeans Control Their Interest Rates?" no. 17 (Brussels: Centre for European Policy Studies, 1984), p. 36.

Table 7. *Effect of Monetary Policy on Real GDP under Fixed and Flexible Exchange Rates, Germany, United States, and OECD*[a]
Percent change

Rate	Germany[b]	United States[b]	OECD Europe[b]	Total OECD
Fixed exchange				
Real GDP[c]	0.3	0.5	0.3	0.5
GDP deflator	n.a.	n.a.	n.a.	0.2
Flexible exchange				
Real GDP[c]	1.7	0.8	1.2	n.a.
GDP deflator	3.4	1.0	2.0	n.a.
Ratio	2.0	1.2	1.7	...

Source: Flemming Larsen, John Llewellyn, and Stephen Potter, "International Economic Linkages," *OECD Economic Studies*, no. 1 (Autumn 1983), pp. 75, 80. Results based on the 1983 OECD INTERLINK model.
n.a. Not available.
a. The monetary policy action is a permanent decline of 2 percentage points in short-term interest rates.
b. Multipliers allow for induced impact on acting country's exports arising from the effects of the action in other countries.
c. Effect in third year.

ciate, assuming that a nominal depreciation can affect the price of exports relative to imports, or of tradables relative to nontradables. Recent European experience suggests this is the case, even for countries with considerable wage indexation. But currency depreciation will have a rapid price-increasing impact not only on imported goods in an open economy but also on domestic goods in competition with imports and, through the influence of consumer price increases on wages, on all costs and prices. For instance, in the OECD INTERLINK model a 10 percent devaluation of the German mark will increase the German domestic price deflator by 2.6 percent after three years before allowance for any push on wages, and by 5.5 percent after allowing for the impact on wages.[80]

A given dose of monetary action influencs real output under flexible exchange rates more than it does under fixed exchange rates, but this additional impact comes largely through the "competitive depreciation" that monetary stimulus produces.[81] For this reason, it has a sharp impact on prices as well, such that the price increase per unit of GDP gain may actually be less favorable under flexible than under fixed exchange rates.

80. Flemming Larsen, John Llewellyn, and Stephen Potter, "International Economic Linkages," *OECD Economic Studies*, no. 1 (Autumn 1983), pp. 82.

81. For example, a sustained 2 percentage point reduction in short-term interest rates increases German GDP by 0.3 percent by the third year, under fixed exchange rates, but 1.7 percent, under flexible exchange rates (see table 7).

By the same token, however, a country wishing to fight inflation can encourage its currency to appreciate, although it thereby incurs a loss in output.

Moreover, currency manipulation for macroeconomic management cannot be easily generalized across countries. For example, the stimulus to German GDP from expansionary monetary policy operating via the exchange rate comes mainly at the expense of the United States and Japan. What is attractive to one country may also be attractive to others. Yet if several countries act sequentially—whether by emulation or to recoup lost competitiveness—they may end up with the worst of both worlds: higher inflation, which comes quickly, with little or no increase in output, since that arrives only with a lag.

A natural response to this conundrum is to coordinate monetary actions among countries. Coordination reduces the impact of a given monetary action on output in a single country by reducing the competitive gain; but the inflation-output trade-off improves. For instance, in the 1983 OECD INTERLINK model, Germany must endure an increase of 2 percent in its price deflator for every 1 percent increase in GDP achieved through sustained reduction in short-term interest rates; if Germany is joined by other European countries in reducing interest rates, depreciation of the German mark is halved and the price level cost per unit increase in output drops to 1.6.[82]

An extreme form of coordination would be to eliminate altogether the exchange rate—and hence price competitiveness—effect of monetary actions by fixing exchange rates among countries, as has been approximated by the European monetary system. Such an action, while greatly reducing the influence of national monetary action on output, also would reduce the inflationary costs of a given impact on output.[83] Under these circumstances monetary action stimulates output in the traditional closed economy fashion by stimulating investment and by stimulating consumption through increased household wealth. Of course, if coordinated monetary stimulus occurs when there is less economic slack than the authorities believe, it could set off a general inflationary boom.

As with monetary measures, fiscal actions to achieve macroeconomic stabilization have unwanted side effects. Both tax and expenditure changes are difficult to reverse, or to alter when the macroeconomic

82. Larsen and others, "International Economic Linkages," p. 80.
83. Simulations on the March 1986 version of the OECD INTERLINK model, incorporating the EMS commitments, are reported in table 8.

Table 8. *Effect of National and Coordinated European Monetary Expansion on Five European Countries*[a]

Percent change

Country	Isolated national action			Coordinated European action		
	Real GDP	*GDP deflator*	*Ratio*	*Real GDP*	*GDP deflator*	*Ratio*
France	0.5	0.4	1.25	0.5	0.3	1.67
Germany	0.5	0.3	1.67	0.6	0.2	3.00
Italy	0.6	1.0	0.60	0.5	0.6	0.83
Sweden	0.8	0.5	1.60	0.9	0.4	2.25
United Kingdom	0.3	0.7	0.43	0.3	0.4	0.75

Source: Based on the properties of the March 1986 version of the INTERLINK model. I am grateful to Pete Richardson of the OECD staff for making this information available, but he bears no responsibility for my use of it.
a. The monetary expansion is a 1 percentage point reduction in short-term interest rates. Data refer to the effect in the third year.

situation changes, because they typically have controversial distributional or allocational effects. For this reason, sensitive governments are reluctant to undertake fiscal action unless the payoff is sufficiently great to make it worthwhile. Yet in open economies the leakages from fiscal action under fixed exchange rates can be substantial, and even under flexible rates the impact on output of the corrective change in competitiveness is delayed compared with the direct effects of increased government spending or reduced taxes. For instance, Britain in the 1978–79 boom experienced a rise in imports equal to 27 percent of the rise in GDP, and France in its expansionary phase of 1981–82 experienced an ex post marginal propensity to import of 23 percent. These figures hardly support the contemporary claim of a "flood of imports" in each case, although the ratio of the growth of imports of manufactured goods to the increase in manufacturing output was greater than these figures suggest, and the concern about imports may not have been about overall policy effectiveness, but rather a thwarted desire to increase output and employment in manufacturing. Nonetheless, the results of fiscal action may be disappointing. Table 9 shows the fiscal multipliers under fixed exchange rates and with accommodating monetary policy that appear in the 1983 OECD INTERLINK model. They are substantially lower than the 2 to 2½ that used to prevail under these assumptions. But, of course, the large leakages do not just disappear; they represent increased exports and production in other countries. For instance, 1 percent of GDP increase in nonwage government expenditure in Germany is estimated to increase German GDP by 1.5 percent in the third year, but it also

Table 9. *Effect of an Increase in Nonwage Government Expenditure Equal to 1 Percent of GDP, with Fixed Exchange Rates and Accommodating Monetary Policy, Four European Countries and OECD*

Country	Real GDP (percent change)		Current account (percent of GDP)	
	First year	Third year	First year	Third year
France	1.1	1.5	−0.5	−0.6
Germany	1.3	1.5	−0.5	−0.5
Sweden	1.1	0.9	−0.7	−0.6
United Kingdom	1.0	1.1	−0.5	−0.6
OECD Europe	1.7	2.2	−0.3	−0.2
Total OECD[a]	1.9	2.9	−0.2	0.0

Source: Larsen and others, "International Economic Linkages," pp. 70, 78. Results based on the 1983 OECD INTERLINK model.

a. "Global" multiplier used here, as opposed to "linked" multipliers in all other cases.

increases GDP in Austria, Belgium, the Netherlands, Switzerland, and Sweden by 0.3 to 0.4 percent, and in France, Italy, and Spain by 0.2 percent.[84] Moreover, fiscal actions in these countries, making due allowance for economic size, also influence German exports and output.

Current account positions can be improved, and fiscal multipliers increased, through collective action. Examples drawn from the OECD INTERLINK model are shown in table 9. If the OECD countries act together in raising their nonwage government expenditure by 1 percent of GDP, with accommodating monetary policy, the output multipliers are increased from 0.9 to 1.5 in the case of individual countries, to 2.2 when European countries act together, to 2.9 if all OECD countries act together. The current account deterioration drops to about one-third the level (relative to GDP) if Europe acts together as compared with individual countries acting alone. So collective action can increase effectiveness in achieving the primary objective of increasing output at a lower cost, in this example measured by the need for net foreign borrowing.[85]

Of course, coordinated action is not usually easy. Countries have

84. Ibid., pp. 72–73.

85. A similar result holds for simulations on the March 1986 version of the OECD INTERLINK model, reported in table 10: fiscal multipers are increased, the inflation cost is somewhat reduced, and the need for net foreign borrowing is reduced.

Table 10. *Effect of National and Coordinated European Fiscal Expansion on Five European Countries*[a]

Percent change

	Isolated national action			Coordinated European action		
Country	Real GDP	GDP deflator	Ratio	Real GDP	GDP deflator	Ratio
France	1.1	0.8	1.4	1.7	1.2	1.4
Germany	0.6	0.4	1.5	1.2	0.8	1.5
Italy	0.8	1.4	0.6	1.3	2.4	0.5
Sweden	1.4	1.1	1.3	2.3	1.9	1.2
United Kingdom	0.7	0.6	1.2	1.1	1.2	0.9

Source: See table 8.

a. The fiscal expansion is an increase in government expenditure equal to 1 percent of GNP, with nonaccommodating monetary policy. Data refer to the effect in the third year.

different decisionmaking processes and timetables. Moreover, countries often find themselves in different circumstances, such that common action is not appropriate. Even if the right conditions exist, it is often more comfortable for small countries to await actions from their larger trading partners. Under conventional ways of looking at the matter, they gain by experiencing export-led rather than domestically generated growth, so they have an incentive to procrastinate. In this connection, it is important for Europeans to appreciate the German phobia about current account deficits. The Federal Republic, the largest country in Europe, is one of the most reluctant to take steps that risk worsening its current account. It would much rather be a caboose than a locomotive.

Finally, there is the possibility of collective error, either about the forecast or about economic structure and circumstances. When ignorance about economic structure and future events prevails, coordinated action can lead to larger and more consequential errors than is likely from independent and partly self-cancelling national actions.

Error about economic structure is especially likely at the current state of understanding of national economies and their interactions. The basic conceptual framework used is one that starts with a closed economy and then opens it through trade and financial transactions. The latter are in general poorly modeled, and exchange rate determination is still only imperfectly understood. Large-scale interactive macroeconomic models are still in an adolescent stage. A comparison of identical policy actions through simulation with twelve global macromodels produced results that differed substantially in magnitude if not in qualitative direction.[86]

86. Ralph Bryant and others, eds. *Empirical Macroeconomics for Interdependent Economies* (Brookings, forthcoming).

The OECD INTERLINK model was one of these twelve, and its results are not radically out of line, but the figures used here must be taken as illustrative rather than definitive.

Despite the evident weaknesses with current global macroeconomic models, the basic thrust of the models is almost certainly correct: in principle, coordinated action can produce better results than independent national action, even if the level of coordination does not go beyond Europe. Whether such coordination passes a cost-benefit test depends on the incremental costs associated with cooperation itself, and those costs can be reduced over time through institutional evolution.

However, the potential superiority of collective action does not mean that nations on their own are hopelessly bound by external constraints. On the contrary, being part of a world market for goods, services, and capital creates, on balance, more opportunities for national action than constraints. By permitting a separation between output and expenditure, it enables a country to sell its excess production abroad or, to put the matter the other way around, to stimulate domestic output through exports. The world market also enables a country to spend more than it produces at home without generating inflation, by drawing real resources from abroad, for example, to be invested domestically. But what each country can do effectively when acting alone is not possible for all countries acting independently in the same fashion. The damage caused by inconsistencies in national action is one of the features that make international cooperation potentially attractive.

Comment by Andrea Boltho

The main thesis of this carefully documented and very well argued paper is that, given a floating exchange rate system and an open international capital market, the external constraint that Europe so often encountered in the Bretton Woods days is no longer present. Individual countries can engage in independent macroeconomic policies and offset any untoward external consequences of their action by altering their exchange rates or borrowing. This conclusion is reinforced by the examination of various post-1975 episodes in which European countries with a balance-of-payments constraint switched from expansionary to restrictive policies. In all those cases, the borrowing option, at least, was open to them, suggesting that the policy turnaround was due to other reasons. Neither analytically nor empirically does the hypothesis of an external constraint stand up.

Yet Europeans may find such a message unconvincing. The perception that each European economy is constrained by its balance of payments is very deep rooted among policymakers, the general public, and economists. Both the alternative strategies suggested by Cooper (depreciation or borrowing) are viewed as suboptimal. The doubts that surround them can best be discussed under two main headings: feasibility and effectiveness.

As regards depreciation, it is not at all certain that in today's world of fickle expectations, unstable foreign currency markets, and limited reserve assets, countries can smoothly reach a particular target for their exchange rate. Both Italy and the United Kingdom tried, in late 1975 or early 1976, to gently depreciate their currencies, but they found that the movement was quickly out of control. The dangers of overshooting have not diminished in the past decade, and many governments would hesitate at present to try to nudge their currencies in one direction or another. As for those countries that have chosen a semifixed exchange rate option, EMS practices show that almost all the realignments so far have at best offset earlier inflation differentials and thus not provided devaluing countries with a competitive advantage.

A second reason for doubting the feasibility of an exchange rate change stems from the fear that real wage resistance will quickly eliminate any possible competitive gain—a fear particularly pronounced in the United Kingdom and Italy in the mid-1970s, when inflationary expectations were high and indexation provisions widespread. The empirical evidence, gleaned from macroeconomic models, does not fully support this idea: pass-through effects from foreign to domestic prices are quite rapid (more so in Italy than in the United Kingdom), but not full, at least within a time span relevant to policy action (two to four years). And this conclusion is likely to be strengthened in the present situation of high unemployment and relatively abundant spare capacity. Nonetheless, the perception that erosion is there and could be relatively quick weakens the temptation to depreciate any currency.

But even if a controlled depreciation could be achieved and "made to stick," there are other European objections to changing the exchange rate. At one very simple level, reference is often made to the successful performance over the past decade of countries such as Germany and Japan (and also Austria and Switzerland) that chose "hard"-currency options. Casual empiricism of this kind is, of course, no proof at all that depreciations are counterproductive, but the demonstration effect provided by these examples nonetheless holds powerful sway over policymakers if not over economists.

At an analytically more interesting level, "elasticity pessimism" remains diffuse (and would seem, incidentally, to receive a measure of support from some of the findings in Robert Lawrence's paper in this volume). For a number of reasons (the increasing weight of trade between branches of multinational corporations, the spread of protectionism, particularly of the voluntary export restraint kind, the rising share of investment and high-technology goods in international trade), nonprice factors have become progressively more important in explaining countries' competitive performances. Elasticity pessimism is also reinforced, in the specific case of the United Kingdom, by the perception that the very sharp real appreciation of the pound at the turn of the 1970s (only partially offset since) may have had some irreversible effect: markets abroad may have been lost forever, or even whole sectors of manufacturing production may have been wiped out. Any longer-run real depreciation may thus fail to generate an adequate supply response—yet another form of the hysteresis phenomenon discussed in several papers in this volume.

In addition, the generalization of floating rates may also have reduced the values of price elasticities. In the Bretton Woods days a devaluation of the currency could have been viewed by most firms as conferring a semipermanent competitive advantage. This, in turn, would have led to long-term changes in strategy as firms reallocated not only production, but also investment, to the more profitable export- or import-competing activities. In the world of floating rates experienced since the early 1970s, the persistence of such exchange rate changes has been limited. Most major currencies have risen and fallen in real terms over the past decade and often by large amounts and in quick succession. In such circumstances risk-averting firms' response to sudden depreciations (or appreciations) that are viewed as temporary may be a quick increase in sales (or sudden withdrawal of purchases) but not a commitment to a long-run switch into (or out of) tradable production. The short-run elasticities may actually be somewhat higher as a result of such behavior than they would otherwise have been, but the long-run ones would be lower.

Therefore, while depreciation is still felt to provide countries with some increase in competitiveness, its benefits are generally perceived to be relatively small and transitory. At best, it can produce a breathing space during which more structural changes are implemented. At worst, it gives a new lease on life to industries or firms that are basically uncompetitive and that, in the interests of long-run improvements in resource allocation, should be run down rather than saved.

With respect to capital movements, the first difficulty that Cooper's paper raises is whether countries can coordinate their fiscal and monetary policies in such a way as to engineer both domestic expansion and a capital inflow. A fine-tuning exercise of this kind may be feasible in theory. In practice, however, considerable institutional problems or credibility problems may impede attainment of the appropriate policy mix. (Recent U.S. experience is hardly a valid counterexample, since the country would seem to have stumbled on rather than chosen its policy mix.)

Even if the mix were achieved, it is not certain that finance would always be forthcoming. With the benefit of hindsight, Cooper thinks that the three expanding economies he examines (those of the United Kingdom, Italy, and France) could have borrowed more. He points to the sharp turnarounds in their balances of payments following the adoption of restrictive policies as indirect evidence that foreign investors were willing to lend to them. Although this does sound plausible in the case of the United Kingdom, whose potential oil-producer status was well known by 1976, it is less likely to have been the case for Italy in the same year or for France in 1982–83. That turnarounds took place is undoubted, but they may well have been prompted not so much by underlying creditworthiness as by the sharp switch toward orthodoxy in policies themselves. This dispelled some of the fears generated by the presence of relatively left-wing governments, by the massive borrowing that had preceded, and by the falls in external reserves that were occurring. Such arguments do not preclude the success of more moderate governments in financing current account deficits in today's conditions, but they raise at least the possibility of a constraint facing more radical ones.

Even if external borrowing could be arranged, a general unwillingness to engage in it permeates Europe and, particularly, continental Europe. As Cooper points out, resource-rich countries such as Australia and Canada may have borrowed for a century or more without apparent negative consequences, yet such evidence is not really relevant to the major European economies. These are neither resource rich nor likely to attract direct investment inflows on a large scale. The only contribution of capital imports could be that of buying time (possibly briefer than that provided by currency depreciation), and this at the cost of a greater future burden of interest payments. Borrowing is, at best, a stop-gap measure. It only postpones the need to take the more painful action required for the correct long-term strategy—namely, "living within one's means," or, even better, running a current account surplus.

Behind this puritanical view of international economic relations lies a deep-seated aversion to borrowing that some would label *mercantilism*. Mercantilism has usually received a bad press among economists, but the same point can be made in another and possibly more acceptable way: European (and Japanese) preferences for current account surpluses translate into relatively high saving propensities. The reason for these high savings, in turn, reflects a much greater aversion to risk than can be found in the United States. Despite superior, even if endangered, social security provisions, European households seem to feel the need to accumulate wealth to a much greater extent than their American counterparts do. And this preference, in turn, is reflected in a national behavior that gives pride of place to external wealth accumulation. Seen in this light, the tendency for European countries to try to run current account surpluses may make greater economic sense than crude references to mercantilism, and could actually be welfare enhancing in a world short of savings.

One could argue that these different tastes will generate particular outcomes for current deficits and surpluses in the world economy that could well be optimal. Yet, as is so often the case in economics, individual wisdom can lead to collective mistakes. If too many households raise their savings, as Keynes pointed out a long time ago, aggregate demand may make everybody poorer at the end of the day. Similarly, if too many European countries plan for current account surpluses, particularly at a time when the U.S. current deficit is expected to decline, the world economy may enter a cumulative deflationary spiral. If there is any truth in this view, the case for international (or at least European) coordination is greatly strengthened. Cooper rightly shows the gains to coordination from higher multiplier values or from lower inflationary repercussions of joint expansionary action. Yet a more important argument for coordinated reflation is that it greatly diminishes the danger that individual countries, following an expansionary policy, will run into what they would all consider to be a genuine external constraint—namely, an intolerable current account deficit.

Comment by Gilles Oudiz

The central thesis of Cooper's stimulating and innovative paper is that European countries no longer face the external constraint on independent expansion that prevailed before 1971. Since exchange rates are now flexible, countries can choose to devalue their currencies to prevent current account deficits, or since capital markets are now highly developed, they can borrow to finance them.

The bulk of the paper is devoted to establishing the absence of external constraints through a detailed and well-documented analysis of policy experiences in the United Kingdom, Germany, Italy, France, Sweden, and Denmark. The episodes selected from the history of the past decade are chosen because they are periods when individual economic strategies appear to have failed.

Cooper draws three major conclusions from his analysis. First, the failures in these episodes reflect internal rather than external constraints. Even though limited capital flight took place in some examples, and governments were concerned about the rise in foreign debt in others, there was no limit on the borrowing ability of the countries under study. Second, European countries are able to pursue independent policies provided they fine tune their mix of fiscal and monetary policies and accept either borrowing abroad or allowing the currency to depreciate (or both). And third, coordinated action is hard to implement. Each of these conclusions will be discussed in turn.

First, European economies do face substantial external constraints. As Cooper himself notes, European countries are much more open than the United States. The share of exports (and imports) in GNP amounts to between 20 and 30 percent compared with about 6 percent in the United States. Most European countries have to deal with very sensitive exchange markets, and consequently they try to limit the buildup of external debt that results from cumulative current account deficits. Furthermore, European countries face disruptive foreign shocks that affect them in different ways, thus causing strains on intra-European exchange rates. The recent upward and downward movements of the dollar affected the major European currencies very differently. This has significantly contributed to the various realignments within the European monetary system since 1979.

The examples discussed by Cooper are all single-country policy experiences. In several cases these policies failed because they were not matched by the main commercial partners of the acting country. In this respect, among others, Europe faces an external constraint unknown to the United States. Among highly interdependent countries, the multiplicity of decisionmakers (individual country governments) has a collective cost that may account for a significant part of Europe's current "deflationary bias."

Second, notwithstanding Cooper's remarks, exchange rates *are* perceived by Europeans as binding constraints. Since the end of the Bretton Woods era, Europeans have been concerned about the risk of competitive exchange rate policies. Since 1971 Europeans have tried to control inter-European parities by agreements such as the "snake" and the EMS. Indeed, for about ten of the past fifteen years the franc and the deutsche mark, for example, have been linked in some way. The exchange rate has thus definitely worked as a binding constraint for most European countries except Germany. The example of France in 1983, which Cooper discussed extensively, is in this respect typical. The Mitterrand government faced a clear choice: withdraw from the EMS and lose credibility on the international capital markets or remain in the system and accept its rules.

On the whole, European exchange rate agreements have worked as an imperfect means of ensuring some kind of monetary coordination in Europe. It should be noted, however, that the goals of such a coordination have evolved markedly since 1971. After the collapse of the Bretton Woods system, European policymakers tried to enforce some kind of a European fixed exchange rate system. They implicitly assumed that exchange rate changes were to be avoided at all cost. But the various versions of the snake eventually failed because the more inflationary European countries—the United Kingdom, Italy, France—found it impossible to follow closely the monetary policy of Germany. Even though its approach was not initially perceived as such, the EMS has allowed a much greater flexibility in the joint management of European exchange rates. The 1979 agreement has proved its ability to cope with both the large appreciation of the dollar and its rapid fall after February 1985.

Third, Cooper's discussion on policy coordination is surprisingly short. In my opinion, coordination is the key to dealing with external constraints on European countries. Far from being an "extreme form of coordination," as Cooper puts it, "fixing the exchange rate among countries" can be an impossible task, as the experience of the European snake in the early 1970s has shown. Europeans have learned at their own expense that policy coordination means confronting differences rather than enforcing uniformity. In this respect, an optimal joint exchange rate policy among countries with different structures, different environments, and different policy objectives can clearly not be a fixed exchange rate policy. On the other hand, frequent exchange rate changes involve adjustment costs and potential instability. Up to now the EMS has dealt reasonably well with this trade-off.

European policy coordination can conceptually be separated into its extra-European (Europe versus the world) and intra-European aspects. Dealing globally with foreign shocks (dollar shocks, oil shocks) implies choosing a European policy in order to achieve average economic objectives: growth, inflation, trade balance. In other words, the Europeans should jointly choose an "optimal" ecu-dollar exchange rate. The appreciation of the dollar in 1980 was, to a large extent, an exogenous shock for the European economies. It seems clear that the joint deflation induced by the authorities was inappropriate: easier monetary policies would have allowed lower average European interest rates and higher growth.

Intra-European exchange rate management, on the other hand, should deal with differences among European countries. In theory, and to some extent in practice, European exchange rates can be adjusted to cope with the distortions induced by exogenous foreign shocks. Going back to the dollar shock example, a globally lower level of European interest rates would in no way have precluded adequate management of interest rate differentials, that is, of exchange rates. In short, the issue of European policy coordination is more complex than Cooper seems to imply in his concluding section.

The empirical models used in Cooper's brief examination of policy coordination are unrealistic. Even though they can provide some empirical evaluations of the impact of fiscal and monetary policies, these macroeconometric model simulations shed little light on the actual policy choices faced by European governments today. The depreciation of the dollar and the fall in oil prices do increase the potential for noninflationary European growth, but the multiplicity of decisionmakers—that is, national authorities—with conflicting interests might well leave Europe at a standstill or at best lead to a modest relaxation of monetary policies. Whatever empirical models show, the prospects of a joint fiscal expansion seem today quite remote.

General Discussion

One participant remarked that Richard Cooper's fiscal multipliers were so small as to imply that the gains from coordination were small. Another noted Cooper had simultaneously observed the decline in these multipliers and yet argued that external constraints were absent. It was stressed that the assumptions of flexible exchange rates and nonaccommodating monetary policy were important in these multiplier estimates, because under such circumstances fiscal policy could induce currency appreciation. In addition, it was noted that revisions of the OECD model between 1983 and 1985 had lowered the average multiplier because of the declining estimated responsiveness of investment to output.

Participants took issue with Cooper's implicit optimism on fine tuning. One questioned the view that the exchange rate can be used as an instrument. In a world with speculative bubbles and portfolio adjustments, the exchange rate can be an independent source of shocks. In addition, the behavior by policymakers abroad who take account only of their national viewpoints can generate exchange rate shocks—an example being U.S. policy in the early 1980s. These kinds of shocks imply a greater need for coordinated responses than is suggested by Cooper's paper.

Some discussants felt that Cooper underestimated European concerns about the inflationary effects of devaluation and had therefore given an inaccurate picture of the ease with which real alterations in the exchange rate can be achieved. Indeed, it was the fear of these inflationary effects that induced the French to remain within the European monetary system.

Cooper's view that fiscal policy can increase domestic growth was also questioned. One participant argued that such effects were temporary and only resulted from misperceptions. In addition, fiscal expansion was based on buying public goods that did not accurately reflect individual preferences.

It was pointed out that available international macroeconomic models give contradictory predictions about the effects of monetary expansion on the current account and fiscal expansion on the exchange rate. Those models in which monetary expansion results in a large exchange rate depreciation generate negative spillovers (that is, monetary expansion at home reduces foreign GNP); those with smaller exchange rate effects have positive spillovers. In several models, therefore, uncoordinated monetary and fiscal expansion does not run into a current-account constraint because the exchange rate depreciates.

One participant pointed out that in 1980 the Germans were relatively sanguine about their current account deficit, but when the deficit increased in 1981 they treated it as a national disaster and acted accordingly. The fear was expressed that the same thing might happen in response to the decline in the German current account that will inevitably occur as a result of the weaker dollar. Since the German economy is Europe's strongest, the most resistant to inflation, and the most creditworthy, it could actually cope well with a period of external borrowing. Its unwillingness to do so could threaten other countries.

A participant complained that relevant institutional factors had been virtually overlooked in discussions throughout the conference. These included not only economic institutions, such as the organization of financial markets, but also more broad-based institutions such as labor unions (whose role in explaining European economic performance should have been examined). He suggested that these omissions reflected the fact that on the whole institutions are not easily changed, at least not in the short run; hence, they are not the sorts of things a Brookings conference (which is policy oriented) would be expected to focus on. In addition, he noted, most of the papers employed time-series as opposed to cross-national analysis: they treated the European nations as if they were independent observations (with essentially identical bias) of a single random variable rather than focused on the differences between countries. He was bothered by the lack of emphasis given to differences among European nations, stating that the homogeneity implied by such analyses was fallacious. Moreover, he added, it is extremely difficult to examine the hypothetical impact of institutional factors in a time-series analysis since those factors do not vary much in the short run. Hence, the conference's predisposition toward time-series analysis would seem to preclude the examination of institutional factors.

It was emphasized that there are dangers in trying to test hypotheses using cross-sectional comparisons without controlling for other variables. Thus, simply because one found no relation between, say, unemployment insurance and unemployment in a cross section did not imply there would be no effect in a properly specified model. Classical bias problems often arise because of the exclusion of correlated variables. It was also suggested that inferences drawn from time-series analyses such as those sometimes made on Germany's performance after the 1978 Bonn summit might be inappropriate today.

Conference Participants

with their affiliations at the time of the conference

Katharine G. Abraham *Brookings Institution*
Robert Z. Aliber *University of Chicago*
Jacques R. Artus *International Monetary Fund*
Martin Neil Baily *Brookings Institution*
Charles R. Bean *London School of Economics*
Andrea Boltho *Magdalen College, Oxford University*
Barry P. Bosworth *Brookings Institution*
Ralph C. Bryant *Brookings Institution*
Willem H. Buiter *Yale University*
Gary Burtless *Brookings Institution*
Richard N. Cooper *Harvard University*
Paul N. Courant *University of Michigan*
Günther Dahlhoff *Embassy of the Federal Republic of Germany*
Ralf Dahrendorf *University of Konstanz and Russell Sage Foundation*
Patrick de Fontenay *International Monetary Fund*
Jacques H. Drèze *Université Catholique de Louvain*
Hermann J. Dudler *Deutsche Bundesbank*
Robert J. Flanagan *Stanford University*
Jeffrey A. Frankel *University of California, Berkeley, and International Monetary Fund*
Robert J. Gordon *Northwestern University*
Armin Gutowski *HWWA Institut für Wirtschaftsforschung*
Bertil Holmlund *FIEF Institut*
Gerald Holtham *Brookings Institution*
Susan Houseman *Brookings Institution*

Alexis Jacquemin *University of Louvain*

Paul R. Krugman *Massachusetts Institute of Technology*

Robert Z. Lawrence *Brookings Institution*

Assar Lindbeck *University of Stockholm and the World Bank*

Stephen N. Marris *Institute for International Economics*

John P. Martin *Organization for Economic Cooperation and Development*

Bernhard Molitor *Bundesministerium für Wirtschaft*

Mario Monti *Bocconi University*

Alain Morisset *Delegation of the Commission of the European Communities to the United States*

Stephen J. Nickell *Oxford University*

G. O'Donnell *Embassy of Great Britain*

Mancur L. Olson *University of Maryland*

Gilles Oudiz *Compagnie Bancaire*

Joseph A. Pechman *Brookings Institution*

George L. Perry *Brookings Institution*

Robert D. Putnam *Harvard University*

Otto Schlecht *Bundesministerium für Wirtschaft*

Charles L. Schultze *Brookings Institution*

Robert Solomon *Brookings Institution*

Jules Theeuwes *Free University of Amsterdam*

Edwin M. Truman *Federal Reserve Board*

Norbert A. Walter *American Institute for Contemporary German Studies*

Alan A. Walters *The World Bank*

Manfred Wegner *IFO Institut für Wirtschaftsforschung*

Name Index

Subject Index